Society, State, and Nation
in Twentieth-Century Europe

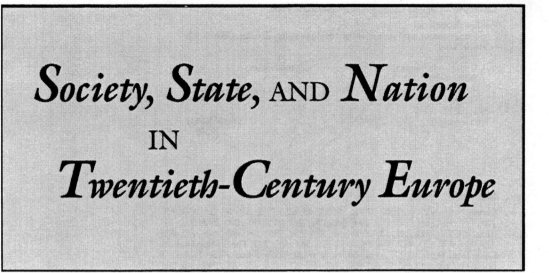

Society, State, AND Nation IN Twentieth-Century Europe

Roderick Phillips

Carleton University, Ottawa

PRENTICE HALL
Upper Saddle River, New Jersey 07458

Library of Congress Cataloging-in-Publication Data

Phillips, Roderick.
    Society, state, and nation in twentieth-century Europe / Roderick
Phillips.
        p.   cm.
    Includes bibliographical references (p.) and index.
    ISBN 0–13–103821–4
    1. Europe—History—20th century.   2. Social change—Europe.
I. Title.
D421.P52   1996
940.5—dc20   95–24431
                                                        CIP

Illustration Credits

Photos.   *Pages 2, 5, 14, 20, 37, 41, 48, 52, 55, 62, 67, 72, 74, 76, 135, 153, 155, 158, 164, 167, 184, 203, 232, 244, 246, 251, 262, 275, 280, 290, 292, 293, 300, 313, 326, 332, 333, 342, 353, 360, 369, 383, 384, 391, 394, 400, 408, 412, 415, 423, 426, 430, 435, 443, 456, 463, 469, 474, 501, 507, 511:* The Hulton Deutsch Collection; *pages 29, 177:* reproduced from the Collections of the Library of Congress; *pages 88, 90, 92, 99, 104, 106, 107, 109, 128, 137, 183, 243, 266, 268, 278, 286, 317, 323, 336, 363, 440:* reproduced by permission of the Trustees of the Imperial War Museum, London; *page 115:* UPI/Bettmann Newsphotos; *page 198:* New York Public Library Picture Collection; *pages 210, 235, 481:* AP/Wide World Photos; *page 222:* Brown Brothers; *page 348:* courtesy of Labour Party Library.

Maps.   *Pages 4, 50, 85, 87, 118, 157, 249, 296, 325, 334, 340, 376, 479, 498, 514, 515:* adapted from James Wilkinson and H. Stuart Hughes, *Contemporary Europe: A History*, 8th ed., © 1995 by Prentice-Hall, Inc.

Acquisitions editor: Sally Constable
Editorial assistant: Justin Belinski
Editorial/production supervision
    and interior design: P. M. Gordon Associates
Cover director: Jayne Conte
Buyer: Nick Sklitsis

Copyright © 1998 by Prentice-Hall, Inc.
Upper Saddle River, New Jersey 07458

Printed in the United States of America
10   9   8   7   6   5   4   3   2   1

ISBN: 0-13-103821-4

Prentice-Hall International (UK) Limited, London
Prentice-Hall of Australia Pty. Limited, Sydney
Prentice-Hall Canada Inc., Toronto
Prentice-Hall Hispanoamericana, S.A., Mexico
Prentice-Hall of India Private Limited, New Delhi
Prentice-Hall of Japan, Inc., Tokyo
Pearson Education Asia Pte. Ltd., Singapore
Editoria Prentice-Hall do Brasil, Ltda., Rio De Janeiro

For Ruth

Contents

3   *The First World War, 1914–1918*   79

4   *The Unstable Peace, 1918–1923*   134

11 *Challenge and Decline, 1970–1985*　*421*

12 *Europe and the Post-Communist Era, 1985–1995*　*468*

List of Maps

Preface

Society, State, and Nation in Twentieth-Century Europe aims to provide a comprehensive account of the main lines of European social, political, and economic history in the twentieth century. While giving a solid account of mainstream political and economic trends and events, it incorporates important recent research on key issues such as the family, gender relations, women's experience, ethnicity, race relations, work, health, population change, and sexuality. Although these subjects are prominent within modern historical research, they are too often either missing from survey histories or treated as subsidiary to the main themes discussed. In this book I have tried to make social change as central as political and economic developments to an understanding of twentieth-century European history.

The book stresses the need to integrate the social dimension into our understanding of political and economic change in order to achieve a more comprehensive understanding of the period. It goes beyond the notion, implied by many surveys, that social change was little more than the "effect" or "impact" of political and economic events. It emphasizes, instead, that changes in the social, political, and economic spheres were so often interrelated that they must be seen in a dynamic relationship.

The chapter on the First World War, for example, avoids discussing the home front experience as little more than the cumulative effects of the military conflict on the economic and social life of civilian populations. Rather, the home fronts and battlefronts are discussed in tandem to demonstrate their intimate and reciprocal relationship. The chapter highlights the importance of the home front experiences—viewed from the perspective not only of economic productivity, but also of class, gender, ethnic relations, morale, diet, and health—to the military and political outcome of the war.

Society, State, and Nation also stresses the importance of understanding the sequence of historical events. As far as possible, the book proceeds chronologically on a series of fronts so that readers can easily appreciate the connections among various events and phenomena. In the chapter on the period following the First World War, for example, the political and territorial arrangements reached at the Paris peace conference are not discussed first, as they generally are. Instead, the chapter sets up the economic, social, and political situation (such as the de facto creation of new states in Central and Eastern Europe) that confronted the conference delegates before they met, and it discusses the way the situation changed in the course of the conference. Readers can thus appreciate that many of the postwar territorial arrangements were imposed less by the conference than by the forces (often armed forces) of nationalism.

Society, State, and Nation provides a comprehensive discussion of Western, Central, and Eastern Europe (including Russia) throughout the twentieth century. The discussion takes account of broad differences between West and East in the spheres of politics, economy, and society. A sense of regional diversity is pursued throughout the text, providing the basis for a discussion of developments in Eastern Europe in the first half of the 1990s.

I have also tried to give due emphasis to the smaller European states, without losing sight of the disproportionate influence and frequent dominance of a small number of major powers. Examples of general social, economic, and political trends and phenomena have been drawn from a wide range of states and regions. Further, the book gives an account of the experience and actions of neutral states in the world wars.

Society, State, and Nation emphasizes that the speed of some trends, often associated with the twentieth century, should not be exaggerated. Industrialization, urbanization, the expansion of women's rights, the spread of democratic institutions, and improvements in diet and health took place at varying paces in the different regions and states of Europe; they did not proceed in a linear path.

A book of this length cannot deal satisfactorily with all issues in all places. Beyond a generally agreed body of material, any survey of a long period must be somewhat idiosyncratic, reflecting the interests and values of its author. In *Society, State, and Nation*, however, I hope to have expanded the base of material that should be thought necessary for a survey. I hope equally that the book's readers, particularly students, will find material here that will make them want to pursue history further.

Acknowledgments

A book of this kind could not be written without reference to thousands of other works, among them general histories, monographs, biographies and memoirs, articles, book reviews, review essays, bibliographies, official documents, compilations of statistics, and conference papers. It is also of the character of this kind of book, which does not provide full reference to the sources of specific information, that the authors of the works used are not explicitly acknowledged. The bibliography includes only a fraction of the works I consulted, and it is limited to reasonably accessible English-language books that students might turn to for more information on some of the key themes. I wish to make a blanket acknowledgment, as inadequate as it might be, to the historians and others whose work enabled me to write this synthesis.

A number of individuals were particularly helpful in commenting on the first draft of the book. They include four of my colleagues and friends in the Department of History at Carleton University, who brought their respective specialties to bear on the text: Alek Bennett, Carter Elwood, Naomi Griffiths, and Franz Szabo. All took time from their own work (which I insisted was not as important as mine) to read and comment on a long manuscript. They have my gratitude for the time, care, and energy they put into the task. I also benefited from the comments of the anonymous readers engaged by Prentice Hall. In all cases I took some of the advice I was offered and decided against heeding other suggestions. Any errors of fact or interpretation in the final text are my responsibility.

The last sections of the book were written, and the whole text revised, in various locations in five countries—not a plan I recommend. Wherever I went, I was made welcome, and I wish to note the hospitality of the staff at the libraries at Carleton University, the municipality of Dijon, the University of Cambridge, the University of Auckland, and the University of New South Wales. In addition, the Bridgewater (Nova Scotia) Public Library and the Birkenhead Branch of the North Shore (Auckland) Public Library gave me space when I needed it. Jill St. Germain located information for me from the Ottawa Public Library. Research for the illustrations was carried out in London at the Imperial War Museum and at the Hulton Deutsch library. At the latter, Mick Farrelly was particularly helpful.

I also wish to acknowledge the hospitality I enjoyed while working on the final phases of the book. In Cambridge I was made welcome by Peter Laslett and members of the Cambridge Group for the History of Population and Social Structure, as well as by the Principal and Fellows of Clare Hall. It was my good fortune that Michael Graves was in Cambridge at the same time, and as usual he added liberal measures of companionship and good humor to my time there.

The editorial and production staff at Prentice Hall have been unfailingly cooperative and efficient. The book was commissioned by Steve Dalphin, who was very encouraging and helpful in the early stages of preparation. Tamara Mann, the College History editorial assistant, dealt efficiently with letters, phone calls, and faxes as I moved from North America to Europe, then to Australasia and back to Europe. Sally Constable gracefully supervised the editorial and production processes. Doug Gordon, with whom I had a number of amiable conversations from phone booths in various parts of Europe, could not have managed the copy-editing and production more smoothly.

Apart from me, only one person was with the book from inception to publication. Ruth Pritchard helped me in a thousand ways, not least by listening to me talk through countless organizational difficulties. Among her other contributions, she checked bibliographies and journal abstracts, and spent days with me in photo libraries looking for illustrations. Her good humor, patience, and tenacity were often astonishing, especially when my own began to wane. I owe far more to Ruth than the dedication and this brief acknowledgment express.

Roderick Phillips

Society, State, and Nation
in Twentieth-Century Europe

· 1 ·

Europe in 1900

Introduction

In the courtyard of the Military Academy of Paris on a cold, wet Saturday morning in January 1895, a French artillery officer, convicted by a military court of espionage, suffered the ritual of extreme degradation that marked dishonorable expulsion from the army. As several hundred soldiers watched at attention, a general on horseback rose in his stirrups, raised his sword, and proclaimed, "Alfred Dreyfus, you are no longer worthy of bearing arms! In the name of the French people, you are dishonored!"

A sergeant-major stepped forward and performed the degradation: The insignia were ripped from the officer's cap and sleeves, his epaulets were torn off, even the red stripes ripped from his trousers; badges indicating his captain's rank were thrown to the ground; his sword was taken from his side and its sheath broken. Ex-Captain Dreyfus, his uniform symbolically in tatters, then returned to prison before being dispatched to serve a life sentence on Devil's Island, the notorious penal colony off the coast of French Guyana.

Although out of sight, Dreyfus was not allowed to fade from the public mind. His wife and family refused to believe that he was guilty, and began a campaign to clear his name. Evidence pointing to his innocence mounted, and in 1898 the novelist Emile Zola published a sensational newspaper article titled "I Accuse" that condemned the army for refusing to look at the evidence and warned that democratic institutions were under threat. France was soon divided into Dreyfusards and anti-Dreyfusards, supporters and opponents, respectively. Political movements were founded on each side, and acrimonious debates sometimes descended into violence. An officer who had forged papers to implicate Dreyfus committed suicide.

In a new trial Dreyfus was again found guilty, though this time only by majority decision with "extenuating circumstances," as if this softened the verdict. In 1904 Dreyfus was granted an official pardon. It was hardly satisfactory because it implied that he was guilty, but Dreyfus, broken by years of forced labor, accepted it. Two years later, justice was done when a court quashed the original verdict as based on error. Yet the end of the case did not dampen the debate, and for decades Dreyfus remained a point of reference for political and ideological allegiances in France. Even as the centenary of the trial was marked in the 1990s, debate over Dreyfus's guilt or innocence flared up again in France.

It is not surprising that the case attracted much public interest at the time, for espionage is a sensational crime. But the Dreyfus case, a legal matter, became the Dreyfus *affair*, a political controversy, because it involved issues of extreme sensitivity, not only in France but also across the rest of Europe. In the first place, espionage meant disloyalty to the nation at a time when nationalist sentiments were running hot. The seriousness of

1

Dreyfus's alleged offense was compounded because he was charged with giving French military information to Germany, a country that not only had defeated France in the 1870–71 Franco-Prussian War, but at the turn of the century was threatening France's political status in Europe. Only the year before Dreyfus was tried, France had entered into a defensive alliance with Russia to protect itself from future German aggression.

Other aspects of the case also bore on the nationalist issue. Dreyfus had been born in Alsace, contested territory that had been annexed by Germany after the Franco-Prussian War. Moreover, Dreyfus was a Jew, charged with espionage at a time of increasing anti-Semitism. Jews, who lived scattered throughout Europe and had no nation-state of their own, were widely thought to be by nature unpatriotic.

Insistence on Dreyfus's innocence called into question the integrity of the military court that had convicted him—this at a time of increasing concern in France about military defense against Germany. Soldiers above all were expected to give up the civil liberties of civilian society and to accept the rougher justice of their peers. (Georges Clemenceau, whose paper had published Zola's article and who was later to become prime minister, is said to have remarked, "Military justice is to justice as military music is to music.") For conservative nationalists, calling into doubt the integrity of the army, the guarantor of France's security, was tantamount to treason. Dreyfus's claim that he was innocent evoked the conflict between individual rights and the national interest that lay at the center of a contemporary debate about society and politics. Many who supported the military court's verdict might well have believed that Dreyfus was guilty, some simply because he was a Jew. Others believed that once Dreyfus was convicted the matter ought to end, even if the verdict was wrong; to overturn the verdict would reflect badly on the army, and it was better for an innocent man to suffer than for the military, representing the nation, to be brought into disrepute. On the other side, those who supported Dreyfus argued not only that he was innocent, but also that individual rights were supreme, no matter what the cost to the army or the nation.

A depiction of the degradation of Alfred Dreyfus, a French artillery officer convicted of spying for Germany.

In many respects the rights and wrongs of Dreyfus's conviction are less important to us than what the affair reveals about political, social, and cultural currents at the turn of the century. Alfred Dreyfus, who only wanted his innocence recognized, found himself at the center of debate over nationhood, national security, the individual's relationship to the state, the status of the military, the impact of social change, and the meaning of ethnicity and race. These were all prominent themes throughout Europe.

People and Nations in 1900

In 1900 Europe's 400 million people were distributed among seventeen significant states and a few minor sovereign territories. While many, like Spain, Portugal, and Switzerland, appear in much the same form on a map of Europe a hundred years later, others do not. The biggest changes occurred in Central and Eastern Europe, regions dominated in 1900 by three great empires that have since fragmented. The German Empire extended from France in the west through northern Poland, as far as present-day Lithuania. To its south and east was Austria-Hungary (also known as the Habsburg Empire), which included modern Austria, Hungary, Slovakia, Slovenia, the Czech Republic, Croatia, and parts of Italy, Romania, Poland, Ukraine, Bosnia, and Serbia. The third was the vast Russian Empire, which stretched east across Siberia as far as the Pacific Ocean and which included, within its European region, not only Russia itself but also parts of Poland, Finland, Lithuania, Latvia, Estonia, Ukraine, Belarus, and Moldova.

Until the late nineteenth century a fourth empire, the Ottoman (or Turkish) Empire, occupied southeastern Europe, but by 1900 the European territory it directly controlled had shrunk to little more than the west side of the Bosporus. In its place had emerged the Balkan States: Greece, Serbia, Bosnia, Montenegro, Romania, and Bulgaria.

In Western and Northern Europe political frontiers in 1900 were much more similar to today's, although the territory now occupied by the Republic of Ireland was part of the United Kingdom, and Norway was part of the kingdom of Sweden. Other states, such as Denmark, Italy, and France, were somewhat smaller in 1900 than today because part of their modern territory was incorporated in neighboring states.

The major changes to the map of Europe during the past hundred years demonstrate a clear trend: the division of larger entities into smaller states. There are twice as many sovereign states in Europe at the end of the twentieth century as there were at the beginning. The process of fragmentation is most evident in the sprawling empires of Austria-Hungary, Germany, Russia, and Turkey, but it also occurred in Sweden and the United Kingdom.

As these changes to the map of Europe suggest, there is nothing natural or sacrosanct about the borders that separate one state from another, although geographical features like rivers and mountain ranges have sometimes been invoked as representing "natural" political boundaries. The French long argued that their country's frontiers were defined by nature as its coastline, the River Rhine, the Alps, and the Pyrenees, which separated it from Spain. But although geography has played an important part in the national defense of many countries, frontiers within Europe have historically been constructed and defined by political elites employing war, diplomacy, and dynastic marriages that united not only ruling families but also the lands that were their personal property.

Europe's frontiers in 1900 were the result of these mechanisms of change. The Habsburg lands of Austria-Hungary were amassed for the most part by advantageous dynastic marriages; the Russian empire was acquired by conquest and annexation; the

MAP 1.1 Europe in 1900.

marriage of the queen of Castile and the king of Aragon united their kingdoms in 1479
to produce Spain; France was pieced together by war, diplomacy, and marriage from numerous kingdoms, principalities, and duchies; Scotland and England were united under one crown in 1707, and Ireland was incorporated into the union in 1801.

Until the nineteenth century (and often after it), state builders gave scant attention
to the aspirations of the populations involved. Nor were there expectations on the part of
the common people, who played no role in state politics, that they ought to be consulted

on who governed the territory in which they lived. When land was conceded by one ruler to another, its inhabitants had as much say in the matter as the cows and pigs with which they shared the land.

The combined effect of shifting borders, resulting from wars, negotiations, and marriages, as well as of large-scale movements of population in response to famines, other disasters, and oppression, was that by the nineteenth century most states included within their frontiers a variety of peoples differing from one another in such respects as language, religion, ethnicity, institutions, history, and customs. One of the most heterogeneous entities was Austria-Hungary, which, in addition to its core populations of ethnic Germans in Austria and Magyars in Hungary, included Poles, Czechs, Slovaks, Romanians, Ukrainians, Croatians, Bosnians, Jews, and Italians. For its part, the 125 million inhabitants of the Russian Empire comprised not only 56 million ethnic Russians but also 22 million Ukrainians, 8 million Poles, 2.5 million Finns, 1.8 million Germans, 1.7 million Lithuanians, and millions from other ethnic populations.

Austria-Hungary and the Russian Empire are widely recognized as having been multiethnic empires, partly because both eventually fractured along ethnic lines, but in fact many other states that appeared homogeneous included a number of more or less distinct ethnic or linguistic groups. In the United Kingdom there were Celtic populations in Wales, Scotland, and Ireland; in France, the Bretons, Basques, and Occitans; in Spain, the Basques and Catalans; in Switzerland, Germans, French, and Italians.

Until the nineteenth century there was little official concern about the presence of different populations within individual states. As a rule, ethnic and linguistic minorities were marginalized within the states they inhabited. Generally they had been conquered or annexed by the dominant group and were treated accordingly, and their different languages and religions could prevent even their elites from participating effectively in state politics. Capital cities and other political centers were generally located in the core territory of the

In 1905 Norway gained independence from Sweden. On June 9 an artillery salute celebrated the raising of the Norwegian flag.

politically and economically dominant population: Vienna in the ethnic German part of Austria, London in England within the United Kingdom, Berlin in Prussia (the dominant region of Germany), and Paris in the Île de France, the core region of the French nation. By law or in practice, minorities in each state were generally treated by the dominant populations as provincial (the word became a moral judgment more than a geographical description) and backward, if not outright inferior.

Nationalism in the Nineteenth Century

During the nineteenth century a new force revolutionized both the way Europeans thought of themselves and the means by which the map of Europe would be drawn: nationalism. One of the several meanings of nationalism is the belief that a specific people constituted a nation in its own right and was intrinsically entitled to establish its own sovereign nation-state. Nationalist ideas came to the fore during the French Revolution (1789–99), and later motivated opposition to the French Empire that Napoleon Bonaparte extended over three-quarters of the continent. In the following decades nationalism became a potent expression of turbulent political, economic, and social forces that underlay the most significant changes in Europe's frontiers up to 1900.

In 1830 Catholic Belgians won national sovereignty and independence from the Protestant Netherlands, and in the same year Greece, which had been part of the Ottoman Empire, became a nation-state. In the 1870s, nationalist revolts in the Balkans against Ottoman control and a war between Russia and Turkey led to a great power agreement (the Treaty of Berlin, 1878) that recognized four new states: Romania, Serbia, and Montenegro became independent, and Bulgaria was granted autonomy within the Ottoman Empire.

In these cases nationalism had a fragmenting effect, breaking down larger political units into smaller national entities, but it could also have the effect of creating larger units. Both Italy and Germany were the result of such processes of national unification. In 1861 Italy was formed from a number of kingdoms, duchies, and other political entities, and in 1870–71 the German Empire (or Reich) was formed from the union of more than thirty political units—duchies, principalities, and city-states. In each case the process of unification was dominated by one state: Prussia in Germany and the Piedmont in Italy.

Various criteria or combinations of criteria could be invoked to define nationality, but the most frequent in the nineteenth century were common language, religion, history, institutions, and culture. Beyond these characteristics a population claiming to be a nation also needed to be able to designate a particular territory as its "homeland," the region where the largest concentration of its people lived.

Establishing criteria for distinguishing one nationality from all others is seldom straightforward. Physical appearance is a poor guide, because differentiating depends upon arbitrary decisions as to which physical traits (such as average height and predominant hair color) are of defining importance; although most Norwegians looked quite different in some respects from most Greeks, there was little difference between most Spaniards, southern French, and Italians. Using these criteria, large nation-states like Germany comprised several physical types.

Linguistic distinctions were often just as blurred, particularly in border regions where people often spoke a blend of languages. Nonetheless, language became a basic criterion of nationality, and many nationalist grievances and policies centered on language, although the fundamental issues at stake were often economic, social, political, and religious. The fact that the majority of people in all parts of Germany spoke essentially the same language was basic to German unification. Czech, Polish, and Finnish nationalisms, among others, were frequently expressed as demands for language rights.

Where nationalism existed in the absence of a common language, efforts were made to create one. In the 1890s there was a revival of Gaelic in Ireland, Norwegian was established as a language distinct from Swedish, and Balkan nationalists worked to forge standard national languages from the many dialects in use. Seven quite distinct Bulgarian grammars were current; Romanians not only spoke various dialects but also employed two different alphabets; Albanians had no commonly accepted script in which to write their language. For its part, Italy unified despite the fact that outside Rome and parts of Tuscany less than 1 percent of Italians knew the Italian language. The first king of unified Italy, Victor Emmanuel II, usually spoke Piedmontese, even with his cabinet ministers, but the first national governments strove to spread the use of Italian.

Like language, a common religion could be an adjunct to nationalism, but it was not essential. Catholicism became inextricably linked to both Polish and Irish nationalism in mainly Orthodox Russia and Protestant United Kingdom, respectively. The fact that the majority of the Romanian population of Transylvania (in Hungary) was Greek Orthodox reinforced their demands for independence from the Magyars, two-thirds of whom were Catholic and one-third Protestant. Italy was almost entirely Catholic, although Italian nationalists were prevented from exploiting this religious uniformity to its fullest extent because the pope declared the church irreconcilably opposed to the unified Italian state when it forcibly annexed papal territory in 1870.

Common economic and social interests also played important roles in nationalism. Most of the states included in the German Empire in 1871 had earlier been members of a customs union that promoted reciprocal commercial ties and increased economic integration. Yet in unified Italy there were vast differences between the urbanizing and industrializing north and the more agrarian, rural, and impoverished south. Nor were there many contacts between the two zones: communications and transportation between them were poor, and the first visit to the south by an Italian prime minister took place only in 1902, forty years after unification.

Nationalists everywhere appealed to history, whether legitimate or bogus, to justify their claims to nationhood. Italian nationalists invoked the unity and grandeur the peninsula had enjoyed as the center of the Roman Empire, a notion that led them to establish the capital in Rome. Polish nationalists dreamed of the reestablishment of their state that had disappeared in 1795, when it was partitioned among Prussia, Austria, and Russia, while Czechs recalled the medieval Bohemian kingdom.

Other aspiring nationalities invented histories and "national" traditions in the nineteenth century, just as states have traditionally promoted versions of their history that best serve their interests. The kilts and tartans associated with Scots were largely sentimentalized creations of this period, and Basque nationalists in Spain coined the name for their region (Euskadi) in the 1890s.

Clearly, there is no one set of criteria that can be applied to all nationalities, and although no nation—existing or aspiring—could be homogeneous in all respects, language, history, and religion were generally key elements. By the late nineteenth century, Germans had the first two in common, Italians the last two, Poles all three. Moreover, the stress on nationality for much of the nineteenth century did not prevent the inclusion of ethnic or linguistic minorities, like the quarter-million French speakers who became citizens of Germany when Alsace and Lorraine were annexed in 1870.

Language, religion, and history could be criteria for a national identity, but what generally motivated nationalism were grievances, fostering the belief that a national group was being oppressed, discriminated against, or could flourish only if allowed to control its own destiny. National populations within larger entities drew on all manner of economic and social grievances. The nationalism of Romanians in Hungary was nurtured by decades of neglect by Budapest, manifested in widespread poverty, high mortality, and low levels of literacy. In Spain, Basque nationalism was not so much resistance to centralizing government (from Madrid) as it was opposition to rapid industrialization and the influx of immigrants from other parts of the country, drawn by new opportunities for employment. In Bilbao, the Basques' largest urban center (where the mortality rate was higher than in any other European city), rapid industrialization had led to the decline of indigenous artisans and forced skilled workers into unskilled jobs.

Nationalism underwent an important shift of emphasis in the late nineteenth century, when greater importance was given to ethnicity—a complex blend of notions about common blood, kinship, and common descent—as the prime defining quality of a national people. The stress on ethnicity reflected the increased influence of ideas about evolution, heredity, and race. Although evolutionary theory as set out by Charles Darwin and others gave an important role to environment, many evolutionary thinkers emphasized heredity alone.

It was not long before scientific arguments were being put forward to demonstrate that inherited or innate differences among nationalities went well beyond appearance, and included emotional and behavioral qualities. Germans were often portrayed as serious, hardworking, and brave, without emotions or a sense of humor. Southern Europeans, in contrast, were depicted as frivolous, afraid of hard work and physical danger, and given to emotional outbursts. Often this line of thinking hardened into racial stereotypes. Although the words *race* and *nationality* were frequently used interchangeably for much of the nineteenth century, race became a narrower biological concept. Social theorists, like Joseph de Gobineau in France and Houston Stewart Chamberlain in Britain and Germany, popularized the notions that there were distinct Nordic-Aryan, Slavic, and Semitic races, each having not only physical but also moral, social, and intellectual characteristics.

Appearance and character were linked in the science of phrenology, which claimed that traits as varied as intelligence, criminality, sexual morality, and insanity could be deduced from the shape and contours of a person's head. The influential Italian anthropologist Cesare Lombroso wrote in 1871 that only what he called "White people" had achieved "the most perfect symmetry of bodily form," recognized "the human right to life, respect for old age, women, and the weak," and had created "true nationalism . . . [and] freedom of thought." But even within the "White people," Lombroso identified what he believed were hereditary physical traits that produced criminality and other behaviors that threatened the social order.

Applied to nationalism, this intellectual trend sharpened perceived distinctions among Europe's various populations. Each ethnic group tried to demonstrate its distinctiveness, which generally took the form of claiming superiority to other groups. (A theory that suggested that the group the theorist belonged to was intellectually or morally inferior would be, for that very reason, suspect.) Defining nationality in terms of ethnicity, however, meant applying more rigid criteria for inclusion in a given nationality. One could not join a nationality defined this way, by learning its language, converting to its religion, or adopting its customs; one could only be born into it.

What made ethnic nationalism so problematic and threatening to political stability was that, especially in central and eastern Europe, ethnic groups did not live in concentrated areas that might easily become ethnically homogeneous nations. Centuries of frontier changes, migrations, and settlement produced a situation where Germans, Magyars,

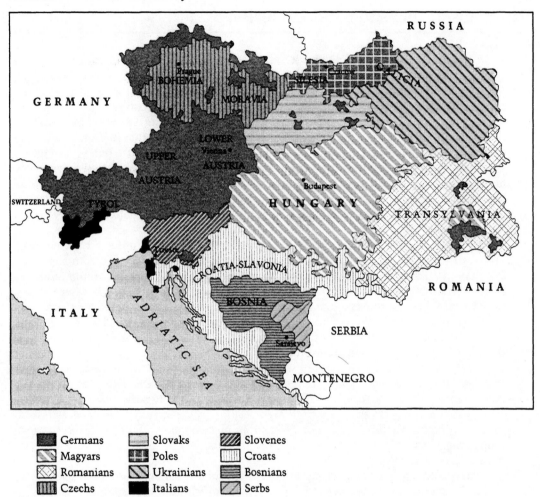

MAP 1.2 Main concentrations of nationalities in Austria-Hungary, 1914.

Russians, Slovaks, Swedes, Poles, and others were scattered across the map. Germans were concentrated in Germany, but they were also a majority in East Prussia, a large minority in Austria, and had significant populations in parts of Hungary and Russia. Romanians lived in Romania, Hungary, Russia, and Serbia, while Poles, who had no country of their own, inhabited Germany, Austria, and Russia.

The redrawing of frontiers to coincide with the distribution of ethnic populations would have required a radical political reorganization of Europe, such as was attempted after the First World War. Even then, individual states would—and did—unavoidably include substantial numbers of other groups. The only way to ensure ethnically homogeneous populations within national borders would be to move masses of people from one state to another. The forcible expulsion of minorities (as distinct from harassing or oppressing them to the point that they left; it is often an unclear distinction) had already begun by 1900; fearing Polish domination of its eastern regions, the German government forced thousands of Poles across the border into Russia in the 1880s and 1890s.

Nationalism: Inclusion and Exclusion

As we have seen, nationalism had both fragmenting and unifying tendencies. By 1900 the Ottoman Empire had experienced the effects of nationalism as Serbs, Bulgarians, Romanians, Montenegrans, and Greeks established their own nation-states. From the late nineteenth century Austria-Hungary was trying to stave off the same process. The two parts of the empire, Austria and Hungary, had reached a "compromise" in 1867 that was itself a result of Magyar national aspirations and resentment at domination by Austria's Germans. Instead of breaking off from the Habsburg Empire, Hungary had agreed to separate but equal status with Austria within the empire. The two states shared an emperor, an army, and the ministries of war, finance, and foreign affairs, but they retained control over internal matters. Each had a parliament, but issues of common importance were discussed by an assembly, to which each state sent delegates, that met alternately in Vienna and Budapest.

In many respects Austro-Hungarian institutions and policies reflected the empire's ethnic diversity. Austria recognized a dozen languages as "official," and minorities like Czechs and Poles had their own political parties. But there were practical limits, and conflicts over language policies broke out continually, especially in Bohemia where almost two-thirds of the inhabitants spoke Czech. German was the language of the Reichsrat (parliament), the ministries in Vienna, the supreme court, the Catholic Church hierarchy, higher education, business, and industry. Germans, 37 percent of the population, held the top positions in all these hierarchies.

In Hungary the core Magyar population, a bare majority of the population in 1900, strove to maintain its status in the empire and resented the fact that German was the language of military command and of the joint Austrian and Hungarian ministries. Within Hungary it attempted to maintain dominant position by measures (called Magyarization) that included the abolition of all non-Hungarian place-names and the compulsory use of Hungarian in schools. Teachers could be dismissed if they or their pupils were deficient in spoken or written Magyar.

Nationalism, particularly among Poles, Finns, and Lithuanians, also made itself felt in czarist Russia in the late nineteenth century. The government became increasingly conscious of ethnic distinctions and began to see ethnic diversity as a source of instability and social disruption. More determined policies of "Russification" were adopted, varying in kind and intensity according to ethnic group. In general Ukrainians and Belorussians were considered part of a greater Russian nation, and their languages declared nonexistent. All printing in Ukrainian (called Little Russian) was forbidden from 1863.

Poles in Russia were targeted for particular attention, especially in terms of language and religion. All schoolchildren were required to use Russian, and storekeepers had to hang signs with Russian characters above or larger than the Polish equivalents. In Warsaw the university was made an instrument of Russification, and a massive Orthodox cathedral was built in the middle of the city, whose Polish inhabitants were overwhelmingly Catholic. Ironically, although Russian was imposed on minorities in the empire (with the exception of the Finns), the language of the Russian imperial court, and of the intimate correspondence between the czar and czarina, was English.

Policies such as Magyarization and Russification had many affinities to attempts by governments in Central and Western Europe to construct national identities within their borders. It may generally be, as E. J. Hobsbawm writes, that "nationalism comes before nations. Nations do not make states and nationalism but the other way round." Nevertheless, nationalism was a sentiment usually confined to political elites in the nineteenth century. Popular nationalism, the sense by the common people that they were part of a nation, often followed, rather than preceded, the establishment of nation-states.

Creating a sense of nationhood was especially important in new states. Italians had to learn to identify with the nation rather than with regions like Calabria or Tuscany. In Italy as elsewhere, education was the favored means of teaching both national loyalty and national language, and there was some success. By 1900 Italian was spoken by one in perhaps every ten Italians, a small proportion but much greater than the one in forty who spoke Italian only thirty years earlier.

Germans also had to learn to be Germans, rather than Saxons or Bavarians. In the 1870s Chancellor Otto von Bismarck, the architect of German unification, confronted the Catholic Church to ensure that education, an important means of social control and national formation, was fully in the hands of the state. For similar reasons, institutions were standardized to rid Germany of internal variations that detracted from the sense of national integrity. A single code of civil law, based on the Prussian model, was imposed on all the constituent states of Germany, even though certain provisions, like liberal divorce, were repugnant to the legal traditions of the states with predominantly Catholic populations. Many of these policies were supported by liberals.

Creating a sense of nationhood was no less important in longer-established states where many inhabitants proved stubbornly resistant to speaking the national language or identifying with the nation at large. In the late nineteenth century the majority of citizens in most departments (the administrative units) in France spoke a language other than French, and loyalties to regions like Brittany and Provence were often as strong as or stronger than allegiance to the French Republic. A policy of "Francisation," intensified during the Third Republic (1871–1940), encouraged them to adopt the language and values of the urban middle class, which included a sense of belonging to the French nation. In Spain the Basque and Catalan populations retained an even stronger attachment to their language and culture. In 1902 the Spanish government decreed penalties against teachers who gave religious instruction in a language other than Spanish.

As nationalism of one sort or another intensified in the late nineteenth century it became clear that two ethnic populations would have difficulty establishing their place in a Europe of ethnically defined nations. Jews and Gypsies, although distinct ethnic groups according to most prevailing definitions (and distinct "races" according to others), had no core European homeland with which to identify. By 1900, Jewish populations were distributed throughout the whole of Europe, the largest single concentration being the 5 million in Russia, most of whom were compelled to live in a region of western Russia and Poland known as the Pale of Settlement. From the 1880s especially, Russian Jews suffered intense discrimination in terms of jobs, education, and place of residence, and were also subjected to periodic pogroms, officially sanctioned outbursts of violence by local people. These conditions contributed to massive emigration: Half a million Jews left Russia between 1880 and 1900, many migrating to Western and Central Europe, others to the United States and elsewhere.

In Central and Western Europe, the migrants joined older established and increasingly assimilated Jewish populations, especially in cities like Vienna and Berlin. By the late nineteenth century Jews outside Eastern Europe had been emancipated from restrictions on education and employment, but anti-Semitism among ordinary people had far from disappeared, and it was particularly strong in Eastern Europe. The Balkan States continued to discriminate against Jews in matters like education and employment despite stipulations in the 1878 Treaty of Berlin that Jews should be granted full civil rights.

Traditional anti-Jewish sentiment was based mainly on religious grounds, Jews being portrayed as not only non-Christian but anti-Christian, and allegedly guilty of killing Christ and of abducting and murdering gentile children for religious rites. But in the later nineteenth century this sentiment was colored by ethnic nationalism and racial thinking. Jews were described as being by nature at odds with the nation-state and even hostile to it; Jews were international or "cosmopolitan" (a word often used as a synonym for "Jewish") who therefore lacked a sense of patriotism. It was no surprise to many French people that Alfred Dreyfus, convicted of betraying France, was a Jew, and as he was stripped of his rank crowds shouted, "Death! Death to the Jew!" The arrival of large numbers of Jewish migrants from the east, more devout than their longer-settled counterparts and distinct in their dress, Yiddish language, appearance, and behavior reinforced and intensified the notion that Jews were outsiders.

Although nationalism was often associated with anti-Semitism, the two were not necessarily linked. The Magyars were better disposed toward the 700,000 Jews in Hungary than to other minorities because Jews learned Hungarian and integrated into Magyar society and politics; a number of Jews were elevated to the Hungarian nobility. Even so, a bill to legalize marriages between Jews and Christians was defeated in the Hungarian parliament in 1883. Given the growing importance attached to nationhood and ethnicity, it is not surprising to find a Jewish nationalist movement at the end of the nineteenth century. Zionism, dedicated to the creation of a Jewish homeland, looked outside an increasingly hostile Europe to Palestine, then part of the Ottoman Empire.

Like Jews, Sinti and Roma (Gypsies) were also excluded from the European nationalist template. Historically an itinerant people with roots outside Europe, probably India (although, as the name "Gypsies" they were given suggests, they were assumed to have originated in Egypt), Sinti and Roma lacked the fundamental prerequisite of nationhood: a homeland. Even though many Sinti and Roma had succumbed to pressure to establish settlements (only 10 percent of the almost 300,000 in Hungary were nomadic by 1900), they were scattered throughout Europe and everywhere lived outside mainstream society. Whether moving about and living off the land, doing odd jobs and selling their handcrafts, or living in settlements where they tended to be self-employed artisans, Sinti and Roma remained on the margins of society and were widely regarded with suspicion and hostility. Just as Jews were believed to sacrifice Christian children, Sinti and Roma were said to steal children. They were sometimes thought to practice cannibalism, were generally believed to be not only poachers, thieves, criminals, and practitioners of witchcraft but also to be prone to spying.

Sinti and Roma were subjected to informal and official harassment throughout Europe, and in the late 1800s many states attempted not only to prevent more Sinti and Roma from entering their territory but also to compel those already there to abandon the itinerant lifestyle that so worried the authorities and respectable citizens. In 1886 Bismarck noted growing complaints "about the mischief caused by bands of Gypsies traveling about the Reich and their increasing molestation of the population."

By 1906 Germany had bilateral agreements "to combat the Gypsy nuisance" with Austria-Hungary, Belgium, Denmark, France, Italy, Luxembourg, the Netherlands, Russia, and Switzerland. Danish authorities deported Sinti and Roma immigrants from the 1870s, and in 1899 the security police in Bavaria created a precedent, soon copied in other parts of Europe, when they opened a central register on Sinti and Roma. Such inordinate concern about such a small population as Sinti and Roma reflected a number of trends at the turn of the century, not least the growing anxiety about the presence of "outsiders" in ethnically defined nation-states.

Nationalism was one of the great political and social traits of Europe in 1900, and it became one of the most powerful forces of the twentieth century. But we should not overstate the breadth or social depth of its appeal at the turn of the century. It was rooted most firmly in the social groups that were active in politics at the state level: the wealthy, the intellectual elites, and the middle classes. The ultra-nationalist, anti-Semitic leagues that developed at the turn of the century in many European countries (see Chapter 2) drew for support almost exclusively from men in the army officer corps, the clergy, the nobility, and the professions.

In 1900 the great mass of Europeans, excluded from formal state politics, still identified less with nations than with the regions and localities where they lived. Many emigrants to the United States before the First World War knew only that they had been inhabitants of a certain community or village, or that they had lived within the jurisdiction of a particular notable or noble. They first learned their European nationality when told by an American immigration officer, and by then they were in the process of giving it up. The sense of identity with a nation was something that was learned, and there was to be no shortage of willing teachers in twentieth-century Europe.

The Governments of Europe

In 1900 many forms of government coexisted in Europe: Autocracies with no system of popular representation contrasted with parliamentary regimes that had narrow- or broad-based male electorates; republics shared frontiers with monarchies; there was a mix of federal and unitary systems. The same variation has existed throughout the twentieth century, during which there have been dramatic fluctuations in almost all countries as empires collapsed and as all manner of democratic, authoritarian, and totalitarian systems have come and gone, some generated within states themselves, others imposed by foreign powers.

With the notable exceptions of the French and Swiss, who lived in republics, Europeans lived under monarchies at the turn of the century. The great empires had emperors at their heads: Kaiser Wilhelm II in Germany, Emperor Franz Joseph in Austria-Hungary, and Czar Nicholas II in Russia. The great ruling houses, like the Habsburgs and Hohenzollerns, traced their lineages back centuries, whereas others were newcomers chosen to head new states, such as Romania and Bulgaria. The dominance of Prussia and Piedmont in their respective nation-states was exemplified by the transformation of the king of Prussia into the emperor (kaiser) of Germany, and the king of Piedmont and Sardinia into the king of Italy. The Serbian monarchy, in contrast, was created from scratch in 1881, when Prince Milan Obrenovic declared himself its first king. In all, some nine new monarchies were created during the nineteenth century (almost all in the second half),[1] a surprising number given the association of the period with increasingly democratic and representative political systems.

Frequently there were family links between the monarchs of the various states, not only because of intermarriage but also because some new monarchs, including those of Belgium, Greece, Romania, and Bulgaria, were drawn from ruling families in Germany's many smaller states and principalities. In the case of Bulgaria a three-man delegation toured Europe for months in 1887 looking for a suitable candidate. Prince Ferdinand of Saxe-Coburg-Gotha finally accepted the offer of Bulgaria's throne, which he occupied for

---

1. Greece, Belgium, Italy, Hungary, Germany, Serbia, Albania, Romania, and Bulgaria.

Old and new dynasties: Kaiser Wilhelm II
(left) with King Ferdinand of Bulgaria,
whose throne dated from the late
nineteenth century.

thirty-one years. Britain's Queen Victoria was grandmother of both the German kaiser and the Russian czar, who were cousins. But family ties were no more a guarantee of harmony at this social level than at any other: At the height of tension between their empires in July 1914, the kaiser wrote to the czar, addressing him as "Nicky" and signing himself "Willy." They were at war within days.

The near ubiquity of monarchs as heads of the European states in 1900 concealed great variations in their powers. Some ruled directly or had the final word in policy decisions. Others were deeply involved in government, but were constrained in their formal authority by constitutions that gave legislative power to representative assemblies. The least restrained was the Russian czar: Nicholas II had a council of ministers and could seek advice wherever he wished, but his was the final decision on any matter of domestic or foreign policy, including declarations of war. In contrast the Reichstag, the lower house of the German legislature, controlled much of the state's budget, even though the kaiser maintained control of the important military budget. Moreover, ministers were answerable to the kaiser, not to the elected members of the Reichstag.

In Austria-Hungary the situation was mixed as a result of the 1867 compromise. Parliaments in Vienna and Budapest had control over domestic policies, but the emperor (to whom ministers were responsible) controlled foreign policy and the military. Within Austria ministers were responsible to the lower house, but they were appointed and dismissed by the emperor, who also summoned and dissolved parliament.

In all cases it is important to make a distinction between the theory and practice of royal government. Although autocrats were in principle able to do as they wished in some or many areas of policy, in practice they had to weigh the consequences of riding roughshod over the expressed will of powerful constituencies that included (depending on the country) large landowners, nobles, industrialists, and peasants. The risks entailed by acting against sectional or public opinion grew as more and more groups demanded influence in the running of their countries.

The representative assemblies that existed in most states had varying powers, and the general tendency was for them to gain power at the expense of monarchs and nobles. Moreover, members of parliaments were increasingly members of political parties representing broad ideological positions or specific constituencies. They ranged from nationalist parties on the right to socialists on the left, with conservatives and liberals occupying the middle ground. In Central and Eastern Europe especially, parties also represented religious, agrarian, and ethnic interests. The Center Party in Germany drew mostly on Catholic support, in Austria there were parties representing Polish, Czech, and ethnic German interests, while in Bulgaria the Agrarian National Union became a powerful force representing peasant farmers.

By 1900 the process of including the mass of adult men in politics was advanced in some countries. France, Spain, Norway, the Netherlands, Bulgaria, Great Britain, and Germany had enfranchised most or all adult males, and progress toward full male enfranchisement was being made elsewhere. There were, however, variations in the definition of adulthood: Men could vote at the age of twenty in Switzerland and twenty-five in Spain. Other qualifications for voting included education, tax status, and property ownership. In Italy men had to be taxpayers or have achieved a modest level of education before they could vote. France, which had almost universal male suffrage (extended in 1884 to the Senate, which had until then been appointive), excluded men in asylums and prisons, and men who had declared bankruptcy in the previous three years. The ability to vote in principle did not always readily translate into practice. In Britain most men were entitled to vote in general elections by 1900, but complex voter registration procedures meant that even by 1911 fewer than 60 per cent of them were actually registered.

In many European states the franchise remained much more restrictive. The exclusion of industrial workers, peasants, and other categories from the franchise in Hungary meant that at the turn of the century only 6 percent of men could vote. Even then many non-Magyars were often effectively disenfranchised as the government rigged elections to minimize the political influence of minorities. In non-Magyar areas, bridges and roads were often declared unsafe during elections to prevent voters from traveling to polling stations, and horses would be put under mandatory veterinary supervision for the same purpose. Those who did vote had to do so openly rather than by secret ballot.

In Russia the absence of a parliamentary system until 1906 precluded the need for any voting qualifications at all. When an assembly (Duma) was established in that year the franchise included all men over twenty-five except for soldiers, nomads, and students, but it was progressively restricted from 1907 on. Even so, the general European trend at the turn of the century was to increase the proportion of men having the vote. The steady but slow progress is exemplified in Italy, where an 1882 reform quadrupled the number of men who could vote, but the two million enfranchised by 1900 still represented less than a quarter of all adult males.

Nowhere in Europe were women able to vote in national elections. There were campaigns throughout the world for women to have equal political rights with men, but by 1900 the only country where women could vote in parliamentary elections was New Zealand, in 1893. A small number of European women, including women property owners in England and Wales from 1894 on, were permitted to vote in local elections. At a more elevated level of political power, most rules of succession in Europe's noble families and to Europe's thrones either excluded women entirely or gave preference to males. The result was a predominance of kings over queens, so that of all the monarchs in Europe in 1900, Queen Victoria of the United Kingdom was the only female.

The gradual male democratization that brought the middle classes increasingly into European political systems necessarily displaced traditional political elites, particularly aristocrats. The proportion of members of formerly noble families in the French Senate plummeted in the 1880s and 1890s, and there was no specific role for Italian nobles in the political institutions of the new nation. In Great Britain, in contrast, the House of Lords continued to play a full role in government; legislation had to pass there as well as through the elected House of Commons. In Great Britain, however, the peerage was increasingly penetrated by families that had made their wealth in industry, as hundreds of peers were created in the late nineteenth century.

This is not to say that nobles lacked political power. As we shall see, despite the revolutions, reforms, and social and economic changes of the late eighteenth and nineteenth centuries, aristocrats retained immense wealth and social prestige that gave them more political influence than their presence in formal institutions might suggest.

The Expansion of the State

Governments of all kinds were extending the purview of their activities by 1900 and concentrating authority in central administrations. From relatively limited activity in matters like public order, foreign policy, administration, and taxation, states began more and more to be involved in issues like education, health, and the regulation of work and morality, with the result that there was an increasing amount of legislation. It was not that these spheres had been unregulated before the nineteenth century, for matters of education, health, and morality had often fallen within the jurisdiction of churches. The difference now was that secular nation-states took control of what we call social policy, and these policies extended further and further.

Across Europe, state or public school systems expanded. During the 1870s, several years' formal education became compulsory in Switzerland, Austria, Great Britain, the Scandinavian countries, Italy, and Belgium; during the 1880s in France and Germany; and in 1900 in the Netherlands. State education systems often served nationalist interests, and they were especially important in imposing linguistic conformity. French children, for example, learned French in school, even if they spoke Breton or Occitan at home.

Thanks largely to the extension of education, there was a general decline of illiteracy throughout Europe, although the ability to read and write depended very much on region, class, and gender. Literacy was higher in the west than the east, among the better-off social classes, and among males because formal education was widely viewed as unnecessary for females. In France, for example, state secondary schools for girls were established in 1880, but unlike boys, whose education was geared toward the qualification that would allow them to enter higher education, girls were given a diploma that was largely honorific.

Estimates of literacy must always be regarded as approximate, for official tests of literacy might require little more than the ability to sign one's name (which can be learned by rote) and read a short passage. More than 85 percent of males in England and France are thought to have been literate by 1900, but in Russia overall literacy remained low; the 1897 census in European Russia produced rates of 36 percent for males and 12 percent for females. The range of literacy rates within a single state is exemplified in Italy where in 1901 the highest rate of combined male and female literacy was 82 percent in Piedmont (up from 58 percent in 1881) and the lowest 21 percent in Calabria in the south (up from 13 percent in 1881). The improvement reflected the spread of schools and implementation of first two, then three, years of compulsory education.

Improved literacy was also produced by education and training in national armies. Europe's permanent military forces at the end of the nineteenth century were larger than ever, and provision was made for reserves that could be mobilized when necessary. The most impressive was the German system (developed by Prussia before unification), which required almost all young men to undergo a short period of military training, ensuring reserve forces that, when mobilized, created an army whose size was quite out of proportion to Germany's population.

In 1900 the major European powers had combined military forces of 3,665,000, a 30 percent increase in twenty years that easily outstripped the growth of population. Yet size alone did not determine effectiveness. The largest single standing force, Russia's 1,162,000 army and navy personnel, was poorly trained and equipped in comparison to the much smaller military forces of Germany (524,000) and Great Britain (545,000). In all cases the trained reserves produced effective forces that were much larger.

Military service exposed young men from different backgrounds to current ideas of nationhood and loyalty; it also instilled discipline and provided rudimentary education, both useful qualities in Europe's industrializing societies. Almost all German soldiers were literate in 1900. Until the 1880s young Italian men who had been conscripted could be kept in the army beyond their initial period of military service if they had not learned to read and write, a provision that produced a high literacy rate among soldiers. Similarly, literacy among Russian army conscripts rose faster than among the population at large, from 21 percent in 1875 to 58 percent in 1905.

Beyond expanding state institutions such as education and the military, governments increasingly intervened in the activities of private enterprise. Legislation to protect the health and safety of workers was passed earlier in the 1800s in Britain, where industrialization occurred first; later in the century it became more widespread. Germany adopted a broad set of social welfare measures in the 1880s, including provisions for pensions and unemployment insurance. The motivation behind these policies was not so much concern for workers as a desire to undermine the attraction of socialist parties and trade unions. In the 1880s Austria followed the German example, regulating work and establishing an eleven-hour working day in factories and a ten-hour day in mines. Similar provisions were enacted in other countries, particularly in Scandinavia.

Private life also fell increasingly within the purview of the state, and in many countries the last decades of the nineteenth century saw the development of state policies dealing with all manner of personal relationships. Marriage, which throughout Europe had fallen within the jurisdiction of churches, was brought increasingly under the control of the state. Secular definitions of marriage and divorce supplanted religious concepts throughout Germany between 1870 and 1900, a federal marriage law was decreed in Switzerland in 1874, and divorce was legalized in France in 1884 over the protests of the church. In Spain, however, the church regained control of marriage in 1875, five years after civil marriage had been decreed.

Sexual behavior was also increasingly regulated. Male homosexuality had long been an offense in church and civil law in various countries, but there had been a tendency in some European law to decriminalize acts regarded as private and not harmful to society. In the late nineteenth century, however, the trend was toward codifying laws against all homosexual acts and making enforcement more effective. Some reforms appeared to reflect a more lenient attitude toward homosexuality, like the abolition of the death penalty for convicted homosexuals in Prussia (1851), England (1861), and Scotland (1889). In fact these extreme penalties were by then not applied, but the fact that they were not even possible penalties made juries more prepared to convict. The German Penal Code of 1875 punished "criminally indecent activity" with up to five years' imprisonment, and in England in 1885 "acts of gross indecency" between men in public or private were made punishable by up to two years' hard labor. The Vagrancy Act of 1898 was also directed in part at male homosexuals and prostitutes. One of the most famous cases was the imprisonment of the writer Oscar Wilde in 1895.

Sexual behavior with a more public face, notably heterosexual prostitution, came increasingly under state regulation. Concerned about what they believed was an epidemic of sexually transmitted diseases and spreading immorality, many governments, including Britain and Germany, subjected female prostitutes to mandatory physical examinations. (Their male clients, who were equally likely to be carriers of disease, were not harassed.) In Paris prostitution was regulated by the Prefect of Police, with whom all prostitutes were required to register. The intention was that prostitutes should work in recognized establishments, preferably in red-light districts, where they could be more easily supervised and subjected to health inspections.

There seemed no limit to the activities the state might consider appropriate for regulation or the services it undertook. They included the provision of mail services, the licensing of motor vehicles, and the issuing of passports. Police forces were expanded to deal with what were believed to be increases in rates of crime and disorder, and most states established secret police services that were often linked to their armies. Newly developed technologies and forensic methods were quickly put to police use, and at the turn of the century Sinti and Roma (Gypsies) were being systematically fingerprinted by the Bavarian police and photographed by the French authorities.

To carry out these widening functions an ever-growing bureaucracy was needed. A desire for efficiency led to public examinations, so that state bureaucracies were increasingly staffed by qualified people—products of the new education systems—rather than by men appointed for reason of birth or influence. The growth of bureaucracies spawned new employment opportunities for both men and women, although a demarcation between "male" and "female" occupations relegated women to lower-paid clerical positions.

By 1900 state bureaucracies were becoming armies in their own right. Germany's civil service more than doubled between the 1880s and 1911, rising from under half a million to 1.2 million, and in the same period Britain's rose eightfold, from 81,000 to 644,000. France's civil service grew more slowly, from 400,000 in 1870 to 600,000 in the first years of the 1900s. In all cases the rate of increase far outstripped population growth. In Austria-Hungary 3 million people, a full 6 percent of the population, were employed by the state in various capacities, so that when their dependents were taken into account a very substantial part of the population, perhaps a quarter, depended directly on the state for its livelihood.

As governments expanded their activities, they increasingly impinged on their citizens. Some of the impact of expanding government was direct and regular, such as the arrival of mail services, increasingly comprehensive military conscription, and the imposition of taxes on income, property, or goods. Income tax, known only in Britain before 1890, had by 1900 been introduced in Germany, Austria, Italy, and Spain.

In order to tax, conscript, and develop social policies of all kinds, states developed increasingly sophisticated statistical offices. Regular national censuses had been conducted in Scandinavia in the eighteenth century but in the nineteenth they were held throughout Europe with varying success. Hungary's first census was taken in 1851, Austria's in 1880, and Russia's in 1897. All provided their governments with a breakdown of the population into ethnic or linguistic groups. Everywhere in Europe states systematically compiled statistics on births, marriages, and deaths, and collected data on such matters as employment, poverty, household structure, and family budgets. They were also able to draw on the fieldwork of a new professional group: social scientists who documented trends in health, work, suicide, sexuality, and other issues. Even granting that many censuses and surveys were incomplete and the analyses tendentious (flaws that persist in their modern counterparts), by 1900 state bureaucracies had far more extensive and reliable information on their citizens than ever before.

In other respects the impact of the state was indirect but nonetheless real. They included fluctuations in prices that resulted from tariffs imposed by governments to protect domestic production from cheaper foreign goods. One effect of spreading state activity that was universal was that people everywhere, even in remote rural areas of their countries, began to be touched by central government, whether in the form of taxes, mail service, or comprehensive conscription. The extension of these and other activities helped to produce a sense of national identity in many places, but a reaction against it in others.

Industry and Agriculture

Political and social developments at the turn of the century were inseparable from economic changes, particularly the progress and impact of industrialization. In all European countries industrial production increased its share of gross national products at the expense of agriculture. Even so, in most of Europe industrialization made slow progress against all manner of economic, social, political, and cultural obstacles. By 1900 there were two Europes in economic terms: an industrializing west and center (albeit with extensive nonindustrial regions) and vast regions in the eastern, northern, and Mediterranean areas that remained almost exclusively agricultural.

The last decades of the nineteenth century saw what is often called the "second industrial revolution." During the first phase of industrialization, from the mid-eighteenth century, mechanization and mass production techniques were gradually applied to traditional products, especially textiles, and output rose to meet the needs of a growing population. Heavy industry, particularly iron production, relied on steam for energy. From the mid-nineteenth century new industries—notably steel, chemicals, and machinery—that employed new technologies grew in importance. Electricity, generated by coal and water, drove more and more of these new industries.

The investment and scale of plant required for mass production meant that heavy industry was generally located in large factories, and as this sector grew it transformed the work experience of industrial laborers. In Germany in 1875, two-thirds of industrial workers worked in small firms of fewer than six employees; by the turn of the century only one-third did. At this time the average factory in London employed more than forty workers. By 1900 heavy industry was well established in Germany, Great Britain, Belgium, and France. Britain and Germany together produced two-thirds of Europe's steel in 1900.

Throughout Europe industry coexisted with agricultural and other economic sectors (notably services), and the degree to which any economy is said to be industrialized depends on the relative importance of industry. Many states not thought of as industrial in 1900 nonetheless included industrialized regions, often where coal provided an immediate source of energy: Slovakia and Bohemia in the Austria-Hungary, Catalonia in Spain, the Donets Basin in Russia, and the industrial triangle bounded by Genoa, Turin, and Milan in northern Italy.

Industry at the turn of the century: women workers in a hat factory in Manchester, England.

Women and men experienced industrialization differently. For one thing, although the older industries like textiles employed many women, the newer heavy industries had no tradition of female employment and tended to hire men almost exclusively. Unions, which became influential in industrial economies only toward the turn of the century, were generally hostile to women workers because their low wages threatened to undercut men's. Reflecting the growing popularity of the notion that women (especially wives) ought to stay home, many men condemned women's work as detrimental to morality and family life. A British chain maker summed it up thus: "I should advocate [women's work-] time should be so limited as neither to interfere with their own health or morals or with our wages."

Although it became a mark of status in industrial economies for a husband to be able to support his wife without her going out to work, few families could afford not to have all their members contributing to the family's survival. As a result, many women worked in domestic situations that combined paid employment with a home environment. By 1900 domestic service was the single largest women's occupation in England, employing 1.4 million women. In Spain more than 300,000 women, a fifth of those in the workforce, were domestic servants.

When hiring practices, their own choice, or their husbands' pride prevented married women from taking employment outside the home, they did domestic work that included taking in lodgers, minding children, and making matches and pins. The connotation of "pin money" as a wife's surplus income to be spent frivolously misrepresents the contribution such work made to a working-class family budget. Because women often worked in hidden areas of employment with irregular hours and no job security, they usually fell outside even the rudimentary safety and health regulations that gave some protection in regular industrial workplaces.

The fact that mass production industry was the leading edge of economic change should not obscure the continuing importance of small-scale and domestic manufacture. In France, where industrialization took place more slowly, half the workers in industry still worked in workshops with fewer than five employees. Throughout Europe small-scale workshops contributed an important, though threatened, proportion of the manufacturing sector.

Agriculture also remained important in most industrial economies, and the food supply had to keep pace with growing populations not immediately involved in its production. Farming employed only 9 percent of British workers by 1900 because Britain imported food from its colonies, but it employed a third of German and French workers and half those in Sweden. The dominance of agriculture elsewhere is shown by the percentages of the labor forces engaged in it: 70 percent in Spain and Hungary, 60 percent in Italy. In European Russia, 84 percent of the 94 million inhabitants in 1897 were peasants.

There was no question whatsoever about the contribution of women to the survival of the peasant family. Women and men had strictly defined tasks, and although women did men's jobs when it was necessary or desirable, the reverse was seldom true. Women's work generally included responsibility for baking, gardening, and any dairy products. There developed a close association between the peasant woman and the family cow, a tangible asset that provided all-important milk for children, as well as perhaps butter. When peasants took to the road, as they were often forced to do during the twentieth century, women refugees frequently took their cows with them.

Just as governments assisted industry by providing investment and tariff protection, so they did agriculture. In the late nineteenth century grain producers across Europe were protected from cheaper foreign imports. A tariff imposed by the French government on imported currants almost ruined Greece's currant producers. There were also continuing difficulties of other kinds. Wine production in France (and later Spain) was badly affected by an outbreak of phylloxera, a blight that attacks grape vines, and vineyards had to be replanted with vines from the United States and Australia.

Despite the obstacles to trade that were thrown up from time to time, commerce within Europe compensated for the unbalanced distribution of industry across the continent. The eastern, northern, and Mediterranean regions provided raw materials and foodstuffs to the more industrialized West. Sweden exported iron ore and timber; Romania grain, timber, and petroleum; and Portugal wine, sardines, cork, and fruit. In return, the industrialized countries exported manufactured products and investment funds for industries and communications. France was an especially active investor in railroad development, financing projects in Russia, Sweden, and Spain.

Despite its apparently limited impact in national or demographic terms, industrialization lay at the heart of the transformation of Europe from the beginning of the twentieth century. Industrialized powers were able to achieve not only economic but also military and political dominance, making economic power more important than such attributes as the size of a country's population and imperial possessions.

Town and Country

The employment opportunities created by industrialization drew an increasing number of peasants, farmers, and agricultural workers from the countryside into urban areas, so that by 1900 most people in Britain and Germany lived in towns and cities. Not all cities were industrial (many were administrative or commercial centers), but in the late nineteenth century most grew as a result of economic development. Only two cities (Paris and London) had more than half a million inhabitants in 1850, but there were seven such cities in 1880, and nineteen in 1900. The number of cities of more than 250,000 grew from thirteen in 1850 to forty-nine in 1900. Within this broad trend, a few cities stood out as giants: London had 6.5 million inhabitants in 1900, Paris 2.7 million, Birmingham 2 million, Vienna 1.7 million, and St. Petersburg 1.3 million. Budapest, Glasgow, Hamburg, Liverpool, and Moscow each had populations of between 700,000 and a million.

The growth of most cities was due as much to migration than to natural population increase (the surplus of births over deaths). This was a period of rapid population growth, and people were simultaneously pushed from rural areas by shrinking opportunities there, and attracted to the cities by employment in the expanding industrial, construction, and service sectors. Cities like Rome, Odessa, Prague, and St. Petersburg would have declined had it not been for migrants.

Growing cities housed an increasingly large working class that presented many social, political, economic, and cultural challenges to the public authorities. To prevent the outbreak of epidemic diseases that had struck European cities in the first half of the century, municipal authorities tried to ensure supplies of fresh water and the disposal of human waste. Large-scale public works programs were started but progress was slow; the sewerage system in Paris was completed only in 1902, and even then only because construction was accelerated after an outbreak of cholera in 1892. Building standards and public health regulations were enforced in French cities only after 1900.

With cities came a distinctly urban culture. Social systems were different and class antagonisms often sharper than in the country, and the different contexts of city life produced varying patterns of social behavior. There was a widespread belief that urban crime rates were higher, something difficult to verify because of inconsistently kept statistics. Urban disorder was often a matter of perception: festivities that appeared innocuous in a small rural community might seem more threatening when they took place in the middle of a city where thousands of people crammed into narrow streets. Middle-class observers, whose comments have often been the basis of our knowledge of social conditions, were fearful of crowds of working people, whom they thought of as "the dangerous classes."

Some social behavior did undoubtedly change: Rates of suicide, marriage breakdown, and divorce were higher in urban centers. In rural areas wives and husbands were economically dependent on each other and effectively locked into marriage. In cities the labor market, despite its fluctuations, gave women and men opportunities that enabled them to strike out on their own. For urban workers, whose main asset was their labor, inheritance was less important than it had been in the country, where family-owned land might be at stake. For these reasons, economic ties between spouses and between parents and children were weaker in cities.

In Eastern and Southern Europe links between town and country remained stronger than in the West, as peasants migrated seasonally to work in industry yet maintained their primary identification with the country. In western and central regions the economic, social, and cultural gaps between town and country grew. Secularization took root in the cities, while religious practices like attending church held up longer in the country. Mutual mistrust between city and country dwellers intensified as people in cities regarded peasants and farmers as ignorant, narrow-minded, and superstitious, while country dwellers looked upon city people as materialistic, atheistic, and immoral.

Not surprisingly, there were symptoms of conflict between town and country. Russian peasants stoned students who came from the cities to disseminate political propaganda. In France middle-class members of cycling clubs who went on weekend rural outings often rode along country lanes at alarming speeds of more than ten miles an hour, frightening livestock and running over poultry. As a result cyclists were often enough shot at by peasants that they eventually took to arming themselves with specially designed cyclists' guns so as to return the fire.

In 1900, despite the progress of urbanization, the overwhelming majority of Europe's people lived in the countryside, but the forces were in place that made isolation less and less viable. The attraction of industrial employment created urban migration; improvements in communications, notably railroads and improved roads for horse-drawn traffic, brought rural areas into closer contact with industrial and urban centers beyond the market towns; and the long arm of the state, its hand holding a letter, a tax demand, or a census form, stretched further and further into the countryside.

Peasants, Workers, Bourgeois, and Nobles

Although the great majority of Europeans lived in rural areas and derived their livelihoods from agriculture in 1900, the proportion of the population that derived its living directly from the land was slowly declining while other groups, especially industrial workers and the middle classes, were increasing.

Throughout most of Europe, peasants either were landless or owned or leased insufficient land to provide for their own needs. They survived by working for large landowners. In southern Italy and Spain, for example, land was generally divided into large estates called *latifundia*. In the southern Spanish province of Andalusia, two-thirds of the land was owned by 2 percent of the population. The Italian census of 1881 showed that for every 1,000 people there were only 59 peasant landowners and another 46 sharecroppers: The great bulk of people were simple laborers with no security of employment and a low standard of living. Similarly in Hungary half the arable land was owned by 3,000 landowners, while three-quarters of peasants owned very small plots.

In Russia the peasants—more than four-fifths of the population at the turn of the century—were scarcely better off. In 1861 Russian serfs had been emancipated from ownership by the state or individuals, but the allotments they were provided with were not enough for survival. By 1900 more than half the peasants could not support themselves from the land they owned. The situation was worst in European Russia, which suffered periodic famines, including a catastrophic one in 1891, and a mortality rate twice that of contemporary England. The situation was eased somewhat only by migration: 5 million peasants left European Russia for Siberia by 1900.

In much of Europe the conditions of peasants deteriorated largely because of population growth. Rural overpopulation, the presence of too many people in the countryside for the work available, was eased somewhat by large-scale emigration outside Europe (see below) and by migration to industrial centers, but the effects of the latter were negligible in many parts of Eastern Europe where industrialization took place very slowly.

The plots available to those who stayed on the land became smaller with the passing of each generation because inheritance rules usually divided land among all the sons rather than passing it on intact to one child. (Women were generally excluded from inheritance.) This process was more severe in Eastern Europe where high birth rates produced more heirs. By 1900 a third to half of Hungary's rural population had no land and survived as day-laborers or seasonal workers. The abundance of labor enabled employers in most regions to pay low wages: In parts of southern Spain average wages for unskilled rural workers in 1900 were a fifth lower than they had been a hundred years earlier.

The decline of living conditions in many parts of rural Europe produced social conflict. Impoverishment could be translated into resentments against other ethnic groups, and in some places underlay an increase in anti-Semitism. Peasant discontent helped inspire the great Balkan revolts against Turkish rule in the 1870s. The departure of hundreds of thousands of Turkish-speaking Muslims from Bulgaria in the 1880s and 1890s made vast amounts of land—perhaps a quarter of the country's arable land—available for purchase. For this reason wage-laborers constituted only 2 percent of Bulgaria's peasants at the turn of the century, a much lower proportion than elsewhere in Eastern and Southern Europe.

Pressures of rural overpopulation helped draw workers off the land into industrial centers, and in countries as diverse as France and Russia agricultural laborers were transformed into industrial workers. Many made a permanent move, altering the character of the society they left and the society they entered. In Bohemia the mass migration of Czech peasants into Prague reduced its German majority to a minority. Everywhere, the industrial labor market attracted younger and single people in particular. About half the migrants to the industrial region of Düsseldorf, Germany, in the 1880s were single men and women, the rest being married couples or larger family groups. Migration altered the character and age structure of rural society and broke family traditions of land-tenure and residence.

Many peasants, however, did not migrate permanently to Europe's towns and cities as much as treat them as another location of seasonal work, turning to factory employment between the peak agricultural labor periods at sowing and harvest in the spring and the fall. These workers did not seek new lives in the city but worked there to raise funds in order to purchase land or otherwise improve their lives in the country. An estimated 50 percent of migrants to Düsseldorf left within two years.

Although many women and men left rural Europe to escape unemployment, hardship, and poverty, the living conditions of most industrial workers were often little better than those experienced by peasants or agricultural workers. Large-scale migration placed intolerable burdens on housing and other facilities and services. Workers tended to live in overcrowded inner-city and suburban tenement buildings within walking distance of their places of work. Facilities were limited, particularly in the newer industrial cities where floods of migrants had swamped existing housing stocks. The situation in rapidly industrializing parts of Germany was especially critical. In 1895 Berlin had 25,000 one-room apartments, each housing six or more people. Another 80,000 single men and women were "sleeping lodgers" who rented a bed in someone else's apartment but had no access to the place during the day, when the same bed (and bedding) was used by someone else. Damp apartments without running water fostered the spread of tuberculosis, influenza, and pneumonia.

There were attempts in some countries to provide good quality, low-cost housing for workers, but they rarely succeeded in meeting the demand. Mining companies in parts of Spain, motivated by the desire for an efficient and docile workforce, initiated housing projects as a way of keeping workers out of taverns where they were exposed to the twin dangers of alcohol and socialism. Completed housing projects rarely met the needs of a tenth of their workers.

Despite a widespread notion that rural life was better than life in the city, the conditions experienced by peasants were also frequently abysmal. Peasants often lived in mud huts, on poor diets, and with polluted water supplies. Garbage and human refuse were dumped near habitations. In southern Italy many communities disposed of their dead in mass graves, where the slowly decomposing corpses were breeding grounds for disease. Cholera, typhoid, scarlet fever, and smallpox ravaged rural populations as they did urban. In southern

Italy malaria was thought to be the cause of 20 to 30 percent of all deaths at the end of the nineteenth century. Conditions in industrial work were also poor. Not only were the safety standards set by governments frequently inadequate but they also were not effectively enforced. Hours of work were long, although they had improved from the seventy-two-hour workweeks (six twelve-hour days) normal in midcentury and by 1900 the sixty-hour week was common in Western European factories. But much production, particularly that carried out by women, took place in small workshops and in domestic settings where hours of work were far longer, often running to eighty or ninety a week. In addition to their industrial workweek, women's labor was extended by household work and child care.

One effect of the growth of the industrial working class was the spread of trade unions whose aim was to protect the wages and working conditions of their members, but in 1900 unions were still quite rudimentary in most of Europe. They were generally confined to a few skilled craft industries (like printing and construction) in the 1880s, and tended to concentrate on mutual assistance programs to help their members and their families in case of accident, illness, or death. During the 1880s industrial workers like miners began to organize, and there were strikes in several countries.

By 1900 unions had really made progress only in Great Britain, where there were 2 million members. Germany, where antisocialist laws prevented unions from organizing effectively until 1890, had 700,000 union members, France had only 250,000, and Hungary a mere 40,000. National unions appeared in Scandinavia in the 1880s and trade union federations in 1898–99. Women, excluded from many jobs in skilled and heavy work, comprised only a small proportion of union members anywhere—5 percent of unionized workers in France in 1900, and 6.5 percent in Britain. There were great variations in salaries between skilled workers, whose incomes rose, and the unskilled whose wages remained depressed by the ready availability of labor.

If the growth of a mass working class can be thought of as a main product of industrialization, so was the expansion of the middle class or bourgeoisie. The middle class (or classes, as some historians prefer) spanned a wide range of occupations, status, income levels, and lifestyles. They included professionals (such as lawyers, doctors, teachers), state employees in the civil and military services, and people in business from small retailers to bankers and merchants. All these categories grew during the nineteenth century, to the point that it is sometimes referred to as "the bourgeois century."

The middle class expanded in tandem with industrialization and the increased activity of centralized states. The growth of the state demanded an increasing number of clerks, secretaries, department heads, inspectors, and functionaries of all kinds. Similarly increased military forces required more officers as well as civilian support staff. The networks of schools, hospitals, prisons, asylums, and other institutions now provided by the state demanded administrative and professional staff at all levels. There were 2,900 secondary school teachers in Austria in 1870, and 6,400 in 1900, while in the Netherlands the figures were 4,800 and 13,100 respectively.

It is the commercial middle class that is often portrayed as the group behind Europe's economic transformation because of its contributions of investment and entrepreneurial skills. We should, however, note the critical contributions by the state in terms of investment in infrastructure like railroads and the erection of tariffs to protect national industries. Bourgeois entrepreneurs came from the upper levels of the middle class, which are often difficult to distinguish from the older landed elite groups with which they frequently intermarried.

At the lower end of the middle class, sometimes shading into the working class, lay artisans, small-scale skilled workers whose activities were progressively taken over by

mass-producing enterprises that could produce cheaper goods. Likewise, small-scale retailers were adversely affected by the development of department stores in many parts
of Western and Central Europe. The livelihoods and traditions of these lower-middle-
class groups were threatened with extinction by economic developments, and they
tended to be politically reactionary, opposed to change and favoring a return to a society that offered them security. The fact that ownership of many of the prominent new
enterprises—like department stores in France and Germany—was dominated by Jews,
tended to reinforce anti-Semitism within the lower middle class.

One of the effects of the growth of the middle class was the expansion of the consumer market. The precursors of late-twentieth-century "yuppies" wanted housing, clothing, furniture, and food that reflected their status. Magazines aimed at women consumers,
in particular, attempted to sell all the accoutrements necessary for domestic bliss. The new
department stores catered to the new trends and shopping was transformed from a necessary and boring chore to a respectable and enjoyable activity for women.

Middle-class couples tended to have smaller families so that their financial resources
would provide them with a higher standard of living and their children with a good education. Similarly, families aspiring to middle class status reduced their family size so as to
increase disposable income for purposes other than simple survival. These ambitions contributed to the decline of fertility rates around the turn of the century, which is discussed
further below.

Yet despite the growth of the middle classes, nobles in most countries continued to
play an important role in all aspects of the new society that only *appeared* to render them
redundant. Nobles frequently owned large estates and fortunes that enabled them to invest in industrial development, although in some places, like France and Russia, there was
a residual belief that it was unworthy for a noble to be involved in trade. Others were unable to play an active economic role: Many old landed noble families in Hungary, for example, failed to adapt to peasant emancipation, fell deeply into debt, and lost all or part
of their estates. Even so, British, Spanish, and other nobilities actively participated in new
economic enterprises. Many of these nobles, it is true, were drawn from the industrial and
commercial elites and elevated to the nobility in the late nineteenth century: This was true
of hundreds of men in Britain. But older-established nobles also took advantage of opportunities to make money from new economic opportunities. A Spanish example is the
Marquis de Argueso, whose family traced its nobility back to the fifteenth century, and
who at the turn of the century had investments in railroads, sugar refining, cork production, explosives, and electricity.

Nobles also continued to play important roles in government and the military despite
the progress of democratization. The British House of Lords was almost entirely the preserve of hereditary nobles (bishops of the Church of England also sat there), and nobles
accounted for about a third of Spain's upper chamber, the Senate. As for the military, in
Germany, 60 percent of all colonels and 70 percent of the general staff were members of
noble families in 1900. Participation in new state structures could even be a matter of survival for nobles. Middle- and lower-ranking nobles in Hungary so often turned for employment to the growing state bureaucracy that it has been referred to as a make-work
project for the nobility. They occupied about half the posts in Hungary's state ministries
and three-quarters of those in county administrations.

Class is not the only way the European population can be divided. Another is into the
broad economic categories of rich, middling, and poor—categories that often crossed
class lines. If we define the poor as those without the resources to eat adequately and keep
warm, then poverty was very likely the experience of half or more of Europe's population

in 1900. Even in England, which had the highest overall standard of living in Europe, and where general prosperity contributed to the expansion of the economy, a third of the population of large cities like York and London were chronically hungry. In Germany a third of family households were destitute, and for those who could just provide for themselves bread and potatoes were the main elements in the diet, as they had been for centuries. In Italy the radical politician Agostino Bertani divided his fellow citizens into two groups: those, the better-off, who ate white bread and those who ate black. Few Italian peasants ever ate meat, and the great majority lived on rice, beans, bread, and pasta.

The widespread poverty in European populations manifested itself in poor health. Vitamin deficiencies meant that anemia and rickets were common in children, while particular occupations produced specific health problems. Miners were notable for the wide range of bronchial maladies they suffered. Of 3,672 Sicilian sulfur miners drafted for military service in the early 1880s, only 203 (6 percent) were judged fit enough to serve.

Poverty had other effects. Women who were unemployed or underemployed frequently turned to prostitution, which was commonly thought to be increasing as the nineteenth century ended. Although middle-class reformers viewed prostitution from a moral perspective and treated prostitutes as "fallen women," there was growing recognition of the effects of economic conditions on social behavior. In the 1890s an Austrian feminist explained that young factory workers took to prostitution because of poor conditions, long hours, and low wages at work.

Population Growth and Patterns of Migration

Industrialization and urbanization and their effects were experienced unevenly across Europe, but one fundamental trend was shared more generally: demographic growth. From the mid-eighteenth century the European population began to increase steadily and in the nineteenth century rates of growth accelerated (see Figure 1.1). The population of Great Britain almost quadrupled, from 10 to 37 million between 1800 and 1900, and Germany's almost tripled, rising from 20 to 56 million in the same period. This was a trend shared by nonindustrial states like Sweden, Italy, and Spain, whose populations doubled during the century.

There were two principal exceptions. Ireland's population was reduced dramatically by a terrible potato famine in the late 1840s that not only resulted in high mortality rates from starvation and disease but also led hundreds of thousands to migrate. By 1900 Ireland's population of 4.5 million was little more than half the 8.2 million enumerated in the 1841 census. France, too, failed to participate in the rapid growth of Europe's population. Although the number of its inhabitants increased by about 50 percent during the first half of the century, it stagnated thereafter, rising by less than 5 percent between the mid-1870s (36.9 million) and 1900 (38.5 million), producing an increase during the 1800s of only 40 percent.

These cases apart, Europe's population increased even more dramatically than census figures suggest, for in the last decades of the century millions of Europeans left their native countries, and therefore do not appear in the statistics of resident population. Eighteen million Europeans emigrated between 1871 and 1900, including almost 650,000 from Sweden and 750,000 from Austria-Hungary. These substantial figures were overshadowed by the 2.5 million Germans, 5 million Italians, and 7 million British who emigrated. In the year 1900 alone, one in every hundred Italians emigrated.

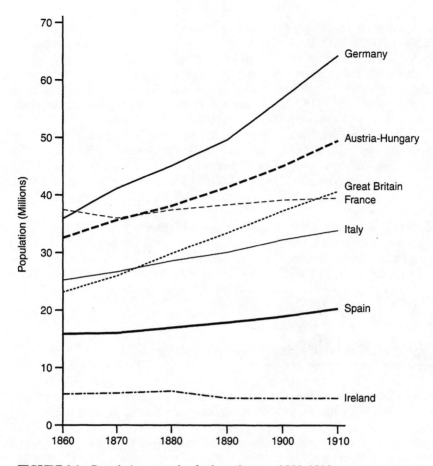

FIGURE 1.1 Population growth of selected states, 1860–1910.

Source: Data from B. R. Mitchell, *International Historical Statistics: Europe, 1750–1988*
(London: Macmillan, 1992), pp. 3–8.

That such massive numbers of people, individuals and family groups alike, should
have uprooted themselves and left for such far-off destinations as the United States,
Canada, Argentina, Australia, and New Zealand is testimony to the impact of the changes
throughout Europe in this period. Leaving family, home, and community at this time was
more definitive than today, for most of the emigrants who went overseas would never
again see or speak to the family and friends they left behind. In some cases emigration was
staggered, a man leaving first, then sending for his wife or having his family choose a local woman to be his wife and send her to him. The migration of many married men produced a larger than usual proportion of single-parent households in Europe. In Sweden,
women whose husbands had migrated to the United States were referred to as "America
widows," and in Stockholm at the turn of the century a third of all households were
headed by women.

Demographic and economic changes within Europe were critical to the mass exodus.
Overpopulation and unemployment in rural areas was a major reason, particularly in
Eastern Europe where industrialization was limited and could not absorb the excess rural

population. An economic depression that increased unemployment in Europe from the 1880s intensified emigration. It was not the very poorest who emigrated, however, but those who could afford to leave. They also tended to be landless laborers, whose attachment to locality was weaker than land-holding peasants, although Italian peasant families sometimes sent sons abroad to avoid having to divide family land among too many children. The aftermath of famine in Ireland led to massive emigration, more than three-quarters of it to the United States. It is instructive that France, which was not suffering overpopulation, produced a disproportionately small share of Europe's migrants.

Only in one case was there mass migration *into* Europe in this period, and that was Spain. Large numbers of Spaniards had emigrated in the mid-1890s, and the 165,000 who left in 1895 and 1896 alone represented almost 1 percent of the country's population. Between 1898 and 1899, however, Spain received 140,000 immigrants as its nationals returned from Algeria and from former colonies annexed by the United States following the Spanish-American War.

There were significant population movements within Europe, not only in the form of migration to the cities but also between countries. In most cases the motivation was economic—the draw of employment opportunities. By 1900 some 80,000 Spaniards had found work in France, where falling fertility had produced chronic labor shortages. Many of the emigrants from Eastern Europe were members of minority populations, like Jews, who sought a more secure life elsewhere. Jews had no place in the schemes of nationalist movements, and anti-Semitism increased in the last decades of the century. After pogroms and official discrimination against Jews intensified in Russia in the 1880s, an average of 20,000

Mass emigration from Europe: emigrants on board a ship en route to the United States.

Jews a year emigrated from the Russian Empire. In 1900, 408 of every thousand emigrants from Russia were Jews, many leaving illegally. Elsewhere, like Galicia in eastern Austria, Jewish emigration was linked less to persecution than to unemployment and poverty.

The migration of tens of millions of people makes Europe's population growth that much more startling, for the continent lost not only the migrants themselves but also their reproductive potential. Many migrants were young men and women and families, all vital to increasing overall population numbers, and this concerned many governments and social commentators. Rather than being alarmed at the social effects of urban overcrowding, they insisted that the security and strength of their states depended on their having robust populations that would provide large workforces and military forces. But most of Europe's populations increased rapidly despite the loss of so many migrants.

Population growth is usually achieved by immigration, a greater number of births than deaths, or a combination of these variables. In the case of nineteenth-century Europe there was far more emigration than immigration, and a tendency of both birth rates and death rates to decline. Because population rose in regions that were economically, socially, and culturally diverse, we should not expect to discover a single explanation to apply to the whole of Europe, but there were common features. Infant mortality—the death of children before the age of one—fell in many countries. In the eighteenth century infant mortality rates of 250 per thousand (one death in every four children born alive) were not uncommon, and even in the 1890s rates above 200 per thousand were still prevalent in Austria-Hungary, Russia, Romania, and Germany. But with the exception of Russia, they had declined during the century. In Norway the rate fell to less than 100 almost every year after 1878, while Sweden's hovered around 100 in the 1890s.

Improved survival rates of infants contributed to a decline in general mortality rates (the number of deaths per thousand population), as Figure 1.2 shows. In Great Britain mortality rates declined from over 20 deaths per thousand in the 1850s to 17 or 18 in the 1890s, in Sweden from over 20 to 15 or 16, in Germany from 25–28 to 20–24. In Austria rates above 30 per thousand were common before the 1860s, but by the 1890s they had settled in the 25 to 28 range. While they appear small, these changes could make a big difference to population numbers: the decline from 30 deaths per thousand in the early 1860s to 23 per thousand at the end of the century in Italy meant that by 1900 an additional 225,000 people were surviving each year.

Declining mortality rates produced an increase in life expectancy, but there were wide variations throughout Europe. Northern Europeans could expect to live longest: to 57 or 58 years in Norway, Denmark, and Sweden, and over 50 years in England and Wales, the Netherlands, Ireland, Switzerland, and France. At the lower end of the scale, where life expectancy was at or under 40 years, were Russia, Austria, Hungary, Bulgaria, and Spain. Everywhere, the average life expectancy was so low because of the substantial number of deaths of infants, and many people lived well beyond the average. In Austria in 1900, for example, a fifth of all males were 45 or older, even though life expectancy at birth was only about 40 years.

Had the decline in mortality been matched by a decline in fertility rates (the number of births per thousand population in a year) the European population would not have increased as it did. But fertility rates remained high for much of the century, over 30 per thousand in Great Britain, Norway, and Austria, over 40 per thousand in Russia and Hungary. The difference between these birth rates and the prevailing death rates produced the natural increase in each country's population. Around the turn of the century, however, birth rates began to fall almost everywhere, starting a fertility decline that continued in most countries throughout the twentieth century. British couples who married

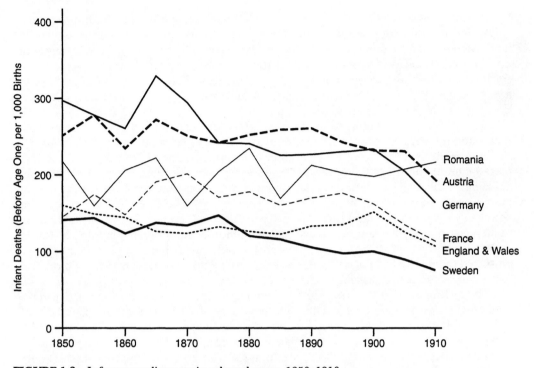

FIGURE 1.2 Infant mortality rates in selected states, 1850–1910.

Source: Data from B. R. Mitchell, *International Historical Statistics: Europe, 1750–1988*
(London: Macmillan, 1992), pp 116–23.

in the 1860s had on average 6.2 children, whereas those who married in the 1890s had
only 4.1. By the 1960s they would have only two.

The Family and Gender

It is easier to describe the trends in mortality and fertility than to explain them. Death
rates fell because of the decline of infectious diseases and improvements in diets, sanitation, and health care. Changes in birth rates—notably the decline in fertility from the
1870s on—require us to look at marriage and the family. The frequency of births outside
marriage (illegitimacy) rose during the nineteenth century, but seldom accounted for
more than a tenth of all children born. In England and Wales it ranged between 4 and 5
percent of all births, in France and Germany between 7 and 9 percent, in Sweden between
10 and 11 percent, and in Austria 13 and 15 percent. Births outside marriage tended to
be more common in cities, with their mass of young, mobile workers, than in rural areas.
Unmarried men and women entered sexual relationships, as they had historically done,
but instead of marrying when the woman became pregnant, as was the custom in settled
rural communities, men were able to escape their responsibilities by leaving town or simply refusing to marry. The frequency of such births depended upon such factors as regional traditions of tolerance and the use of birth control.

For the most part, children were born within marriage, and having children was a decision that married couples made (implicitly or explicitly) in the context of their economic and social environment. To this extent the fertility decline means that throughout Europe couples decided to limit the size of their families. The precise methods varied according to place, class, and gender. In Ireland, which had Europe's lowest birth rate (and a very low marriage rate), births were limited by delaying marriage, thus reducing the period during which couples could have children.

Within marriage the most common methods of limiting family size were sexual abstinence and the practice of coitus interruptus (the male withdrawing before ejaculation), but both techniques required physical discipline and the latter (and often the former) placed men in control of the process. The exception was the diaphragm, which became available in the 1880s and gave women some control over conception. It seems that in most cases the initiative to limit family size came from women, even if the realities of power in marriage prevented them from having as much control as they should. Many women resorted to abortion: It was the most common form of family planning in Russia at the turn of the century, and was so common in Germany (where some contemporaries estimated there were 300,000 abortions a year) that it was referred to by some doctors and social commentators as an epidemic.

The technique of vulcanizing rubber (making it more elastic) allowed the mass production of latex condoms by the 1860s, but there were obstacles to their use. Condoms in various natural forms (such as sheep's intestines) had been used for centuries, but for the prevention of venereal disease rather than as a means of contraception. Long associated with prostitutes, who often used them, condoms suffered from what might be called a negative image. Even when cultural reservations were overcome, condoms were expensive and beyond the reach of many people. In Germany they cost five marks a dozen in 1900, about a half-day's pay for a skilled male worker.

Other obstacles to limiting family size included the opposition of states (which wanted large populations), and churches (Protestant and Catholic alike), which were universally opposed to contraception and abortion. Some Catholic priests in Italy observed the old canon law and permitted abortion within forty days of conception, but they were few. Equally small was the number of doctors anywhere who were prepared to provide information or assistance on any kind of family limitation. Women, who have historically been more favorable than men to birth control, were only just beginning to enter the medical profession in some countries in 1900.

Despite these obstacles, couples throughout much of Europe began to have fewer children than their parents and grandparents had produced. They did so for reasons like the costs and benefits of children. Children took on a different meaning and value as economies shifted from agriculture to industry, and as rural regions began to experience population surpluses. In agrarian Europe work was generally performed by families as a whole, each member of the family contributing according to her or his age and sex. Children worked from young ages, learning to perform the tasks deemed appropriate to them: boys to work the fields, girls to cook, do laundry, and look after children, as well as carry out tasks on the farm. The contribution of each enabled the family to survive, and it was important to have enough children so that even after high infant mortality rates had taken their toll, there would be enough members to do the necessary work.

By the second half of the nineteenth century industrial employment was becoming more common and agrarian societies were experiencing the overpopulation that contributed to mass migrations—to nearby cities, other European states, or across the world.

Many states introduced labor laws restricting the work children and women could do and the hours they could work, and children were increasingly required to attend school. The need for, and desirability of, large families diminished. Among working-class couples there was a delay of almost five years between marriage and the birth of the first child; the delay was two and a half years in the middle classes.

In France, where mortality rates fell from the 1820s and fertility rates from the 1830s—a good fifty years earlier than elsewhere in Europe—inheritance might have played a part: The law required land to be divided among all children, and peasants might have limited the number of offspring so as to avoid excessive subdividing of family property at each generation.

Each couple or each woman—whether from the industrial working class of Moscow, the middle class of Vienna, or the peasantry of Italy—made an individual decision based on its specific economic circumstances and taking heed of religious, social, and cultural considerations. There was a wide variety of responses, not only between regions of Europe, but also within individual communities. The fertility decline that began in the 1870s lay at the intersection of individual, familial, communal, and broad systemic variables, and it played an important role in the political and social history of the twentieth century.

Other aspects of family behavior changed, too. In northwestern Europe the majority of people spent most of their lives in nuclear family households, typically consisting of parents and their children. Extended family households, which included kin like grandparents, cousins, aunts, and uncles, were more common in Southern and Eastern Europe, although even there they were generally only a small minority of households. Migration patterns often modified households because men and women who migrated to towns and cities frequently lived with relatives who had moved earlier. This led to an increase in extended family households in industrial centers of England and elsewhere during the periods of intense urban migration. Economic changes also undermined the *zadruga*, the extended-kin community that was found in parts of the Balkans.

Industrialization and urbanization fragmented the family economy characteristic of preindustrial families. Instead of working as a unit in the interests of collective survival, family members began to be employed as individuals earning their own wages. To the extent that they were able to work, children and women, who had had less freedom of action in the preindustrial society, began to gain a measure of financial independence. We should not exaggerate the liberating effects of employment, however, for work was hard, days were long, and the wages paid children and women were poor. At best women earned two-thirds an adult male wage. In Paris in the early 1890s average wages were 6.15 francs for men and 3.00 francs for women; in the provinces they were 3.90 and 2.10 francs, respectively.

In Western Europe legal changes reflected the new economic patterns. From the 1870s married women, traditionally under the control of their husbands, were gradually given the right to own property and to keep their wages. A series of laws in England between 1870 and 1882 recognized women's property rights, while in France married women were permitted to have their own savings accounts in banks (1881) and control their own property (1893), although not until 1907 were they given control over their own wages. Norwegian women gained control over their personal incomes in 1888.

Laws also began to be enacted to limit the right of husbands to beat their wives. Traditionally European law permitted a married man the power of "moderate correction" over his wife: the right to correct (or punish) her physically as long as it was done for good reason and "moderately." That is, he could not beat her randomly, nor could he beat her with a deadly weapon or so severely that he drew blood. Laws to punish violence against women passed in several Western European states reflected the spread of the "cult of femininity," the notion that women were fragile and innocent, and needed to be protected.

It was one thing to pass such laws, another to have them observed. Domestic violence against women continued because men's attitudes toward women were unchanged and because, despite increasing state regulation, many aspects of married life were considered private. The courts were reluctant to intervene in domestic conflicts, even though women generally suffered by their reluctance. There were also class biases in attitudes toward women. Women of the better-off classes were thought to be more in need of protection than working-class or peasant women. The latter were believed to be inured, by the very circumstances of hardship and labor, to physical and verbal abuse.

But expectations of behavior in marriage rose in this period, a trend reflected in legal reforms that, depending on the country, legalized divorce for the first time, liberalized existing divorce laws, or provided other remedies for unhappily married couples. Divorce had been available for centuries in all European states that were officially Protestant (notably northern Germany, the Scandinavian states, the Netherlands, Switzerland, and Scotland). The first English divorce law came into effect in 1858; France, where divorce had been legalized during the French Revolution, then abolished in 1816, legalized it again in 1884; divorce was extended to all states of the German Empire (in restrictive form in the mainly Catholic regions) in 1875, before being standardized in 1900. In Catholic Spain divorce remained unavailable, but legal separation was made easier. Attempts to legalize divorce in Italy provoked the clergy to organize huge petitions opposing legal reform; the 1902 petition contained 3.5 million signatures.

Where divorce was permitted, divorce rates began to rise in the late nineteenth century, although they were very low compared with those a hundred years later. There were only 590 divorces in England a year at the turn of the century, but that was almost three times the number in the early 1870s. In France the annual number of divorces doubled between the legalization of divorce in 1884 and the turn of the century. European divorce and separation rates were far lower than in the United States, which had already established itself as the world leader in this respect.

More liberal divorce laws were only one reason for rising divorce rates, however. More divorces were sought by women than men, and the rise in divorce reflected expanding opportunities for women outside marriage. There were increasing opportunities for employment in industry, retail, and professions like nursing and teaching. Women had more legal rights, including power over their property and incomes and rights to have custody of their children; before the nineteenth century, fathers had sole legal rights over children. Social attitudes, although far from favorable to divorce, also began to change. Moreover, as the state took over the regulation of marriage, the hostility of the churches to separation and divorce mattered less and less.

Changes in the family lay at the heart of a complex set of social, economic, and political shifts that were under way at the beginning of the nineteenth century. They had far-reaching effects that included a slow-down in population growth and a tendency for European populations to age as older age groups became proportionally more significant. In France, where the birth rate was especially low, women and men aged 60 years or more made up 13 percent of the population by 1900, compared with only 10 percent in 1850. Such changes, documented by state statisticians and academic researchers, alarmed governments and social commentators to whom they represented a weakening of labor and military strength.

Churches and Religion

The expansion of state activities was often at the expense of the churches that had for centuries had overriding influence in areas like social welfare, education, the family, and sexuality. In the nineteenth century, education was frequently a battleground between state and church, as each sought to have prime influence over young minds and bodies. In France the church fought a fierce rearguard battle in the 1880s when a national system of secular schools was established, and in Italy the major educational debate was not over the high level of illiteracy but religious instruction; primary education was the responsibility of local authorities, and Catholics fought local elections in order to ensure that curricula included religious instruction. There was a major confrontation (known as the *Kulturkampf* or Culture Struggle) between state and church in Germany in the 1870s, as the state (supported by liberals) asserted primacy over education.

The extension of state regulation over family relations and sexuality was also frequently at the expense of churches that had a long tradition of overseeing public and private morals. In 1857 the Church of England's control over marital separations and morals offenses was taken over by the state. Under the terms of an 1855 concordat, jurisdiction over marriage in Austria was transferred to the Catholic Church, but it was restored to the state in 1868. In other cases the church resisted successfully. In Spain the introduction of civil marriage in 1870 created such a controversy that in 1875 obligatory religious marriage was restored.

The arrogation by the state of functions that had been carried out by the church was one aspect of a broad process of secularization. The churches, through their clergy and courts, played a diminishing role in social control and policy, and by 1900 the churches in many countries were virtually limited to performing strictly spiritual and pastoral functions. As they ceased playing vital roles in law, education, the family, and social welfare, they lost some of their practical importance for Europeans.

Although historians often point to an important trend of intellectual secularization in European societies during the nineteenth century, its social impact varied greatly. There is no doubt that people in the western regions of Europe, particularly the growing working class in large towns and cities, became more and more indifferent to religion and less inclined to attend church services. In England the decline set in during the 1880s. Chapels in Liverpool that in 1881 were 40 percent full during morning services and 58 percent full in the evening were only 13 and 28 percent full, respectively, by 1908. In 1902 Anglican churches in central Liverpool were only 16 percent full. There were other signs of secularization as well. In England and Wales the proportion of couples choosing civil over religious marriages rose during the century, until by 1900 almost one in five weddings was secular.

Mainstream denominations like the Catholic and Anglican Churches were often perceived as hostile to workers because they opposed socialism (which they associated with atheism) and often condemned strikes. Socialists, for their part, condemned the class bias of the churches; one French socialist referred to the Catholic Church as "the eternal accomplice of the Rich."

For such reasons church attendance in towns and cities tended to be higher among the middle class, and it was also generally higher in rural areas, where people had stronger ties to their communities. Women were usually more observant than men, in part because women's social lives were much more limited than men's, and attending church provided an opportunity for women to socialize with other women. It is possible that men considered singing hymns and praying for divine help as signs of weakness to be avoided as inconsistent with the independent masculinity that was increasingly in vogue.

Yet there were important exceptions even to the qualified trend of secularization in much of Central and Western Europe. Among Poles and in Ireland adherence to the Catholic Church held up, partly because the church was a strong nationalist force. For Poles outside Austria, dominated by Orthodox Russians and Protestant Germans, and for the Irish dominated by the Protestant majority in the United Kingdom, Catholicism distinguished them from the dominant majority. For a similar reason German Catholics supported the Center Party as a counterweight to the dominance of Lutherans in the empire. Religiosity also seems to have been strong among Russian peasants, for whom the church and czar were inextricably linked, and among Muslims in the Balkans. Jews in Eastern Europe also tended to remain actively faithful, but their co-religionists elsewhere modified their observance as they integrated into non-Jewish society. Orthodox Jewish practices, like wearing distinctive clothing, were widely disregarded in Western and Central Europe, and the proportion of Jews marrying non-Jews was as high as one in three in some German cities by the turn of the century.

It is difficult to measure a trend like secularization, when we can turn to little more than outward signs, like church attendance, for evidence of religiosity. People attend church for as many reasons as they do not attend church, among them habit, social pressure, and spiritual commitment. Overall we should have to say that although secularization made progress, it was greatly qualified by gender, geography, and class. As far as laws and other social controls were concerned, however, the trend was clear, for jurisdiction over such critical spheres as private and public morals, the family, education, and the maintenance of social order was progressively transferred from church authorities to secular governments.

The Ideologies of Change and Their Adherents

Three ideologies are commonly associated with the changes that took place during the nineteenth century. For liberalism, socialism, and conservatism, the state was a central concern, and all responded to societies being transformed by industrial and demographic expansion. Other ideologies, notably fascism and anarchism, began to take shape at this time, but they reached a more mature form in the twentieth century. In all cases we must be aware that ideologies are not fixed, but evolve and at any given time may encompass a wide range of variations. Moreover, terms often change their meanings over time, so that modern definitions and associations are rarely applicable to the late-nineteenth-century phenomena.

The great contest in political thought at the end of the nineteenth century was between liberalism and socialism. Characteristic of classical nineteenth-century liberalism was the value it placed on the individual, along with its concern to ensure that all individuals enjoyed equal liberty. In political terms this was often interpreted as meaning freedom from arbitrary restrictions of behavior, although liberals conceded that there should be limits. They generally drew the limit of freedom at the point where the actions of one individual began to interfere with the freedom of another. Applied to economics, liberalism led to the doctrine of laissez-faire, which advocated an economy in which market forces of supply and demand have free play and individuals enjoy unrestricted freedom to produce, trade, and consume.

Liberal principles triumphant: This cartoon shows the Law giving the Army a kick in the face after the charges against Alfred Dreyfus were revised in 1898.

Liberals took aim at any institution that had the power to limit freedom. This included organized religion because liberals insisted that individuals could be free only when they were able to develop their critical faculties, their reason, free of prejudice. An educated person, they believed, would achieve a broad harmony between the individual and the social interest so that there would be few conflicts between individual actions and the broader public interest. External controls might be necessary in theory, but in practice they would be redundant. This optimistic view derived from the Enlightenment, the wellspring of liberal thought, which believed in the perfectibility of human beings. The importance liberals attached to reason explains why they were prominent advocates of universal and secular education.

A prime source of anxiety for liberals was the state, which, as we have seen, was in the process of extending its influence and authority into a wide range of political, social, and economic matters. Even so, liberals were generally positive toward the state's roles in maintaining the rule of law, private property, and external security. The state could also guarantee freedoms of conscience, expression, and religious belief.

From the late 1880s a new school of liberal thought gave greater stress to the social dimension of individuals. The growth of the social sciences had demonstrated that human behavior was influenced by social forces of all kinds. They called into question the notion of pure individual freedom and made the stark separation of the individual from society appear naive. New liberals argued that liberty entailed more than being left alone, for individuals could not enjoy the liberties available to them unless they had the appropriate economic and social conditions.

In contrast to the older liberals like Herbert Spencer, who thought that the British state was going too far when it legislated on such matters as the poor, safety in factories, and public health, new liberals had a more positive view of the state. They supported state intervention and activity where it enhanced or protected freedoms: State-sponsored education was permissible and desirable because an educated populace was better able to exercise freedom, and state assistance to the poor, ill, and unemployed was justified as enabling the disadvantaged to enjoy liberty.

Unlike liberalism, which focused on the individual, socialism focused on society or the collectivity. Individual happiness and well-being were to be ensured by seeing that there were broad social institutions to protect the disadvantaged. Socialists thus concerned themselves with practical matters like social welfare, education, pensions, and housing. Unlike liberals, for whom the state was often a last resort to protect individuals from the worst effects of inequality, late-nineteenth-century socialists advocated state intervention on a broad scale, including state ownership of key industries and services.

There were and are many different varieties of socialism, but at the end of the nineteenth century two were dominant. One followed the thinking of Karl Marx, the German political economist who was a major influence within and beyond Europe in the late nineteenth and throughout the twentieth centuries. Marxist socialists saw history as a series of struggles between classes, defined in terms of their relationship to economic power. The state and social system existing at any given time represented the economic interests of the class that was dominant.

For Marxists the ruling class in nineteenth-century Western Europe was the bourgeoisie, which had seized power from the aristocracy when capitalism replaced feudalism and the industrial economy rose to its position of dominance. All the attributes of society—laws, social structure, social status, the family system, and religion—supported the bourgeoisie and its interests. Thus the law protected property owners from theft of material goods, but not workers from exploitation and "theft" of the value of their labor. Similarly, bourgeois religion advised the poor not to protest against oppression or resist exploitation, but rather to bide their time in expectation of heavenly rewards.

Although Marxists believed that the struggle between workers (the proletariat) and owners would inevitably lead to a working-class victory, they wanted to hasten the inevitable. Many Marxists believed that a revolution was necessary, and tried to organize workers to strike and even plan uprisings that would overthrow bourgeois society. This was especially so in Eastern Europe where the bourgeoisie was not yet in power and where parliamentary activity was generally impossible.

Other socialists, although still much influenced by Marx, argued for an evolutionary process rather than change by revolution. Sometimes calling themselves social democrats, they believed that socialist policies could be implemented within existing or reformed political institutions. Political parties along these lines included the Social Democrats in Germany, Austria, and Scandinavia, the Labour Party in Britain, and the Socialists in France. They pressed for universal male suffrage (and often for women's suffrage as well), and supported social welfare, universal education, and reforms in labor laws to protect workers' health and safety.

The third of the dominant political ideologies of this period was conservatism. Nineteenth-century conservatives were not necessarily die-hard opponents of all change as the name suggests, but argued for slow, organic evolution of political and social institutions. This placed them at odds with socialists, who had a particular vision of social, economic, and political relations, and attempted to achieve them by reformist or revolutionary means. Conservatives were generally at odds with liberals because they tended to support traditional institutions like monarchies, aristocracies, and the church (which they often portrayed as the "natural" leaders of society) and were opposed to the broadening of political participation and to key liberal tenets like universal secular education. Being rather more pessimistic than liberals about the possibility of enlightening the masses, conservatives thought that strong leadership was necessary and that the trend toward democracy was dangerous.

It is wrong to think that certain social classes consistently supported particular ideologies, but there were general tendencies. On the whole social democrats won support from workers (whose interests they claimed to represent), although when it came to voting many workers supported nonsocialist parties. Catholic workers in Germany, for instance, often voted for the Center Party, which had a generally liberal platform. The middle classes were the core of support for liberal parties, although some strata (like the lower middle class) often saw conservative parties as better representing their anxieties about change. Conservative parties drew much support from the elites that had most to lose from change, but because they were often more vigorously nationalistic than either socialists and liberals, they were also able to draw support from a wide social spectrum. It is important to recognize that just as ideologies changed in response to conditions, so did patterns of support.

Fin de Siècle: Confidence and Anxiety

As the nineteenth century ended and the twentieth began, a period often referred to as *fin de siècle*, there were manifestations of both confidence and anxiety in Europe about the direction of political, social, and economic changes. Depending on one's class, nationality, wealth, and gender, the future might look rosy or bleak. The predominant sentiment among the middle and upper classes, those who had most influence on government policies, was anxiety in the face of what appeared to them changes for the worse. Of the many issues that gave rise to this feeling, one of the most important was a generalized belief that society was in decline because institutions and beliefs perceived as the bedrock of the social order were crumbling.

Churches were aghast at the increasingly secular society that was being constructed. In 1864 Pope Pius IX issued his "Syllabus of Errors," a condemnation of the "errors" of the age that ended with the declaration that the Pope would not accept "progress, liberalism, and modern civilization." The syllabus expressed thoroughly conservative, if not reactionary, alarm at the decline of religion and growth of secular institutions that would leave society morally rudderless. Specific errors included the spread of democracy and state encroachments on church power.

If Christian beliefs were thought central to morality, marriage and the family were believed fundamental to the social order. An 1880 encyclical letter published by Pope Leo XIII deplored the secularization of marriage and the spread of divorce, both of which harmed children, broke up homes, and lowered what he called "the dignity of womanhood." The pope emphasized what conservatives of all religions and ideologies believed—that any erosion of the family threatened society generally: "Divorces are in the highest degree hostile to the prosperity of families and States, springing as they do from the depraved morals of the people, and, as experience shows us, opening out a way to every kind of evildoing in public as well as in private life."

Concern for morality and the family in general led to campaigns against specific activities and perceived threats to the social order. As we have seen, a campaign against what was viewed as a plague of venereal disease led to prostitutes in many countries being rounded up and imprisoned under health regulations. Their male clients, who shared responsibility for spreading whatever sexually transmitted diseases were current, were not touched. A campaign was also mounted against the "white slave trade," which supposedly abducted young European women and sold them as concubines and prostitutes in the Middle East. Pornography, which flourished in the late nineteenth century, was also the object of vigorous public campaigns and legislation.

Other social problems also attracted attention. The most important was alcohol, which was blamed for common drunkenness and a wide range of additional problems. Men were said to drink their wages away and leave their wives and children hungry. In many cases it was scarcely an exaggeration; a British worker who was no more than a moderate drinker, consuming two pints of beer a night and an extra one on Saturdays and Sundays, spent money that could feed a family of five for two or three days.

Drinking was a way of life for men especially, whether it was in British pubs or bars in European cities, or the drinking houses scattered throughout the countryside. In London at the turn of the century there was one pub for every 400 people, and that was the least favorable ratio (to drinkers) of all large English cities. Women were less likely than men to drink, and when they did they tended to do so at home. While there is abundant evidence that male violence was often associated with drunkenness, the extent of alcohol abuse is unclear. The evidence of people who lived in an English fishing community at the turn of the century suggests that drunkenness there was rare: "There weren't no drunkenness and that like there is now. No. They'd go and have a pint before they came home but you never heard of a fisherman around here being drunk."

Not only was working-class drinking alleged to harm families, it was also linked to other vices. Men were said to use alcohol to seduce respectable young women, and it was noted that drinking accompanied such activities as gambling and prostitution. Temperance unions, established in many countries in Europe and elsewhere, represented a broad anti-drink front dominated by women and including churches and other organizations.

Coupled with concern about the decline of society was a belief that Europeans were in decline physically. As we have seen, the later nineteenth century attributed increasing importance to heredity, not only for personality traits and medical conditions like epilepsy, mental retardation, and insanity, but also for behavioral and moral characteristics such as indulgence in alcohol and gambling, crime, or adultery. One effect of this intellectual trend was the growth of the eugenics movement, which set out to promote populations that were physically and morally strong and create societies free of crime, insanity, prostitution, alcoholism, adultery, and divorce. For these goals to be achieved, men and women with "undesirable" traits had to be discouraged or even prevented from having children. Failure to take action against what was often called the "breeding of the unfit" would lead to what eugenicists termed "race suicide."

Eugenics movements were founded throughout Europe. They disseminated their ideas through books and public meetings, and called on governments to stop the "unfit" from marrying or having children. Eugenics concerns attracted widespread support across the political spectrum and from doctors, social scientists, and natural scientists. In 1899 the future British Prime Minister, Winston Churchill, wrote that "the improvement of the British breed is my political aim in life." In 1908 he wrote that "the unnatural and increasingly rapid growth of the feeble-minded and insane classes constitutes a national and a race danger which I find impossible to exaggerate."

The women's rights movement that rose to prominence in the decades before 1900 was an integral part of the sense of anxiety about the state of society. Feminists at this time argued against the double standard of sexual morality that focused on prostitutes but not their clients, and against inequalities in family law. The English divorce law, for instance, enabled men to divorce their wives for adultery, but did not make a husband's adultery a ground for divorce. In Spain a husband was guilty of adultery only if his extramarital sexual relationship became a "public scandal," and any man who discovered his wife or unmarried daughter having sexual intercourse was permitted to kill her for staining the family honor. In Italian law adultery could be committed only by a woman, and in a famous judgment in 1903 the country's Supreme Appeals Court ruled that a woman could commit adultery with a man "even if he lacked, through amputation, his male organ."

Equality in the law of sexuality, feminists argued at the turn of the century, would improve morality. It was not that they wanted the same rights to commit adultery with impunity, for most reformers were conservative on issues of family and morality. They did want men brought within the law as much as women, however. Such reforms were opposed by legislators, middle-class men who wanted to locate moral problems among other groups, like women and workers, rather than among themselves.

The enfranchisement of women was also portrayed as a reform that would improve society and morality. Women were depicted as repositories of moral virtues that men did not have; women were chaste, generous, and altruistic. Giving the vote to them would project these qualities into public life. Many advocates of women's suffrage argued their case on the ground that women were essentially different from men.

Reaction against moral and social reform, 1908: Marchers (mainly men) wind their way down the Embankment, in London, to protest against the Licensing Bill, an attempt to reduce the number of liquor licenses in England.

There was no unanimity in the various movements of protest and improvement that spread during the last decades of the nineteenth century. Support for some of them, like temperance, spanned the political spectrum; alcohol could be viewed by conservatives as a cause of working-class crime, and by socialists as a drug that anesthetized workers to their conditions and prevented them from becoming politicized by them instead. Many women in the anti-drink and anti-sex campaigns did not support equalizing divorce laws but wanted divorce abolished as detrimental to the family.

But the protest movements reflected two characteristics of *fin de siècle* Europe. The first is that social changes like industrialization, urbanization, and secularization evoked a good deal of anxiety, even if the proposed means of dealing with them varied. Second, although many of the movements were led or dominated by the political elites, they drew large numbers of people, especially women, into the public arena. Many of the reformers might not have had the vote—yet—but they were able to cut their political teeth by going to public meetings, participating in conferences, and organizing petitions. Within the mass society that developed in the late nineteenth century, the reformers were one element that tried to loosen the grasp of gender and class elites on the handles of political power.

Conclusion

In 1900, Europe was in the grip of a series of changes that were transforming the relationships between men and women, among social classes, between town and country, and among nations. No sphere of human activity was immune to the great transformations whose effects included shifts in the balance of industrial and agrarian economies, massive movements of people within Europe and from Europe to the rest of the world, and increasing nationalist sentiment.

It is important to appreciate that these various lines of change were not independent of one another, but intimately connected. Ethnic nationalism was spurred on by declining rural living conditions that were produced, in part, by population growth and by inheritance practices that had led to the progressive subdivision of family farms into plots that were so small as to be unviable. Anti-Semitism, which became an adjunct of nationalism, was reinforced by pressures on small producers and shopkeepers who saw Jews as representing the new economic forces of mass production and mass retailing; it was given intellectual legitimacy by the rise of pseudoscientific theories of ethnicity, race, and heredity.

It is difficult to point to any area of change that could exist independent of any other, whether it was the large population that industry needed, both for its labor force and markets, or the decline in fertility that resulted from changes in the economy. As we survey Europe in the twentieth century it is important to bear in mind the interrelatedness of spheres of historical change that at first glance appear self-contained.

Before the Deluge: Europe from 1890 to 1914

Introduction

The First World War (1914–18) was one of the defining events—many historians would argue *the* defining event—of the twentieth century. As we shall see in the next chapter, it was far more than a military conflict. It led to widespread political, economic, social, and cultural changes that included a fundamental reorganization of political boundaries, shifts in the balance of European and global economic power, an increase in state authority, increased political conflict, and a reorientation of social relationships of many kinds.

Only by appreciating the immense and wide-ranging *results* of the war can we understand why so much energy has been spent—starting the very day the war began—trying to define its causes.

Yet if there is no neat account or explanation of the causes of the First World War that has gained general support, it is at least partly because historians are not agreed on what is to be explained.

There is a fundamental division between historians who focus on the critical months of June to August 1914 and those who look at the longer-term origins of the war. An explanation that focuses on the crises of mid-1914 is likely to give overwhelming weight to diplomacy, government decisions, and the ever-narrowing range of options open to the states involved, as ultimata, warnings, mobilizations, and intergovernmental discussions led to one declaration of war after another. An explanation of the background to these critical months is likely to give greater weight to longer-term political issues: imperial rivalry, military build-ups, and the threats that nationalism of varying kinds posed to the internal stability of states as well as to the balance of power.

We are led to yet other sets of explanations if, instead of focusing on the reasons war broke out, we direct our attention to why the war took the shape it did and why it had such cataclysmic consequences. What is there in the history of Europe before 1914 that throws light on the collapse of empires, the growth of the states, changes in work patterns, and the course of wartime and postwar fertility?

For the most part political and diplomatic policies have been given primacy in discussions of the origins of the First World War. This is partly because wars are generally conceived as instruments of foreign policy, and because of the overwhelming bias of the evidence most readily available to historians. Following the war, the main powers involved published political papers, diplomatic correspondence, and ministerial minutes, all designed to present each state's role in the most favorable light. The sheer volume of evidence and their complexity led many historians to ignore other areas of evidence that might clarify the origins of the war.

On the domestic side of things, economic change has been well analyzed, generally as it related to the growth of Germany's power and to the ability of various states to expand their military production. Less attention, however, has been given to the social aspects of the period 1890 to 1914. Yet it is clear that as much as political leaders focused on foreign policy—in times of crisis it monopolized their attention—they also had to deal with domestic developments. All states, as we have seen, faced challenges of one sort or another, from groups as diverse as workers' organizations, women, and dissident ethnic populations, and from the effects of structural changes like industrialization, urbanization, declining fertility rates, and sharpening class antagonisms.

These developments formed part of the universe within which social and political policies were developed, and foreign policies were no exception. Although there were periods when diplomatic concerns were clearly dominant, understandings of national interests and the domestic consequences of foreign policy decisions were refracted through governments' perceptions of internal political, economic, and social conditions.

The great difference between the political and social levels of explanation is that while the political factors seem explicit and clear, the impact of social and economic trends is diffuse and often indirect. It is frequently difficult to know where to draw a line: which social trends were relevant to the origins of the war and which were not. In the sense that everything is connected to everything else there is a temptation to bring all trends everywhere to bear on the origins of the war, but that would introduce so many variables as to make a coherent explanation impossible.

This chapter examines a number of trends in Europe from 1890 to 1914, giving a dynamic perspective to structural characteristics outlined in the previous chapter. Here we develop an understanding of the origins of the First World War, but try to avoid the implication that the only trends that are important are those that led to war; for every trend of this kind there was a countervailing one. It is important to remember that although there were warnings and fears of an impending war on many occasions between the late 1890s and 1914, there was no point before August 1914 that war can be said to have been inevitable.

Shifts in the Balance of Power, 1890 to 1911

The few changes to the map of Europe in this short but eventful period reflected the continuing influence of nationalism, especially in the Balkans where the Ottoman Empire, its government distracted by internal political problems, ebbed dramatically. In 1908 nationalists in Bulgaria, which already had autonomous status within the empire, declared complete independence. In the same year Austria-Hungary annexed Bosnia and Herzegovina, former Ottoman territories that it already administered, in order to forestall the creation of a south Slavic state on its borders. Outside the Balkan area, Norway gained independence from Sweden in 1905.

These relatively minor changes in political frontiers on the margins of Europe masked immense shifts in its balance of power. At the turn of the century a nation's power was measured in terms of several variables, especially population size and growth, industrial strength, the extent of overseas empire, and military record and potential. It was the combination of variables that was important. Despite having a large population and vast territory, for instance, Russia would not become a major political and military power until it industrialized. Similarly, France's substantial African and Asian empires did not compensate for its sluggish demographic performance and the blow its military reputation suffered in the Franco-Prussian War.

In the nineteenth century, Great Britain had combined these variables most success-fully, having a growing population, a well-developed industrial economy, and a vast em-pire that provided raw materials and food. Although Britain's military establishment was numerically small, its navy (all-important for the defense of island Britain and its overseas empire) was the most powerful in the world, and its demographic and industrial strength gave Britain the potential to create a major land army.

But British preeminence in Europe was challenged and in many respects surpassed by Germany between 1890 and 1914, a fact that transformed the balance of power. Germany's rapid rise to the status of great power began with its defeat of France, followed by national unification in 1871. A strong centralized government with ambitions to be-come not only a force to be reckoned with in Europe, but also a global power, encouraged a course of economic development that soon made up for a late start in industrialization.

One of the best indicators of the level of a nation's industrialization is the amount of energy it consumes from modern sources (notably coal, petroleum, natural gas, and elec-tricity). In 1890 Britain consumed the equivalent of 145 million metric tons of coal, twice Germany's 71 million metric tons. Only twenty-four years later the energy consumption of the two powers was almost equal, with Britain at 195 million equivalent tons, and Germany at 185 million. As Figure 2.1 shows, in terms of steel production, an indicator of potential military power as well as actual industrial strength, Germany surpassed Britain in the late 1890s. By 1913 Germany was producing 17.6 million tons of steel a year, more than twice Britain's 7.7 million tons. In 1890 Britain's share of world manufacturing output was twice Germany's; by 1913 Germany's 14.8 percent share was greater than Britain's 13.6 percent.

Germany was not the only state where industrialization accelerated from the turn of the century, but only Germany achieved an absolute level of industrialization that promoted it to the first rank of industrial powers. Lesser economies such as France, Austria-Hungary, Russia, and Italy actually had faster growth rates in some sectors, but that was largely because they started from very low levels of industrial development. By 1914 they formed a distinct second rank of economic powers. France's share of world manufacturing declined steadily,

FIGURE 2.1 Steel output in selected countries, 1880–1910.

Source: Data from B. R. Mitchell, *International Historical Statistics: Europe, 1750–1988* (London: Macmillan, 1992), pp. 456–62.

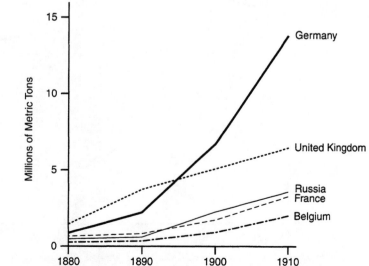

while Russia, Italy, and Austria-Hungary barely managed to hold their own. On the other hand, by 1913 Austria-Hungary produced more coal and almost as much steel as Russia or France, and had a faster-growing industrial potential than Russia.

Smaller states, including Spain and Portugal, the Low Countries (Belgium and the Netherlands), and the Scandinavian and Balkan states continued to industrialize at varying rates, but could not be thought of as economic powers. In specific cases industrial activity even declined for part of this period. When Bulgaria achieved independent status within the Ottoman Empire in 1878, the departure of Turkish residents affected the luxury goods market, and the Bulgarian textile industry, which had sold extensively to the Turkish army, also went into decline.

Although economic strength was a critical variable in international relations, it was not the only one, and it was not strictly in economic terms alone that Britain began to lose ground to Germany. Britain's birth rate began to decline rapidly from the 1880s, falling from 34.2 per thousand in 1880 to 26.2 in 1910 (see Figure 2.2). Germany's birth rate not only was higher but also began to decline somewhat later: It stood at 37.6 per thousand in 1880 and 29.8 in 1910. In 1880 Great Britain's population was 66 percent of Germany's; by 1910 it had slipped to 63 percent.

FIGURE 2.2   Birth rates in selected countries, 1850–1910.

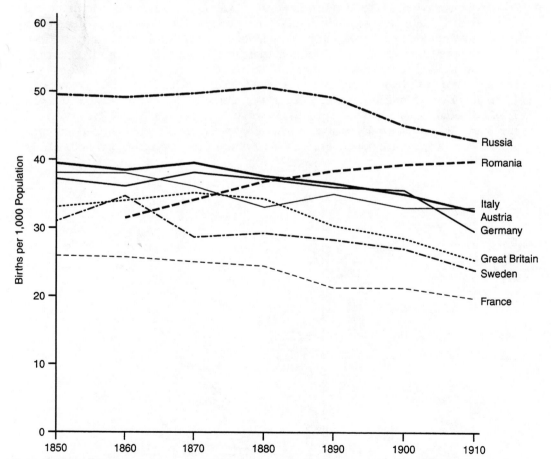

Source: Data from B. R. Mitchell, *International Historical Statistics: Europe, 1750–1988* (London: Macmillan, 1992), pp. 94–106.

France was even worse off than Britain in comparison with Germany. Its economy grew steadily but was increasingly outpaced by Germany. Although France's population had begun to increase after stagnating in the 1870s, birth rates remained alarmingly low. In 1910, 20 children were born for every thousand inhabitants in France, compared with 30 in Germany, 25 in Britain, and even higher rates elsewhere, such as 33 in Austria. Between 1880 and 1910 France's population plummeted from 83 to 60 percent of Germany's.

In military terms, too, Britain and France had suffered blows. For decades the French agonized over their defeat in the war with Prussia, seeking the explanation not only in government incompetence and economic weakness, but in the physical and moral decline of the nation. Pierre Toulement, a Jesuit priest, announced that God had inflicted the defeat on the French as punishment for the sin of using contraception. Be that as it may, the sagging French birth rate hampered the improvement of France's military position. In 1906 France was able to call up only 368,000 men. Germany was not only able to draft 1.2 million but also could even afford to demobilize more than half of them so that they could contribute to national strength through their civilian work.

As for Britain, it had defeated Dutch settler challenges in the South African (Boer) War of 1899–1902, but only with great difficulty. The conflict had begun with a series of humiliating defeats for the British, and in the course of the conflict, joined by imperial troops from several countries, they suffered 25,000 deaths, though more by disease than in action. Official investigations after the war pointed to fundamental problems in the army and society at large that called into question Britain's military capabilities.

Economic, demographic, and military problems in France and Britain led to growing anxiety over the buoyancy of Germany's economy and population, and the military strength it implied. The French were not reassured by German delight at their declining fortunes. Theodor Mommsen, the prominent German historian of the Roman Empire, who presumably recognized a state in decline when he saw one, was reported as declaring, "Another German invasion, and all that will remain of France is a bad memory." The likelihood that France would recover Alsace and Lorraine from Germany seemed to recede steadily.

French anxiety was amplified by the alliances Germany had forged with Austria-Hungary (1883) and Italy (1889). This Triple Alliance, as it was known, was in part designed to isolate France diplomatically. Unable to attain security through their own economic and demographic resources, the French also turned to diplomacy, and began to create alliances intended to deter German aggression. The first was an 1894 agreement with Russia obliging each to help the other if Germany or Austria-Hungary launched an aggressive war.

Anxiety over an ascendant Germany rose another notch in 1898 when Kaiser Wilhelm II announced his intention to pursue a global policy (Weltpolitik) that would extend German interests beyond Europe itself. A latecomer to imperial expansion outside Europe, Germany lacked the extensive empires held by Britain and France; its overseas possessions included scattered territories in Africa (modern Togo, Cameroon, Namibia, and Tanzania) and some Pacific islands. Echoing the British boast that the sun never set upon its worldwide empire, Germany claimed "a place in the sun" as its right as a great power. In 1898 a navy law revealed Germany's intention to construct a fleet that would challenge British naval supremacy.

Global ambitions also reflected domestic pressures in Germany. Powerful industrial and commercial lobbies wanted an expansionist foreign policy so as to develop overseas markets for German goods and a more powerful navy to protect Germany's present and future global economic interests. They gained the support of the powerful agrarian lobby, representing large landowners, in exchange for supporting higher tariffs on imported

A French nationalist view of the result of the 1870–71 Franco-Prussian War. France, a
dagger held at her breast, is forced to sign an agreement giving Alsace and Lorraine to
Germany. Reflecting French anxiety about population decline, the cartoon shows
France's children either killed or abducted by Prussian soldiers.

food. Parties representing these groups in the Reichstag easily outvoted the socialists.
Socialists opposed both policies because the indirect taxes on such items as bread, beer,
and tobacco, which financed rearmament, fell more heavily on workers than any other
group, and workers were also hit harder by higher food costs resulting from the protective tariffs that benefited large landowners.

Although much attention is paid to its imperial ambitions, Germany was far from
alone in espousing such policies. Existing imperial powers like Britain and France were
determined to hold on to their overseas possessions and commercial interests, and even
extend them where possible. To compensate for their low fertility rate, the French looked
to the indigenous people of their African colonies for additional soldiers.

Italy, like Germany a late entrant in the race for colonies, had been even less successful and set out to rectify the situation. After setbacks in North Africa, Italy focused on
Abyssinia (Ethiopia), but its campaign of occupation ended with a disastrous defeat at
Adowa in 1896 that cost the lives of 6,000 Italian soldiers. This was the first time indigenous African forces had defeated a European power in a major battle. The Abyssinian fi-
asco prevented Italy, still a weak industrial state, from becoming an immediate threat to
the balance of power.

Germany's ambitions had to be taken far more seriously. To assert its great power status, the German government had not only begun to increase its naval strength but also
opened a series of diplomatic, military, and commercial initiatives abroad. The port of

Kiao-Chow in China was seized to provide a refueling station in the Far East for the expanding German navy. Closer to Europe, during a state visit to the Ottoman Empire in 1898, the kaiser declared himself protector of the world's Muslims, an implied threat to British and French interests in the Middle East and North Africa. In 1899 Germany obtained permission to build a railroad through Turkey to the Persian Gulf.

The extension of German influence into the Mediterranean, Middle East and Asia fostered closer ties between Britain and France, both of which had colonial and commercial interests in those regions. In 1904 the two countries settled outstanding disagreements over their respective authority in North Africa, and at a conference of imperial powers two years later Britain supported France against German claims on French-controlled Morocco. Early in 1906 the British and French began discussions on coordinating strategic plans in the event of a general war in Europe. Although Germany had attempted to isolate France, which would be an enemy until it recovered Alsace and Lorraine, Germany's Weltpolitik had instead brought France back into the thick of European international affairs.

Russia also stepped back onto the European diplomatic stage at this time. While other European powers were consolidating their overseas empires, Russia's interests were directed to the Balkans and Asia, partly with the aim of obtaining year-round ports for its navy and merchant marine. Black Sea ports were ice-free in winter, but ships using them could reach the Mediterranean only through Ottoman-controlled straits. To break this stranglehold Russia attempted to expand into Ottoman territory, and championed Slav nationalism in the Balkans in order to undermine Turkish hegemony there.

These Balkan policies brought Russia into conflict with Austria-Hungary, which was keen to repress Slav nationalism for fear that it would weaken its authority over its own Slav populations. When it became clear that Germany supported Austria-Hungary, Russia agreed to preserve the status quo in the Balkans (a treaty was signed in 1897), thus temporarily resolving what was known as "the Eastern question."

As its Balkans policies faltered, Russia looked farther east, to southern and eastern Asia. Attempts to penetrate Persia (modern Iran) and Afghanistan commercially were frustrated by British determination to contain Russian expansion and protect British interests in India, but the Russians were successful in extending their political and economic influence in the Far East. In 1891, with French financial help, construction began on the economically and militarily important Trans-Siberian Railroad between European Russia and Vladivostok, the Pacific Ocean port that had been acquired in 1860.

Russia's expansion in the Far East coincided with the collapse of central authority (under the Manchu dynasty) in China, and Russia was able to lease a warm-water port, Port Arthur, and gain commercial concessions in the Chinese province of Manchuria. In 1900, after European forces suppressed the antiforeign Boxer Rebellion in Beijing, a Russian army remained in Manchuria to protect Russian interests. Plans were also made to extend Russian penetration into Korea.

Again, however, the extension of Russian influence was blocked by another power, this time Japan, which was emerging as the political, economic, and military force to be reckoned with in East Asia. Lacking adequate indigenous raw materials for its industries and food supplies for its rapidly growing population (which rose from 40 to 51 million between 1890 and 1913), Japan had invaded Korea and part of Manchuria in 1894–95 to secure coal and other resources. Conflict over Korea resulted in a war between Russia and Japan in 1904–5. Not only was Russia's army in Manchuria and its Far Eastern fleet defeated but also its Baltic fleet, which had sailed almost nine months to join battle, was promptly wiped out by the Japanese navy.

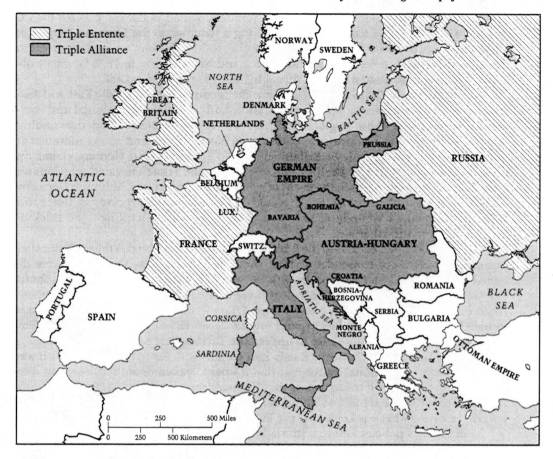

MAP 2.1   The alliance system in Europe, 1914.

This military debacle in the Far East had important repercussions in Russia, not the least as a catalyst for the 1905 revolution (which is discussed below). It also refocused Russian attention on Europe, especially the Balkans. This policy coincided with a British concern to secure its control over India in light of growing German economic and military power in Europe. Both Russia and Britain perceived Germany as a threat: It challenged British preeminence in Europe and colonial interests abroad, and it backed Austro-Hungarian policy against Russia in the Balkans.

Spurred by common anxiety about Germany, and encouraged by France, which wanted to foster an anti-German coalition, Britain and Russia settled their differences in southern Asia in 1907. Russia conceded Afghanistan as a British interest, both recognized Chinese authority over Tibet, and Persia was divided into zones of British and Russian influence. In addition, both powers agreed to block German attempts to extend its commercial and political influence into Persia, where extensive exploratory drilling was on the verge of proving vast oil reserves.

Although its formal scope was limited, the 1907 treaty established a cooperative (and anti-German) spirit between Russia and Great Britain. Before long they and France were perceived as acting in concert in what became known as the Triple Entente, a de facto counterweight to the Triple Alliance that linked Germany, Austria-Hungary, and Italy.

The two tripartite coalitions formed the background to European affairs in the following years, although they were sufficiently loosely framed (especially the Entente, which did not obligate Britain formally to France and Russia) that they did not inevitably lead to multipower confrontations whenever there were conflicts among member states. When Russia protested against Austro-Hungarian annexation of Bosnia and Herzegovina in 1908, Britain and France stood by, and Russia was compelled to accept the annexation after Germany insisted it do so or suffer the consequences.

It was not by chance that Germany was involved directly or indirectly in most confrontations among European powers in the decades before the First World War. In this period Germany emerged as a great power without the empire and global influence it believed were its right. Its geographic position at the center of Europe symbolized its geopolitical position. Germany could not expand its territory within Europe without encroaching on other nations, and the adoption of a global policy could not but produce conflict with other states that wanted to protect their established interests.

Nationalism in an Unstable Climate

As the major states jockeyed for the most advantageous position in the changing configuration of power in Europe, they wore the colors of nationalism. A potent force for political change in the nineteenth century, nationalism became if anything even more powerful an appeal in the decades before the First World War, especially as its connotations changed. For most of the nineteenth century it was liberals who had championed the nation-state and national institutions as the best means to attain the freedoms, education, and general improvement in the human condition that they sought. But from the late nineteenth century, nationalism became associated instead with intolerance, authoritarianism, and beliefs in national superiority.

Like earlier nationalists, those of the prewar generations stressed the common characteristics and interests of their fellow citizens; unlike their predecessors, they increasingly proclaimed the superior virtues of their own countries. Other nations were portrayed as inferior in critical respects (usually morality) and, frequently, as potential or real threats. The emphasis on national unity remained but more often as a part of defense against outsiders. By stressing alleged differences between nations, nationalism became a force for international misunderstanding and even conflict. This kind of crude, blustering nationalism is often called *jingoism*.[1]

The German government certainly appealed to nationalist sentiments in this way. Germany, it argued, was a great power whose destiny was frustrated by foreign interests trying to prop up an outdated status quo. Chancellor Bülow's famous "hammer or anvil" speech of 1899 expressed this frustration: "We cannot let any foreign power, any foreign Jupiter, tell us: 'What can be done? The world is already divided up.'" Yet nationalism of this sort was by no means confined to Germany, and was expressed by nationalists in Britain, France, and elsewhere with equal vigor. The British press waged a campaign against the sale of German-made goods in British stores.

Sentiments of pride in one's country, belief in its superiority, and fear or dislike of other nations were often expressed by political and military leaders. They extended beyond each

1. After a British music hall song that became popular during the 1878 eastern crisis: "We don't want to fight, yet by Jingo if we do, / We've got the ships, we've got the men, and we've got the money too."

country's political elites, at least as far as the middle classes, for which nationalism appeared to be a substitute for any concrete social or political program. There is less evidence that the working classes, sections of which were more receptive to theoretically antinationalist and internationalist ideologies like socialism, rallied to nationalism to the same extent.

Children were exposed to nationalism through state and private education systems. German students learned from one of their history texts that "the Empire is unified, powerful, and respected throughout the world. There are no longer divisions among different classes." British children learned that their country bore the light of civilization to dark corners of the world, carrying "the white man's burden." In Italy a popular children's book, set in a primary school in northern Italy, exemplified the nationalist morality. Students in the book write essays on patriotic subjects (such as "Why do you love Italy?"), and in one story a bully is expelled for laughing during a ceremony in honor of the king. National unity is stressed when a teacher warns students not to make fun of a new boy from Calabria, a region regarded as backward by urban northern Italians.

The storyline of one French textbook (*The Tour of France by Two Children: Duty and Fatherland*) appealed to nationalistic sentiments. Two boys lose their parents when their mother and father die, and their symbolic father when Lorraine, the region where they were born, is annexed by Germany. The orphans tour France in search of an identity and finally discover their long-lost Uncle Frantz. They are thrilled to be able to identify with Frantz and France, a father figure and a country whose names sounded almost identical. When Uncle Frantz suggests erecting a French flag, one of the boys exclaims, "I love France with all my heart!" The message was clear: French citizens were children of the Fatherland (as the first line of the French national anthem proclaims[2]), and links to country were as strong and natural as those within a family. The book went through 209 printings up to 1891.

Young people also learned love of country in youth organizations. One of the best known was the Boy Scouts, founded in 1908 by General Robert Baden-Powell, hero of the British defense of the town of Mafeking against a Boer assault during the South African

A drawing by General Baden-Powell of Lord Cecil's Cadet Corps at Mafeking, during the South African War. These cadets became the model for the Boy Scout movement.

---

2. The first lines of the *Marseillaise* are: "Children of the Fatherland, arise, / The day of glory has arrived!"

war. Scouting was designed to prepare boys to serve their country under arms. The Scout handbook informed boys that just as no one had ever thought Mafeking would be attacked, "it just shows you how you must be prepared for what is possible . . . and so, too, we must be prepared in Britain against being attacked by enemies."

The Scout movement stressed discipline, religion, and patriotism, and although Baden-Powell later hoped that as his organization spread to other countries it would foster international understanding, he emphasized that the British Empire had to be defended against "bully" nations. By 1910 the Scouts had more than 100,000 members. Most were middle-class boys; not only were their working-class peers less attracted to displays of patriotism, but they were less able to afford luxuries like uniforms.

Middle-class members were also predominant in German youth organizations. It is notable that although these bodies were set up in the later nineteenth century by private sponsors, particularly churches, the state became increasingly involved. Edicts encouraging the establishment of youth associations were issued in 1901, 1905, 1908, and 1911, the last providing a subsidy of a million marks. Major institutions that encouraged youth activities included the army, churches, the Prussian Soldiers' Federation, and the Trade and Industry Convention. Organizations were pledged to instill in young people "community spirit and fear of God, love of home and Fatherland," and a prime aim was to combat socialism.

Nationalists concerned for the future of their country quite understandably directed their message toward boys who would grow up to serve their country's armies. Girls were not expected to be nationalistic in the same way as boys, who were encouraged to express their love of country in military or other public ways. The author of *The Tour of France by Two Children*, whose heroes were two boys, wrote another textbook in which a teacher assures girls that "a woman's life is entirely interior, and her influence on society occurs in a nearly invisible manner." The author of the textbooks, Augustine Fouillée, embodied the idea, for she wrote under the gender-neutral pseudonym G. Bruno.

Although parallel female organizations to the Scouts and German boys' movements were soon formed, the emphasis in the Guides and other girls' organizations was on preparing them for the particular roles that women were expected to play in their nation's destiny. Stress was placed on first aid, cooking, and child care, reflecting the prevailing belief that the most important role for a woman was to be a good wife and mother. This implied producing children and raising them for the good of the country.

Nationalism and Fertility

Increasing concern was expressed in many countries before the war at declining birth rates and persistently high infant and childhood mortality rates. In England in 1899, 163 in every thousand children died before reaching the age of one, and the rate was considerably higher among the poor. The combined effect of falling birth rates and recalcitrant mortality rates presented an alarming prospect for the human resources that would be available for future British industrial and military needs.

In 1904 a government report on the physical deterioration of Britons, prompted by concern at the ill health of many volunteers for military service in South Africa, pointed to infant mortality as a national problem. Ignoring the fact that many poor women simply lacked the resources and environment to raise healthy families, reformers pinned primary responsibility on mothers, whom they portrayed as ignorant or neglectful of their children's needs. A speaker at a 1906 conference on infant mortality called for society to make the death of a child "something of a social stigma as well as a racial sin." (The word *racial* was used in the eugenic sense, as in "race suicide.")

Similar fears and attitudes were expressed in France and Italy, even in Germany, despite its robust population growth. In the first decade of the century about 18 percent of babies in Germany and 13 percent in France died before reaching the age of one year. Speakers in the French Senate debates on child protection legislation in the early 1900s referred to "the grave national peril" of depopulation, to France's need of babies "for its defense and maintenance," and of the "national advantage" that providing maternity leave would give France. Pronatalist policies, encouraging population growth, were an integral part of nationalist programs to improve their countries' economic and military status.

Governments in many countries responded to such concerns by enacting legislation and policies to promote fertility and to improve maternal skills and women's and children's health. In Britain a 1902 law required midwives to be trained, another (1906) provided for meals for poor children, while yet another (1907) established medical inspections in schools. Myriad voluntary societies to promote the health of mothers and children sprang up, inquiries and congresses were held, and prizes offered by municipalities for healthy babies and babies that survived their first year.

In France organizations like the League Against Infant Mortality supported campaigns for maternity leave, baby clinics, and assistance for new mothers. In Germany legislation was enacted to provide for maternity leave and promote children's health. In Sweden, beginning in 1900, most women were forbidden to work in industry for four weeks after giving birth, a period increased to six weeks in 1912.

As state interest in children's health increased, compulsory education was seen as a means of monitoring and ensuring that children received an adequate diet. In the Netherlands, France, Great Britain, and Italy, school feeding became an integral part of the educational system. The 1900 Schools Act in the Netherlands went further than most by providing for clothing, as well as food, to be given to children of poor families if it was necessary for them to be able to attend school.

There were also nationalist campaigns against all kinds of family limitation, and across Europe there was growing concern at the frequency of abortion. This is difficult to measure because in the absence of legal provisions, most abortions were performed illegally by unqualified people or by women on themselves, frequently using lead or phosphorus as abortifacients. Phosphorus, an ingredient in match-heads, was involved in 90 percent of abortions in Sweden where, as elsewhere in Europe, women would swallow hundreds of match-heads, or scrape the phosphorus off and insert it vaginally. In 1903 an international conference discussed a ban on phosphorus matches, and although no concerted action was taken, Germany enacted a unilateral prohibition in 1907. Doctors' estimates of what some termed an "epidemic" of abortions in Germany ranged from 100,000 to 300,000 a year before the war. In Russia the prewar debate on population growth focused even more on abortion, which was frequently used as the main form of family limitation. Attempts were made to tighten the law, despite the fact that population was growing faster than food resources and that almost a third of all children born died before reaching the age of one.

Anxieties about the state of the population were generally expressed in nationalistic terms: pronatalism (policies favoring births) and nationalism were inseparable. Motherhood, wrote one British doctor, was "a matter of Imperial importance." The survival of the greatest number of English babies was essential, another noted, because if Britain and its colonies were not inhabited by "people of British stock [they] would sooner

Reflecting growing concern about declines in public health and fertility in Great Britain, a 1913 Liberal Party poster shows plans for state-assisted health insurance, including a maternity grant.

or later be occupied by other people." A bestselling book on domestic hygiene that went through numerous printings between 1897 and 1913 noted that "since national health depends upon the health of individuals, patriotism and a desire for self-preservation ought equally to prompt each person to keep well."

Growing fears of national degeneration embraced homosexual men, whose stereotyped effeminacy contrasted with the virile masculinity thought appropriate for militaristic nationalism. The worst offense homosexuals committed was to "waste" male reproductive potential, but other objections were raised to them as well. Gay men were thought to have little energy, weak nerves, and to be prone to hysteria, and because these conditions were primarily associated with women, homosexuals blurred the stark distinction between men and women that conservatives thought essential to the social order.

What made things worse was that homosexuality became more visible, especially in big cities, from the 1890s onward. In England gay men wore a green carnation, in Paris gay men and lesbians publicly defended their sexual orientation, and in Berlin the number of homosexual bars doubled between 1904 and 1914. In the first decade of the twentieth century, homosexual scandals eddied around the most elevated places. From 1907 to 1909 there was a series of courts-martial that drew attention to homosexuality in the German army (half a dozen officers committed suicide after being blackmailed), and five trials highlighted the homosexuality of prominent members of the kaiser's court. Other homosexual scandals implicated prominent nobles and members of the British and Swedish royal families. Collectively, they suggested to conservatives that the moral "rot" that had set into European society had spread to the highest levels.

Nationalism touched every facet and institution of major European societies in the prewar period. The struggle for national survival and success was not confined to men or to the public spheres of politics, industry, and the military. It involved women, the family, domestic life, and children. In Britain General Sir Frederick Maurice alluded to his country's main rival when in 1903 he wrote approvingly of "the view of the Emperor of Germany that for the raising of a virile race, either of soldiers or of citizens, it is essential that the mothers of a land should be mainly devoted to the three K's—*Kinder, Küche, Kirche* [children, kitchen, church]."

Nationalism and Ethnicity

Although nationalism took on new jingoistic associations in some parts of Europe, it remained a different kind of threat to political stability elsewhere. In the great multiethnic entities that dominated eastern Europe—Russia, Austria-Hungary, and Turkey—nationalism remained a force for disintegration. The most troubled was Turkey, which by the end of the nineteenth century had seen its European territories crumble steadily, and such a process was the aspiration of nationalists within the other empires.

Regionalism and ethnic difference were essential facts of Austria-Hungary, and they became more prominent in the prewar years. Austria and Hungary, sharing a monarch and dominating the empire, bickered repeatedly from the 1890s over such issues as Hungary's claim that Magyar (Hungarian) should replace German as the language of command in the Hungarian part of the imperial army. To preserve the preeminence of German and prevent the division of the Habsburg army, which would surely have followed a linguistic division, the emperor blocked the proposal.

The conflict produced a constitutional crisis in 1905 when a coalition of Hungarian nationalist parties won control of the Hungarian Diet. Although the Diet voted no confidence in a loyalist ministry appointed by the king (who was also emperor) the ministers remained in office. In the stalemate that followed, freedoms of expression and assembly were curtailed and parliament was first prorogued, then dissolved. Foreign observers feared that the empire might collapse and there was concern that Germany might try to annex Austrian territory. The Austrian general staff prepared plans for the invasion of Hungary in case the conflict escalated. Eventually the anti-imperial coalition collapsed under a threat to introduce a wider suffrage in Hungary that would allow other ethnic minorities to swamp the Magyars electorally. In 1910 nationalists demanded the creation of a Hungarian national bank that would issue its own currency.

Ethnic tensions intensified within, as well as between, the two parts of Austria-Hungary. Austrian pan-Germans advocated the dissolution of the empire so that the territories of the old German Confederation could unite with Germany, and by 1900 over a thousand local associations in Austria were devoted to maintaining the purity of German language and culture. Not the least of the Germans' concerns was that the non-German birth rate was higher than their own, making them not only a minority in Austria but also a shrinking minority. The Polish population was especially worrying, having increased from 15 percent of Austria's population in 1880 to 18 percent in 1910.

German domination produced chronic conflict over education and language issues with Czech speakers in Bohemia. Italians in the empire objected to Germanization and looked to union with Italy. In the south the Slav populations were particularly restive. Independent Slav states had arisen from the collapse of the Ottoman Empire, and in order to forestall the spread of separatist sentiments among its own Slav populations, Austria first gained control over, then in 1908 annexed, Bosnia and Herzegovina.

Nationalist conflicts were even more serious in Hungary where the Magyars attempted to shore up their predominant position by repressing other ethnic populations. Unlike the Germans in Austria, the proportion of Magyars in Hungary grew steadily, from 49 percent to a bare majority of 51 percent in 1900, and to 55 percent in 1910. Magyarization intensified from 1900. In 1907 Hungarian was decreed the only language of instruction in elementary schools, and non-Magyar cultural and religious organizations were harassed and suppressed and replaced by Hungarian cultural societies. Warning signs in public places were printed only in Hungarian.

Even the German-speaking minority in Hungary felt threatened enough by Magyarization to form its own political party in 1905. But when they looked outside Hungary for protection, it was still within the empire, to Austria. In contrast, when members of other minorities looked for support, it was outside the empire entirely, as when Romanians in Hungarian Transylvania agitated for union with Romania. Even traditionally loyal populations like the Croats began to look beyond Austria-Hungary as a result of increasing Hungarian persecution.

Russia, also a great multinational empire, increased its Russification policies from the mid-1890s, although their intensity varied from region to region. The use of Russian was strictly enforced in Polish areas, for example, but in Finland it was required only in girls' schools, and then from 1900 on. The policies met resistance of varying strengths. When in 1901 the separate Finnish army was dissolved and its soldiers ordered to be incorporated into Russian units (because of Finland's strategic importance in a time of rising international tensions), there was widespread resistance to conscription.

Finns and Poles in Russia participated in the wave of strikes that washed through the empire in 1905, and benefited from the extension of civil liberties that resulted from the pressure on the tsarist regime after Russia's humiliating defeat in the war with Japan. For two years Russification was relaxed: Poles were allowed to establish private schools where children could be taught in Polish. In 1906 Finns established Europe's most democratic parliamentary system in which all adults, female and male, voted for a unicameral legislature. Hundreds of thousands of Finns demonstrated their national attachment in 1906 by changing their Swedish family names into Finnish. (Ironically, however, the success of Finnish nationalism also created anxiety in many members of Finland's Swedish population, who promptly formed their own political party.) But minority gains in Russia, like political liberties, were rolled back from 1908 as the czarist autocracy reasserted its power. The brief experience of a more liberal policy, however, sharpened nationalist aspirations for greater freedom and sovereignty.

Pressure for Irish independence grew in the prewar period, too, and divisions grew between the predominantly Catholic southern counties and the overwhelmingly Protestant province of Ulster in the north. By 1912 a volunteer force was created in Ulster to protect the region from the possibility of being ruled from Dublin, the expected result if the British Parliament granted home rule to Ireland. A parallel paramilitary force was established in the south to fight for home rule. The question of Irish nationalism was now complicated by the willingness of part of the population to fight for it and part to fight against it. Pressure to resolve the issue grew after 1912, and although it dissipated when war broke out, it was revived both during and after the war.

Nationalism in all its forms was an important ingredient in the instability of Europe in the years before the First World War. It contributed to the rise of the new great power, Germany, and to the defense of the powers whose status it threatened, notably Great Britain and France. At the same time it was a factor in the virtual disappearance of the Ottoman Empire's European territory and the weakening of Austria-Hungary and Russia.

The Rise of Right-Wing Extremism

Ethnic nationalism found its most extreme expressions in right-wing movements that were the ideological precursors of twentieth-century fascism. Fascism is one of the more difficult ideologies to define, but in concrete political terms it generally describes movements that were ultranationalistic, populist, and which stressed the notion of a corporative national community implying the exclusion of one or more specific groups. Within this last category, fascists were especially hostile to Jews as well as to other "outside" groups like Sinti and Roma and Freemasons.

In many cases fascism was a reaction not only to liberalism (which stressed individuality over community) and socialism (which stressed the importance of classes over community) but also to the broad social, political, and economic trends of the late nineteenth century. Fascist ideology often evoked a mythical and mystical age of rural bliss and harmony in which men and women knew their places in the social hierarchy. To this extent fascists can be seen as both revolutionary and reactionary.

Every expression of fascism seems to challenge any single definition, although late-nineteenth-century forms seem somewhat more homogeneous than the variants that developed after the First World War. One of the most prominent expressions of turn-of-the-century fascism was Action Française (French Action), which was formed in France in 1898 during the turmoil surrounding the Dreyfus Affair. Action Française was rabidly nationalistic, backed the army against its pro-Dreyfus detractors, and supported the Catholic Church against the secular policies of the Third Republic. It was strongly anti-Semitic as well as hostile to Freemasons and Protestants, all of which were seen as representatives of "anti-France." Action Française also opposed democracy, which it portrayed as "feminine" and "weak" in contrast to a virile, strong monarchy, a reminder of the importance of gender and sexuality to political language in this period.

The organization, which attracted thousands of supporters, mainly professionals (especially teachers and lawyers), priests, and army officers, formed paramilitary groups of young people to harass anyone suspected of being unpatriotic. In 1908 one professor was attacked and his lectures disrupted because he had taken students on a study-tour of Germany, and another in 1909 because he had made comments about Joan of Arc that were considered offensive to nationalists. Jewish teachers were frequent targets.

A number of similar ultranationalist and anti-Semitic leagues were founded in Germany, but there a distinctive ingredient was added: the belief in the superiority and destiny of the Germanic *Volk*, or racially defined people. The *völkisch* or racial element was stronger in German right-wing ideology than elsewhere, and was directly against Jews in particular. In much German fascist writing, Jews were condemned for being associated with democracy, liberalism, and capitalism, but they were also portrayed as a threat to the survival of racially defined Germans. Julius Langbehn, an influential ideologist of the German right, wrote "Germany for the Germans. A Jew can no more become a German than a plum can turn into an apple," and he called for racial ancestry to be made a criterion of German citizenship.

Although many German organizations of the right did not necessarily possess all the elements of fascist movements, their antiliberalism, extreme nationalism, hatred of "outsiders," and strong attachments to authoritarian social and political systems endow them with affinities to interwar fascism. Like them, many nationalists evoked a mythic past, drawing on pre-Christian paganism and mysticism to construct a history of Germany and Europe that stressed the purity of the so-called Teutonic and Aryan races from which "true" modern Germans derived.

Movements with fascist characteristics emerged in the prewar period in many countries, but most achieved little success beyond limited middle-class appeal. In Austria they were represented by some of the pan-German organizations that promoted the unification of the ethnic German regions of Austria with Germany. Many other Austrian parties were anti-Semitic to varying degrees, and in 1911 they won two-thirds of all the votes cast by ethnic German Austrians. It was in this environment that Adolf Hitler (who was born in Austria in 1889 and was twenty-two years old in 1911) grew up.

Although we should be careful not to portray prewar movements in Austria and Germany as Nazi, they did provide the ideological foundations of the program Hitler later developed, and many of their members became prominent Nazis in the 1920s and 1930s. It is important to note, however, that they also drew on mainstream intellectual and cultural currents such as the fears of social and physical degeneration, ideas about ethnicity, anxiety about industrialization and urbanization, and eugenics.

Finally, extreme right organizations developed in prewar Russia. They have often been overlooked, partly because the czarist regime seemed to occupy the right wing of the political spectrum quite adequately on its own, partly because the success of the Bolshevik revolution in 1917 directed attention more consistently to the history of the Russian left.

From 1905, when short-lived reforms were introduced in Russia, right-wing associations collectively known as the Black Hundreds agitated in favor of autocracy and against Jews. At their peak in 1906–7 they had 3,000 branches, drawing their leadership from the aristocracy and church hierarchy, and gaining support from across the social spectrum, especially the lower middle class. The Black Hundreds were behind the widespread pogroms in 1905–6 in which hundreds of Jews were killed and thousands wounded.

In Russia as elsewhere in Europe, the belief in a Jewish conspiracy to take over the world took root from the late nineteenth century. It was reinforced by the publication of *The Protocols of the Elders of Zion,* which purported to be a record of secret meetings of the leaders of a Jewish conspiracy to control the world. According to the *Protocols,* Jews had produced all disasters and problems in history, including the French Revolution, political assassinations, strikes, infectious diseases, alcoholism among workers, and increased food prices. As absurd as the work was, it became a key reference point of anti-Semites in Russia and, after the First World War, in Germany.

Reactions to Nationalism

Although nationalism goes a long way to explaining the popular enthusiasm for war in many countries in 1914, it would be misleading to ignore attempts to reduce nationalist fervor and the military preparations that often accompanied it before the war. In 1898, after the announcement that Germany planned to construct a new fleet, Czar Nicholas II called for a conference to discuss ways of stopping the competition between states to build up their armies and navies. He was motivated less by a spirit of internationalism than by a realization that participating in an arms race would place unbearable strains on Russia's already shaky economy and finances.

Two conferences were held in The Hague (in the Netherlands) in 1899 and 1907, and although there was no agreement on arms limitations, restrictions were placed on certain new weapons that industrialization had made possible, such as poison gas and weapons launched from balloons—bombs. In addition an international court was established in The Hague to arbitrate disputes between nations.

Other manifestations of internationalism included the regular declamations of Europe's socialist parties, decrying nationalism as inimical to working-class interests. Not only did nationalism blur class distinctions, but workers, whether German, French, Austrian, or British, had more in common with one another than either had with the middle class and wealthy elites in their respective countries. The Second International, an international organization of socialist parties, called upon its members to refuse to vote for war credits in case of war.

Many women's rights organizations also deplored nationalism, stressing the common interests of women everywhere and insisting that the struggle for women's rights crossed political borders. It was frequently argued that wars would diminish or end once women were able to vote, enter government, and influence domestic and foreign policy. International rallies of women were held to coincide with The Hague conferences in 1899 and 1907. Women's activities were part of a broader peace movement that dated from the nineteenth century. It was reinforced by bodies such as the Inter-Parliamentary Union, an association of legislators from many nations, and the Nobel Committee, which began to award its famous peace prizes in 1901.

One attempt to replace growing national rivalry was the organization of the first modern Olympic Games in 1896. But the original plan for young men (women were initially excluded) to compete with one another as individuals was subverted by the division of competitors into national teams. Before long the Olympics became an occasion for nations to demonstrate the strength of their youth and, by implication, themselves. Olympic contestants were a denial of the mass physical decline so many nationalists feared: young runners, fencers, shooters, and gymnasts, wearing national insignia and marching behind national flags, were the physical elite of the generation each country could draw on for its armies.

Other innovations that might have eroded the differences between nations and promoted international understanding also failed to do so. In the 1890s a Polish Jew, L. L. Zamenhof, devised an international language that he called Esperanto, meaning (in Esperanto) "the hopeful one." It was telling that an attempt to develop a language that would allow people of all nations to communicate with one another should have emerged from a place and time when linguistic and national conflicts were intensifying. The International Esperanto Society was formed in 1908, but despite some enthusiasm for it, the language attracted only a small following.

Even learning a genuine foreign language, which had the potential to help young people bridge Europe's linguistic divides, was an occasion to make points about nationality. The standard French text used in English schools in the early 1900s required children to translate passages such as: "The Russians used to plunder everywhere. When they were in Italy they plundered the Italians. The Scotchmen and Englishmen near the border were enemies, but now Scotchmen are the good friends of the English," "English horses are generally better than French horses," and "The French are the most brilliant talkers; the Germans are the most painstaking writers; the Americans are the cleverest inventors; and the English are the most capable rulers of the world."

International tourism took off in the late nineteenth century, allowing the middle classes, at least, to visit foreign places. But instead of broadening horizons, tourism tended as much to narrow them and confirm national stereotypes. The Thomas Cook travel agency warned its clients against the moral dangers of France, including the nightclubs of Paris, lax attitudes toward alcohol, and widespread disregard for the Sabbath. Invidious comparison between nations extended to food, with one English health manual commenting that outside England "it is impossible to avoid the greasy dishes which are apparently preferred by all except our own countrymen; and a frequent consequence is rancid indigestion, with a nauseous taste in the mouth, and flatulence or diarrhoea."

The comment of one Rev. E. J. Hardy in the 1890s, that English tourists returning home "give one the impression that they are returning from war, rather than a pleasure trip," was sadly prescient. In the increasingly tense international climate before World War I, appeals to common humanity and international understanding and cooperation lost ground to the attraction of flag, nation, and preparations for war. Nothing, it seemed, could turn back the rising tide of nationalism. It became much more potent a force in the prewar years when it was linked to broader political, social changes, and to the needs for entrenched elites within the various states to defend their political and economic interests.

Preparing for War:
Militarization and Its Discontents

Military strength was a critical consideration in international relations before the war, and between 1890 and 1914 almost all European states' armed forces grew. Military budgets were increased and armies and navies were expanded and professionalized. This trend is sometimes seen as contributing to the outbreak of war in 1914, but it is important to bear in mind that the existence of armed force is different from its use. Although it could well be that politicians and military commanders with bigger armies and new equipment more readily undertake wars—if for no other reason than to justify or try out their new acquisitions—the arms buildup of 1890–1914 did not make war inevitable.

There were great variations in the sizes of regular military establishments (excluding reserve forces) on the eve of the war. Russia's 1,350,000 army and navy personnel, which represented almost twice the number under arms in 1880, were by no means the most efficient, and they lacked modern equipment. On the other hand the 890,000 German forces (more than twice the 1880 figure) were well trained and equipped. Britain's relatively small force of 530,000 reflected the priority given to the navy. In all, the major European states had 4.5 million men in their permanent forces in 1914, compared with 3.7 million in 1900 and 2.8 million in 1890. Military personnel doubled in a quarter of a century, compared with an increase in population of less than a third.

European armies were mostly composed of conscripts (Britain's volunteer force was the exception), who were called up in large numbers. By 1900, Germany called up 280,000 a year, France 250,000, Russia 335,000, and Italy and Austria-Hungary about 100,000 each. Continental states copied the German system of drafting large numbers of young men for short periods so as to provide an extensive pool of reservists. Military service was not universally welcomed by conscripts, though in most states there were few ways of avoiding it. In Spain, where it was possible to purchase an exemption, the rate of avoidance of military service rose steadily from 2.7 percent in 1895 to 10.5 percent in 1908 and 22 percent in 1914.

Beyond the simple size of military forces, there were significant differences in the quality of the soldiers. The spread of formal education, which exposed increasing proportions of national populations to learning and discipline, made for better-trained soldiers. Literacy was immensely useful for military training and command, and an advantage that some countries had over others. The proportion of literate men among recruits ranged from two-thirds in Italy and Russia, and three-quarters in Austria-Hungary, to more than 90 percent in France and 99 percent in Germany.

The period also saw increases in the weaponry available to armed forces. The tonnage of warships possessed by the major European powers doubled between 1880 and 1900, then more than doubled again by 1914. The greatest increases were posted by Britain and Germany, which together possessed well over half of Europe's warship tonnage. This was largely the result of a naval arms race that began in 1898 when Germany announced a program to build a generation of super-battleships. The British, wanting to maintain naval superiority, quickly launched their own naval construction program,

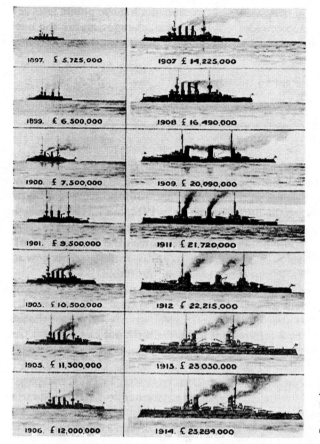

A diagrammatic representation of the growth of the German navy from 1897 to 1914. The figures reflect Germany's annual expenditure.

notably of the large Dreadnought class of battleships. Even though the British were able to maintain naval superiority, the gap between British and German navies narrowed dramatically. From having the world's fifth largest navy in 1890, Germany had the second largest by 1914.

Aircraft were also added to military forces, although more for reconnaissance than combat purposes. Britain established the Royal Flying Corps and added air power to the navy. Both Germany and France were also quick to apply the new flying technology to their military preparations. Germany forged ahead of its rivals in airship technology, however, and at the outbreak of war had eleven available for military use.

Military preparations tested a nation's economic strength, and here, too, Germany outdid its allies and rivals with the exception of Great Britain. The German army budget more than doubled between 1910 and 1914, to the equivalent of $440 million. Its main ally, Austria-Hungary, chronically underfunded its military establishment, and conflicts over the language of command hampered its development even as international tensions rose. In Italy, the third member of the Triple Alliance, the situation was little better, despite the fact that a quarter of all state expenditure between 1867 and 1913 was on the army and navy. Italy's navy, the world's second largest in the 1880s, declined relative to other European powers, and a 1911–12 war to win territory in Libya, although successful, was so costly that it created a huge budgetary deficit.

British governments financed their military with relative ease. The land army was small, but even with a heavy increase in naval spending Britain allocated a smaller percentage of its national income to defense than any other major European power. In contrast France, which tried desperately to modernize and increase its military strength, was barely able to allocate $200 million in 1914, less than a 5 percent increase over 1910. For its part the Russian army and navy remained outmoded and inefficient despite attempts to modernize both after the fiasco of the Russo-Japanese war.

Expansion of military forces was not confined to the great powers, and some smaller states improved their military positions. The growing demand in Norway for complete independence from Sweden led both to prepare for a conflict. Sweden extended the term of military service in 1901, while Norway ordered warships, bought field artillery, and constructed defenses along the common border with Sweden. In some states, however, the costs of building and equipping modern armies were too much for budgets to bear, and they contributed to financial crises in Serbia and Bulgaria between 1895 and 1901.

Militarization went well beyond the narrow scope of armed forces and included what is sometimes called *popular militarism*, the militarization of society more generally. Youth groups that sprang up at the turn of the century were part of this process. There was emphasis in the Scout movement and its counterparts in France, Germany, and elsewhere on activities and skills that were in effect basic military training: camping and survival, marching, drilling, and map reading, all within a context of loyalty and martial discipline. The middle-class boys who experienced the Scouting life were well prepared for officer training in the military in later life. Churches set up their own youth organizations based on military models, like the Anglican Church's Church Lads' Brigade, the Methodists' Boys Brigade, and the Girls' Brigade in England.

The military model extended to other spheres as well. The Salvation Army, founded in England in 1890 to work and proselytize among the poor and working classes, was organized on a military basis. Members had ranks and wore uniforms with the appropriate insignia. It is possible that its military appearance made the Salvation Army more acceptable to the working-class men it tried to persuade to abandon their "manly" pastimes of drinking and gambling, but it nonetheless figured within an increasingly pervasive military cast of mind.

Military preparedness echoed loudly, too, in debates on population and motherhood in the prewar period. Because children—male children, anyway—were the soldiers of the future, women could be portrayed as performing a national service by being mothers. The Swedish feminist Ellen Key, who was influential in Scandinavia and Germany, argued that women's training and activities as mothers were equivalent to military training for men. In France a 1906 bill to guarantee women their jobs after maternity leave was modeled on a law that guaranteed army reservists their jobs when they had completed a period of active duty. Broad formulations of military service such as these established the conceptual framework for the "home front" of the First World War, the notion that the contribution of civilians, women and men, at home and work, were as crucial as the efforts of soldiers on the front lines.

Military themes, enriched with nationalist aspirations and fears, increased their profile in European culture from the turn of the century. In Britain, France, and Germany especially, there was an outpouring of novels, for adults and young people alike, that dealt with foreign invasions and espionage. A 1904 German novel called *The World War: German Dreams,* which painted a picture of a combined German-Russian invasion of Britain, caused alarm when it was published in English translation as *The Coming Conquest of England.* The sheer improbability of a combined German-Russian enterprise of any kind in this period was overlooked. The apprehension of Britons was not allayed when one of their field marshals wrote an introduction to a 1906 novel, *The Invasion of 1910,* warning that the country's failure to prepare its military defenses laid it open to invasion by Germany. Novels in all three countries described spy networks, frequently run by Jews, who were assumed to be loyal to no nation. They helped prepare the ground for the suspicion of people with accents or "foreign-sounding" names that was widespread during the 1914–18 war.

Military expansion, popular militarism, and suspicion of foreigners were not universally welcomed, however. Just as a sentiment of internationalism coexisted with increasing nationalism, so there was an antimilitarist spirit abroad as states everywhere armed for war. Many of its bearers were those who supported internationalism over nationalism.

One of the prominent antimilitarist forces in prewar Europe were socialists, who frequently used their elected representatives to oppose conscription and increases in military budgets. The French Socialist Party called for a radical reform of defense, with the army of conscripts replaced by a volunteer militia. Because military service fell most heavily on young men, the youth sections of socialist parties were often quite strong and in many countries tended to be even more internationalist in their outlook than older party members. A youth group was expelled from the Swedish Social Democrats in 1908 after it was found to have connections with Finnish and Russian terrorists.

Opposition to military activity was also widespread among women's organizations. Socialist women espoused internationalism, and others expressed more strictly pacifist views, arguing that women, who suffered through the deaths of their husbands, fathers, brothers, and sons in battle, had a special duty to speak out against war. There were massive peace marches by women in 1899 and 1907. Nor were women's organizations universally delighted by the prevailing view of motherhood as a national (or explicitly military) duty. In France, Nelly Roussel proclaimed women's rights to control their own fertility, and even threatened a kind of labor strike: "Beware, Oh Society! The day will come . . . when we will refuse to give you . . . your ration of cannon-fodder, of work-fodder, and fodder for suffering! The day, at last, when we will become mothers only when we please."

There was also a reaction to the supposedly scientific justifications of war, particularly against "social Darwinism," which suggested that humans had to struggle against one another to survive. Against the notion that Darwinism supported imperial rivalry and racial conflict, protagonists of peace used it to support the idea that humanity advanced by acting cooperatively. There were also eugenicists who insisted that hostility and bellicosity could be bred out of humans to create a peaceful world.

Governments were wary of pacifists and antiwar activists, suspecting them of being at best misguided women and men who would not defend their country, at worst potential traitors who would turn their fellow citizens over to the enemy. Socialists were often singled out, not only because they opposed war but also because they threatened the prevailing social order more generally. Efforts were made to shield soldiers from socialist and pacifist ideas, and German soldiers were forbidden to attend left-wing political meetings in their spare time.

Challenges to the Status Quo
Within European States

Opposition to military preparation, although unsuccessful and for the most part abandoned once war began in 1914, reveals the growing importance of new political forces within European social and political systems. They were represented by groups such as unions, socialist parties, and women's organizations, all manifestations of the mass society that distinguished the twentieth from the nineteenth century.

In many countries pressure on elite control of political systems resulted in broader participation by the extension of voting rights. Before 1890 adult men had the right to vote in very few states. Male suffrage took its most complete form in France, while in Britain there were anomalies that disenfranchised some men. All German males over twenty-five could vote for the lower chamber of the empire (the Reichstag) but the upper chamber (Bundesrat) was appointed. Moreover, although adult males had the vote in state elections in most of Germany, Prussia's electoral system was weighted to give the wealthiest citizens a disproportionate influence.

Between 1890 and 1914 the trend in much of Europe was to extend the franchise to more and more men. Spain, where universal male suffrage had existed from 1869 to 1875, restored it in 1890, and virtually all adult men were granted the vote in Belgium (1893), Norway (1898), Finland (1906), Austria (1907), Sweden (1909), and Portugal (1910). There were some general exceptions, notably men in jails and asylums, and individual countries specified other disqualified men; in Norway men on poor relief could not vote, and in Sweden men who had not been taxpayers for at least three years were disenfranchised. In Italy, where there was an educational criterion for voting, the franchise was extended in 1912 to men who could not satisfy the requirement yet had reached the age of thirty or had completed their military service.

In Russia, too, political participation expanded folllowing a revolution in 1905, the result of growing opposition to the czarist autocracy combined with the collapse of the government following Russia's defeat by Japan. One of the concessions made by Czar Nicholas II was for a Duma, an elected assembly. But thereafter Russia bucked the trend of widening political participation: The almost universal male suffrage established in 1906—even though voting procedures favored some social groups (like large landowners) over others (especially city dwellers)—was progressively reduced by subsequent decrees. By 1907 it included only 15 percent of the adult male population, and by 1914 scarcely one in a hundred men in major cities like St. Petersburg and Moscow was enfranchised.

Universal male suffrage is not the same as universal suffrage, for women were almost everywhere excluded from voting in national elections, although in some places they could vote municipally or regionally. The exceptions were Finland, where women were enfranchised in 1906, and Norway, where they were granted the vote in stages between 1907 and 1913. In most countries women were excluded by implication because laws explicitly enfranchised men of a certain age, but the Portuguese, reacting against increasing demands by women wanting the vote, specifically excluded them in 1913. In most German states women not only could not vote, but until 1908 they also were barred from belonging to political organizations.

The gradual, though sex-specific, extension of the franchise in much of Europe was accompanied here and there by constitutional changes that opened up the political process. Lower houses, elected by a widening constituency, gained power at the expense of upper chambers that were appointive or hereditary. In France the upper chamber (the Senate) was made elective in 1884. The power of the British House of Lords was limited in 1911 and members of the House of Commons began to receive salaries, enabling men other than the independently wealthy to take up a political career. In Denmark minsters were made responsible to Parliament, rather than the king, in 1901. Secret balloting was also introduced in a number of European legislatures to protect representatives from political pressure and prevent bribery; there was no point in paying a deputy to vote a certain way when one could not see that he did.

Elsewhere, however, pressures for constitutional reform in a democratic direction were resisted. The czar progressively undermined the powers of the Duma and within a few years of its creation had reduced it to a tool of the autocracy. The kaiser (who was also king of Prussia) resisted any attempt to alter the Prussian voting system that would dislodge the landed elites from their dominant position. The Magyar minority in Hungary opposed any reform that would endanger its political dominance over other ethnic groups.

Despite the uneven progress of constitutional reform, the political spectrum throughout Europe broadened as new constituencies clamored for inclusion in the political system, some in order to change the system radically. Left-wing parties of various kinds, notably socialists and social democrats, fielded candidates and won increasing numbers of seats. The Labour Party won 29 of the 670 seats in Britain's House of Commons in 1906, socialists won a quarter of the votes in the 1912 Norwegian election, and in the German election the same year the Social Democrats attracted 35 percent of the votes cast and became the largest party in the Reichstag.

The growing influence of social democrats, who often pooled their votes with liberals, was reflected in the spread of social legislation in the prewar period. Laws were passed in many countries to regulate conditions of work, set up unemployment and sickness insurance plans, and introduce old-age pensions. In France, for example, a six-day week was made law in 1906 and an insurance plan introduced in 1910. Germany, which had led the way in sickness, accident, unemployment, and old-age insurance in the 1880s, extended some programs to include middle-class occupations. Even in Russia there were workers' insurance schemes from 1912.

Some of the prewar social legislation was designed to do more than improve the lives of citizens. In Germany the various programs to assist workers were intended to undercut growing support for socialism and trade unions by showing that they were unnecessary. Much of the social legislation to improve the health of women and children was, as we have seen, designed to increase population for nationalist and state purposes.

Increasing success brought new problems to socialists. As they gained positions of power within political structures many socialists began to act like other politicians, and to support established practices and policies rather than seek to reform or replace them with socialist alternatives. Every socialist party was torn by conflicts between those who wanted rapid transformation of the social and political systems and those who were satisfied with gradual change. In most Western European states the moderates gained the upper hand, sometimes leading radicals to break away and form their own parties or movements.

Labor unions were often associated with socialist parties, and they, too, became forces that the elites had to reckon with more and more. Union membership rose rapidly between 1900 and 1914; it doubled to 4 million in Britain, more than trebled to 3 million in Germany, and quadrupled to 1 million in France. Even so, unions represented only a quarter of British workers, a fifth in Germany, and an eighth in France, and their representation of women was minimal.

The classic form of pressure that a union could exert was the industrial strike, and strikes became far more common in the early 1900s than they had been in the late nineteenth century. For the most part strikes centered on issues of wages and conditions in specific industries, rather than being political strikes. Although there were examples of general strikes to add pressure for political reform, it often proved difficult to mobilize workers for political action. A 1912 poll of German miners and textile and metal workers found that only a small proportion were concerned about broad political and social change; most aspired to higher wages, more plentiful food, and a better life for their children.

A third source of pressure on political structures was women seeking rights of participation in the full range of social, economic, and political activities. Women's rights organizations throughout Europe sought equality with men, in itself a qualified demand because

The struggle for women's suffrage: A
British suffragette is arrested in 1913.

men were fully enfranchised in only a few states before 1914. The 1905 program of the
Union of Women's Associations in Germany expressed the aspirations of many women's organizations throughout Europe: equal education, equal pay, equality in marriage, equal
rights of political participation.

The vigorous struggle for women's rights in other spheres met with gradual success.
Although women were admitted to medical schools in Britain and Russia in the 1880s, the
same right was not extended to women in Germany, France, and Switzerland until the
1890s, and elsewhere even later. Italian women could go to law school, but were forbidden to practice. Women's rights activists used all means available to communicate their
message and put pressure on governments to change the laws. Meetings and rallies were
held (one of the largest was the quarter-million-strong assembly in London's Hyde Park
in 1908), and pamphlets were written and distributed. Legislatures were disrupted by
demonstrators, and when imprisoned for their actions, some women went on hunger
strikes and were force-fed.

Many women activists looked further than obtaining the vote and declared war on un-
regenerated men. In England Emmeline Pankhurst and her daughter Christabel declared a
kind of separatism, denouncing marriage as dangerous as long as men were morally corrupt,
and condemning the general domination of women by men. In 1913 and 1914 women's

rights activists in England carried out an arson campaign, setting fire to stations, churches, and cricket pavilions, causing tens of thousands of pounds of damage each month.

Revolution in Russia, 1905

Prewar political systems found themselves under growing pressure to include new constituencies: women almost everywhere, workers in many countries, and middle-class citizens in states where traditional landed and hereditary elites continued to exercise disproportionate power in political structures. For the most part the pressure was steady but uneven so that governments could respond piecemeal, granting a concession here and a new law there, just enough to keep pressure below a critical point and maintain the appearance that the prevailing system was responsive to its citizens and capable of change, however glacial its speed.

In all cases, however, compromises and concessions were made at the expense of the existing elites, and the result was to sharpen social and political conflicts in many European countries. But in some states circumstances and pressures created situations where compromise proved impossible. In Russia the spread of socialist and liberal ideas in the wake of industrialization, combined with widespread famines in the 1890s, led to increasing criticism of the regime. In 1905 moderate liberals, including republicans and constitutional monarchists, formed the Constitutional Democratic Party (known as the Cadet Party after the initials in Russian). On the left the most important parties were the Social Democrats, a Marxist party formed in 1898 to work among the urban proletariat, and the Socialist Revolutionaries, an agrarian socialist party.

The rise of these parties reflected the period of turmoil that Russia entered at the turn of the century. The number of strikes increased, students protested, and there were widespread peasant disturbances. Complaints ran the gamut from the food supply and agrarian reform, to specific legal and social reforms and broad constitutional change. While strikes, conferences, and demonstrations were the usual means of applying pressure, the Socialist Revolutionaries adopted terror, and assassinated a number of public officials including two of the czar's ministers and the commander of the Moscow military region.

Pressure mounted from 1902 and culminated on Bloody Sunday (January 22, 1905) when police fired on workers in St. Petersburg, killing or wounding several hundred. (The czar noted in his diary that night, "It's been a difficult day.") In the following months demands for serious reform increased, despite attempts by the government to appease specific groups by proclaiming religious tolerance, easing discrimination against ethnic minorities, and promising to establish a consultative assembly. There were mutinies in the military, including a famous rebellion on the battleship *Potemkin*, and a massive general strike in October.

At the end of October 1905 the czar announced sweeping reforms, including civil liberties, a promise of more reforms to follow, and the establishment of a Duma with full legislative powers. While this response satisfied the moderates in the opposition, socialists were wary of Nicholas's promises, and called for an assembly that would draw up a new constitution. Their suspicion proved justified when the following May Nicholas promulgated Fundamental Laws by which he retained immense powers, including the right to dismiss the Duma and veto its legislation. Almost half the state budget would remain at the czar's disposal, ministers were responsible to him, and up to half the members of an upper house would be appointed by him.

The first election to the new legislature suggested the breadth of desire for change. The liberal Cadets won 38 percent of the vote and held 184 of the 497 seats, while socialists held 124 seats, despite a general boycott of the election by the Social Democrats and Socialist Revolutionaries. A stalemate between the czar and Duma over constitutional reform led to his dismissal of the assembly. Elections to the Second Duma, in 1907, resulted in an even stronger representation for the opposition: Left-wing deputies held 216 seats, close to an absolute majority.

Unable to win the game, the czar changed the rules, insisting that he had authority from God. The suffrage was modified so as to favor the land-owning gentry over peasants and workers. From 1907 the vote of a member of the gentry was worth, in electoral influence, the same as 65 middle-class men, 260 peasants, or 540 workers. This system produced a much more compliant Duma, but it frustrated the evidently widespread desire for political and social reform.

The Russian Revolution of 1905 represented only a temporary setback for the czar, although it was undoubtedly a milestone on Russia's road to the more fundamental transformation of the Bolshevik Revolution during World War I. Before the war, however, other states went through revolutions of one sort or another.

The czar survived—for a few more years, at least—but two European monarchs were overthrown in the prewar period. In 1903 the Serbian king Alexander and his wife were killed in a military coup. A provisional government established a constitutional monarchy under a king drawn from the other of Serbia's two preeminent families. In 1910 there was a revolution in Portugal, in which King Manuel II was toppled and a republic proclaimed.

On their way to an international crisis of the greatest magnitude, the powers of Europe were involved with internal problems, which in some cases had the dimensions of crises. Austria-Hungary was facing increasing ethnic strain, in Germany the growing strength of organized labor and the socialist parties alarmed the imperial government and its supporters among the agrarian and industrial elites, and in Russia the autocratic reaction that followed the liberalization of 1905 created immense political frustration. The more democratic powers, notably France and Britain, experienced their own problems but they did not approach the critical levels of those in the empires to the east.

The Crises Mount, 1911 to June 1914

In the quarter century before World War I, Europe's social and political institutions came under pressure from shifts in the balance of power and from the nationalist aspirations of states as different in size and power as Germany and Serbia. Individual countries were to varying degrees beset by the challenges posed by rapid social change and the problems of accommodating or containing new political forces.

To understand why this volatile mixture ignited and produced the war in August 1914, we must focus on the critical phase from 1911. This short period saw an acceleration of the existing trends, increasing tensions, and rising expectations of war. In these conditions the assassination of the heir to the Austrian throne in June 1914, a relatively minor event compared to its consequences, was enough to set off a series of decisions that culminated in a world war.

Hostility between Serbia and Austria-Hungary over influence in the Balkans was central to this process, but only because the Balkan area was important to the great powers more generally. Russia's continuing preoccupations were to become the dominant influence in the Balkans and to obtain a permanently secure passage from the Black Sea to the Mediterranean. With the increasing possibility that the Ottoman Empire might collapse entirely, Russia tried to ensure that the straits came under the control of a friendly power, if not under direct Russian control.

The main obstacle to Russian expansion in the region was Austria-Hungary, but from 1911 Germany entered the picture more directly. The global policy announced by the kaiser in the late 1890s had failed. The last attempt to expand German influence in Africa provoked the Second Morocco Crisis when in 1911 Germany protested against French occupation of the capital of Morocco, and sent a gunboat to the port of Agadir to force the French to make concessions. Although the French did concede a small amount of territory in exchange for German recognition of French authority in Morocco, Germany's action badly misfired. While its Habsburg ally offered no support whatever, Britain gave unexpectedly strong backing to France. The incident indicated the tension that had developed between Britain and Germany and the understanding between Britain and France. The episode convinced the German government to moderate its global policy and concentrate on the already volatile region of the Balkans and Asia Minor.

The French-German confrontation over Morocco had other immediate consequences. The compromise was opposed by nationalists in both countries. Germans felt they had been humiliated by having to back down and by being given some colonial crumbs; their French counterparts were enraged that Germany should have been given any French crumbs at all. Britain and France reopened defense discussions, and in 1912 agreed on joint naval strategy. The state of French feeling was indicated by the election in early 1912 of Raymond Poincaré, a fervent nationalist and native of Lorraine, a region regarded by the French as being under German occupation.

The result of the 1911 Morocco crisis persuaded the Italian government that the age of colonialism in Africa was not over, and in September that year Italian troops invaded the Ottoman province of Libya in north Africa. Reactions to Italy's venture had the effect of reinforcing the alliances and understandings that linked the great powers. Germany calculated that the Triple Alliance was more useful than any link with Turkey, and not only supported Italy but also persuaded Austria-Hungary to do the same. There was no objection from either when Italy also occupied the Dodecanese Islands in the Aegean Sea in the heart of the Balkan region. Britain and France, on the other hand, opposed Italian expansion. Britain was alarmed at the potential threat an Italian Libya posed to British-controlled Egypt, and France was embroiled in conflict with Italy over the arrest of two French steamers in January 1912.

The Turkish government's preoccupation with Italian aggression led Serbia, Bulgaria, and Greece, encouraged by Russia, to form a Balkan League against Turkey in 1912. Russia saw the league as a bulwark against Austria-Hungary, but the league's members intended to cooperate in seizing additional territory in Ottoman Europe. In 1912 the window of opportunity opened wide when the Turkish government, weakened by foreign setbacks, fell. Its successor purged the army officer corps, and the Balkan League seized the moment to invade Macedonia and other Ottoman territory. Serbian troops seized territory as far as the Adriatic coast (occupying what is now Albania), while Bulgaria annexed land in its south, and Greek forces moved into territory to its north.

It was the Serbian gains that were most sensitive to outside powers. Italy and Austria-Hungary were determined that Serbia should not keep the coastal areas it had seized, not only because it gave Serbia so much territory but also for fear that Russia might be given access to the ports. For a while in late 1912 it seemed that the issue might draw the great powers into conflict. Russia delayed the demobilization of a levy of conscripts, and the

Austro-Hungarian army was increased. In December 1912 the Triple Alliance of Germany, Italy, and Austria-Hungary was pointedly renewed before its term expired. On the other side, France and Russia extended their alliance to include a war resulting from a Russian attack on Austria-Hungary.

Against the polarization of European powers over the Balkans, and Serbia's policies in particular, must be placed great power cooperation in settling the issues without resort to war. At a London conference it was quickly agreed that Serbia should relinquish territory along the Adriatic coast, and that an independent Albania should be created. This settlement disappointed Austria-Hungary most, for it established a relatively weak Albania that would be little guarantee against future Serbian encroachment. Nor were the Balkan States ready to comply speedily or entirely with the arrangements imposed on them at the London conference. Austro-Hungarian threats were needed before Serbia evacuated some of territory designated for Albania.

National policies throughout the crisis of 1912–13 are open to varying interpretations, but some appear more ambiguous than others. In most cases the policies served both foreign and domestic purposes. The Austro-Hungarian government was clearly determined to stop the development of a powerful southern Slav state with Serbia at its core. The objection was founded as much on the repercussions such a state would have on the stability of Austria-Hungary as it was on any threat such a state might pose externally. A strong Slavic state would almost certainly have reinforced nationalist sentiments among Slavs in Hungary who would readily give up Magyar rule to be part of a Slavic nation.

German policy was more diffuse. Germany's cosponsorship of the1912 London conference, and its support of Britain against its Austro-Hungarian ally on a number of issues (like the size of Albania) might be interpreted as evidence of moderation among ruling circles in Berlin. But it must be read in light of a German decision to foster cooperation with Britain to try to ensure British neutrality in the event of a war pitting Germany against France and Russia.

From 1912 there were sound domestic reasons for the German government to contemplate at least a limited war. In the election that year the Social Democrats won a third of the vote and 110 of the 397 seats in the Reichstag, an achievement that reflected growing divisions within German society. Before the election the conservative-dominated Reichstag had rejected a proposal that part of Germany's increased military spending be paid for by a death duty, which would have affected the wealthy in particular. Instead it devised a plan for indirect taxation, which hit workers and the poor, who used the election to translate their anger into votes for the Social Democrats. Political conflict sharpened in 1913 over renewed proposals to finance part of the army budget by a new direct tax borne mainly by the well-off. Conservatives again reacted; there was talk of dire threats to national stability, the imminence of civil war, and there were even proposals for the suppression of democratic government. As paralysis struck the German legislature, policy decisions fell increasingly to the Army General Staff.

French policy also reflected domestic conditions, though it was steered by the overwhelming anxiety about Germany that had been reinvigorated by the 1911 confrontation over Morocco. The years 1912–14 were marked by political turmoil over issues like taxes and military reform, to the extent that there were seven different ministries under six different prime ministers in less than three years. Under Poincaré's presidency, however, socialist opposition to army reform was overcome and in 1913 the period of military service was increased from two to three years. But reluctance to commit more resources to military preparedness led many to doubt France's readiness to go to war. The German ambassador in Paris reflected a common outside view when he reported to Berlin that in

THE DIVISION OF THE EARTH.
(From "Kladderadatsch," Berlin.)

RUSSIA

& ENGLAND DIVIDE PERSIA

ITALY GETS ALBANIA

& AUSTRIA - MACEDONIA

FRANCE GETS MOROCCO,

BUT ONLY THE KINGDOM OF HEAVEN REMAINS FOR GERMANY !

A German nationalist view of Germany's place in the world. As the other European states divide the earth among themselves, Germany is promised heaven.

France "the bellicose desire for revenge . . . is now outmoded. . . . Nobody is inclined to risk his or his son's bones for the question of Alsace-Lorraine."

This assessment might have been what the German government wanted to hear, but it underestimated French nationalism, especially its anti-German form. Parisians flocked to patriotic plays and cheered when actors spoke anti-German lines. In April 1913, a German airship made a forced landing in northern France, raising fears of invasion and leading to attacks on some visiting German businessmen.

The French were not alone in their apprehensions, for there was a widespread sense from 1912, well before the final crises of summer 1914, that war was inevitable. A Serbian nationalist paper declared in 1912 that "war between Serbia and Austria is inevitable. If Serbia wants to live in honor, she can only do this by war. [The whole Slavic race] must stand together to halt the onslaught of these aliens from the north." In February 1913, the professor of modern history in the University of London observed in a lecture: "When I survey the energy, the single, devoted purposefulness throbbing everywhere throughout Germany, her forward-ranging effort, her inner life, her army, her fleet, I seem to hear again the thunder of the footsteps of a great host. . . . It is the war-bands of Alaric!" He concluded with a call to the English that echoed that of Demosthenes to the citizens of Athens: "Rouse yourselves from your lethargy! Cease to hire your soldiers! Arm and stand in the ranks yourselves—as Englishmen should! And thus, dying you shall die greatly, or, victorious, yours shall be such a victory as nothing England's past can exceed or rival."

It was not that people necessarily wanted war, rather that they believed it was either necessary or preferable to any alternative. Opinion in Russia was mixed. Some conservatives feared that war would revive revolutionary sentiments, as it had in 1905, while others believed that a war—by which they meant victory—would help the czarist regime recover the prestige it had lost in the Russo-Japanese conflict. Russian liberals were keen to strengthen ties with France and Britain, even at the risk of being drawn into a war, in the hope that they would be a liberalizing influence.

All these positions reflected assessments of the impact of foreign policy on domestic conditions. There was general agreement that Russia should maintain its interest in the Balkans, although there was a difference in that conservatives intended Russia to dominate the region, and liberals foresaw Russia providing leadership in a region of sovereign states.

Russia, in fact, was the great power that Germany was most likely to encounter when it pursued its policies in Asia Minor, a likelihood realized in early 1913 when Germany undertook to reorganize the Turkish army. Russia's vehement objection to this German role in Turkish affairs might seem an overreaction, but it reflected concern that the vital straits to the Mediterranean might come under the control of an enemy, which Germany certainly had the potential to become. By the beginning of 1914 Russia had begun to prepare its Black Sea fleet to fight for access to the straits.

All this time there was a contest for influence in the Balkan region. The French and Russians actively courted support by commercial and political means. The French extended loans to Bulgaria and Greece, and the czar made a state visit to Romania. Germany, its resources thoroughly committed to domestic economic development, was unable to match France's capacity to lend and invest abroad, while Austria-Hungary had alienated the Balkan States by its hard-line policies against Serbia. Relations within the Triple Alliance were not particularly strong: Germany evinced little sympathy for Austro-Hungarian anxieties about Serbia, and relations between Austria-Hungary and Italy were set back in August 1913 when Italian nationals were forbidden to hold local office in Trieste, an Adriatic port in Austria that had a predominantly Italian population.

Between 1911 and 1914, then, the international tensions rising since 1890 rose several more notches. Major states had increased military spending considerably, and governments were beginning to consider the domestic and foreign policy implications of war. The inevitability and even the desirability of war—ideas expressed in the rhetoric of excited nationalists—were being discussed quietly by mainstream politicians.

The Outbreak of War, June to August 1914

It was in this context of volatility that the Austrian Archduke Franz Ferdinand, heir to the Habsburg throne, visited the Bosnian city of Sarajevo on June 28, 1914. It was a poorly conceived visit: Bosnia had been annexed in 1908 and the visit to its capital was scheduled on a date, sensitive for nationalists, that marked the Turkish defeat of Serbia in 1389. There had been warnings of an attack on the archduke, and he was understandably reluctant to proceed. Astonishingly, a planned motorcade through Sarajevo continued even after a bomb was thrown at it. Changes were made to its route, but they had the opposite effect to that intended, for when the archduke's car hesitated at an intersection because the driver was uncertain about the new directions, a young student, Gavrilo Princip, rushed forward and shot and killed both the archduke and his wife.

It was quickly assumed in Vienna that Princip had not acted alone, but that the assassination was conceived by a Serbian nationalist movement called National Defense, which had links to the Serbian government through well-placed members of the Serbian army. At

Austrian Archduke Franz Ferdinand and the Duchess Sophie shortly before they were assassinated in Sarajevo in June 1914.

the time there was no unambiguous evidence that the Serbian government knew in advance of the attempt on the archduke's life, although it is now evident that plans for the attack were known about. It is likely that the Serbian government declined to intervene for fear of appearing pro-Austrian.

Despite the lack of clear evidence in mid-1914, a chain of reasoning and prejudice led the Austrian government to fix responsibility where it wanted to: in Belgrade, the Serbian capital. Instead of reacting unilaterally, however, the Austrian government asked Germany to support a plan to exploit the assassination to destroy Serbia as a power factor in the region. Although Germany had until then moderated Austrian-Hungarian policies in the Balkans, the kaiser now assured the government in Vienna that Germany would support whatever action it deemed fit in the circumstances, even if war with Serbia led to hostilities with Russia.

The assurance of unqualified support is often referred to as Germany's "blank check." In fact Germany went further than offering contingency support, and Chancellor Bethmann Hollweg encouraged the Austro-Hungarian government to pursue a policy that would produce war with Serbia. Austria-Hungary was widely perceived as an empire in decline and Germany hoped that a military victory (even over a small state like Serbia, which was perhaps all the Austro-Hungarian army could hope to defeat) might at least arrest the collapse of its ally's international reputation and status.

The Germans thought it quite possible that Russia would not intervene on behalf of Serbia if Austro-Hungarian policy led to war. Russia seemed too divided and weak internally, and had drawn back from confrontation when Bosnia was annexed in 1908. Moreover, it was thought unlikely that France would join the conflict even if Russia did declare war against Austria-Hungary. France had not declared war on Japan during the Russo-Japanese War, nor rushed to Russia's side in the 1908 dispute over Bosnia.

German planners believed that even if a broader war broke out, German military might could deal with Russia and France, both of which were in the midst of army reforms in 1914. German military strategy, in fact, was predicated on simultaneous war against the two powers. The Schlieffen Plan, named after the chief of the General Staff who drew it up in 1905, called for a quick strike against France by the main German forces while the Russian army was still mobilizing. Following a rapid defeat of the French, the bulk of German forces would then turn east and deal with Russia. Contingency planning of this kind does not mean that the German leadership actually wanted war against France and Russia, but its encouragement of Austria-Hungary certainly entailed that risk.

The Austro-Hungarian government waited until July 23, more than three weeks after the assassination, before taking action against Serbia, and then it was in the form of an ultimatum. The delay was to avoid a confrontation during a visit to Russia by the French president and prime minister, which would have allowed instant coordination of French and Russian policies. It also allowed more of the Austrian and Hungarian harvest to be taken in before it was interrupted by mobilization of reserves. (Of the two, only Hungary's output fell markedly in 1914.)

The ultimatum began with a declaration that Serbian toleration and protection of terrorists gave the Austro-Hungarian government no option but to step in to end the menace to itself. There followed ten demands, including the banning of anti-Habsburg propaganda, suppression of nationalist movements, and tightening of border controls. Other demands were clear infringements of Serbian sovereignty: Serbia should dismiss specified officials, and Austrian officials should be permitted to participate in the investigation of a Serbian conspiracy leading to the assassination. The Serbians were given forty-eight hours to accept the ultimatum in its entirety; failure to do so would mean war. It was, said the British foreign secretary, "the most formidable document I had ever seen addressed by one State to another that was independent." As soon as it received the ultimatum, Serbia began to mobilize its army.

Serbia's official response, delivered just before the deadline on July 25, was conciliatory; it accepted all the demands except the one relating to Austrian participation in the investigation. As soon as he received the reply, the Austro-Hungarian ambassador in Belgrade broke diplomatic relations with Serbia and within hours was on a train to Vienna. Ignoring attempts by Great Britain to find a peaceful solution, and encouraged by Germany, which wanted a limited conflict, Austria-Hungary declared war on Serbia on July 28, and the next day began to shell Belgrade from ships on the River Danube.

Because of Germany's active backing, more than two states were implicated in the war between Austria-Hungary and Serbia from its very beginning. The question was whether the conflict would be localized geographically. The chances of that diminished when Russia mobilized its army on the border with Austria-Hungary the day hostilities against Serbia began. Russia's complex mobilization plans, however, allowed only a simultaneous mobilization against both Germany and Austria-Hungary. Realizing that a general mobilization (the only sort possible) might provoke war with Germany, the czar ordered military preparations to cease twelve hours after they had begun. Then, after a night of warnings and appeals from his advisers that failure to mobilize at once would leave Russia vulnerable to a German attack, the czar ordered mobilization to start again on the morning of July 30.

The confidence of the Russian government (the czar apparently excepted) was buoyed by the recent visit of the French leaders, who had given the impression of being fully behind Russia in the Balkan dispute. When President Poincaré reached Paris on July 29, he confirmed that France would stand by its treaty obligations if Russia were attacked by Germany or by Austria-Hungary with German support. France had already begun to move troops from Morocco and discreetly recall soldiers on leave. On July 30 French frontline forces were mobilized, but kept six miles back from the German frontier to avoid incidents. Britain, too, had begun to think in terms of war: Its fleet had just completed exercises in the North Sea, but instead of dispersing, it remained on station and all shore leave was postponed.

Even at this point a wider war was preventable. Britain proposed mediation, and Russia promised to halt mobilization if Austro-Hungarian forces withdrew from Serbia. But the German and Austro-Hungarian leaderships were unwilling to return to the earlier status quo, although they offered what they saw as compromises: Germany suggested that Belgrade be held but only as a hostage to put pressure on Serbia, and the Austro-Hungarian government indicated that although it planned to pursue its aims (to rid Serbia of anti-Habsburg elements) it would not actually annex any Serbian territory. This was not a real concession, for Hungary had already declared itself opposed to any annexation that would bring even more troublesome Slavs within its borders.

These last-minute proposals were superseded when on July 31 Germany issued two ultimatums: Russia was given twelve hours to halt its mobilization, and France was given eighteen hours to declare its neutrality in the case of a German-Russian war. Russia refused to comply and Germany declared war on August 1. There were now two separate but linked conflicts: between Austria-Hungary and Serbia, and between Germany and Russia.

Just as Germany declared war on Russia, the French, believing that Germany would not respect French neutrality even if it were offered, ordered full mobilization. It was known that the German military plan involved an initial invasion of France followed by an attack on Russia, and it was thought unlikely that the German General Staff would change the plan and leave their western border vulnerable to a French attack. At the very least, the French thought, Germany would insist on holding French border forts as a guarantee of French nonintervention.

In preparation for hostilities, Germany issued yet another ultimatum, demanding on the evening of August 2 that neutral Belgium allow German troops free passage through its territory. The demand was promptly rejected, and the next morning German troops

BRAVO, BELGIUM!

A British cartoon showing "Brave Little Belgium" defying the German bully, August 1914.

were ordered to enter Belgium. Later the same day, claiming that French forces had violated its territory, Germany declared war on France.

Britain was the only great power not directly involved. In the critical week of ultimatums and mobilizations, the British concentrated on mediation. Although Britain had no formal obligation to enter a war on the side of either France or Russia, economic and military considerations made British neutrality unthinkable. Victory by Germany and Austria-Hungary would upset the balance of power that was favorable to Britain not only in Europe but also globally, and British interests in the Middle East and Asia would be vulnerable. An earlier arrangement whereby France's navy was concentrated in the Mediterranean and Britain's in the Channel and North Sea meant that a French defeat would endanger British access to India through the Suez Canal.

Britain's wider interests therefore pointed toward participation in the conflict, but they were too diffuse to justify a declaration of war. The German invasion of Belgium provided just the reason that was needed, however, for Belgian neutrality had been guaranteed in 1830 by Britain and other powers. On August 3 Germany received an ultimatum for a change, this from Britain demanding its withdrawal from Belgium. When Germany failed to comply, Britain declared war on August 4.

Although the series of declarations of war had begun with the Austro-Hungarian attack on Serbia, the center of attention quickly shifted to Germany, the real military and economic threat, leaving its Habsburg ally marginalized and almost forgotten. Austria-Hungary did not declare war on Russia until August 6, and then justified its action by falsely claiming that Russia had attacked Germany. For their part, France and Britain declared war on Austria-Hungary as late as August 12. The chronology of declarations of war shows how marginal the Balkan conflict quickly became.

Of the major powers only Italy stood apart from the war, despite membership of the Triple Alliance with Germany and Austria-Hungary. Not only was Italy in poor financial and military condition after the Libya campaign, but by 1914 it had begun to look to Austro-Hungarian lands on the north and west of the Adriatic for more territory. An Austro-Hungarian defeat offered the prospect of territorial advantage, an important consideration to Italy's expansionist government. When Italy did join the war, in 1915, it did so against its former allies.

Conclusion

Perhaps the most straightforward way of understanding the origins of World War I, both in terms of its outbreak and the form it took, is to consider long-, medium-, and short-term factors. Among the first we might place industrialization, population growth, and the evolution of the European balance of power up to 1870. The medium term, the quarter century covered by this chapter, comprised the rise of Germany to challenge France and Britain, and the decline of the eastern empires that were in part due to the regional impact of population and economic trends. These shifts in the balance of power were expressed as imperial rivalry, growing nationalism, official and popular militarism, and challenges to the political and social systems from new political forces.

The result was a sharpening of tension within and between states, a process marked by the rise of extreme ideologies and sporadically punctuated by revolutions and wars. By 1912 there was a general crisis in domestic affairs and international relations, such that there was widespread readiness, in governments and populations at large, for war, even a belief that war was inevitable. The short-term events included heightened international conflict, culminating in the Balkan crisis in the summer of 1914. In this sense the war was the legacy of a quarter century and more of growing conflict in all spheres, as much among economic interests, social classes, political parties, ethnic groups, and visions of social development, as it was a conflict among nations.

Such a diffuse explanation might remove responsibility for the war from any government or country, just as does the notion that Europe "drifted into war" because of the alliance system. Structural explanations need not, however, prevent historians from attributing responsibility to policymakers who operated in their historical context.

· 3 ·
The First World War,
1914–1918

Introduction

The war that broke out in August 1914 was soon known as the Great War, a name more than justified by the scale of hostilities alone. Armed forces from almost every continent participated in the conflict, troops coming from countries as scattered as the United States, Senegal, Australia, and India. Although the main battle zones were located in Europe, theaters of war included the Middle East, Africa, China, and the Pacific islands, not to mention the air and the high seas. The extent of military mobilization was without precedent, and by 1918 some 70 million men were under arms. The toll in casualties was correspondingly great—almost 10 million men killed in action and 20 million more wounded or listed as missing.

Beyond these military aspects, the war had far-reaching social, political, economic, and cultural effects that also warrant calling it "great." It shattered the four great empires that ruled from Berlin, Vienna, St. Petersburg, and Constantinople, devastated national economies, and ended Europe's preeminent status in the global economy. The war demanded unprecedented state activity in such matters as industrial activity, labor, conscription, social welfare, and censorship. It propelled women into new areas of employment, and had immediate and enduring effects on social relationships, the family, and population trends. It disrupted existing patterns of political allegiance and created the conditions that nurtured totalitarianism.

The Great War was such an upheaval, cutting across and upsetting the course of European history, that many historians prefer to think of the nineteenth century as ending in 1914 and the twentieth century beginning in 1918. From this point of view, the war itself is a period that belongs in neither century, the unwanted child of one era and rejected parent of the other.

We should not exaggerate the novelty of all the effects of the war. Even though it seems that nothing was quite the same after the war as before it, many of the changes were foreshadowed in the prewar decades. Both the Russian and Austro-Hungarian Empires, for example, were riven by ethnic and political divisions before 1914. We cannot say whether they would have collapsed when they did, in 1917 and 1918 respectively, had there been no war (it is possible that the Russian Empire's life was actually extended by the war), but we can reasonably view the war as a catalyst that brought existing stresses to a critical point. Similarly, the expansion of state activity in many countries in wartime, as governments organized war production and food supplies, had its origins in preexisting policies of conscription, taxation, and welfare, but it was a process intensified and accelerated by conditions of war. The entry of women into previously male-dominated or male-monopolized areas of employment had also begun slowly by 1914, and took off during the war.

Of other consequences of the war, on the other hand, there was no warning. The most obvious was the loss of millions of men from their late teens to their mid-forties, and its consequences for family structure and population growth in postwar Europe. Other unforeseen results were economic. Before the war Europe, considered as an economic bloc, was an international creditor and industrial power that appeared to be going from strength to strength. After the war European nations, victors and vanquished alike, were heavily in debt, their economies and trading relationships in tatters. Living standards, rising before the war, fell precipitously after 1914 in most of Europe.

As catalyst of change, accelerator of trends, or simple cause of the political, social, economic, and cultural transformations, the First World War stands as a critical period. The military conflict at its center was only the core of a broad process whose repercussions were felt throughout the twentieth century, making an appreciation of this period indispensable for an understanding of the following eighty years of European history.

Reactions to the War, August 1914

The declaration of war in August 1914 involved not only European states. Outside Europe the imperial links of Britain and France created more combatants, and before the war was over almost 3 million soldiers were mobilized in Canada, Asia, Africa, Australia, and New Zealand. The nineteenth-century flow of armed forces from Europe to the outposts of empire was suddenly reversed.

Most European countries did not hasten to enter the war in 1914, however. Belgium and Luxembourg, both neutral before the war but invaded by German forces in August 1914, became unwilling participants. Other powers, notably the Netherlands, Spain, Switzerland, Norway, Sweden, and Denmark, remained neutral throughout. Yet others—Greece, Italy, Portugal, Romania, and Bulgaria—entered the war in 1915 or 1916 for strategic and political reasons; all but Bulgaria joined the Allies. Non-European powers that declared war on the Central Powers included Japan and, more important, the United States, which dispatched forces to Europe in 1917.

Despite the reluctance of most European countries to join the conflict in its first months, enthusiastic support for war was expressed by important sections of the populations of the combatant countries. A European war had long been expected, and in the heightened international tension following the assassination of Archduke Ferdinand, demands for a war to settle the international disputes became increasingly common and strident. By the end of July, with its exchanges of ultimatums and threats, and diplomatic and military posturing, war seemed unavoidable. The opening words of the London *Times* editorial the day Britain declared war—"The European war has finally begun"—convey the sense of an expectation fulfilled.

But the eagerness for war that was expressed in the capitals, cities, and towns of Germany, Britain, France, Austria, and Russia went well beyond mere relief that the tension was finally broken. Nor was it simply a desire for something different, for a bit of armed combat as a diversion from the boredom of everyday life and work. Rather, there was a positive enthusiasm for national honor and glory in battle. Throughout Europe millions of young men, volunteers and conscripts alike, marched proudly to their troop trains past crowds of cheering, flag-waving civilians. Brilliant warm weather at the beginning of August in 1914 encouraged crowds to gather. The British consul-general in Moscow expressed the spirit of the time, writing that the Russian troops, "bronzed by the summer sun, looked formidable as they sang their martial songs and swung through the streets on their way to the railway stations."

In some instances pro-war demonstrators took the offensive as soon as war was declared. In St. Petersburg the German embassy was ransacked, and everything from a great portrait of the kaiser to a grand piano was thrown from the upper windows and burned. In Graz, Austrian crowds shouting "Death to all Serbs! Long live the Emperor! Down with traitors!" set upon and killed men they believed were Serbian spies.

Even men and women not this enthusiastic about engaging the enemy in person rallied to their national cause once the war had begun. They included socialists who had opposed increases in military spending before 1914 and who had been committed to opposing war credits if war was declared. As war moved from an abstract possibility to reality, most European socialist leaders put down the red flag of internationalism and rallied behind their respective national colors.

In Germany the Social Democratic Party abandoned its slogan "To this system, no man and no penny," and adopted instead "In the hour of danger, we will not leave the Fatherland in the lurch." The party's leaders voted 78 to 14 in support of the government's declaration of war on Russia, and its deputies in the Reichstag voted unanimously for the necessary war credits.

In France, the Socialist Party reversed its opposition to war and swung behind the government; the socialist leader Jean Jaurès, vilified by the nationalist press as effectively an accomplice of Germany, was assassinated by a nationalist the day before France mobilized. The British Labour Party also did an about-face on war, and two of the party's leaders who would not suspend their pacifism (one of them was Ramsay MacDonald who later became the first Labour prime minister) were forced to resign. In Russia, Social Democratic and some Labor deputies in the Duma voted against the war (a number were later imprisoned or sent into exile), and in Serbia the socialists split on the issue.

On the whole, however, socialists took a pragmatic view of the new political conditions in August 1914, and decided that their interests were best served by supporting their governments' war policies. Most workers backed the war, and on the eve of hostilities French and German trade unions canceled planned strikes designed to disrupt preparations for war. Both union movements justified their change of heart by insisting that the impending conflict was a defensive war, not an imperialist one. The growing strike movement in Russia came to an abrupt halt in August 1914. Socialist parties were anxious to avoid a conflict with rank-and-file workers on such an important issue as national safety. As one Austrian socialist leader put it, "It is better to be wrong with the workers than right against them." Socialists also hoped that by showing themselves patriotic and by being part of the war effort, they would win support for their policies when the war was over.

Moreover, socialists were genuinely alarmed at the consequences should their countries lose the war. German socialists feared that a victory by autocratic Russia would set back the progress of workers' rights, while French socialists contemplated with horror the prospect of living under a political system as undemocratic as Germany's.

Women's organizations exhibited a similar change of mind when faced with the reality of war, putting aside internationalism and pacifism, and rallying behind their governments in the summer of 1914. French feminists canceled congresses, meetings, and lectures calling for women's suffrage, and instead called on women to participate in the war any way they could. "We will claim our rights," the feminist paper *Le Droit des Femmes* wrote, "when the triumph of Right is assured." In 1915 Emmeline Pankhurst, one of Britain's most famous suffragettes, organized a demonstration supporting women's "right to serve" in the war effort, and some feminists called for women to be allowed to do combat duty. Like the socialists, women's rights advocates feared isolation if they opposed war, and they hoped that if they shared the burdens of war women would make political gains and get the right to vote. "Let us show ourselves worthy of citizenship," a prominent British women's rights leader declared.

Finally, the churches in each country fell into line, some more reluctantly than others. Most regretted the need for war, but few expressed doubts (especially after August 1914) that its nation's declaration of war was just and necessary. Theological problems did arise, however, from the fact that there were Catholics and Protestants on both sides. The Vatican adopted a position of neutrality in this situation, and consistently called for a peaceful resolution of disputes. Pope Benedict XV's declaration that the church "must extend the same charity to all combatants" or expose "the tranquillity and internal concord of the Church to serious risk" angered many French nationalists. They argued that peace and the status quo in 1914 would favor the Germans by legitimating their annexation of Alsace-Lorraine after the Franco-Prussian war. Georges Clemenceau, who became French prime minister in 1917, sneered at the Vatican's advocacy of peace: "It would be a Boche's [Germans'] peace, O Pontiff of the Holy Empire!"

It was to be expected that national or established churches would support the war. In Britain the Church of England regretted but understood that war was necessary to hold militaristic powers like Germany to their international obligations. In Russia in August 1914 a special chant was sung in all Orthodox churches: "Most Gracious Lord. Crush the enemy before our feet!"

Churches that were in chronic conflict with the state rallied with equal enthusiasm. For the French Catholic Church, which had fought the Third Republic tooth and nail over issues like education, the archbishop of Paris proclaimed quite clearly, "Our country calls her children to arms. . . . Let us pray that our arms may vanquish, as they have so often in the past." French Protestants joined in, calling on French Jews to support the war on the ground that German Protestantism had given birth to anti-Semitism, stressing that French Protestants had nothing in common with their German co-religionists. German Lutherans, with traditionally strong links to the Prussian state, clearly felt the same way, and threw their spiritual weight behind the kaiser. The Catholic Church in both Germany and Austria supported their governments' policies wholeheartedly. The Austrian church and its chaplains to the Austrian-Hungarian armies implied that loyalty to God and to the emperor were not that easily distinguishable.

Despite the progress of secularization in nineteenth-century Europe there was a distinct religious overtone to August 1914. All over Europe young men were dispatched to battle as if they were setting off on a crusade to save the world for God and justice. To help them in their endeavors, military chaplains went along as well, at first in small numbers but later by the thousands.

So it was that in all combatant countries the war carried a broader spectrum of support than might have been anticipated only weeks before it was declared. If the German government had hoped that war would close social divisions, it must have been very satisfied. The kaiser declared a "fortress truce" (*Burgfrieden*), the internal truce that was traditionally observed in a fortress under siege. The French government declared a sacred union (*union sacrée*) of all French people in the face of a common enemy. Both had the same purpose: to set aside existing political and social conflicts for the duration of hostilities, so that all energy could be directed at the external foe.

The British declined to adopt any lofty ideal like a sacred union to rally the people. "Business as usual," which became for the first year of the war a quasi-official slogan was, if anything, a call to inaction. Even so, the British government tried to paper over the divisions in society. Jailed suffragettes and trade unionists were released in a spirit of reconciliation that was echoed by Mrs. Pankhurst, who said of the British that "as soon as we were attacked from outside we agreed to adjourn our quarrels."

Conflict and war among nations instantly produced a semblance of domestic unity and peace in each country. But as Mrs. Pankhurst said, the social quarrels were adjourned, not canceled. The social consensus that greeted the declaration of war would prove so fragile that some governments later resorted to compulsion in attempts to maintain it.

Even in August 1914, at the height of enthusiasm for war, there were some dissidents, pacifists as well as feminists and socialists who disagreed with their colleagues' new pro-war position. In the face of popular and official hostility, some continued to speak against the war even after it had begun and numbers of them were jailed. The British philosopher Bertrand Russell was dismissed from his lectureship at Trinity College, Cambridge, and later served a jail term for antiwar activities, while the left-wing French novelist Romain Rolland suffered public odium for his campaign against the war, conducted from neutral Switzerland. In Russia a number of Social Democrats were exiled in Siberia for persistent opposition to the war, while in Germany prominent socialist women like Rosa Luxemburg and Clara Zetkin continued their opposition to the Social Democrats' policy as far as government suppression of antiwar opinion allowed.

Neutral governments looked on with anxiety as most of Europe's citizens enthusiastically prepared to kill one another. In light of Belgium's fate they could only hope their neutrality would be respected. King Christian of Denmark issued a message to Danes expressing the hope that "no one will by an untimely display of feelings, by rash demonstrations, or in any manner will violate the dignity and peace" that would create confidence in Denmark's neutrality. But in August 1914, voices raised against war and in favor of moderation were easily drowned by choirs singing victory masses, by military bands and marching songs, and by the tramp of soldiers marching to their trains.

Nationalism, popular militarism, and a long period of anticipation of hostilities go some way to explaining why there was such willingness to go to war. Another important reason was the nearly universal conviction that the conflict would be brief. This rather puzzling belief was based on the experience of the previous century. The few international wars in Europe since the defeat of Napoleon in 1815 had been short: The most recent, the Franco-Prussian War (1870–71), had lasted six months from beginning to end, and the actual fighting occupied an even shorter period. Wars outside Europe that involved European forces, like the Crimean War (1854–56) and the Boer (South African) War (1899–1902), had lasted longer, but it seems that they did not count.

The war was welcomed by generals, politicians, and common people alike in August 1914. It was expected to be a military venture that would deal the enemy a short, sharp lesson and set the international state system to rights. It was widely described as "the war to end all wars." Military specialists were confident that weapons like machine guns, hand grenades, and artillery, together with transportation by railways and motor vehicles, would produce a brief and mobile war. Politicians, recognizing the economic interdependence of European states, could not conceive of a long war, and one French economist proved statistically (to his own satisfaction, at least) that a war could not possibly last more than six months.

Predictions of an even shorter war were legion. Bernard Montgomery, later a field marshal but in 1914 a lieutenant in the British army, was an optimist among optimists. "At least," he wrote, "the thing will be over in three weeks." Others thought it might take a little longer. Men from eastern France set off to war expecting to be in Berlin four weeks later, while other conscripts knew they would miss the grain harvest but still expected to beat the Germans in time to be home for grapepicking. For their part, German soldiers thought victory would be theirs by September.

One of the few who doubted that the troops would be home by Christmas was Lord Kitchener, the British secretary for war. His thinking was hinted at in the very first appeal for 100,000 volunteers on August 6, which set out the terms of service as "a period of three years, or until the war is concluded."

The First Months of Battle, August to December 1914

The general expectation of a short war was the first of many illusions attending the outbreak of the First World War to be shattered, although the first weeks seemed to confirm that the war would be quickly won by the Central Powers. On August 4, five of the eight German armies, more than a million strong, invaded neutral Belgium with the intention of driving through it and then into France, thus avoiding a direct assault on the French defenses along the border with Germany. The original Schlieffen Plan called for German forces to swing west from Belgium into France, then south to besiege Paris before heading east to attack the rear of French forces that were expected to have moved to the border as soon as war broke out. A quick victory over these prime French armies and the capture of Paris would allow Germany and its allies to attack Russia before its large, unwieldy, and poorly equipped army was able to mobilize, a process expected to take two months.

The French strategy, Plan XVII, envisaged a crippling attack on German forces in the center of the frontier, quickly followed by an attack on Germany's eastern frontier by Russian forces. Under French pressure, Russia had agreed to send its armies into action on the sixteenth day of mobilization, whether or not they were ready. The double blow, French strategists calculated, would have Germany suing for peace within weeks, and France would recover Alsace-Lorraine.

The first indications were that it was the Schlieffen Plan that would succeed. The German armies thrown into Belgium swept everything before them on the route to France. Ignoring the Belgians' plea that they were a country, not a road, the German army devastated towns and villages; the medieval university at Louvain and part of the town itself were burned. Thousands of civilians were killed, some incidentally to military operations, others deliberately. These acts provided instant material for Allied propaganda to portray the Germans as barbarians who had no respect for the law of nations.

Much was made of the heroism of the Belgian forces, which defended the country as best they could—Belgians were not the "chocolate soldiers" the German forces had been led to expect, but they were no match for the large, mechanized German force that swept in. After two weeks of fighting, Brussels was occupied and the Germans reached the French-Belgian frontier.

Yet the very success of the German army posed problems, for the infantry, covering up to twenty and even thirty miles a day, sped ahead of its supplies and artillery. Telegraph and telephone links between the front and headquarters proved troublesome, and the pace of the advance was slowed. Then the Schlieffen Plan was modified. Vital units were transferred to the east when Russia attacked East Prussia. Then, instead of continuing the drive west toward Paris, the overextended First German Army under General von Kluck

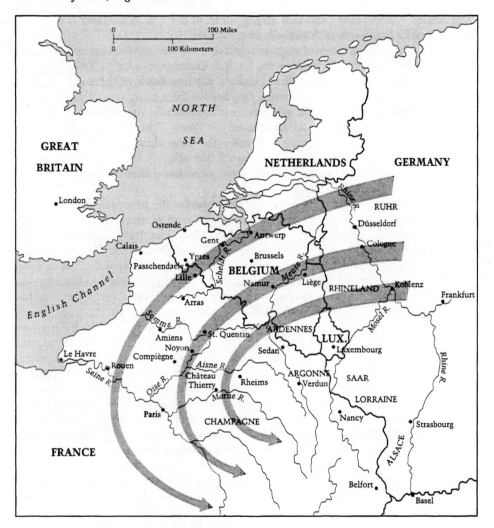

MAP 3.1 The original Schlieffen Plan.

(whose name gave British soldiers an excellent opportunity for derisive rhymes) wheeled southeast to attack the rear of the French forces that had, in line with Plan XVII, already attacked in Lorraine and been repulsed.

On September 6, as the right flank of the German armies was exposed to the direction of Paris, already deserted by 500,000 civilians and the national government, which had decamped to Bordeaux, the French forces in the capital were ferried to battle in hundreds of requisitioned taxis. It was not quite what had been intended by a war of mobility, but Paris taxi drivers proved equal to the task; perhaps, even then, driving in Paris was excellent training for armed combat.

Aided by units of the British Expeditionary Force that had been rushed to France, the French troops pushed the German armies back to the River Marne by September 10, and Paris was freed from immediate danger. The Battle of the Marne, really a succession of small battles, was the first extended engagement of the war. It involved millions of men and resulted in hundreds of thousands of casualties.

It was followed by a series of engagements as each side tried to outflank the other, all the time moving closer and closer to the English Channel in what became known as "the race for the sea." In the second half of October, the first Battle of Ypres was fought, as the Germans tried to break through French and British lines using tens of thousands of university and high school students who had enthusiastically volunteered in August. The Germans later called the battle *der Kindermord von Ypern*—"the massacre of the children at Ypres"—but the Allies could equally well call it the same thing. Among the terrible casualties, the British 7th Division lost more than 9,000 of its 12,400 officers and men in the eighteen days of fighting. Total British losses[1] were more than 50,000; the French lost 190,000, and the Germans 140,000.

In many respects these early battles set the tone for the next four years of conflict on the western front. The German armies occupied Belgium and economically important parts of northern France, but the modified Schlieffen Plan had failed. The French and British forces had held Germany to limited territorial gains and had deprived them of the quick victory that would have allowed them to deal definitively with Russia. From the English Channel south for 500 miles to Switzerland, both sides dug in—literally—and established the parallel lines of trenches, in places only hundreds of feet apart, that have become the hallmark of the First World War.

The first months of battle on the 800-mile-long eastern front followed a course not much different from that in the west, although trench warfare was never as extensive there. Two Russian armies invaded East Prussia on August 15, but despite surprising and outnumbering the Germans, their effectiveness was limited. After some early gains, Russia lost 100,000 men—killed, wounded, or taken prisoner—in the Battle of Tannenberg in the last week of August. After two months of advance and retreat, retreat and advance, the German and Russian armies faced each other roughly where they had begun. But the apparent stalemate disguised significant German victories over the Russian forces at Tannenberg and the Masurian Lakes. The German armies, although outnumbered, were better trained and equipped than their Russian opponents, and their tactics better planned. The results of these first months on the eastern front made the reputation of the two German commanders, Gen. Paul von Hindenburg and Gen. Erich Ludendorff, both of whom would play important political roles in Germany later in the war and after it.

Farther south on the eastern front, the Austro-Hungarian armies were much less successful. In August they invaded Serbia but were forced to retreat. Although subsequent attacks in September and November promised better results—Belgrade was occupied for a few days—the troops were forced out again by mid-December. Austro-Hungarian losses against Serbia totaled 200,000. Farther north, they made initial progress into Poland and hoped to capture Warsaw. They were confronted by four Russian armies, however, and eventually succumbed to the sheer weight of Russian numbers, and even assistance from German armies made little difference. By November the Austro-Hungarian-Russian front had, like the others, settled into immobility and stalemate after early weeks of massive troop movements and deadly but indecisive battles.

---

1. "Losses" generally include the total killed, wounded, missing, or taken prisoner. The figures for losses in the First World War vary from source to source. Statistics kept at the time are often unreliable, and the dead were often so badly mutilated that it was impossible to tell which army they belonged to.

MAP 3.2　The western front, 1914–15.

Only outside the European theaters of war did events seem less ambiguous. From August 1914, German colonies scattered throughout the world were successfully occupied by the Allies. Tsingtao in China was invaded by an ad hoc force of British, Indian, and Japanese troops, German New Guinea by Australians, and German Samoa by New Zealanders. British forces occupied German colonies in Africa.

But these gains and losses were marginal to the main task, which was to win the territorial advantage in Europe itself. There the best that could be said was that all sides had managed to avoid defeat in the first months of the war, and that at the cost of unprecedented casualties. By the end of 1914, the French and Germans had each suffered 800,000 casualties (killed, wounded, missing, or taken prisoner), and the British 90,000. Austro-Hungarian casualties, a proportionally higher 550,000, were inflated then, as throughout the war, by thousands of soldiers from ethnic minorities who deserted or surrendered;

Trench warfare in the First World War: a British trench on the Somme.

early in 1915, 1,850 of the 2,000 Czech soldiers of a Prague infantry regiment joined the Russians, and 1,600 soldiers of another Czech regiment allowed themselves to be captured. In all armies, the early casualties were suffered by the best trained and equipped units, those thrown into the war first in hope of ensuring a quick victory.

Despite the high casualty figures, morale in most forces seemed almost as high at the end of 1914 as when they set off in their respective blazes of glory in August. Many poems written by soldiers—especially British soldiers—in these early days of the war depicted battle as a noble and purifying enterprise. Some wrote of combat as a joyous event, and portrayed death as a rather abstract or even pleasant experience, as being embraced in the wings of the angel of night. But other soldier-poets had a harsher, less rosy judgment. They predicted (often accurately) a quick death for themselves, and seemed resigned to it rather than overjoyed at the prospect. Others described life, dying, and death in the trenches in anything but abstract terms, dwelling on the stench of gangrenous wounds and the moaning of dying men.

War poetry was a remarkable phenomenon of the First World War (it did not occur to nearly the same extent in the Second), adding a cultural dimension to the period. It has been suggested that more than 3 million war poems were written by Germans during the first six months of conflict, but it is difficult to verify. Some 2,225 English war poets (most of them civilians writing nationalistic verse) have been identified, although only perhaps a dozen are at all well known, most of them for having written while in service.

In the circumstances of 1914 the pessimistic and negative expressions are understandable, and it is the optimistic poems that are striking for their incongruity. Equally bizarre was the camaraderie that developed on some parts of the western front between German and British forces dug in only hundreds of feet from one another. There were tacit agreements to refrain from shooting during mealtimes and to ignore one another's night patrols. On Christmas Day, 1914, fraternization reached an astonishing point when, on some sections of the front, opposing troops met in no-man's land to exchange gifts of chocolate, tins of bully-beef, biscuits, and cigarettes. At midnight, however, the troops returned to their respective trenches and got on with the war. The episode is intriguing, but it was no more representative of the war as a whole than the enthusiasm of some poems was indicative of most soldiers' attitudes toward the carnage of the first five months of battle.

Creating the Home Front

One of the terms that the First World War contributed to the English language was "the home front," the civilian societies that were not sites of military combat but were nonetheless integral parts of the war effort. European societies and economies had seldom been unaffected by far-off wars in the past, having been subjected to taxation, requisitioning, recruitment, conscription, and economic blockades. But seldom before had home fronts and battlefronts been as explicitly interdependent as they became from 1914 to 1918.

As the number of battle casualties began to mount and it became clear that the war would not be over in a matter of months, all the belligerents had to act quickly to replace the dead, disabled, missing, and captured soldiers. That meant recruiting and conscripting men and stepping up the production of weapons and munitions they needed. Certainty that the conflict would be brief had led governments to neglect the most elementary preparations, like stockpiling reserves of equipment and ammunition.

As the expected war of movement slowed to immobility in the winter mud and snow on all battlefronts, the home fronts became the primary sites of activity and decisive change. For the next four years the experiences of war on the battlefronts and the home fronts were so intimately connected that we must understand both in order to understand either. Indeed, the war was won and lost in the fields, factories, and houses of Britain, Germany, France, Russia, and Austria, as much as in the trenches and headquarters of their respective armies.

The first imperative in each country was to tap the human reservoir to fill the trenches. In order to hold their positions, armies needed to replace their losses, and in order to contemplate improving their positions they needed to increase their forces beyond their initial strength. Raising armies was no problem, however, even where there was no conscription. Britain, for example, had planned to mobilize only 100,000 men in addition to its standing army, but increased that target to 4 million by the end of 1914. By then a million men had volunteered, and another million and a quarter did so in 1915. Thousands of friends and workmates formed what became known as Pals' Battalions, following a promise that those who joined up together would serve together.

The heavy losses of late 1914 (the original British Expeditionary Force of 84,000 had been effectively wiped out) made rapid and constant replenishment of the forces essential, and normal physical requirements for military service were relaxed. The minimum height of 5 feet 8 inches was reduced to 5 feet 5 inches, then to 5 feet 3 inches. When miners, many of below-average height, enlisted, they were formed into special units with a

Raising mass armies: A British recruitment poster shows how the Boy Scout movement was seen as training boys to be future soldiers.

height requirement of between 5 feet and 5 feet 3 inches. Yet despite the number of volunteers, which at times overwhelmed supplies of arms and uniforms, Britain had to resort to conscription halfway through the war.

France, by contrast, had introduced conscription before the war and maintained a standing army of 900,000. General mobilization was announced on August 2, and in a matter of days more than 3 million men joined their units. The rate of resistance to conscription was far lower than authorities had predicted, and within a year some 6 million French men were in uniform; by the end of the war the French had mobilized 8 million men, almost every male of military age (eighteen to forty-six years) in the country.

The third major power of the Allied forces, Russia, had a standing army of a million in August 1914, but mobilized by way of conscription an astonishing 15 million troops by late 1917. It was the largest single national force, but was so poorly equipped, trained, and commanded that its armies could be neutralized by smaller and better-armed forces, as they were in August 1914.

The European troops on the Allied side were augmented by colonial forces from all parts of the world. The British Empire, notably Canada, India, South Africa, Australia, and New Zealand (which alone sent 40 percent of its military-age males abroad), contributed 2.5 million soldiers. The French drew half a million from their African colonies, particularly Senegal and Morocco.

The Central Powers were equally successful in raising large armies. Germany's permanent force of 850,000 was swelled by volunteers and conscripts until by the end of the war over 13 million men—three-quarters of the country's men between the ages of fifteen and sixty years—had been mobilized. Similarly the Austro-Hungarian army of 400,000 in August 1914 was expanded by conscription to 9 million by 1918. As such figures suggest, getting men into the armies was the least of the challenges facing governments. They were able to draw on huge reserves resulting from the steady growth of population almost everywhere during the previous hundred years.

Women were also integral to the military forces, for the most part serving in auxiliary branches as telephone operators, clerks, and typists. Some 150,000 women were employed thus in the British armed forces by the end of the war, and thousands more women served closer to the front lines as nurses and ambulance drivers. Most nurses worked in field hospitals several miles or more behind the lines, but nurses were sometimes called in to be stretcher bearers at the front and to collect the wounded from the no-man's land between the lines. Women were generally not employed in combat roles, although thousands of them did serve in the Russian and Serbian armies. Some disguised themselves as men, while others appear to have enlisted with the knowledge of company and regimental commanders. One woman, Princess A. M. Shakhovskaia, who had a private pilot's license, joined the Russian air force.

But it was men who comprised the bulk of the armed forces, and the sheer magnitude of male mobilization had far-reaching economic effects, some of which, in turn, had implications for the effectiveness of the burgeoning military forces that soon began to congregate on the battlefronts. In the general euphoria of August 1914, little thought was given to the consequences of suddenly withdrawing millions of men from the labor force. They were, after all, expected to return home before long. Although there were some attempts to exempt key workers in some sectors (such as railroads and mines) from military service, too many exemptions would have undermined the effect of general mobilization. Anticipating a short war, governments and military authorities were confident that existing stocks of weapons and munitions would suffice, and did not envisage the need to raise production above prewar levels.

It was soon clear that massive enlistments had drawn off too much of the vital workforce and left mines and factories underproducing just at the very time when there was an urgent need for production to be stepped up. As early as September 20, 1914, the French government called on industrialists to increase military output. The run on artillery shells had been far higher than foreseen (120,000 shells a day instead of the expected 13,000) and it was estimated that within a month there would remain only 200 shells for each 75-mm field gun. A production target of 100,000 shells a day was set.

Men made up the great majority of workers in industries crucial to the war—coal mines, iron and steel, arms and munitions—but just as it was impossible to restore and step up production overnight by instant improvements in technology, so it was out of the question to demobilize all the workers who had enlisted. In most countries key male workers who had signed up for service or were already serving at the front were placed on reserve and ordered to return to industrial work. This reverse flow of essential workers from the trenches and army camps to their workshops, benches, and mine faces in France, Britain, Germany, or Russia, began within months of the war breaking out. By the end of 1915 some half-million French servicemen, mechanics, and metalworkers prominent among them, were back at work. Their dual roles, as workers and reserve soldiers, made visible the interdependence of home front and battlefront.

The industrial workers who remained in military service were replaced primarily by women, as well as by young people and retired employees. The employment of women in

Women in a British munitions plant filling machine gun belts.

the French metal industries illustrates how labor patterns changed: They had numbered 17,731 before the war, but there were 104,641 by mid-1916, and 132,012 by the beginning of 1918, an eightfold increase in less than four years.

The entry of women into heavy industry through Europe from 1914 onward is often thought to have changed the status of women by enabling them to break out of the constraints of domesticity. Their new employment, however, often did little more than compensate for female unemployment in other sectors of the wartime economy. Soon after the war began many nonessential businesses and consumer industries reduced their activity or closed down entirely, throwing hundreds of thousands of women out of work. In France, for example, 61 percent of women in textile industries and 67 percent of those in the garment industries lost their jobs early in the war. Massive orders for uniforms did not counterbalance the decline of civilian consumer demand.

Women's employment in heavy industry in France and elsewhere was largely a matter of redistribution within the workforce, not of women finding work for the first time. It was based on the need for women to work, rather than on a patriotic urge to help the war effort by making rifles and ammunition. It was not part of a policy to break the traditional gender division in employment; women were still paid far less than men in equivalent jobs, and trade unions were anxious that male workers would recover their jobs after the war.

In Britain the war produced immediate unemployment among women who had worked in textiles (which reduced production by 43 percent) and clothing (21 percent) and as domestic servants. But the increased production demanded from war-related industries soon provided employment opportunities to replace those lost. In 1914 some 212,000 women worked in munitions (metal and chemical) industries in Britain; the figure rose to 256,000 by mid-1915, 819,000 by 1917, and 947,000 by 1918. In industry as a whole, the number of women employed rose from 2,178,000 in July 1914 to 2,970,000 four years later, an increase of more than a third.

Yet even in the munitions industries most women did traditional women's tasks. In Britain more than 700,000 of the women employed in this industry (three-quarters of the total) performed work that women had done there before the war. In effect, women who had worked in the industry before 1914 were promoted to "male" tasks, and were replaced by the newcomers. In other industries, like steelmaking and shipbuilding, women were employed not in the main workforce but to sweep floors and check stock. In some industries, like coal mining, men were not affected by the intrusion of women at all.

Outside industry, in the commercial and service sectors, women replaced men in significant numbers as the war went on. The number of women in transport (as drivers and bus conductors) increased sixfold during the war, from 18,000 to 117,000, and there were massive increases in the employment of women as clerks and tellers in banking (1,500 to 37,600) and as clerks in various levels of government (262,200 to 460,200). Unlike their counterparts in industry, women employed in these jobs tended to hold on to them after the war.

In Russia a quarter of Moscow's labor force was inducted into the army in 1914, although the most essential skilled workers were later recalled from the front. The demand for additional labor was filled by those exempted from military service: women and young people (including children under twelve years). During the three and a half years that Russia participated in the war, women increased their participation in the workforce from 25 to 38 percent, and young people (seventeen years old and younger) from 15 to 26 percent, so that together these groups made up two-thirds of workers. Women were also employed in paramilitary police forces in Russian cities.

German women, too, found work in industry during the war: Their numbers grew from 1,406,000 to 2,139,000, an increase of more than 50 percent. By the end of the war a third of the industrial workforce was composed of women, compared to a fifth before the conflict. Even so, most of the women who got industrial employment for the first time during the war had been employed before the war, many in agriculture, domestic service, and in sectors of the economy that had declined as the war economy developed. Female-intensive industries like textiles cut staff and rendered 40 percent of their employees unemployed. The simultaneous growth of war industries (which increased their workforce by 44 percent) provided opportunities for unemployed women, thus redistributing women within the German labor force.

As in industry, so in agriculture women were to the fore in taking up the slack when men went to war. The conflict erupted just as farmers across Europe were preparing for the harvest, the most labor-intensive phase of the agricultural year, and the departure of millions of men from the countryside might well have jeopardized the vital crops. Throughout France and elsewhere, however, reports noted that "the women have replaced the men in the fields" and that "women, children, old people, all set to work . . . to take the place of men." In Britain a Women's Land Army was formed to provide farmers with young middle-class women who volunteered to do agricultural work.

In various ways, then, the war had an immediate impact on women in work, although it was not the dramatic break from housework to replacing men in factories that is often portrayed. At no point did industrial employers regard the additional women as anything more than stop-gap employees; they were readily identifiable when it came to dismissing them in 1918. It was men who did better from the expansion of heavy industry during the war. The need for more skilled workers and supervisors created promotion opportunities for men who would otherwise have remained in the lower ranks of industry.

The most immediate and dramatic effect of the war on the home front was to create a dramatic imbalance in the sex ratio in the military age groups. By the end of the war the main European powers had fielded more than three-quarters of their men between their late teens and mid-forties, leaving women numerically preponderant in this broad age group. Because roles and responsibilities at work, in the family, and in society generally were differentiated by gender in the early twentieth century, the war could not but affect the most fundamental aspects of European society.

The State and Economic Activity, 1914 to 1915

Although state intervention in the economic and social spheres had increased from the late nineteenth century, most governments espoused essentially laissez-faire ideologies and defended such activities as regrettable but necessary exceptions to the rule. A long war, however, required governments to organize not only personnel for the armies but also the production of everything from uniforms and rifles to artillery and trucks, and the requisitioning of horses and transportation systems. Civilian populations, the producers, also needed to be sustained. Victory, it soon became clear, would depend on the successful exploitation and management of all human, social, and economic resources for total war.

In Britain the governing Liberals had been elected in 1906 on a platform of minimal interference in social and economic matters. Although they had implemented some social policies, when the war broke out they did not envisage state controls beyond what was immediately and demonstrably essential. The privately owned railroads, a vital transportation system for troops and supplies, were brought under government control (the owners' profits were guaranteed) and imported commodities like sugar (which had come from the Central Powers before the war) were regulated.

In 1915, however, the British government was forced by conditions like a critical shortage of shells to begin what became a veritable revolution in state activity. David Lloyd George, who was to become prime minister in 1916, was put in charge of a newly created Ministry of Munitions, and he set about marshaling the personnel, technology, and capital necessary to sustain a long and expensive war. Legislation in 1915 also nationalized Britain's coal mines for the duration of the war and gave the Ministry of Munitions power to take over factories if owners refused government terms for war contracts. The terms included limits on profits, the resolution of labor disputes by arbitration (to avoid loss of production by strikes), and restrictions on the movement of workers from one job to another.

Additional legislation in 1915 regulated more foods and imposed rent controls to cushion the effects of price increases. Finally, the state took a role in building housing for workers and government employees. The housing was certainly needed because the scale of the war effort and centralized government controls led to the growth of a huge state bureaucracy in London. In 1914 the Army Contracts Office, which had overseen military procurements before the war, had twenty clerks; by 1918 the Ministry of Munitions employed 65,000 to supervise a sprawling network of plants with more than 3 million female and male workers.

France followed a pattern broadly similar to Britain, bringing military production under state direction only when it became apparent that existing supplies and production levels would not see French forces through a prolonged conflict. Thereafter, requisitioning transportation, controlling factories, and regulating the prices of raw materials, wages, and profits enabled France to increase its military production such that the target of 100,000 shells a day, set in September 1914, was being met within a year. This achievement was the more remarkable because France was less industrialized than either Britain or Germany, and because early in the war Germany had occupied territory producing 40 percent of France's coal and 80 percent of its iron and steel.

France was slower to regulate the supply and prices of food and consumer goods, in part because it was virtually self-sufficient and anticipated no shortages on account of interrupted imports. Although Germany had occupied land that grew a fifth of France's grain, it was more than a year before grain was requisitioned at fixed prices, and rationing was introduced only in the last months of the war. Adherence to laissez-faire policies was also stronger in France because of hostility to state powers in the National Assembly and by Georges Clemenceau, prime minister from 1917.

Germany had not prepared for a long war because of confidence in the Schlieffen Plan, and when war was declared the German armies had only six months' supplies. But unlike Britain and France, Germany had a longer tradition of bureaucratic centralization and economic planning, partly a result of policies designed to make the Reich economically self-sufficient and able to act as a free agent in world affairs. The organization of the war effort, or "war socialism" (*Kriegssozialismus*) as it became known, was less a matter of state control than a state-sanctioned partnership of the military and big business.

It began late in 1914 when all companies engaged in particular categories of military production—munitions, rifles, and so on—were grouped into corporations or cartels. Each cartel bought raw materials and allocated them to the member firms that were judged most efficient, a procedure that favored larger companies that could achieve economies of scale. The whole system was devised and run by Walther Rathenau, a prominent businessman who had headed the AEG electrical firm, and it was supervised by the Raw Materials Section of the army.

The main differences between this setup and the state-run system in Britain was that in Germany industries were not nationalized or controlled by the government, and effectively decided among themselves how best to meet the requirements specified by the army. The larger firms that dominated the cartels were able to direct most contracts to themselves at the expense of smaller enterprises, which either went bankrupt or were forced to merge with the big companies. Profits went largely unregulated.

The German government did try to regulate food supplies early in the war because one of the first strategies adopted by the Allies was to place an economic blockade around the Central Powers to choke off imports. Germany was far from self-sufficient in food production, and as early as January 1915 bread was rationed, followed by meat and fats. The prices of all foodstuffs were regulated, and in October 1915 Germans were instructed to observe two meatless days a week. But the policies could not prevent shortages. The Allied blockade cut imports, and domestic production fell as scarcities of farm labor, fertilizers, and horses made their impact. A vigorous black market in food sprang up alongside the official market, enabling those who had money to continue to eat as well as ever.

Germany's attempts to maintain economic production and food supplies were to prove ineffective in the face of more than four years of war, and its main ally was even less successful. Austria-Hungary's constitutional organization was not promising for the kind of centralized regulatory system that was progressively imposed in Britain, France, and Germany. Not long after the war began it became clear that national rivalries would undermine the common war effort. At the heart of the empire the industrial strength of Austria complemented the agricultural strength of Hungary, but in practice there was little cooperation. In 1915 the Hungarians closed their border with Austria, declined to reveal grain production figures, and refused to export grain to Austria except to pay for industrial products. The imperial administration was constitutionally paralyzed because the Hungarian Diet was autonomous. So great were fears of aggravating national rivalries in wartime that the Austrian parliament did not meet from 1914 to 1917, and the parliament building was put to use as a military hospital.

For want of centralized coordination, Austria-Hungary's economy foundered. Grain production fell dramatically: The 1914 harvest of 9.2 million tons was just enough for self-sufficiency, but it declined to not much more than half that by 1918. Industrial production was low outside limited regions like Bohemia, and even there it declined as the Allied blockade created shortages of raw materials for the factories and of food for workers. Food rationing, introduced early in the war, was extended over time to include more and more items in smaller and smaller allotments. Price inflation, much of which resulted from the government's printing money to pay for the war, effectively placed an adequate diet beyond the reach of a growing number of families.

As bad as the Austro-Hungarian position was, it was exceeded by conditions in Russia, where the government proved quite unable to mobilize resources for war. Men were an exception, for the Russian armies grew by millions each year, but we cannot say that these soldiers were "in uniform" or "under arms" because many fought in civilian clothes and in some units at times in 1915 only one in four soldiers had a rifle. The others were instructed to arm themselves from their dead comrades; it was not an arrangement likely to boost morale.

The problem was not that Russian industry could not expand its productive capacity—by 1914 Russia was producing more coal, iron, and steel than France—but the czarist government had failed to prepare for an army of the size it fielded. Wartime initiatives to coordinate economic activities were more often made by individual industrialists than by the government, and they proved reasonably successful. In addition, the Duma set up war industry committees, composed of representatives of workers, management, and government, to improve war production. Between 1914 and 1916 the output of rifles increased 11-fold, artillery pieces 10-fold, and shells 20-fold. But Russian transportation networks often proved unequal to military needs so that military operations were jeopardized by shortages of materiel at the battlefront.

Ensuring food production and distribution was equally beyond the administrative ability of the czarist government. Peasants refused to sell their produce for paper money because the industrial goods they wanted were no longer available once industry turned to military production. The result of government inactivity was that in the cities, swelled by newcomers who had migrated to work in the expanding military industries, workers suffered chronic shortages of food and fuel. When goods were available, it was often at prohibitive prices.

That policies of regulation reflected necessity more than ideology is suggested by the way food supplies were regulated in Germany and Austria-Hungary well before they were in Britain and France. The 1914 harvest was variably affected by the declaration of war. Austria's wheat and rye output fell by a third, and Germany's by a quarter. In France, however, the decline was marginal, at a little over 10 percent, whereas in Britain output of almost all crops rose. The first months of the war established what would become critical patterns of food shortage in the Central Powers and relative plenty in Britain and France.

Prodded by necessity and circumstances and guided by political conditions and philosophies, the major European powers thus embarked at different speeds on the process of centralizing and coordinating wartime economic production. Almost all abandoned laissez-faire as a fundamental principle of government, and once they began to intervene in economic and social matters it was not easy to establish limits. This was a total war that demanded all resources for the military effort, and there was in theory no area of economic or social life that could be exempt from regulation.

Many governments, for example, showed increasing appreciation of the arguments advanced by the temperance societies, and began to regulate the production, distribution, and consumption of alcohol so as to minimize drunkenness that would interfere with military effectiveness or industrial productivity. Beer production in Germany was cut by a quarter, the consumption of alcohol was forbidden in Russia for the duration of the war, and in England bar hours were restricted, often to lunchtimes and two or three hours at night. The British royal family was persuaded to set an example by abstaining from alcohol for the duration. The output of beer in Great Britain, where it was the workers' staple drink, fell by a sixth between 1914 and 1915.

Whatever their methods of ensuring war production, however, all states quickly had to face the problem of how to pay for their war supplies. Again, the solutions differed. Britain and France both liquidated their investments abroad, then borrowed (mainly on the American market) to purchase raw materials and equipment. In addition the British increased personal tax rates and levied duties on goods like tea and beer. The French government, still hostile to income taxes, relied more on sales taxes and war bonds. Germany, denied access to U.S. money markets soon after the war began, financed the war primarily by sales taxes and bond issues, a strategy that would cause problems both during and after the war.

Russia, however, reaped the storm of its war financing earlier, in the 1917 revolution. Introducing prohibition reduced absenteeism among workers, but the loss of state revenues from taxes on alcohol deprived the government of a third of its income at a time when the war imposed massive new expenses. Reluctant to raise taxes on better-off citizens, the Russian government instead floated loans and printed money to cover its costs, and one result was that by the end of 1916 inflation had pushed prices to four times their mid-1914 level.

The economic organization of the home fronts that was undertaken soon after the war began was one of the most important aspects of the expansion of state activity during the First World War. The success or failure of war management of this kind was not just a matter of political will and administrative ability (although they helped); it depended also on the particular traditions and the political and economic conditions in each state. If historical experience made it easier for the German government than the French to tax, France was favored with better access to raw materials and food supplies. However, success in managing the home front was critical for the outcome of the war. Military strategy, leadership, and equipment were undoubtedly necessary, but they could be neutralized by the failure of the home front to supply the resources for battle, and those resources could be produced only by an adequately fed and supportive civilian population.

Society and Morale on the Home Fronts, 1914 to 1915

The importance of keeping up morale at home as well as on the front lines was understood better by some governments than others, but all attempted to sustain the initial enthusiasm for the war. Extensive use of propaganda, censorship, and political repression to this end was further evidence of state activity and the marshaling of all resources for total war in democratic societies. In autocratic states, where such practices had predated the war, the onset of conflict saw renewed attempts to suppress dissent.

In Britain the government had invoked the Defence of the Realm Act as early as 1914, enabling it to censor and even suppress newspapers. In fact the British press was relatively compliant because of the close personal and social relationships between newspaper proprietors and politicians. The government took repressive action against dissidents, however, and in 1915 a special security service was developed to investigate antiwar groups in Britain. The British government's zeal in curbing dissent was demonstrated in 1915 when it confiscated the passports of twenty-four women who had planned to attend the International Congress of Women in the neutral Netherlands.

Similar powers were used extensively in France, where the freedom of the press was curbed ostensibly to prevent the publication of sensitive military information. Political debate and discussion of the causes of the war and the merits of continuing it were discouraged or quashed outright in Germany, Austria-Hungary, and Russia, as governments tried to maintain national unity. From the start of the war, German reporters were briefed by the military, and in 1915 a War Press Office was set up under the General Staff to centralize censorship and news distribution. The German authorities, unlike the British, treated the press as an adversary.

All governments spread false news of the military situation, exaggerating victories and enemy casualties and minimizing the importance of defeats and their own losses. The press, working in this environment of nationalism and control, began to practice self-censorship by writing stories that would be acceptable. French newspapers were far from atypical in printing hopelessly optimistic war reports. One Paris paper in 1915 described the abysmally outfitted Russian army as "admirably equipped with everything it needs for modern battle," and four months later another paper put a brave face on a Russian retreat: "The Russian army . . . is retiring in good order. . . . Geographical lines mean nothing. . . . Time is on our side." In fact the French press tended to give readers the impression that no Allied forces ever retreated. Commenting on a failed British offensive, one paper wrote: "It has to be clearly said, because it is the truth, that this slight [British] withdrawal was not dictated by the enemy, but simply reflected the wishes of the British command." The French authorities are known to have deferred the call-up of journalists who wrote positively about the war, and this might well explain the upbeat tone of much French reporting.

Photographs in newspapers were often deceptive. In one British paper, a picture of a pogrom against Jews in Russia in 1905 was described as showing German atrocities in Belgium. Another, in the London *Daily Mail*, purported to show "three German cavalrymen, loaded with gold and silver loot." In fact it was a prewar photograph of the winners of a cavalry competition holding their trophies.

In Britain, posters (which became the preeminent propaganda medium of the war) were widely used to keep up morale in general, as well as for specific purposes like encouraging men to enlist and women to work for victory in their own spheres. The most famous poster of the war showed Lord Kitchener in military uniform, pointing directly at the viewer with the slogan "Britain needs you." For men who needed to be shamed into service, one poster depicted a man sitting comfortably at home while his son played on the floor with toy soldiers; his daughter is shown asking, "Daddy, what did YOU do in the Great War?" Another poster showed a wife and her children at an open window, watching soldiers march off. The bold slogan read, "Women of Britain say—GO!"

Many posters were directed specifically at women to highlight their contributions to the war effort. One portrayed a housewife in her kitchen, holding a steaming pot. The caption read: "The kitchen is the key to victory. Eat less bread." Another of the war duties of British women in their homes was set out in a Department of Food poster that made as clear a statement as one could want of what was meant by "the home front." Showing a housewife in her kitchen, it read: "The British fighting line shifts and extends and *you* are in it . . . it is in *your* larder, *your* kitchen, and *your* dining room. Every meal *you* serve is now

Women in war propaganda. The German poster, depicting women's role in the war effort, shows a wife arming her husband with a hand grenade. The British poster was designed to foster hatred of German women by British women. Many women were active in internationalist and peace organizations, and there was an official effort to combat the notion of a sisterhood that overrode national frontiers.

RED CROSS OR IRON CROSS?

WOUNDED AND A PRISONER
OUR SOLDIER CRIES FOR WATER.

THE GERMAN "SISTER"
POURS IT ON THE GROUND BEFORE HIS EYES.

THERE IS NO WOMAN IN BRITAIN
WHO WOULD DO IT.

THERE IS NO WOMAN IN BRITAIN
WHO WILL FORGET IT.

a battle." This was intended not to reflect on the quality of British cooking but to create a sense of the home as an extension of the trench.

There were also attempts to carry the spirit of duty to the bedrooms of the nations, as propaganda everywhere encouraged men and women to marry and have children. Once it became clear that the war would result in hundreds of thousands of casualties among young men, the very group relied on to father the future population, many governments took a surprisingly long-term view and adopted pronatalist policies. In a period when it was thought essential for a strong nation to have a robust population base, the immediate demographic effects of the war were alarming. The departure of hundreds of thousands of young men reduced marriages in almost every combatant state: Between 1914 and 1915 marriages fell from 205,000 to 86,000 in France, from 461,000 to 278,000 in Germany, and from 136,000 to 61,000 in Hungary. England was different; marriages actually rose in 1915 (to 361,000 from 294,000 in 1914) partly because enlistment was voluntary and slower, giving couples time to marry before men left for the front.

Many couples everywhere accelerated their marriages (there were thousands of emergency marriages in Germany in the first days of August 1914) so that men could leave for war as husbands. The practice produced, of course, many young war widows. Ironically, the very reason that caused a decline in marriages during the war (the departure of men) also reduced divorce rates everywhere, as the enforced separation of unhappily married couples by war service temporarily resolved marital differences. War deaths resolved many of them permanently.

Birth rates also declined, partly because marriages fell, partly because so many husbands and wives were separated, partly because, despite the urging of governments, many couples decided to postpone having children in the uncertainty and difficulty of war years. The effect was very pronounced in France, where the number of births in 1915 was more than a third lower than in 1914, but declines in births were registered everywhere: by almost a tenth in Britain, a quarter in Germany and Austria, and almost a third in Hungary.

Little wonder that all governments, though some more than others, encouraged marriage and procreation as a matter of urgency. The French, with their history of anxiety about population, were especially worried, and produced thousands of posters and postcards that portrayed marrying and having children as national duties. One, titled "Marriage at the Front," showed Marshal Joffre marrying a couple in a trench (all three stand taller than the breastworks and would certainly have been shot). It bore the caption, "By your valiant union you do France a twofold service," a reference to the couple's contribution both to the war and to population growth. Other postcards were more to the point. One showed a French soldier's cap, a voucher for a six-day leave from the front on "special duty," and three babies, each in a bag and all dangling from a bayonet. The caption read, "A good thrust."

In Germany the campaign for births became coercive, as from 1915 the military authorities banned the advertising of contraceptives and their distribution by door-to-door salesmen. But there were also inducements in the form of care for mothers and children: In 1914 expectant and recent mothers were paid weekly allowances, and the next year conservative notions of family and sexuality were put aside when allowances were offered to any mother who could prove that the father of her child was a soldier. For a government wanting to encourage fertility, this was an odd qualification.

The attitudes of many women's and feminist organizations toward the marriage and birth campaigns show how they abandoned their earlier policies and threw their weight behind the national war effort. One French feminist paper that had opposed pronatalist demands on women before the war urged its readers in 1915 to answer the call to have "children, lots of children, to fill the gaps" caused by war losses. German feminists across the political spectrum talked of the need "to strengthen the sacred will to motherhood," and of "women's natural duty toward family and society."

Complementing such efforts to create a sense of duty throughout all sectors of the home front was propaganda designed to give a sense of urgency to the civilian war effort. One technique was to show that the war was a fight for civilization, decency, and morality against an inhuman enemy. Capitalizing on the German attack on neutral Belgium, the Allied propaganda machinery set the tone for much wartime reporting. In France the government-financed Press Bureau, which controlled the dissemination of war news, circulated reports that the kaiser had ordered his troops to kill the Belgian king's children, and had offered bonuses to submarine crews that sank ships carrying women and children.

In Britain a prestigious committee of historians and lawyers produced an account of German "murder, lust, and pillage" in Belgium "on a scale unparalleled in any war between civilized nations during the last three centuries." The report detailed mass rapes in the marketplace of Liege, described how eight German soldiers had bayoneted a two-year-old child, and how another had sliced off a peasant girl's breasts. Belgian civilians were indeed assaulted, raped, and killed by German troops, but a postwar Belgian commission was unable to find evidence corroborating any of the major offenses alleged in the British report.

Much wartime rhetoric was racist, attributing to one nation or the other inherent qualities both good and bad. German academics portrayed Germans as the repositories of culture and civilization, and dismissed other Europeans as mere barbarians. They were countered by the French ultranationalist Charles Maurras, who wrote of "the instinctive savagery of German flesh and blood." Homophobia also came into play. The prewar homosexual scandals in the Germany army were recalled, and cartoonists and writers portrayed it as effeminate, weak, and easily defeated.

Less sensationalist efforts were also made to encourage distrust of the enemy. The London *Daily Mail* carried prominent advice to its readers, recommending that they should "refuse to be served by an Austrian or German waiter. If your waiter says he is Swiss, ask to see his passport." The same spirit lay behind purging English of actual or apparent German references. Sauerkraut became known as "liberty cabbage," and people with German-sounding names had them changed; Battenbergs became Mountbattens, and later in the war the British royal family, which descended from the German house of Saxe-Coburg-Gotha renamed itself Windsor. The German name of the Russian capital, St. Petersburg, was Russified to Petrograd.

Much of the socialist and trade union press, we might note, opposed blanket national characterizations. In France socialists condemned the wave of anti-German feeling that had led to mobs in Paris ransacking and looting shops allegedly owned by Germans. The socialists, consistent to this extent at least with their prewar position, insisted that it was not the German people who were the enemy, but Germany's government and industrial elite. In Russia the Bolsheviks refused to change the name of their Petersburg Committee to Petrograd Committee until 1918.

Efforts to convince civilians that the war was necessary, and that they were a vital part of the struggle were successful only to a point. While civilians were prepared to make certain sacrifices for the war effort, sharp declines in living standards could easily undermine people's spirits. Hence the attempts to regulate the supply and price of staple foods such as bread, potatoes, meat, eggs, and milk. Despite state intervention, price inflation occurred everywhere in 1914 and 1915. In Germany average real wages (the buying power of wages) of workers fell by 20 percent between March 1914 and September 1915 because of price increases. Higher-paid workers (especially women) in the war industries suffered less (their real incomes declined only 5 to 10 percent), but those in the consumer sectors like clothing and food production saw inflation wipe out a quarter of their purchasing power in eighteen months. The war thus ended the prewar trend of a slow but steady rise in German workers' real wages. Middle-class Germans, such as civil servants, experienced a 20 percent decline in real income between 1914 and 1915.

In France workers actually experienced a reduction in nominal wages in the early period of the war, and although wage levels were restored in 1915, incomes lagged behind prices. In Austria, where inflation reached 121 percent in 1915, workers' real wages fell by 20 to 40 percent in the year starting in July 1914. In Britain, by contrast, inflation was only 28 percent in 1915, and, more important, there was no appreciable decline in real income.

Besides attempts to cushion the impact of inflation by regulating vital foodstuffs, governments also compensated the families of men in military service for their loss of income. Expecting a short war, the British government initially made no provision of this kind, and in the first months of the war the Royal Hospital for Soldiers at Chelsea gave needy dependents help at the rates paid during the Boer War fifteen years earlier. By October 1914 the government stepped in, but even then the allowances were not generous: A soldier's wife (legal or de facto) and two children would receive sixteen shillings and six pence a week, two-thirds the average male industrial worker's wage. The absence of the husband, however, did reduce his family's food costs.

In France separation allowances were paid from the day war was declared. Wives were paid at a rate of 1.25 francs a day plus 0.50 francs for every child under the age of sixteen, when boys were eligible for military service. The adequacy of these sums depended on local food and housing costs; in large cities, and especially Paris, the allowance was less than an industrial worker would make, but for many rural workers it represented an improvement in income and living standards. There were complaints that some women were using the allowances to lead idle, dissolute lives with frequent visits to bars, patisseries, and dress shops. But while the allowances protected many families' standards of living, they were hardly enough to support a life of luxury.

In the Central Powers, similar provisions were made, but they proved poor protection against rapid price inflation. German soldiers' wives received 67.50 marks a month, two-thirds the average industrial wage. But when German soldiers died, the allowances paid to their families were reduced by a third. Similarly the effectiveness of allowances paid to dependents of Austrian and Hungarian soldiers (a maximum of 1.5 crowns a day) were quickly eroded by inflation.

War widows not only had to look after a household and perhaps raise children alone (sometimes with reduced finances) but had to bear emotional burdens as well. It was considered wrong for them to grieve openly, too much, or for too long for their dead husbands because doing so only drew attention to their country's suffering. A patriotic war widow would be stoical and ensure that her demeanor did not lower morale among her neighbors and workmates.

In the first year of the war the longer-term pattern of experiences on home fronts became discernible. The living standards of civilians in France and Britain were less seriously affected than those of their counterparts in the Central Powers. The gap between them grew wider as the war went on and had a significant impact on the result of the war.

The War on the Battlefronts, 1915 to 1916

While politicians and bureaucrats organized the home front for total war, the challenge facing the generals was how to break the stalemate that had developed on all the European fronts by December 1914. The strategic reality was that consolidating forces in trenches was essentially defensive, a conservative posture. Of the various strategies and tactics used in efforts to break out of it, the most dramatic (and costly) were repeated attempts to breach the enemy lines by using the massive manpower the generals had at their disposal.

Military commanders could not believe that such huge numbers of men would fail to overwhelm the enemy. They could order hundreds of thousands of men at a time to go "over the top": to surge out of the trenches at a whistled command, charge toward the enemy, and risk death in what was ironically called no-man's land—ironically, because it was quickly populated by the dead, dying, and wounded. Mass assaults of this kind were generally preceded by artillery bombardment and often accompanied by a barrage (strategic shelling that crept progressively toward the enemy, ahead of, and supposedly protecting, the infantry advance). They were attempted sporadically by both sides on the western front during 1915, but the results were inconclusive.

At the end of the year the German command decided that a breakthrough had to be made and that it could best be accomplished by throwing as much weaponry and as many men as possible at the historically important fortress of Verdun, a critical point in the prewar French defense system and a key element in the protection of Paris. The assault began on February 21, 1916, when 1,200 German artillery pieces opened fire with what the commander of the defense, Philippe Pétain, called "an avalanche of steel and iron, of shrapnel and poison gas shells." But again, instead of a quick rout the battle evolved into a standoff, one that lasted ten months. The German forces almost encircled Verdun and laid siege, pounding the fort's defenses day and night and attempting periodic mass assaults. Verdun's defenders finally prevailed, but at a cost of 350,000 lives. Besides saving Verdun they could console themselves that the Germans, who had intended "to bleed France white of all able-bodied men" by taking the fortress, had suffered more than 330,000 deaths during the siege. They had advanced their lines by two or three miles.

The assault on Verdun led to another major engagement, the Battle of the Somme, which lasted from July to November 1916. It was an attempt by the Allies to win ground by using mass manpower and weaponry, and it was timed to relieve pressure on Verdun. The British forces, led by Gen. Sir Douglas Haig, planned to weaken the German lines with a week-long artillery bombardment, then push forward with infantry so as to clear the way for three cavalry divisions to advance and smash the military deadlock. The Allies did push forward, but their best units gained only seven miles and the attack stalled before the cavalry saw action. The scale of casualties in the battle outdid even the siege of Verdun that it was designed to relieve: 400,000 British soldiers, 500,000 Germans, and 200,000 French troops were lost, more than a million men in all. The first day of the infantry assault, when the British alone suffered 60,000 casualties, was one of the bloodiest days of the war.

On the eastern front in 1915 and 1916 there was initially little alteration in the standoff achieved in late 1914. In December 1915, the Russian army attacked Austrian forces in Galicia, but gained little ground and lost 50,000 troops. Then in the spring of 1916, under pressure from their French allies who wanted action in the east to divert German resources from Verdun, the Russians opened an offensive against the German armies near Vilna. It was a disaster, the Russians losing 100,000 soldiers to the Germans' 20,000.

The battlefield on the Somme, 1916.

Later in 1916, however, Russian forces under General Brusilov scored an important blow against Austrian forces. Mounting a rapid and wide-scale offensive preceded by an artillery bombardment on June 1, the Russians advanced so effectively (they took 200,000 prisoners) that the strength of Austro-Hungarian armies in the east was halved in the space of a week. But attempts by Brusilov to advance even further foundered, partly because of supply problems and partly because of German intervention to prop up their allies. Even so, by the end of September 1916 the Russians had managed to reestablish the stalemate farther west than it had been four months earlier.

It was partly to break these stalemates on both land fronts that in 1916 the German leadership brought naval forces into play. During the preceding year the German navy had kept the bulk of its surface ships, especially the big battleships built during the arms race with Britain, in port so as not to expose them to the superior British navy. Instead the Germans turned to their submarine fleet in order to impose their own marine blockade of Britain and France. In February 1915 a free-fire zone was declared in the Atlantic around Britain, Ireland, and northern France, a zone in which any ships, including those of neutral countries, could be torpedoed without warning. But although a number of merchant ships carrying raw materials and food to the Allies were sunk, the most important sinking, in May, was the Cunard Line's *Lusitania*, which was carrying passengers and munitions. More than 100 of the 1,200 who died with the *Lusitania* were Americans, and the sinking so inflamed American public and political opinion that German submarine activity was curtailed so as not to cause further diplomatic waves between Washington and Berlin.

In May 1916, when the land war appeared to be no closer to resolution, the commander of the German High Seas Fleet, Admiral Scheer, proposed engaging the British in a major sea battle that would alter the balance of naval forces and thus change the overall military picture. A decoy fleet of German battle cruisers was dispatched to the coast of Norway to entice the British fleet from its base in Scotland, while the main German fleet waited off Denmark to intercept the British. The resulting engagement, the Battle of Jutland, lasted from May 31 to June 1 without a decisive strategic result. The Germans, aware of British superiority in numbers and guns, kept their distance, while the British, fearful of submarine attack, were equally cautious. If there were a naval equivalent to trench warfare—each side shooting at the other from as safe a position as possible, and neither side winning a definite victory—the Battle of Jutland was it.

The scope of hostilities on land also expanded in 1915 and 1916 as countries that had remained aloof in August 1914 were courted by both sides in the hope that additional pressure on the enemy would force a resolution of the intolerable deadlock. The Ottoman Empire had joined the Central Powers on November 2, 1914, and on October 15 the following year Bulgaria joined the same alliance with the intention of gaining territory from Serbia. The other European countries that entered the war in 1915 (Italy) and 1916 (Portugal, Romania, Greece) all opted for the Allied side. High moral principles were rarely involved, each state's decision to enter the war a calculation of what it might gain and which side was likely to win. Under the Treaty of Bucharest, for example, the Allies promised Romania Austro-Hungarian territory that would have doubled its size.

Italy, the most important of the additional European combatants, had been linked with Germany and Austria-Hungary in the Triple Alliance before the war, but had declined to join them in 1914 on the ground that their war was offensive rather than defensive. Right from the start of hostilities, however, both sides courted Italy. Fearing another front and realizing that Italy might well join the Allies, Germany even pressed Austria-Hungary to offer Italy part of its territory occupied by 700,000 Italian-speaking inhabitants—not as an inducement to join the Central Powers, but merely to remain neutral.

There was, in fact, strong neutralist sentiment in Italy's government, and a majority in parliament, including the Socialists, wanted to stay out of the war. But the prime minister, Antonio Salandra, favored entering the war on the side of the Allies, who offered extensive returns for Italian support: territory and population from Austria-Hungary, as well as Albania, Libya, and other territory in Africa. Large and often violent pro-war demonstrations took place in major cities, influenced by nationalists like the poet Gabriele D'Annunzio and the prominent Socialist (and later Fascist leader) Benito Mussolini. As a result of the extra-parliamentary pressure, an interventionist cabinet was formed, and on May 23, 1915, Italy signed the Treaty of London and declared war on Austria-Hungary. War on Germany was declared later, in August 1916.

As valuable as the opening of a new front was to the Allied cause, it was expensive for the Italians. The military command had expected Italy to join the Central Powers, and were given only three weeks' notice to redeploy their forces. The army, moreover, had been run down in the Libyan campaign and in 1915 was still poorly equipped and suffered low morale. Worse, Salandra was convinced that the war would not last beyond 1915, and had sought no military or economic assistance from Italy's new allies. Thanks to this combination of disabilities, the Italians suffered 250,000 casualties (a quarter of their forces) in their first engagements with Austro-Hungarian forces between June and December 1915. They made no headway in their attempt to cross the Isonzo River so as to link up with their new allies, the hard-pressed Serbian forces in Trieste.

Adding to the pressure on the Serbian army in 1915, German and Austro-Hungarian forces had attacked on October 7 and, with the assistance of the Bulgarians (who formally declared war after the fact), occupied Belgrade within days. The half of the Serbian army that survived these battles made its escape to the Albanian coast, and was evacuated by the Allies to the Greek island of Corfu.

Allied concern about the course of the war in the Balkan region and further afield was amplified by the alliance of the Ottoman Empire with the Central Powers. Ottoman forces controlled the straits vital for shipping supplies to Russia's Black Sea ports, and moving Russian grain exports out. Ottoman forces were also in a position to threaten French and British imperial interests in the Middle East, South Asia, and North Africa. There was particular concern about possible threats to the security of the Indian subcontinent and the vital supply route through the Suez Canal.

In February 1915, a joint German and Ottoman assault on the Suez Canal was beaten back by British, Australian, and New Zealand forces. Two months later, combined forces of the same countries landed at Gallipoli in the Dardanelles with the intention of opening access to Russia, but the venture was a debacle reminiscent of the bloodbaths of the western front. The British and imperial troops sustained 250,000 casualties, and were forced to withdraw.

The second and third years of the war, then, offered no great promise of an imminent resolution. If anything, the war looked increasingly like a huge, deadly maelstrom, sucking in more and more countries and soldiers and spewing out death and destruction without any hint that it might soon be satiated.

Serbian refugees, predominantly women, take their livestock with them as they flee ahead of the advancing Austro-Hungarian and German armies.

Weapons for Mass Destruction

The battles that took place on all fronts from 1914 to 1916 were notable for the weaponry deployed for the first time or deployed on a large scale for the first time. The single most important weapon was the machine gun, whose mass use from 1914 was largely responsible for the stalemated trench warfare. Men stumbling across the unprotected space between lines of trenches could be mown down easily by machine gunners, whereas defenders firing single shots from rifles were much more likely to be overwhelmed by massed troop assaults. A good rifleman could fire fifteen shots a minute, a machine gunner 600 rounds.

The other important category of weapon was artillery, mobile guns of various calibers used in sieges, to bombard enemy positions before the infantry was sent in, and to provide the barrages that accompanied infantry attacks. Artillery ranged from portable trench mortars of varying sizes to naval and fortress guns mounted on carriages and pulled by trucks, to heavy guns mounted directly on railway rolling stock. The biggest of all—the supergun of the war—was a 42-cm (16-inch) caliber monster developed by the Krupp arms firm for the German army. Variously called the kaiser's gun, the Paris gun, and Big Bertha, it fired 264-pound high-explosive shells, and, mounted on a railway flatbed, was used to bombard Paris from a distance of seventy-five miles.

But as important as machine guns and artillery pieces were, they seemed only to contribute to the deadlock on the western front and, for lack of new tactical ideas, military leaders looked for new weapons that might help them win the war. The Germans employed chlorine gas for the first time at Ypres, and poison gases of various kinds (such as phosgene

The use of gas in war: a line of men blinded by tear gas at an Advanced Dressing Station during the Battle of Estain, 1918. Each man has his hand on the shoulder of the man in front.

and mustard gas) were afterward used by both sides. Flamethrowers were also deployed by all armies after the Germans initially used them at Verdun in February 1916. They were essentially hoses that projected a jet of oil that was ignited. Flamethrowers had limited effectiveness because of their restricted range, but when they could be used they could set fire to tanks and usefully created terror and terrible injuries when directed into machine gun emplacements and trenches.

Tanks were deployed by the British for the first time in the Somme campaign in September 1916, and more extensively in later battles. But their effectiveness, even in the last stages of the war, is unclear. Some critics point to apparently high loss rates as evidence that tanks were too vulnerable to enemy fire and too susceptible to mechanical problems to be a reliable weapon in the First World War. In the first five days of the August 1918 Battle of Amiens, for example, the number of tanks deployed fell from 414, to 145, to 85, to 38, and finally to 6. Even if the decline was not due entirely to tanks being put out of action, the rate of attrition speaks loudly to the notion that tanks were of limited value.

At sea the major innovation of the war was the extensive use of submarines by both sides. Their most notable success was as a German weapon against ships bringing supplies to the Allies, and as a result the Germans devoted a great deal of energy to improving the strength, weaponry, and range of their U-boats. An unusual use of seapower was the shelling by German cruisers of English east coast towns in December 1914; 137 civilians were killed and almost 600 injured.

War was also carried to the air. In the first two and a half years of the war, airplanes were used primarily for reconnaissance purposes, although they were often armed with machine guns installed in the observer's cockpit behind the pilot. When in 1915 the Dutch engineer Anton Fokker designed a mechanism that permitted bullets to be fired between the blades of a spinning propeller, machine guns were mounted facing forward and reconnaissance aircraft became fighter planes. Even so, the much celebrated dogfights between fighter "aces" flying British Spads, French Nieuports, and German Fokkers contributed more to morale and the legend of wartime gallantry than to the military struggle on the ground below. More potentially useful to the war was the use of bombers and airships to bomb military and industrial targets, but the extent of such activity was limited. In all there were 51 airship raids on London between 1915 and 1918, causing almost 2,000 casualties, and 57 airplane raids causing some 3,000 casualties.

A characteristic common to the weapons widely used in this war was that they were designed for mass killing at the expense of precision. While a rifle had to be aimed and fired at each individual target, a raking machine gun sprayed bullets generously over a broad area in the reasonable expectation that if enough rounds were fired, some of them would hit something, or better, someone. Machine guns placed at regular intervals along front-line trenches, each one traversing a section of no-man's land so that no part of it was not covered, effectively defeated mass infantry assaults and prevented the front lines on the western front from moving significantly from late 1914 until the middle of 1918.

Massive, sustained artillery bombardments were designed to kill and wound in the same indiscriminate way. In the first seven days of the Allied offensive on the Somme (June 24–30, 1916), for example, the British fired 1.5 million shells at the German positions. Other innovations of the war, such as the use of bombers and submarines, may be counted as means of killing and wounding large numbers of people in single attacks.

In the final analysis the effectiveness of the various weapons for most of the First World War can be measured in terms of their ability to put enemy soldiers permanently or temporarily out of action. It is estimated that edged weapons (notably bayonets) ac-

The effects of bombardment. Aerial photographs show the Belgian village of Passchendaele before (top) and after the battle in 1916. The community was entirely obliterated and the land reduced to cratered earth.

counted for less than 1 percent of all wounds, bullets (usually from machine guns) accounted for 30 percent, and shells and bombs accounted for the rest. This distribution points to the extent to which warfare had ceased to be close one-on-one combat and had become a distant mechanized process. Techniques of mass production, an achievement of the industrial revolution, had resulted in techniques of mass destruction.

The Home Fronts at Midpoint: 1916

It is hardly surprising that morale on the home fronts everywhere began to falter during 1916. At the beginning of the year, people were living through their second wartime winter and could reflect that millions of dead and wounded sons, husbands, and brothers had produced a military stalemate. By the end of the year the stalemate remained unbroken, and all that had changed was that people were living—and many dying—in a third and even more difficult winter, and that millions more husbands, brothers, and sons had been killed or wounded.

In Central and Eastern Europe especially, 1916 was a pivotal year: Increasing numbers of civilians began to suffer the effects of escalating prices and inadequate supplies and services. The British and French, able to produce or import relatively plentiful supplies, nonetheless regulated prices on such goods as eggs, milk, and sugar. These controls checked inflation and prevented too great a gap developing between the cost of living and incomes. In Britain, in fact, the gaps between prices and wages was effectively closed once the full range of economic controls was imposed in mid-1916, and some groups of workers (especially the lowerpaid) experienced improvements in their real wages. Significantly the number of strikes fell to 672 in 1915 to 532 in 1916, and the number of workers involved in them declined even more, from 448,000 to 276,000.

How well the British fared during the war is underscored by children's health. The percentage of children with subnormal nutrition declined consistently, the number of children fed by municipal agencies fell, and there were even improvements in hygiene, as indicated by the rising proportion of boys and girls found by medical officers to have clean bodies and heads free of nits and vermin. The French did not do nearly as well as the British, but at least the decline in real wages slowed in 1916 as the gap that had opened between wages and prices in 1914 and 1915 began to close. It is indicative that the number of strikes increased, from 98 in 1915 to 314 in 1916, but even then only 41,000 workers were involved.

The German experience by the middle of the war was quite different. Faced with the prospect of shortages due to interrupted imports and declining domestic production, the government resorted to rationing rather than price controls. Prices began to rise as demand for increasingly scarce commodities grew, and the purchasing power of most incomes fell appreciably. Workers in war industries, who had more bargaining power, held their own reasonably well; compared with 1914, men's real wages had declined 22 percent by September 1916, whereas women, benefiting from nominal wage increases that narrowed the gender wage gap, saw their real incomes fall only 8 percent. For workers in other industries, however, purchasing power had dropped by more than 30 percent during the war to that point, and the real incomes of professionals like civil servants had declined by 40 percent.

More important than price inflation in Germany were shortages. In May 1916, the War Food Administration was established to regulate supplies and distribution, but it was too late to avert a disaster at the end of the year. During what became known as the "turnip winter" shortages of food and fuel were rampant, and turnips replaced potatoes as the main item in the working-class diet. Three-quarters of a million Germans, mainly infants, the elderly, and the poor, died of starvation or hypothermia.

Under such conditions German schoolchildren could hardly fare as well as their British counterparts. A survey in the Saxon town of Weissenfels showed that those starting school in 1916 were appreciably less healthy than those who started the year before. In the twelve months that separated the cohorts, the average weight of boys fell 1.3 kg (2.9 pounds) and of girls 0.5 kg (1.1 pounds). Children who started school in 1916 were shorter than those who preceded them by a year, and their overall nutritional score was lower. Such indications of hardships of the war on children were echoed by an examination of boys at two schools in Saxony that showed more than a third of them suffering from anemia.

Austrian civilians also began to reel under war conditions by 1916. Food production and imports declined, and rationing was introduced in 1915. These measures did not prevent a price inflation exceeding 200 percent in 1916, however, far above wage increases. From mid-1915 to mid-1916 real incomes declined by half or more, compared to a decline of a third or less in the preceding twelve months. Late in 1916 a central food agency was established, but working-class people, living on the inadequate diets prescribed by rationing and unable to purchase extra food at the exorbitant black market prices, increasingly took action themselves. Forty percent of industrial strikes in Austria in 1916 were protests about food supply.

The privations of war also sharpened ethnic antagonisms within Austria. The predominantly Czech-populated province of Bohemia was subjected to a harsher rationing regime. Not only were food supplies to Bohemia halted, but the province was expected to provide grain for the rest of the country. Official rations in Bohemia declined progressively from 9.5 pounds of bread and flour a week in 1915 to 5 pounds in 1918.

Italians, although late entrants to the war, began to suffer its effects as early as 1916. Price inflation began within months of the declaration of war, and workers in major industrial cities like Turin and Milan struck for higher wages. Deteriorating domestic conditions together with the Italians' poor military performance in the first year of their war, led to the collapse of the government and the installation of a broad-based coalition cabinet.

We should also note conditions in the Balkan States, key to the crisis that led to war in 1914, but often forgotten in accounts of the war itself. All suffered high military and civilian casualties, Serbia losing a higher proportion of its population than any other belligerent. Much of the country was subjected to a ruthless occupation by Austro-Hungarian forces that included some units with substantial numbers of Serbs and Croats. An estimated 650,000 Serbian civilians (out of a population of 3 million) died of the combined effects of malnutrition and disease.

Mobilization throughout the Balkan States had interrupted harvests, and all their populations suffered terrible privations. Germany and Austria made such great demands on their Bulgarian ally in 1916 that many areas were deprived of grain for sowing the next year's crop. Starvation led to widespread riots, including what became known as the "women's revolt," a wave of protests by women. There were increasing demands for Bulgaria to withdraw from the war unconditionally, and even the premier acknowledged that Bulgaria was treated by its allies more like a defeated enemy than a partner.

Home front administrations elsewhere also began to show signs of stress under worsening conditions in 1916, and there were changes to the administrations that had led the first two years of war. The most dramatic took place in Germany, where the military was given a formal role in government. From the beginning of the war the army General Staff had been more influential than other armies in their respective countries, and this influence was consolidated when in August 1916 the kaiser appointed two prominent generals, von Hindenburg and Ludendorff, to coordinate all aspects of the war effort. One of their first important measures, the Auxiliary Service Law of December 2, 1916, mobilized labor to an extent unprecedented in Europe. It required all males between the ages of seventeen and sixty to work in the war economy, and limited the freedom to move from job to job.

Germany's Austro-Hungarian ally, inadequately centralized to establish an administration that could coordinate policy effectively, foundered in 1916. In October the Austrian prime minister, Count Sturgkh, was assassinated, and the following month the old emperor Franz Joseph died. He was succeeded by his great-nephew the Archduke Karl, who had the wit to recognize the effects two years of war had had on his empire and its people: The army (which by the end of 1916 was conscripting fifty-five-year-old men) was near exhaustion, the empire's war effort was increasingly dependent on Germany, and civilian suffering could not be ignored.

It might also be argued that by this time Austria-Hungary had achieved enough of its war aims to quit the conflict: With their allies they had finally defeated Serbia, they had access (with Germany) to the coal and grain reserves of Romania, and their main rivals, Italy and Russia, had both been weakened by the war. In 1917 the new emperor put out peace feelers, but by that time the Germans so dominated their partnership that he had no freedom of independent action. He feared, too, that if a separate peace were pursued, the Germans might invade or the ethnic-German parts of Austria would secede and join Germany.

Russia's government experienced a quite different sort of change in 1916. Having failed to create an effective war administration from the undoubted political and techno-cratic talent available in the Duma and other bodies such as the Union of Towns, Czar Nicholas relied increasingly on his wife Alexandra and her strange (and arguably mad) personal adviser and spiritual guide, Gregory Rasputin. Having to all intents and purposes abdicated his political responsibilities, Nicholas proceeded to remove himself from the center of power: Over the protests of almost all his ministers he left Petrograd to take personal command of the Russian forces. The result was an even more unstable administration than before, as ministers came and went at Rasputin's whim. The chaotic process ended only when Rasputin was murdered by conservative forces in December 1916, and by then the po-litical situation in Russia was so volatile that two months later the czar was overthrown.

Compared with such upheavals, the change of leadership in Britain seemed almost trivial. Herbert Asquith, Liberal prime minister when war was declared, was under in-creasing pressure to resign two years later. The *Manchester Guardian* expressed the opin-ion of many when it wrote of his leadership: "Nothing is foreseen, every decision is postponed. The war is not really directed—it directs itself." In December 1916, Asquith was replaced by David Lloyd George, who had made a name for himself first as minister of munitions and then (when Lord Kitchener was drowned at sea in 1916 en route to Russia) as minister of war.

Lloyd George promptly formed a coalition cabinet to run the war, and under his lead-ership the pace of state activity was accelerated. In 1916 conscription was introduced to re-place the voluntary system that the British army had relied on for the preceding two years. Running counter to tradition and laissez-faire principles, it was not wildly popular but was generally accepted as necessary: It had been determined that as of 1916, some 2 million el-igible men had not enlisted. By the end of the war the men conscripted (who were often regarded by officers as shirkers, unfit, and the dregs of society because they had not rushed to the colors) represented 50.3 percent of all British men enlisted during the war.

In the face of continuing military stalemate and signs of restiveness among the peo-ple, the German and British governments in particular began to regroup in the middle of the war. Others, notably France and Russia, would do so the next year. All did what they could to position themselves for victory. Their plans were tested in 1917, the critical year of the war.

The Western Battlefronts in 1917

Desperation, disenchantment, or a desire for fresh ideas led to some changes in military leadership in 1916 and early 1917. The French commander-in-chief, Marshal Joseph Joffre, was replaced by Gen. Robert Nivelle, who had had some successes at Verdun. Nivelle promised to "break the crust" with a decisive offensive in Champagne, but the new leader merely modified the old method of an artillery bombardment followed by an as-sault with massed infantry. The results of the offensive, which involved 1,200,000 French troops together with British, Canadian, and other forces, looked as familiar as the strategy. In the first few days of the attack, 40,000 French troops were killed, and by the time the action was abandoned in early May, French casualties numbered 150,000 for insignificant territorial gain. Nivelle was fired.

One result of the failure of Nivelle's offensive was a wave of mutinies that washed through the French forces. Conscripts refused to advance when ordered, and in some cases attacked their officers. Others talked of commandeering a train and taking it to Paris. All told, as many as 40,000 men were involved in collective acts of insubordination, and 23,000 were disciplined in some way. Just over 400 death sentences were ordered, and 23 were actually executed.

Undeterred by the results of the spring French offensive, and not entirely informed about the extent of French losses, the British under Gen. Haig organized the next attempt to breach the German lines. The plan was to attack in Flanders, where the flat countryside made defense more difficult, so as to expel the Germans from Belgium and northern France. Besides the obvious advantages that would accrue from this, the British wanted to terminate the use of Belgian ports as bases for the German submarines harrying the Allied shipping routes.

Haig's offensive, known as the third Battle of Ypres, began at the end of July, but was dogged from the start by poor planning. The by now conventional artillery bombardment, designed to soften up the enemy positions, instead softened up the terrain by destroying the dikes and drainage system built to turn the area from swamp to farmland. British shelling, combined with abnormally heavy rains in August 1917, restored the countryside's previous swampy character and the whole advance bogged down. Many men, weighed down by heavy packs, drowned in mud-filled craters. Minor gains were made in September and October, but they contrasted dismally to the 300,000 Allied casualties that were sustained.

For their part the Germans' strategy on the western front was consolidation. In some areas they even pulled their lines back so as to intensify their defenses without committing more troops or equipment. Although the Germans suffered extensive casualties defending the western front in 1917, they were fewer than those of the Allies, and the Germans could envisage letting the French and British exhaust and demoralize themselves by throwing their armies into a series of futile offensives.

It was increasingly argued in the German leadership that the strategy of letting the Allies lose the war by exhaustion and attrition would be accelerated by stepping up submarine action against their supply routes. Although the sinking of neutral vessels risked retaliation from the United States in particular, it seemed inconceivable to leaders like Gen. Ludendorff that the potential power of submarine warfare should not be used to its fullest advantage. Even if the United States declared war, they calculated, choking off supplies might force Britain out of the war before American forces could be effectively deployed in Europe.

In February 1917, Germany resumed unrestricted submarine warfare, attacking Allied and neutral shipping in designated zones. The immediate results were impressive: Almost 1,140,000 tons of shipping went to the bottom in the first two months of the campaign. But several of the losses were American ships, sunk without warning, and on April 6 the United States, which had cut diplomatic relations with Germany at the renewal of the submarine campaign, declared war.

President Woodrow Wilson was clearly inclined to enter the conflict, and the sinking of a United States ship might have been reason enough for the isolationist Congress to endorse a declaration of war. But as it happened, at the beginning of 1917 the Americans were already outraged to learn, thanks to British interception of a cable message (known as the Zimmerman telegram), that Germany was proposing a military alliance with Mexico in the event of U.S.-German hostilities. The German proposal, which came to nothing, aimed to force the Americans to fight on two fronts, the bonus for the Mexicans being recovery of the land lost to the United States (notably Texas, Arizona, and New Mexico) in the Mexican-American War of 1846–48.

The immediate impact of the American entry into the war was minimal: The American government had expected to provide supplies, naval support, and money, and was taken by surprise when its new allies called for combat forces. The United States military numbered only a little more than 200,000, and the government quickly inducted the National Guard and adopted conscription. Within a month of the American declaration of war, 9.5 million men had registered for military service. The first units of 2 million American troops to serve in Europe arrived in June. In the meantime the American navy played a vital role escorting the convoys of merchant ships supplying the Allies, and the high shipping losses began to decline: From a monthly average of 420,000 tons sunk from April to July 1917, losses were more than halved to 196,000 tons in September.

By 1917 certain social patterns had developed within the European armies. Although the armies flung 3 million men into one another's company over long periods of time, gender and sexual relationships remained important issues. Every British soldier who enlisted received a personal letter from the commander-in-chief warning that "in this new experience you may find temptations . . . and while treating all women with courtesy, you should avoid any intimacy. Do your duty. Fear God. Honour the King." In fact it was not so much God the authorities feared as venereal disease, and with good reason: By the end of the war, one in five British soldiers had contracted it.

Soldiers were sexually active with women in the localities where they spent breaks from the front lines, either as casual relationships or as clients of prostitutes. On some fronts, such as the Austro-Hungarian occupation of Serbia, rape was relatively more widespread. In 1917, after resisting pressure to do so for three years, the British army issued condoms to reduce the incidence of sexually transmitted diseases. The French military authorities set up official brothels, which gave them some control over the spread of these diseases.

The presence of thousands of nurses near the front lines created difficulties for the authorities. The official image of the nurse was a combination of a nun and a mother, both asexual categories of womanhood. Nurses were depicted as looking after wounded soldiers as if they were their children; a nurse who promoted the sexual side of her femininity, by flirting with soldiers was considered deviant and a menace to the war effort. Besides these images, of course, nursing could be seen as paralleling service in the trenches. Nurses worked to the same rhythms of assault and defense, endured terrible work conditions (often aggravated by poor administration), and had to deal with the most appalling injuries. Nurses were decorated for service and particular bravery, although there are few memorials to them as a part of the national service.

Revolutions in Russia:
March and November 1917

As buoyed as the Allies were in early 1917 to have the United States as a partner in arms, they were concerned that growing political instability in Russia might threaten the viability of the eastern front. The First World War can hardly be said to have caused the two revolutions that rocked Russia at the beginning and end of 1917, but the stresses and strains of the conflict were important elements in the collapse of the czarist regime.

In March[2] 1917 there were large demonstrations by women and men in Petrograd to protest shortages of coal and bread. Demonstrations of this kind were scarcely unprecedented, and they paralleled the growing anger and despair among civilians elsewhere in Europe, especially Germany, Italy, and Austria-Hungary. Conditions were severe in Russia: By December 1916, prices were four times the level they had been at the outbreak of war, and supplies of goods were held up by the reluctance of farmers to sell and by the breakdown of the transportation system. The government, seemingly inspired by a death wish, added to the misery in 1916. First it introduced new taxes—too late to halt inflation, but a new source of grievance; second, because military casualties had reached disabling levels (3.6 million dead, wounded, or very ill, and another 2.1 million taken prisoner), it called up the second category of recruits, men who were their families' sole wage earners.

Unnerved by the estimated 200,000 restive people milling through the streets of Petrograd in March, Czar Nicholas ordered his troops to disperse them. Shots into the crowd outside the palace on March 11 killed some forty people, but then the soldiers sent to put the crowd to flight began instead to fraternize with the demonstrators. Without moral or military force to sustain him, the czar was isolated, and the following day the Duma stepped in and set up a Provisional Government drawn from its members. Despite their preference for a liberal state with a constitutional monarchy, these men realized that only a completely new political system had any chance of winning public support. Nicholas was persuaded to abdicate in favor of his brother Michael, but Michael declined to accept the position and turned authority over to the Provisional

Petrograd, March 1917. Demonstrators are fired on by the czar's troops, an act that provoked the downfall of the Russian autocracy.

2. February by the old Julian calendar that was then in use in Russia. Dates in this book are given in terms of the modern calendar so that they can be related to events in other parts of Europe.

Government until a new legislature could be elected. With Nicholas's abdication, Russia ceased to be a monarchy.

There was no certainty that the Provisional Government, a group of men from the gentry and middle class who had been elected to the Duma on a very narrow suffrage, could successfully assert authority over an increasingly restive population of peasants and workers. Its first acts were to promulgate a mixture of structural reforms (including universal male suffrage and freedom of the press), and equally important measures to rally specific groups to it. Workers were guaranteed an eight-hour workday, peasants were promised that monastic and royal estates would be expropriated and redistributed to the needy. Soldiers were to benefit from a military code of civil rights, including abolition of the death penalty for military offenses. By such measures the government hoped to limit the revolutionary activity among workers, halt the seizure of lands by peasants that had already begun, and arrest the decline of discipline and morale in the Russian armies.

But the Provisional Government was not the only claimant to the authority abandoned by the czar. No sooner had the Duma acted in March than a Petrograd soviet made its appearance, a reincarnation of the committee of workers that had led the 1905 general strike. The leaders of the soviet drew their authority from having served on the War Industries Committee, and they quickly gained support from workers suspicious of the Duma and the Provisional Government. Equally important, the soviet was able to demonstrate a socially and geographically broad base of support, as hundreds of soviets were set up in other towns, as well as in the country and in many army units.

It was from the disheartened army that the Petrograd soviet hoped to draw particular support. On March 5 it issued Soviet Order No. 1 on its own authority, effectively placing the Petrograd garrison under its own control. The order abolished the power of officers to impose punishments, and instructed army units to form committees to control the distribution and use of weapons, to settle differences between officers and men, and to exercise political authority over the troops. Although this order was initially limited to forces in the Petrograd area, its understandable popularity ensured that it was observed throughout the Russian armies. Citing its authority, troops in many areas refused orders, while some units deposed (and a few lynched) their officers.

Besides issuing an order that had rendered the army unreliable and potentially mutinous, what made the soviets a threat to the Provisional Government (rather than a partner in political reform) was that they were dominated by socialists who wanted much more fundamental social and economic change than envisaged by the liberals of the Provisional Government. Workers in the cities, especially those employed in large factories, distanced themselves from the liberal intellectuals. A number of issues were at stake, including the reluctance of the Provisional Government to impose controls so as to ensure that workers had a secure supply of food. The main point of conflict, however, was the war; the Provisional Government planned to continue Russian participation, while socialists wanted Russia to withdraw from the war. This disagreement in particular produced a polarization of the revolutionary forces in mid-1917.

Although the Bolsheviks were later to seize control of the revolution, their role in the events of the first half of 1917 was slight. The increasingly important Petrograd soviet drew membership and support from a spectrum of social democratic and socialist groupings. The Bolsheviks themselves were not the tightly organized revolutionary organization that they later portrayed themselves as being; their internal organization was decentralized, relatively democratic, and scattered.

One of the Bolshevik leaders, Vladimir Lenin, had been living in exile in Switzerland and could not participate in the events in Petrograd because the only direct route there ran through the Central Powers. Calculating that Lenin's presence in the Russian capital could only increase revolutionary activity, aggravate the confusion in the country's government, and derail its war effort, the Germans allowed him to make the journey across their territory and through their lines in a sealed train.

Soon after his arrival at Petrograd's Finland Station in April 1917 (an event later treated by the Communists like the coming of a messiah), Lenin set out the variant on Marxism that bears his name, Leninism. Russia, he declared, did not have to go through full industrialization in order to reach socialism; the peasants could be considered proletarians, and the fact that much land was already held communally by them meant that evolution toward a communist society was already under way. Lenin promptly called for "all power to the soviets," a clear summons to reject the Provisional Government's claim to authority, and he put forward a program of "peace, bread, and land"—an end to Russian participation in the war, control of the economy by workers, and the seizure of landed estates by peasants.

Lenin's reformulation of Marxism at a time of deepening political, economic, and social crisis gave some impetus to the revolutionary movement in Russia. It armed Marxists with a rationale for embracing more rapid change, and the straightforward agenda of peace, bread, and land would attract mass support in a country where war had brought only exhaustion, massive loss of life, and terrible suffering. Even so, workers lacked the ability and confidence to challenge the Provisional Government, and instead cooperated with it in order to prevent a right-wing reaction.

Not only was Russia's home front fragile in the spring of 1917, but its battlefront began to unravel. The troops were unnerved by the news from home: It was no longer clear for whom they were fighting, and conscripted peasants were worried at the thought that land might be redistributed in their absence. Confusing reports of political turmoil apart, almost three appalling years of war, defeats, stalemate, massive casualties, hunger, and cold had understandably taken their collective toll on morale. The only positive development was that the Germans refrained from attacking the Russian lines in case it revived their fighting spirit.

The Provisional Government, on the other hand, was anxious to resume military activity, partly from fear that idle troops would be susceptible to soviet influence. It had reassured the Allies that Russia would fight "to the end, unswervingly and indefatigably," and the Allies had welcomed the political change in Russia because it gave more credibility to their claim to be fighting for democracy. Choosing to believe reports that the armed forces were in good heart, rather than more accurate accounts of widespread despair and defeatism, the government decided to mount an offensive against Austro-Hungarian forces in Galicia in July 1917. But it was indicative of the Russian morale that although their offensive met with initial success (the Austro-Hungarian forces were themselves weakened by internal conflicts among nationalities), they retreated in confusion when reserve units appeared.

This latest setback on the battlefront echoed loudly in Petrograd, where living conditions continued to deteriorate: Prices had almost doubled in the previous six months, a trend that did not increase support for the Provisional Government. On July 16 there was a popular insurrection by workers whose March grievances had not been resolved and who were now even more incensed that the government had let more men die for no apparent reason.

This time it was the Provisional Government that ordered soldiers to fire into the crowd; they outdid the czar's effort by killing five times as many demonstrators as his troops had in March. A general repression of the government's opponents followed, and Lenin, who had openly supported the uprising, took refuge in Finland, where virtual autonomy

MAP 3.3 The eastern front, 1914–18.

from Russia had been unilaterally declared. Following the suppression of opposition, and in the face of deteriorating conditions, support for the Bolsheviks rose. Opposition to the government grew within the Petrograd garrison when the death penalty was again applied to soldiers on the front lines.

The government's war policy also dissolved what was left of discipline in the Russian armies. By the fall of 1917, attacks on officers became common, reserve units behind the front lines threw in their lot with the soviets, and the front-line troops began to experience mass desertions. Believing that strong government had to be restored, one of the Russian commanders, General Kornilov, attempted a military coup in September. It failed, mostly because his troops were unreliable, but not before the moderate leftist leader of the provisional government, Alexander Kerensky, had turned for help to his other adversaries, the soviets and the Bolsheviks, and their Red Guard paramilitary units.

The Kornilov coup failed, but it doomed Kerensky's administration anyway. The government had demonstrated its isolation by falling back on the soviets and Bolsheviks for help, and shown its desperation by protecting the Winter Palace (seat of the government) with a garrison of military cadets and a unit of young middle-class women. During September the government was paralyzed by ministerial crises. It failed to act on any of the pressing issues that had brought it to power in the first place, such as land reform and ensuring the food supply, and did not respond to other demands that included a guarantee that garrison troops would not be sent to the front.

From that point, collaboration between the government and the workers ended, and as the government's support and authority dissipated, the strength of the Bolsheviks increased. The Bolsheviks were assisted by evidence of the government's resistance to opposition. There were rumors that the government was going to be moved to Moscow, the ancient Russian capital, partly to free it from radical pressures. The government also attempted to repress the Bolsheviks; their newspapers were closed and the Bolshevik-dominated Military Revolutionary Committee (an organ of the Petrograd soviet) was ordered to disband. Members of similar-minded groups, like the left wing of the Social Revolutionaries, rallied to support the Bolsheviks, strengthening their position within the antigovernment socialist forces.

In these circumstances the Bolsheviks planned and executed the insurrection that began on the night of November 6–7 (October 25 by the old calendar), when the seat of the Provisional Government in the Winter Palace was attacked. The sailors of the naval base at Kronstadt, drawn from the working class (unlike soldiers, who were mostly peasants) threw their lot in with the Bolsheviks. The cruiser Aurora was brought within range of the palace, but fired blanks because its guns could not be brought to bear. Two or three shots (of some thirty fired) from the Peter and Paul Fortress struck home. Finally Bolshevik forces stormed the palace and the Provisional Government was disbanded. A Council of People's Commissars, all of them Bolsheviks, was installed as head of a new Soviet government. A week later the Bolsheviks took power in Moscow, too. This was achieved with considerably more difficulty, and the Kremlin was seized only after serious fighting.

Although depicted by Soviet historians as a tightly planned revolution, the Bolshevik seizure of power reflected the weakness and mistakes of the Provisional Government as much as the strength of the revolutionaries. By late 1917, too, the traditional institutions of authority, such as the police, civil service, army, and municipal councils, were in disarray, and there was evidence of widespread social collapse and crime in the cities and countryside. At the same time, the policies espoused by the Bolsheviks—an end to the war, land reform, and bread—had considerable appeal.

The October Revolution had immediate implications for the war, for one of the Bolsheviks' first acts was to end Russia's participation. Although the Germans could easily have advanced through the disintegrating Russian forces in the final months of 1917, their priority was to develop a new offensive in the west. On December 15 the Russians and Germans agreed to a provisional armistice on the basis of existing positions, and began work on a comprehensive peace agreement. As for Russia's former partners, they could anticipate increased German pressure on the western front following the cessation of hostilities in the east.

One historian (J. A. S. Grenville) has suggested that by 1917 Italy, Austria-Hungary, and Russia were in a race to see which would collapse first. It is hardly an exaggeration, for the political structures of all three (and Germany might also be considered a fourth contender with an outside chance) began to give way under the sustained pressure of waging total war. Russia's regime was not the only one to succumb; it was merely the first.

War Aims and Political Warfare

As we have seen, the objectives of German foreign policy before the start of the war have long been debated. But early in September 1914, when Germany's armies seemed to be driving to a quick victory, a memorandum prepared by the German chancellor set out ambitious war aims. After a German victory, Europe would be reorganized to give Germany political and economic control of west-central Europe (Mitteleuropa). Various parts of France, including the coast as far as Boulogne, and Luxembourg would be annexed. Belgium would be placed under German control. The raw materials, resources, and strategic ports of these states, as well as the Netherlands, Denmark, and Austria-Hungary, would make Germany self-sufficient. Britain would be denied any influence on the continent, and Germany would be protected from a weakened Russia by a buffer state under German protection. Germany would add French and Belgian colonies in Africa to its own, giving Germany an empire befitting Europe's most powerful state. These aims, driven as much by economic and military, as by political concerns, guided German war policy. They go some way to explaining why Germany pushed on with the war in early 1918 instead of trying to reach a settlement that consolidated the gains in Eastern Europe that it made under the peace treaty with Russia signed in March 1918.

The war aims of Germany's main partners were less ambitious. Austria-Hungary sought to destroy Serbia as a factor in the Balkans and to strengthen its own security by weakening Italy and Russia. The Ottoman Empire was concerned with events in Europe mainly insofar as they distracted France and Britain and provided an opportunity for the Turks to extend their dominion over French- and British-controlled areas of the Middle East, Asia, and North Africa.

On the side of the Allies, early wartime aims were no more homogeneous. The French wanted to recover Alsace and Lorraine, and to weaken Germany permanently so as to secure France's eastern border. British intentions were broadly conservative at first: limiting the power of Germany and restoring the balance of powers on the Continent. This meant liberating those parts of France (including Alsace and Lorraine) and Russia invaded by the Central Powers, and restoring the political integrity of Belgium and Serbia.

Although Britain and France had limited ambitions, they agreed to the territorial aims of their partners. Both Russia and Serbia wanted to secure territory at the expense of Austria-Hungary, and the the other European states that joined the Allies in 1915 and 1916 (notably Italy and Bulgaria) were motivated by the desire to win territory.

As the war bogged down from late 1914, the war aims of the major belligerents changed to reflect the growing importance attributed to the home fronts. If the enemy could not be defeated quickly by arms, they might be weakened politically from within. To this end initiatives were taken to encourage dissident national and political groups, particularly in the three land-based empires at war. By 1916 the Allies were giving assistance to restive nationalities in Austria-Hungary, notably the Italians, Romanians, Slovaks, Czechs, and Poles. Early the same year Hussein, the grand sherif of Mecca, agreed to raise an Arab revolt against Turkish dominion in exchange for British guarantees of independence for most Arab provinces after the war.

The Central Powers pursued similar policies where they could. They tried to weaken Russia by encouraging national movements among Poles and in Finland, Ukraine, Crimea, and the Baltic provinces. German agents attempted to foment dissent in various French and British colonies in North Africa, where they portrayed themselves as defenders of Muslim interests. German assistance to Irish nationalists in their struggle against

Britain paid slight dividends when in March 1916 the Easter Rebellion took place in Dublin. The rebellion was soon crushed by British and Irish forces; its leaders were tried and fourteen of them executed under the Defence of the Realm Act that was enacted in 1914 to deal with threats to Britain's war effort. Germany also tried to ship arms to revolutionary nationalists in India.

The Allies' ad hoc attempts to weaken their enemies politically were elevated to policies of principle when in December 1916 President Wilson, seeking a basis for a peace settlement, asked the European belligerents to specify their war aims. The British and French replied that their intention was to create a stable Europe based on respect for nationalities. That meant not only the liberation of countries and provinces occupied by the Central Powers, but also the liberation "from foreign domination" of national groups like Czechs, Slovaks, and Romanians, and the emancipation of populations "subject to the bloody tyranny of the Turks."

The dismemberment of the Austro-Hungarian and Ottoman Empires thus appeared on the Allied war agenda by early 1917, by which time internal forces had made the achievement of the goals much easier. During that year and the next, the march toward national independence, especially for nationalities in Austria-Hungary, received tacit and open Allied support. In July 1917 the Declaration of Corfu envisaged a unified kingdom of Serbs, Croats, and Slovenes, and laid the basis of postwar Yugoslavia. In Rome in April 1918, a Congress of Oppressed Nationalities pledged support for national self-determination for the nationalities in Austria-Hungary. Thereafter the Allies recognized various national committees (notably the Poles and Czechoslovaks) as governments-in-exile, and their military forces as autonomous armies.

But Allied policy was less than transparent. While talking openly of national independence, they had constructed a web of agreements dividing territory among themselves. The Treaty of London promised Italy lands that included hundreds of thousands of non-Italian inhabitants. The 1915 Constantinople Agreement promised Russia the Turkish capital and control of the Dardanelles. The May 1916 Sykes-Picot Agreement gave territory and influence in the Middle East to Britain, France, and Russia, despite earlier commitments to Arab nationalists. In November 1917 the British further muddied the prospects for postwar order in the Middle East by agreeing to the Balfour Declaration. Named after the foreign secretary, it expressed British support for the Zionist aim of creating a Jewish homeland in Palestine, which at that time contained 60,000 Jews in a total population of 750,000.

The substantial gap between the Allies' public policies and their secret promises was revealed to the world by the new Bolshevik government in Russia as it attempted to reach an armistice agreement with Germany. Leon Trotsky, people's commissar for foreign affairs, denounced the secret agreements as a means by which capitalists deceived, traded, and enslaved working people. One of the documents showed that the Allies had promised one piece of land in Dalmatia to both Italy and Serbia.

Trotsky's revelations of clandestine deals and his call for open diplomacy and a democratic foreign policy were followed by a flurry of principled justifications for the war. In January 1918, Lloyd George announced British policy as being guided by the principle of government with the consent of the governed. This meant the liberation of occupied territory and the creation of an independent Poland. He denied wishing to dismember Austria-Hungary, but insisted that the principle of self-determination must be applied there. At the same time, Lloyd George's support or the "legitimate" claims of Italy and Romania implied limits to the principle of self-determination when other claims conflicted with it. Finally, British policy called for an international organization to lessen the probability of war in the future.

Lloyd George's statement was followed three days later by Woodrow Wilson's declaration before Congress of his famous Fourteen Points, his principles for a lasting peace. The most important were the first five, which included replacing secret diplomacy by "open covenants of peace openly arrived at"; freedom of the seas in peace and war; ending barriers to international trade; reducing armaments to the lowest level consistent with each nation's security; and national self-determination. The remaining nine points were more specific, such as the restoration of occupied Belgium, Russia, Alsace-Lorraine, and Serbia, and national self-determination for the peoples of Austria-Hungary and the Ottoman Empire. The final point called for the establishment of an association of nations to guarantee the political independence and territorial integrity of all states, great and small.

The French made no declaration of war aims except in the familiar terms of regaining Alsace and Lorraine, putting an end to German militarism, and securing reparations to pay for the war. In March 1918, Clemenceau described his foreign and domestic policies succinctly: "I make war. I keep making war. . . . I continue to make war, and I will continue to make war until the last quarter hour."

The Allies' commitment to political independence and territorial integrity was soon tested. When Russia signed its peace treaty with Germany in March 1918, the British sent forces to the Arctic port of Murmansk and later to Archangel, ostensibly to ensure that military materiel supplied by the Allies did not fall into German hands. Later in the year France, the United States, Canada, Italy, and Greece also dispatched forces to these ports and to Odessa and Vladivostok, until more than 100,000 troops of Russia's former allies were on its soil. (Japan, hoping to benefit from Russia's internal turmoil, sent forces into Siberia in 1918.) The initial justification for intervention in Russia, to secure military supplies, ended with Germany's surrender in November 1918, and for a year after that Allied troops aided anti-Bolshevik forces (the "Whites") in the civil war that broke out soon after the Bolsheviks (the "Reds") seized power.

The European, Canadian, and United States forces quit Russia in late 1919, a year after World War ended, but kept up a maritime blockade until early 1920, when it was clear that the Bolsheviks were on the verge of victory. Japanese troops left Siberia in 1922 and the Russian part of Sakhalin in 1925. Allied intervention in Russia did little more than reinforce Bolshevik hostility toward the West. The fact that France wanted to carry on the war against Russia, while Britain was reluctant to extend hostilities, highlighted the disunity among Allied foreign policies that made postwar peace-making so difficult.

Neutrals and Nonbelligerents

Too often it is forgotten that many of Europe's states declined to join the 1914–18 war. Norway, Sweden, Denmark, the Netherlands, Spain, and Switzerland remained nonbelligerents throughout. Belgium and Luxembourg had no option but to participate, if only briefly in an active sense, because they were invaded by Germany on the first day of war. Both were neutral and would almost certainly have stayed out of the war if they could.

How did the neutral states fare during the conflict? Clearly, none had to endure the most direct effects of the war. They did not have to raise and equip massive armies, nor did they face the social and economic dislocation resulting from the withdrawal of huge numbers of men from the economy. In theory, at least, the neutrals ought to have been able to carry on as usual, but in fact they soon experienced the side effects of the massive conflict going on elsewhere. The hostilities very quickly had economic implications, initially positive ones for the Scandinavian countries, which sold to both sides. Sweden, a major producer of iron ore and high grade steel, found a ready customer in Germany; despite attempts by the Allies to place a blockade on Sweden, the value of exports to Germany more than doubled during the war. Denmark traded across the border with Germany and by sea with Britain. Norway at first sold its export fish production to Germany, helping to treble its exports there in 1915 and 1916.

In the first half of the war Scandinavia's economy boomed as demand for primary and industrial products pushed up prices. By 1916, however, Britain was placing economic pressure—notably by withholding coal supplies—to gain greater access to Scandinavia's produce. From 1916 the great bulk of Norway's export fish went to Britain, and Norway was pressured to allow most of its merchant shipping fleet to be used on the trans-Atlantic supply route. The resumption of German submarine attacks led to the loss of half the shipping tonnage, along with the lives of 2,000 Norwegian seamen, and the country's merchant fleet fell from fourth to sixth largest in the world.

In the last two years of war Scandinavians suffered hardships because food imports were interrupted by war and a disastrous harvest in 1917. Controls on food were introduced and in 1917 the flour ration in Norway was half a pound a day, and in Sweden potatoes were rationed. Dairy products were in very short supply, despite imports from Denmark, which suffered no significant food shortages. Norwegians resorted to making a substitute butter by mixing mutton fat with honey.

The Netherlands also experienced a decline of living standards during the war because of interrupted trade. Unemployment rose, food supplies declined, and municipal governments established programs of school meals for children and communal kitchens for the poor.

Spain, in contrast, appeared to have benefited from the war. The value of Spain's exports, especially to France, rose substantially, and exports of cotton and wool textiles did especially well. With increased demand for products, new factories were built and employment expanded. Coal production, stagnant before the war, had increased by a third by 1916, by two-thirds in 1918. The wartime boom in Spain's economy produced vast profits for some entrepreneurs, but its benefits trickled only a little way down the social scale.

The fate of Belgium was entirely different, as was its status during the war. Neutral in terms of international law, Belgium had resisted invasion in 1914, and thereafter most of the country was occupied by Germany; some of the most devastating battles on the western front were fought in Belgium. German occupation policy was to exploit Belgian resources to the full. Livestock, agricultural production, and coal were requisitioned, and whole factories were dismantled and moved to Germany. Even before the war Belgium depended on imported grain, although it was self-sufficient in meat, potatoes, and dairy products. But the cessation of imports and the imposition of German requisitioning led to a food crisis as early as the end of 1914. Despite international relief efforts, welcomed by the Germans as removing responsibility for Belgians' welfare from them, caloric intake fell. Mortality rates rose in 1917 and 1918.

Beginning the End:
The Battlefronts to August 1918

The decline of Russian strength in late 1917 took pressure off German and Austro-Hungarian forces and had repercussions on all fronts. The most immediate was on the frontier with Italy, south of the Alps, where Italian and Austro-Hungarian forces had been engaged in a campaign of attrition, punctuated by a dozen major battles, from the day Italy entered the war. Each side had lost about 100,000 dead. In October 1917, however, six German divisions were diverted from Russia to join the nine Austro-Hungarian divisions in place on the Italian front, and together they attacked in the region of the small town of Caporetto.

The assault, preceded by a bombardment of heavy artillery and poison gas, routed the Italians, and for three weeks (until November 12) they were pushed back as far as the River Piave. Only that natural barrier—the river was in its autumn flood—stopped the Austro-Hungarians and Germans from proceeding further and taking more of the Italian province of Veneto. The Battle of Caporetto was not only a major military defeat for Italy, but also a humiliating one. When the attack began, confusion broke out, discipline broke down entirely, and hundreds of thousands of soldiers ran from the lines, many simply abandoning their weapons. Some 200,000 soldiers lost contact with their units and 300,000 surrendered or were captured.

By early 1918, the weight of the war had tilted dramatically toward the west, the focus of German attention once Russia[3] had sued for peace. The Allies, however, were welcoming the fresh troops from the United States just in time to offset the advantage Germany should have gained from being able to transfer its forces from the eastern front. But although the American Expeditionary Force looked fresh and ready for battle, it was also inexperienced. The German High Command calculated this would counterbalance what the Americans added to the Allies in numbers (still a relatively small 175,000 soldiers by the beginning of 1918), and prepared an offensive for the late spring.

The Germans need not have opened this new campaign in the west had they been satisfied with the extensive gains of their peace agreement with Russia, the Treaty of Brest-Litovsk, signed on March 3, 1918. So desperate was the new Bolshevik government to get a breathing space so that it could consolidate its authority, quickly challenged by anti-Bolshevik armies, that it agreed to give up non-Russian territories in Europe that had been part of the czarist empire. Poland, Lithuania, Latvia, Estonia, and Finland, as well as Trans-Caucasia (Georgia, Armenia, and Azerbaijan), were granted independence, Ukraine was occupied by Germany, and a strip of territory in Trans-Caucasia was ceded to Turkey. These territories included a quarter of the old empire's population, a quarter of its arable land, a third of its crops and manufacturing industries, and three-quarters of its iron industries and coal fields. In addition, the Bolshevik government agreed to pay Germany compensation for Russia's war, effectively paying for the policy the Bolsheviks had repudiated from the very beginning.

The independence of most of the formerly Russian-controlled states was qualified by their agreeing to German protection, so that by Brest-Litovsk, Germany achieved two

---

3. Russia was renamed the Russian Soviet Federated Socialist Republic (or Soviet Russia) in July 1918. In 1922 it became part of the Union of Soviet Socialist Republics (USSR, or Soviet Union), along with the Ukrainian, Belorussian, and Trans-Caucasian Soviet Socialist Republics.

goals: ending the Russian threat to German interests in Europe, and extending German economic and political domination to include areas with vast reserves of raw materials and food. These stunning gains might have enabled the German leadership to consider negotiating an end to all hostilities, but it was driven by the vision of a German-dominated Europe. This, plus the fact that the French were unlikely to agree to a compromise peace, convinced the Germans to fight on in the west.

Their strategy envisaged an attack where the Battle of the Somme had taken place in 1916. Instead of using the conventional (and unsuccessful) method of a lengthy artillery bombardment, which only announced the impending massed attack, Ludendorff planned a short, sharp period of shelling followed by assaults by small and well-equipped infantry units. His aim was to split the Allied forces, driving the British north to defend the Channel and the French south to defend Paris, and enabling the German forces to drive through the gap. The strategy was initially successful, forcing the British back forty miles at one point and causing confusion and squabbling between the French and British commands. But a coordinated leadership for the Allies was agreed upon for the first time in the war, their forces rallied, and the German advance was halted. At 150,000 the Allied casualties were high, but the German offensive was not decisive.

An attempt by German forces to repeat the attack in Flanders the following month also met with brief success before petering out, but a third try looked more promising. At the end of May 1918 German troops broke through French and British lines on the Aisne River and reached the River Marne, only forty miles from Paris. At this point the influx of fresh American forces (275,000 in June alone) began to have an impact, and the German armies were beaten back.

By mid-July the German armies in the west, depleted by 800,000 casualties in four months, were not the fighting force Ludendorff needed to execute his strategy. From July 18 they were driven back across the Marne by American, French, and British forces using infantry and tanks. In early August 1918, the same troops, augmented by forces from other parts of the British Empire, and using aircraft as well, defeated the Germans near Amiens and took 15,000 prisoners. Ludendorff informed the kaiser that the German army could no longer be considered an effective force.

The Home Fronts, 1917 to 1918

The German people at home were no longer an effective force, either. Industrial production declined through 1917 and 1918, until by the end of the war it was only two-thirds the 1913 level. Attempts had been made to shore up the workforce by releasing almost 2 million soldiers from military service in mid-1917 and by using the forced labor of foreign civilians and many of the 1.7 million prisoners of war taken by Germany. But productivity declined in the face of shortages of raw materials and the steadily deteriorating living conditions that workers and their families had to endure. The official food ration provided for only about two-thirds the calories needed for light work, and half those needed for medium to heavy work.

In 1917, even before rations hit their lowest point, German workers were becoming desperate. A worker in a Berlin armaments firm reported that conditions "were such as they must have been under early capitalism. . . . There was no night without the collapse of one or more women at the machines, because of exhaustion, hunger, illness." Although arms factories provided their workers with free or subsidized food, it was not enough to make a difference. In the same Berlin plant "the canteen served turnips twelve times a week. . . . In the canteen women had almost daily screaming fits, and sometimes depressing fights amongst themselves, because they alleged 'the ladle was not full.' "

By August 1918, one union issued a plea to the government: "It cannot go on like this . . . our colleagues suffer want. They cannot afford black market prices, and rationed goods cannot fill their stomachs. . . . We can no longer go on. We have come to the end. . . . Our children are starving. . . . It is simply beyond our strength." Strikes more than doubled from 240 in 1916 to 562 in 1917. A wave of strikes in Berlin and other cities in January 1918 was crushed by the police and army and a prominent labor leader tried and sentenced for treason.

As German living standards fell, so did morale, and by 1918 there was no good news from the battlefront to reverse the decline. People began to talk openly of peace, unconditional peace if necessary, and to look for targets on which to vent their frustration. Already in 1917 the chief of the Frankfurt Army Corps reported frequent protests about profiteering and black market activities, and complaints that the wealthy could provide for themselves "as well, and sometimes even better, than in peacetime." In fact the wealthy continued to eat well and enjoy ostentatious luxuries like vacations at the beach, right through the war. It did not help that work on public projects like the crown prince's new stately home outside Potsdam continued while ordinary citizens starved.

The very way the German war was financed reinforced the inequalities. Instead of raising income taxes, which could have spread the burden throughout society, there were increases in sales and other indirect taxes that fell more heavily on the middle- and low-income groups. By 1918 revenue from consumption taxes alone (on such items as beer, spirits, and tobacco) exceeded 2 billion marks, three times the 1913 level, despite a decline in consumption. Better-off Germans did have an opportunity to support the war by buying war bonds, and while they did so by oversubscribing the issues early in the war, they held back when the fortunes of war turned in 1917 and 1918, leaving bond issues undersubscribed by tens of millions of marks. The growing perception of unequal burdens tended to destroy the sense of common purpose that had been carefully nurtured at the beginning of the war. Just as needy citizens criticized the "haves," so city dwellers condemned farmers for selfishly hoarding or withholding goods from the open market. A reader wrote to a Mainz newspaper in 1917 that "the larders of farmers and the well-to-do are filled with bacon, ham and sausages, while my family's food consists mainly of potatoes and turnips." After prices on pigs were regulated, the number sold on the open market plummeted (from 61,000 to 15,000 a week between 1915 and 1916) as farmers obtained higher prices on the black market. For their part farmers resented the high wages they believed industrial workers were earning. In fact the decline of real wages did slow down in 1917 and 1918, but critical shortages and rationing meant that there was nothing to buy. In these conditions other familiar antagonisms were expressed. There were accusations that Jews were profiteering from food and other shortages and getting out of military service, and there were complaints that "the Jews have not yet earned enough, that is why the war has not yet ended."

As disturbing as dissension and falling morale were, it was even more worrying to the German government that disenchantment with the war increasingly took political form. As early as the "turnip winter" of 1916–17, a rumor circulated to the effect that "the crown princess bathed in milk, while infants were not given any." In the worsening conditions of 1918 it was a short step from criticizing the elites of politics and wealth to condemning wholesale the system from which they profited. Revolutionary groups, such as the Marxist Spartacist League (named after the leader of a slave rebellion in ancient Rome), exploited bitterness to convince workers that the war was being fought only in the interests of big business. When workers struck in early 1918, their demands were not solely economic but political as well: a quick peace, worker representation at the peace talks with Russia, release of all political prisoners, and more democracy in Germany.

Conditions in Austria-Hungary toward the end of the war paralleled those in Germany. As harvests declined year by year and shortages became acute, already inadequate rations were reduced such that workers received a quarter of the calories they consumed in peacetime. Children increasingly suffered rickets, tuberculosis, and anemia, and in Hungary infant mortality rates increased. The food available, it was said, was "too little to live on, but too much to die on."

By mid-1918 the effects of price inflation had cut real wages in Austria to a mere 15 percent of those on the eve of war. Almost three-quarters of all strikes were classified as hunger strikes in 1917, and their proportion rose in 1918. When flour rations were again reduced at the beginning of 1918, workers at the Daimler auto plant in Vienna went on strike, and within days were followed by nearly a million workers throughout Austria and Hungary.

In Vienna starving citizens raised small livestock, such as pigs, goats, and rabbits, in their gardens and even in basements and on balconies. Others grew what vegetables they could in small allotments on land made available by the emperor: Some 34,000 people were involved in this "war gardens" movement in 1917, nearly 160,000 in 1918. But domestic production was marginal, and in late 1918 tens of thousands of people, mainly women and children, invaded the countryside around the capital to forage for the potatoes the farmers would not sell. After clashes with farmers, the foragers were dispersed by troops and police.

Deteriorating conditions without any purpose (there was certainly no evidence that they led to military success) combined with rising casualties to make for serious political consequences. Officials now feared for the life of the emperor when he occasionally visited soup kitchens, and army officers were attacked by soldiers on the streets. In one incident a crowd attacked the minister of war's car. When in 1917 the Reichsrat was convened for its first time during the war, Czech delegates called for the Habsburg monarchy to be turned into a federal union of "free and equal national states." Over the next year, however, there were increasing demands for nationalities within the empire to be granted outright independence.

Separatist sentiments were reinforced by the sense that the minority-populated regions were paying a higher price than the German core of the country. In Czech-populated Bohemia, rations declined sharply from 1917 to 1918, when the combined meat, potato, bread, and flour allotment amounted to only 774 calories a day. Supplies were not always available, and in Prague in July 1918 bread was not baked for three weeks. Anti-Austrian sentiment increased when emergency food programs were seen to give preference to provisioning Vienna.

Demands for independence were strengthened when the Allies accepted the principle of national self-determination and recognized various governments-in-exile. By the middle of 1918, the empire was breaking up under internal and external pressures, the army was in disarray and was being propped up by German forces, and the political leaders who had brought war on the people were being repudiated.

In contrast, the home fronts in Britain and France held up well. Rationing of some foods was introduced in Britain only in the last year of the war, when two meatless days were also encouraged. While cereal and vegetable output on the Continent had fallen, Britain's had increased. When inflation began to spark discontent, prices were regulated. Overall it appears that British wages not only kept up with, but might have outpaced prices

British children receiving a midday meal at a canteen, 1918.

in the last stages of the war, and a government inquiry determined that a family income in 1918 purchased food with the same nutritive value as in 1914. There is some evidence, indeed, that citizens in some of the older age groups (beyond military age) in Britain actually improved their life expectancy because of wartime food and welfare policies. Important indices of health like infant and childhood mortality continued to decline steadily in Britain during the war.

This is not to say that there was no discontent or frequent demands for peace in Britain, particularly after Russia withdrew from the war. In November 1917, Lord Lansdowne, a member of the cabinet, called publicly for a negotiated peace. It is no coincidence that a Ministry of Information was created in early 1918 to ensure that the British people received news and views that would keep their fighting spirits up. Strikes increased as the war drew to an end, and included a stop-work by women bus conductors for pay equal to that of men doing the same work.

Conditions and morale in France in the last two years of the war were not as good as those in Britain, but still nowhere near as bad as in the Central Powers. In mid-1917 (soon after the mutinies in the French armies), the minister of the interior asked the prefect of each department to report on public opinion and social unrest. He also asked what police or military reinforcements they might need to ensure public order. The prefects' responses indicated a general decline in civilian morale, but that people in half the departments were in good or fairly good spirits and that the great majority of peasants were quite buoyant. Most important for the government was the almost unanimous assessment of the prefects that there was no need to fear a breakdown of order.

But threats to order seemed to rise the next year, when there was widespread worker discontent and an increase in strikes. Many workers, influenced by the example of the Bolsheviks, wanted an end to the war. It is notable, though, that the large-scale strike actions of 1918 petered out before gaining any revolutionary momentum, not least because they faced broad public opposition and the willingness of the government to take repressive measures. In addition many workers were content with their lot: Even if their real wages had declined, the war had seen the establishment of social welfare measures sponsored by the state and private enterprise. They included canteens with subsidized food, child care facilities, medical care for women and children (part of the concern for population), and the sponsorship of cooperative stores where goods were available at reduced prices.

Italy, the third major European ally, was in much worse shape. Government instability (a different prime minister supervised each year of the Italians' war) and inability to control food supplies and prices led to bread riots by the summer of 1917, with forty-one deaths in the disturbances in Turin alone. Resentment grew, directed not only toward the government of the day, but also toward "sharks" (war profiteers). As hardships increased, familiar social cleavages between workers and employers, and between the northern and southern sections of the country began to manifest themselves. Italy also began to experience the demographic effects common to other European combatants with the exception of Britain: declining marriage and birth rates, and rising mortality, particularly among infants.

What is striking about conditions and morale on the main European home fronts in the last year of the war is the difference between Britain and France on the one hand, and the Central Powers and Italy on the other (Russia was no longer a belligerent). Without minimizing their difficulties and grievances, the British and French were better fed, more productive, in higher spirits, and appeared much more able and willing to carry on than their German, Austrian, and Hungarian opponents. The fact that Italy, the Allies' junior partner, was struggling did not much alter the imbalance because its main adversary, Austria-Hungary, was in such poor condition too. Stalemate on the western front might have given the appearance that the war was an even match, but in the equally important battle of the home fronts, the Central Powers began to fail.

The Last Months of the War

From August to November 1918 the Central Powers' armies and home fronts, always interdependent, became inextricably trapped together in a spiral of disintegration. The internal collapse of Austria-Hungary was sharpened by the defeat of an offensive on the Italian front in July. The attacking forces, poorly fed, equipped, and led, sustained more than 14,000 casualties and never recovered their morale. The rate of desertions increased, and there were demands that Hungarian units be removed from what was seen as inept and deadly Austrian command.

By October the Austro-Hungarian army had deteriorated even further, so that when Italian troops attacked they engaged a fighting force much reduced in strength and effectiveness. Uniforms were in tatters, equipment inadequate, and food rations so inadequate that on sections of the front the average weight of soldiers was only 120 pounds. Learning that a separate Hungarian state had been proclaimed in Budapest, two Hungarian divisions refused to fight any longer, and soon the mutiny spread to other non-Austrian units. The result was that when the Italians mounted a major offensive at Vittorio Veneto on October 24, they won a comparatively easy victory.

In October 1918, the besieged government in Vienna ordered the remaining supplies of grain and coal to be removed from Bohemia. This act convinced many Czechs that they no longer had a secure future within Austria. The first act of the Czech national committee, which assumed government powers, was to ban the export of any food supplies from Czech territory.

With the multinational empire and army unraveling together, the Habsburg emperor appointed a new cabinet on October 25 and sued for peace. While it was being negotiated, the new Hungarian state declared its neutrality and ordered its forces to cease hostilities (many already had) and return home. Now isolated, the Austrian units surrendered more than 300,000 soldiers to the Italians until an armistice was signed on November 4. A week later Emperor Karl renounced first the crown of Austria and, two days afterward, that of Hungary.

The Austrian armistice had been preceded a few days earlier by the Ottoman surrender. From September 1918, British, Imperial, African, and Arab forces had scored major military successes, and by the end of October they occupied such important cities as Damascus and Aleppo. On October 30 the Turkish government, now in control of a much reduced territory, signed an armistice.

The German armistice, the most important of all, took a little longer. By August the outcome of the war in the west seemed certain, but it remained for the Allies to inflict decisive defeats on the Germans, the only remaining viable military force of the Central Powers. The Allied strategy was to attack in as many places as possible, isolating German units and cutting their supply lines so as to defeat the army bit by bit. The Allied offensive began in late September, and even though progress was not as rapid as had been hoped, progress it was. Ludendorff concluded that a German defeat was unavoidable and that an armistice should be sought before the war was carried to German territory. He communicated this assessment to the kaiser on September 29, and Wilhelm agreed to appeal to President Wilson for a cease-fire and peace negotiations on the basis of the Fourteen Points. Wilson was perceived as less likely than Lloyd George or Clemenceau to want retribution against Germany.

The kaiser also bowed to the unavoidable by agreeing to introduce parliamentary government, just as he had agreed in Easter 1917 to reform the suffrage when political discontent had risen at home. In the fall of 1918, however, political pressure came from the majority bloc in the Reichstag, composed of Social Democrat, Progressive, and Center (Catholic) Party deputies. Wanting constitutional reforms but reluctant to force a political showdown while the military authorities retained effective control, they had waited for the right time to make their demands.

When the kaiser announced parliamentary reform and a search for armistice terms on September 29, his hard-line chancellor, Count Hertling, resigned and was replaced by Prince Max of Baden, a moderate conservative who had opposed the resumption of submarine warfare and the 1918 offensive. Max's tenure as chancellor was as eventful as it was brief. Responding to the Reichstag majority, he assembled a broad-based cabinet that included Social Democrats in government for the first time. Max also oversaw the end of military dominance of political affairs. When General Ludendorff forced the issue in October by insisting that peace negotiations be broken off and the war fought to the last man to preserve German honor, he was dismissed by the kaiser and sought refuge in Sweden.

The renewal of government and restoration of civilian authority in Germany was a revolution carried out from above, sometimes known as Germany's October Revolution. Parliamentary reform had been achieved without great damage to the monarchy, and for a short time it seemed that the kaiser had succeeded in riding the tigers of military defeat and political change. But as October turned to November it became clear that change was a rogue tiger impossible to control.

Military and civilian disintegration accelerated in the last days of October when the German fleet at Kiel and Wilhemshaven was ordered to sea for a last battle to ensure that the navy's honor was preserved. Units of the fleet refused to obey the command, and when the leaders were arrested there was an uprising of sailors, soldiers, and workers at Kiel. Their potpourri of demands were military and political, including amnesty for the mutineers themselves, more democracy in the armed forces, a peace settlement, and the abdication of the kaiser.

More important, the Kiel uprising was quickly emulated as news of it spread. Throughout Germany, councils (akin to the Russian soviets) composed of workers, sailors, and soldiers were formed, public buildings were occupied, and republics were proclaimed in the constituent states of the empire. In Bavaria a people's republic was declared under the leadership of Kurt Eisner, a Socialist writer. In Berlin, where the revolutionary wave crested on November 9, mass demonstrations convinced Prince Max that radical reform could not be avoided. In an effort to contain the revolution he urged the Kaiser to abdicate and appoint the Social Democratic leader Friedrich Ebert as chancellor. Wilhelm tried to minimize the damage to himself by abdicating as emperor while retaining his title as king of Prussia, but he finally capitulated to reality. On November 10 the former Kaiser Wilhelm II, the last of the Hohenzollern rulers, left Germany for exile in the neutral Netherlands. In contrast to Germany's October revolution from above, November's was a revolution from below.

Wilhelm left behind a struggle for authority among several groups. Social Democratic leaders, including Ebert, tried to consolidate their authority in a provisional administration they called the Council of People's Commissars. Having been appointed by the kaiser, Ebert had some claim to legitimate authority, but the repudiation of the monarch simultaneously weakened that claim. The revolutionary Spartacists, led by Karl Liebknecht, refused to have anything to do with Ebert's government. They tried to form an alternative power center, drawing on support from the soldiers' and workers' councils, but they were generally outmaneuvered by the majority Social Democrats who worked closely with the well-organized trade unions.

Outside this struggle for authority within the center-left and left groups, was the right wing, a disparate coalition of nationalists, conservatives, monarchists, and the military that believed that the army could have suppressed the November revolutions had the kaiser called on it. They blamed left-wing politicians for bringing about the German defeat, and promoted the notion that the German army, although unbeaten in battle, had been "stabbed in the back" by liberal and left-wing politicians on the home front.

As if to confirm this, Ebert's socialist administration authorized German negotiators to sign what nationalists considered a humiliating armistice agreement with the Allies. Under the pact, signed on November 11, 1918, Germany agreed to repudiate the Treaty of Brest-Litovsk, evacuate all occupied areas including Alsace-Lorraine, surrender most cannons, machine guns, and aircraft, and deliver to the Allies all submarines and the High Seas Fleet. They were also to withdraw all forces from French-German border areas.

The idea that the German army was undefeated but betrayed begged a number of questions, notably (as Ludendorff himself had recognized as early as August) that the army was unable to fight effectively any longer. But it also contained an element of truth: that the First World War was won and lost as much on the home front as on the battlefront.

Conclusion: Europe in November 1918

There is no easy way to summarize what happened in and to Europe between August 1914 and November 1918. All facets of political, social, economic, and cultural life had been affected in some way, some more radically and permanently than others. As a general rule, conditions became worse from west to east.

The war had dramatically redrawn the political map of Europe. By late 1918 Central and Eastern Europe were still in the throes of political and nationalist turmoil, and it was conceivable that Germany itself would break up into several republics. Austria-Hungary had disappeared as a single entity, Russia's territory was ill-defined, and the Ottoman Empire had fallen. New states had been formed or were in the process of formation: Austria and Hungary (both much diminished in size), Poland, Czechoslovakia, Yugoslavia, Finland, Latvia, Estonia, and Lithuania. Europe had never seen such a radical realignment of borders in such a short period.

The political and constitutional make-up of Europe was also in flux. While it was clear that the autocracies of 1914 had been swept away, it was still not clear what would replace them. New political forces were making their presence known. The most potent were the Russian Bolsheviks, whose achievement inspired revolutionary communist movements throughout Europe. But there were also signs of activity on the right, from nationalist conservatives to extremists who would later call themselves fascists.

Economic, social, and demographic conditions in Europe in 1918 are discussed in the next chapter. In the economic sphere, we need note here only that Europe had lost its preeminent place in the world economy, and that apart from war-related production, industry and agriculture had declined dramatically. These conditions affected the whole of Europe, not only the states involved in the war.

Europe's population had also fallen, reversing a long-term trend of growth, thanks largely to massive numbers of military and civilian deaths (Table 3.1), while marriage and birth rates were well below prewar levels. Despite this population drop, millions of Europeans found themselves without homes, in the material and other senses, in 1918. The hundreds of thousands of Belgians who had fled before the invading German armies in August 1914 began to return home, as did the 3 million French women, men, and chil-

TABLE 3.1   War-Related Deaths in the First World War

	Number Mobilized	Military Deaths	Total War-Related Deaths (Military and Civilian) as Proportion of Population
Austria-Hungary	7,800,000	1,200,000	1:50
Belgium	267,000	13,715	1:170
Bulgaria	1,200,000	75,844	1:200
France	8,410,000	1,350,000	1:28
Germany	11,000,000	1,808,546	1:32
Great Britain	8,904,000	908,000	1:57
Greece	230,000	5,000	1:22
Italy	5,615,000	460,000	1:79
Russia	12,000,000	1,700,000	1:107
Serbia	707,343	125,000	1:12
United States	2,000,000	54,000	1:2,000

dren who had left the regions invaded by Germany. The million foreigners who had been forced to work in Germany—260,000 Poles, 500,000 from Russian territory, and 210,000 Belgians—began to make their way home. There were some 8 million soldiers held prisoner throughout Europe. Without counting military forces, as many as 20 million Europeans had been involuntarily uprooted from their homes by 1918, and by the end of the year most were on the move.

For countless millions more, especially women and children in Central and Eastern Europe, 1918 was yet another year of poverty, malnutrition, and deteriorating health. Women who had charge of families were preoccupied with sheer survival, and spent their "leisure" time standing in line and foraging for ever-scarcer food and supplies. Despite the frequent depictions of British and French women flourishing as munitions workers and ambulance drivers, most European women would not have thought of the war as in any sense a liberating experience.

Four years of total war had touched every facet of political, social, economic, and cultural life in Europe, and in most cases the result was deterioration rather than improvement. The young men who were killed in the war are often referred to as the "lost generation," but it could as well be argued that many other elements of prewar Europe had been lost as well. The task of postwar reconstruction, like the war itself, would encompass every aspect of life and leave no European unaffected. If 1914 marked the end of one age and 1918 the beginning of another, the intervening years have all the characteristics of a no-man's land of history. It was a period traversed by European states that set off with all the blind bravery of men going "over the top." Like the soldiers, some states never made it to the other side, and those that did got there in a state of disorientation and near collapse.

· 4 ·

The Unstable Peace, 1918–1923

Introduction

Between 1918 and 1923 the immediate results of the war interacted with longer-term conditions in Europe to produce immense problems in every imaginable sphere. The collapse of empires produced a radical redrawing of borders in Central and Eastern Europe that in some cases reflected, and in others frustrated, long-held nationalist aspirations to sovereign statehood. The war had drained the industrial and agricultural economies of the European belligerents, and had damaged those of nonbelligerents as well. Four years of total war had resulted in millions of military and civilian deaths, millions more wounded, and even more millions malnourished and in ill health.

To say that this was not a promising environment for a lasting peace is an understatement, and peace of any kind was a long time coming to many parts of Eastern and Southern Europe. Border wars persisted for years. Soviet Russia settled its frontiers with the Baltic states and Poland only in 1921; Greece remained at war with its neighbors until 1922. Within individual states the absence of legitimate administrations, or even of administrations that could exercise control over its territory, led to struggles for power. They took the form of revolutions, military coups, civil wars, and even elections.

Political turmoil was inextricably related to the social and economic problems created or aggravated by the experience of four years of total war. Social grievances were expressed as industrial strikes in Britain, Italy, and France, and as demands for agrarian reform in the agricultural economies of Eastern and Southern Europe. Across Europe workers and peasants took reform into their own hands, seizing factories and occupying large estates. Many demobilized soldiers, discovering that service to their countries was paid in the coin of unemployment and poverty, gravitated toward extremist political parties and paramilitary organizations.

Yet, by 1923, border disputes were grudgingly and at least temporarily settled, revolutionary movements on both left and right seemed to have run out of steam, and a sort of stability had descended almost everywhere. In many regions it was a depressed stability, however, for the social effects of the war persisted. The deaths of millions of men condemned their families to chronic poverty.

The peace treaties signed in Paris in 1919 and 1920 addressed only a few of the problems of postwar Europe. They gave legal recognition to new borders of many old states as well as of the new nations. Yet much of the postwar settlement fell beyond the power of the

Paris peace conference to control. Europe's new states had already proclaimed their existence and were widely recognized as legitimate by the time the conference convened, leaving the conference to adjudicate border disputes, many nonetheless important. Many of the conflicts over borders that erupted after 1918 were outside the jurisdiction of the Paris conference; Soviet Russia's borders with Poland, Finland, the Baltic states, and Romania were settled bilaterally, by force and negotiation. Moreover, although the peace treaties imposed democratic constitutions on a number of European states and required them to respect the rights of minorities, many such stipulations were ignored and never enforced.

This is not to say that the treaties signed in Paris were of little purpose. They were clearly important in giving international legitimacy to Europe's new borders, determining the political and military strength of Germany and its former allies and establishing the principle that they should pay reparations. Nor should the establishment of the League of Nations be overlooked, although its effectiveness in the interwar period is much debated.

Even so, in Central and Eastern Europe especially, the actual course of immediate postwar political development owed less to the decisions made in Paris in 1919 and 1920 than to other traditional mechanisms of political change: war (both international and civil), revolution, coup d'état, and repression. As we will see in this chapter, the experience of Europeans in these years varied according to nation, class, and gender. If there was one more or less common factor, it was that Europeans were disappointed by the peace. States—and within them constituencies like workers, women, nationalists, and ethnic groups—went to war with explicit or implicit intentions and expectations. The results can have satisfied few of them, even in the victorious countries. Italians referred to the

Return of German troops to Berlin after the armistice, 1918. They were greeted as heroes as they passed through the Brandenburg Gate and along the decorated Unter den Linden.

peace as "mutilated," while Germans condemned the peace treaties as "dictated." British soldiers, who had been promised a land "fit for heroes," found that conditions in Britain after the war were if anything worse than before it. Conservatives found the old hierarchies weakened or swept away entirely; liberals were confronted by powerful state apparatuses that showed all the symptoms of permanence. Populations like the Poles, Czechs, Slovaks, and Estonians found that nationhood alone was no solution to political, economic, and social problems. In some countries women gained the vote, but in others they were still denied it, and the social and economic conditions of most European women showed no improvement to compensate for the hardships war had inflicted.

This chapter looks at the way the immediate results of the war interracted with conditions in various regions of Europe, and how they impinged on people, depending whether they were women or men, children or adults, lived in town or country, and were peasants, industrial workers, or members of the better-off classes. The manifestations varied, but there is reason to believe that in this period a general crisis gripped Europe's social system, economy, political institutions, and culture.

Mortality and Recovery

The most arresting characteristic of the war was the extent of military and civilian mortality. The global statistics of war-related deaths set out at the end of the preceding chapter only hint at the impact such losses had on European society and economy. The impact was serious in a practical sense because unlike the civilian dead, who included women and men, young and old, the much more numerous military deaths were specific to males in limited age groups that were important for population growth, a persistent preoccupation of European governments. Sixty percent of British soldiers killed were between 20 and 29, and fully 40 percent of the German military dead were in the narrow range of 20 to 25 years. More than a quarter of French men aged between 20 and 25 died during the war.

These cohorts represented men who were either recently married or could be expected to marry soon. The average age of bachelors at marriage before the war was 28 in England, and not much different elsewhere in Western and Northern Europe, though it tended to be somewhat lower in the east. Among the military dead, the proportion of the men who had been married (many of them recently married) varied widely: 28 percent in the British army, a third in the German forces, half of those in the French army, and 70 percent of Viennese soldiers in the Austrian armies. The war left millions of war widows and orphans, all deprived of their main income earners. In 1920 600,000 widows in France were eligible for state pensions, and 750,000 orphans were officially "adopted" by the state.

As if the ravages of the war were not enough, a deadly influenza epidemic swept through Europe and the rest of the world, beginning in late 1918. First identified in Spain, the epidemic was called the Spanish flu or Spanish lady, a name that stuck despite the efforts of a medical commission, set up by the Spanish government, to prove that the epidemic had originated in Russian Turkestan. The waves of infection resulted in more than 2 million deaths in Europe and added to the anxiety and confusion that attended the end of the war.

In absolute numerical terms Russia suffered most from influenza, with 450,000 deaths, but 225,000 died in each of Germany and Britain, and some 170,000 in Spain and France. Italy had the highest per capita rate, its 375,000 deaths representing more than 1 percent of the country's population. Ironically, unlike most epidemics of this kind, the Spanish flu did not prove most deadly to the conventionally vulnerable groups, the very

A poster highlighting the suffering of women and children in Austria in the postwar period.

young and very old, but killed a disproportionate number of healthy, robust young men. To this extent it amplified the effects of the war.

Throughout Europe the war deaths of husbands and fathers damaged family economies and altered household structures, as the proportion of households headed by women alone increased. Many men who did return home did so in ill health. A million French soldiers were permanently disabled; Of them 125,000 had lost at least one limb and more than 40,000 had been completely or partially blinded. Incalculable numbers of soldiers of all armies suffered the traumatic syndrome known as shell shock. In such cases men who returned home were a mixed blessing, for they could be a drain on family resources rather than a contributor to them. Social welfare schemes existed in some countries to protect families from the worst effects of poverty, but in much of Eastern and Southern Europe survivors of men killed in the war, and the families of those permanently disabled, had to rely on an economy of makeshifts that included low-paid drudgery and charity.

The prospects of remarriage by widows were reduced by the massive number of male deaths during the war, which had skewed normally balanced sex ratios and created an excess of marriageable women in many European populations. In Britain in 1911 there were 990 marriageable women (that is, single, divorced, or widowed) in the 25-to-29-year age group for every thousand marriageable men; in 1921 women outnumbered men by a ratio of 1,154 to 1,000. In Austria the sex ratio in the 25-to-34-year age group widened from

106 to 117 women per 100 men between 1910 and 1923. By 1924, 250,000 French widows had remarried, and another 12,500 did so by 1928.

In many countries there was a marriage "boom" right after the war, lasting from 1919 to 1921 or 1922 (see Figure 4.1). In Germany, for example, marriages from 1919 to 1922 averaged 792,000 a year (a rate of 25.4 per thousand population) compared with 511,000 each year in the period 1910 to 1913 (15.6 per thousand). In Romania marriage rates rose to 24 to 26 per thousand in 1920 and 1921, compared with average rates of 19 per thousand before the war. These postwar marriages went only some way toward compensating for the marriages that had not taken place during the war and those that had been ter-

FIGURE 4.1 Marriage rates (marriages per 1,000 population), selected countries, 1910–39.

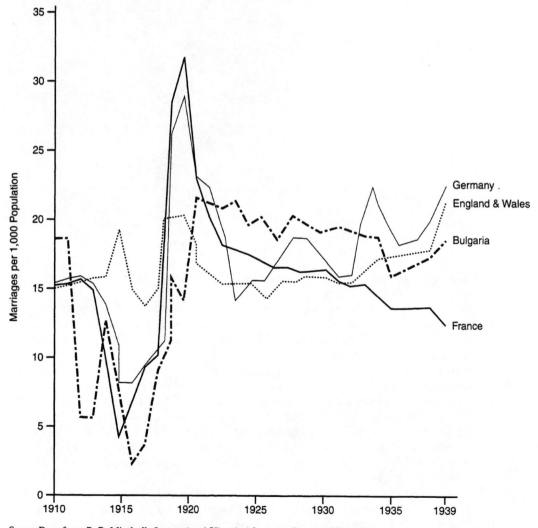

Source: Data from B. R. Mitchell, *International Historical Statistics: Europe, 1750–1988* (London: Macmillan, 1992), pp. 94–111.

minated by the wartime deaths of married men and women. Approximately 1.3 million marriages were "lost" to France when the marriage rate fell during the war, more than 600,000 marriages were terminated by the death of a husband on active duty, and thousands more ended when married women were killed. The marriage boom of 1919–23 contributed 840,000 more marriages than the projected prewar figure would produce, leaving France's marriage shortfall at close to half a million. By a similar reckoning, the war cost Germany some 400,000 marriages.

The excess of women resulting from overwhelmingly male mortality meant that thousands of women in that generation would not find marriage partners. In Britain more than a quarter of women in the 30 to 34 age group in 1921 had not married, and almost one-fifth of them never did.

The record number of marriages in many countries right after the war did not translate into births. Although birth rates everywhere rose from their depressed wartime levels, they tended to be no higher than the immediate prewar years, so that the long-term fertility decline continued. In Germany the birth rate peaked in 1920 at 26 per thousand population, compared with the 1913 rate of 27.5. This was the case also in Austria, Hungary, Romania, and Russia. In other states, including Britain, France, Italy, and Bulgaria, there was a slight increase in the birth rate in one or two postwar years before fertility resumed its downward path. Governments did all they could, including using coercive powers, to prevent the use of birth control. Their efforts failed. Although it is possible that malnutrition played a role in producing low fertility rates in some countries, many couples simply refused to have children in the political and economic uncertainty of the postwar period.

The Postwar Economies

The war had a devastating effect on both Europe's standing in the world economy and on the economies of individual states; the two are, of course, related. In global terms, the major European states, which had been world leaders in investment, production, and commerce, were reduced to indebtedness and industrial stagnation. In order to finance their wars, Britain and France had resorted more to borrowing than taxation. After liquidating and exhausting their extensive investments in the United States, both countries borrowed on domestic and United States markets. By 1918 they had amassed huge debts to the United States. Initially the French, at least, hoped that the debts would be forgiven by its ally, and when that proved groundless, both countries turned to reparations by the Central Powers to cover their astronomical war costs.

Italy was in similar straits. State expenditure had shot from 2.3 billion lire in 1913 and 1914, before Italy entered the war, to 30.9 billion lire in 1918 and 1919. Italy's participation in the war for less than four years cost more than twice all state expenditure since national unification, a period of fifty years.

As bad as these cases were, finances were in worse shape in Central and Eastern Europe. There, states had been unable or unwilling to tax their inhabitants to pay for war, and had resorted to loans or, more frequently had simply printed money to cover their expenditures. The foreign value of their currencies began to fall rapidly, and price inflation began to increase. An early example was Austria, where the exchange rate of the crown against the U.S. dollar fell from 5 to almost 84,000 by mid-1922. In 1920, 30 million crowns were in circulation, and the national bank issued more than 7 billion more in the next three years. Whirlwind inflation shot prices up 14,000 times the prewar level in Austria,

23,000 times in Hungary, and 2.5 million times in Poland. In each case the League of Nations (discussed later in this chapter) stepped in to provide loans and supervise the stabilization of currencies.

The fundamental economic challenges faced by Europe immediately after the war cannot easily be generalized because they differed from region to region. In Britain the end of hostilities was followed by a brief economic boom as factories were flooded with orders for consumer goods that had been unavailable during the war. The demand for workers and production facilitated the shift from war to peacetime industry and enabled the British to demobilize quickly. Four million soldiers were demobilized by the end of 1919, but unemployment remained low at 2.4 percent.

In 1920, however, when imported goods arrived to compete with British products and pent-up demand had subsided, factories began to scale production back and lay workers off. Unemployment rose rapidly to 15 percent in 1921 and 1922, representing 1.5 million workers. Thereafter until the Second World War, official unemployment in Great Britain remained above 10 percent, two or three times the level common before 1914. As unemployment began to grow, social tensions erupted. In England and Wales the presence of thousands of blacks, soldiers from the British colonies in the Caribbean who remained after the war, produced racist violence. Believing that the newcomers were taking jobs and housing, workers in several cities attacked blacks and killed several of them. The British government responded by paying the passages for 2,000 blacks to return home, an example of ethnic repatriation outside Eastern Europe.

The difficulty that Britain and some other European countries experienced in recovering economically after 1918 was a reflection of their inability to recapture their prewar markets. The diversion of Europe's resources into war had given non-European states four years to develop their own economies. India expanded its own cotton industry, Australia and Canada increased grain production, and the United States extended its industrial and agricultural sectors across the board. Europe's dominance in merchant shipping was eclipsed by the United States and Japan. Unable to reestablish its prewar markets, Europe found its industrial production stagnating, with the result that many countries experienced high unemployment rates after their armies were demobilized.

There were other specific economic obstacles. The great majority of military deaths were of workers and farmers, and their loss had varying effects on Europe's economies. These effects were perhaps most dramatic in France, which even before the war had suffered labor shortages, but which by 1919 was estimated to need 3 million more workers than were available. The shortfall could have been made up by the employment of women, but government policy was to encourage women to stay home and raise children. Instead, large numbers of foreign workers—a million by 1924, most from Poland, Belgium, Spain, and Italy—were admitted into France. France's severe labor shortage was atypical. In contrast, Britain and Germany experienced postwar unemployment, which would have been much more serious had it not been for wartime mortality. In several Eastern European countries the demographic loss relieved rural overpopulation, although we should not assume that it was in any sense welcomed for that reason.

In almost all countries (the notable exception was Great Britain), industrial output in 1918 was at least a third lower than before the war. German industrial production in 1918 was only 57 percent of the 1913 level, although certain sectors like chemicals had experienced tremendous increases in output. Hungary's industrial production in 1920 was only 30 percent of the 1913 level, leaving a third of industrial workers unemployed. The worst affected was Russia, where by war's end industry produced little more than a tenth of its prewar output.

In the industrial areas of France and Belgium where the war had been fought there was extensive damage to housing, factories, mines, and communications. In France some 20,000 factories had been destroyed, and most coal mines had been flooded, much of this destruction inflicted by the retreating Germans. Iron and steel production in the occupied departments at the end of the war was only 5 percent of the 1913 level. Towns and cities in the battle areas were ruined. Reims had only 17,000 inhabitants left from a prewar population of 117,000; Soissons, before the war a substantial industrial community of 18,000, was reduced to the size of a village with 500 inhabitants. Some towns had been entirely obliterated.

Throughout Europe communications and transportation networks that were vital for the recovery of industrial production and trade were in poor shape. The proportion of railroad rolling stock fit for service in 1920 ranged from 70 percent of locomotives and 90 percent of wagons in Poland, to 27 percent and 76 percent respectively in Hungary, and 37 percent and 56 percent in Bulgaria. A League of Nations report described the situation of railroads in the Baltic states as "chaotic."

The creation of new states and the redrawing of national boundaries (discussed below) also led to economic dislocation, particularly in Central and Eastern Europe. Austria-Hungary, which had been a single economic unit, was broken up into smaller units: principally Austria, Hungary, and Czechoslovakia, with territory also going to Italy, Romania, Yugoslavia, and Poland. The prewar railroad network had been built with Vienna and Budapest as its hubs, so that many lines had to be redirected to new national centers. Industrial regions were cut off from traditional markets and sources of raw materials. Austria's iron works, for instance, were crippled because after the war half the coal resources necessary to power them were located in Czechoslovakia and Poland.

For similar and additional reasons, many countries' agricultural economies also fared poorly immediately after the war. In substantial areas of rural France, intense bombardment had repeatedly torn up the ground and made 8 million acres of land useless for cultivation or pasture until the shrapnel and live shells were removed. Some 900,000 sheep, 840,000 cattle, 400,000 horses, and 330,000 pigs had been pillaged. France's rural workforce saw 700,000 peasants killed, and 500,000 wounded.

The recovery of agriculture was slow everywhere. Farms had run down during the war, and the lack of fertilizer had exhausted the soil as large landowners tried to maximize crops so as to benefit from high wartime prices for food. After the war there were problems with markets as well as continuing shortages of livestock and fertilizer. Border changes often make pre- and postwar comparisons difficult, but in Germany production of important crops like potatoes, rye, and oats recovered their prewar levels only in the late 1920s. The war and border changes (such as the loss of East Prussia) led to a decline in the importance of agriculture to the German economy; agriculture had produced 23.2 percent of the national wealth in 1913, but by 1925 it had fallen to 15.7 percent.

If there was a positive aspect to the postwar period in much of Europe outside Russia, it was that many peasants were able to obtain land. In France this was less a matter of policy than good fortune. Postwar inflation, which increased agricultural prices in 1919 to four times their 1913 levels, led to a period of prosperity for farmers, enabling many to pay off debts and purchase additional land. Inflation benefited Italian peasants in much the same way.

Eastern European peasants also improved their position, though under different circumstances, as prewar demands for agrarian reform were revived. Some governments had offered land as an inducement for peasants to fight, and from late 1918, when armies began to demobilize, there were demands for these promises to be kept. For peasants, land was usually preferable to a payout at demobilization or to a war pension. All Eastern

Europe states began the process of agrarian reform, most by stipulating maximum sizes for land holdings. In Yugoslavia the maximum was set at 30 hectares, and over time some 650,000 families received land. In Romania land reforms eventually benefited some 1.4 million families; in Bulgaria 173,000. In Estonia the number of landowners was doubled, and landless agricultural laborers declined from 65 to 13 percent of the population.

When land redistribution seemed to be proceeding too slowly, peasants took action to speed it up. In 1919 the liberal regime of Count Károlyi in Hungary collapsed in the face of mounting problems that included chronic food shortages and widespread rural disorder, as peasants burned manor houses and seized land. Károlyi's communist successor, Béla Kun, alienated peasants by trying to turn large estates into state farms, and one of the first measures introduced by the following regime, led by the reactionary Admiral Horthy, was a program that provided land to over 400,000 people, most of them peasants who had had virtually no land at all.

But land redistribution did not always mean a redistribution of economic power. Most of the small plots given to Hungarian peasants were a little over half a hectare in size, so small and economically unviable that within a few years 80 percent of the new owners sold them. On the other hand the Horthy regime awarded farms of up to fifty hectares to members of the newly created Order of Heroes, which was restricted to ex-soldiers, civil servants, professionals, and others who could demonstrate patriotic values. Elsewhere land reform served ethnic policies. In Czechoslovakia, for example, large estates owned by Germans were subdivided before those owned by Czechs.

Gender: Work, Society, and Family

Just as the war years had called into question the assumptions current in prewar Europe about the different roles of women and men, so gender relations remained a lively issue when the war ended. The most dramatic change during the war was the redistribution and increase in women's employment, but it soon became clear that this did not mean a permanent shift of values and policies. Beginning in war-related industries like munitions plants that sharply reduced production, hundreds of thousands of women were fired from their jobs, although in some specific industries, like metalworking, women were kept on in reduced numbers to do low-skilled, repetitive tasks.

German women who had worked in war production received no unemployment benefits when they were declared redundant. In France tens of thousands of women were reduced to poverty when employers refused to pay them the unemployment benefits the government recommended. One woman wrote to a newspaper in April 1919: "My husband has been in the army for the last six years. I worked like a slave at Citroën during the war. I sweated blood there, losing my youth and my health. In January I was fired, and since then have been poverty-stricken."

Many (but not all) of their British counterparts received modest and declining benefits, but they were often condemned for it. In early 1919 London's *Evening News* commented on women who received unemployment payments: "These women are not wearing out their shoe leather to any great extent looking for work. Many of them would do their best to avoid a job if they saw it coming. A holiday on 25 shillings a week is quite good enough for them."

Women removed from the areas of employment opened to them during the war frequently found that there were few jobs in the much-reduced consumer industries many had previously worked in. The number of women working in the French textile industry, for example, was 18 percent lower in 1921 than in 1906. The extent of women's unemployment brought about by the end of the war is generally underrecorded by official statistics because women were often excluded from the benefits on which numbers were based. Those who did remain in industry often found that wage differences between men and women, which had tended to narrow during the war, widened after it. In France, by 1921, women earned between 20 and 40 percent less than men doing the same work, the actual difference depending on job and region.

As women were compelled to leave the industrial workforce, opportunities increased in occupations defined as female: secretaries, typists, retail clerks, kindergarten and elementary school teachers, nurses, and librarians. Such jobs in the tertiary sector were service occupations with relatively low status, but unlike much industrial work they required education and often some professional training. Many were perceived as extensions of women's domestic roles of caring for the sick, looking after or serving men, and raising children. In 1921, 863,000 women were employed in clerical posts in commerce and banking in Great Britain, a fivefold increase since 1911, while the number in manufacturing fell 10 percent. In France the number of women in the tertiary sector rose from 344,000 in 1906 to 855,000 in 1921.

A numerically smaller but yet important set of occupations also opened for women in the professions. In Britain a 1919 act removed legal barriers to employment in the professions and public service based on gender or marital status. Women were admitted to take degrees at Oxford and Cambridge Universities in 1919; the first woman justice of the peace was appointed in 1920, and the first woman barrister in 1922. In 1919 French women were given equal access to secondary and higher education. These were advances for women as a whole, though they benefited only a small number of women directly and hardly compensated for the mass layoffs in industry after the war.

Being deprived of work could be disastrous for many women and their dependents, but women's unemployment was seen by many middle-class men as a good thing because it would allow more women to become full-time mothers and wives. There had been anxiety about the effects on women of wartime work, notably a fear that they would become masculinized by exposure to male work conditions. There was a revival of nineteenth-century alarm about the harm that young women's morality would suffer if they worked side by side with young men, doing the same jobs, mouthing the same curses. Such anxieties had been expressed during the war, when women in the better-paid industries, such as munitions, were sometimes criticized as war profiteers for earning what were regarded as excessive salaries.

A blurring of the traditional distinctions between men and women was reflected in wartime and postwar fashion. Some women had worn military or military-style uniforms for several years, and so fashionable did uniforms become that some women whose jobs did not call for a uniform designed their own. Short hair replaced long, in part a residual effect of the practicalities of work during the war. Postwar women's clothing stressed a more masculine than feminine figure, with designs that flattened the breast and concealed the waistline. Clothing in general was looser, lighter, and permitted greater physical mobility, in contrast to the traditional tendency for women's clothing to restrict their movement.

But the historic distinction between women's and men's clothing, speech, and behavior was so fundamental an element of European culture that any undermining of it was widely viewed as a sign of incipient social collapse. In Britain the Association of Moral and Social Hygiene set up a commission in 1919 to investigate the moral effects of the war, especially the perceived decline in women's morals that was produced by greater freedom during the war. Sir Charles Tarring, a medical adviser to the Ministry of National Health, told the commission, "I have seen more cases of promiscuity among girls in the last five years than in all the rest of my practice, which now extends over forty-three years."

Similar fears were expressed in France. The right-wing politician Pierre Drieu la Rochelle lamented of postwar France's cultural and social conditions, "This civilization no longer has clothes, no longer has churches, no longer has palaces, no longer has theaters, no longer has paintings, no longer has books, no longer has sexes." Asked about the "modern girl" produced by the war, a young Paris law student said, "These beings—without breasts, without hips, without underwear, who smoke, work, argue, and fight exactly like boys—these aren't young girls! There are no young girls anymore! And neither are there any women anymore!" These were alarming thoughts: that in Western Europe at least, much of the cream of the male population had been killed during the war, and that those who remained were confronted with young women who no longer behaved like females, and who appeared to be either sexless or like males.

In Western Europe many social policies aimed to reassert the difference between women and men, and the clearest way to achieve that was to confine women to home and family as much as possible. There was renewed stress on women's "natural" roles as home-makers and mothers, and there was particular hostility to the notion of mothers working in paid employment. In France, two days after the armistice with Germany, the minister of munitions published a bulletin informing women in the arms industries that they were no longer needed: "Now you can best serve your country by returning to your former pursuits, busying yourselves with peacetime activities." Few could have doubted what this meant.

The drive to keep women out of work coincided with the desire to increase fertility rates. Fears of population and physical decline were reasserted. One woman trade unionist in Britain declared in 1919 that mothers ought to be paid to stay home and raise children: "We have got to encourage motherhood. . . . I honestly believe that the institution of pensions for mothers would go a long way towards checking the race suicide that is now going on."

In France, where the loss of hundreds of thousands of young males at peak reproductive ages only aggravated the long-term decline of fertility, governments adopted draconian legislation. A July 1920 law stipulated a fine and jail for up to six months for anyone distributing birth control information or making contraceptives available. In March 1923, abortion was removed from the disposition of often lenient juries and came under the jurisdiction of far more conservative judges; all parties involved in an abortion (including the woman) became liable to imprisonment. The government established an advisory council on fertility, and also institutionalized Mother's Day. Women who had given birth to five living children were awarded bronze medals, those who had eight were awarded silver medals, and those with ten children won the gold.

Another development in the postwar family created anxiety: a rapid increase in divorces that began in the last phase of the war. In Germany before the war there had been about 13,000 divorces a year, but between 1919 and 1922 there were 33,592 annually. In England, where divorce was more difficult to obtain, the average 701 a year from 1910 to 1913 rose more than fourfold to an average 3,183 a year between 1919 and 1921. France experienced a similar pattern.

The rise in divorces reflected several tendencies. Many of the marriages that couples rushed into just as young men were going to war were unwise and soon regretted. Even marriages of longer standing were weakened by years of separation during which husbands and wives experienced the war differently and failed to adjust to life together afterward. It is possible that domestic violence increased after the war, but the most common direct reason for divorce was adultery by wives in their husbands' absence. It is not that women were necessarily more likely to commit adultery, but that their affairs were more likely to become common knowledge, especially among neighbors. Pregnancy, of course, betrayed a woman's part in an adulterous liaison, and many men returned home to find children they could not possibly have fathered. The sexual activity of husbands while on military service was less likely to be discovered, although many must have returned home still suffering from sexually transmitted diseases. By the end of the war, a fifth of all British soldiers had contracted venereal disease, and there is no reason to think that the rate of infection was much different or lower in other national armies.

The picture of the family throughout much of Europe at war's end cannot have been encouraging to those who saw it as the foundation of social stability. In France, as we have seen, various policies were enacted to promote fertility, and in Britain the 1918 Maternal and Child Welfare Act added to earlier policies aimed at looking after mothers and children. But while such governments tried to reinforce the family, Soviet Russia's seemed bent on destroying it. Marx and Engels, whose writings were fundamental to the new Bolshevik regime, had condemned the family as reinforcing bourgeois social values and as an instrument for oppressing women and children. In the *Communist Manifesto* they had predicted that as capitalism disappeared "the bourgeois family will vanish as a matter of course." To help it on its way the Bolsheviks quickly legalized abortions and made them freely available in public hospitals, removed all restrictions on contraceptive information and sales, secularized marriage, and made divorce readily available.

Any Soviet citizen or couple wanting a divorce had only to file a petition to obtain one. A letter from a German visitor to Moscow in 1920 noted that "marriages in present-day Russia are interesting. . . . Divorce is as easy as marriage. It takes five minutes." Another commentator condemned the Soviet system that resulted in people lining up for divorces, "as compunctionless as those in bread queues." Divorce in fact became very popular, far more so than secular marriages. In Moscow in the first four months of 1918, only 214 marriages but 2,516 divorces were registered, and by the end of year there had been 6,000 marriages and 7,000 divorces. The most striking comparison was with the prewar (and pre-Bolshevik) period. Between 1911 and 1913 the crude divorce rate in European Russia (the number of divorces per thousand people) was so small as to be hardly worth calculating at 0.0002; by 1924 it was 1.4 and rising. This was the highest rate in Europe—three times that of Germany and five times the Swedish divorce rate—but nowhere near the high rate of divorce in the United States.

News of the Bolshevik family policies only intensified the view that communism was inimical to social order and morality. It did not help that many Western European intellectuals praised the new policies as intelligent, enlightened, and (as George Bernard Shaw wrote) a good example to follow. Conservatives and liberals throughout Europe saw in Bolshevik Russia the future of their own societies if they did not combat socialism at home.

One sphere in which women made gains in some states during or immediately after the war was in voting rights. Women won the franchise in Denmark, Iceland (1915), Britain (in stages between 1918 and 1928), Luxembourg, Russia (1918), the Netherlands, Poland, Czechoslovakia, Sweden, Germany, Austria (1919), Hungary (1920), and Ireland (1922). In a number of countries, however, the franchise soon became meaningless when democratic institutions were abolished. Italian women almost got the vote: The lower chamber overwhelmingly supported women's enfranchisement in 1920, but the government of the day fell before the vote could be ratified by the Senate. The Fascist government of Benito Mussolini, which began to assume power in 1922, declined to enfranchise women and, in fact, soon disenfranchised men as well. That was not the kind of equality Italian feminists had in mind.

In a few cases, women's voting rights were qualified, as in Britain, where Parliament had enfranchised some women over the age of thirty and men over the age of twenty-one. The distinction (removed in 1928) was made to prevent women from having a majority of votes. There were usually more adult women than men in modern European populations, but the imbalance was aggravated by the heavy male mortality during the war. About a quarter of British women over the age of twenty-one could not vote because of the discriminatory terms.

It is often argued that it was women's wartime service that persuaded male legislators that women deserved the vote. While the participation of women in all facets of the war effort was widely (if often equivocally) recognized, it can hardly be an explanation for the spread of women's voting rights across Europe. For one thing, half the states that enfranchised women during and soon after the war were nonbelligerents, and for another, some belligerents did not give women the vote. Moreover, support for women's suffrage had been increasing before 1914, that is, before women had the opportunity to serve their countries in time of war. In a number of states where women were given the vote in national elections after the war, they had been able to participate in local, provincial, or state elections before it.

Changes in governments are important in understanding the enfranchisement of women. Liberal and socialist parties had long favored giving women the vote, and their coming to power goes a long way to explaining why women were enfranchised. In Germany the Social Democratic Party (SPD) had endorsed women's suffrage since the 1890s, despite some concern within the party's leadership whether women would vote for the SPD. In November 1918, in discussions on reforming Germany's constitution, SPD delegates proposed giving women the vote but then agreed to delay it in order to get Liberal and Center Party agreement on universal male suffrage in Prussia and elsewhere. When revolution broke out shortly afterward, the Liberals and Center Party agreed to women's enfranchisement and other democratic measures, not on principle, but in order to appease the massed demonstrators and to reduce the attraction of the far left.

In Great Britain the granting of partial women's suffrage in 1917 was also a compromise among the various political parties. Although politicians of all stripes were full of praise for women's contribution to the war effort, they did not give the vote to any women under thirty years of age, who were the bulk of workers in industry. If women's contribution to the war effort were in itself an adequate explanation for women's suffrage, French women would not have had to wait another thirty years before they could vote in national elections. As it was, the issue was debated but anticlerical deputies voted against enfranchising women, who they recognized as generally more religious than men, for fear that they would use it to elect clerical deputies. The one case in which some women explicitly received the vote because of the war was Belgium, which enfranchised war widows, mothers with sons killed in the war, and women who had been imprisoned by the Germans. In this case, however, women were enfranchised not because of their active service to their country, but for reason of their awful wartime experiences.

In the new European states, women obtained the vote because the Paris peace conferences insisted that it be included in their constitutions, even though women were not enfranchised in two of the main Western allies, France and Italy. Similarly, the peace treaties provided for women to vote in plebiscites that determined which states disputed territories were to belong to. There were, however, limits to equality. Whenever individuals had the option of choosing one nationality or another, married couples had to opt for the same one, and that one was the nationality chosen by the husband.

The Nations of Eastern Europe, 1918–20

For two or three years after the Great War officially ended, there were armed conflicts throughout Central and Eastern Europe as states attempted to establish their new borders. There was little dispute about the core territory of each state, those regions where national populations were concentrated and formed an overwhelming majority of the inhabitants. Thus the heart of the new state of Czechoslovakia consisted of Bohemia and Moravia, where Czechs were the preponderant ethnic group, and Slovakia and Ruthenia, where most inhabitants were Slovaks. Even in these core regions, however, other ethnic populations existed in large numbers; within Czechoslovakia as a whole there were more ethnic Germans than Slovaks.

The most difficult disputes arose over regions where ethnic populations were mixed in more even numbers, where no single group represented a clear majority of inhabitants, and where two nationalities might reasonably stake a territorial claim. Nor was it easy to establish exactly how many Czechs, Poles, Germans or others there were in any given area. Border disputes were further complicated by the fact that, despite the rhetoric of national determination that filled the air after the war, some territorial claims were based on arguments that overrode the criterion of nationality. A notable case was the conflict between Czechoslovakia and Poland over Teschen, a small mining area where just over half the people were reported as Polish-speaking, a quarter spoke Czech, and a fifth spoke German. Poland had a stronger claim on linguistic-ethnic grounds, but Teschen had historically been considered part of Bohemia, a core part of the new Czechoslovakia. Traditional relationships, not to mention economic interests and national grandeur, could easily undermine the principle of ethnic nationalism. Teschen remained in dispute between Poland and Czechoslovakia for decades.

Nationalist passions and expectations were too high immediately after the war to allow for easily or quickly negotiated resolutions. Even if the new states had had the will to settle their disputes peacefully, they lacked the necessary political and diplomatic mechanisms, and instead turned to armies—often the only substantial national institution that existed right after the war—to seize and hold disputed territory.

Poland's borders were established only after a war with Russia that began when German authority in East Prussia collapsed, and ended when a treaty establishing Poland's eastern frontier was signed in 1921. At the same time, Poland was engaged in border conflicts with two other new states, Czechoslovakia and Lithuania. In the end, Poland became an independent state as a result of the collapse of the Russian Empire, then added former Austrian and German territories in 1918. Between 1919 and 1923 it expanded eastward at the expense of Ukraine and Bolshevik Russia.

For its part, Romania enlarged its territory by force, under a prior agreement with Britain and France. In early 1919, Romanian troops occupied Transylvania, part of Hungary but having a preponderantly Romanian population. Later that year Romanian forces launched a full-scale invasion of Hungary to weaken it and to consolidate their territorial gains. Having seized additional territory from Austria and Russia, postwar Romania was twice the size it had been in 1914.

With the exception of Poland's border with Russia, the general shape of the new territorial arrangements became clear within a year of the end of the war. The collapse of the Russian Empire had allowed Poland, Ukraine, Estonia, Lithuania, Latvia, and Finland to proclaim independence, while former Russian territory was occupied by Poland and Romania. In the region previously occupied by Austria-Hungary there were now Austria,

Hungary, and Czechoslovakia. Serbia had incorporated former Austro-Hungarian territories, notably Croatia and Bosnia-Herzegovina, and created the Kingdom of the South Slavs, eventually called Yugoslavia.

Creating new states and rearranging political frontiers were only two ways by which greater harmony between nationality and statehood was achieved in Europe after the war. Although nationality and statehood could never be perfectly congruent, the process was advanced by massive migrations of ethnic populations toward the states that were now designated their "homelands." Countless women, men and children, individuals and families alike, took to the roads of Europe, driven by fear and drawn by hope, both emotions inspired by the territorial changes that accompanied the end of the war.

Millions left states where they feared persecution and migrated to places where they would be among their own ethnic kind. Thus more than a million Poles left Russia for the new Polish state, and displaced and demobilized Finns, Estonians, Latvians, and Lithuanians set off for the states that were in the process of seizing independence from Russia. But many members of minorities, we should note, stayed put, preferring to take their chances rather than leave the homes, communities, and livelihoods to which they were accustomed. Members of nationalities that had lorded it over others before the war were especially likely to move once their dominance was gone. Magyars in Romania, Czechoslovakia, and Yugoslavia now found themselves at the mercy of ethnic groups they themselves had oppressed. By 1921 almost a quarter of a million Magyars had fled from these states, so overwhelming Hungary that in 1921 and 1922 the government closed its borders to refugees. The arrival of Magyars in Hungary was partly offset by the departure of many of Hungary's ethnic Germans, but in 1921 tens of thousands of refugees still lived in camps in Budapest and elsewhere.

Ethnic Germans, blamed for the war and resented by minorities in the former German Empire, East Prussia, and Austria-Hungary, were no more welcome outside their own nation states (Germany and Austria). In Hungary and Poland, boycotts of German businesses were quickly mounted. Half a million ethnic Germans abandoned what they expected would be hostile futures in the Baltic states, a quarter of a million left Alsace and Lorraine after they reverted to France, and others left regions annexed from Germany by Belgium and Denmark. In all, Germany received almost a million German refugees.

While countless Europeans traveled to new territories where they hoped they would be "home" in an ethnic sense, others returned to the places the war had forced them from. Hundreds of thousands of French and Belgians returned to the homes from which they had fled in 1914. The end of the war also meant the repatriation of prisoners of war— there were 2 million in Germany alone—and forced laborers.

Jews formed a particular group of migrants, as social and political turmoil and heightened nationalism combined with traditional anti-Semitism to produce widespread pogroms and outbursts of violence directed at Jews and Jewish property. Between 1917 and 1921, an estimated 30,000 Jews were killed in Russia and Ukraine by pogroms that destroyed 28 percent of Jewish homes and left half a million Jews homeless. Polish nationalism became associated with anti-Semitism (Jewish officers in the Polish army were interned during the Russian-Polish war as suspected traitors) and there were government-sanctioned pogroms in Hungary in 1919. Hundreds of thousands of Jews began to move westward. Many left Europe entirely—some 136,000 in 1921 alone—but when the United States and Canada began to restrict immigration from Europe in the early 1920s more and more Jews settled where they could in Western and Central Europe.

Throughout 1919 and much of 1920, national boundaries were debated and determined by the Allied nations as part of the overall Paris peace settlement. The results and implications of the decisions are discussed in a later section, but it is important to note that when the delegates met in Paris they were already faced with a number of faits accomplis, and that even while they conferred, the situation in Central and Eastern Europe was constantly changing.

State-Building in Central and Eastern Europe

The destruction of prewar states and the weakening of old political elites in many countries created a political vacuum, the absence of a political authority that could either claim legitimacy or even exercise authority over its territory. The liberal parliamentary systems adopted by almost every Central and Eastern European state looked good on paper, but they were implanted in political cultures that had no tradition of political toleration. Many governments came under direct pressure from movements dedicated to the destruction of democracy, and all had to deal with immediate problems of hunger, poverty, social conflict, and public order before engaging in the formidable tasks of reconstructing agriculture, industry, and communications.

A major challenge was posed to many governments by communists, encouraged by events in Russia to believe that revolution was possible in the rest of rural, agrarian Europe. Workers' and soldiers' committees, modeled on the Russian soviets, were organized to direct revolutionary activity, and from 1918 onward communist parties were established in most countries.

Nowhere did left-wing revolutionaries seem to have a better opportunity to gain power than in Germany. As the kaiser's last chancellor, Prince Max of Baden, left office on November 9, 1918, he handed control to Friedrich Ebert, the leader of the moderate Social Democrats (SPD). What seemed an orderly political transition had, in fact, no constitutional force whatsoever. The viability of Ebert's administration rested not on Max's blessing but on a pragmatic agreement the same day between the SPD and the Independent Social Democrats (the USPD, which had broken from the main party in 1917) to cooperate in governing Germany until elections could be held to draft a republican constitution.

The socialist coalition was fragile, however, for the USPD contained factions like the Spartacists, Marxists led by Rosa Luxemburg and Karl Liebknecht, who wanted revolutionary change rather than evolutionary transformation by constitutional means. The tension within the coalition was graphically demonstrated by two declarations on November 9, 1918. At 2:00 p.m. Philipp Scheidemann of the majority SPD announced a parliamentary republic from a window of the Reichstag; two hours later, Karl Liebknecht appeared at a window of the royal palace and declared Germany a revolutionary socialist republic.

In the competition between moderate and revolutionary socialists, the moderates prevailed. They acted quickly to consolidate support from the growing trade union movement: On November 15, an agreement was reached with employers that recognized unions as bargaining agents for workers and gave unions extensive rights. An eight-hour working day was decreed. In return the unions agreed not to try to alter existing property structures, effectively renouncing the revolutionaries' policy of worker control of industry. Even the workers' and soldiers' committees that had sprung up throughout Germany were dominated by moderate socialists.

Ebert's government also won immediate support from an unexpected source, when on November 9 General Groener, the chief of the General Staff, offered the army's help if it was needed to maintain law and order, by which it meant suppressing the revolutionary left. The army was not sympathetic to Ebert and the SPD administration, but it recognized that they exercised de facto authority, and it was more anxious to suppress any revolutionary stirrings than concerned about any temporary alliance it might have to make in order to achieve that end. It was a condition of the army's support that army officers had command authority.

It did not take long for the socialist coalition to begin to break down. In late December, Marxists led by Luxemburg and Liebknecht left the USPD and formed the German Communist Party. The real crisis occurred in early January, when Ebert removed Berlin's police chief, who had the support of radicals in workers' committees in the capital. Revolutionaries took to the streets, threw up barricades, and occupied public buildings. Ebert's government had not had time to organize its own police or military force, and so resorted to the existing army, together with groups of right-wing military volunteers, many of them demobilized soldiers, known as the Free Corps (Freikorps). Battles were fought in Berlin's streets, but the communists and their supporters were no match for the trained and well-armed troops. In the suppression of the uprising, hundreds were killed, and Luxemburg and Liebknecht, who had assumed leadership of the rebellion and had been arrested, were murdered by Free Corps members.

There was a brief respite from civil unrest in Germany later in January as elections were held for an assembly to draft a new constitution. This election, Germany's most democratic to that time, was based on universal suffrage that included women for the first time. More than three-quarters of the voters supported the three moderate parties, the SPD (which won 38 percent of the vote), Catholic Center Party (20 percent), and the liberal German Democratic Party (19 percent). In contrast, the militant socialists of the USPD won 8 percent and right-wing nationalist parties 15 percent. The assembly met at Weimar, a small town in Saxony, that gave its name to the liberal democratic constitution under which Germany would be governed until it was abrogated by the Nazis in 1933.

The victory of what are known as the Weimar parties in 1919 reflected expectations that moderate politicians could lead Germany into a prosperous peace. Unionized workers, who rallied to the SPD, were an increasingly important voting bloc: By 1918 union membership exceeded 2 million, and during 1919 it more than tripled. The real incomes of many workers, including lower-level civil servants, began to improve, and despite demobilization, unemployment in early 1919 was not significantly higher than it had been in 1913.

Improving conditions did not prevent further revolutionary activity in Germany. In March 1919, there was a second communist uprising in Berlin, this one suppressed at a cost of more than a thousand deaths. The following month a communist republic was proclaimed in Bavaria, the important southern German state where Prussian domination of Germany had never fully been accepted. An independent Bavarian socialist republic had been proclaimed by the socialist Kurt Eisner in November 1918, but his assassination in February 1919 threw the moderate socialists into disarray, and communists seized the opportunity to take power.

Chancellor Ebert, anxious to reestablish central authority over Bavaria, again called on the army and the Free Corps to suppress the communist insurgents. The authority of moderate socialists was restored in Bavaria as it had been in Berlin, but again thanks to army and paramilitary forces that were fundamentally hostile to socialism. This uneasy alliance against the communists boded ill for longer-term political stability in Germany.

The sputterings of communist revolt in Germany in the six months after the armistice were echoed elsewhere in Central and Eastern Europe. In Hungary a parliamentary republic with liberal freedoms and land reform had been proclaimed in November 1918.

But the regime that proclaimed it, headed by Count Michael Károlyi, a liberal aristocrat, was unable to survive in the face of debilitating challenges, including the territorial claims that Romanians, South Slavs, and Slovaks began to make on Hungary. In January 1919, Romanian forces occupied parts of Hungary, and in the hope that the Russian Bolsheviks would help a fraternal state defend its borders, a new Hungarian regime was formed by socialists and communists.

Real power in this regime lay with the communist commissar for foreign affairs, Béla Kun, who soon expelled the socialists from the coalition and began to create a regime modeled on Lenin's. A Red Army was created, private property confiscated, large estates expropriated, and produce requisitioned. These policies served only to antagonize the peasants who hoarded or destroyed their crops rather than surrender them.

Kun's expectation that Lenin would help the Hungarian communist government against external threats came to nothing. In the spring of 1919 the Russian Bolsheviks were still preoccupied with political and ethnic challenges to their own power. Under Kun, Hungarian troops invaded Czechoslovakia in March 1919 and proclaimed a soviet state in Slovakia. At this the Romanians, aided by the French who were nervous at the extension of communist power in Europe, launched a full-scale invasion of Hungary in July 1919, occupying Budapest in August, and forcing Kun to flee to Russia.

After the Romanians withdrew from Budapest (but not from all Hungarian territory), a new regime was set up under the reactionary and anti-semitic Admiral Miklós Horthy, former commander of the Austro-Hungarian navy. His regime began with a period of repression in which thousands of socialists and Jews were killed. Horthy's authoritarian regime had a parliamentary facade, but the franchise was restricted and the secret ballot eliminated in many areas. Peasant grievances were appeased by a policy of land distribution, and quotas were placed on Jewish students in Hungarian universities, the first of many anti-Jewish laws that would be passed in the inter-war period.

The Bulgarian government also defeated challenges from the left wing. Strong opposition to the government developed in the towns, which had been swollen by refugees and demobilized soldiers. Food and jobs were scarce, and many people were kept alive by foreign aid. Social Democrats and Communists organized a week-long general strike in 1919, but premier Alexander Stamboliski consolidated his power by interfering in the 1920 elections so as to produce a majority for his Peasant Party.

Perhaps the most formidable challenges were those facing the Poles, who re-created their nation-state from Russian, Austrian, and German territory. Two-thirds of the country's population had lived in Russia, a fifth in Austria, and 12 percent in Germany, and although Poles shared a language and religion, it was necessary to create national institutions of all kinds. At first Poland had six different currencies, and four different legal and fiscal systems, and economic development was hampered by an incoherent railroad network based on the previous frontiers. There were regional disparities of all kinds, reflecting the previous imperial administrations; agriculture was most productive in the former German lands, least in the poorly developed eastern areas, and literacy levels reflected the superior German system over those of Austria and Russia. Finally, although 70 percent of Poland's 27 million inhabitants were Poles, the country contained 5 million Ukrainians, 3 million Jews, and a million Germans, an ethnic composition with rich potential for conflict. To these obstacles were added a period of war as Poland stabilized its borders with Czechoslovakia, Lithuania, and Russia.

Poland adopted a democratic constitution, based on France's, in 1921, though it came into force only in late 1922. Until then a series of administrations wrestled unsuccessfully with economic problems, agrarian reform, and the competing claims of interest groups from peasants to army officers. In the first elections under the new constitution, no party won a majority in the Sejm, the Polish parliament. There was an almost even four-way split among the parties of the right, center, left, and national minorities. A shaky coalition was formed, but it fell in 1923 in the face of a collapsing currency, spiraling inflation, a general strike, and widespread civil disorder. Other administrations tried their hand, but the days of democratic government in Poland were numbered.

The political turmoil of Central and Eastern Europe reflected the multilayered conflicts that had long simmered in the authoritarian empires. Although they appeared ideological, the struggles for power were more fundamentally contests between social groups and ethnic populations, all seizing the unprecedented opportunities the postwar period offered for national power.

Political Unrest in Western Europe

The political unrest experienced by the major Western European states after the war was dramatically different in kind and scale from the turmoils of Central and Eastern Europe. In narrowly defined terms, in fact, it seemed like politics as usual in France and Britain. In the first French election after the war, Clemenceau's conservative National Republican bloc won a majority of seats. In Britain, voters in what was called the khaki election (because of the participation of so many uniformed citizens) gave an overwhelming victory to Lloyd George's wartime coalition of Conservatives and Liberals.

In both major Allied countries, the emphasis on continuity over change reflected popular satisfaction with the outcome of the war and optimism about the future. But the election results did not mean that there was no discontent in Britain and France. Both wartime governments had held elections within weeks of the armistice so as to capitalize on the popularity associated with victory. But the euphoria of November 1918 rapidly gave way to the hangover of postwar conditions.

One manifestation of unrest in both countries was an increase in strike activity. In Britain, strikes involved 2.5 million workers in 1919 (double the 1918 number), and in France 1.2 million, six times the number who had struck the year before. The breadth of the strike movement reflected a substantial growth in the number of unionized workers. In France the General Confederation of Labor (CGT), which represented many trade unions and, increasingly, professional associations, had a million members by 1919, compared with under 700,000 in 1914. British trade union membership peaked at 8.3 million in 1920, when it represented almost half the workers who could join unions.

Many strikes in Britain and France were political, and some workers expressed solidarity with the Russian Bolsheviks by trying to stop Allied support for anti-Bolshevik forces in Russia. British dock workers, especially those on the Clydeside in Scotland, refused to load supplies bound for Russia, set up workers' councils, and ran up the red flag. In France similar action culminated in a general strike on May Day (May 1), 1919. On the whole, however, the immediate experience of war did not convince significant numbers of French or Britons that fundamental political and social change was necessary or desirable.

There was one major exception, an echo of the national reorganization farther to the east, and that was the growing demand for Irish independence. Eighty of the MPs elected to the British Parliament in 1918 were Irish nationalists, and a war of liberation had broken out in Ireland. Paramilitary forces called the Black and Tans and auxiliary troops, many of them demobilized soldiers, tried to maintain British control, but by 1921 an

The struggle for independence in Ireland: barricades in the streets of Dublin, July 1922.

agreement was reached that predominantly Catholic southern Ireland should become an independent state within the British Commonwealth, while the mainly Protestant northern counties (Ulster) should remain within the United Kingdom. In 1922 southern Ireland was proclaimed the Irish Free State. The division of Ireland into two separate political entities did not satisfy nationalist aspirations, however, and the Irish question dogged Britain throughout the twentieth century.

In Italy, postwar conflicts were not so quickly resolved, even on paper. Although Italy had been on the winning side and had had a shorter war, there was little satisfaction at the outcome. The public debt had skyrocketed; wartime price inflation of 400 percent accelerated, rather than slowed, immediately after the end of hostilities, and depressed real income even more; and political and social conflict had intensified. More than 1.5 million workers were involved in strikes in 1919, compared with an average of 230,000 a year in the preceding decade. Many strikes, especially in northern industrial cities like Milan and Turin, were in support of Lenin's regime; the government had given diplomatic recognition to the anti-Bolshevik White forces.

Discontent spread to the rural areas of Italy as well. To encourage support for its war policies, the government had promised veterans land. When the promise was not immediately fulfilled, many peasants and farm workers, veterans and nonveterans alike, simply occupied vacant land. They were supported by veterans' organizations, left-wing Catholic activists, and socialist farm workers' unions.

Despite sporadic manifestations of support for the Bolshevik struggle against counterrevolutionary and reactionary forces, no Western European state other than Germany was threatened by a powerful communist movement. Lenin's Bolshevik regime at first attracted the support of many socialists throughout Europe, and intellectuals and union leaders from around the world visited Russia. Many reported in more or less glowing terms on the prospects for building a new society based on equality, freedom, and common ownership of property, but many others came away disillusioned.

The preference of most Western European socialists for parliamentary change was demonstrated when Lenin founded the Communist International, an organization of socialist parties that would spearhead the revolutionary movement in each country. Parties could belong to the Communist International only if they satisfied stringent conditions that included repudiating reformist policies in favor of promoting a revolutionary seizure of power, reorganizing themselves on the Bolshevik model with its tightly knit structure, and agreeing to combat reformist socialism as vigorously as opponents on the right.

All the major European socialist parties split. In some cases, such as Britain, Sweden, and Austria, a small minority broke away to form communist parties. A third of the Italian socialists rallied to the Communist International, as did the same proportion of the Independent Social Democrats in Germany. The Norwegian Labor Party joined the Communist International but later withdrew. The major success for Lenin was the decision by most members of the French Socialists to join and rename themselves the French Communist Party.

The split within the socialist movement between communists and reformist socialists had long-term implications. In a number of countries the division of the left was to have critical results, as in Germany ten years later where it facilitated Hitler's rise to power. Although the Bolshevik form of government had limited support in postwar Europe, socialist parties generally continued their prewar trend of increasing popularity. The French Socialist Party, founded in 1918, had 36,000 members in December that year, and 133,000 twelve months later. As we shall see, reformist socialist parties took increasingly prominent roles in governments during the 1920s.

The Paris Peace Conference, 1919–20

Wars, invasions, nationalist upheavals, and revolutions in Central and Western Europe; a Bolshevik regime in Russia that inspired revolts and labor unrest throughout Europe; industrial dislocation, ruined agricultural economies, a collapse of trade; millions of Europeans uprooted from their homes. This was the background to the conference in Paris that was to draw up permanent peace settlements.

The first of the three broad aims of the conference was to fix the status, borders, and military strength of the defeated states. Separate treaties, each named for the location in or near Paris where it was signed, set out peace terms with each of the Central Powers. Second, the conference established new political frontiers and accorded them legal recognition. It is important, however, to remember that even as the conference convened, only months after formal hostilities ended, the political map of Europe had already been sketched quite firmly by national armies, often with the assistance of the Allies. As discussions and negotiations continued in Paris for a year and a half, the situation continued to evolve. The third task of the conference was to set up an international organization designed to prevent another world war.

The Paris peace conference was a conference of victors. The defeated states were not invited to negotiate the peace terms as equals, but were ordered to accept what was offered. Neither was Russia, by 1919 considered an enemy of the Allies, invited to participate. The twenty-seven countries actively involved comprised the United States, the European Allies, their non-European colonies and other wartime partners, and representatives of the emerging nations of Central and Eastern Europe. Of the twenty-seven, however, the five major powers—Britain, the United States, France, Italy, and Japan—formed themselves into a Supreme Council that effectively made the decisions.

The peace conference in Paris, 1919: from left, British Prime Minister David Lloyd George, Italian Premier Vittorio Orlando, French Premier Georges Clemenceau, and U.S. President Woodrow Wilson.

Even then, agreements were not easily reached, for each power had its own agenda. The British and French were primarily concerned with reestablishing a workable balance of power on the Continent. Both Lloyd George and Clemenceau negotiated with one ear tuned to domestic public opinion, which in both countries wanted revenge against Germany. There were widespread demands for the kaiser to be tried. The Japanese wanted to maintain their territorial gains, whereas the Italians were anxious to get legal title to the land they had been promised as an inducement to join the Allies in 1915.

The Americans seemed to have more abstract aims, having no direct interest in acquiring territory and stressing the importance of Woodrow Wilson's Fourteen Points as the bases of any agreements. Wilson, who led the U.S. delegation in person (he was the first American president to travel abroad while in office, and he stayed in France for almost six months), wanted priority given to the establishment of an international organization to keep the peace.

This was, in fact, the first task completed by the conference. The League of Nations was agreed upon in principle by January 25, 1919, and the details of its constitution (the Covenant) on April 28. The League's members agreed to respect each other's territorial integrity and to submit disputes to the organization's Council. The Council was to consist of the five great powers that had formed the Supreme Council at the peace conference, together with four other states elected by the League's General Assembly, which was to consist of all the member states. Thus the League gave representation to all members, but primacy to the great powers.

Insofar as member states were required to submit disputes to the League for investigation and inquiry, the maintenance of peace was voluntary. The Covenant empowered the League to impose sanctions (in the form of a blockade or even military action) against a recalcitrant state. But the League had no military force of its own, and could take action only with the unanimous agreement of the Council. Taking a longer-term view of peace, the Covenant also called for general disarmament. In addition, the League had a role in supervising colonial possessions. The overseas territories of the defeated states (notably Germany) were not given unreservedly to the victors but were to be administered by them under mandates issued by the League.

The League involved itself in social issues in addition to the immediate political and diplomatic issues. It entered into agreements with states having large minority popula-tions to protect them from discrimination. It established an International Labor Office to oversee conditions of work and wages worldwide; specific aims included the elimination of unemployment, equal pay for women, pensions, and a maximum working week. Other agencies were established to deal with health and other humanitarian issues.

For the French the central issue of the peace conference was security against what they perceived as an innately militaristic and expansionist Germany. Having twice been in-vaded within fifty years, the French were anxious to weaken Germany as much and for as long as possible. Clemenceau floated the idea of breaking Germany up into the states that existed before unification. Although Britain and the United States opposed that option, they were sympathetic to French demands for secure borders.

There was no dispute (even among most German politicians) that Alsace-Lorraine should return to France, but other border issues were more contentious. Clemenceau wanted the Rhineland, the strategically important German border region on the west bank of the River Rhine, turned into an independent republic under French military pro-tection, but the idea was opposed as likely to be a continuing source of friction. A com-promise was reached whereby the Rhineland, together with a fifty-kilometer-wide zone on the east bank of the Rhine, would be demilitarized and occupied by Allied forces for the following fifteen years.

Clemenceau compromised on the Rhineland in the hope that the British and Americans would agree to France's annexing the German Saarland, a major coal-producing area. This, the French argued, would compensate for the Germans' destruction of coal mines in the north of France during the war, and help France's economic recovery. Again a compromise was reached: France would have access to the region's resources for fifteen years (during which time it would be administered by the League of Nations). After that period, the inhab-itants would vote to be incorporated into France, return to Germany, or become independent.

The French also had a direct interest in the border between Germany and Poland, see-ing in the latter a future ally against both Germany and Soviet Russia. To ensure that it had access to the sea, Poland was eventually awarded a "corridor" of former German territory that had a predominantly Polish population. The German port city of Danzig was made a free city under League of Nations supervision, but the Poles were given extensive rights over it.

To the territory Germany lost on the Continent was added its overseas colonies. Almost all had been occupied during the war, and none of the occupying states was eager to relinquish its acquisitions. The Americans were appalled by attitudes toward conquest that accorded poorly with Wilson's ideas of the new world order, and in order to accom-modate these notions the occupiers were permitted to retain control of the former German territories under League of Nations mandates. These mandates bound the con-trolling states to prepare the territories for eventual independence, in line with the ideal of creating sovereign nation-states.

Under this system Britain consolidated control of the former German East African colonies, as well as parts of Togoland and Cameroon in West Africa, France kept most of Togoland and the Cameroon; Belgium and Portugal obtained small African territories; and South Africa extended its control over South-West Africa (Namibia). Beyond Africa, Japan replaced German influence in parts of China and retained the German Pacific island colonies north of the equator, while Australia took German New Guinea and shared the is-lands south of the equator with New Zealand.

This scramble for territory was reminiscent of the old imperial days, not a new world order that respected national aspirations. A Pan-African Congress met in Paris during the

Legend:
- ·········· 1914 Boundaries
- ──── 1923 Boundaries
- ▓▓ New Nations
- ░░ Former Austro-Hungarian Empire

Scale: 0 — 250 — 500 Miles / 0 — 250 — 500 Kilometers

MAP 4.1 The territorial settlement after the First World War.

peace negotiations and attempted to have written into the mandates the obligation of the controlling powers to recognize the rights of indigenous populations to self-government. The point was noted, but no action was taken.

To ensure that Germany did not threaten European stability, restrictions were placed on its armed forces. Germany was permitted only a volunteer army of 100,000. A minimum twelve-year term of service prevented the building of a larger force of trained men through short periods of recruitment. The army was to have no heavy artillery and only 288 pieces of light artillery. There was to be no air force, and the navy was to have no submarines or ships larger than 10,000 tons. No new fortifications were to be constructed.

The final issue relating to Germany was the reparations that should be paid to compensate the European Allies for the costs they sustained during the war. Although the French are often portrayed as the hardliner on reparations, the French initially expected that financial assistance for reconstruction would come not from Germany but from France's war partners, especially the United States. Only when it became clear that the Americans had no intention of continuing their wartime aid—in March 1919 the United States terminated government loans to its partners—did the French turn to Germany as the prime source of revenue.

While there was general agreement among France, Britain, and the United States that Germany should pay reparations, there were differences over the amount. The Americans proposed a minimum of 100 billion marks and the French 124 billion, but the British demanded 220 billion to be divided among the Allies proportionately to the damage they suffered to civilian property, including industry. Included in the British sum was the cost of war pensions.

Because of the complexity of the calculations, it was impossible to reach a decision on reparations when the rest of the treaty dealing with Germany was complete, and the con-

A German tank being broken up in compliance with the Treaty of Versailles, which stipulated low limits on the levels of German military capacity.

ference appointed a commission to establish Germany's financial liability. In order to justify it, a clause establishing German moral responsibility for the war was inserted in the treaty. Clause 231, known as the "guilt clause," held Germany responsible "for causing all the loss and damage to which the Allied and Associated Governments and their nationals have been subjected as a consequence of the war imposed upon them by the aggression of Germany and her Allies." This clause (a similar one was included in the treaty with Austria) would lie at the heart of German grievances about the treaty, and it would become a major political issue in Germany in the next two decades.

Although the German representatives who signed the Treaty of Versailles were later condemned by nationalists for doing so, they were wholly opposed to its terms. The German delegation of almost 200 experts, led by the foreign minister, expected to negotiate the terms of peace. Even though they represented a former enemy, they thought of themselves as representing a regenerated and democratic Germany that had renounced the evils of its imperial past, and as partners with the Allied powers in the fight against communism.

Instead they were treated as if they were unrepentant supporters of the kaiser. This was not entirely without justification, for the SPD, the majority party in the government, had voted for war in 1914, even if it did later revert to its antiwar policy. The Germans were given a single copy of the draft treaty and allowed two weeks to submit comments in French or English. News of the draft treaty provoked outrage in Berlin where the SPD chancellor, Philipp Scheidemann, declared that Germany would never sign it as it stood.

Given an extra week to frame a response, the German delegation in Paris concentrated on showing, line by line, how the draft failed to meet the principles set down in Wilson's Fourteen Points. Suspecting that the German government might indeed refuse to agree to the treaty, Britain, France, and the United States considered a joint invasion of Germany's western region to demonstrate their resolve.

The German delegation presented its objections to the conference at the end of May 1919. On June 16, the Supreme Council announced that apart from allowing plebiscites in some of the German territory being transferred to Poland (without obstructing the corridor to the sea), the draft treaty would not be altered. The German government was given five days to agree to it or face a resumption of the war.

Faced with this ultimatum, the cabinet in Berlin resigned. The treaty was condemned by politicians across the political spectrum, and there were declarations that Germany would never sign it. But when the treaty was put before the National Assembly only hours before the deadline expired, it passed by 237 votes to 138, with 5 abstentions. Signed in the Palace of Versailles on June 28, 1919, the Treaty of Versailles ended the war with Germany but became a defining document for political divisions and conflict within Germany itself.

Separate peace agreements were reached regarding Austria (the Treaty of St. Germain) and Hungary (the Treaty of Trianon). Austria was treated by the conference much as Germany was, but with the difference that Austria was much weaker politically and economically, having lost the vast empire from which it drew power and prosperity. Like Germany, Austria was held responsible for the war and was required to accept a guilt clause, despite the insistence of the social democratic government that it had repudiated the imperial policies that had led to war. Austria was required to cede territory such that it was reduced to an ethnically German state half its 1914 size. It lost the South Tyrol (with a German population of a quarter-million) to Italy, the Sudetenland (with 3 million Germans) to Czechoslovakia, but gained the mainly German Burgenland from Hungary.

Like Germany's, Austria's military forces were reduced. It was to have an army of only 30,000 long-service volunteers, no air force, and a navy of three patrol boats on the

Danube. With the collapse of the empire, Austria was landlocked and could have no seagoing navy, in any case; the Austrian-Hungarian fleet was seized by the Allies. Austria was also to pay reparations, but until the final sum was set, it was to make payments in kind—sheep, cows, horses, and merchant ships—to Italy, Romania, and Yugoslavia.

Finally, the Treaty of St. Germain forbade Austria ever to join politically with Germany, despite the fact that when the Austrian republic was proclaimed in 1918, its founders declared it a "constituent part of the German Republic." Although the treaty contradicted the principle of national self-determination that was supposed to underlie the reorganization of the European state system, the French and Italians especially were opposed to allowing Germany to gain from the incorporation of Austria. In effect, Austria became the state inhabited by those German residents of the Habsburg Empire who had not been allocated to Italy, Czechoslovakia, or Yugoslavia; as Clemenceau put it, Austria was "what was left over."

The Hungarian delegation in Paris attempted to portray Austria as domineering and militaristic, and Hungary as a hapless junior partner in Habsburg war policy. Their case was not helped, however, by the establishment of Béla Kun's communist state in March 1919, while the conference was in session. That alone was enough to alienate the Allies, and Kun's subsequent attack on Czechoslovakia did not strengthen the image of Hungary as a peace-loving nation.

It was not until the end of 1919, when Admiral Horthy's reactionary regime was in power, that the peace terms with Hungary were decided. Hungary lost some two-thirds of its former territory and population. Transylvania was transferred to Romania; Slovakia and Ruthenia to Czechoslovakia; Croatia and Slovenia to Yugoslavia; and the Burgenland to Austria. These transfers excluded many non-Magyars from Hungary, but they also meant that more than 3 million Magyars were living outside Hungary.

There remained two other Central Powers to be dealt with: Bulgaria and Turkey. Under the Treaty of Neuilly (November 27, 1919), Bulgaria's territory was sharply reduced. It was forced to return all land occupied during the war, and transfer other territories (and Bulgarians) to Greece and Yugoslavia. In addition, Bulgaria was ordered to pay reparations of 2.25 billion gold francs to the Allies and make other payments in kind (mainly coal, railway rolling stock, and livestock) to neighboring Yugoslavia, Romania, and Greece. Its army was limited to 20,000 volunteers.

Many of the details of the peace agreement with Turkey (the Treaty of Sèvres, signed October 20, 1920) do not concern Europe proper. By 1920 Turkey occupied less than a third of the territory and had about 40 percent of the population of the former Ottoman Empire. Much of the territory in the Middle East was placed under foreign control: Britain was granted a mandate over Palestine; France and Britain shared control over Syria and Mesopotamia (now Iran); Greece received western Thrace and some islands in the Aegean; and Italy was awarded the Dodecanese islands. Turkey, restricted to territory on the Anatolian peninsula, was required to recognize Armenian independence. Finally the Allies dealt with the strategic problem that had defeated them during the war: They declared the straits between the Mediterranean and the Black Sea an international waterway, and demilitarized the land on each side of them.

Much of the work of the conference, carried out by separate commissions, was to arbitrate border disputes in Eastern and Southern Europe. Representatives of the Allies listened to representations from the various parties and took into account the various agendas of the Allies. Harold Nicholson, a member of the British delegation, recorded the trading and negotiations in a diary. An example (the entry for March 4) reads in part: "At 4.0 we have our penultimate meeting of the Greek Committee. (1) Frontier with Albania.

We give way to French about Loritsa. Americans insist on modified line south of Voiussa. Italians want 1913 frontier. (2) With Bulgaria. . . ."

The redrawing of Europe was, then, a compromise among principles, legal obligations, and the pragmatic concerns for security, as the major powers tried to establish states large enough to resist a resurgent Germany and the new Bolshevik power in the east. All states, new and old, ended up with a numerically preponderant ethnic group and several minority groups; this had been the situation in the great empires before the war, but now it was on a smaller national scale. Czechoslovakia, for example, comprised 6 million Czechs and almost 2 million Slovaks, but substantial minorities—nearly 4 million Germans, 750,000 Magyars, and 500,000 Ukrainians. The result was the creation of a number of states that were vulnerable to continued nationalist challenges.

The Paris peace treaties were contentious from the very beginning, and have often been blamed for creating the conditions that led to political volatility, the rise of totalitarian states in Europe, and the Second World War. Particular attention is given to the apparent harshness of the Treaty of Versailles, which is portrayed as having so embittered Germans that the drive to revise the treaty, especially what became known as the guilt clause, led to their turning to Hitler in order to retrieve national self-esteem.

Some of the implications of the new boundaries were unavoidable (like the disruption in economic and commercial patterns) while others were unplanned. It was not only the national map of Central and Eastern Europe that was redrawn, but the religious map as well. The dissolution of the Habsburg Empire, which was vigorously opposed by the Vatican, broke the Roman Catholic dominance over much of the region, and shattered what looked like a Catholic bastion wedged between Protestant Germany and Orthodox Russia. Although Austria and Poland remained overwhelmingly Catholic, as was Lithuania, fewer than two-thirds of Hungarians were; Lithuania was Lutheran, and the Protestant Czechs dominated the Catholic Slovakians in Czechoslovakia. Catholics made up 32 percent of the population of Weimar Germany, compared with 37 per cent of Imperial Germany's inhabitants. Overall, the Catholic Church lost from the settlements; the Vatican was excluded from participation in the peace conference despite asking to take part and dispatching a representative.

Some of the greatest flaws in the agreements could not have been anticipated. A major blow was the failure of the U.S. Senate to ratify the treaties or U.S. membership in the League of Nations. This meant that from the beginning the League excluded not only the world's most powerful state in 1919, but two other major powers, Russia and Germany, neither of which was invited to join. From its beginning the League failed to be the truly international organization its effectiveness largely depended upon.

Insofar as the treaties were only one influence on the reorganization of Europe after the war, it would be wrong to place overwhelming emphasis on their part in the causation of the Second World War. Perhaps their more important role in the following twenty years was as a permanent source of grievance that could be exploited by nationalists.

Postwar Italy and the Rise of Fascism

Of all the Allied powers, Italy was least satisfied with the treaties. Although Italy was awarded some Austro-Hungarian territory guaranteed by the Treaty of London, it failed to obtain land promised later in the war: territory in Africa, in the Middle East, and in Dalmatia on the eastern shore of the Adriatic Sea, including the port of Fiume. Moreover, although included on the Supreme Council at Paris, the Italian delegation felt patronized and at one point had walked out of the negotiations. From the process and results of the negotiations grew the notion of a "mutilated peace," for which Italian nationalists blamed both the major Western powers and the government in Rome.

The image of an Italy insulted and cheated in Paris was promoted by nationalist opponents of the government. This sentiment was reinforced in September 1919 when a nationalist poet, Gabriele D'Annunzio, led a band of veterans and seized Fiume in the name of the Italian people. D'Annunzio's bravado captured the imagination of Italians and kept the issue of dissatisfaction with the treaties alive in Italian politics. The occupation of Fiume received some covert official aid, but in the end it undermined the government by highlighting the weakness of its resolve to promote Italy's interests.

The government's apparent failure in foreign policy compounded popular dissatisfaction with its handling of domestic problems. The war, as we have seen, crippled Italian finances and led to widespread social unrest that was manifested in strikes by industrial workers and land seizures by veterans and peasants. There were chronic food shortages and the standard of living continued to decline through 1919. Italy looked more like one of the defeated nations than a victor.

The country's parliamentary system, long regarded as corrupt and ineffective, was soon implicated in the prevailing discontent. Cabinets had changed in rapid succession during and immediately after the war, and the perception grew that national recovery depended not on one parliamentary party or another (it seemed that they had all been given a chance) but on an entirely new system where political rivalries would not quickly lead to government paralysis. By late 1919 two main groups offered an alternative to what appeared a futile succession of centrist administrations: the Communists and the Fascists.

The Italian Fascist movement was officially inaugurated in Milan on March 23, 1919. Its founder and leader, Benito Mussolini, had been a Socialist before the war, but he had been expelled from the party when he rejected its noninterventionist policy in 1914 and called for Italy to join the Allies. Mussolini's socialism was deeply influenced by syndicalism, which eventually informed key aspects of the Italian variety of fascism. Syndicalism shared socialism's stress on workers' rights, but instead of aiming to install a strong central state power, it looked to a decentralized political and economic system in which syndicates (workers' associations) exchanged products and services among themselves. The utopian characteristics of syndicalism were part of the socialist tradition, but they were at odds with mainstream twentieth-century socialist programs.

Although many Fascist policies changed over time, the movement was consistently nationalist. Its 1919 program called for territorial expansion, including the seizure of more land from Austria and parts of Dalmatia from Yugoslavia. On domestic issues the early Fascists were social radicals, calling for women's suffrage, a republic, abolition of the senate, an eight-hour workday, worker participation in management, confiscation of church property, and land redistribution in favor of peasants.

The Fascists' status as a party was ambiguous. Mussolini ran as an independent in the first postwar election in November 1919 (he received only 5,000 votes out of 270,000 cast), and Fascists contested the next election in 1921. At the same time they behaved as an extraparliamentary force, seeking power by violence in the streets and fields of Italy more than by votes in parliament. The Fascists drew on sympathetic, unemployed veterans to form commando groups known as *arditi*, which quickly saw action against their Socialist opponents. In April 1919, Fascist squads destroyed the offices of the Socialist Party newspaper.

During 1919 the Fascists were a small marginal political force, probably numbering fewer than a thousand. By the end of 1920, however, their numbers had risen to 30,000, and their presence was widely felt. Strikes for higher wages increased, and in August and September half a million workers in the northern industrial cities, locked out by employers, occupied the factories and formed councils, soviet-style, to direct production. The government's decision to let the workers' movement run its course was interpreted by employers as weakness. They turned to Fascist direct-action squads (*squadristi*) to harass, intimidate, and attack their workers.

Rural landowners similarly engaged the *squadristi* to evict squatters from land and to break up agricultural labor unions and peasant cooperatives. Although they inflicted relatively few severe physical injuries, the Fascists destroyed hundreds of buildings, houses, and newspaper offices. Gradually the Fascists were drawn into de facto alliances with big industrial and agricultural interests. Employers and farm owners did not find Mussolini's initial policies—such as worker participation and land redistribution—attractive, but they saw in the Fascists a useful force against organized labor and communism.

Still harboring parliamentary ambitions, Mussolini attempted to reduce the level of Fascist violence from late 1920, as the party prepared for the May 1921 election. As usual the electors gave no single party a majority, but in 1921 it proved impossible even to form a workable coalition. Two of the largest parties could not be included in a centrist administration: The Socialists, with 123 seats of the 535 seats in parliament, would not enter a bourgeois administration, while the left-wing Catholic Popular Party (Popolari) embraced social reforms like land redistribution that were unacceptable to centrist parties. The prime minister, Giolitti, constructed a fragile coalition that included the thirty-five Fascist deputies in his government, but his administration lasted only a month.

For more than a year thereafter, the pace of cabinet changes accelerated, and in February 1922 the political crisis reached the point that for three weeks there was no government at all. Discontent with the political system drove support to groups that seemed to offer a radical alternative, and during 1922 the Fascists increased their membership from 30,000 to 300,000. As parliament became less and less relevant to government, direct action increased. Fascists carried out local coups, dislodging Socialist and Communist administrations in towns and cities. In May 1922, Ferrara and Bologna were taken over by Fascists, in July and August dozens of other towns, including Milan. The Fascists began to look more and more like a government-in-waiting.

In October 1922, the Fascist leadership decided to seize national power using paramilitary forces that would converge on Rome from different directions. King Victor Emmanuel III's uncertainty about the reliability of his troops was increased by the assessment of the army commander: "Your Majesty, the army will do its duty; however, it would be well not to put it to the test." On October 29, the king invited Mussolini to form a government. Although seizure of power by a "march on Rome" entered Fascist mythology, Mussolini was already in office when his forces arrived (by train) in the capital.

In strict terms Mussolini became prime minister of Italy constitutionally, for it was the king's prerogative to invite any member of the parliament to form a government. In a broader sense the Fascists had come to power illegitimately, for they had set out to aggravate political instability and paralyze constitutional government.

In the short term, Mussolini's government looked like a conventional, unstable Italian coalition. Only four of the fourteen members of cabinet were Fascists, but they held key posts. Mussolini himself was prime minister, foreign minister, and interior minister, the last one giving him control of the police. Other minor posts were held by liberals, nationalists, and even social democrats. This broad-based coalition was merely a smokescreen for the development of a one-party state, however, and from 1922 to 1926 Mussolini created a political system that consolidated his power.

Germany from the Treaty of Versailles to 1923

While Italians regarded the peace settlements as "mutilated," Germans regarded the Treaty of Versailles as a "dictated peace." Anger at the terms was exacerbated by the failure of the treaty to specify the reparations that would have to be paid. Germany had signed an agreement binding it to pay a sum yet to be determined, in effect the second blank check the country had signed in five years.

Resentment at the peace terms signed in June 1919 was superimposed on living conditions that were scarcely much better than during the war. The Allies continued the economic blockade of Germany until March 1919, making food suppplies scarcer and scarcer. Prices continued to rise, and unemployment grew as soldiers were demobilized. These were not promising conditions for social or political stability. Lloyd George had tried for a milder treaty for fear that very punitive terms would unleash a political crisis that communists could exploit to seize power in Germany.

Up to the middle of 1919, indeed, it seemed that communists represented the greatest threat to the center-left coalition elected in January. Communist revolts in Berlin, Munich, and Leipzig had been suppressed by the army and the Free Corps. But these reactionary military allies of the Weimar government in turn posed their own equally serious threat. Although apparently doing the bidding of the Social Democratic authorities, the volunteers of the Free Corps had little time for socialists of any stripe. In March 1920, when the government attempted to demobilize some of the Free Corps units, one unit

Women provide refreshments to one of the sailors brought into Berlin to suppress disturbances in January 1919.

marched into Berlin. Anti-republican politicians saw the opportunity for a coup against the government, and one of them, Wolfgang Kapp, tried to seize power. The army did not support what became known as the Kapp Putsch, but neither would it take action against the Free Corps, and the government was forced to flee Berlin. The coup petered out after only four days, however, because career civil servants refused to acknowledge Kapp's administration and because a general strike by workers paralyzed the economy.

But the Putsch had resonances elsewhere in Germany. In Bavaria the army command deposed the Social Democratic government in Munich and installed as governor Gustav von Kahr, a conservative supporter of Bavarian autonomy. In the industrial Ruhr, on the other hand, the left raised an army of 50,000 to counter the right-wing forces, and a brief civil war flared before the army suppressed the insurgents.

The army's actions in 1919 and 1920 clarified its political position. It would suppress the revolutionary left, but would support the revolutionary right actively (as in Munich) or passively (as in Berlin). Clearly the army command, with its tradition of influence over the political process in Germany, had no intention of supporting the republic in its own right.

The military coups of 1920 were part of a broader, but uncoordinated right-wing nationalist movement that emerged as a public force in the postwar years in addition to the mainstream nationalist parties that had contested the 1919 election. One of these groups was the small German Workers Party, founded in Munich in January 1919. It attracted conservative nationalists, including demobilized soldiers, and stressed the need to regenerate the German *Volk* (racially defined people) by eliminating the power of those it blamed for Germany's defeat: mainly Jews, but also Freemasons, communists, and socialists.

In 1920 the German Workers Party was joined by Adolf Hitler, an Austrian who had fought with distinction as a corporal (he was awarded the Iron Cross for bravery) in the German army. Hitler had taken on the mix of nationalist German ideas and anti-Semitism that circulated in prewar Austria, especially Vienna. When he was assigned by the army's political section to investigate the German Workers Party, he found it so compelling that he resigned so as to devote himself full time to the party. Under his leadership the party merged with another and took the name National Socialist German Workers Party (NSDAP or Nazi Party, the latter drawn from the German word *Nationalsozialist*).

The Nazi Party adopted as its symbol the swastika, an ancient symbol of continuity and rebirth, and in February 1920 set out its program. Specific points were nationalist and anti-semitic: repudiation of the Treaty of Versailles, union (*Anschluss*) with Austria, and denial of citizenship to Jews. The economic policy of the party reflected the status of many of its members, and favored small artisans and merchants over big business. War profits were to be confiscated, trusts nationalized, and department stores broken up into premises for small-scale retailers.

These policies reflected the fear for their way of life that artisans and small entrepreneurs felt was represented by the growth of large firms. The growth of large corporations and department stores, many owned by Jews, and the wartime system of giving contracts, had only furthered the process of concentration of ownership by driving many small enterprises out of business. The decline of the self-employed was marked by the increase of salaries and wages to 56 percent of Germany's national income in 1925, compared with 43 percent in 1913.

The Nazi Party assumed importance as the vehicle on which Hitler rode to power in Germany in the early 1930s, but in 1920 it was but one right-wing fringe group among many. The popularity of extreme groups and parties of both left and right grew in the five years following the war. Despite the evidence of optimism in the January 1919 election that center-left parties could manage the social and economic problems produced by the war, continuing hardships, aggravated by anger at the Treaty of Versailles, provided conditions that made extreme solutions more appealing.

Postwar conditions in Germany were mixed. Rates of unemployment certainly increased in 1919 and 1920 as Germany's huge army was reduced to the level specified by the Treaty of Versailles. But male unemployment was kept reasonably low by economic expansion and the removal of many women from the occupations they had held during the war. A degree of industrial peace was achieved by the Works' Council Act of February 1920, which gave workers a consultative role in matters like working conditions and welfare. A system of collective bargaining was introduced, and the number of unionized workers began to increase dramatically from 1920 onward. Although the number of strikes in 1920 (3,800) and 1921 (4,500) rose slightly in comparison with 1919 (3,700), they involved many fewer workers and lost days. The workers' situation was helped by legislation providing social security and unemployment benefits, and the overall aim and effect were to promote social peace.

In general, workers and employees maintained their real wages in 1920 and 1921, and the continuation of rationing and rent controls, together with controls on heating and fuel costs, helped protect many working-class families. Some workers, like unskilled railway workers, were as well off in 1921 as they were before the war, while others, like miners, improved their position over 1918. But other occupational groups, especially in the middle classes, like civil servants, saw their real wages continue to decline. Professional soldiers had their career expectations guillotined by the limitation on the size of the German army imposed by the Treaty of Versailles.

The war had produced a particular category of poor: war widows and their children. A third of the 1.8 million German soldiers killed had been married, and their surviving families lived on meager pensions. Millions of other soldiers were physically disabled or emotionally disturbed for varying periods of time that affected their ability to work, and many were reduced to begging.

On a more general level, German finances were in serious trouble. The war had been financed largely by loans and the sale of bonds, rather than by taxation, on the assumption that Germany would win and obtain reparations from the Allies. By 1919 the accumulated national debt was almost 160 billion marks, although the inflationary effects of indebtedness were largely concealed in the initial postwar period.

Conditions did not deteriorate badly until 1921, but even before then popular confidence in the center-left parties—the "Weimar coalition"—began to erode. In the June 1920 election they lost almost half the votes they had won eighteen months earlier, and their combined 44 percent of the vote gave them 206 seats in the 459-member Reichstag. The main right-wing parties—the German National People's Party, the German People's Party, and the Bavarian People's Party—garnered a third of the vote and 157 seats, while on the left the Communist Party and Independent Socialists won a fifth of the vote and 87 seats. Social and economic conditions, conflict between left and right, and resentment at the Treaty of Versailles had polarized voters. If it is true, as it is often said, that the Weimar Republic became a republic without republicans, the process was first evident in these elections in which the parties that created the constitution failed to attract the support of the majority of Germans.

Disenchantment with the republic increased from 1921 to 1923 as inflation began to rise and the value of the mark fell. The reasons were the way the war had been financed (by bonds and loans rather than taxes), and increases in the money supply after the war to pay for reparations and government programs. In 1914 one U.S. dollar was worth 4.2 marks, but by July 1919 it could buy 14. The exchange rate fell to 65 marks by the end of 1921, 192 by January 1922, then plummeted to 18,000 marks to the dollar in January 1923.

In the course of 1923, Germany fell behind in deliveries of timber and coal to France that were required under the reparations terms. The French and Belgians dispatched armed forces into the Ruhr—one of Germany's most important industrial regions—to ensure that coal deliveries were made. The German government ordered workers to resist passively, and France and Belgium were compelled to increase their forces' strength to 100,000 (the size of Germany's reduced army) and to run the mines and railroads themselves. While the occupation of the Ruhr achieved its limited goal of extracting goods, it also provoked active resistance and sabotage and led to clashes in which German workers were killed.

The German currency, already tottering, collapsed entirely so that by the end of 1923 there were 4,200,000,000,000 marks to the dollar. Paper money became virtually useless as a means of exchange; prices of goods were raised many-fold several times a day; postage stamps, which had previously cost a few pennies were overprinted with new prices in millions of marks. Although many workers were able to survive the inflation by securing wage rises that kept up with the falling mark, Germans on fixed incomes suffered terribly. The middle classes were particularly badly hit, and their savings—for their children's education and their own retirement—became suddenly worthless.

Under the impact of foreign invasion, which Germany had been spared during the war, and the collapse of the currency, the parties of the extremes saw an opportunity. The Communist Party in the Ruhr gained strength and entered coalition governments in Saxony and Thuringia. In Bavaria the radical right flexed its muscles. The state's governor, Gustav von Kahr, was a nationalist whom the Nazis hoped to persuade to lead an armed revolt

The German inflation of 1923 made paper money virtually worthless. Here children play with wads of bank notes as if they were blocks.

against the Weimar government; a threat to do this in Italy had catapulted the Fascists there into power the previous year. Von Kahr was unwilling to challenge the government head-on, but on November 8, 1923, Hitler and his supporters invaded a political meeting in a Munich beer hall and, in an emotional confrontation during which Hitler leapt onto a table and fired a shot into the air, persuaded the governor and others present to support an insurrection. The following day Hitler, who had found an ally in General Erich Ludendorff, a war hero and by 1923 leader of a racist political movement, led a march to the government buildings in Munich. By then, however, von Kahr and his conservative colleagues had decided that a revolt against Weimar was premature. Troops fired on the marchers, killing several. Hitler was arrested, tried, and eventually imprisoned.

There was one more burst of rebellion, by the communists in Hamburg in November 1923, but it, too, was suppressed, and by the end of the year there was some cause for republicans to be optimistic. During five stormy years of revolts, attempted coups, and counterattacks from both left and right, the center parties had retained authority. The republic had survived a disastrous peace treaty, an invasion, and a currency crisis that would have brought down many regimes. From late 1923 the Weimar Republic entered a period of relative calm and stability.

The Bolsheviks Consolidate Power, 1918–23

The most extensive and prolonged turmoil occurred in Russia where the Bolshevik Revolution, instead of settling issues, had aggravated conflicts, and the region descended into four years of war and civil unrest. The overthrow of the Provisional Government in November 1917 was broadly accepted, not least because the Bolsheviks were expected to respect the results of the elections to a constituent assembly at the end of the year. But voters in the most democratic of elections in Russia up to that time—all adult men and women were enfranchised—gave 419 seats out of 707 to the Socialist Revolutionaries (who were agrarian socialists but not Marxists), and only 168 seats to the Bolsheviks. Threatened with losing power, the Bolsheviks used their Red Guard military forces to have the Assembly dispersed on January 10, 1918, the day after it met. This act set the tone for Bolshevik intolerance of opposition and for the wide-ranging and multilayered conflict that was to follow.

Initially Bolshevik policies rallied some support. A February 1918 decree, distributing large estates and church property to local people, responded to peasant land hunger, and legitimated many land seizures that had already taken place. The Treaty of Brest-Litovsk, despite its harsh terms, satisfied the desire for peace. On the other hand the dissolution of the constituent assembly broadened political opposition to the Bolsheviks, adding non-Marxist socialists to liberals, Mensheviks (socialists), national minorities, and supporters of the czar. The very spectrum of opposition contributed to its eventual failure, for common hostility to the Bolsheviks was not enough to overcome the differences between such diverse groups. The name "Whites" that is generally applied to the anti-Bolshevik forces gives a misleading impression of unity.

The civil war that raged from the summer of 1918 until the Bolshevik victory in 1920 was several conflicts in one. To the political conflict, expressed now in armed form because the Bolsheviks had rejected parliamentary change, was added the struggle of various national groups of the old Russian Empire to win or retain their independence. The Treaty of Brest-Litovsk had separated Ukraine and the Baltic states from Russia, although it effectively placed them under German control. When Germany's defeat made the treaty a dead letter, the Bolsheviks reversed earlier declarations of national autonomy and insisted on the integrity of the Russian Empire's territory.

In Ukraine, nationalists attempted to retain their independence, but were able to attract little support from the great majority of Ukrainians who were peasants and more concerned with agrarian matters than national politics. A 1918 German report noted that Ukrainian nationalism "has no true roots in the country. . . . The people as a whole show complete indifference to national self-determination," a conclusion echoed by another the same year; a British colonel suggested that Ukrainian peasants thought of themselves not as Ukrainians but as Greek Orthodox peasants who spoke "the local tongue."

Nevertheless, some councils of peasants, soldiers, and workers pushed for Ukrainian independence, particularly after the January 1918 Bolshevik seizure of power in Russia made political association with Russia inconceivable to them. Whatever passive or active support the Bolsheviks gained among Ukrainians, they lost it whenever they took control, by interfering with peasant communities and by harsh requisitioning policies. The final Bolshevik victory in Ukraine was won over the opposition of Ukrainians, and with the support of the largely Russian urban workers and the power of the Red Army.

In contrast the Baltic states—Estonia, Latvia, and Lithuania—retained their independence. In no case was it a matter of a mass nationalist movement seizing the opportunity to achieve a long-held aspiration of nationhood. In all instances, occupation by Germany in the period between the Russian Revolution and the end of the war gave nationalists an opportunity to establish themselves and to take advantage of the initial weakness of the Soviet state. Russian agreement to Lithuanian independence was secured after Polish forces invaded the capital, Vilnius, in 1919; the Russians considered an independent Lithuanian nation preferable to a greater Poland, with which it was already involved in border disputes.

Another dimension of the civil war was the intervention of Allied forces. Although justifying their initial presence on Russian soil in March 1918 as necessary to prevent the Germans from seizing supplies that would help their war effort, the Allies wanted the Bolsheviks defeated so that Russia would reenter the war. Once the general armistice was signed, the Allied aim became solely to defeat the Bolsheviks, who were regarded as expansionist and as a dangerous model for revolutionaries elsewhere in Europe. As the civil war deepened, more and more Allied troops were dispatched, and by mid-1919 fourteen countries had a combined force of 100,000 concentrated in eastern Siberia, the northern ports, and Crimea.

Despite the urging of politicians like the British war minister Winston Churchill and the French premier Clemenceau, the Allies were reluctant to pursue a war in Russia. Allied soldiers were war-weary, and their populations were in no mood to undertake another war just as one had ended. In the end the Allies did little more than provide funds, arms, and other supplies to White forces. Most of the Allied troops were withdrawn by the end of 1919, although Japanese forces remained in the Vladivostok region until 1922. The real legacy of Allied intervention was not the defeat of the Bolsheviks, but the enduring belief of Lenin and his successors that the Western nations were irreconcilably hostile to Russian communism and would even invade Russia to defeat it.

By the time most Allied forces left Russia in late 1919, the Bolsheviks were virtually assured of victory. The Red Army, organized by Leon Trotsky as commissar for war, had developed into an impressive force of more than 5 million, the great majority of them conscripted peasants. The Bolsheviks had been quite pragmatic, keeping on a large number of officers from the czarist army, though making sure that each was accompanied by a Bolshevik political commissar who countersigned orders. The White armies proved no match for the Reds. Not only were they unable to coordinate their activities, but they also were unable to offer a coherent political program. Nor was there a mass uprising against the Bolsheviks that the Whites had hoped would take place. The czar was eliminated as a rallying point for the right-wing opposition. He, Czarina Alexandra, and their children were removed from Petrograd to Siberia, and then to the Urals region. In July 1918, on orders of the Urals soviet, they were all killed.

The Bolsheviks used terror more broadly to consolidate authority within the territory they controlled, which had shrunk in early 1919 to the size of Muscovy in the sixteenth century. A secret police force known as the Cheka, originally formed to deal with disorder and looting after the October Revolution, carried out mass arrests and thousands of summary executions: almost 8,500 in the eighteen months to the end of 1919, according to the Bolsheviks themselves. On the whole, however, the Bolsheviks probably behaved no more ruthlessly than the Whites in the territory they controlled, so that the people at large had no reason to oppose one side more than the other for this reason alone.

In some respects at least, peasants, the overwhelming majority of Russia's population, probably thought of the Bolsheviks as the lesser of two evils. They at least supported the redistribution of land, while the Whites included elements committed to the virtual restoration of the czarist regime. On the other hand, there was resistance to the requisitioning of food that was instituted during the civil war, and to the conscription of peasants for the Red Army.

It was not that the peasants were singled out, for the civil war period witnessed the extension of state powers across the economic board. In 1918 a policy known as war communism brought large-scale industry, followed later by small-scale enterprises, under state ownership. The intention was to create a command economy to enable the government to control labor, resources, and manufacturing. There was to be no free trade in food, but instead a state-run distribution network. In many sectors Russia's cash economy began to fade, and increasingly wages were paid partly in food and other goods. Although aspects of war communism were superficially similar to the communist society envisaged by Marx, Lenin adopted it for pragmatic rather than ideological reasons. When it failed, he abandoned it.

More permanent tendencies did appear, however, such as the authoritarianism that became entrenched in the Soviet system. This was an early predisposition of the Bolsheviks, as their refusal to accept the 1918 electoral result showed, but it was no doubt reinforced in the following three years. The Bolsheviks' first experience of governing took place in a context of civil war and foreign intervention, and the primacy of the Red Army, the most successful institution of the new regime, put a military stamp on the Communist Party. For years afterward, army tunics and boots were the clothes of choice for many party members, a sartorial reminder that the regime had been born in battle. The Cheka, although formed before the civil war, became an agent of mass political repression during the conflict.

The Bolsheviks adopted authoritarian and repressive policies for both pragmatic and ideological reasons. As far as the latter are concerned, it was a tenet of Marxism that in a society divided into classes, one class would dominate and repress others. For the Bolsheviks, the October Revolution had catapulted the proletariat to power, and it was historically necessary for nonproletarians to be dominated, not only by force but economically and politically. The 1918 constitution reduced the universal franchise to include all "workers," which excluded categories such as employers, people living off private incomes, and priests. A 1919 manifesto, *The ABC of Communism,* described the application of class rule to justice: "In the old law-courts, the minority class passed judgment upon the working majority. The law-courts of the proletarian dictatorship are places where the working majority passes judgment upon the exploiting minority."

The Bolsheviks' desire to transform society was evident in other policies adopted during the early years. They were anxious to establish large-scale agriculture, and during the civil war some state and collective farms were established to replace smaller privately owned properties. This was accompanied by criticism of peasant individualism—for example, of the way peasants would sit down to eat as a family, rather than dine communally with other members of their communities.

This criticism reflected continuing pressure on the family, considered a bourgeois institution, and a source of women's oppression, inappropriate for the new society. Communal kitchens, laundries, and child-care centers were established to free women from household responsibilities so that they could engage in other work. Edicts on marriage and divorce were brought together into a new family code adopted in October 1918. In some respects, like its provisions for civil marriage and divorce, the code was similar to reforms in Europe (although divorce was much easier to obtain under the Bolshevik code). But in other respects, the 1918 code broke entirely with prevailing European legal trends and Russian legal tradition by abolishing the concept of illegitimacy, and giving women absolute legal equality with men. Adoption was banned on the ground that children whose families could not bring them up were better looked after by the state.

Some of the policies put in place in the early years of Bolshevik rule (like the secret police) became permanent fixtures, others (like the family policies) were less durable. But the first to go, after the civil war had been won, was war communism. By 1921 the Russian economy was in a state of chaos. Industrial production was a fifth the 1913 level, a result of shortages of raw materials, the Allied blockade, the breakdown of the transportation system, and poor management. There was a severe shortage of food, in part because peasants preferred to hoard or destroy crops rather than turn them over to the state, but also on account of a major drought in 1920. In 1913, when Russia produced 28 million tons of wheat and 26 million tons of rye, it had been a major grain exporter; by 1921 production of these two crops alone had fallen by 70 percent, to 6 and 10 million tons, respectively.

By 1921 starvation, epidemics, and the civil war had killed an estimated 20 million people, more than the Russian army lost in World War I. The famine, which was directly responsible for over 5 million deaths, was one of the worst in European history. People tried to escape its effects, but often with little success: One train that left Russia with 1,948 refugees on board reached Poland with only 649 alive, the rest having died of exhaustion, starvation, and infectious diseases.

In the area most affected by drought, between 90 and 95 percent of children under three died, as did a third of those older. Fridtjof Nansen, who coordinated postwar population exchanges for the League of Nations, reported that "hundreds of thousands of these poor little creatures are wandering about . . . in conditions of incredible suffering, want and destitution. Thousands of them die by the roadside or in the streets from hunger and disease." The government mounted an emergency plan to evacuate abandoned and orphaned children from the worst famine areas and place them in state-run homes. In 1918 these institutions housed 75,000 children; by 1921, 540,000. The government also organized public kitchens and sent relief by train, but even though millions were fed, millions more continued to starve.

In addition to demographic and economic devastation and widespread starvation, extensive social disorder broke out. It took the forms of strikes, food riots, and mutinies in the army and navy. There was a wave of banditry in the countryside, much of it by former Red Army soldiers (2 million were demobilized by early 1921) who faced unemployment and hunger.

In 1921 the government replaced war communism, whose results had been disastrous, and adopted new policies that became known as the New Economic Policy (NEP). Instead of having their grain requisitioned by the state, peasants would pay a 10 percent tax in kind on their produce, but were permitted to market the surplus, and individuals and cooperatives were allowed to lease and operate nationalized industries. The result was a rapid increase in both agricultural and industrial production, the former being helped by climatic improvements. Between 1921 and 1924, cereal production doubled and the potato crop not only recovered but exceeded the 1913 level.

There were costs, however, because the shift to the NEP led to mass unemployment as concern for profitability grew. State employees like teachers and medical personnel were laid off in large numbers. Most of the unemployed were women, who by 1922 constituted two-thirds of the registered unemployed.

But the revision of economic policy was not matched by a shift toward political toleration. The repression of opposition parties continued, with prominent members being executed, imprisoned, or exiled from Russia entirely. Lenin also reversed the Bolshevik practice of allowing free discussion of policies *within* the party. Even though it was a rule that, once adopted, a party policy would be supported by all members, Lenin was concerned about the development of permanent factions. With the assistance of Stalin, his right-hand man, Lenin persuaded the 10th congress of the party to ban factional activity. This effectively put an end to the party's tradition of allowing a relatively high degree of internal democracy, and helped establish the conditions for dictatorship. Stalin became general secretary of the party in 1922, soon after Lenin suffered a major stroke, and was well placed to assume leadership when Lenin died in January 1924.

Conclusion

The five years following the outbreak of the First World War had far-reaching social, economic, and political repercussions. There is no easy way of summarizing the period, although it might be said that it saw the resolution, albeit often temporary, of social and political conflicts that had long been undercurrents in Europe. Some, like demands for women's enfranchisement, had been more vigorous issues before the war than during it. Others, like nationalist aspirations, developed sharper form during the war than they had before.

One thing is clear, however: Mass participation in political change arrived in the immediate postwar period. This refers not only to the enfranchisement of women in many countries (though they remained excluded in others), but also to the intervention of workers, peasants, and the bourgeoisie, not just as voters but as rioters, revolutionaries, and squatters, all on an unprecedented scale. As elitist as their leaderships might be, political movements across the spectrum, from communists to Nazis, would draw on mass support.

The postwar period gave Europe's aspiring leaders a new set of social and economic grievances to exploit, for if the outcome of the war left Europeans shaking their heads, the following years saw them shaking their fists. Unemployment and poverty were more extensive than before, and threatened to engulf even members of those social classes that had thought themselves safe. The reorganization of political frontiers resolved some national disputes, but in doing so created others.

If a sort of peace and stability had settled over most of Europe by 1923, it seemed to have come from exhaustion rather than any conviction that the disputes were resolved, the grievances satisfied, or the tensions calmed. Nonetheless, at the end of 1923, in contrast to the preceding years, it must have seemed that peace had finally reached Europe, ten years after its departure, and fully five years after its return had been announced. Putting the best possible face on things, Europe's leaders began to talk about achieving normality.

· 5 ·

Attempts at Normalization, 1923–1929

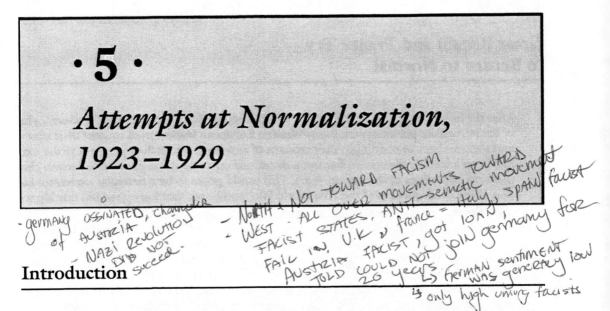

[handwritten annotations:]
- germany ossinated, chancelor of austria. Nazi revolution did not succeed
- North + west - Not toward facism. All over movements toward anti-semitic movement. facist states, Italy, spain facist
- Fail in U.K, France = Austria facist, told could not join germany for 20 years. got loan. German sentiment was generally low → only high among facists

Introduction

By 1923 the aftershocks of World War I had dissipated. If revolutionary activity had not entirely vanished, it was at least far less troublesome for the established authorities. The elevated marriage and birth rates (which were welcomed) and divorce rates (which were not) were falling. After being battered by rapid inflation and currency crises, Central and Eastern European economies had begun to stabilize. From about 1923, Europeans thought they might begin to return to normal and in some senses put the war behind them.

The very idea of normality—the word was used frequently to describe political aims—is an interesting one. It clearly did not mean a return to the status quo before the Great War, something that Eastern European governments in particular had no desire to see. For the most part the word *normality* was a value-laden concept that meant whatever the user wanted it to mean. In many cases it referred simply to a stabilization of political, social, and economic forces, a diminution of the volatility that had characterized the immediate postwar period. In other contexts normalization referred to a specific balance of social and economic forces in a specific state, such as the secure enjoyment of dominance by one class or one ethnic population.

In international affairs, normality certainly did not mean a return to the past, but rather attempts to create a quite different international political climate. There were attempts to create mechanisms for limiting armaments and negotiating between states in conflict. Compared with the decades that preceded and followed, the 1920s were in fact years of peace.

The period of normality, or attempts to return to normal, was to prove short lived, because in 1929 the global recession produced another set of economic, social, and political shocks to much of Europe. The Great Depression, which by 1930 began to affect Europe's economies, then its social and political structures, did not come completely out of the blue or even wholly from the United States. Throughout the 1920s there were fundamental social, economic, and political weaknesses that explain the transformations a number of states experienced between 1929 and 1934. Beneath the surface of relative normality and stability, in short, ran currents that would again lead Europe into turmoil.

Great Britain and France Try
to Return to Normal

After the immense upheavals of the First World War and the political and social aftershocks of the immediate postwar years, many Western European leaders tried to steer their states and societies back to conditions they thought of as normal. From their perspective the war had been a terrible aberration but not a disastrous one, and it was possible to recover the practices and values of the prewar years. This would prove to be a dramatic underestimation of the consequences of the First World War, and hopes that Europe would quickly recover the relative stability it had had before 1914 were soon dashed.

In both Britain and France voters flirted briefly with left-wing governments before returning more conservative administrations to power. The first socialist government in Britain, the Labour Party administration that took office in January 1924, had a minority of seats in the House of Commons and governed only because it was supported by the Liberals. Led by Ramsay MacDonald, it set out to extend social security programs, establish a minimum wage, and introduce progressive taxation. In order to maintain Liberal support, the government tried to distance itself from communism by avoiding Marxist terms, but it nonetheless embraced socialist programs, by advocating the nationalization of key industries like coal mines, railways, electricity, communications, and the manufacture and sale of alcohol. Little progress was made in any of these areas because the Labour administration fell after only ten months. Its main domestic achievements were to reduce tariffs on imported basics like tea and sugar, and encourage the construction of housing for low-income families.

Conservatives, who had painted the Labour Party as communist, were not reassured by the government's comparatively moderate program. Their worst fears seemed justified when one of the first acts of the new government was to extend British recognition to the Soviet Union, on February 1, 1924. This was followed by steps to improve relations between the two countries: A commercial treaty gave the Soviet Union most favored nation status, and attempts were made to settle British claims for property confiscated by the Soviet authorities. Although the Labour government felt some ideological affinity to the Soviet government, the party had in 1920 decided that Bolshevism was incompatible with British democratic traditions. The policy of improving relations with the Soviet Union was largely motivated by the hope that exports to the huge Soviet market would stimulate the British economy.

In 1924 industrial production in Britain was still sluggish as traditional markets were supplied by the non-European producers that had come to the fore during the war. Despite rising world demand for textiles, coal, and iron and steel, British production and exports stagnated or declined. In the mid-1920s more than half Britain's steel-making capacity was idle. The main result of these doldrums in the highly industrialized British economy, whose technology was rapidly becoming outdated, was continuing high levels of unemployment. Throughout the 1920s the number of unemployed remained over a million, more than 10 percent of the workforce and two or three times the rate common before the war. Increased employment in newer but smaller industries like chemicals and automobiles made little impact on the unemployment figures.

A combination of Labour's closer relations with the Soviet Union and other issues such as an allegation that the prime minister had accepted a limousine for his personal use, led the Liberals to withdraw their support from the government in October 1924.

This third general election in less than two years provoked little public interest until a week before voting when the *Times*, which supported the Conservatives, broke a story that purported to link Labour's Soviet policy with communist aims. According to the *Times*, Gregory Zinoviev, the Soviet head of the Comintern (the Communist International organization run from Moscow), had instructed the British Communist Party to support Labour's policies because they would further the cause of Bolshevism in Britain. The "Zinoviev letter" was later shown to have been forged by a Polish anticommunist, but it played a critical role in the 1924 election. Both Labour and Liberal parties lost support and the Conservatives, led by Stanley Baldwin, regained power and held it for the rest of the decade.

In contrast to Labour's plans, the Conservatives set out to regenerate the economy by restoring prewar liberal economic policies. This was part of their notion of getting back to normal. In April 1925, the British pound returned to the international gold standard and was fixed at its prewar level. Prominent economists like John Maynard Keynes argued that this overvalued the pound in relation to the dollar and would lead to deflation in Britain and make British goods expensive abroad.

But the basic weakness of the British economy lay in the loss of vital markets during the war and its inability to recover them by competing efficiently. Coal mining was especially sensitive because it was the largest single employer in the country. But coal exports were poor: There was a world glut, and British mines suffered low productivity because of outdated equipment and because the fragmentation of ownership among many small companies prevented economies of scale. In 1925 a confrontation developed when mine owners repudiated their contract with the miners. Fearing wage reductions, miners argued that the owners should use their wartime profits to improve equipment and management. Fearing a strike, the government paid the owners a temporary subsidy to maintain wage levels, and set up a royal commission to inquire into the coal industry.

The commission's report in March 1926 satisfied neither side. Among other things, it called for less profitable companies to be merged with stronger firms, for profit-sharing and housing schemes to help workers, and for miners to accept wage reductions during the transition. Negotiations between workers and owners broke down, and on April 30 the coal miners went on strike. When the government declared a state of emergency, the TUC (Trade Union Congress, the federation of individual unions) declared a general strike on May 4, which brought workers in other key industries out on strike as well.

As many as 4 million workers were involved in the strike, which affected critical industries and services like mining, the railways, buses, electricity, gas, and newspapers. The government employed the armed forces to maintain electrical and gas services using stockpiled coal supplies, and middle-class men and women volunteered to operate the buses and trams. The TUC quickly recognized that a prolonged strike would be futile, and called it off on May 12, after only eight days. The coal miners stayed on strike until December, when financial hardship forced them to give in.

The 1926 general strike was a victory for the government, which consolidated its position by outlawing general strikes and sympathy strikes, and by restricting union activities in other ways. Allegations that the Soviet Union had contributed to the coal miners' strike funds gave the government an opportunity to reverse Labour policy and sever diplomatic and trade relations with Moscow. The general strike was portrayed by many Conservatives as an attempt by communist-influenced workers to seize state power. For their part, unions, which had joined the strike for economic not political reasons, recognized that economic recovery was to be achieved at their expense. Embittered industrial relations in Britain were the legacy of the general strike.

France experienced superficially similar political trends in the 1920s, although in a different economic context. In elections in May 1924 the conservative administration of Raymond Poincaré, whose hardline policy toward Germany had been discredited, was replaced by a coalition of moderate left-wing parties, the Cartel des Gauches (Cartel of the Left). The main partners were the generally liberal and fiercely anticlerical Radicals, and the moderately Marxist Socialist Party. Although the two were able to agree on some policies, they differed profoundly in matters such as the extent to which the state ought to be involved in the economy. The achievements of the government elected in 1924 and led by premier Edouard Herriot, a Radical, reflected the extent of common ground: Diplomatic recognition was given to the Soviet Union and education was reformed to reduce elitism and church influence.

But these policies were cosmetic when compared with the financial problems France confronted. By 1924 industry in France had bounced back from the war more effectively than in Britain, but the costs of reconstruction placed immense burdens on the treasury. The Cartel's term in office was littered with failed attempts to reduce the budget deficit. New or increased taxes on real estate, incomes, and tobacco were rejected, and the United States refused a request to link payment of French war debts to receipt of German reparations, which were already seriously in arrears. Financial and political crises intensified in tandem (Herriot resigned in April 1925 and the Cartel went through seven ministries in a little over a year), inflation rose, and confidence in the franc fell, until the Bank of France refused to lend the government money for its ordinary operating costs.

In desperation the president of the republic asked Raymond Poincaré to form a government of National Union to save the French franc from the kind of disaster that had befallen the German mark in 1923 (thanks in part to the invasion of the Ruhr that Poincaré himself had ordered). Such was the new premier's reputation as a solid manager that the franc began to recover before any new policies were introduced, and the National Assembly gave him emergency powers to deal with the financial crisis. Poincaré's thoroughly conservative remedies included raising interest rates to attract investment and increasing indirect taxes (which hit workers harder than the better off). In 1928, when the franc had recovered much of its lost value, it was returned to the gold standard.

Despite the financial problems, the French economy in general grew through most of the 1920s, thanks in part to state investment in key areas like transportation, electrification, and housing. From 1924 to 1929 industrial production grew by 5 percent a year, a rate that would quickly erase the productivity lost during the war and immediate postwar years. Several sectors showed remarkable growth. One was automobile manufacturing, which was able to benefit from converted munitions and aircraft factories. By 1928 France was producing a quarter of a million cars a year, and associated industries like rubber production and oil refining experienced a parallel boom. The chemical industry also grew dramatically, thanks in part to a clause in the Treaty of Versailles that allowed it to use German formulas and research without paying royalties.

The war had intensified regional disparities in industrial development. A few restricted areas, notably Paris, had been chosen for the relocation of industries during the war, but after the war funds were granted for industrial reconstruction only when it took place in its original location. The result was that the west, southwest, and center of France remained chronically bereft of industry.

Nor did agriculture flourish in these regions, and productivity per unit of land in France was far lower than elsewhere in Western Europe. The explanations lay in the multitude of small farms, low levels of mechanization, and failure to use advanced methods of production. The 1920s saw a steady migration of young people from the countryside to the towns and cities. Between 1919 and 1931 almost a million people made the move, contributing to France's finally becoming a country with a predominantly urban population.

Attempts to normalize political arrangements and stabilize economies and financial systems after the disruptions of the war interacted with entrenched social trends. Unemployment in Britain throughout the 1920s remained at levels unanticipated by unemployment insurance plans. Although benefits were extended in 1924 and again in 1927, many of the unemployed remained outside the scope of the plan and had to fall back on the Poor Law. In the nineteenth century this had meant being institutionalized in a workhouse. Even though this was no longer the case in the 1920s, recipients of welfare were stigmatized by having to report to a workhouse (euphemistically renamed "Poor Law institution") for a medical inspection and classification. The inability of the old system to cope with the new demands led to the abandonment of the Poor Law in England in 1929 and in Scotland in 1930.

Chronic unemployment and poverty affected a substantial proportion of the British population. General mortality rates were higher in poorer regions of Great Britain, especially in areas of high unemployment like Scotland, Wales, and northern England. Children of poor families suffered from rickets, anemia, and other effects of malnutrition, and infant mortality was markedly higher among poor families. Whereas overall infant mortality rates fell in England during the 1920s (the trend was less clear in Scotland where poverty was more extensive), the maternal death rate began to rise in 1925. A 1929 investigation concluded that half the deaths were attributable to poor prenatal care and methods of delivery.

Growing concern about widespread poverty and ill health and the role played by unrestricted fertility led to the development of more tolerant attitudes toward birth control. In 1923 Marie Stopes, one of the most prominent birth control activists, filed a libel suit

A German Communist Party poster promoting the right to abortion in order to spare women the burden of children for which they could not care.

against a Catholic doctor who had accused her of "experimenting on the poor" in her clinics. Stopes lost the case but won on appeal, and the case gave the birth control campaign unprecedented publicity. By the end of the decade the Church of England had softened its stand against contraception.

The gradual acceptance of contraception, to the point that it would soon become an integral part of health advice, marked a shift from the official preoccupation with encouraging fertility in Britain. This occurred despite the continued decline of the birth rate, which by the late 1920s was a third lower than its prewar level. The acceptance of a lower fertility rate was an indication that, in the short term at least, Britain's economy could not accommodate unrestricted population growth. Even with declining fertility, population rose more than 5 percent from 37,887,000 in 1921 to 39,952,000 ten years later.

In contrast to Britain's declining birth rate, France's stabilized in the 1920s at between eighteen and nineteen births per thousand population, the same as in the prewar years. It is possible that the decline was slowed by draconian laws passed in 1920 to penalize abortion and even publicity about contraception. But because of high mortality (about seventeen per thousand), the fertility rate was barely enough to maintain a stationary population, and three-quarters of France's demographic growth in the 1920s resulted from the arrival of nearly 2 million immigrants. Half came from neighboring countries, especially Italy, where unemployment was high.

Weimar Germany Between Inflation and Depression

Securing normality was even more urgent in Germany after four years of war followed by five years of political and economic turmoil. In August 1923, a broad coalition government was formed under the leadership of Gustav Stresemann, its members ranging from the left-wing Social Democrats to the moderate-right People's Party. It dealt quickly with the monetary crisis by creating a new currency, the rentenmark (each worth a trillion old marks). Because of lack of gold to back it, the new currency was supported by a mortgage on Germany's land, industry, and assets. At the bottom of Germany's financial problems were war reparations, and Stresemann (who became foreign minister in November 1923 and remained in the post until his death in 1929) set about the task of obtaining a revision of the payment schedule. By late 1923 even French premier Poincaré, whose Ruhr venture had backfired politically, was forced to support the idea of an international commission to investigate how German reparations should most effectively be paid.

The commission, headed by an American financier (and later U.S. vice president) Charles Dawes, reported in August 1924. It recognized that more would be lost than gained if Germany were weakened economically and thereby exposed to political turmoil, and it concluded that reparations should be based on Germany's ability to pay, not on Allied needs or revenge. Under what became known as the Dawes Plan, payments would be derived from new taxes and income from the German railways. In recognition of the fragile state of Germany's economy, payments in the first years would be modest, and foreign loans would be extended.

In practice the Dawes Plan helped promote German economic recovery: Between 1924 and 1930 $4,500 million was invested, most from American sources. This inflow of money made it relatively easy for Germany to pay its reparations debts and to finance central and local government without recourse to higher taxes. In 1924 another new currency was introduced, this one based on gold. Germany looked increasingly prosperous but American financial penetration made the German economy more and more dependent on the United States. The risks this entailed became clear in 1929.

More broadly the reorganization of German finances after 1924 produced a restructuring of the economy. Controls on money forced many small and marginally profitable businesses to close or merge with larger firms, resulting in huge cartels with control of much of the market. I. G. Farben, a conglomerate formed in 1925, dominated Germany's chemical and dye industry, and the United Steel combine, created the next year, produced half the country's steel.

The recovery of the German economy was accompanied by a shift to the right in its governments. In 1925 the Social Democrat president was replaced by Paul von Hindenburg, a seventy-eight-year-old Prussian field marshal, monarchist, and war hero. He failed to win a majority of the popular vote, but his 48 percent was enough to beat the candidates of the Center and Communist Parties who attracted 45 and 6 percent respectively. In the 1928 Reichstag elections, support for the left increased, but votes were still so scattered across the political spectrum and representatives scattered across the assembly by the system of proportional representation that the new Social Democrat chancellor Hermann Müller was compelled to govern with a coalition that included centrists and conservatives.

On the surface, at least, Germany achieved political stability within the Weimar system after 1924. Political assassinations, attempted coups, and factional street fighting were markedly less common.

But important political leaders and groups remained hostile to the very existence of the republic. Even such a dominant political presence as Gustav Stresemann supported Weimar for pragmatic rather than ideological reasons. His German People's Party originally campaigned against the republic, but became a key participant in coalition governments in order to contain the Communists and the more extreme among the Social Democrats. Although Stresemann was instrumental in having reparations revised, as a conservative nationalist he remained essentially committed to undoing the Treaty of Versailles and even to revising the borders Germany had been forced to accept in 1919. President Hindenburg himself was not committed to the republic, and his advisers prepared various contingency plans for the use of emergency powers to establish a presidential dictatorship.

Nor was the far left, in the form of the Communist Party, reconciled to the Weimar Republic, which had been born not only in the defeat of Germany and its army, thus alienating conservative nationalists, but also in the defeat of communist revolutionary uprisings. Throughout the 1920s German Communists came more and more under the direction of the Soviet Union, which discouraged cooperation with the Social Democrats in defense of the republic. Even the so-called Weimar parties, such as the Center and Social Democrats, although committed to the republic's constitution, wanted some changes. All, for example, favored some revision of the Treaty of Versailles.

Beyond political parties and personalities, key institutions in Germany had little time for the Weimar Republic. The civil service remained a hostile elite. The judiciary showed its colors when it dealt with Weimar's opponents: Those who challenged the republic from the right were treated with far more leniency, when they were dealt with at all, than Communists. One Communist was jailed for four weeks for calling the Weimar state a "robbers' republic," while a right-winger who called it a "Jew's republic" was merely fined

70 marks. For his attempted Putsch in 1923, Adolf Hitler was sentenced to light detention in a fortress, where he received visitors and wrote, rather than a term in jail.

The army, much reduced in size and effectiveness and deprived under the Weimar constitution of the domestic role it had played before and during the war, was loyal to Germany not the republic, and remained committed to the destruction of the Treaty of Versailles. Working contrary to government policy, the army made secret arrangements with the Soviet Union to acquire weapons forbidden under the Treaty of Versailles. In 1926 the army chief of staff approved a memorandum arguing that Germany needed to acquire territory (including Austria), rearm, and regain its European and global position by peaceful or military means.

German universities were also notable centers of anti-republic sentiment, just as they were of anti-Semitism. Students were drawn predominantly from the middle classes, which had suffered most from the 1923 inflation and blamed the republic for their losses. Students, whose employment prospects after graduation deteriorated during the 1920s, gravitated toward right-wing nationalist groups, like the Nazis, that offered radical solutions. Farmers, too, laid their grievances on Weimar's by now rather crowded doorstep. Increased agricultural productivity had not produced prosperity because global surpluses had sent international prices plummeting. Between the periods 1919–22 and 1927–30, the price of wheat fell 40 percent, and milk and meat fared little better. Political support in agricultural regions, especially Protestant areas, shifted to right-wing parties.

Many of the economic and social conditions of the time tended to weaken the Weimar Republic. Despite the recovery of the economy, unemployment remained high at around 8 percent, although it rose to 18 percent in 1926. The number of long-term unemployed began to increase, partly as a result of technological changes as German industry modernized. An example is mining, where in 1913, 98 percent of the coal was extracted by hand and pickax, but by 1929 only 7 percent was mined this way, and 87 percent by more efficient pneumatic drills. With the new equipment, each miner's annual output rose from 255 to 350 tons between 1925 and 1929 alone, and the result was a decline in the number of miners, from 545,000 in 1922 to 353,000 in 1929.

The general modernization of German industry marginalized many workers, particularly the large cohort of young men born early in the century when birth rates were still high. Too young to fight in the war, they had survived it intact, and suffered the economic problems of the Weimar Republic. Young people experienced especially high rates of unemployment and their plight worsened when social benefits to the young were reduced. Many looked for political solutions at the extremes, both of which were hostile to the republic.

Entrenched male unemployment focused criticism on married women who worked and contributed a second income to their families. Although the criticism was based on the notion that married women ought not to work, there was broad acceptance of women's employment in occupations that were defined as female: as elementary school teachers, social workers, shop assistants, secretaries, and assembly-line workers. Such jobs were generally poorly paid, and where women did perform the same tasks as men they received lower wages.

In some respects women benefited during the Weimar Republic. They were able to vote, and in the 1920s they increasingly attended universities and other institutions of higher education, accounting for 12 percent of students in 1925. But even more than their male counterparts, women found limited employment opportunities after graduation, and many appear to have accepted the notion that they should cease paid employment once they married. The proportion of women in the German workforce remained relatively stable throughout the 1920s.

Marriage was an increasingly popular option, because in contrast to countries like Italy and France, where the marriage rate fell after the postwar marriage boom, in Germany the long-term decline was reversed and the rate rose from 14.2 per thousand in 1924 to 18.4 five years later. In numerical terms this meant that there were 446,000 marriages in 1925 and 597,000 four years later, a significant increase. To the despair of pronatalists, however, the rising marriage rate was not matched by the birth rate, which continued to fall: From 20.6 per thousand in 1924 it reached 18 in 1929, only half the rate at the turn of the century. They were all the more despairing because Germany had in 1927 implemented the Maternity Protection Act, which included provisions for maternity leave, breast-feeding breaks at work, maternity benefits, and protection from dismissal during the six weeks either side of giving birth.

But the impact of such policies was limited by economic realities. Women workers were entitled to maternity leave at half the basic wage (increased to 75 percent in 1929), but most pregnant women could not afford to take leave at any level of reduction. Many women, including domestic and agricultural workers—about a fifth of all employed women—were not covered at all. Clearly, German women and couples increasingly chose not to have children. Despite concerns about population, Weimar governments tended to relax laws against contraception and abortion. From 1926 those convicted of being involved in an abortion served their sentences in low- rather than high-security jails, and the next year abortions carried out in the interests of the mother's health were decriminalized.

There was a vigorous public debate in Weimar Germany on issues of family and sexuality, with currents running in various directions. One current called for the demystification of sexuality and its recognition as a natural attribute about which there ought to be no embarrassment or shame. The nudist movement, which had become prominent as part of the emphasis on health at the turn of the century, gathered strength in this period, particularly after vitamin D was discovered in Germany during the war and exposure to sunshine was declared beneficial to health.

Not only bodies but also sexuality became more public. There were discussions of sexuality in the press, and in Germany as elsewhere sex manuals began to sell in large numbers. Berlin became famous (or infamous) for its nightlife, which included risqué nightclub acts and pornographic shows. By 1929 the capital also had a thriving homosexual culture that was more open than those of other European cities. There were an estimated eighty gay and a dozen lesbian bars. Male homosexuality was punishable by law, but prosecutions were rare and there was a vigorous campaign to have it decriminalized.

Positions in the debate on sexuality in Germany often coincided with political ideologies. Many right-wing nationalists embraced nudity, especially male nudity, as part of a doctrine that promoted an ideal of a healthy, bronzed body as representative of the regenerated German race. Here nudity was associated with rural health, and often involved the rejection of smoking and drinking alcohol. Conservatives took pains to distinguish their ideal of nudity from representations of nakedness that they considered pornographic or decadent. A vast ideological gulf was constructed between rural, vegetarian nudism and urban cabaret striptease acts that were portrayed, together with pornography and homosexuality, as signs of the moral decline that was accelerating the physical degradation of the German people. Nudism also had supporters within the socialist movement. For them the principal merit of nudism was that it enhanced egalitarianism by stripping people to their common bodies and removing the external signs of status and rank provided by different styles of clothing.

The debate on sexuality also intersected with concerns about race, and particularly the place of Jews in German society. Right-wing politicians had an easy target in the form of Magnus Hirschfield, founder of the important Institute for Sexual Science and a campaigner for homosexual rights. Jewish men were often depicted as physically weak sexual perverts given to seducing or raping Christian girls, and corrupting the morality of Germans more generally.

These were not the only charges leveled against Jews in the 1920s when anti-Semitism continued to imbue many sections of the population and influenced the programs of a number of political parties on the right. Jews were targeted because they tended to be active in liberal and left-wing politics and to be overrepresented among professionals and intellectuals compared with their proportion in the population. As such they represented a secular and international culture that was anathema to nationalists. Jewish integration, in the forms of intermarriage and simple apathy toward their religion, was perceived by the right as a threat. Jewish leaders also deplored it for its effect of weakening the identity of the Jewish community.

Nonassimilated Jews and other ethnic groups were also regarded as "outsiders" dangerous to German society. After the war, many east European Jews, whose clothes, accents, and behavior were quite distinctive, and who did not assimilate, migrated to Germany in search of work. During the 1923 economic crisis, when unemployment first began to rise, the Bavarian government expelled all Jewish migrant workers and there were riots in those parts of Berlin where Jewish communities existed. Sinti and Roma (Gypsies), with their international itinerant culture, were also repugnant to nationalists. Although the Weimar constitution specified equality before the law, a 1926 Bavarian law forbade Sinti and Roma to move about or camp in bands (which included any group living together like a family). It also specified that Sinti and Roma unable to prove regular employment could be sent to a workhouse for up to two years.

Although anti-Semitism and the persecution of Sinti and Roma, homosexuals and other perceived threats to German society and culture were soon to be associated with the Nazis, they were widely diffused sentiments that were concentrated but by no means confined to nationalist and conservative parties during the Weimar period. The Weimar Republic was portrayed by them as not only tolerating but even encouraging "outsiders" and immorality that would lead to "the death of the race." The right-wing opponents of the republic were thus able to draw on long-standing tensions within German society, and to appeal to social and occupational groups that experienced declining fortunes during the 1920s.

Adolf Hitler's National Socialist Party, which was to come to power in 1933, set down its foundations during the apparently stable period of the Weimar Republic. After he was released from confinement in 1924, having written up his ideas in *Mein Kampf* (My Struggle), Hitler created the structure of the Nazi party, with himself as *Der Führer* (The Leader). Individual Nazi doctrines—anti-liberalism, anti-Semitism, and anti-communism—were common to right-wing parties, as were specific policies like its virulent hostility to the Treaty of Versailles. What was new (and what eventually drew voters to it from the older nationalist parties) was its youthful energy (Hitler was only thirty four at the time of the 1923 Munich Putsch) and its vision of national renewal.

The Nazis drew support from a broader social spectrum than any other party. The largest single group (about a quarter of the members) were workers but while they were underrepresented in the party in terms of their numbers in Germany, the middle classes were overrepresented, as were young men. Many members came from the groups that had suffered economically and socially during the 1920s or whose expectations had been dashed. They tended to be downwardly mobile Germans who saw Nazi policies as a way of stopping their decline. Many Nazi supporters categorized as workers were artisans who had been displaced by changes in the economy. The Nazi Party had made little headway by the 1928 elections, when it won only 2.5 percent of the popular vote and returned only twelve members to the Reichstag. But the Great Depression had a dramatic effect, and in

Adolf Hitler (right) at a Nazi
Party rally in 1927.

elections only two years later, the Nazis won 18 percent of the votes and, with 107 deputies,
became the second largest party in the German parliament.

In the years before the Depression, the republic was able to hold its own, although
there were clear signs of trouble. There was pressure from left and right, and a large pool
of residual sympathy for the regime that was toppled in 1918. In 1926 a national referendum defeated a proposed law that would confiscate the property of the former ruling
house. Disenchantment with politics produced in 1928 the lowest voter turnout (74.6 percent) of any Weimar election, and on the left the anti-republic Communists picked up half
a million more votes than in the previous election. It is often said that Weimar was a "republic without republicans." That was certainly not so, but by 1929 the constitutional and
ideological compromises on which the republic was founded had begun to break down.
The depression would administer the fatal blow.

Italy Under Mussolini, 1923–29

Mussolini, leader of the Italian Fascists, came to power in 1922, initially heading a coalition government that included members of liberal, conservative, and Catholic parties. But
the most important posts, including foreign affairs and the ministry of the interior, which
controlled the police, were in the hands of Fascists. Soon after Mussolini was installed as
premier, the Chamber of Deputies granted him authority to rule by decree for a year, a
not uncommon practice during the war, but one Mussolini used to undermine the democratic system itself.

A Fascist rally in the Piazza Venezia, Rome. Mussolini (barely visible at top center) takes the salute.

Fascists were soon appointed to key positions in the regional administrations, civil service, and the police. Other nationalist parties and movements, notably the monarchist and conservative Nationalist Association, were merged into the Fascist Party. To replace the undisciplined *squadristi*, a Fascist militia was formed in January 1923 and paid for from state funds, even though it was little more than Mussolini's private army. Members swore allegiance to him rather than to the king. By following conventional economic policies and reining in extremists (some party bosses were expelled or given posts in the colonies), the Fascists began to appear a respectable political movement. Mussolini personified the transformation, eschewing his black-shirt uniform for formal attire when he attended social occasions as premier, and taking lessons in deportment and protocol.

Fascist policies also changed as the party ceased being a fringe movement and began to court particular interest groups and constituencies and as it was influenced by its new Nationalist members. Mussolini distanced himself from many of the policies the Fascists had embraced immediately after the war. In place of earlier support for women's suffrage, by 1923 his government's commitment was to a watered-down policy of enfranchising only some categories of women, and then only gradually, beginning with the right to vote at the municipal level. An earlier commitment to legalize divorce, strongly opposed by the Church, was abandoned; in 1923 the minister of justice declared that the Fascist Party shared the Italian people's "profound and general repugnance to the institution of divorce." Mussolini's anticlerical and antimonarchist rhetoric was softened to the point of being inaudible.

For all that the Fascists looked like a conventional party pragmatically trimming its sails to the prevailing political winds, they were not prepared to operate within the law or constitution. Opponents of the government were regularly harassed or physically assaulted on Mussolini's orders, and some died of their injuries. Nor was Mussolini prepared to put up with the political uncertainties of Italian democracy. In 1924, in preparation for an eventual election, changes were made in the system of proportional representation that had produced perpetual deadlocks and frequent changes in government. The new law stipulated that the party with the largest share of the popular vote, providing that share was at least 25 percent of all votes, would get two-thirds of the seats in the Chamber of Deputies.

This law, designed to give Mussolini's coalition a comfortable majority, proved unnecessary, because in the April 1924 election, the Fascist-dominated National Bloc won 66 percent of the vote and 374 of the 535 seats in the Chamber. This was an impressive result; in the previous election (1921) the government parties had attracted 48 percent of the votes, and the Fascists had won only thirty-five seats. The 1924 election campaign was characterized by widespread intimidation and violence by the Fascists, which undoubtedly increased their share of the vote. Even so, the result also reflected Italians' disillusionment with the constantly changing governments, and many people were evidently impressed by Mussolini's first eighteen months in office.

The vote should not be seen simply as support for the Fascists, however, because the National Bloc included several other parties, including the Liberals. Nonetheless, Mussolini's policies attracted support from the middle classes because they promised to protect the status quo. The government coalition was also very popular in the agricultural regions of central and southern Italy, where chronically poor farmers hoped it would improve their lives. In the south, where the Fascists' Liberal partners were especially popular, Mussolini's ticket received 82 percent of the votes cast.

But Mussolini's success at the polls was almost immediately undone when Giacomo Matteotti, a Socialist deputy who had condemned the election as invalid because of Fascist violence, was abducted and murdered. Suspicion quickly and logically attached to the Fascists, not least because Mussolini had remarked of Matteotti, "That man . . . should not be allowed to go around." The men suspected of the killing were former Fascist squad members, believed to be members of a group operating from the Ministry of the Interior (which Mussolini headed) that specialized in attacks on the opposition.

In response to Matteotti's murder, which became a focal point for grievances against Mussolini's policies, opposition deputies and some Liberals walked out of the Chamber, vowing not to return until law and order were restored and the constitution respected. The crisis might have brought Mussolini down, but despite some misgivings the king was persuaded to keep him on as premier, and Mussolini was able to ride the crisis out by making some modest concessions. He surrendered the Ministry of the Interior to a Nationalist, and a well-known professor of law was named to the Justice Ministry. The militia was required to swear loyalty to the king, and Mussolini called on his party to distance itself from violence and illegality.

These conciliatory moves, designed to appease the outrage at Matteotti's death, provoked a reaction among hard-liners within the Fascist Party who called Mussolini's leadership into question. At the end of 1924, demonstrations by thousands of Fascists in several cities declared loyalty to Mussolini but on condition that he take decisive measures against opponents, "if necessary, by dictatorial action." Mussolini, who had either to try to conciliate the opposition and risk losing the support of his party or maintain his party leadership by acting decisively against opponents, chose the latter. In January 1925, the militia was mobilized, arresting scores of the government's opponents and searching offices and houses for evidence of antigovernment activities. Some anti-Fascist organizations were suppressed.

Thereafter, the Fascists were able to consolidate their power with relative ease. Opposition deputies who tried to return to parliament to fight the government were prevented from taking their places, and the Chamber of Deputies gave Mussolini almost unlimited power to rule by decree. The Senate, Italy's upper house appointed by the king, proved generally compliant. The opposition was further weakened by internal divisions, not least because the pope, impressed by Mussolini's pro-Church measures, had warned the Catholic political movement, the Popular Party, not to make common cause with the Socialists against the Fascists.

After 1926 Mussolini was able to establish an authoritarian regime with himself as dictator. Mussolini became known as *Il Duce* (The Leader) and surrounded himself with all the trappings of power, including an ornate uniform and large carefully orchestrated military rallies. Gradually the Fascist Party and state institutions were merged, a process culminating in 1928 when the Grand Council, the supreme body of the party, became an organ of the state. No longer made up of party bosses, its members from 1928 were ministers and top government officials, and its mandate was to advise Mussolini on constitutional issues. Although the monarchy was retained, the king was deprived of the authority to nominate premiers, the authority that had brought Mussolini power in 1922. Victor Emmanuel thus reaped the consequences of having failed to dismiss Mussolini during the Matteotti crisis in 1924.

By late 1926, Mussolini had seriously weakened Italy's democratic institutions: Local elections were canceled and Fascists appointed as mayors with increased powers; independent socialist and Catholic trade unions were suppressed; press restrictions and censorship were imposed and Fascists were appointed editors of important dailies; Masonic lodges, many of whose members were prominent anti-Fascists, were suppressed.

Several attempts on Mussolini's life in 1925 and 1926 contributed to growing demands for law and order that gave the government the opportunity to further the task of destroying Italy's democracy. All passports were withdrawn, opposition parties and newspapers were banned, and the mandates of opposition deputies were declared to have expired, depriving them of parliamentary immunity. A special tribunal was established to deal with antigovernment (now equated with anti-Fascist) activities, and the police were permitted to banish suspects to islands or to southern provinces, a reminder of their persistent isolation from the political heart of Italy.

In such ways Mussolini consolidated the authority of his authoritarian regime over a wide range of institutions between 1925 and 1929. The regime's slogan was "Everything within the State, Nothing outside the State, Nothing against the State," but even so the degree of coercion needed was light compared with that employed by many other authoritarian regimes in the 1920s and 1930s. The courts and justice system operated much as before, and although the new political police were very active, carrying out as many as 20,000 searches, arrests, or investigations a week, opponents of the regime were imprisoned or exiled rather than executed. The special tribunal ordered only nine executions between 1926 and 1940.

The development of an authoritarian regime did not lead to a comprehensive "fascistization" of government, and there was a high degree of continuity in Italy's administration. Civil servants could be fired if their beliefs were "incompatible with the general policy directives of the government," but few were. Little was done to fulfil pledges to cut the size of the bureaucracy, partly through fear of a backlash from those who would lose their jobs. The number of prefects (regional governors) was increased from seventy eight to one hundred. The military retained a great deal of independence, and many officers declined to join the Fascist Party. The autonomy of the three branches was strengthened when Mussolini took over all the responsible ministries himself; unable to run these plus the other ministries he headed (as well as being overall head of government), Mussolini effectively turned over control to senior bureaucrats.

Part of Mussolini's success lay in his ability to weaken potential rivals within the Fascist Party itself. When parliament became irrelevant, so did the Fascist deputies within it; the militia was brought under regular army control; the prefects, appointed by Il Duce, had more power than provincial party bosses. The Fascist Party itself was transformed as new members were admitted, many of whom joined not for ideological reasons but because they had occupations (like government clerks) in which party membership could be an advantage. At the same time thousands of old party members left or were purged. The new members swamped the old, their numbers depleted by 150,000 resignations or expulsions, and by 1927 more than half the party membership of 938,000 (up from 600,000 in early 1926) were new adherents.

As he consolidated power, Mussolini began to translate Fascist aims into concrete economic and social programs. One of the keys was the reorganization of economic relationships. Independent unions were replaced by Fascist syndicates, which by 1927 had more than 2 million members. But the Fascists aimed to "discipline" labor above all; syndicates were prohibited in key sectors, and strikes were forbidden. Some progress was made in setting up a system of "corporations" to replace the antagonistic system of industrial relations that pitted workers against employers. Corporations combined employees and employers, stressing the shared interests of both and echoing a key tenet of Italian fascism, that the common interests of Italians were more important than the narrow interests of specific groups, whether they were workers or employers, farmers or town dwellers, men or women.

But employers were initially treated more gently than workers: Some sectors (like life insurance) that had been nationalized were returned to private ownership, and taxes on excess war profits were reduced. State funds were used to help private companies. Between 1921 and 1925 industrial production rose by more than 50 percent, largely because of strong exports. But the low value of the lira (about 150 to the pound sterling) persuaded Mussolini in 1927 to revalue it at the *"quota novanta,"* 90 lire to the pound. The result was to raise the cost of Italian exports, while imports of foreign goods, which the new exchange rate ought to have increased and made cheaper, were depressed by high tariffs and by wage cuts that reduced buying power.

As imports and exports declined, the Italian economy turned inward. Certain industries, like steel and shipbuilding, which depended on imported raw materials, flourished but lacked external orders. The Fascists intended that Italy should become economically self-sufficient, a policy in which they had mixed success. By 1929 the chemical industry was producing all Italy's needs, and compressed natural gas was increasingly used in place of gasoline in automobiles so as to reduce Italy's reliance on oil imports.

Self-sufficiency in food production was more difficult to achieve. From 1925, after a poor harvest forced Italy to import 2.3 million tons of wheat, Mussolini declared a "battle for wheat." Tariffs on imported wheat were increased so as to raise prices, which both cut consumption and encouraged production. Although the policy succeeded in its narrow aims (production in 1926–29 was 12 percent higher than in 1922–25), it diverted resources from other areas of agriculture, reducing livestock numbers and forcing Italy to become an importer of olive oil.

Redefining the state's relationship with the Catholic Church proved more straightforward than reorientating the economy. Although initially anticlerical, Mussolini early recognized the importance of gaining the support of the Church. Many policies in the early 1920s, such as banning Freemasons, abandoning plans to tax church property, and restoring the crucifix to schoolrooms, were designed to attract Church support. The plan paid off, and the pope abandoned the Popular Party, which might have played an important role in blocking the Fascists' rise to power. Mussolini again personified the shift in principle: Although he had earlier condemned religious marriage and had himself married civilly in 1916, he went through a religious wedding ceremony (with the same woman) in 1925 and had his children baptized.

Such actions and policies were the public face of a long process of discreet negotiations between the regime and the Church that culminated in a concordat and other agreements. The Lateran Accords (named after the palace where they were signed in February 1929) ended the more than half-century-long refusal of the Church to recognize the Italian state. The Vatican City in the center of Rome was recognized as having sovereign status under the authority of the pope, with full diplomatic rights. For territorial losses after 1870 the pope was compensated with 750 million lire and a further billion lire in state bonds. Under the Concordat, which regulated state-Church relations, Mussolini agreed to allow religious education in all schools, recognize Church marriages provided they were followed by civil ceremonies, and permit Catholic organizations as long as they confined themselves to religious purposes and abstained from interference in political matters.

The Lateran Accords benefited both sides, though historians debate which gained more. The Church in Italy won a measure of territorial and financial security it had been denied since Italian unification. On the other side, not only did Mussolini's regime gain implicit recognition by the Church, but Pius XI hailed him as "the man sent by providence." Such blessings could only increase popular support and strengthen the Fascist regime. The Lateran Accords were ambiguous, however, and although they resolved some major disputes between state and Church, they also gave rise to new problems after 1929.

Among the disputes that had dogged state-Church relations were the roles each should play in education of young people. The Church's traditional claims in these areas were confronted by the Fascists' insistence on their right to influence young people so as to produce a generation of right-minded citizens. In 1926 a Fascist youth organization (the Balilla) was set up for boys and girls, combining sports, political indoctrination, and (for boys) elementary military training. Rival bodies, including the Boy Scouts and Catholic sports organizations, were closed down to ensure a Fascist monopoly.

In terms of education, indoctrination was most effectively achieved in the lower grades, where textbooks recounted Italian history from the Fascist perspective, including Italy's poor treatment after the war. Less concerted efforts were made to interfere with high school curricula, and in the universities little was done beyond creating new Faculties of Political Science that expounded Fascist ideas. University teachers were required to swear an oath of loyalty to the king and the Fascist regime, and to vow to train citizens who would be devoted to their country and the regime. More than 99 percent of them (1,189 of 1,200) swore the oath of loyalty. Similarly, most students joined the Fascist University Youth organization, which held social events and sponsored interuniversity debating competitions. On the whole, the acceptance of Fascist requirements by students and teachers probably reflected a pragmatic acquiescence in the minimum necessary to avoid harming their careers, together with a realization that, in the 1920s, Italian fascism was authoritarian but relatively benign.

The regime's attempt to control ideas went well beyond young people. As we have seen, the press quickly came under censorship. An even more effective medium, especially given widespread illiteracy in many rural areas, was radio. State radio stations, the only kind permitted, began to operate in 1925. Although radios were not common household items, they were often set up in cafés or town squares where each set could be heard by scores or even hundreds of people.

The Fascists quickly realized the political uses of sport and recreation, too. A national Dopolavoro ("after work") scheme was established in 1925 to provide recreational facilities such as sports grounds, billiard halls, bars, and space for plays and concerts. Dopolavoro provided summer holidays for children as well as organizing tours and trips for adults and families. From 280,000 members in 1926, the movement increased to over a million in 1929 (and 4 million ten years later). While there was little overt propaganda involved in these mass leisure activities, the point was not lost on members that they were subsidized by the state. In some areas Dopolavoro distributed food to the poor.

The standard of living was a constant concern. The vagaries of industrial relations contributed to fluctuations in workers' incomes, which generally declined from the mid-1920s, a process accelerated by a general wage cut of 10 percent in 1927. Agricultural wages also declined. At the same time, unemployment rose from 110,000 in 1925 to 324,000 in 1928. Many workers left Italy to work in France where there was a labor shortage. Changes in the marriage rate, often a guide to prosperity, suggested that there were problems. Following the postwar marriage boom, the marriage rate settled back at its prewar level by 1924, but by 1928 had begun to sink even lower.

The birth rate, meanwhile, did not recover its pre-1914 level, but continued the decline that had begun at the end of the nineteenth century. The rate fell throughout Italy, but it was lower in the more urban and industrial northern and central regions than in the rural and agricultural south and islands. Between the beginning and the end of the 1920s, the birth rate fell from 29.9 to 27.1 per thousand in the north, and from 36.3 to 33.8 in the south. In northern industrial cities rates hovered above 20 per thousand. White-collar families everywhere had smaller families than manual workers, whereas agricultural workers had larger families than industrial workers.

Ignoring the social variations of fertility by social group, an investigation was launched into the physical characteristics of men and women who had large families. Its findings, that women who had borne numerous children tended to be short and wide-hipped, was not helpful for the development of policy. Potentially more effective were measures such as prohibiting the advertising or use of contraception, banning abortion, and imposing a punitive tax on men who had not married by the age of twenty-six. Priests were exempt from the last measure.

Despite declining fertility, Italy showed signs of overpopulation, especially after United States quotas stemmed the flow of Italians to America from 1921. There was a shortage of land to settle rural families on, widespread poverty among large families, and rising unemployment. Yet Mussolini adopted a vigorous pronatalist stance (he declared a "battle for births"), in 1925 insisting that Italy needed to increase its population (then 40 million) by 50 percent, to 60 million within twenty-five years. Rapid population growth would serve a number of Fascist purposes. It would provide a rationale for territorial expansion as well as the human resources, in the form of soldiers, necessary to achieve it. A robust fertility rate was also linked in Italian Fascist doctrine to masculinity and national strength. The virility that births demonstrated was compared to the impotence and weakness betrayed by France's drooping birth rate. The connection of national power and the birth rate, not to mention Mussolini's notions of gender, was encapsulated in his declaration that "War is to man as motherhood is to woman."

Mussolini's population policy emphasized the role of women as mothers and wives first and participants in the wider social sphere afterward. With the abandonment of democracy, the issue of the women's vote became redundant (as did the men's vote), and the new policy became clear when in 1927 Mussolini told a delegation of Fascist women, "Go back home and tell the women I need births, many births." To assist mothers and help reduce infant and childhood mortality, the National Agency for Maternity and Infancy was established in December 1925. It was geared especially to help unmarried mothers and their children and to look after abandoned children. The effectiveness of the agency is unclear, for infant mortality rates were already declining and continued to do so.

In rural areas, the picture of women's employment is complicated by the division between those who worked for wages and those who worked as part of the family economy. There was a general decline in the first category, but the others had little option but to continue to play a full part in agricultural work. The official calculation in 1926 was that a woman's labor contribution was 60 percent of a man's, but that did not include the four or more hours a day women spent on household tasks, especially cooking and child care.

Despite forays into population policy and education, in the 1920s Mussolini tended to be more concerned with consolidating his regime than with remaking Italian society. Many of the social policies that were implemented, especially as they affected women, were not startling departures from mainstream European doctrine and practice. Although threats to his authority from the left and within the Fascist Party were repressed or neutralized, major institutions such as the Church, monarchy, military, large corporations, and the civil service, were conciliated rather than confronted. The revolutionary element in Italian fascism, although implicit in such innovations as a mass party and the leader principle, became much more evident in the 1930s.

The Smaller Western and Northern European States

Although many of the smaller Western European states had been neutral during the war, they experienced postwar disruptions of varying dimensions because of their economic relationships with the combatants. This was true in Spain, which had benefited from increased wartime exports, and where the end of hostilities led to falling demand, rising unemployment, and widespread unrest compounded by military setbacks: In 1921 a Spanish army of 20,000 suffered 12,000 casualties at the battle of Anual in Morocco. The result was political turmoil and fifteen governments between 1917 and 1923. Spaniards became so disillusioned that half the voters (only men were enfranchised) abstained from participating in the April 1923 elections.

The apparent collapse of the political system led to a coup mounted by General Miguel Primo de Rivera, the army chief in Catalonia where especially acute labor disputes had resulted in a number of deaths. Primo de Rivera, quickly appointed president of a military directory by King Alfonso XIII, declared that he would regenerate the constitutional life of Spain "so that normality can be established as soon as possible." Normality here meant ensuring respect for the Catholic Church and the monarchy within a populist nationalism. Although he adapted some ideas from Mussolini, his regime was not motivated by a coherent ideology, fascist or otherwise.

At first government was by officers (which, it was pointed out, saved additional salaries), but in 1926 civilians were added. Primo de Rivera, convinced that leaders with Spain's true interests at heart would emerge once corrupt and self-serving professional politicians were removed, was disappointed. He created the Patriotic Union, with the slogan "Spain, united and great." It was intended to be a mass movement of nationalists who would rally to the tasks of moral and economic regeneration, but attracted few adherents. Instead of arousing widespread support, the regime rested on extensive repression and disunity among its opponents. The press was censored, juries were abolished, and a paramilitary police force established. But it was a comparatively light repression, and enemies of the regime were more likely to be imprisoned than executed. Some moderate Socialists cooperated with the regime, which established compulsory arbitration boards to set wages.

An overriding aim of Primo de Rivera's regime was to make Spain economically as self-sufficient as possible. Import tariffs and government intervention, employed to promote industrial and agricultural output, combined with favorable external conditions to produce modest but real results: Between 1923 and 1929 annual coal production rose by 20 percent and cotton output more than doubled. Major capital projects vital to industrial development, like hydroelectric schemes and railways, were hampered by lack of capital. A plan to raise funds by reforming the tax system so that the wealthy paid their share collapsed in the face of opposition from those who would have been affected. When the government resorted to loans, inflationary pressures rose, and the value of the peseta fell. Still, the output of electricity from all sources doubled from 1923 to 1929 and communications were improved.

Social reform was modest. An extensive school-building program made some impact in a country where in the early 1920s almost half of the women and a quarter of the men remained illiterate. Low-cost housing schemes were undertaken and social welfare, notably maternity benefits, improved. The infant mortality rate, one of the highest in Western Europe (it was twice as high as Britain's) continued its steady decline. The regime's policy toward women was not confined to their maternal and familial roles, but it was guided by them: In 1924 women who headed families were given the vote in local elections. The 1920s saw a vigorous debate on gender, sparked in part by a 1927 feminist article provocatively titled, "Woman, Man's Problem."

But fundamental economic problems were not addressed. Agrarian reform amounted to little more than encouraging large landowners to sell small plots to peasants. The living conditions of industrial workers were scarcely improved and real wages probably fell during the period. As for the chronic problem of regional opposition to state centralization, Primo de Rivera's government appears to have encouraged Catalan nationalism rather than suppress it by abolishing the local government conceded in 1912 and by banning the public use of the Catalan language and the display of the red and yellow Catalan flag. The one notable success of the regime was external—the consolidation of Spanish control of Morocco by 1927.

In 1928 and 1929, opposition to Primo de Rivera's government began to widen in reaction to various policies. The universities became centers of opposition largely because of plans to allow Jesuit colleges to grant degrees. Sections of the army were disaffected by plans to reform the system of promotion. Moderate Socialists, who had cooperated with the regime, backed away. In January 1930, when the depression began to affect Spain's economy, Primo de Rivera, in declining health and two months away from death, resigned.

The economic crises that weakened his regime also produced political change in Portugal, whose participation on the Allied side from 1916 resulted in a huge debt, postwar inflation, and widespread industrial unrest. Although the economy stabilized by the middle of the 1920s, the middle classes had been affected adversely, and opposition to the government of the republic developed among key groups like army officers.

Ideologically, fascist ideas began to gain popularity among some Catholic intellectuals, particularly the faculty at Coimbra. In 1926 a group of army officers seized power and a mixed military-civilian regime governed for two years. One of its key members was

Antonio de Oliveira Salazar, a professor of economics at Coimbra who had written an influential criticism of Marxism, and by 1929 he had emerged as its leader. He subsequently ruled from 1932 to 1968, making him one of the longest surviving authoritarian leaders in twentieth-century Europe.

Under Salazar's direction, education improved and within four years of the coup the number of children attending school had increased by a quarter. Women attended school in larger numbers, but although Salazar was not sympathetic to women's rights, the freedom to divorce (introduced by the republic) was initially maintained intact because it was popular among middle-class Portuguese.

The historical trajectory of Ireland in the 1920s reflected attempts to achieve normality after the crisis provoked by the treaty granting southern Ireland independence from Britain. The treaty was opposed by many Irish republicans because it allowed Britain to retain control of Ulster, the northern part of the island. In 1922 and 1923 a civil war had raged, during which as many as 4,000 died and 80 rebels were executed by the government of the new Irish Free State.

The Irish state shared some characteristics with those created after the war in Eastern Europe; like them it was racked by civil war in the period 1919 to 1923. But its social, political, and economic character allowed it to establish a more stable government. The standard of living was comparable to the rest of Western Europe, and the virtual stagnation of the Irish population (the birth rate was far lower than in any Eastern European country) meant that there was little pressure on land. Most farmers owned their land and the minority who were tenants were enabled from 1923 to purchase their holdings. Education at the primary level was widespread and literacy almost universal, and the level of university attendance, only slightly lower than in Britain and France, provided recruits to the professions, civil service, and commerce. A well-developed political culture drew politicians and administrators from rural and small-town Ireland as much as from the cities. All adult women in the Irish Free State were enfranchised in 1923, five years before women's enfranchisement was completed in Britain.

Nor was the Free State plagued by the ethnic problems of its counterparts among new Eastern European states. The main division was religious, and that had been largely dealt with when Ireland was partitioned into a Protestant north and a Catholic Free State. Protestants amounted to about 5 percent of the Free State's population, and despite attacks by some ultra-Catholic groups, they were treated equally in law; it was partly to protect Protestants that the 1922 constitution embraced a system of proportional representation.

During the 1920s the Free State's predominantly agricultural economy was affected by falling world prices. The value of exports peaked in 1924 then declined, and a recovery in 1929 was cut short by the depression. The wages of farm laborers (a fifth of the workforce was in agriculture) fell steadily throughout the decade, and their numbers declined. Despite official statistics to the contrary, unemployment rates were high and very likely rose throughout the 1920s. Little was done to help those in need. In a drive to cut government spending, even pensions to the old and blind were reduced. In order to reduce what was perceived as a high level of alcohol abuse, the government tried to pass legislation restricting drinking hours and reducing the number of taverns; there was one liquor license for every 200 people in Ireland, compared to 1:400 in England and 1:700 in Scotland. But public pressure and the liquor interests combined to force its withdrawal.

Catholicism played an influential role in some areas of law. Divorce, which in Ireland had been available only by each couple getting a private Act of Parliament dissolving their marriage, was abolished entirely in the Free State. A 1929 censorship law targeting "indecent and obscene" work was used not only against pornography but also to ban works by

Irish writers including James Joyce and Sean O'Casey, and encompassed any literature advocating birth control.

Social inequalities produced divisions within Irish society, as did the unresolved conflict over partition into the Free State and Northern Ireland. In 1925 the Irish Republican Army (IRA), which had demobilized the year before, revived its army council. A new republican political force that emerged in 1926, the Fianna Fáil led by Eamon de Valera, attracted the support of many IRA sympathizers. Fianna Fáil campaigned in the 1927 elections, winning fifty-seven seats compared with the government's sixty-two. Taking the oath of loyalty to the British Crown, required of all Free State members of Parliament while the state remained in the British Commonwealth, posed a moral problem for republicans, but it was solved by covering the words of the oath while signing one's name, and placing the Bible, face down, as far as possible from the signing ceremony. This done, the party opposed to the Free State's constitution entered Parliament.

The Smaller Central and Eastern European States

Almost all the Central and Eastern European states, including the Baltic and Balkan nations, shared a common trend in the 1920s in that they began or completed the process of becoming authoritarian regimes. These regimes ranged from monarchies to civilian and military dictatorships, and whereas some were unambiguously fascist, others were authoritarian administrations motivated by no overriding ideology. The specific reasons for this broad tendency toward dictatorship varied from state to state, but certain obstacles to the development of democratic and liberal institutions were general throughout Eastern Europe.

A number of these states had been created after the war, and despite the long-standing aspirations of nationhood, their dominant ethnic populations possessed neither traditions of national statehood nor any real consensus on the way a sovereign state should be governed. Moreover, ethnic rivalries persisted where minorities remained within the nations established after the war; minority rights were seldom respected, and ethnic groups in some states wished to secede and join other states, turning national strife into international tension. Few Eastern European states had stable political cultures, and in the 1920s churches, armies, traditional elites, and peasants jockeyed for power. Governments faced what seemed intractable social, economic, and administrative difficulties. Finally there were persistent social and economic problems, notably the dominance of agrarian populations at a time of declining prices and rural overpopulation. Various combinations of these characteristics produced volatile political and social conditions that authoritarian regimes attempted to resolve by means ranging from conciliation to outright coercion.

Hungary, Austria's former partner in the Habsburg Empire, had by 1923 established an authoritarian regime after the tribulations of revolutionary government under Béla Kun in 1919. From 1921 Admiral Miklós Horthy, former commander of the Habsburg navy and one of the military officers who replaced Kun, presided over a quasi-parliamentary regime, with Istvan Bethlen as his prime minister. The franchise, open to all adult males in 1919, was restricted, and the abolition of the secret ballot in rural areas as well as some towns and industrial suburbs tended to dissuade workers from voting for parties opposed by the large landowners. The aim was to restore power to the landed elite.

Although parties like the Social Democrats that were opposed to the regime were able to elect deputies the parliament had few powers and was little more than a consultative assembly. The left wing, even the Social Democrats, had been discredited by its association with the Kun regime. The government regularly ignored constitutional guarantees of free speech and other liberties, and was guided by a policy of "Christian nationalist" regeneration. It was often expressed in ethnic or racial terms, in which liberalism, democracy, and socialism were portrayed as alien to the "Hungarian spirit."

Also regarded by the right as "alien" were Jews, who made up 6 percent of the population, and were especially prominent in the professions in Budapest and other urban centers. Bethlen himself opposed demands for anti-Semitic measures, partly because he feared that expropriation of Jewish property would undermine the legal security of private property and provide a model for assaults on non-Jewish wealth. For the same reason agrarian reform, the breakup of large estates and the distribution of land to small holders, was resisted.

The Catholic Church, to which 63 percent of Hungary's population belonged, supported the regime following an agreement giving it influence in government. (Both Horthy and Bethlen were among the 28 percent of the population who were Calvinists.) The Church had a say in the appointment of judges and other officials in regions that were predominantly Catholic, and retained control of the education of Catholic children. It had a virtual veto over the choice of education minister.

Hungary's economy survived the 1920s largely by means of loans. Some of the borrowed money was used to stimulate industry, which grew modestly between 1924 and 1929, but half was used to pay debts, including Hungary's share of the outstanding Habsburg debt. Despite a growing economy, unemployment remained high at between 10 and 15 percent, real wages were low, and from 1926 to 1928 there was a wave of strikes and hunger marches.

In Poland the postwar period witnessed civil war, a war with Soviet Russia, and political crises that included the assassination of a president in 1922. An elongated economic crisis culminated in the collapse of the Polish mark, dragged down by its German counterpart from an already atrocious 53,375 to the dollar in May 1923 to 6 million to the dollar seven months later. A general strike in 1923 led to clashes between police and workers and the deaths of several of the latter, and in December the government resigned.

There followed a period of normalization under Wladislaw Grabski, who had been a member of Sikorski's administration. Given a mandate by the Sejm to continue his work, Grabski established a national bank and created a new currency, the zloty, which was pegged to the Swiss franc. He also introduced land reforms, setting a maximum size for holdings of between 180 and 300 hectares (depending on region), and reached a concordat with the Church. As in Hungary, the Church won influence over education, an important issue in a country that was more than three-quarters Catholic.

In 1925 Poland experienced an economic crisis when Germany, a major market for Polish coal, declined to purchase any Polish goods at all until the Germans in Poland (4 percent of the population) were granted concessions. As exports and production fell (coal production declined 20 percent) and unemployment rose, the value of the zloty fell, and Grabski was forced to resign. The following year Marshal Jozef Pilsudski, the socialist soldier who had led Polish nationalist forces against the Russians at the end of the war, staged a coup d'état with the assistance of sections of the working class. Some 500 lives were lost during the coup.

Pilsudski created a government committed to a policy of "cleansing" (*sanacja*). What Pilsudski wanted to achieve was a clearing out of the tensions and conflicts within Polish politics and society. Political action had been reduced to stalemate by the multiplicity of parties (thirty two were represented in the Sejm) and pressure groups ranging from unions to nationalists. Ethnic tensions rose, partly because of a systematic Polish effort to colonize non-Polish parts of the country, and working-class and peasant discontent was on the increase. Workers suffered from inflation and unemployment; peasants were frustrated by the slow pace of agrarian reform.

Between 1926 and 1929, the economy recovered quickly, helped in part by the 1926 British miners' strike that gave Poland access to the Scandinavian market. Workers were helped as unemployment declined by two-thirds to 5 percent, and peasants benefited from a program of land redistribution and an extension of rural credit facilities. Equality among ethnic groups was pursued, particularly in educational opportunities, although it did not go as far as establishing a Ukrainian university, as Ukrainians wanted, or ending the quota on Jewish students in Polish universities. The progress made was enough to give Pilsudski and his allies on the noncommunist left 53 percent of the vote in elections in 1928.

In Romania, the democratic 1920 constitution had soon been abandoned, and it was replaced by another in 1923, which maintained universal male suffrage but limited some freedoms. It was followed by laws designed to maintain the power of the Liberals, elected in 1922, and to ensure that Romania remained a firmly centralized state despite demands for local autonomy in newly annexed regions like Transylvania and Bessarabia. In 1925 Romania was divided into seventy-one administrative units, each run by a prefect appointed by the government in Bucharest. In 1926 proportional representation was modified to give any party with 40 percent of the votes half the seats in parliament, the other half being divided among all parties, including the largest. Thus a party that won exactly 40 percent of the votes was guaranteed 70 percent of the seats. Both these measures echoed policies adopted in Fascist Italy to overcome the inherent instability of proportional representation where there were many parties.

Attempts were made to stimulate Romanian industry by raising high tariff barriers, and Romania became one of the most protectionist states in Europe. Foreign economic influences were restricted: Only Romanians could own land, foreign capital investment was limited to 40 percent of any undertaking, and with one exception Romania avoided borrowing abroad. Such measures hit the peasants (who made up 70 percent of the population) hard. In 1926 a National Peasant Party (NPP) was formed from two smaller parties, and it gained additional support when poor harvests in 1927 and 1928 placed additional pressures on farmers. In December 1928 elections, the NPP won 78 percent of the votes which, under the constitution, gave them 95 percent of the seats.

During 1929, the National Peasant government made concessions to regional autonomy, allowed more foreign investment, reduced export tariffs, and made credit easier for rural cooperatives. Relaxation of restrictions on the size of land purchases, which had helped break down the dominance of large estates, allowed a wealthy peasant stratum to emerge. But although there was potential for agricultural renewal in Romania, its export markets soon disappeared as the depression struck Europe.

In neighboring Bulgaria the overwhelming peasant majority had been represented by Alexander Stamboliski's regime until his policies so alienated important constituencies (notably Macedonian separatists, the urban middle classes, the Church, and the army) that he was killed and his regime deposed in June 1923. Within six months the coalition government that replaced Stamboliski's was challenged by an attempted Communist coup, and in the following years there was a savage repression of the Bulgarian left, marked by mass imprisonments and executions.

Throughout the period Bulgarian agriculture deteriorated but industry prospered. Major crops like cereals and even tobacco declined in value, giving way to industrial crops like sunflowers (for oil) and sugar beets. The size of land holdings fell, partly because of the pressure of rural overpopulation. Industry, on the other hand, was promoted by tough import tariffs, and enterprises increased in both number and size. Between 1921 and 1930, textile, cement, chemical, and metallurgical output grew by 25 percent or more each year, while sugar and paper production rose more than 10 percent annually.

From 1926 a new government reduced state controls, relaxed censorship, and even allowed the Communists to become active again. But Bulgarian politics were dominated by ethnic issues. Macedonian nationalists—some wanting a united Macedonia within Bulgaria, others wanting an autonomous state—were active inside and outside Bulgaria, leading to retaliation from both Greece and Yugoslavia.

Nowhere were ethnic relations more complicated than in Yugoslavia, known until 1929 as the Kingdom of Serbs, Croats, and Slovenes. Attempts were made to forge a workable political agreement between the main Serb and Croatian parties, and in 1925 a coalition government was formed, but there was continuing instability until 1928 when the Croatian leader was assassinated by a Montenegran terrorist. On January 6, 1929, with the support of the army, King Alexander abolished parliament and suppressed all political parties, trade unions, and religious and regional associations.

Two states stood apart from the general Eastern European trends: Austria and Czechoslovakia. In the years immediately following the war, Austria was racked by economic disruption, high inflation, and social unrest. When the dust had settled, it became clear that the country was politically and socially divided. Vienna, with its various ethnic populations, contained just over a quarter of Austria's 6.5 million people and supported the Social Democratic Party, which had its own paramilitary force, the Schutzbund. Beyond "Red Vienna," as it became known, Austria was largely rural and ethnically German. There the dominant political group was the Christian Social Party, a Catholic right-wing party that had its own paramilitary force, the Heimwehr.

The antagonism between the two dominant parties was exacerbated by the fact that neither could obtain a majority of votes in the country. Between 1923 and 1927, however, the Christian Social Party, led by a priest, Father Ignaz Seipel, governed with the support of smaller right-wing and peasant parties. In 1927 there were violent demonstrations in Vienna over the lenient treatment given right-wingers who had killed a veteran and a child during clashes. The justice building was set on fire and when demonstrators refused to let the fire engines get near the blaze, the police opened fire and killed almost a hundred people.

Social reform varied throughout Austria during the 1920s because the loose federal structure gave regional and local governments extensive administrative powers. In Vienna the governing Social Democrats introduced a wide range of social welfare schemes and low-cost housing. The most extensive project, housing 1,500 families, was provocatively called Karl-Marx-Hof; much of it was destroyed by the army in 1934 when a workers' uprising was suppressed by the government. In the rural areas and at the national level, however, conservative policies reflected the ideology of the Christian Social Party.

Czechoslovakia was an island of relative calm in the noisy sea of Eastern European normalization. Despite the large number of political parties vying for power, coalition governments throughout the 1920s provided stability. Between 1922 and 1926 they consisted of socialists and agrarians, between 1926 and 1929, agrarians and conservatives. Various mechanisms developed to reinforce the continuity and stability of governments. Specific ministries tended to be held by individuals of the same party year after year, and a convention developed whereby the leaders of the main parties, whether or not they were in the coalition, met with the prime minister to sort out government business. A level of consensus thus existed to parallel the rivalry of the individual parties.

The Czechoslovak governments had mixed success in dealing with the massive ethnic issues that the settlement of its frontiers had produced. Slovaks bitterly resented Czech numerical domination and its economic and cultural echoes. Although 17 percent of the population, Slovaks held under 2 percent of posts in the central administration. Slovaks' salaries were lower than Czechs', and their unemployment rate higher. Religious conflict was especially sharp: The predominantly Catholic Slovaks resented the decline of religious instruction in schools, the legalization of divorce, and the demolition of a huge statue of the Virgin Mary in Prague. In 1925 the government even declared that one of the national holidays would honor Jan Hus, a church reformer put to death as a heretic by the Catholic Church in 1415. Slovak disaffection was demonstrated in the 1925 elections, when the Slovak nationalist party and Catholic clerical parties won more than 50 percent of the vote in Slovakia.

In contrast the German population of Czechoslovakia—a fifth of the national population and concentrated in the Sudetenland, which was to become the issue that destroyed the country in 1938—rallied to the government in the 1920s. In the same elections that the Slovaks used to register their discontent, 80 percent of ethnic Germans voted for parties well disposed toward the Czechoslovak state. It was not that the Germans got their share of the benefits of Czechoslovak citizenship, for there were persistent grievances over language, education, and budgets, but they were optimistic and, besides, could expect no help from Austria or Weimar Germany.

The Soviet Union

If any state tried to normalize in the early 1920s it was the Soviet Union. Since 1914, people had experienced a terrible war, followed by revolutions, civil war, foreign intervention, famine, and the disruptions of war communism. The abandonment of centralized state control of the economy, and the adoption of the New Economic Policy in 1921, signaled an attempt to reduce social and economic tensions.

The Communist leadership reached a watershed as 1923 gave way to 1924. Lenin died in January, leaving the question of succession open, and by that time it was clear that the Russian revolution was not about to be emulated anywhere else in Europe. The last communist rising, in Hamburg in November 1923, had subsided under army repression. The dissipation of revolutionary energy outside the Soviet Union had repercussions on the Soviet Union itself. Instead of being preeminent among a number of communist states as the Bolsheviks had expected to become, the Soviet Union was alone and would have to adjust to a Europe whose states were variously democratic or authoritarian, but decidedly and explicitly not only not communist, but anti-communist.

For much of the 1920s the leaders of the Soviet Communist Party debated the way in which they ought to proceed. There was general agreement that the country had to industrialize. Lenin might have portrayed the peasants as a progressive force, enabling Russia to sustain a revolution before the development of a mature working class, but industry was needed if the Soviet Union were to maintain and improve its position.

Two broad alternative roads toward that goal were proposed in what is known as the industrialization debate. The first, which was supported by a "left" group headed by Leon Trotsky, the commissar of war, insisted that industrialization should be carried out at the expense of the peasants. The peasants were able to produce excess wealth that could be purchased at low prices to finance industrial development. That potential, Trotsky argued, should be used to the benefit of the state, even if the peasants' income and living standards suffered.

Against this a "right" group, headed by a communist theorist Nikolai Bukharin, argued that bringing the peasantry into a cooperative relationship with industry would be more productive. Peasants were the mass of the population, and if they were allowed to produce for the market and increase their incomes, they would provide a huge domestic market for industrial and consumer goods.

Although they represented different approaches, both left and right operated within the same basic assumptions. There was agreement that economic development should be financed within the Soviet Union itself. On a broader level, the leadership was united on the character of Soviet government: The Communist Party was to be the only legal political entity. In other words, no matter what toleration there was of private enterprise and production for the market, the government would remain centralized and authoritarian.

This did not mean that a "successor" to Lenin had to be found. Not only was there no rule that one person ought to be preeminent within the party leadership, but the notion of a single leader, so common in fascist thought, was offensive to most Bolsheviks. Lenin himself was sometimes criticized for abusing the authority his name carried, and there was general agreement that the Russian Revolution should not degenerate into "Bonapartism," as the French Revolution had been appropriated by Napoleon Bonaparte in 1799.

During Lenin's illness, following his first stroke in May 1922, his duties were gradually taken over by the seven-man Politburo (Political Bureau) of the Central Committee of the Communist Party. Although it was pledged to collective leadership, and there were affirmations that no one member could possibly replace Lenin, a struggle for power took place, notably between Trotsky and Stalin. Stalin, a Georgian, was born Joseph Djugashvili, but in 1913 adopted the pseudonym that means "man of steel." He was the only working-class member of the top Communist leadership, and by 1924 had come to dominate the

Early (1910) photographs of Stalin, taken by the czarist police.

party apparatus, even though Lenin had expressed serious reservations about his personality ("too rude") and fitness to lead the party. In the following years he used his control of the party machine to isolate and remove his opponents. In 1925 Trotsky was dismissed as war commissar, and the next year Zinoviev was fired as head of the Comintern. Greater centralization was introduced into the Communist Party itself, and the power of local and regional organizations weakened, thus undermining the power bases of Stalin's rivals.

The culmination of this process came when the 1927 congress of the Communist Party condemned all "deviation from the party line," which by then was largely decided by Stalin himself. Opposition leaders were expelled from the party for breaking the rule against factionalism that had been implemented by Lenin. Trotsky and his colleagues were first sent into internal exile, and in 1929 Trotsky was stripped of Soviet citizenship and expelled from the country.

Historians debate the relationship between Lenin and Stalin. On the one hand, neither was in favor of democracy within the Communist Party, and both worked toward the creation of a centralized, bureaucratic party machine and state. On the other hand, Stalin took Lenin's methods much further than Lenin had; Lenin's critics would say that it was not that Lenin would not have done so, merely that by the time he became seriously ill he had not had the opportunity to do so. Although there were strong lines of continuity between the form of government under Lenin and Stalin, the use of the instruments of control was different in degree; Lenin was in favor of centralizing power but not necessarily in using it as Stalin did.

But although the clear tendency at the political level was toward greater centralization and less tolerance of divergence from party policy, there remained ambiguous trends in the Soviet economy and society. Additional concessions were made to the peasants, and in 1925 the liberalization of the economy reached its peak. By then private trade accounted for 42 percent of the country's economic activity, and represented 54 percent of national income. By 1928 the Soviet Union showed signs of a general economic recovery; production of key industrial products (like coal) and foodstuffs (rye, wheat, and potatoes) had more or less recovered to prewar levels.

In the late 1920s, policies restricting private enterprise began to be applied. Taxes on some profits were increased, private ownership of flour mills was limited, and personal taxation on better-off peasants (*kulaks*) was increased. Stalin was particularly hostile to this group, seeing it as a peasant bourgeoisie that was essentially hostile to communism. An amendment to the criminal code provided three years' imprisonment for "evil-intentioned" individuals who increased prices by hoarding or withholding goods from the market. The government also reduced the prices it paid for agricultural products and introduced policies of confrontation with the peasants. Barns were searched for hoarded grain and roadblocks thrown up to stop peasants moving their grain to any but the official markets, where peasants received lower prices for their produce.

The result of such policies was a gradual reduction in the activity of the private sector. By 1929 its contribution to national income was 39 percent, compared with 54 percent four years earlier, and by 1932 it would fall to 9 percent. Under Stalin, the New Economic Policy was disemboweled. It was intended to be an interim policy to support the economy until the state had the means to take control, but Stalin's opponents argued that Lenin would not have abandoned it so quickly. Stalin, who had never been convinced of the need for the NEP, replaced it in 1928 with the First Five-Year Plan, which imposed production targets on all sectors of the economy.

While there was a tightening of discipline in politics and the economy, certain spheres of social life remained unregulated. In the case of the family, in fact, the liberalism of the

Bolshevik period was reaffirmed in a new family code enacted in 1926 and put in force in 1927. Contested divorces were shifted from the courts to administrative bodies, and the procedures simplified and shortened. The code eliminated the distinction between couples formally married and those living in de facto unions. All the rights attached to marriage were granted to free unions, and a marriage registration had no legal significance except as evidence that a marriage existed.

In some senses family policy ran counter to other trends, for the new code effectively deregulated the family and removed the state from family affairs. The state no longer defined the personal status of men and women, but left them to arrange their own relationships. At the same time the code showed awareness of the negative effects of the NEP, such as the high rate of female unemployment. Under the code, a housewife who divorced was entitled to a share of the property acquired with her husband's wages, and unemployed women were entitled to support payments.

One effect of the new code was to increase the divorce rate, particularly in the cities. In Moscow the number of divorces per thousand population rose steadily from 3.5 in 1922 to 6 in 1926, but leapt to 9.3 in 1927 and 10.1 by 1929. There was a similar effect in Leningrad, where the divorce rate rose from 3.6 in 1926 to 9.8 the following year. The marriage rate showed no such consistency, however. In Moscow it declined slightly in 1926 and then stabilized, but in Leningrad it rose steadily throughout the 1920s.

In the cultural sphere, too, there was more latitude than one might expect from a regime that gradually tightened political control. During most of the 1920s Soviet art, literature, and music flourished. There were restrictions, and the government attempted to coordinate artistic activity, but nonetheless a great deal of experimentation was allowed in the visual arts, theater, music, and dance. Throughout the period, however, there was an undercurrent of opinion within the Communist Party that artists ought to serve the revolution. Realism in style and tradition in content were considered most appropriate, but by the end of the 1920s the state began to seize total control of culture in the Soviet Union and to impose rules regarding content and style on artists, writers, composers, and performers.

Finally there was the secret police. The Cheka (Extraordinary Commission for Combating Counter-Revolution, Sabotage, and Speculation), established by Lenin, was replaced in 1923 by the OGPU (Unified State Political Administration). On the whole its repressive activities were relatively light until 1927 when there was a war scare, a widespread fear that the Soviet Union was about to be invaded by the capitalist powers. At that time the OGPU rounded up and interned suspected enemies, but even then its activity during the 1920s pales against the terror it implemented during the 1930s.

Normalizing International Relations

Efforts to distance Europe from the war also took diplomatic form in the mid-1920s, when various attempts were made to forge new understandings that would reduce international tensions. One direction was the growing acceptance that the Soviet Union was a permanent fixture on Europe's landscape. The first state to recognize it officially was Weimar Germany, a case of two pariah nations finding common interests despite vast ideological differences. The agreement between the two states was struck in Rapallo, Italy, in 1922 when their foreign ministers were attending a conference on economic problems, including the obligation of the Soviet government to pay the debts of the czarist regime. Under the Treaty of Rapallo, Germany and the Soviet Union agreed not to make economic claims against each other, but to cooperate in the economic sphere. Later the new relationship was used to enable the German army to use Soviet facilities and resources in order to train troops and rearm secretly in contravention of the Treaty of Versailles.

In 1924 France, Britain, and most other European states followed Germany's lead and recognized the Soviet government. The next year Japan removed its last troops from northern Sakhalin Island and extended recognition as well. The changes of policy reflected desire on the part of the British and the French to reduce the risks of war. They began to work for the entry of Germany and the Soviet Union to the League of Nations. The process of detente was pushed further with the signing of the Locarno agreements, in October 1925. The most important of these was a declaration by France and Germany that they accepted their common border as determined under the Treaty of Versailles. Britain and Italy, as cosignatories, undertook to intervene if either French or German forces breached the frontier or if Germany sent troops into the demilitarized area of the Rhineland.

The Locarno accord meant that Germany renounced its claim on Alsace and Lorraine and surrendered its right unilaterally to remilitarize the Rhineland. To compensate Germany for these concessions, which were bound to anger nationalists, France agreed to sponsor German membership of the League of Nations and to begin withdrawing its forces from the Rhineland in advance of the schedule set down in the Treaty of Versailles. France also renounced its right under the treaty to send armed forces into Germany (as it had done in 1923).

The significance of the Locarno agreements was more than the sum of concessions on both sides. The accords were hailed throughout Europe as the symbol of a new spirit of international understanding and harmony. The day after the agreements were signed, the *New York Times* ran the headline, "France and Germany Ban War Forever." The German and French foreign ministers, Gustav Stresemann and Aristide Briand, were awarded the Nobel Peace Prize in 1926. Although the praise and the cheering were excessive and premature, the Locarno agreements created a momentum of peacemaking. In 1927 preparations began for a World Disarmament Conference, an event announced in 1919 but neglected until the spirit of Locarno breathed life into it. In the event it did not take place for another five years, by which time the inflated expectations of Locarno had lost a lot of their air. Still, the push for peace seemed to gain ground in August 1928, when the main European states, together with the United States and Japan, signed the Kellogg-Briand Pact (Frank Kellogg was the U.S. secretary of state). The signatories promised "to renounce war as an instrument of national policy."

Underneath all the rhetoric about peace, international understanding, and disarmament was a spirit of hard realism about the balance of power in Europe. Agreement had been reached, at the 1922 Washington conference, on the relative size of fleets of capital ships that the major powers should have. For every 5 tons in the British or United States navies, Japan was to have 3 tons and France and Italy 1.75 tons. But when attempts were made in 1927, in the afterglow of Locarno, to regulate the relative tonnage of other vessels, like submarines and cruisers, France and Italy refused to be limited. Even when Britain, the United States, and Japan agreed to ratios, they reserved the right to ignore them if they felt threatened by a nonsignatory state.

The "spirit of Locarno" was a fragile and short-lived thing, as much a product of wishful thinking as anything of substance. No doubt the settlement of grievances between France and Germany was an important step, but it was too flimsy a base upon which to construct a lasting European peace, let alone a global peace. Ironically, it was not long before European international relations *were* normalized; but the normality in Europe was conflict and war.

Women in the 1920s

Accounts of women in the 1920s frequently dwell on the freedom they enjoyed following World War I. This was the decade of "flappers" and good-time girls, young women who let their hair down although they cut it short, and enjoyed life unrestrained by parents, morals, or religion. There were dramatic shifts in physical appearance as women abandoned long hair for short styles and began to wear lipstick and other cosmetics. More of the female body became visible as skirt lengths contracted. In their leisure hours women went to dance halls and the cinema, where they smoked and socialized freely with young men. At weekends on the beach they wore one-piece backless bathing suits instead of bathing suits with skirts, and on the tennis courts they wore shorts instead of long skirts. The introduction of tampons and disposal sanitary napkins only added to their freedom from traditional constraints.

But like the images of cheerful young women driving ambulances during the war, "vamps" and "flappers" were only a small part of the larger picture of women's life during the 1920s. There might have been many of them among middle-class or well-off young women in the larger towns of Europe, especially Western Europe, but they represented a tiny fraction of women in Europe, even in Western Europe.

The 1920s did see changes designed to benefit women. As we have seen, women gained the vote in many states, although Polish, Soviet, Hungarian, and Spanish women lost it when their respective countries abandoned democratic political systems, and others would follow suit in the 1930s. Although men also lost political rights in these cases, the withdrawal of political rights had different implications for women. It was usually part of a more general policy of reemphasizing women's functions within the family.

There were, nonetheless, legal reforms that benefited women, including changes to family law. In 1923, English women were put on an equal footing with men in access to divorce. While men had been able to obtain divorces (as many had after the war) if their wives committed adultery, women had been able to divorce adulterous husbands only if the offense was compounded by desertion or violence against the wife, or if it involved incest or bigamy. From 1923, men were placed on the same legal basis as women with respect to adultery. In 1924, a reform reduced the inequalities in parenthood by stipulating that both parents had guardianship of small children. In 1926, a new property law gave all women, married and single, the right to own and dispose of property on the same terms as men.

Economic dependence prevented most women from taking advantage of legal reforms. The right to own property in their own right was meaningless where there was no property to speak of. Most working-class wives could not use divorce because they lacked the financial resources to survive, especially with their children, without a male wage. Refuges for battered women did not exist, so despite laws and policies, women who suffered physical or emotional abuse could do little about it. Most of the relatively rare divorces throughout Europe in the 1920s were obtained by middle-class women and men, a small percentage of the population.

Meaningful emancipation for women depended upon comprehensive social welfare, which no state had implemented, or employment that paid women a living wage, which no economy provided. Neither condition was met in the 1920s, for not only did women earn less than men doing equivalent work, but women were concentrated in low-income occupations. Even when much of Europe went through a period of relative prosperity from the mid-1920s, women experienced high rates of unemployment.

In the Soviet Union, hundreds of thousands of women lost their jobs when the New Economic Policy was adopted in 1921. Even when the Soviet economy began to improve in the mid-1920s, and employment rose, unemployment also increased because of peasant migrants looking for work in the cities. Although twice as many women worked in factories in 1929 (804,000) as in 1923 (416,000), in the same year women accounted for 29 percent of the employed and 50 percent of the unemployed. The number of women looking for work far exceeded official unemployment figures, which included only workers who had lost one job and were seeking another. Women who had never worked for wages before, such as wives of workers and peasants who wanted to enter the workforce, were not included.

There were various reasons for the continuing problems of women who wanted to work. Some were specific to the Soviet Union, like the government's desire to employ demobilized soldiers to prevent them from turning to crime. There was also the enduring attitude, found throughout Europe, that it was less important for women than men to be in paid employment. Many unions, led by men, saw female employment as a threat to male jobs and wage levels. Managers saw women employees as an added expense because of the costs of paid maternity leave and legal restrictions on the kind of work that could be performed by women, especially pregnant women and nursing mothers.

The problem might have been resolved by repealing protective legislation, but that would have run counter to the state policy of ensuring the health and welfare of mothers and children. Soviet legislation and policy forbade sexual discrimination in employment, but managers were under pressure in the 1920s to increase industrial productivity and cut costs. When the ideology of sexual equality conflicted with more pragmatic economic and demographic policies, it lost out.

International Women's Day in Moscow, March 1925. Working women march to Lenin's tomb carrying a banner that reads, "In the Soviet land the woman slave is building a new life."

Women experienced continuing difficulties with employment in many European countries throughout the mid-1920s, a period generally described as prosperous. In Italy, women's employment was legally restricted before the advent of Mussolini's Fascist government; under Fascism they were excluded from more occupations deemed "male," such as teaching history. In 1928, state agencies were instructed to give preference to male heads of households in hiring and promotion, and educational opportunities ensured that women were sparsely represented in the medical and legal professions. On the other hand, women predominated as elementary school teachers, social workers, and librarians, and opportunities for women secretaries expanded with the bureaucracy. In these respects Fascist Italy was little different from other European societies in maintaining quite rigid divisions between "male" and "female" occupations.

In Germany the years of so-called prosperity saw overall unemployment rise to between 6 and 10 percent of the workforce between 1926 and 1929, and women's unemployment rose faster within it. In Britain the government passed legislation excluding women from certain occupations in order to protect male employment. On the other hand, there were attempts to encourage unemployed women to train as domestic servants; a state agency trained 25,000 women in this way between 1920 and 1924.

The Politics of Leisure

One of the characteristics of postwar Europe was the involvement of the masses, not only in politics but also in many spheres of economic, social, and cultural life. This was not a phenomenon that suddenly appeared, but the war seemed to accelerate a process that had been evolving for some time. Mass armies and mass death ushered in changes that we now take for granted.

Perhaps the most evident form of mass culture—because it bears the word in its name—was the development of mass communications. The potential for communicating with large numbers of people was inherent in printing, but its realization largely depended upon the achievement of general literacy, something associated with the late nineteenth and early twentieth centuries.

The circulation of newspapers grew before the war, but really took off afterward. In Britain in 1920 there were only two newspapers with circulations of more than a million, but by 1930 there were five. The largest selling papers were the "popular" press, the forebears of modern tabloids, such as *The News of the World* and *The People*. The so-called quality press, such as the *Times*, had relatively small sales. Wider circulation of newspapers created mass consumer markets and exposed people to news on a regular basis.

Even more effective was radio. Private transmissions between individuals had been possible from the late nineteenth century, and radio was used extensively for military communication during the war, but in 1920 it became possible to broadcast live to countless radio sets. Within a year broadcasting facilities were established in many European states and the mass production of radio receivers began. The popularity of the wireless, as it was known in England, was instant. By the end of the 1920s there were 3 million sets in Great Britain, about one for every four households, and the same number in Germany, which represented one for every six households.

Although the first radio stations were private, a number of state broadcasting systems were established in the 1920s, some of them having monopolies on the radio waves. The

British Broadcasting Corporation, the first major public corporation formed in twentieth-century Britain, was granted exclusive broadcasting rights in 1926.

As a new technology, radio and radio sets were initially expensive, and in some countries a license had to be purchased to operate a set. This priced radios out of reach of the poorer sections of all societies. But just as illiteracy had historically been overcome by public readings of newspapers and other written material in cafés and taverns, so radio listening became a collective activity until the cost of radios fell far enough that people could listen within their own homes. In Germany in the 1920s, where the rate of radio ownership was lower than in Britain (there was one set for about six households), people often gathered in bars and clubs to listen. Mussolini's regime ensured that a radio was installed in every community so that no one would have to miss one of Il Duce's long speeches. Radio could encompass two senses of mass activity. Like newspapers directed at a mass readership, radio was directed at a mass audience, but unlike reading, which was essentially a solitary activity, radio-listening could be a mass or collective experience.

There were even larger collective experiences available on a regular basis. After the war a series of massive stadiums were built throughout Europe, generally to accommodate the crowds that packed in to watch soccer games. Facilities like the Wembley Stadium in London, completed in 1923, and the Lenin Stadium in Moscow held more than 100,000 people, but even they were dwarfed by stadiums built in Central Europe in the 1930s, some of them as public works projects designed to pull faltering economies out of the depression. The largest was the Strahav Stadium in Prague, which held a quarter of a million people.

The time that workers had at their disposal in order to enjoy these activities increased, although they were still more limited in the rural areas than in the cities and were less significant among the poor than the stable employed workers and middle classes. During the 1920s pressure grew for workers to be granted annual vacations, similar to extended summer holidays. Until then workers had holidays scattered throughout the year (such as Christmas and Easter), as well as longer breaks when factories closed for particular local or regional festivities. Relatively few workers won vacation rights before the 1930s, but those who did included printers and bakers in France (a week's annual holidays), British and French civil servants, and specific categories of workers in Germany, Czechoslovakia, and Austria. In Russia workers were declared to be entitled to a forty-hour week.

Most of the adult population of Europe was excluded from the benefits of restricted work hours. Farmers and those engaged in agricultural labor worked the necessary hours to produce what they needed. Cows produced milk every day, not five or six out of seven, and at peak labor periods like the harvest, work went on throughout and beyond the daylight hours. Working-class women in households everywhere, whether town or country, in agriculture or industry, had to shop, clean, cook, and look after children as well as perform any paid labor they might be involved in.

To this extent the much-vaunted revolution in leisure that occurred between the world wars tended to be largely confined to urban males. They were the vast majority of spectators at soccer matches as large-scale sports events took off in the 1920s. When the first Football Association Cup final was held at Wembley Stadium in 1923, an estimated 150,000 people turned up, about 50,000 more than there was room for. Not only was there a boom in watching sports, but participation picked up, too. In 1929 the London County Council estimated that it had some 350 cricket pitches, but more than a thousand clubs applying to play on them.

Urban men were also behind other kind of leisure activities. Throughout Europe it was clerical and skilled workers who were responsible for the growth of the hiking and camping movement. The Youth Hostel Association was founded in 1929, and the first French youth hostels opened that year. In Britain the Workers' Travel Association was founded in 1921, and the British Camping Club in the mid-1920s.

The growth of mass sports had political implications. As we have seen, the Italian Fascist Dopolavoro organization sponsored leisure activities for workers, and the Nazis would establish a similar agency, Strength Through Joy, in Germany in the 1930s. Western European socialists generally objected to state-organized leisure, but they insisted on the importance of workers to have leisure time (hence their demands for a forty-hour week), and there was no shortage of activities with which to fill it.

Conclusion

Although domestic and international tension lessened during the 1920s, there was something tenuous and fragile about the settlements that were reached. Few, whether in international relations, the economies, social policies, or constitutions, addressed fundamental issues. It was as if ten years of preparing and waging war, then waging peace until 1923, had exhausted Europeans across the board.

The Weimar Republic was arguably the clearest example, a state that retained basic conflicts between supporters and opponents of the republic itself, an apparently prosperous economy with high unemployment, and deep-seated social antagonisms that did not disappear when the spirit of revolution ebbed in 1923. The problems percolated away during the 1920s, which simply stored up the issues that would burst forth at the next opportunity. The next opportunity knocked after a remarkably short time, when the Great Depression descended upon Europe in 1930. The pressure of the economic crisis was more than enough to shatter the compromises that had emerged, and plunge Europe into another period of turmoil.

·6·

The Depression Era, 1929–1934

Introduction

Historians often debate whether the fundamental causes of specific historical events were political, cultural, economic, social, intellectual, or a combination of some or all. But in the five-year period from 1929 to 1934, the period known as the Great Depression, there is no doubt that economic events were of prime importance. The very name of the period refers to a phase in the economic cycles of prosperity and depression (meaning a major decline in production and trade) that had been characteristic of European economies for centuries.

The depression of the early 1930s was called "great" because, like the Great War, it was unprecedented in scope and scale. The interdependence of many economies and financial systems meant that once the depression had begun, it spread from country to country like an epidemic. The symptoms—a decline of international trade, low domestic demand, industrial stagnation, and high levels of unemployment—affected most of Europe, although some countries suffered more than others. Recovery was generally slow, and some economies had not regained their 1929 standard of health when the Second World War began ten years later.

Yet if the depression was essentially economic, its effects were much broader. Massive levels of unemployment alone increased Europe's already substantial numbers of poor, and placed immense strains on social welfare programs. Governments struggled, with mixed results, to deal with the worst effects by introducing emergency work and food plans.

Some administrations and regimes survived the crisis, but others fell as voters turned to radical alternatives in the search for solutions to the extraordinary problems the depression brought. The fall of the Weimar Republic and rise of Nazism is the most dramatic example. Yet there was no neat correlation between the easily measurable effects of the depression (like unemployment rates) and political disruption. The depression interacted with other existing social and cultural conditions in each country to produce the political developments of 1929–34.

The depression had immediate and long-term social consequences. Patterns of marriage, birth, family life, education, and work were affected, as were social relationships more broadly. Women and men experienced the depression differently. Ethnic tensions and conflicts became sharper as scapegoats for suffering were sought. Those who grew up in the period constituted what became known as the "depression generation," with values different from those who matured in more prosperous times.

In this chapter we examine the causes and course of the Great Depression, the various attempts to mitigate its worst effects, and its direct and indirect social and political consequences up to 1934. This is not to suggest that the depression ended in 1934, but that the five years from 1929 represented the core of the phenomenon.

The Depression and Europe's Economies

The single event most often associated with the Great Depression is the crash of the American stock market on October 29, 1929. On that "Black Tuesday" there was such an extraordinary frenzy of share and bond selling that in eight hours $18 billion disappeared from the value of stocks on the New York market. A week later the losses reached $60 billion.

The magnitude of the losses was not anticipated, but the fall itself was. Prices on the stock exchange had risen rapidly since 1926, and by the time of the crash (when the index was more than double the 1926 level) stocks were priced at levels out of relation to their real values. The market was due for what is sometimes called a readjustment, and in order to prevent one of disastrous proportions, authorities had tried unsuccessfully since 1928 to limit speculation.

As shocking as the Wall Street crash was to investors who lost their speculative earnings, it did not "cause" the depression. By late 1929 there were already key signs of a slowdown in the United States economy. Construction had begun to decline the year before, and industrial production started falling in 1929 before stock values plummeted. World prices for agricultural products had been slipping from the mid-1920s, as we have seen. The price of a bushel of wheat, $2.76 in 1919, fell to $1.25 in pre-crash 1929, and to $.60 in 1930.

What the crash did was to alert investors and manufacturers to underlying weaknesses in the American economy. The result was an instantaneous change of business policy from expansion to contraction, and industries began to reduce production and run down their inventories. Industrial output in December 1929 was 10 per cent lower than in October, orders for foreign imports quickly declined, and foreign lending fell off almost entirely.

These reactions had implications for European economies, but again there were trends in place before Black Tuesday. The boom in share prices in U.S. markets up to October 1929 induced many American investors to withdraw from foreign markets so as to benefit from profits at home. This affected many investments in Europe, where they had assisted postwar economic reconstruction. American lending abroad in the second half of 1929 was only half the total of the previous six months, and after Black Tuesday it dried up almost entirely. In addition, prices for agricultural and primary products like grain and coal had fallen steadily, undermining economies that depended on primary exports. By 1929 there were already huge surpluses of foods and agricultural products, and the conditions for a precipitous fall in demand were in place.

The recessionary policies adopted in the United States after October 29 could not but affect Europe (and other parts of the world) because of the centrality of the United States to the global economy. The United States was the world's largest industrial, trading, and financial power. It produced 40 percent of the world's manufactured goods, purchased 12 percent of the rest of the world's exports, and was the world's largest foreign investor.

October's turmoil in American financial markets and its immediate effects on American production and trade accelerated a trend already in place. The rapid decline in American imports in late 1929 deprived many foreign export producers, already suffering low prices, of a vitally important market. The application of high tariffs under the 1930 Smoot-Hawley Act, designed to discourage imports and protect American producers, led to a further decline in trade. In 1930, British exports to the United States were worth 29 million pounds, less than two thirds of the 46 million pounds earned the year before. German exports to America fell almost 30 percent (from 685 million to 488 million marks) in the same period. In each case 1930 represented only the beginning of a precipitous decline in exports.

Production by the United States' main European trading partners declined. Workers were laid off, reducing domestic demand and leading to further reductions in production. Compared with 1929, British industrial production was down 8 percent in 1930 and 16 percent in 1932; in Germany the decline was much more severe, at 14 percent and 53 percent, respectively. There were significant declines in important indices of industrial health, like coal and steel output, and lower consumer demand for goods such as cars led to cuts in production. Italy produced 52,000 private automobiles in 1929, many for export, but only 42,000 in 1930. These early declines in production were, however, only the beginning. Every ton of coal not mined, every car not built, meant that European economies needed less productive labor, and the steady decline in production that began in 1930 added millions more to the millions of men and women who were already unemployed when the depression began to bite.

The commercial links among European states meant that the depression spread from country to country. As unemployment rose, consumer demand fell, and imports were cut, affecting exporting countries. Europe's vast agricultural economies were deeply affected. The steady decline in world prices for agricultural products accelerated after 1929, when they fell by a half or more. Even then many farmers were unable to find markets for their produce.

There was also a financial dimension to the depression. With the withdrawal of investments, many banking systems became vulnerable to collapse, taking with them not only business funds but also small savings deposits and public confidence in the monetary system. Banks were left further exposed to insolvency by the inability of many of their borrowers to make payments. All across Europe small and large enterprises foundered during the depression, leaving lenders with real estate, buildings, and unsold inventory to sell in a depressed market.

In Eastern Europe, rural debt was a particular problem. Wishing to promote agricultural growth, and responding to peasant demands, Eastern European banks and states had extended credit to farmers to enable them to buy more land or improve their existing farms. Indebtedness made Eastern Europe's rural population extremely vulnerable, because a significant drop in farm income would render them unable to pay their debts. This would affect not only the landowners and their families but also the day-laborers they employed.

All these problems of finance, production, and trade were aggravated and institutionalized by tariff barriers that individual states raised against imports. Britain raised existing tariffs in 1931, and in 1932 placed a general tariff of 10 percent on all imports from outside the British Empire.

The collapse of agricultural prices and the decline of international trade had the devastating effects that might be expected. An example was Hungary, where more than half the population earned a living from agriculture. Even though the price of wheat fell by three-quarters, there was no foreign market for it, and by 1932 production was less than half the 1929 level. Export income from Hungary's main trading partners, which had amounted to 387 million pengos in 1929, was halved to 189 million in 1932.

A crowd outside one of Berlin's savings banks in July 1931, after the government allowed them to reopen.

Rural incomes plummeted, and farmers who had borrowed were unable to pay their debts and had their farms seized. More than 60,000 small holdings of less than two hectares (one in twenty) were auctioned off. The fortunate half of the country's million rural day-laborers found work for wages that were seldom adequate to feed their families; the unfortunate ones sank into utter destitution.

The economic, financial, and commercial interrelations between the United States and Europe, and among the European states, meant that once the depression had begun it was virtually impossible to contain. It affected everything from coal production at the heart of industrial Europe to agricultural crops on the periphery. For example, Greece's main exports—olive products, tobacco, and currants—were nonessentials, and demand for them fell. Tobacco output in 1932 was less than half the amount throughout most of the 1920s, and currant production was down about 40 percent. Other sectors of the economy were drawn into the vortex. To compound Greece's economic difficulties, the decline in world trade left the Greek merchant fleet underemployed. Retailers laid off staff as demand for goods classed as nonessentials fell. Demand for items like new furniture, clothing, tobacco, and alcohol declined.

There were exceptions to the general trend, notably states that were insulated by being relatively independent of foreign investment and for which foreign trade was less important. In France the effects of the depression were not felt until 1931 because much of the economy was self-financing and not vulnerable to the withdrawal of capital. But

French products, especially in the luxury area, were overpriced on world markets, and exports began to fall as its main trading partners experienced problems and raised barriers. French exports to the United Kingdom earned 8 billion francs in 1928, but less than 2 billion a year between 1932 and 1935.

The Scandinavian states also fared relatively well because the raw materials they exported were still in demand during the slump. The only state to escape the depression entirely, however, was the Soviet Union, which is discussed later in this chapter. With this single exception, the depression gripped Europe solidly from 1930 to 1932 and later, making not just a short-term impact, but an enduring mark on Europe's economic, political, and social history.

Unemployment and Government Policies

Unemployment became the human face of the depression, and sluggish and stalled economies could be measured by the millions of workless. The unemployed are usually pictured as men lined up outside labor exchanges, crowding city squares, and forming hopeless knots on street corners. But this is only a partial picture. Women who lost their jobs were discouraged from registering as unemployed; they looked for work in the secondary, less visible sectors of the economy. Neither should we forget that, especially in the east, Europe's population was rural and agrarian. Peasants who lost their farms, those who cut production because there was no market, and the millions of day-laborers thrown out of work, suffered unemployment as extensively as industrial workers. But they were more diffused geographically throughout the countryside and, like women, less visible.

The depression did not create unemployment, for there were already millions of jobless in the major European industrial societies: 1.2 million in Britain in mid-1929, and 1.4 million in Germany. But the depression accelerated the trend: By 1930 the number of registered unemployed in Britain grew by more than a half to 1.9 million, and in Germany their ranks doubled to more than 3 million. National economies that were even more vulnerable, like those of Belgium and Romania, experienced a threefold rise in unemployment in the space of a year. France was spared an immediate surge in unemployment: There it rose only marginally, from 10,000 in 1929 to 13,000 in 1930.

As the unemployment crisis deepened throughout Europe during the next two years, record levels of unemployment were posted (see Figure 6.1). In 1932 the 5.5 million German unemployed accounted for 30 percent of the workforce, and the 2.75 million British workers without work represented an unemployment rate of 23 percent. By 1932 even France had joined the trend, its 300,000 unemployed being a 25-fold increase over 1930 figures.

Across Europe the aggregate figures were staggering. If we take the major industrial countries of Western Europe (France, Britain, Germany, and Italy), unemployment rose from 1,540,000 in 1929, to 5,431,000 in 1930, 7,948,000 in 1931, and 9,627,000 in 1932. The smaller states of Central and Eastern Europe suffered no less. The combined official unemployment of Austria, Hungary, Czechoslovakia, Romania, and Yugoslavia was 264,000 in 1929, but it reached 425,000 in 1930, 685,000 in 1931, and 1,052,000 in 1932.

Aggregated figures such as these, and even national unemployment statistics, underestimate the real extent of unemployment and conceal important patterns, because unemployment did not strike workers randomly. Even though few sectors were not affected, some parts of the labor force were hit much harder than others. Heavy industry

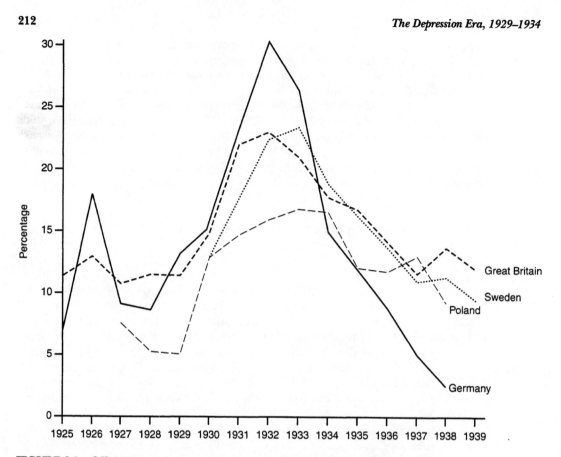

FIGURE 6.1   Official unemployment as a percentage of the workforce in selected countries, 1925–39.

Source: Data from B. R. Mitchell, *International Historical Statistics: Europe, 1750–1988* (London: Macmillan, 1992), pp. 159–66.

everywhere suffered first and most. In Britain, for example, the 1932 unemployment rates of 60 percent in shipbuilding and 50 percent in the iron and steel industries were more than double the overall industrial jobless rate of 23 percent.

The fact that women were less represented in these hard-hit heavy industries meant that women were initially less directly affected by unemployment than men. In Germany, for example, the actual *number* of women in the workforce *fell*, but their overall *proportion rose*, because men were thrown out of work at a faster rate. Given a choice, employers often preferred women workers, who were paid only about two-thirds the wage of men doing equivalent work. Yet women were frequently made scapegoats for male unemployment. In Germany and elsewhere, policies were enacted to reduce women's employment, and married women in the civil service were dismissed. France was unusual in not dismissing married women from its civil service, although entry to the service was closed for several years.

The notion that women, married women especially, ought to stay at home rather than work outside the home for pay was widely shared by policymakers throughout Europe. A British royal commission on unemployment insurance noted in 1931 that, "in the case of married women as a class, industrial employment cannot be regarded as the normal condition." In France the Nobel Prize–winning physician Charles Richet called for all women to be removed from the workforce, a move he said would solve both the birth rate crisis and the problem of male unemployment.

Women who lost their jobs were often denied unemployment insurance and excluded from unemployment statistics. This was especially true of women in unregulated employment: domestic servants, part-time workers, and women who earned income at home. In Britain by the end of 1931 an estimated 134,000 married women who had lost their jobs were barred from receiving unemployment benefits.

In Fascist Italy, too, policies designed to reduce women's work outside the home were intensified as male unemployment rose. In 1934 policies to restrict women's employment were decreed. The number of women permitted to take civil service entry tests was limited, and quotas were placed on the proportion of women in various occupational sectors. Within the Italian civil service, women could hold no more than 5 percent of senior posts or more than 20 percent of lower positions. In the private sector, women were limited to 12 percent of bank employees and 15 percent of workers in insurance companies.

The depression gave the Italian government the opportunity to promote male work at the expense of women, as it had talked of doing earlier in the 1920s. There were gender and populationist motives at play here, as Mussolini revealed in a 1934 speech: "With women replaced by men, legions of men would raise their humiliated heads, and hundreds of new families would immediately become part of the nation's life. . . . The very labor which in women causes loss of generative attributes, brings out in men a powerful physical and moral virility."

Other governments might have been less explicit about the motivations for their employment policies, and few would have expressed them as Mussolini did, but nonetheless throughout Europe there was this difference between the experience of male and female workers: Men lost their jobs because of the economic conditions, while women were put out of work not only by economic trends but also by deliberate government policies.

If women were forced out of work, governments also ensured that foreigners did not enter the workforce. In the 1920s France, suffering labor shortages because of high war mortality, had encouraged immigration by hundreds of thousands of foreign workers, especially from Eastern Europe, Italy, and Spain. When the depression began to bite in France, many were laid off and encouraged to return to their countries of origin, and in 1932 restrictions were placed on immigration. These policies, together with policies against women working, kept male unemployment relatively low; from virtually none in 1929, the number of jobless rose to 260,000 in 1932 and 426,000 in 1934. These policies that protected French workers from the scale of unemployment experienced by Britain and Germany raised rates elsewhere as foreign workers were forced to return home.

No state had anticipated unemployment of the magnitude the depression created, and governments and private institutions scrambled to find ways of mitigating the worst effects. Unemployment funds that had been adequate to cover the levels of unemployment current in the 1920s, were soon threatened with exhaustion. Early in 1929 the German government tried to stave off the crunch by reducing unemployment benefits, but was prevented from doing so by Social Democratic opposition. This precipitated a government crisis, and for more than two years, beginning in March 1930, President Hindenburg governed by decree, as the constitution permitted in times of emergency.

Hindenburg's Chancellor Heinrich Brüning, a conservative Catholic, cut unemployment benefits twice, but also reduced civil service salaries and lowered wages to January 1927 levels. Brüning hoped that these measures, together with reductions in prices, rents, and government spending, would lead to deflation and create confidence in the German economy. The result, however, was to deepen the depression even more, and unemployment rose.

In Britain stringent regulations introduced in 1931 lowered unemployment benefits by 10 percent and restricted entitlement to it. Married women were generally barred, and a means test was introduced for anyone who wanted unemployment benefits beyond an initial 26-week period. Officials could investigate the homes and family lives of the unemployed and require them to live off resident children's wages, use up savings, or even sell furniture before they would receive relief from the state. The means test became a focus of much working-class resentment because it treated the unemployed not as respectable workers who had lost their jobs through no fault of their own, but as paupers in need of charity.

Initially the French government was able to draw on considerable budget surpluses to moderate the effects of the depression. Public works projects were undertaken, including the construction of the Maginot Line, a series of fortifications along the border with Germany. Taxes on land and businesses were lowered or even abolished outright, and between 1930 and 1933 all school fees for secondary education were removed.

In Czechoslovakia the "Ghent scheme" of unemployment relief became operative in 1925, under which unions were made responsible for unemployment relief, with the government contributing half the cost. Because only a third of workers were unionized, this scheme proved quite inadequate to the demands placed on it after 1929, and direct state payments were instituted. The destitute received coupons entitling them to food and clothing, and in 1932–33 the state established a central grain-purchasing agency and floated a loan to fund public works projects to reduce unemployment.

Unions throughout Europe were generally unable to defend the interests of workers during the depression. Unemployment weakened their bargaining power as many workers were prepared to take work at any wage and in any conditions. Compared with the 1920s, the number of strikes declined, and fewer and fewer of those that did take place were successful; in France more than half the strikes between 1922 and 1929 achieved their aims, compared to a third between 1931 and 1935.

Unable to get help, apart from organizations or governments, many of those who suffered the effects of the depression took direct action. Thousands of unemployed took part in hunger marches in Great Britain, making their way from the worst-hit areas in Scotland, Wales, and the English Midlands to bring their plight to the attention of policymakers in London. In agricultural regions grievances were sometimes expressed in riots, as in Normandy and the Somme in France. Farmers occupied the prefect's offices in Chartres, near Paris, in 1933.

The Social Dimensions of the Depression

If the most immediate social implication of the depression was unemployment itself, unemployment in turn had wider social consequences. As men and women lost their jobs, families lost their sources of income. Where they were available, unemployment benefits (the "dole," as it was called in Britain) compensated to some extent, but nowhere did they match what had been earned from work. Attempts were made in many countries to freeze basic costs like rents and food prices, but they were usually unsuccessful and seldom compensated for declining incomes.

Real incomes, whether from work or unemployment benefits, fell. In Germany families living on employment income were 15 percent worse off in 1932 than two years earlier, but those who depended on unemployment benefits fared even worse than that. In many countries ad hoc welfare schemes were set up by public authorities and private charities, both religious and secular. They included the distribution of clothing for the poor and the provision of emergency meals in soup kitchens. The police in England provided clothing for the desperately poor, marking it so that it could not be pawned. Women, discouraged from active paid employment, were the core of many volunteer staffs. In Italy, for example, women had not been encouraged to join the Fascist women's organization until the early 1930s, when they were urged to do so to staff soup kitchens and welfare agencies established to assist the destitute.

Family economies were rocked by the depression. When unemployment struck, the burden of "making do," of providing enough food for their children and husbands, fell primarily on women as it traditionally did. Women, whether or not they had been employed before, took on any kind of work they could find. Young Fascist volunteers in Italy noted with shock—because it was a reversal of accepted gender roles—that the wives of unemployed construction workers became the main breadwinners of their families, mainly by taking cleaning jobs. The fact that in 1931, 45 percent of Italian families depended on two or more income earners suggests the magnitude of the hardship caused by growing unemployment. Throughout Britain, women took on any work they could to supplement the dole: laundry, sewing, baby-sitting, cleaning, and taking lodgers, as well as small-scale domestic work like box making, painting tin soldiers, or putting the hooks on Christmas tree decorations.

There seemed no end to the ways of making do. In the English port city of Liverpool, families emptied urine from their nighttime chamber pots (indoor toilets were rare in working-class homes) into a receptacle at the back door each morning. There it was collected by an employee of the local copper works, because uric acid was used in the production of copper. The families were paid each week with a packet of tea (which presumably stimulated production and kept the whole process going).

Women in the most distressed regions sometimes resorted to public demonstrations in order to put pressure on the authorities to provide basic food for their families. In 1934 there were such demonstrations by women in both northern and southern Spain, in the Basque region and in Andalusia. They harked back to the bread and grain riots of the eighteenth century and earlier in which women were prominent.

In England it was widely noted that women suffered in order to provide for their families during the depression. Typically mothers and wives looked after their children and husbands before themselves, and the health of women of families struck by unemployment declined. One English periodical ran a series on "Hungry England" in 1933, after Annie Weaving, a 37-year-old London woman, died as a result of starving herself in order to provide food for her seven children. Maternal mortality rates, already rising in the late 1920s, peaked in 1934 (at 4.6 deaths per thousand live births) as poor nutrition, stress, and reductions in health services contributed to the death of an estimated 3,000 women a year in childbirth.

The health of adult women, and adults generally, was overshadowed by medical and public concern about children. Overall infant mortality continued to decline in England (and elsewhere in Europe), but there were great disparities among social classes. In the upper and middle classes in 1930–32, the infant mortality rate was 33 per thousand births, but among skilled workers it was 58 and among unskilled workers more than twice as great, 77 deaths per thousand.

Of the poor children who survived their first year, many were dogged by ill health, and the depression aggravated the situation. Medical inspections of schools in England in the early 1930s showed that about one in ten children had a "slightly abnormal" nutritional assessment, and one in a hundred was classified as "bad," or malnourished. In areas of particularly high unemployment, however, like northeastern England and southern Wales, the proportion of malnourished children was between a quarter and a third. A 1933 medical survey in Newcastle-upon-Tyne showed that poorer children were eight times more likely to have pneumonia, ten times more likely to have bronchitis, and five times more likely to have rickets.

Governments were not always forthcoming about the effects of the depression on their citizens' health. The British Ministry of Health tried to suppress any data that appeared to compromise the government, and in 1932 Sir George Newman, the chief medical officer of health, censured any of his officials who tried "to define the relationship between economic change and local mortality rates." The ministry was keen to show that malnutrition among children was as much a question of ignorance as of lack of money. This conclusion echoed explanations of infant mortality earlier in the century, which blamed women for poor motherhood skills rather than the material circumstances in which they lived.

Health differences between the poor and better off did not appear for the first time during the Great Depression, of course, but the depression expanded the number of poor and produced a widening and deepening health problem. Some efforts to assist malnourished children were made by state and municipal governments. In England and Wales, funds for school meals were increased in areas of highest unemployment, and in 1934 the Milk Act provided for a third of a pint of milk a day for all children in elementary schools. The number of children in school-feeding programs in the Netherlands doubled from 20,000 to 40,000. There, as elsewhere, however, many parents preferred not to have their children receive free meals at school because it identified them as poor. The sense of being stigmatized this way was especially acute for families that before the depression had provided for themselves and that resisted the notion of receiving what they perceived as charity.

The depression not only enhanced class differences in health and mortality, but affected other aspects of family life. Throughout Europe the annual number of marriages declined in the early 1930s. There were 52,000 marriages in Austria in 1930, but only 44,000 in 1933, a drop of 15 percent. In Germany they fell from 570,000 in 1930 to 517,000 in 1932, a loss of 10 percent. In other countries the decline was less marked, but there was a tendency for women and men to postpone marrying until their financial positions were more secure.

The decline in marriages contributed to a decline in births, strengthening the longer-term trend, as couples decided to limit their families, at least temporarily, until their family finances improved. In Germany the annual number of births fell 15 percent between 1930 (when 1,144,000 children were born) and 1933 (when there were 971,000 births). In Great Britain the number of births fell by 11 percent in the same years. The French birth rate, long a source of anxiety for nationalists, dropped dramatically, from 18.2 per thousand in 1926–30 to 16.5 in 1931–35.

The continued decline of Italy's birth rate (which fell below replacement level in some urban centers in the early 1930s) reinforced the Fascist government's determination to reverse the long-term trend. Loans were made available to newly married couples, and in the 1931 penal code a whole section was devoted to crimes against "the race," such as contraception and abortion. Male homosexual activity was punished, not only for conservative moral reasons but also because gay men did not contribute to population growth; they were lumped together with bachelors as men who failed to perform their national duty to reproduce.

If the depression made single men and women think twice about marrying, and made couples hesitate to have children, it also made many married people reluctant to divorce. Divorce rates had risen during the later 1920s, but they either stabilized or fell during the early 1930s. Some married couples might well have been brought together by shared adversity, but in most cases it is likely that depression conditions made separating and divorcing too problematic. Women filed for most divorces at this time, and unemployment or the impossibility of getting a job deprived many married women of the resources necessary for life alone or with their children. Until they could survive on their own, divorce had to be postponed. This probably explains why divorce rates rose later in the 1930s, when the worst of the depression was over.

There is no evidence that the fall in the depression-years divorce rate meant an improvement in marital relationships. On the contrary it is likely that families under severe economic stress experienced more conflict and violence. Men who were unemployed were often embarrassed by being supported by their wives. Since the nineteenth century fathers and husbands had been defined essentially as breadwinners, and joblessness deprived them of their reason for being. A young social worker in Italy described unemployed husbands at home as being in a "horrible temper," and it is likely that this was the general demeanor of men who felt victimized and humiliated. It is equally likely that domestic violence against women increased.

On the other hand, alcohol consumption, which is often linked to male domestic violence, fell as unemployed men were forced to cut back. The output of beer in Germany and Great Britain dropped 20 percent between 1927–29 and 1931–33, whereas in Austria it fell by half. Men still drank, of course, one English woman explaining that her unemployed husband sometimes found casual work at a fruit market and "the coppers [pennies] he made on the side meant he could go out for a drink or have a little bet."

Not only marital relationships came under increasing pressure—the depression accentuated social tensions and conflicts of all kinds. One was the grievances of the newly dispossessed against those they perceived as responsible for their hardships. There was, however, no consensus about who was responsible, and the targets ranged from diffuse, abstract economic "forces" to specific groups and individuals.

There was a widespread, if often poorly expressed, sense that "the system" was at fault and needed to be radically changed if not replaced entirely. Some saw the problem as the capitalist system, others blamed the political system of their country, which seemed to favor one group over another. One result of the depression in many nations was a shift of support from the parties that had supervised the postwar economies and thus were regarded as responsible for the depression, to those that seemed to offer alternative policies. The parties of the extremes were often the political beneficiaries of this movement.

It was, however, often more satisfying to blame something more concrete than an abstract system, and in the early 1930s long-standing ethnic, religious, and other conflicts emerged. In Scotland the slump aggravated conflict, which had increased since the war, between Protestant and Catholic communities. It culminated in a riot in Edinburgh in the summer of 1935 when a Catholic Eucharistic Congress was surrounded by a Protestant mob estimated to be 30,000 strong.

Throughout Europe Jews were a popular target because they were often associated, in fact or in the public mind, with banking and commerce. Anti-Semites in many parts of Europe evoked a sympathetic reaction when they blamed the Jews for precipitating the depression in their own interests. Jews loomed large as alleged profiteers when banks seized farms whose owners had defaulted on loans, and Jews were widely perceived as doing too well during the depression. In Poland, often associated with anti-Semitism, Jews made up only 10 percent of the population, but accounted for half the lawyers and almost half the doctors. But apart from these professionals and a few large industrialists and estate owners, most Jews were poor, being involved in the least modern sectors of the economy: small business, trade, and crafts. Nonetheless, manifestations of economically based anti-Semitism increased in Poland in the 1930s, and there were demands that quotas be placed on Jews in universities. Most non-Jewish university students supported right-wing or fascist parties, and anti-Jewish incidents were frequent.

Ethnic tensions increased more generally as the depression brought renewed consciousness of the presence of "outsiders" in European states. In Estonia, which had one of the best records in Eastern Europe in terms of its treatment of minorities, rising German nationalism led to policies against the country's small ethnic German population of 17,000. English replaced German as the first foreign language in Estonian schools, and German street names were banned.

In Poland, beginning in 1930, "pacification expeditions" were dispatched to deal with growing unrest among Ukrainians and in Galicia as farmers' incomes fell. The net return per acre for Ukrainian peasant land holdings declined by three-quarters during the depression. Almost 1,800 arrests were made, special taxes were imposed, and non-Polish cultural organizations were suppressed. Appeals to the League of Nations under the Protection of Minorities Treaty backfired, because in 1934 the Polish government announced that it would no longer cooperate in monitoring the operation of the treaty.

Depression also exacerbated ethnic stress within Czechoslovakia, where unemployment was far higher among ethnic Germans and Slovaks than among Czechs. Half the country's unemployed were Germans in the Sudetenland, and there were more unemployed in the Sudetenland than in the whole of France. One result was that in the 1935 elections, Germans voted overwhelmingly for the fascist Sudeten German Home Front, which had ties with Nazi Germany.

Nor were refugees and foreign workers welcomed in depression-affected states. This worked a particular hardship on Jews who wanted to leave Germany after Hitler came to power. There were some havens, such as Switzerland, where one border crossing alone processed 10,000 refugees from Germany between April and September 1933. For the most part, however, government policies kept immigrants and refugees out, just as tariffs excluded foreign products. The number of people leaving Poland fell as if it were an index of any other kind of export: from 243,000 in 1929 to only 21,000 in 1932.

Germany: The End of the Weimar Republic

Nowhere in Europe was the depression more closely linked to political change than in Germany where 1929–33 saw Adolf Hitler's National Socialists, a hitherto marginal party, sweep to power, dismantle the Weimar Republic, and create the Third Reich. The relationship of the depression to these political developments is complex. The Nazis gained significantly in the elections held between 1929 and 1933, and the economic depression was an important context within which voting patterns changed.

Hitler was not simply elected to dictatorial office, and it is important to consider other political forces, elite as well as popular, that contributed to Hitler's gaining power. For some Germans the depression was less important in itself as for what it represented to them: the final evidence that the Weimar experiment had failed.

The end of the short-lived republic began in March 1930 when the Social Democratic chancellor, Hermann Müller, resigned following his failure to restructure the already hard-pressed unemployment insurance fund. Müller was the last supporter of the Weimar system to lead the German government. President Hindenburg's choice for new chancellor was Heinrich Brüning, a conservative Catholic who used the emergency powers provided by the Weimar Constitution to govern without majority support within the Reichstag. Brüning tried to counteract the effects of the depression by cutting wages, raising protective tariffs, and all but destroying the social security provisions built up during the 1920s.

Although the social and economic programs associated with the Weimar Republic were rapidly unraveled, few politicians raised serious opposition. The parties of the extremes were delighted, albeit for quite different reasons. Right-wing parties had opposed the social democratic Weimar policies all along. On the left, the Communists, guided by Moscow, took the view that the worsening economic crisis in Germany could only create the kind of turmoil, similar to the postwar period, where a revolution might succeed. Meanwhile the parties that might have defended the republic, notably the Social Democrats and Center, were paralyzed by the fear that opposing Brüning's measures would create even more political instability. In practical terms both left- and right-wing enemies of the republic had the upper hand.

The Reichstag elections of September 1930 suggested that popular feeling was running clearly against the republic, too. Compared to the previous (1928) election, the Weimar parties (Social Democrats and centrist Catholic parties) saw their support slip from 45 to 39 percent of votes cast. The parties of the extremes gained: The Communists increased their share slightly from 11 to 13 percent, and support for the Nazis soared from under 3 to more than 18 percent (see Figure 6.2). In 1930 the Nazis became the second largest party in the Reichstag, with 107 deputies to the SPD's 143.

FIGURE 6.2 Elections for the German Reichstag, 1928–33: percentages of the total vote won by the major parties.

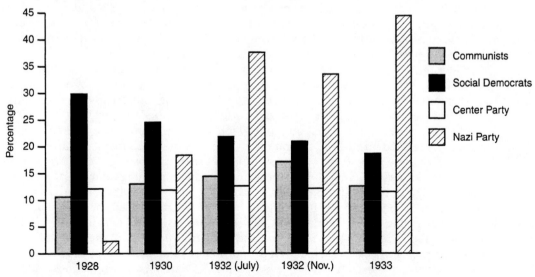

Source: Data from V. R. Berghahn, *Modern Germany: Society, Economy and Politics in the Twentieth Century,* 2nd ed. (Cambridge: Cambridge University Press, 1993), p. 301.

The four German elections of the depression period (1930, July 1932, November 1932, and 1933) have been intensively studied by historians trying to identify the groups that deserted the republic or rallied to the Nazi Party. Although there is no exact relationship between class, religion, and voting preference, Nazi electoral strength appears to have rested heavily on Protestant middle- and lower-middle class voters, rural and urban. Workers continued to support the Communists and Social Democrats (the latter gradually lost ground to the former), and Catholic voters stayed loyal to their Center Party, but in 1928 no single party had attracted Protestant middle-class and peasant interests. Their votes were spread among the parties of center and right, such as the Democratic Party, the National People's Party, and the Nazis.

But whereas in 1928 the five main non-Catholic, nonworker parties attracted an impressive 35 percent of the votes cast, they were divided by ideology and did not form a coherent voting bloc in the Reichstag. The big difference in 1930 was not just that these parties increased their overall voter support slightly to 37 percent, but that one party, the Nazis, cornered half of it.

Voting trends from 1928 to 1930 intensified in the elections in the next two years. Social Democrat support slipped in favor of the Communists, who by November 1932 had 17 percent of the vote. The Center Party retained and even increased its Catholic support slightly. But the big winner was the Nazi Party, which in July 1932 won 37 percent of the vote, and in November of that year won 33 percent. The shift in voter preference was clear: away from the centrist parties that had been the core of the Weimar Republic, and toward the extremes that were hostile to it. Both the Communists and Nazis opposed Weimar, and they even collaborated at times to defeat the Social Democrats.

The Nazis successfully attracted the huge bloc of voters both dismayed by the fortunes of Germany under the Weimar Republic and repelled by Bolshevism. The Nazis, like fascist movements elsewhere, presented themselves as being above party, class, religious, and sectional politics. They insisted that they were supported by men and women of all parts of society and all regions of the country. It is true that the Nazis attracted some working-class voters, but the bulk of their support came from the middle classes and rural population (especially artisans), who had been battered in turn by a pointless and humiliating war, by the 1923 currency debacle, and most recently by the depression. Beyond strictly economic considerations, these strata feared being relegated to the working classes, and felt trapped between powerful trade union and big business interests.

Professionals rallied to the Nazis in considerable numbers because they had suffered financially and in terms of status in the Weimar period. A growth in university enrollments had created an oversupply of men (and a few women) looking for work in the professions, especially law and teaching. It is estimated that each year in the later 1920s, about 30,000 new graduates were produced, but only 10,000 job openings appropriate to their qualifications. Between 1918 and 1932 the number of lawyers doubled, rising from 11,000 to 20,000, and of these some 6,000 earned so little that some commentators began to refer to a "legal working class." There were complaints of women pushing men out of work, although by 1932 only seventy-nine women had been admitted to the bar in Germany. Meanwhile teachers were forced into early retirement or had their salaries rolled back.

Disenchanted with the Weimar Republic, a few professionals turned to the left, but more chose the right. Non-Jewish doctors and lawyers in particular could identify with anti-Semitic policies because such a high proportion of these professions (29 percent of lawyers in Prussia, for example) were Jews. From 1932 Nazi-backed associations for doctors, lawyers, teachers, and engineers were formed. In that year they attracted the support of 9 percent of Germany's doctors, 7 percent of lawyers, 5 percent of teachers, and 2 to 3 percent of engineers. Although initially small percentages, professionals came to be significantly overrepresented within the Nazi movement.

Protestants also rallied in disproportionate numbers to Hitler, giving the Nazis more support in the north than the south. They had no tradition of loyalty to a major confessional party like the Catholic Center or (in Bavaria) the People's Party. Within the Protestant church, moreover, there was generally more sympathy than among the Catholic clergy to the Nazis. In 1932 a pro-Nazi organization, German Christianity, was founded. Hailing Hitler as "the redeemer in the history of the Germans," members of German Christianity were elected to a third of committee positions in the local parish elections in the fall of 1932.

Women were generally more reluctant than men to support the Nazis. Catholic and Social Democratic women voters stayed loyal to those parties longer than their male counterparts, but Protestant women of the middle class and peasantry, like men in these groups, turned in large numbers to the Nazis. In the 1932 election, the Nazis made an unprecedented effort to attract women's votes by setting up a new national women's organization and stressing that Nazism stood for "God, nature, family, nation, and homeland." The plan paid off, for although Catholic women remained suspicious of the Nazis, women in Protestant districts threw their support behind the Nazis in greater numbers than men.

Why did women vote for a party that clearly represented male interests and was openly hostile to paid employment and political activity by women? The answer must be that most middle-class and rural women shared these views of women's roles (as did the churches). During the depression, male unemployment was often blamed on working women, and Nazi policy neatly complemented prevailing concerns. The Center Party itself was on record as supporting the exclusion of women from the workforce in order to provide jobs for men.

The Nazi success in elections during the depression can be partly attributed to policies that responded to the resentments and anxieties that swirled through Germany. German electoral turnout improved during the depression (75 percent of eligible voters voted in 1928, 81 percent in 1930, and 88 percent in 1933), and the Nazis seem to have attracted the lion's share of the new votes: young people who had recently turned twenty-one, and men and women who had previously not bothered to vote.

In the early 1930s, we must remember, Nazism did not carry the appalling connotations it was to earn ten years later. In 1932 Hitler was clearly no democrat, but in its brief life in Germany, democracy had not produced such political or economic miracles that it was widely viewed as indispensable or even desirable. The Nazis seemed to stand for concrete advantages: strong government instead of the prevailing political chaos; national renewal instead of national humiliation; and moral regeneration instead of moral decline. It was not that the Nazis won support entirely by default, or simply as the beneficiaries of a negative protest vote against the conventional parties. Economic and social conditions worsened as the number of unemployed soared to 6 million, and the political process and leaders seemed unable to do anything. Increasing numbers of Germans saw Hitler and the Nazis as positive solutions to their country's problems.

Some of the Nazis' words (like their anti-Semitism) and deeds (like the violence of the Brown Shirt paramilitary squads) might have seemed regrettable, but many of their early supporters were prepared to give the Nazis a chance. They expected that the Nazis would tone down their rhetoric and that Hitler would rein in his overzealous supporters once he was in power.

Reflecting these considerations, German voters in the November 1932 election gave the Nazis a third of the seats in the Reichstag, making them the single largest party. Hitler refused to give his party's support to a government he did not control. In terms of the popular vote and seat distribution, Hitler had a better claim than any other party leader to form an administration: The second largest party, the Social Democrats, had only 121 of the seats, compared to the Nazis' 196.

After several months of frustrated efforts to create coalitions of various parties, Chancellor Schleicher was forced to recommend Hitler as his successor. The former chancellor, Franz von Papen, believed that Hitler could be controlled, and had himself named vice chancellor, with equal rights of access to the president. President Hindenburg named Hitler chancellor on January 30, 1933.

Papen's mistake was the same misunderstanding of the Nazis that many German voters made. The Nazis were not a conventional political party that intended to govern by democratic and parliamentary means. They were a fundamentally anti-democratic movement that used parliamentary methods to gain power so as to destroy the Weimar Republic and its institutions. The nonparliamentary outrages and the anti-democratic extremism of the Nazi gangs and political leadership were not the exuberance that an inexperienced party would slough off once it assumed the responsibility of government. They were intrinsic to the Nazi movement, and the proof of that rapidly became evident.

As soon as Hitler was appointed to lead a coalition government, he set in motion a strategy that would eliminate all opposition to his party. The immediate tactic was to gain secure control of the Reichstag, and to that end Hitler persuaded Hindenburg to call new elections for early March 1933, a mere five weeks after he was appointed chancellor. Much of this election campaign was literally fought in the streets; Nazi Brown Shirts fought with Communist paramilitary forces, as they had done during the preceding few years. On both sides people were killed and injured, and property destroyed.

A week before the election, the Reichstag building was set on fire, apparently by an emotionally disturbed Dutch Communist, although there were suspicions at the time and since that the Nazis themselves were behind it in order to reinforce the sense of a civil crisis. Either

German President Paul von Hindenburg with Chancellor Adolf Hitler.

way, Hitler took advantage of the fire to allege that there was a Communist plot to take over the state. He persuaded Hindenburg to declare a state of emergency, under which the police were given extended powers to search and detain suspects. The emergency powers were used against the Nazis' opponents, especially the Communists and Social Democrats, whose leaders were arrested, offices ransacked, and newspapers closed down.

Badly battered, the democratic process was not entirely destroyed. Both the Communist and Social Democratic parties lost some support in the 1933 election, but together they attracted 31 percent of the vote, a drop from 37 percent in November 1932. The Center Party held its support almost intact. The Nazis, however, saw their share of the vote increase from 33 to 44 percent (see Figure 6.2), giving them 288 of 647 seats in the Reichstag, which was forced to meet in a Berlin theater because of the fire.

Hitler was able to create a majority with the support of the National People's Party, which gained 8 percent of the vote and 52 seats, and with this he enacted a "Law for Terminating the Suffering of People and Nation." The effect of this law was to give the Nazi cabinet the power, for four years, to legislate, govern, and even make changes to the constitution, without reference to the full legislature. By the time the law was passed, on March 23, 1933, the Communists had been banned, and the only votes against the legislation came from the Social Democrats. The other parties voted for it out of fear, or in the expectation that they would benefit by supporting the now preeminent Nazis.

Having suppressed the Communists, Hitler then banned the Social Democrats, while his right-wing allies and the Center Party saved him the trouble of dealing with them: They voluntarily dissolved themselves. A law of July 14, 1933, declared the Nazis the only political party in Germany. This was not only descriptive but also prescriptive, and jail terms were stipulated for anyone who tried to maintain or found an alternative party.

In possession of extensive power, Hitler began to put into action his repeated insistence that unlike ordinary political parties, which saw power as the zenith of their desires and existence, the Nazis considered power as nothing but a prerequisite for fulfilling what they thought of as their true mission. One aspect of this was the removal of what Hitler referred to as "Jewish corruption" from German life. As early as April 1933, a national boycott of Jewish businesses by Aryans (as Nazis called people of "pure Nordic blood") was declared. Jews were barred from public office and from employment in the civil service and education, and were restricted in terms of employment in the media.

Many organizations willingly complied with the requirements. The German Mathematical Association declared in September 1933 that it "unconditionally and joyfully" placed itself at the service of Hitler, and adopted the Hitler leadership principle for its own organization. Moreover, the mathematicians agreed that the "requirements of Aryan ancestry in their strictest form" should be observed when their association's council was appointed, meaning that Jews would be excluded.

The broader Nazi agenda was under way when the death of President Hindenburg in 1934 enabled Hitler to complete his dictatorship at the constitutional level. A law of August 1 changed the constitution to merge the powers of president and chancellor so that Hitler held all executive and legislative authority. This law was the first to refer to Hitler as *der Führer* (the Leader), his title in the Nazi Party. As such it marked an important point in the merging of the Nazi Party and the German state and the formation of a totalitarian regime.

Hitler's seizure of power had all the appearance of a legal process. The Nazis won large proportions of the vote, were appointed to govern, and proceeded to pass legislation that cemented their hold on power. In strict terms, little of this was contrary to the law or the Weimar constitution, which did not protect itself against its own destruction.

The illegal methods employed by the Nazis at various stages—intimidation, violence against persons and property—probably made little difference to the overall result. Hitler's ability to construct a dictatorship rested on the paralysis of the Weimar political system in the face of repeated crises, of which the depression was only the last, and the willingness of millions of Germans (though never a majority of voters) to give Hitler and the Nazis a chance to do better.

Northern and Western Europe: The Pull to the Extremes

Germany was the most striking example of political change that emerged from the depression, but economic instability and its social consequences produced political shock waves that reverberated through other countries as well. Financial and economic systems had proved fragile, and the question was widely asked if political systems were made of stronger stuff.

In Britain the economic crisis produced no real threat to the political system, although there was a shift in party fortunes. In 1931 the Labour government, in power when the depression began, gave way to a multiparty coalition—a "National Government" of Labour, Liberals, and Conservatives—to promote nonpartisan policies. Even though the Conservatives won a record majority in elections late in 1931, they maintained the National Government until 1935. The leaders of all three major parties were able to cooperate because they shared a commitment to orthodox measures such as devaluation and protective tariffs.

The practical alternative to these policies was offered by a Labour Party renegade, Sir Oswald Mosley. Mosley had been a minister in the 1929–31 government, but broke with the Labour Party when it refused to endorse his proposals to get Britain out of the depression. Mosley's prime focus was on unemployment: Lower that and provide a living wage, he argued, and spending, demand, and production would rise in turn. In the short term his plan required the government to run a deficit (something unthinkable for Labour economists at that time) and insulate Britain from international financial pressure.

Frustrated by the refusal of his colleagues to listen to these ideas, Mosley left the Labour Party and founded his own movement, the New Party. Although it attracted some left-wing support initially, Mosley's party won no seats in the 1931 election. The next year he transformed the party into the British Union of Fascists (BUF), which not only called for radically different economic policies but also insisted that a reform of the British political system was needed before there could be a true national recovery. In Mosley's system, the monarch would name a prime minister after consulting a National Council of Fascists, while a Chamber of Corporations, composed of various economic interests, would oversee the economy. Every five years the people would vote to ratify the prime minister's work. Although clearly inspired by Mussolini's regime, Mosley saw his program as specifically British, and he insisted that the capital necessary for his program should be generated within Britain itself. His fascism, like Mussolini's, stressed the common interests of capitalist and worker alike. Beyond these policies Mosley stressed Britain's imperial role and expressed a generally anti-Semitic ideology.

The BUF also adopted the style of continental fascist movements. Young male supporters were formed into uniformed squads of Black Shirts and turned loose on Labour opponents and east-end London Jews. The Union's rallies were characterized by martial accouterments and behavior—floodlit flags, black uniforms, fascist salutes, and the presence of a leader—that would not have been out of place in Italy or Germany.

The BUF never attracted a mass membership, and it peaked early, in late 1934. At that point it had an estimated 50,000 members and won the backing of one of London's newspapers, *The Daily Mail.* Much of its early support came from unemployed workers in Britain's urban centers, mainly young men disillusioned by economic conditions and frustrated by the inability of mainstream parties to do anything. But Mosley attracted uppermiddle-class followers as well, men from the professions and former army officers who had seen their fortunes decline.

It is perhaps surprising, given the devastation wrought by the depression in Britain, that radical alternatives like the BUF and the Communist Party attracted such little support. There were certainly widespread protests against government economic and social policies, like the famous marches of the unemployed and massive demonstrations in 1935 by hundreds of thousands of workers protesting against changes in unemployment benefits. But they were not transformed into formal political action (partly because the Labour Party was suspicious of the 1935 demonstrators' motives), and they were never successfully exploited by proponents of radical solutions. The writer George Orwell suggested that the availability of cheap luxuries like silk stockings, tinned salmon, chocolate, the movies, strong tea, and soccer pools had combined to avert revolution in Britain. This explanation was proposed half-jokingly; it is worth taking half-seriously, for it reminds us of the relative prosperity of the British compared with the rest of Europe.

Across the Channel the situation in France was a contrast in halftones. There the effects of the depression were mitigated by the relatively low profile of industry in the economy and the ability of the government to keep unemployment low by removing immigrants from the workforce. Once the depression began to bite in 1932, voters opted for a left-center coalition of Radicals (who were liberals), Socialists, and several small reformist parties, headed by Edouard Herriot. By 1934 the coalition had broken down over economic policy, and a new coalition brought together Radicals and other centrist parties. Even so, France had vigorous movements at the political extremes, in part reflecting the country's long revolutionary and counterrevolutionary traditions.

Added to the government's inability to deal effectively with the deepening depression from 1932 to 1934 was anxiety about the resurgence of Germany under Hitler. The old French semi-fascist movement Action Française had no time for the Nazis, which it called "one of the greatest dangers for France," and as long as the extreme right was nationalist and showed no affinity to similar German movements, it was able to benefit from the volatile mix of increased national feeling and economic anxiety. This did not, however, prevent the French fascists from sharing anti-Semitic beliefs.

Action Française not only increased its membership, newspaper sales, and income between 1931 and 1933, but did so despite being joined on the right of French politics by several new organizations that espoused the kinds of policies associated with fascism: corporatism, nationalism, and anti-Semitism. Perhaps the largest of these was the Croix du Feu (Cross of Fire), which claimed to have a million members, but other groups (calling themselves leagues to distance themselves from conventional parties) were also important. The perfume manufacturer François Coty, who had financed fascist organizations in the 1920s, began his own movement in 1933. Called Solidarité Française, it had its own stormtroopers, but attracted only a few thousand adherents. Nineteen thirty-three also saw the formation of Le Francisme, a movement that self-consciously copied the uniforms (blue in this case) and martial organization of German and Italian fascists.

Although the street activist wings of these groups, together with other organizations like the Jeunesses Patriotes (Patriotic Youth) that were dedicated to fighting the Communists, made their impact through public violence, they posed no great threat to French political stability until early 1934. At that time the right-wing leagues were galvanized into action by the revelation of political corruption surrounding the business activities of a Russian emigré, Alexander Stavisky. Among the politicians implicated were several Jews, and when Stavisky was found dead—almost certainly he committed suicide—it was alleged that he had been killed to protect politicians.

On February 6, 1934, the leagues mounted a massive demonstration against the government's handling of the issue. In a violent confrontation of demonstrators and armed police, more than a dozen were killed and thousands were injured. The riot, the worst civil disturbance in France in peacetime during the century, shook the government but not the political system. The prime minister Edouard Daladier resigned despite majority support for his handling of the affair. A broad-based government of national unity was formed, spanning the parliamentary spectrum from the Radicals to the conservatives, and including prominent figures from outside parliament, such as Marshal Pétain, the hero of the Battle of Verdun. The French body politic had absorbed the blow.

Across the Pyrenees, Spain's politics were also disturbed by the depression. The authoritarian administration of General Primo de Rivera that had come to power in 1923 had coped poorly with the agricultural and industrial slump during the 1920s. After he lost the support of the army, he resigned in 1930, leaving King Alfonso XIII without an effective government.

Although Spain's economy was largely isolated from general European currents, and prices and wages stayed relatively steady, the depression gradually made itself felt. From 1930, and especially after 1932, agricultural and industrial exports (such as oranges, olive oil, and iron and steel) fell. Unemployment rose as producers laid off workers. When the municipal elections of April 1931 indicated widespread support for republican and socialist parties, especially in the cities, Alfonso XIII abdicated rather than test the loyalty of his armed forces. In national elections in June 1931, voters gave a majority to parties of the center and reformist left, a coalition that promptly established a republic (the Second Republic) with a secular, liberal, democratic constitution.

This administration, which governed until the elections of November 1933, began to put in place sweeping reforms in all spheres of Spain's economy, society, and political makeup. The Church and army, mainstays of the former regime and of the Spanish social and political order, but now regarded as the main obstacles to democracy, were tackled head-on. Catholic schools were ordered closed by 1933, and the government began a massive program of state school construction. The Jesuits were dissolved, members of other religious orders limited in their teaching and other activities, and religious property was subjected to taxation. Secular legislation repugnant to the Church, such as a very liberal divorce code (1932), was adopted. The size of the army, especially its officer corps, was reduced, and the army staff college was closed.

As the government alienated these powerful groups, it sought to reinforce its support among workers and to attract peasants to its side. The province of Catalonia, fiercely independent and Spain's industrial heart, was granted extensive autonomy. Labor laws were revised in favor of workers, and social security introduced. A redistribution of property to landless peasants was begun, although it never achieved its potential. Such measures were resented and opposed by sections of the Spanish population. The clergy and the military were quite rightly anxious about their status in the new state, while large property owners (stung by new taxes) and the middle classes feared what appeared to be the growing power of peasants and workers.

Worsening economic conditions and political antagonisms increasingly led to vigorous confrontations in parliament (the Cortes) and in the streets. Marxist and anarchist movements had strong support among miners and workers, and they expressed a militant impatience with the slowness and moderation of the very same reforms whose radicalism and speed appalled conservatives. By moving ahead firmly but carefully, the government alienated the powerful political and social forces on both extremes, and the extremists increasingly did battle directly.

In August 1932 right-wing forces led by a prominent general, José Sanjujo, attempted a coup. It failed, but in the following year the right wing gained strength. Its most notable expression was an organization called Falange Española (Spanish Phalanx, a reference to a type of military attack formation), founded by José Antonio Primo de Rivera, son of the general who had headed Spain's authoritarian regime in the 1920s. The Falange attracted only a few thousand adherents, but it occupied an important position on the political spectrum, and would later be co-opted by the military leadership as its political wing.

Increasingly divided over how far and how fast to carry out its program, the governing left-liberal coalition collapsed in 1933. In the elections of November that year, the voters gave no clear mandate to any one party, but the conservative CEDA (Spanish Confederation of the Autonomous Right, a coalition of conservative and right-wing parties) won the single largest number of seats in the Cortes. By the end of 1933 an unstable liberal-conservative government was formed, and under it many of the reforms of the previous government were either explicitly canceled or simply not implemented.

This about-turn radicalized many reformist socialists and persuaded others to rally to the revolutionary camp. The administration of Catalonia refused to recognize Madrid's authority over land reform. Left-wing and regional opposition culminated in a series of poorly planned uprisings in Madrid, Catalonia, the Basque country, and the Asturias in October 1934. The government was quickly able to restore its control in all but the Asturias, a mining area on the Bay of Biscay that had a strong sense of regional identity and that had been badly hit by the depression. There a separatist Socialist Republic was declared in October 1934, and the workers, formed into a "Red Army" militia, fought elite units of Spain's Moroccan army for two weeks before being defeated. In the course of the revolt, they attacked symbols of the Spanish regime, destroying many churches and police stations, and suffered 4,000 dead and wounded.

The uprisings of late 1934, particularly the virtual civil war in the Asturias, reinforced conservative fears of an imminent workers' revolution, and in reaction the Spanish government swung firmly to the right. It systematically reversed the reforms begun in 1931–33, reinstating Catholic education, suspending Catalonian autonomy, restricting freedoms of expression and organization, and reinforcing the army and police, now viewed as more important than ever. The depression period in Spain thus witnessed the beginning of the kinds of political trends evident elsewhere in Europe to varying degrees: political polarization and increased readiness to resort to direct, often violent action in place of electoral politics.

Elsewhere in Western and Northern Europe, the political repercussions of the depression period were minimal. Even in Scandinavia, where unemployment skyrocketed, voters tended to remain loyal to centrist parties, ranging from Social Democrats to Conservatives, that were committed to democratic principles. Social policies like unemployment benefits and comprehensive health care (all paid for by progressive taxation that was widely regarded as equitable) deprived the parties of the extremes, communist and fascist alike, of the ability to benefit from depression conditions. In Sweden the Communist vote increased slightly between 1928 and 1932 (from 6 to 8 percent). The largest vote for a Scandinavian right-wing party was the combined 4 percent won by the semi-fascist National Liberal Party and the fascist National League (headed by Vidkun Quisling) in the 1933 Norwegian election.

Authoritarian Regimes in Central and Eastern Europe

The eastern half of Europe, more agricultural than the west, was especially affected by the decline of demand and prices for primary products. The relatively small industrial economies fared no better. As in Western Europe the effects of the depression on politics varied, and there was no neat correlation between such phenomena as unemployment and declining production on the one hand and shifts in political allegiance on the other. Nonetheless, the widespread misery caused by unemployment, rural bankruptcy, and general impoverishment could not but help sharpen social and political conflict everywhere.

In Austria the depression aggravated a situation that was already in the mid-1920s marked by political instability and the growth of right- and left-wing political armies within the state. In elections in 1930 the Social Democrats won over 40 percent of the vote and the largest number of seats, but no one party had a majority. A conservative-right coalition was formed, and in order to widen its support it opened discussions with Germany in 1931 (that is, before Hitler came to power) on a customs union between Austria and Germany. Developing closer relations with Germany was popular across the Austrian political spectrum, but the negotiations looked to other states like the beginning of Anschluss, the full-scale union of the two countries that was forbidden in the Treaty of St. Germain.

Even though Europe was by 1931 in the grip of economic crisis, France was relatively well placed to apply pressure against closer Austrian-German ties. The substantial French deposits in the largest Austrian bank were withdrawn, forcing its closure. This action added to Austria's economic problems (unemployment increased from 182,000 in 1928 to 300,000 in 1931) and strengthened the appeal of the extremes. In September 1931, the Home Guard attempted a coup; it failed, and although the leaders were convicted, they were set free. In local elections in April 1932, when unemployment had climbed another 100,000, the Austrian Nazi Party made impressive gains throughout the country, including winning fifteen seats on the Vienna municipal council.

In May 1932, Engelbert Dollfuss, a minister in earlier administrations, was appointed Austrian chancellor, the sixth since 1929. He was immediately forced to turn to the League of Nations for a loan, which was granted with conditions: that Austria should form no links with Germany for the next twenty years. Broad opposition to the government's acceptance of these terms, together with pressure for new elections he knew he could not win, led Dollfuss to dissolve parliament. "Nobody can say when it will be allowed to take up its dubious activities again," he announced.

Dollfuss governed under a 1917 act giving the administration emergency powers to deal with economic problems. Freedoms of speech and assembly were immediately restricted, and challenges from both sides of the political spectrum confronted. Dollfuss was concerned at the growing strength of the Austrian Nazi Party (which had 43,000 members by 1933), especially after the appointment of Austrian-born Adolf Hitler as German chancellor. Pressure for political union now came from Germany as much as from Austria's

"Greater Germany" supporters. Relations between the governments deteriorated. When the German minister of justice entered Austria for a propaganda tour in May 1933, he was immediately expelled, and in retaliation Hitler imposed a 1,000-mark tax on German visitors to Austria, weakening the tourist industry. In June 1933, Dollfuss suppressed the Austrian Nazi Party. Dollfuss was nothing if not even-handed, however, and also destroyed the Social Democratic opposition. Its 80,000-member armed force was disbanded, its newspaper censored, and strikes suppressed.

Hostility to Nazi Germany's claims on Austria, and its interference in Austrian affairs through the Nazi Party, led Dollfuss to closer ties with Mussolini's Italy. Visiting Rome at Easter 1933, he was advised by both Mussolini and Pope Pius XI to establish a corporative state. Encouraged by Italian promises of support against Germany, Dollfuss established a Fatherland Front that would lead a "social, Christian, German Austria, on a corporative basis and under strong authoritarian leadership."

The last episode of internal resistance to the development of Dollfuss's fascist state occurred in February 1934, when the Social Democrats organized armed opposition and a general strike against arrests and weapons searches. A socialist center of resistance in a working-class housing project, the Karl Marx Hof, was overcome by government artillery. More than 300 were killed on both sides during the uprising, and 10 of its leaders were executed. The Social Democratic party was outlawed. On May Day 1934, a new authoritarian constitution was issued, making Austria a one-party fascist state on the Italian model.

In Hungary, too, the economic crisis of the early 1930s aggravated social and political problems. As we have seen, Hungary's agriculture was badly affected, and the country's small industrial sector was also ravaged. Production fell by a quarter, 15 percent of factories closed down entirely, and a third of the labor force was thrown out of work. There were no unemployment benefits or welfare schemes to help the jobless and their families. Official unemployment figures, which grossly understate its extent, show 66,000 out of work in 1932 (more than 10 percent of the labor force), a fourfold increase over the 14,000 in the mid- to late-1920s. Again, the fortunate ones kept their jobs, but with lower wages and longer hours.

Unable to overcome the financial crisis by foreign loans, and facing increasing unrest, including the blowing up of a Vienna-Budapest express, Hungary's government resigned in 1931. The new government obtained French assistance only on the condition that Hungary abandon its aim of revising the Treaty of Trianon, another example of France using economic leverage to achieve political gains. Opposition to the new administration came from agrarian lobbies that wanted agricultural subsidies, and nationalists who believed that Hungary was being sold out to France and to Jewish interests. In October 1932, another government took office, headed by Gyula Gömbös de Jafka, an anti-Semitic nationalist with expressed sympathies for the new Hitler regime and Mussolini's Italy.

Gömbös, who had organized armed squads to oppose Béla Kun's communist regime in 1919, had the support of the army officer corps and the bureaucracy. Although he declared hostility to the traditional political structure of Hungary (his was only the second cabinet in Hungary's history—Kun's was the first—to include no aristocrats), many aristocrats also supported him for his nationalism and anti-democratic ideas.

Yet despite proclaiming a 95-point National Work Plan that was supposed to get Hungary out of the depression, from 1932 to 1935 Gömbös adopted economic and social programs carefully designed not to alienate any important sector of the population. A three-year moratorium of debt repayments benefited a few farmers, and in 1934 a program was begun to settle 37,000 landless families in the following twenty-five years. For workers, Gömbös offered an 8-hour day and a 48-hour workweek.

All the while, however, his administration was undermining independent organizations, like trade unions, and creating the infrastructure of a one-party state under his Party of National Unity. State apparatus and party organizations were merged, government newspapers created, and a paramilitary force of 60,000 set up. Gömbös attracted support for his party by frequent attacks on popular targets, including aristocrats, Jews, foreigners, and communists. Elections in March 1935 gave Gömbös control of the parliament and would have allowed him to consolidate his one-party state had he not died the next year.

The depression also heightened political problems in Poland, whose economy was heavily dependent on exports. Industrial production fell 39 percent by 1932, one of the worst declines in Europe, and the value of exports fell to a quarter of the level in the 1920s. Unemployment embraced more than a quarter of the industrial workforce by 1931, real wages fell 22 percent, and peasants suffered from falling incomes that left them unable to pay taxes or make loan payments.

These conditions put increasing pressure on the regime of Marshal Pilsudski, who had come to power by a coup d'etat in 1926. Although Pilsudski had maintained Poland's democratic constitution while increasing the power of the executive, by 1929 there was fear among center and left-wing parties that a constitutional revision toward more authoritarian government was in the offing. A worrying sign was the installation of a fourteen-man cabinet in 1929 that included six army officers.

By 1930, challenges to Pilsudski emanated from various quarters. Parties of the center and left formed a common opposition and large antigovernment demonstrations took place. In response to government measures that included mass arrests and the demolition of Ukrainian community centers and libraries, a terror campaign by Ukrainian nationalists intensified later in the year. The worsening economic situation, which slashed government revenues and produced widespread unrest in cities and the countryside, aggravated the deepening political crisis. The government responded by arresting thousands of its opponents, including sixty-four deputies of the Sejm, the Polish parliament. Most of those arrested were Ukrainians and members of other minorities.

In the following four years, Pilsudski's regime increased its authority. Some opposition parties were banned, and the government extended its power to rule by decree and restricted the right of assembly. A new constitution, drafted in 1934 and enacted the next year, provided for a Sejm much reduced in power and size. The bulk of the powers would be vested in a president, directly elected by universal suffrage every seven years. The president would be responsible not to the Sejm, but to "God and history." Democratic government in Poland had receded another step.

All three Baltic states had experienced political instability in the 1920s—Estonia had twenty-one governments between 1919 and 1933—but the climate of economic suffering and political instability during the depression increased the attraction of extreme parties and movements of both left and right. Of the three, Latvia and Estonia also experienced a shift toward authoritarianism when the depression cut their export income and increased unemployment.

In Lithuania, the odd state out, power had already by 1928 been concentrated in the presidency to the point that the parliament ceased meeting. In 1929 President Smetona dismissed his prime minister and began a period of personal rule with the support of the army. Increasing repression of opponents culminated in the banning of all but Smetona's National Party in February 1934.

In contrast, when economic troubles hit Estonia, the country's liberal constitution, which gave all power to parliament, was still largely intact, despite the banning of the communist party and restrictions on extreme right-wing movements. Attempts to change the constitution to provide a stronger executive failed to get popular support in referenda until 1933, when the economy was suffering and the currency was devalued 35 percent. A new constitution created the office of president, and correspondingly diminished the power of parliament. Faced with challenges from the extreme right-wing Freedom Fighters, who controlled Estonia's three largest towns, the new president took determined action. In March 1934, the army was used to disband the Freedom Fighters and parliament was prorogued. The next year all political parties were banned.

The Peasants' League government in Latvia also came under increasing pressure in 1933 from economic stress and growing political extremism. In late 1933, seven communist deputies were arrested on charges of planning a revolution, but the fascist Thunder Cross movement, which emulated Nazi political style and policies, was left alone. In May 1934, however, the political and economic pressure rose so high that President Ulmanis banned both the communists and the Thunder Cross, then all parties except the Peasants' League.

The path of authoritarianism was trod by the states of southeastern Europe, too. In Romania, the National Peasant Party (NPP) swept to power with almost 80 percent of the votes in December 1928, just in time to supervise the collapse of the economy. The government's policies included reducing state involvement in mining and industry, removing restrictions on land purchases, and making rural credit more accessible. To attract outside capital, limits on foreign investment in Romania's economy were removed.

These policies, relying on trade, foreign loans, and investment, were put in place just as the depression dried up investment and closed foreign markets to Romanian agricultural products. Agricultural income declined by almost 60 percent. Frustrated by economic forces beyond its control, and weakened by internal divisions between peasants and nationalists, the NPP administration resigned in 1930. That year a new factor entered, or rather, an old factor returned. In 1925 the heir to the throne, Prince Carol, had renounced his right to succession, but in 1930 after his father's death he was permitted to return as king. As monarch, Carol began to dominate the government, and by 1934 he had established an authoritarian regime.

Bulgaria's trajectory through the depression years was somewhat different. After authoritarian regimes from 1919 to 1926, a period of democratization began. Censorship was relaxed, and those communists left (many were killed after an abortive coup in 1925) were allowed to become politically active again. In 1931 a relatively free election was held, and a centrist administration formed with members of peasant parties.

The first task of the new government was to deal with the effects of the depression on peasants, whose income fell more than 50 percent. To prevent the seizure of land needed for peasant survival, debts were immediately reduced by 40 percent, loan periods extended, and families were guaranteed five hectares of land that could not be seized if debts were called in. Subsidies were granted farmers who would grow export crops, even though export market prospects were poor.

These policies alleviated some problems, but many peasants, together with urban workers who also suffered as the economy declined, turned to the Workers' Party, as the communists were now called. In the 1931 election the Workers' Party won thirty-one seats, and in 1932 it gained a plurality in city elections in Sofia, the capital. More alarming was the growth of right-wing nationalism, which gained support especially in the army and among intellectuals. Offended by political wheeling and dealing, these nationalists saw party government as destructive and looked to a nonparty regime.

In May 1934 army officers staged a coup and set up an administration headed by two colonels. Parliament was dissolved, the state given a greater role over the economy, as well as in education, and the press came under controls. Only one trade union was permitted, and corporations were established to represent groups such as peasants, industrial workers, and professionals. It was not a full-fledged fascist regime, but it drew on the ideas promoted by contemporary fascist movements.

In Yugoslavia parliamentary government had survived during the 1920s despite curbs on extremist parties, but the political situation deteriorated from 1926 in the face of persistent tensions between the main ethnic groups, the Serbs and Croats. In late 1928 it seemed that the federation might break up, and to forestall this the monarch, King Alexander, seized power on January 6, 1929. Parliament was suspended, political parties and regional or religious organizations banned. The king assumed all power to rule, and made the commander of the palace guard his prime minister.

Alexander set about creating a unitary state from the federation. A single national flag was adopted, a standard legal code replaced regional laws, and taxation was made uniform. A new constitution, promulgated in 1931, provided for a bicameral parliament elected by universal male suffrage, but without a secret ballot. Alexander's regime failed to generate any great support, especially among Croatians who saw it as a Serb-dominated administration. Nor was it able to overcome the devastation wrought by the depression on Yugoslavia's economy. Alexander's personal rule ended in October 1934 when he was assassinated by a terrorist with connections to Croat nationalist extremists.

Throughout Eastern Europe the changes in political systems that occurred during the depression had an impact on their international relations. In general the changes that took place involved a shift to, or the intensification of, authoritarian political systems. But

Political extremism: the assassination of King Alexander of Yugoslavia, in Marseilles, France. The French foreign minister was also killed. The assassin, his coat held by the king's chauffeur, is trying to ward off a saber thrust by an officer on horseback.

it is important to recognize that even though they can generally be classified as right wing, and many as fascist, there were great differences among them.

Unlike the extremes on the left wing that looked to the Soviet Union and were generally controlled by the Communist International, the right-wing regimes were invariably nationalist. Although they often drew on Hitler's Nazis and Mussolini's Fascists for inspiration and policies, they had no desire to be dominated by them.

This was, in fact, rarely an issue. The notable exception was Austria, where the idea of union with Germany (*Anschluss*) was current among people of all political positions before the Nazis came to power. After Hitler's accession it is likely that Austrians' enthusiasm for inclusion in a Greater Germany waned somewhat, except among Austrian Nazis, and thereafter the main impetus for Anschluss came from Germany.

When Dollfuss established his one-party state under the Fatherland Front in 1934, Hitler attempted to overthrow him and install a Nazi regime. On July 25, 1934, Austrian Nazis in police uniforms entered the chancellery in Vienna and shot and killed Dollfuss, but despite this and scattered Nazi uprisings in other parts of Austria, Austrian forces regained control. For the time being Hitler abandoned the idea of Anschluss, not least through fear of provoking a response from Mussolini, who saw Austria as a vital bulwark between Italy and Germany.

In Poland, Marshal Pilsudski adopted cautious policies toward his country's German and Soviet neighbors; called the "doctrine of the two enemies," it reflected Poland's vulnerable position. In 1932 a nonaggression treaty was signed with the Soviet Union, and in 1934 another with Germany. Although Pilsudski was disdainful of Hitler's regime, he sensed that as Germany's position improved, Polish guarantees from France became less reliable, making a pact with Germany a useful asset. It also improved German-Polish relations for a while and the Germans suspended the assistance they had secretly been giving Ukrainian nationalists.

Although fascist governments throughout Europe agreed on certain policies, such as opposing Soviet influence (hence their concerted effort against the left in the Spanish civil war from 1936), they were almost universally nationalistic. The spread of fascist and non-fascist authoritarian regimes of the right throughout Central and Eastern Europe reflected not a conspiracy or a concerted program, but the intersection of general economic and social crises and the specific conditions in each state.

The Soviet Union: Industrialization, Collectivization, and Terror

The Soviet Union was the only European nation to escape the ravages of the Great Depression, largely because its economy was insulated. Even under the New Economic Policy adopted in 1921, foreign investment in Soviet industry and agriculture was so limited that foreign concessions in 1928 accounted for only half of 1 percent of industrial production. Soviet industry was largely unaffected by the contraction of investment that damaged so many European economies. Moreover, international trade was less important to the Soviet economy than to many others in Europe; by 1925 imports were a little more than a third the 1913 levels, and the Soviet Union's share of world trade was less than 3 percent, about the same as Switzerland's.

In 1928, as the rest of Europe was on the verge of industrial and agricultural decline, Stalin's regime determined to accelerate the sluggish pace of Soviet economic development. Seven years after the abandonment of "war communism," agricultural production just matched typical prewar levels; wheat production in 1926–29 was a shade under 22 million tons, compared with an output of a little over 22 million tons in 1909–13. Industrial performance was little better. Coal output was about a fifth higher than before the war, while steel production was about the same. Performances like these were disastrous for a state that aimed to become a major political and military power.

In order to catch up on lost time and to return to the principle of public ownership of production, Stalin introduced in 1928 a five-year plan for economic development. Known as the First Five-Year Plan when others followed, it set targets for increased productivity in all spheres of the economy. Two sets of goals were presented to the Communist Party conference in 1929 (after the plan was in progress), and the conference chose the more ambitious of them. Among other things, it called for an increase of 40 percent in the labor force between 1927–28 and 1932–33, and growth of 136 percent in industrial production, 55 percent in agricultural output, and 178 percent in wool textiles. The overwhelming emphasis was on construction of an industrial infrastructure (including energy production) and on heavy industry, especially steel and machinery.

Such ambitious targets were based on uncertain base figures and optimistic forecasts of labor availability, efficiency, and even weather. It was, however, intended to be a flexible plan, allowing targets to be decreased or increased according to conditions that could not be foreseen in 1928. In practice, however, the agency overseeing the Five-Year Plan always revised targets upward, making them even more difficult to achieve.

Integral to the economic modernization that Stalin was determined to force the Soviet Union through, was an increase in agricultural production. Not only was agriculture to finance industry, but in order to sustain the projected growth of the industrial labor force it was necessary to have plentiful, reliable, and cheap supplies of food, especially grain. Even before the Five-Year Plan was put into effect, Stalin had confronted the failure of peasants to produce adequate crops. He attributed this to peasants withholding grain from the markets until scarcity produced price increases. Relatively wealthy peasants called *kulaks*, those who had larger farms and who often employed other peasants as laborers, were identified as the prime culprits. Although the 1927 census showed kulaks making up only 5 percent of the peasantry, the government alleged that they had the power to hold the state to ransom and force it to pay higher prices for grain, and in turn that they could undermine the Soviet Union's drive toward industrialization.

The regime was driven by the logic of its ideology to adopt a policy of collectivizing agriculture, that is, of depriving peasants of their private land and forcing them to farm state-owned land on a collective basis. Not only did the notion of collective farming respond to Marxist ideology, but it was expected that collectivized agriculture would be more efficient, just as mass production in industry achieved economies of efficiency and scale. Collectivization would thereby produce a surplus rural population that could be employed in the new industrial plants.

The kulaks were to be excluded from the collectivization campaign that began in 1929. Communist officials visited local communities, where they persuaded or, if necessary, forced poorer peasants "voluntarily" to sign onto a collective farm. Land for the collective was obtained not only from the poorer peasants but also by driving kulaks out, and livestock was procured by seizing whatever was available in the locality.

The collectivization drive was an outright assault on the delicate modus vivendi the regime and peasantry had achieved, and the peasants resisted. They had successfully fought Bolshevik agrarian reforms before, when they contributed to the abandonment of war communism and the adoption of the more tolerable NEP. In 1929 officials were attacked, and peasants—poor and rich alike—slaughtered or sold their livestock rather

The official Soviet portrayal of the collectivization of agriculture. Collective farmers, most of them women, on their way to work. The banner denounces kulaks, the stratum of wealthy peasants.

than turn it over the collective farms. Many peasants who had been forced into collectives fled from them at the first opportunity to find work in the towns.

Women were prominent in riots against collectivization, not least because it threatened the familial basis of peasant life. Some might have believed reports that children would be taken from them, and that women would be shared collectively, but they were more often motivated by concrete economic concerns. Women were at the forefront of opposition to the seizure of domestic livestock, generally a woman's responsibility within the peasant household and vital for the family's well-being.

By the end of 1928, under 2 percent of peasant households were in any way collectivized, and by October 1929 only 4 percent had been. This was slow progress, and in late 1929 a commission proposed a program of total collectivization region by region, including the lower Volga by the autumn of 1930 and the whole of Ukraine by the spring of 1932.

In order to accelerate progress, a terror campaign was begun. Hundreds of thousands of peasants were arrested, others deported, some executed. The question of the kulaks was addressed. If whole regions and populations were to be collectivized, were kulaks to be included? After some debate among the Communist leadership and in the party press, Stalin decided that the kulaks should be "liquidated as a class." In Stalin's mind, kulaks were too dangerous to include in collective farms in case they dominated them, and from late 1929 the deportation of kulaks from their homes began.

Terror had mixed results. By early 1930, 21 percent of peasant households had been forced into collective farms, and by March 1930, 58 percent. In the process the peasants had slaughtered huge numbers of livestock. The Soviet Union's cattle and swine herds were reduced by about 30 percent between 1929 and 1931, and sheep and goats by almost 50 percent. These losses, combined with the prospects of peasant resistance and disruption during spring sowing in 1930, presented the possibility of an agricultural disaster that would derail the Five-Year Plan. Stalin pulled back. In an article titled "Dizzy with Success," he claimed that the terror and atrocities were the fault of local authorities who had exceeded their authority. To appease the peasants, Stalin ordered confiscated live-stock to be returned to their original owners (kulaks excepted). As soon as the pressure to collectivize was off, half the peasants who had joined collective farms quit them.

Over the next years collectivization was achieved by slow, steady persuasion and pres-sure. Peasants were allowed to keep their cows and chickens, and each family was permit-ted a plot of land for private use, including growing produce for private profit. By 1934, collectivization encompassed 71 percent of peasant households and 87 percent of the Soviet Union's cultivated land.

It was not only peasant cultures and social systems that were under attack. There was a shift in nationality policy and campaigns against non-Russian education and culture. Ukraine came under particular pressure, and in Kazakhstan nomadic populations were forcibly settled. Religion, too, came under increasing pressure, and thousands of churches, mosques, and synagogues were closed. In response rumors of the Apocalypse spread through the countryside. It was said that anyone who joined a collective farm would be signed over to the Antichrist, and after the church in one Ukrainian village was closed it was reported that a miraculous light emanated and a sign appeared on the cupola, reading, "Do not join the collective farm or I will smite thee."

During 1930 and 1932, however, the deportation of kulaks continued. *Kulak*—by now used in a political rather than a socioeconomic sense—denoted any peasant who was hos-tile or would not cooperate with the regime; some teachers, for example, were subjected to anti-kulak measures, and women who behaved in a disorderly manner (sexually and otherwise) were sometimes condemned as kulaks. The breadth of the term makes it diffi-cult to estimate the number of better-off peasants subjected to persecution. Estimates of the number of peasants deported in the late 1920s and early 1930s range as high as 15 mil-lion men, women, and children. Perhaps as many as 2 million were sent directly to work on the new industrial projects, causing havoc because they were unskilled and not used to living in an industrial environment. Another million adult men were sent to labor camps, where they performed forced work in mining and forestry. The remainder were sent to remote areas in the north, where they had to establish their own habitations and food sup-plies. An estimated 15 to 20 percent of the deportees died on the way, in cattle trucks or on forced marches.

Even these deaths paled against the mortality inflicted upon Ukrainian peasants in 1932–33. Each year the government decreed the amount of grain the peasants had to de-liver to the state, but in 1932 the demand was for an amount that exceeded the actual yield. The reason was an official overestimation of the size of the crop, based on projec-tions from land under cultivation rather than the actual harvest. Refusing to believe that the crop was smaller than government officials had estimated, Stalin insisted that the de-liveries be made. Many regions of Ukraine were stripped of their entire grain harvest, in-cluding seed for the next year, fodder for livestock, and the year's food requirements of the peasants themselves.

In the ensuing winter of 1932–33, between 4 and 5 million people died of starvation and disease in Ukraine alone. This was not the inadvertent result of a massive bureaucratic blunder; had it been so, enough of the requisitioned grain could have been returned to feed the hungry. Not only was that not done, but steps were taken to prevent starving peas-ants from entering towns in search of food and assistance. The famine was Stalin's way of reducing peasant opposition to collectivization, and Ukrainian opposition in particular.

Despite the effort put into collectivization, deportations, and killing—all of which were successful—the main thrust of Stalin's economic policy was rapid industrialization. It, too, was successful, even though many of the original targets of the Five-Year Plan, not to mention the hopelessly ambitious revised goals, were not met. There is probably little to be gained from comparing results to goals, except to demonstrate the unrealistic state of mind of contemporary Soviet planners and political leaders, and the subordination of statistics and forecasting to ideology within the Soviet bureaucratic culture.

From the perspective of industrialization, however, the results were impressive. The vast Dnieper Dam was constructed, providing power for more industries, and the production of oil and coal rose healthily. Massive engineering, steel, chemical, and automotive plants were constructed, not only in existing industrial regions but also in the more remote and agrarian regions. Precise and reliable figures are not always available, but it seems that between 1928 and 1933 petroleum output doubled, the amount of electrical energy generated increased threefold, and steel production rose 40 percent.

The program had drawn in vast numbers of workers, even to the point of creating some labor shortages. Work on construction and production was carried on seven days a week, with workers having a seven-hour day and a five-day week, which meant four days at work followed by one day off. This eliminated Sunday as a universal day free of work, which tied in with the campaign against religion that intensified in the early 1930s.

Food rationing was introduced in 1929 because of shortages and the government's need to export increasing amounts of grain on a depressed world market in order to purchase machine tools and other equipment for Soviet industrialization. Within the rationing system, urban populations were favored over rural inhabitants in the allotment of food. Between 1928 and 1932, the per capita consumption of bread and potatoes in cities rose substantially, by 20 percent; in rural areas consumption fell about 12 percent. Urban populations increased rapidly and new cities appeared on the countryside, placing immense pressures on housing and services. Several families were forced to live in single apartments, and there were shortages of fresh water.

The mobilization of the Soviet people also increased the employment of women in industry, reversing a decline in 1929 and 1930. In the fall of 1930, large numbers of women entered the workforce, not because of a specific state policy to encourage women's work, but simply because more labor was needed. By the end of 1931, more than 400,000 women had begun paid work for the first time. In just eighteen months, between January 1930 and July 1931, the proportion of women in heavy industry rose from 14 to 24 percent, and in light industry from 51 to 58 percent. Many peasant women, accustomed to hard labor in the country, joined the unskilled industrial workforce, and some professions, notably medicine and teaching, were almost entirely filled by women.

The growth of women's work had an immediate impact on the Soviet family. The fertility rate fell, and household family size declined from an average of 4.7 members in 1927 to 3.8 in 1935. The state's need for all adults to work meant that child-care facilities had to be expanded. Between 1928 and 1934, facilities for infants rose 20-fold from 257,000 to 5,143,000, while day-care centers for older children had places for over a million children by 1935. Full employment failed to give women independence within the family, however, because real wages in the Soviet Union fell so fast in the early 1930s that two adults working earned no more than one had in the late 1920s.

The First Five-Year Plan was also accompanied by a "cultural revolution" designed to instill, in young people especially, a proper ideological orientation, and to create a reliable managerial stratum. The rapid creation of so many new industries, plants, and bureaucracies required new managers and administrators at all levels. Many workers were promoted from the shop floor to management; about a sixth of top-level administrators in 1933 had been manual workers five years earlier, and in all half a million people moved from blue- to white-collar occupations in the period of 1930–33.

The vast number of technicians required by the new economy promoted the growth of education, particularly engineering schools. Some 150,000 workers and Communists entered institutions of higher education during the plan's existence. Many of them would emerge later in the country's elite, and they included three future chairmen of the Council of Ministers (Khrushchev, Brezhnev, and Kosygin). At times the cultural revolution got out of control as young enthusiastic members of Komsomol, the communist youth organization, harassed professors whom they regarded as having "bourgeois" attitudes, campaigned for collectivization in the countryside, disrupted performances of plays they considered insufficiently proletarian, and pressed for harsher policies against the enemies of the state.

The experience of the Soviet Union was quite different from that of the rest of Europe in the depression era. In economic terms the Soviet Union could be portrayed as a sparkling success; Soviet propagandists in the early 1930s contrasted Soviet achievements with the depressed economies of the Western democracies to demonstrate the superiority of Stalin's regime. Economic development was accompanied by immense tragedies, however; not only were traditional peasant cultures destroyed, but millions of women, men, and children were deported to uncertain lives or certain deaths, and of those left behind, millions perished from starvation.

Conclusion

In the five years from the onset of the depression to 1934, the political map of Europe changed dramatically. States like Italy and the Soviet Union that were already authoritarian were not affected, but they were joined by others: Germany, Austria, Hungary, Yugoslavia, Poland, Estonia, Romania, Lithuania, Latvia. Spain was in turmoil. Although this period, and the years immediately following, are associated with the spread of fascism, not all the new regimes were fascist or even semi-fascist. Some regimes, like those in Austria and the Baltic states, were anxious to forestall the success of fascism, although not as anxious as they were to prevent a Communist victory.

The depression, as a strictly economic phenomenon, played a variety of roles in the political changes. It did more than merely provide a context within which political changes took place, but neither was the depression the sole cause of change. Rather, we must appreciate the way in which the manifestations of the depression—unemployment, falling incomes and living standards, anxieties about the future, resentment at the failure of political systems to prevent such catastrophes—interacted with the political, social, economic, and cultural traditions and conditions of each state in this period.

· 7 ·
The European Dictatorships, 1934–1939

Introduction

The short five-year period from the Great Depression to the outbreak of World War II was marked by the consolidation of existing authoritarian states and the creation of new ones. Prominent among the former were Germany, where Hitler's young dictatorship became unassailable, and the Soviet Union, where Stalin entrenched his personal dictatorship. Prominent among the latter was Spain, whose democratic system collapsed after a brutal civil war that became a symbol for the conflicts that divided Europe in the 1930s. In Eastern Europe more authoritarian right-wing regimes, royal and republican, civil and military, were established.

In all cases, there were social and economic consequences. In Germany the Nazis sketched the outlines of the racial state that they would draw more firmly after the war began. In the Soviet Union totalitarian policies had some success in achieving social and economic goals.

The mid- and late-1930s also witnessed a shift in the balance of military and political power in Europe. Within twenty years from the end of the First World War, Germany emerged as the major force to be reckoned with. Under Nazi economic and social policies, Germany recovered more rapidly than any other major nation from the depression. In the Soviet Union a crash program of economic modernization had uncertain results; Great Britain and especially France recovered more slowly.

In general it was Germany that set the agenda for the 1930s, not only in terms of international relations but also in terms of domestic policies in many states. The Nazis' drive to overturn the Treaty of Versailles encouraged other challenges to the postwar settlement, and the assertion of German military power from 1935 on affected most of Europe.

Germany, 1934–36:
The Nazis Consolidate Power

In the first years of his regime, Hitler's principal concerns were to consolidate his position to the point that it was unassailable, and to restore the German economy to its former strength. The two goals were not unrelated, for the Nazis had won considerable popular support in the expectation that they could perform the economic miracles that eluded others. Rapid economic recovery would prevent that support from slipping away. Between

1933 and 1936, these goals were pursued rigorously in ways that also indicated the Nazis' other priorities. Much of Germany's economic growth was military, in contravention of the Treaty of Versailles that Hitler was committed to overturning. Anti-Semitic measures were introduced, and social policies were put in place that indicated the direction of social and cultural change under the Nazis.

By 1934 the Nazi regime had consolidated its political position, using a policy of *Gleichschaltung,* meaning "coordination" or "bringing things into line." In mid-July 1933, all remaining political parties were suppressed or, in the case of nationalist right-wing parties, incorporated within the Nazi Party. Independent trade unions were abolished and replaced by the German Labor Front (DAF), which was supposed to represent the interests of all workers. Professionals, peasants, and artisans all had their own state-sponsored organizations. All Germans were to think of themselves as members of what the Nazis called the "national community."

To rally Catholics to the regime and give it an appearance of respectability internationally, Hitler also signed a concordat with the Vatican in 1933. Hitler was, besides, a Catholic and was never excommunicated by the Church. Under the terms of the concordat the Center Party, which was in effect a Catholic party, dissolved itself, and the Church and clergy were bound not to interfere in German politics. Many members of the Lutheran church, Germany's other main denomination, had already rallied to Nazism.

The structure of German government was also brought into line. The Reichsrat, parliament's upper chamber, was abolished, leaving the lower chamber, from which all non-Nazis had been removed, in a state of limbo. It had no function but to support the regime's decisions, which were not referred to it in any case. Germany's federal system was also abolished, leaving power concentrated in Hitler and his cabinet. When President Hindenburg died in August 1934, Hitler merged the offices of president and chancellor, and gave himself the title "Führer [Leader] and Reich Chancellor." The military and state services now had to swear oaths of loyalty not to Germany but to Hitler himself.

For obvious reasons it was important for Hitler to have the army on his side, and it rallied to him largely because his policies coincided with its own interests. Hitler promised to destroy the Treaty of Versailles, which not only insulted Germany but institutionalized the army's humiliation by reducing it to a size and effectiveness of a third-rate power. The regime quickly put rhetoric into practice when in July 1933 a program of tank construction began in the guise of building tractors for agricultural use. By 1934 ships, aircraft, and munitions were in production, all in contravention of the Treaty of Versailles.

Hitler took further action to win the support of the army. It was reassured by the destruction of the SA, the brown-shirted Nazi paramilitary force, which had become a large organization, difficult to control and a rival to the regular military forces. Beginning on the night of June 30, "the night of the long knives," the leaders of the SA, as well as scores of Hitler's prominent rivals, were killed. To give the murders the semblance of legality, a law was passed on July 3 stating that the measures taken were justified "acts of self-defense by the state."

The repression of opponents of the regime had begun as soon as the Nazis gained power. Communists, socialists, Catholic activists, and others were arrested and held without trial by the thousand in makeshift prisons, called concentration camps. (They should not be confused with the death camps the Nazis later established.) Prisoners were held in appalling conditions and often forced to work on construction projects.

The Nazi government also began its official persecution of Jews with legislation in 1933 that excluded Jews from the civil service, law, medicine, schools, universities, and culture. These policies reinforced and extended the support the Nazis received from non-Jewish professionals. At the same time regional and local party organizations harassed Jews in various ways, particularly by encouraging boycotts of Jewish-owned businesses and stores.

Anti-Semitism was central to Nazism because the Germany Hitler planned to create would include only "Aryans" or "pure" Germans, to whom Jews were perceived as a real threat. Not only had Jews undermined Germany economically and culturally, Hitler thought, but they represented a biological threat, much as a virus threatens an otherwise healthy organism. Nazi rhetoric referred to Jews as "vermin" and a "plague," and propaganda films made the point by juxtaposing images of Jews in ghettos with shots of rats swarming in sewers and granaries. To call Jews vermin was not a metaphorical device; it was meant to draw attention to the actual harm the Nazis insisted could be suffered by Aryans who came into contact with Jews. At the very least, these ideas implied the need to exclude Jews in particular, and non-Aryans in general, from the political nation.

It is often pointed out that Jews were more assimilated in Germany than elsewhere in Europe, as if full participation of Jews in German political, economic, and social life, and the frequent intermarriage between Jews and Christians or Gentiles, should have reduced the level of anti-Semitism. For the Nazis, however, it was the very progress of Jewish assimilation into German society that was alarming. The anti-Semitic policies they devised and carried out were intended to reverse the historical trend.

Despite the centrality of anti-Semitism to the Nazi vision, Hitler hesitated to implement full-scale persecution in the first years of the regime. Against the urging of radicals in the Nazi party like Julius Streicher and Joseph Goebbels, Hitler paid more heed to bureaucrats and advisers who warned that too vicious an attack on Jews could disrupt the German economy and harm the new Nazi regime's international reputation. For Hitler this was a difference of priority and timing, not of policy. Action would be taken against the Jews, but it could wait until other goals had been attained.

The main thrusts of Nazi policy in this period were to bring Germany out of the depression and to reverse some of the most repugnant terms of the Treaty of Versailles. The first was achieved with remarkable speed by stimulating the economy with massive public works projects and state investment, taking control of wages, prices, and resources, and protecting the German currency and economy from outside influences.

The kinds of projects that were favored reflected the longer-term policy of the regime: achieving economic and military autarky, or self-sufficiency, that would enable Germany to expand its territory and acquire *Lebensraum,* additional "living space" for Germans in Central and Eastern Europe. One of the first projects undertaken was the construction of the autobahns, superhighways of the time that linked major cities throughout Germany. Many were designed with military purposes in mind, but they also assisted the economic development of the country and brought peripheral regions into closer contact with the center. Like many major projects, the autobahns provided the infrastructure for the development of military industries, without themselves contravening the Treaty of Versailles.

The vast building program, together with policies that encouraged women to leave the paid workforce, rapidly reduced unemployment. It was an achievement that provoked in other countries, still mired in the depression, a mixture of admiration, envy, and fear. Official unemployment in Germany fell from its peak of 5.6 million (30 percent of the workforce) in 1932 to 1.6 million (7 percent) in 1936. But although many more workers had jobs, wages in sectors of industry not connected to rearmament lagged behind price increases until 1938. In order to ensure continuing popular support, the production of consumer goods was promoted, but from time to time the conflicting demands of heavy industry led to shortages.

Social policy in the first years of the Nazi regime was also harnessed to Nazi economic and race goals. Not only did Germany have to be cleansed of non-Aryan (especially Jewish) influences, but the Aryan population had to be strengthened in number and quality. The Nazis drew on the language of eugenics that had been spoken by mainstream political and social leaders in Europe for decades, but they emphasized race over more general biological qualities.

In 1933 a loan system was established to encourage young, healthy, and "racially pure" Germans to marry and have children. The interest-free loans, for furniture and other household goods (which stimulated those sectors of the economy), had to be repaid in full only if the couple did not have at least four children; with each child, a quarter of the loan was forgiven. About one in five marriages in the 1930s was assisted by these loans. They might well have contributed to the increase in the marriage rate in Germany, although there was a general increase in marrying throughout Europe as economic conditions improved.

Encouraging marriage and fertility had implications for German women, whose prime function was regarded by Nazis as bearing and rearing children. Young single women were urged to quit paid work and marry (until 1937, recipients of marriage loans were forbidden to work), and some companies gave women cash bonuses as a further incentive. Despite the Nazi stress on women's familial roles, they did consider certain occupations, like agriculture and domestic service, suitable for them. Employment in heavy industry, however, was considered "biologically" dangerous for women. The departure of thousands of women from industrial work created vacancies for men, and was a substantial factor in reducing unemployment, not least because women who left paid work in industry were excluded from official unemployment figures.

The social and economic policies enacted early in the Nazi period laid the ground for the development of an authoritarian regime in which the government abandoned liberal economic principles in favor of state control, and undermined the private sphere of social life by making marriage an instrument of state policy. The process was carried a step further in September 1935 when a set of race laws, known as the Nuremberg Laws, was announced at one of the Nazis' massive rallies in Nuremberg. A scheme was concocted to classify men and women as Aryans, Jews, and those of "mixed race." Among those who were considered Jews were people having three Jewish grandparents. Anyone who had two Jewish grandparents and who belonged to the Jewish religious community was also considered a Jew; so was anyone married to a Jew. All those with one Jewish grandparent (or two, as long as they themselves were not members of the religious community) were considered "part-Jews" to one degree or another. These definitions bore no relation to definitions of Jewishness in Orthodox Jewish law.

The Nuremberg Laws identified Jews for the purpose of removing them from mainstream German society. They were the legal foundation of subsequent anti-Semitic policies, for they enabled the authorities to determine which individuals were subject to discriminatory legislation. The 1935 law dealt with the civil status of Germany's Jews. They were no longer considered citizens, but "state subjects" without civil rights. (This was the minimal form of exclusion implied by Nazi ideology.) Jews were not permitted to identify with Germany by displaying the national flag or colors.

Marriage between Jews and Aryans was prohibited by law, and extramarital sexual intercourse between Aryans and Jews, which was also forbidden, was referred to as "race defilement." Echoing the frequently asserted sexual slander that Jewish men lusted after and sexually assaulted young Aryan women, Jews were forbidden to employ non-Jewish women under the age of forty-five. For the same reason, Aryans were warned not to let Jewish doctors treat them, even though in some large cities most doctors were Jewish.

Illustration from a German children's book, showing a Jew trying to seduce a young "Aryan" woman. The picture expresses the allegations of anti-Semites that Jewish men lusted after non-Jewish women.

By 1936, Hitler's policies were moderate compared with the demands of radicals that Jewishness be defined even more broadly to encompass more people. The Nuremberg Laws appeased some anti-Semitic extremists in the party, and Hitler distanced himself from activists at the local level who attacked Jews and Jewish businesses. In these respects Hitler's policies toward Jews were carefully modulated so as to avoid aggravating the international reaction to his plan to overturn the Treaty of Versailles.

In 1935, as provided for in the treaty, a plebiscite was held in the Saarland to determine its political future, and the inhabitants voted in favor of union with Germany. Apart from this instance, where the treaty favored Germany, Hitler proceeded deliberately to break the treaty. Using Austrian Nazis, Hitler had attempted a covert takeover of Austria in 1934, an unsuccessful attack that killed Chancellor Dollfuss. Rearmament had begun covertly as early as 1933, but in 1935 Hitler announced the existence of an air force, a program of general rearmament, and the introduction of conscription to create an army of half a million men, five times that allowed under the Treaty of Versailles.

The reaction of Germany's former enemies appeared firm. At a meeting in Stresa (Italy), a month after Hitler announced rearmament, France, Britain, and Italy declared their united opposition to any unilateral repudiation of treaties that endangered the peace of Europe. In May, Hitler responded by renouncing war as a means of achieving policy goals, and reaffirming Germany's commitment to the Locarno Treaty. He did not, however, cancel the rearmament program.

Apart from condemning Hitler's actions, Britain, Italy, and France were unwilling to take action; nor was any of them in any political, economic, or military position to do so. Britain and France embarked on the policy that has become known as "appeasement," which is discussed in the next section. Within months of its protest at German rearmament, Britain's government signed an agreement allowing Germany to build a surface fleet a third the size, and a submarine fleet half the size, of its own. The agreement was an open breach of the Treaty of Versailles, but the British calculated that because there was no politically acceptable way to stop Germany rearmament, it was best contained within bilateral international agreements. They anticipated that the Nazis would respect agreements they entered into freely, more than the dictated terms of the Treaty of Versailles.

In March 1936, Hitler took advantage of international preoccupation with Italy's invasion of Ethiopia (described in the next section) to take a dramatically daring step forward in the destruction of the Treaty of Versailles. A force of about 12,000 soldiers and home guard troops was dispatched into those parts of the Rhineland that had been ordered demilitarized in 1919 to provide security for the French border. Even though the German forces involved were minimal, the French decided not to attempt to expel them and reestablish a demilitarized zone (as they were entitled to by the Locarno Treaty). Although some members of the French government wanted to mobilize the army, most civilian and military leaders were uncertain whether such a response would be successful.

The French had constructed a system of defensive fortifications (the Maginot line) along the border, making the continued demilitarization of the frontier region less pressing than it had been immediately after the war. In 1937, however, Belgium declared that it was reverting to neutral status. This posed a new problem for France because the Maginot line extended north only as far as the Belgian border, and there was no guarantee that French troops would be allowed passage through a neutral Belgium in the event of hostilities with Germany.

It did not seem likely that Britain would support a French military response in the Rhineland. The British took the view that the Rhineland was, after all, German territory, and that remilitarization was unlikely to threaten peace in Europe. Again there were protests, and again there was no military response. The act was, however, immensely popular in Germany itself, where Hitler was praised for undoing some of the injustices inflicted on Germany and restoring national honor.

In the short period of 1933 to 1936, Hitler had not only consolidated his position in Germany and begun the transformation of German political, social, and cultural life. He had also magnified Germany's position in Europe, and put in place the policies that would extend the Nazi shadow beyond the borders of the Reich.

The remilitarization of the Rhineland, 1936. German soldiers entering Heidelberg are presented with flowers by some of the inhabitants.

The Balance of Power Shifts, 1934–36

It was not a coincidence that Hitler was able to pursue his domestic and foreign policies aggressively without much more than token resistance from the major European powers. The same depression that weakened them politically had brought him to power. Attitudes toward Hitler's regime varied throughout Europe. In many respects Germany appeared to be following the path toward authoritarianism that was by 1934 being followed by most Central and Eastern European states. On the other hand, there was a realization that a resurgent Germany had far different ramifications from an economically strong Estonia or Bulgaria.

The apparent unity of the "Stresa Front" that condemned Germany's breaches of the Treaty of Versailles was a "front" in another sense, too, for it concealed widely different national policies. By signing a naval agreement with Germany in mid-1935, the British signaled their acquiescence in the destruction of the treaty. The French, mindful of the threat that a new powerful Germany might again pose, were less sanguine, but were unable to act alone. France's economy, affected later than others by the depression, suffered the effects longer; in 1935–36, just as Hitler announced that Germany was rearming, unemployment in France was at unprecedented levels, and industrial production was at its lowest point during the slump. Even though general unemployment in Britain had fallen, jobless rates in key military industries like coal mining, steel, and shipbuilding were over 25 percent.

Mussolini's government was less concerned with Germany than with its own plans to create an empire in Ethiopia. Italian interest in Ethiopia dated from the nineteenth century, although it had waned after the humiliating defeat at Adowa in 1896. Mussolini resuscitated plans for imperial expansion there in the early 1930s for several reasons: Ethiopia, a sovereign state, was not controlled by any European power; it lay adjacent to existing Italian possessions in Eritrea and Somaliland; an imperial success would boost Italian morale and the popularity of the Fascists, both of which had sagged during the depression; and nationalists would be heartened by the revenge of Adowa.

Italian forces based in Eritrea and Somaliland invaded Ethiopia in October 1935. With a quarter of a million troops supported by aircraft and tanks, they were almost assured of victory, but it still took seven months before the capital, Addis Ababa, was captured. Italian casualties, about 2,000, were few compared with the almost 300,000 suffered by the defending forces, which were not prepared for bombing and poison gas.

As soon as the invasion began, Ethiopia's emperor Haile Selassie appealed to the League of Nations, which condemned the attack and recommended economic sanctions against Italy. However, the sanctions were ineffective. They were limited to military supplies, did not include vital resources like oil, and were to be applied by states individually. There was, in fact, no real desire by the major powers to confront Italy in such a way as to provoke a war or even a diplomatic crisis. Britain and France in particular had no wish to alienate Italy, which they considered a partner in the loose Stresa Front against Germany, and they tried to work out an arrangement that would give Italy half of Ethiopia outright and economic rights in the remainder. When the British press publicized the deal, which conflicted with the British government's declared support for the League of Nations, it was abandoned, leaving Mussolini to seize Ethiopia without British or French acquiescence.

By the end of 1935 it was clear that the League of Nations was politically impotent and that both Britain and France, the only great powers that were still members, were reluctant to risk war by trying to stop Italian or German breaches of international law and treaties.

By the spring of 1936, significant changes had taken place in the European balance of power, although their implications were not necessarily evident at the time. In Italy, Mussolini had launched an aggressive foreign policy. In Germany, Hitler had consolidated the Nazi dictatorship to the point that he could simply ignore the Treaty of Versailles. Britain and France had adopted policies that have become known as "appeasement." These policies permitted Germany to redress its grievances emanating from the Treaty of Versailles in exchange for German cooperation in international affairs. In effect, however, appeasement allowed Germany to commit one breach of international law or treaty obligations after another, each success encouraging Hitler to move to the next.

Whether Britain and France ought to have acted more decisively against Hitler was a matter of fierce debate at the time, and has been a matter of vigorous historical argument since. In 1936 there was general agreement throughout Europe that the Treaty of Versailles was unjust, and that Germany ought to be allowed to take its place in the community of nations as a major industrial power. The Nazis' repression of its opposition aroused concern, but many national leaders thought the Nazis at least preferable to the Communists, who seemed to be the main alternative. The policies of discrimination against Germany's Jews did not worry too many European leaders. Physical attacks on Jews, frequently reported in the Western European and international press, were often dismissed as the acts of extremists and hooligans rather than as reflecting the thrust of official policy.

The fact that Hitler still, in 1936, wanted to court international opinion is shown by his determination to make the Olympic Games, held in Berlin in August, a showcase for his regime. The Olympic effort exemplified the residual contradictions and uncertainties of Nazi policy in this period as it tried to balance ideology, political consolidation of the regime, and good international relations. A 1934 Nazi booklet on sports condemned international meetings that allowed "Frenchmen, Belgians, Polaks and Jew-Niggers [to] run on German tracks and swim in German pools. . . . There is no room in our German land for Jewish sports lead-

Hitler is presented with flowers at the opening of the 1936 Olympic Games in Berlin.

ers and their friends infested with the Talmud, for pacifists, political Catholics, pan-Europeans and the rest. They are worse than cholera and syphilis, much worse than famine, drought, and poison gas." But in answer to the question, "Do we then want to have the Olympic Games in Germany?" the booklet gave an enthusiastic, "Yes, we must have them! We think they are important for international reasons. There could not be better propaganda for Germany."

To help the Olympic public relations exercise, anti-Semitic posters and newspapers disappeared from Berlin's streets for a few weeks. Books that had been previously censored and even burned suddenly reappeared in bookstores along with foreign newspapers. Jazz, which had been ruled decadent because of its black (and allegedly Jewish) origins, could be heard again. Germans were encouraged to be friendly to foreign visitors "even if they look like Jews." The German Olympic team included a fencer, Helene Meyer, whose father was a Jew. Meyer won a silver medal and, in a very controversial act, gave the Nazi salute from the podium as other German medal winners did during the games.

The Berlin Olympics were a cynical exercise in giving Nazism an acceptable face. A few miles from the vast new Olympic sports complex, one of the public works projects that helped Germany out of the depression, lay another creation of the Nazi regime: the Sachsenhausen concentration camp, which was filled with socialists, homosexuals, Jews, Sinti and Roma ("Gypsies"), and other real or supposed enemies of Hitler's Germany. The young, healthy "Aryan" gymnasts who entertained the crowds in the impressive, swastika-festooned stadium, and the political prisoners who performed forced labor in their grim camp, were two of the faces of Nazi Germany.

The Spanish Civil War, 1934–39

Even as the Berlin Olympics were taking place in August 1936, a civil war had broken out in Spain after the army mounted a coup against the elected government. From November 1933, when the left-wing government of the Spanish Republic was defeated in elections, to February 1936, Spain had been governed by coalition administrations drawn from parties of the center and right. In contrast to the "red biennium" of 1931–33, when Socialists dominated the government, this period is known as the "black biennium." It was marked by a gradual undermining of many of the liberal and secular reforms introduced during the republic, a breakdown of public order, and the growth of extraparliamentary movements at both ends of the political spectrum.

Although the cabinet sworn in after the 1933 elections was made up of moderate centrists who supported the republic, they relied for parliamentary support on a bloc of right-wing parties known as CEDA (an acronym for Spanish Confederation of the Autonomous Right). CEDA was anti-democratic, authoritarian, and in favor of replacing the republic with a regime that rested on the traditional pillars of political power in Spain: the Church, army, and large landowners.

In its first year, the new government acted moderately, although it reversed some earlier reforms: The death penalty was restored and the closure of Catholic primary and secondary schools was suspended. But when three CEDA members were added to the cabinet, the Spanish left feared there would be a wholesale abandonment of all the gains they had made, and revolts broke out in October 1934 in Madrid, Catalonia, the Basque provinces, and the Asturias. All were suppressed quickly except in the Asturias, where rebellious miners were defeated only after bloody battles with units of the Foreign Legion from Morocco, commanded by General Francisco Franco.

As 1935 opened, the tensions in Spanish politics and society that had been evident since the establishment of the republic were polarized more than ever before. Seeing the October 1934 revolts as evidence that Spain was on the brink of communist revolution, the government adopted increasingly conservative and authoritarian policies. It began to undo social welfare policies, halted agrarian reform in favor of peasants, and introduced press censorship. The Civil Guard was strengthened and thousands of left-wing activists arrested. Believing that only military force could contain future revolts, the government made plans to increase the strength of the army and root out leftist elements within it. On the left wing, the belief that the government was planning to replace the democratic republic with a clerical authoritarian state pushed support to the extremes.

The political polarization of Spain was neatly encapsulated in the election of February 1936, when both left and right formed coalitions to avoid fragmenting the votes of their supporters. The left-wing Popular Front included groups that had previously been antagonistic to one another: Communists, Social Democrats, Catalan nationalists, and left-wing Republicans. The right-wing National Front similarly included mutually hostile groups such as CEDA, monarchists supporting different branches of Spain's royal family, and Agrarians.

Given the situation, the election result could hardly have been worse, for although the Popular Front won, it did so by a slender margin, attracting 4,176,000 votes to the right's 3,784,000. The new government, headed by the Socialist leader Manuel Azaña, who had been prime minister during the red biennium, promptly released leftists imprisoned after the October 1934 revolts, restored autonomy to Catalonia, and pressed ahead with agrarian reform so aggressively that within three months more than 100,000 peasants had been settled on their own land. He governed a country, however, that was descending into violence as activists on both sides attacked one another. There were widespread strikes and, despite the pace of official agrarian reform, tens of thousands of peasants occupied land belonging to their employers.

The specter of disorder and national disintegration, including the assassination of the monarchist leader by the security police, prompted military officers to join with right-wing leaders to overthrow the government. Their aim was to install a conservative regime that would maintain a republican form of government, with the army guaranteeing internal order. One of the key figures was General Franco, whose Morocco-based troops had suppressed the Asturias rebellion at the end of 1934.

The military revolt began in Morocco on July 17, 1936, and spread to Spain the next day when garrisons in many major centers seized control of their localities. Franco and thousands of legionaries were ferried across the Strait of Gibraltar. By the end of the month the insurgents controlled a third of Spain, including important towns such as Seville, Cordova, Zarazoga, and Burgos. As the most prominent military commander, as well as having the best-trained and most effective troops, Franco became de facto leader of the rebellion. At the end of September he assumed the title of Chief of Government in those parts of Spain under the control of the Nationalists, as the rebels became known.

The Spanish civil war set off by the military coup lasted for two and a half years, during which the Nationalists (rebels) and Republicans (supporters of Popular Front and the Second Republic) fought for control of the country. Each side, claiming to be the legitimate government, adopted a full range of policies. In 1937 Franco established a party, the Spanish Traditional Phalanx, as the political wing of the rebellion, although the army maintained firm control. In the Nationalist zones, left-wing reforms like land redistribution and the secularization of education were reversed, and the status of the Catholic Church restored.

Republican-held Spain was divided into three broad areas, each governed by a different group. The region around Madrid was administered by the main socialist trade

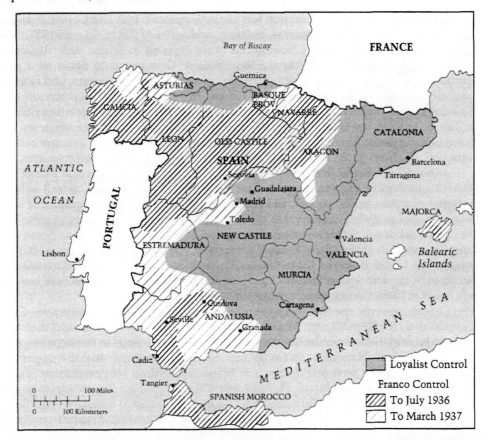

MAP 7.1 Territorial control during the Spanish civil war.

union federation, Catalonia (and its capital Barcelona) by Catalan nationalists who included strong anarchist and syndicalist representation, and the Basque country by Basque nationalists. The character of internal administration varied. In Barcelona major enterprises like banks and factories were placed under the control of workers' committees modeled on soviets. Throughout Republican Spain the reforms of the Second Republic remained in force.

What made the Spanish civil war important for the course of European history was not simply the eventual victory of Franco and the establishment of yet another authoritarian, if not fully fascist state, but the intervention of external forces in the conflict. From the very beginning of the coup, Franco's armies were assisted by Italy, whose aircraft ferried troops from Morocco. Mussolini saw in the military rebels kindred ideological spirits, and supported the establishment of another dictatorship in the Mediterranean region as a counterweight to French and British influence.

Although the Spanish government appealed for British and French assistance, it met with prevarication. The French cabinet was split on the issue, and the British feared the consequences of a diplomatic clash between the major powers over Spain, let alone a military one in Spain. Both sponsored a proposal that outside powers should not intervene in the civil war, and it was eventually endorsed by Germany, Italy, and the Soviet Union.

But the policy of nonintervention was blatantly ignored. Italy and Germany provided Franco's Nationalists with resources, training, and military forces. In mid-1937, 50,000 Italian troops, all classified as "volunteers," were fighting in Spain, while Italian submarines attacked ships supplying the Republicans. Germany used Spain as a testing ground for the weapons it had begun to build in its rearmament program, and as a way of providing combat training for German troops. In April 1937, German aircraft of the Condor Legion practiced the technique of saturation bombing by obliterating Guernica, a historic town in the Basque country that had no military significance whatever. Apart from helping fascist forces and gaining valuable military experience, Germany benefited economically from its aid to Franco by getting access to Spain's iron ore resources.

Although the Republican government was not assisted by Britain and France, it received considerable external support. The Soviet Union sent advisers, as well as limited supplies of trucks, tanks, aircraft, and artillery, although much of the equipment was obsolete. It also provided considerable aid in recruiting foreign volunteers to serve in the International Brigades that were one of the enduring legacies of the civil war. Some 40,000 men and women from across Europe (especially France, Germany, Austria, Italy, and Britain), as well as from the United States, Canada, Australia, and other countries, were inspired by the war against fascism. They included workers, professionals, and intellectuals, many of them Communists recruited by national parties.

Overall, however, the Nationalists received much more—and more effective—foreign support than the Republicans. Despite a number of important victories and their ability to hold Madrid to the end, the Republicans gradually lost ground to the better-equipped and better-trained Nationalist forces. By late 1938, Franco clearly had the upper hand, and in February the next year Britain and France recognized his government. The civil war ended definitively on March 28, 1939, when Madrid, the last Republican stronghold, fell. The war cost half a million lives, and another half-million Spaniards had fled the country, most of them to France. In the aftermath of the conflict, Franco's government held mass trials and executed tens of thousands of those who had opposed him.

The polarization of political forces in Spain and the ensuing civil war, spanning the whole of the 1930s, serves almost as a model of what was happening more broadly in much of the rest of Europe. In many respects the battle between left and right in Spain reflected the options as they were widely perceived and portrayed throughout Europe: a choice between fascism and communism. The fact that communists and fascists fought face to face in Spain only reinforced the image.

Western Europe Between Depression and War

Although they survived the various economic and political crises of the depression period, several of the Western democracies remained vulnerable throughout the 1930s and had not fully recovered when a European war broke out again in 1939. France was perhaps the critical case, a major power that remained mired in the aftereffects of the depression more deeply and longer than other states. After the riots of February 1934, a centrist coalition governed for two years, but its economic and financial policies had the effect of slowing the French economy just as other countries were beginning to pull out of the depression. Wage cuts in the public and private sectors angered workers, and paved the way for a left-wing victory in the 1936 elections.

The administration elected in 1936 was a Popular Front coalition that included Socialists and Radicals, and had the backing of the Communists. The support of the French Communist Party, which won a million and a half votes (about 15 percent of all those cast) represented a change in Comintern policy. From 1928, European communist parties had been forbidden to cooperate with bourgeois socialist parties, but by 1934 it became clear to Stalin that the policy was counterproductive; it had actually helped the Nazis gain power in Germany by fragmenting the left-wing opposition. By 1934, too, Japan was beginning to extend its power in China, presenting the Soviet Union with the threat of war on two fronts.

The election of the Popular Front government in 1936 unnerved French conservatives, and it did not help that Léon Blum, France's first Socialist premier, was a Jew. The election was followed, moreover, by a massive general strike and widespread demonstrations, giving the appearance of a France on the verge of working-class revolution. In view of this, business interests were willing to give Blum's Popular Front a chance to restore order.

The new government posed itself three main tasks: to undertake a broad program of social reform, revive the economy, and weaken the fascist organizations, which by the mid-1930s had the support of 2 million members. The first proved much easier than the other two. Blum brought representatives of labor and owners together and hammered out an agreement that, together with subsequent legislation, vastly improved workers' conditions: wage increases, a forty-hour week, two weeks' paid vacation each year, the right to join unions without repercussions.

The economy proved far more recalcitrant to change. Increased purchasing power did not lead to an increase in productivity, and exports continued to fall because the franc was overvalued. Social reforms and an increase in defense spending led to a bud-

French women block a street in support of demands for women's suffrage. France did not enfranchise women until 1946.

get deficit. In order to reassure middle-class voters, Blum had promised his government would not devalue the currency, but by September 1936 he reneged on the promise. Blum also nationalized the Bank of France and created an agency to oversee the armaments industry.

The Popular Front lasted a little more than a year, partly because the Socialists' partners found Blum's policies unpalatable. The Radicals were concerned at the trend toward nationalization, whereas the Communists accused the government of doing not enough to fight the fascists at home and abroad. The perception that the police favored the right seemed confirmed when, during a confrontation between fascists and Popular Front supporters in a Paris suburb in March 1937, police shot and killed six leftists. On the right activists repeated the slogan "Better Hitler than Blum."

In foreign policy Blum was unable to mobilize support for France against Hitler. Belgium revoked its alliance with France and declared neutrality, while several of the increasingly authoritarian Eastern European states drifted further into Germany's or Italy's orbits. France and Italy were at odds over the invasion of Ethiopia. Although France had signed an alliance with the Soviet Union in 1935, Blum was not interested in pursuing it. France was perceived as impotent to act when Hitler ordered troops into the Rhineland, and the French government intervened in the Spanish Civil War only to the extent of sponsoring a conference at which the main powers agreed not to intervene.

Blum's administration was thus pressed from right and left, and in June 1937, when it was clear that the Socialists had lost control of parliament, Blum resigned. In strict terms the Popular Front remained in power until the 1938 elections, but in reality government devolved upon the moderate Radicals. Hoping to restore business confidence, the new government proposed reversing some of the social reforms enacted by Blum, and in response there was a general strike in November 1938. The government called in the army to end the strike, and by the beginning of 1939 the old class hostilities had been reasserted.

France's gains between 1934 and 1939 were minimal. By 1938 production was still lower than it had been in 1929. Unemployment had been reduced to 600,000 from 800,000 in 1936, but the wage increases in 1936 and 1937 had been largely neutralized by price rises.

Great Britain escaped political turmoil in the depth of the depression. In the mid- and late-1930s, despite persistent high levels of unemployment, even the marginal appeal of the extremes declined. In part this was due to the passage of measures like the 1934 Unemployment Insurance Act, which in spite of its shortcomings provided some support for workers who had exhausted their unemployment benefits by being out of work more than 156 days. The government also acted against the British Union of Fascists by banning uniforms and party standards at outdoor meetings, a measure that undercut much of the BUF's martial appeal.

On the whole, however, Britain's economic position improved, and the unemployment rate in 1939 was half what it had been in 1932. Industrial production rose by more than a third between 1931 and 1939, with chemical, electrical, and synthetic fabric industries growing particularly fast. A sign of growing consumer demand was the output of private automobiles, which increased from 171,000 in 1932 to over 400,000 in 1939.

The government that presided over Britain during the 1930s was a coalition dominated by Conservatives and headed (until 1937) by Stanley Baldwin. Much of the government's attention was diverted from domestic and foreign problems in the latter part of 1936 by a crisis involving King Edward VIII. Before he was crowned, it became known that Edward was romantically involved with one Wallis Warfield Simpson. She was unacceptable as a queen because she was an American, a commoner, and—worst of all—she had been divorced twice. Even though Parliament was at the very time liberalizing divorce in England, it was unthinkable that the king should marry a woman of such dubious qualities. When it became clear that the proposed marriage was unacceptable not only to Parliament but to the empire (Canada hinted that it might have to sever its links with the monarchy), Edward chose to abdicate rather than give up the woman he loved. The couple went into exile in France, where they married. George V's younger son succeeded under the title George VI.

The smaller democratic nations generally rebounded better from the depression. In Scandinavia unemployment rates fell considerably during the 1930s, though by 1939 they remained at 9 percent in Sweden and 18 percent in Denmark and Norway. In other respects, apart from Denmark, Scandinavian economies recovered during the 1930s. Sweden's GNP rose 50 percent, and Norway's industrial output expanded steadily. Denmark's recovery was hampered by restrictions on access to the British market for its dairy products. There was no great attraction to extremist parties in any of the Scandinavian countries, largely because their Social Democratic governments had enacted a broad program of social welfare measures that prevented great hardship.

In the Netherlands the depression peaked in the mid-1930s (unemployment rose from 25 percent in 1932 to over 30 percent in 1935 and 1936), and support for authoritarian parties increased. In 1935 the Dutch National Socialists won 8 percent of votes in an election for the upper house of parliament, but in an election for the lower house the next year their support declined.

In neighboring Belgium a more serious threat arose in the form of the Rexist movement. Formed along the lines of the fascist Action Française in France, the movement called for national regeneration and had a strong Catholic emphasis. It formed paramilitary groups and was responsible for street violence in the 1920s. In 1936 Rexists stood for election to parliament and won 11 percent of the popular vote, giving them thirty-three seats. This result was all the more surprising because the worst of the depression was over in Belgium. In subsequent years Rexist support declined, however, and by 1939 their representation in parliament had declined to four.

All the Western European states also came under pressure from an external source, the masses of refugees fleeing persecution in Central and Eastern Europe. As increasing numbers of refugees strained social resources and threatened to sharpen social tensions, most governments reconsidered their entry policies. A meeting in Evian, France, failed to produce international coordination, and countries adopted their own responses.

France had accepted more refugees than any other country, but after the fall of the Popular Front administration the rules were tightened and refugees could be summarily turned back by border guards. Switzerland, which like France had a tradition of welcoming exiles and refugees, also tightened its policy in 1938, partly because after the Anschluss, Austrian Jews were being transported to the Swiss border in large numbers and being pushed across.

In contrast, Britain continued to accept relatively large numbers of refugees from Germany, about 50,000 between 1933 and 1939. Britain was also responsible for access by Jewish refugees to Palestine, which it administered under a League of Nations mandate. Jewish emigration to Palestine soared after 1933, reaching 62,000 in 1935; by that year the 400,000 Jews in Palestine represented a third of its population. Palestinians reacted violently to a trend that threatened to make them a minority, and the British government set quotas on Jewish immigration.

External forces, notably the rising power of Nazi Germany, placed additional burdens on much of Western Europe, including the need to rearm in case of war. The British spent

1.2 billion pounds on military equipment between 1933 and 1938, most on ship and air-craft construction. In 1936 plans were announced to double the number of frontline air-craft, and in 1938 when international tensions sharpened, a crash program to modernize the army was put in place.

In France expenditure on defense had fallen slightly in the early 1930s, but it began to rise steadily from 1934 (18 billion francs) until 1938 (29 billion), before accelerating in 1939, when 89 billion francs were allotted. The French military had a major program of modernization to complete in the 1930s; in 1934–35 four times as much was spent on horse fodder as on gasoline. Moreover, interservice rivalry and outdated notions of war-fare ensured that even when substantial sums were devoted to armaments, they were not allocated in the most useful manner.

The Scandinavian countries reaffirmed unqualified neutrality in the 1930s. Sweden, which had an important armaments industry, built up its air force and navy, and increased the military training period from 140 to 175 days. In Finland the armed forces were reor-ganized as early as 1932, and between then and 1938 the military's share of the budget rose from 12 to 24 percent. In both Norway and Denmark, however, there was consider-able public opposition to rearmament, and it was not until the international situation be-came critical that they acted. In Norway the military training period was extended from 72 to 84 days in 1938, and in 1939 extra funds were provided for equipment, including aircraft purchases from the United States.

Central and Eastern Europe: Authoritarianism Deepens

By 1934 most of the Eastern European states that had introduced democratic institutions after World War I had abandoned them. At the outbreak of the Second World War the re-gion was, almost without exception, dominated by regimes that were thoroughly authori-tarian and in some cases fascist. A number had been brought, by ideological affinity or by the sheer pressure of proximity, into the orbits of Nazi Germany or Fascist Italy.

While granting the specific circumstances that influenced each state's political evo-lution, there were several broad reasons for the attraction of fascist or conservative au-thoritarianism in Eastern Europe. Right-wing regimes tended to be nationalistic and for the most part supported traditional institutions such as the army and church. The right was also widely viewed as the only effective counter to communism. There were con-cerns about the rise of Nazism, but Soviet power was more threatening to the middle classes, which linked it to domination by workers, and to Eastern Europe's numerous peasants, to whom communism meant collectivization of their farms. Finally, the loss of democratic institutions in Eastern Europe was little mourned; democracy was widely seen as a foreign imposition that prevented things from getting done and feathered the nests of politicians.

In Hungary the regency of Admiral Horthy continued, but his premier Gömbös died in 1936. Under different administrations, policies wavered between the conservative and radical right wing, but tended toward fascism. The fascist Arrow Cross movement gained support steadily, winning a quarter of the national vote in the 1939 elections. In 1938 the first anti-Jewish law was passed, limiting the number of Jews in the civil service. The draft of a second, the same year, widened the definition of "Jew" and imposed a quota of 6 per-cent in the professions and 12 percent in business.

In foreign policy the Hungarians were primarily concerned to overturn the Treaty of Trianon, which had cost Hungary so much territory. This goal led Horthy into an ambivalent relationship with Nazi Germany, which was an obvious ally. Later Hungary would be rewarded with territory and 10 million people seized by Germany in Czechoslovakia.

The personal regime of Marshal Pilsudski in Poland ended with his death in 1935, but its general line persisted during the following four years, with disastrous results. Per capita output in 1939 was still less than that of the region in 1913, and successive governments failed to modernize Poland's armed forces. Pilsudski's attachment to the cavalry stood in the way of creating an effective air force, and little was done after his death, so that when Germany invaded Poland in 1939 its defenses were easily overcome.

The administrations that followed Pilsudski upheld the primacy of the military in politics, and moved increasingly toward fascist ideologies and policies. As the economy foundered there was increasing unrest in the countryside, including peasant strikes. Pandering to middle-class anti-Semitism, the government in 1938 proposed depriving Jews of Polish citizenship. The overriding concerns of the regimes, however, were the growing threats posed by Germany and the Soviet Union. As a low-cost measure of self-defense, Poland obtained British and French guarantees of its sovereignty in March 1939.

The Baltic states pursued different courses in domestic and foreign policies. All entrenched right-wing regimes in the 1930s, although none attempted to introduce fascist policies. Given that all three states were strategically vulnerable, lying between Germany and the Soviet Union, there was a remarkable failure to coordinate foreign policies. By the end of the 1930s Latvia was attempting to achieve strict neutrality, whereas Estonia's policies were primarily anti-Soviet and Lithuania's anti-German.

Both Romania and Bulgaria drifted into the German sphere of influence from the mid-1930s. In Romania King Carol, who assumed personal rule, allied himself with the fascist Iron Guard movement, but then gradually distanced himself from it as he was able to strengthen the authority of the state. In 1938 Carol abolished the 1923 constitution and established a personal regime, partly because of the electoral strength of the Iron Guard and its allies. Along with all parties, the Iron Guard was then banned, leaving the king's Front for National Rebirth as the only legal political movement. Ironically, having destroyed the fascist movement and killed its leaders (ostensibly "while trying to escape"), King Carol introduced a system based on Mussolini's Fascist state. Despite these policies, Romania gradually developed a strong commercial relationship with Germany. The country's oil reserves made it a valuable trading partner for Germany, and a March 1939 financial agreement gave Germany considerable influence in the Romanian economy. Germany took more than half Romania's exports and provided more than half its imported goods.

The monarchy also played a role in Bulgaria, where King Boris in 1935 issued a manifesto banning all political parties and installing himself as leader. Anxious to draw off support from the left and the right, the government created a curious representative system to give an illusion of "slow but steady progress" toward "tidy but disciplined" democracy. Unmarried women and widows were enfranchised, but educational qualifications were imposed; voting was staggered to allow the police to be concentrated wherever elections were taking place; and deputies could be elected only as individuals, not as members of parties. The Bulgarian parliament (which was purged of some elected members) had few powers, and Boris effectively created a police state.

In order to revive the Bulgarian economy, the king abandoned close cooperation with Italy and entered into extensive trade agreements with Nazi Germany. By 1939 Germany was Bulgaria's main trading partner, taking two-thirds of its exports, providing two-thirds of its imports, and supplying most of its weapons. This relationship drew Bulgaria into a de facto political relationship with Germany, despite attempts by the British to include it in an anti-German alliance.

In Yugoslavia the government devolved upon the prime minister, Milan Stoyadinovich, after the assassination of King Alexander in 1934. His main goals were to protect Yugoslavia's position internationally and to resolve the tensions between Croatians and Serbs. In the foreign sphere, neutrality pacts were signed with Bulgaria and Italy, and closer relations established with Germany. The administration adopted some of the outward symbols associated with fascism, including a youth movement whose members wore green shirts.

Attempts to reconcile Croatian nationalists failed as Croatians took heart from the apparent success of Slovaks in escaping from Czech domination, after Germany dismembered Czechoslovakia and created a separate Slovak state. In 1938 the Croatian and opposition Serb parties won 45 percent of the vote despite questionable voting procedures. But events outside Yugoslavia led to a temporary reduction in Croat-Serb tensions. The German Anschluss with Austria and the Italian annexation of Albania brought Nazism and Fascism to the borders of Yugoslavia. Afraid that internal weakness would make the country more vulnerable to external pressure, the government in August 1939 agreed to extensive internal autonomy for Croatians. The arrangement proved unsatisfactory, not only to Serbs who thought it had gone too far and radical Croatians who thought it had not gone far enough, but eventually also to Croatian moderates who feared that the government's foreign policy would drag Yugoslavia into war.

In Albania King Zog's regime lasted throughout the period. Although it retained some of the forms of representative government, it was dictatorial and repressive. Albania became increasingly dependent on Fascist Italy for economic assistance, and by the end of the decade had become in many respects subordinated to Italy. The process was completed when Italy invaded and annexed Albania in September 1939.

In Greece the years between the depression and the war began with attempts by republican army officers to seize power from politicians who, they feared, would restore the monarchy and replace them with royalist officers. In 1935 royalist officers seized power from civilians and organized a referendum that returned a vote of 97.8 percent in favor of restoring the monarchy. Presumably it was a desire for credibility that prevented the regime from reporting a result of 100 percent in favor.

In November 1935, King George II ascended the Greek throne. When elections the following year produced a deadlock, the king appointed the minister of war, General Metaxas, premier. Before long Metaxas declared a state of emergency and dissolved parliament, and with the support of the king and army, he became a virtual dictator. Political parties were outlawed, opponents imprisoned, the press censored, and education closely supervised. At the same time Metaxas introduced some social reforms: a minimum wage and two-week vacation for workers, and economic aid to villages. Following the example of Mussolini (*Il Duce*), Hitler (*Der Führer*), and Franco (*El Jefe*), Metaxas took the title *Archigos* (Greek for Leader). His corporatist and nationalist regime promoted values of piety and family stability. Metaxas also modernized the armed forces and strengthened the frontiers so that, initially at least, Greece was able to fend off invasion once war began.

The major exception to the drift to authoritarianism in Eastern Europe was Czechoslovakia, but it was a fragile democracy that came under increasing pressure from without and within. The major external threat emanated from Germany, not least because of the pan-German aspirations of the 3 million ethnic Germans in the Sudetenland. A defense pact had been signed with France soon after the First World War, but the accession of the Nazis to power also led the Czechoslovak government into a treaty with the Soviet Union in 1935.

This arrangement aggravated internal tensions by angering ethnic Germans, Slovaks, Ukrainians, and peasants (who associated the Soviet Union with the destruction of peasant ownership). The depression had sharpened ethnic conflicts in multinational Czechoslovakia, because Slovakia and the Sudetenland were worse hit than the Czech lands; more than half the country's unemployed were Sudeten Germans. Not surprisingly, the 1935 elections showed increased support for ethnic nationalists. There were demands for partial autonomy for Slovakia, but they were resisted by the government in Prague.

The German nationalists, who gained two-thirds of the votes cast in the Sudetenland in the elections, were more problematic because they had the backing of Germany. In the spring of 1936 the government passed an act allowing it to declare martial law in any part of the country where the state or its democratic, republican character was threatened. Soon after, the leader of the nationalist movement, Konrad Henlein, called for laws to protect racial groups, and in February 1937 the government made concessions. They guaranteed ethnic proportionality in the civil service, an equitable distribution of state spending among regions, allocation of funds to German cultural and welfare organizations, government contracts for German-owned firms, and more widespread use of the German language.

But the Germans inside and outside Czechoslovakia were not content. Nor were they likely to be, because the ethnic Germans were bent on separating from Czechoslovakia, and the Nazis on incorporating them. In February 1938, Hitler declared himself protector of all Germans wherever they lived, and thereafter the Sudetenland became central to the dismemberment of Czechoslovakia and the process that led to war.

Stalinism: State and Terror, 1934–39

The history of the Soviet Union during the 1930s is dominated by repression. It took its most spectacular forms in the forced collectivization of agriculture and the famine that opened the decade, and in mass purges, executions, deportations, and deaths that occupied the five years from 1934 to 1939. Social and cultural policies were also repressive, as Stalin's regime altered the terms of life in the family, at work, and in the cultural spheres. The overall picture of the period is a grim drive to construct a regime that tolerated no opposition to its often idiosyncratic and inconsistent policies.

The role of Stalin himself is crucial to an understanding of the period. Stalin had not been the only candidate to succeed Lenin as the leader of the Soviet Union, nor was there any party rule that Stalin was entitled to hold office for life. Throughout the 1920s he faced open and covert challenges from within the Communist Party itself, and maintained control by centralizing party authority and defeating his rivals one by one on specific issues.

Stalin's actions in the 1930s are sometimes portrayed as motivated by paranoia, a desire for revenge, cruelty, and sheer madness. Perhaps such characteristics had a role to play, although the personality traits of a single man can go only so far to explain the success of policies that controlled a nation of 170 million inhabitants for more than two decades.

To the extent that the dreadful repression he initiated in 1934 was motivated by insecurity about his own position, Stalin had some justification. A number of leading Communists believed that, following the crisis of collectivization and mass deaths, Soviet life ought to be normalized. Stalin, they believed, was too militant to lead this phase, and they conceived the idea of promoting him to a largely honorific post and giving the general secretaryship of the party, held by Stalin, to the head of the Leningrad section of the party, Sergei Kirov. Kirov declined to have anything to do with the plan, but in the secret ballot for the new Central Committee of the party, 300 of the 1,225 delegates crossed Stalin's name off the ballot, and all but three voted for Kirov.

Stalin looked upon Kirov as a threat, a possible rallying point for dissent within the party, and in December 1934 had him murdered. Claiming distress at what appeared an assassination, Stalin promptly announced measures against terrorism, allowing him to round up those he perceived as his enemies. They included Gregory Zinoviev and Lev Kamenev, two of Lenin's original Politburo, and their close associates. All were eventually tried in secret and sentenced to varying terms of imprisonment. Kirov's assassin, a party member put up to the job by the secret police, was executed, along with several members of his family and various party members accused of constituting a terrorist center in Leningrad.

In 1935 the repression continued, with large numbers of purges, arrests, deportations to labor camps, and some executions. One coercive measure was an April 1935 decree that extended adult criminal punishments to children as young as twelve. This was part of a general attack on a perceived increase in juvenile delinquency, but it also served the purpose of pressuring victims of the political repression who had children. It became a common pattern for family members to be arrested with enemies of the regime, and the 1935 law implied that failure to cooperate could lead to even young children being jailed or executed.

A new constitution, passed in 1936, added new legal force to the continuing repression. The constitution prescribed the existing political reality, notably the power of the Communist Party alone to nominate candidates for election to public office. It also set out classic liberal civil liberties for Soviet citizens, including the freedoms of speech, religion, the press, and assembly. Sexual and racial equality were decreed, as well as the right to work, leisure, housing, welfare, and education. Individuals were guaranteed inviolability of the person and the home, and the privacy of correspondence.

All these rights were conditional, however, because the constitution stipulated that they could be enjoyed only "in conformity with the interests of the working people, and in order to strengthen the Socialist system." This was broad enough to be interpreted in any way, and under Stalin it was interpreted in the most restrictive sense.

It is possible that the 1936 constitution was drawn up at least partly to put an acceptable international face on the Communist regime, for Communist parties in Europe were beginning to participate in popular front governments. The constitution was also designed for domestic consumption: It was given a great amount of publicity in the Soviet press just as the main phase of Stalin's terror campaign was launched.

The public face of the terror, the main phase of which ran from 1936 to 1938, was a series of show-trials of prominent Communists, many alleged to have conspired with Trotsky or unnamed fascists to commit sabotage and espionage. The trials were carefully designed to demonstrate to the Soviet people that there existed a treasonous conspiracy at the highest levels, and that only Stalin had been able to identify it and root it out. The first trial, of those arrested after Kirov's assassination, took place in August 1936. In return for promises that their lives and those of their families would be spared, the defendants admitted the charges, and even urged the Soviet people to follow Stalin loyally. All the accused were sentenced to death, and the sentences were carried out despite Stalin's guarantee. Their families also disappeared, either killed or deported to labor camps. In the aftermath of the trial, several thousand prisoners were also executed by the secret police. The following year a second public trial was held, this one also including former associates of Lenin. Of the seventeen defendants, thirteen were executed, and the other four, sentenced to imprisonment, were never heard of again.

At this point Stalin turned on the personnel of his own terror. The chief of the secret police, Genrikh Yagoda, and his team of interrogators were arrested, as well as leading generals. The generals were tried by a military court, found guilty of treason, and shot. Yagoda was included among the defendants in the third great show-trial, in 1938, along with Nikolai Bukharin, a leading party theorist, and nineteen other prominent Communists.

The show-trials, however, were only the tip of an enormous program of terror and killing that took place between 1934 and 1939. It was directed not only against those Stalin could identify as his "enemies," but at the Soviet people more generally. On the basis of information relayed by individuals, suspicion reinforced by incomplete evidence, trumped-up charges, and malicious investigations, millions of people were imprisoned or killed. They included workers who accidentally damaged machinery and who were shot for "sabotage," and ordinary citizens who received gifts from relatives outside the Soviet Union and were thereby suspected of being foreign agents.

Of greater importance to Stalin himself were those in positions of influence who might challenge his authority or even criticize his policies. Special attention was given to those who had been close to Lenin, and by 1939 only two of the seven men in Lenin's original Politburo were still alive. Lenin himself had died, and four had been shot on Stalin's orders or had died in prison camps. Of the two survivors, Trotsky would be killed the next year in Mexico, and Stalin would live on.

More broadly, almost half the members of the Communist Party, 1.25 million of 2.8 million, were eliminated. More than half the delegates to the 1934 party congress, where Kirov's name had circulated as a replacement for Stalin, were executed or sent to camps. The terror also cut a swath through the Soviet military hierarchy, for it claimed the lives of three of the five army marshals, all but one of the army commanders, all the corps commanders, almost all the brigade commanders, half the regimental commanders, and thousands of other officers. The navy lost nineteen of the twenty-five senior admirals.

Between 5 and 10 percent of the Red Army's officers and commissars were discharged from 1937 to 1939. Among the charges they faced were associating with conspirators, Poles, Lithuanians, or other foreigners, and offenses such as drunkenness and moral depravity. Others were dropped from the rolls for medical reasons or death by natural causes. Of the 18,658 discharged in 1937, 4,661 (25 percent) were reinstated by 1939, and the rate of reinstatement rose to 39 percent of the 16,362 officers discharged in 1938.

The precise number of people who suffered arrest or death during the terror is uncertain, not least because it is difficult to put dates on the phenomenon and because records are unreliable. Should we, for example, include labor camp deaths in the 1940s as part of the terror of the 1930s? Some estimates put the number of arrests between 1937 and 1939 at more than 8 million people, one in every twenty men, women, and children in the Soviet Union, or one in ten adults over the age of nineteen. Estimates of deaths due to the terror, but excluding the famine of the early 1930s, range into the millions. The Soviet secret police (KGB) estimated in 1990 that almost 800,000 people were shot during the period; others, of course, died in other ways that included being worked to death in labor camps.

There is more agreement on the demographic profile of the victims. The great majority were men in their thirties and forties, the age at which they might be expected to have achieved some experience and influence and thereby constitute a "threat" to Stalin. The loss of males in their forties is evident in Table 7.1, which shows the number of men for every 100 women in specific age groups in 1939.

If the preponderance of males among victims of persecution is taken into account, the estimate of 8 million arrests suggests that one in every two or three adult men was detained, which is highly unlikely. Such rates are not supported by the recollections of those

**TABLE 7.1   Men per 100 Women by
Age Group in the Soviet Union, 1939**

30–34 years	91
35–39 years	83
40–44 years	79
45–49 years	78
50–54 years	82
55–59 years	82

Source: Data from F. Lorimer, *Population of
the Soviet Union* (Geneva, 1946), p. 143.

who lived through the period, though doubtless there were variations in the intensity of
repression according to class and region.

Some estimates suggest that the number of prisoners in the Gulag, the Soviet system
of forced-labor camps, ranged between 1 and 1.3 million at any given time in the period
1937–39. These figures are far lower than those proposed by other historians, but they are
bad enough. It might seem unimportant whether Stalin's regime was directly responsible
for 1, 2, 5, or 10 million deaths, for all are deplorable. But unless historians are to give up
the task of providing precise figures and fall back on generalizations like "many" or "millions," they attempt to be as accurate as their data allow. Under the circumstances, however, it is still difficult to reach firm conclusions.

Although most of the victims were men, women were not spared torture, assault, imprisonment, and deportation at the hands of the secret police, and thousands, perhaps
hundreds of thousands, of women were killed. The fact that the higher ranks of Soviet hierarchies were predominantly male, despite affirmations of sexual equality, partly explains
the sexual imbalance among victims. Women members of the party were purged and liquidated, and many women were arrested as wives and daughters of condemned men. The
few women at the top, however, survived the terror rather better than their male counterparts, partly because of Stalin's apparent reluctance to condemn women to death. Unlike
the males, Lenin's female colleagues, one of whom was his widow Nadezhda Krupskaya,
were spared. So were the two female members of the 1934 Central Committee of the
Communist Party, although more than two-thirds of its sixty-nine male members were shot.

Apart from the terrible human price of the terror, there were institutional costs, as the
depleted officer corps of the Soviet military forces discovered. It took twelve years to train
a major and twenty to train an army commander. The purges left the armed forces bereft
of experienced officers at the top, something Stalin (and Hitler) bore in mind in the
diplomatic and military maneuverings that took place from 1938 to 1941. The compensation was political, and it benefited Stalin alone. By 1939, terror had eliminated anyone
of any consequence around whom dissent might gather. At the party congress that year,
97 percent of the delegates were new; they were men, and a few women, on whose loyalty
Stalin expected to be able to count.

There remains no wholly satisfactory explanation for the extent of the terror, which
represented a wide-ranging onslaught on the Soviet population no matter what the different estimates of arrests and deaths. Many historians see the terror as little more than a
grand plan by Stalin to eliminate any threat to his own position. Other historians suggest
that the terror served the interests of other entities in the Soviet political structure. The
central party authorities used it to eliminate regional and local leaderships that were becoming too independent, while rival groups in the provinces attempted to eliminate one
another. Long-term social currents came into play, as when party functionaries purged

women schoolteachers in some regions, not because of any evidence of disloyalty, but because of traditional hostility to women in professional positions. The central government had to order a halt to the persecution of teachers. We cannot rule out the importance of the climate of fear and suspicion that developed, producing waves of denunciations. Functionaries at all levels must have felt impelled to expose "enemies" if only to demonstrate their vigilance in order to protect their own positions and lives.

The terror brings into relief the structure of government that developed in the Soviet Union in the 1930s. It appeared to be a monolithic and highly centralized bureaucracy where the state apparatus and Communist Party were merged. Stalin undoubtedly achieved extensive personal control, particularly during the purges when he took an active role in drawing up lists of higher-ranking victims. He was elevated to superhuman status in party pronouncements, a practice denounced by his successors as a "cult of personality."

But no one man could keep abreast of all events, let alone determine them, in a country that spanned a sixth of the world's land surface and had a population of 170 million. The Stalinist state was more pluralistic than it appeared. The sheer geographical extent of the Soviet Union and its division into republics produced fissures between the center in Moscow and the peripheral regions. Powerful individuals in the regions created their own small regimes that often protected them from too much interference from Moscow. In addition, Stalinism as an ideology was more a general line than a set of detailed policies, allowing the heads of large bureaucracies enough room to devise policies.

Perhaps the most powerful bureaucracy was the secret police (NKVD, or People's Commissariat for Internal Affairs), which constituted a quasi-autonomous entity within the Soviet state. In addition to being responsible for internal security and guarding the frontiers, the NKVD operated forced labor camps and through them controlled much of the Soviet Union's economic productivity. The NKVD watched for signs of opposition to the regime, employing networks of informers who monitored and reported the conversations and activities of their friends, neighbors, and colleagues at work. The show-trials were public knowledge and there was general awareness of arrests and interrogations of ordinary people. Fear of repression, as much as repression itself, acted as a deterrent to even mild dissent, let alone outright condemnation of or resistance to the regime.

Soviet Society Under Stalin

Beyond the reality and the implied threat of coercion, the institutions of the Stalinist state attempted to shape the thoughts and behavior of the population at large, not merely to ensure a docile citizenry, but to foster positive support for the regime and its policies. In order to bind the Soviet people to its ideology and goals, the Stalinist regime exploited all the means of mass persuasion at its disposal. The emphasis was on each individual's membership in the collective, and people in the millions participated in massed gatherings to celebrate Soviet achievements. They reached their fullest form on the two most important dates in the Soviet calendar: May 1, which celebrated labor, and November 7, the anniversary of the 1917 Bolshevik Revolution. On those days there were massive demonstrations of Soviet military and political might, expressed in parades of weaponry and personnel, as well as formations of workers and children.

In the early 1930s, the mausoleum containing Lenin's embalmed body became the focal point of these demonstrations in Moscow's Red Square. Stalin and other members of the Politburo watched the parades from the top of the mausoleum, demonstrating to all

A May Day celebration in Red Square, Moscow. The Red Army parades in front of
Lenin's tomb, while Soviet leaders look on.

the world that they were Lenin's rightful successors. To accommodate the massive events,
Red Square itself was enlarged in the 1930s by the demolition of many buildings, including several churches.

Throughout the period there was a great deal of emphasis on the *Soviet* people, in order to stress their common citizenship over any regional, national, or linguistic variations.
Stalin himself was a Georgian, not a Russian, and he spoke Russian imperfectly and with
a heavy Georgian accent. The stress of the regime was on the integrity of the whole nation, rather than on the dominance of Russia within the federation, which had been the
emphasis of Russification under the czarist regime. It implied, nonetheless, the decline of
national cultures and languages, and those who promoted national sentiments over Soviet
patriotism were prominent as victims of the terror.

The Stalinist message was conveyed to the masses by all the means available. Mass
communications were controlled by the state, and the press, movies, and radio produced
a continuous stream of propaganda. As they were elsewhere, posters became a popular
medium of propaganda in the Soviet Union; they were cheap to produce and could be
put up anywhere. Cultural expressions, whether literary, visual, or musical, that did not reflect the glory of the regime were suppressed as bourgeois, fascist, or merely decadent. In
this respect Stalin's regime was far removed from the Soviet Union of the 1920s, when a
wide range of artistic expression was permitted.

Young people were an especially important target group. Communist youth organizations were established for boys and girls, Young Pioneers for the younger children and Komsomol for the older. Education was given a high priority, and the proportion of children attending school increased steadily. The ideological demands of the regime required changes in the school syllabus, although the imposition of the Russian language in all Soviet schools remained constant. Although there was a strong emphasis on technical and scientific education, subjects like history were considered important for imparting a sense of the place of Stalin in the Russian tradition. Toward the end of the 1930s, history texts placed emphasis on two czars, Ivan the Terrible and Peter the Great, both of whom established centralized administrations and defended the Russian state. The Russian war against Napoleon was portrayed as a great patriotic event, and even the czarist annexation of foreign territory was forgiven on the ground that it eventually exposed more people to the benefits of the Bolshevik Revolution.

Not only distant but also recent history had to be revised. Historians employed by the regime developed skills in quickly and frequently rewriting history since the Bolshevik Revolution, so as to minimize the roles of Stalin's rivals and inflate the importance of Stalin and his relationship with Lenin. Trotsky was depicted as having done little more than produce chaos in the Red Army, but at least his name remained in the history books; many of those who were eliminated in the 1930s disappeared from the past record as well. Technicians ensured that their images disappeared from photographs of the period, even though this sometimes produced awkward gaps in group portraits.

There were purposes to these policies, other than the creation of a docile population and a hierarchy that presented no challenges to Stalin's position. The rise of fascist regimes and movements that declared themselves implacably opposed to communism and the Soviet state made it imperative that the Soviet Union should prepare for war. The purges of the trained military and economic elites seem utterly inconsistent with these goals, but they were pursued nonetheless.

One aim of the regime was to increase the Soviet population, not only to provide military personnel but also for economic labor. This populationist goal led to radical changes in Soviet family policies and had a particular impact on women. The Bolsheviks had regarded the family as bourgeois and doomed to extinction along with capitalism, and in the 1920s Soviet policy had been generally liberal; marriage was easy to enter and exit, suggesting that the state would not try to shore up a moribund institution. By 1930 "Soviet family policy" seemed like an oxymoron. Spouses in de facto relationships had the same rights as those formally married. Divorce was available easily and quickly, and any alimony obligations ceased a year after divorce. Bigamy was decriminalized, although polygamy was banned as part of an attack on Islam. Laws regarding sexual relationships were similarly relaxed; adultery, incest, and homosexuality were decriminalized.

It is difficult to separate the effects of these laws from the social and economic upheavals the Soviet Union experienced in the early 1930s, but the picture was worrying to state planners. By 1934 more than a third of marriages in Moscow ended in divorce. The birth rate had fallen considerably since the late 1920s; in 1927 there were 45 births per thousand population, in 1935 only 30 births per thousand. In concrete terms that meant a deficit of some 2.5 million births a year. Abortion, which even before the revolution was a principal form of family limitation in Russia, became the main means of birth control, especially in the cities. By 1934 in Moscow there were almost three times as many legal abortions as births, a ratio that would be widened by the addition of countless illegal abortions. The most common reasons given for having abortions were poverty and illness, although some women wanted to avoid having children so that they could pursue careers or have an uninterrupted income. Under these circumstances it is not surprising that the birth rate fell.

Despite the declining births, a severe social problem was caused in some cities by the presence of unwanted children, the children of easily dissolved marriages, and children left behind after their parents died in the famine or were deported. Thousands, mainly teenaged boys, roamed the streets and engaged in crime. In 1935 children above the age of twelve were ordered to be treated the same way as adults if they were found guilty of serious crimes. The result was a wave of arrests, mostly of teenagers for theft or hooliganism.

Crime could no longer be attributed to poverty because poverty had officially disappeared from the Soviet Union. Stalin himself announced that workers' living standards were rising all the time and that "anyone who denies this is an enemy of Soviet power." In these circumstances no one was very anxious to deny it, and juvenile crime was therefore attributed to the disintegration of the family. Concerned at the effects of existing family patterns on Soviet society and population growth, the regime opened a campaign to bolster the family and promote family responsibility.

In 1936 a new family code was introduced, making divorce more difficult to obtain. Both parties had to appear in court, and an escalating scale of fees was introduced for successive divorces; it cost 50 roubles for a first divorce, 150 for a second, and 300 for a third. Alimony provisions, for some time a subject of public debate, were tightened up. The noncustodial parent had to pay a third of his or her salary for one child, half for two children, and 60 percent for three or more. In the light of evidence that many men defaulted on their alimony obligations, the new code stipulated imprisonment for two years for failure to make payments.

The new code banned abortion; any person performing one was subject to two years in prison, and any woman having an abortion was subject to a fine. On the other hand, women who bore children received favorable treatment in the workplace, increased child support payments, and pregnancy leave. Bonuses were offered to women who had large families, and women who produced ten or more children were awarded the title "Hero of Socialist Motherhood." Provision was made for more child-care facilities, health clinics for women and infants, and milk supplies. The immediate effect of these measures, particularly the criminalization of abortion, was a small increase in the birth rate. It lasted only two years, however, before declining again.

Part of the explanation lies in the reason women most often gave for having abortions: poverty. Soviet women worked in massive numbers; 82 percent of people entering the workforce for the first time in the 1930s were women, and by 1939 71 percent of women between sixteen and fifty-nine were in paid employment. But although women found their way into jobs that had previously been closed, like managerial positions, the great majority worked in low-status and low-paid employment.

Real wages declined during the 1930s as the prices of basic goods like potatoes, milk, and meat rose, particularly after rationing ended in 1934–35. Moreover, there were extensive housing problems because priority was given to other construction projects. A 1935 survey of renters (which included families and individuals) in Moscow showed that 6 percent had more than one room, 40 percent lived in one room, 24 percent occupied a part of a room, 5 percent lived in kitchens and corridors, and 25 percent lived in dormitories. Adding to families under these conditions cannot have been an attractive idea.

Beyond reproduction, the Soviet regime urged workers to increase industrial production. Workers in general, female and male, could be reduced to sullen compliance with official requirements. Collective action by workers was rare because the only unions permitted were staffed by party officials. Division and competition, rather than solidarity and cooperation among workers was encouraged by bonuses for productivity. In 1935 the government launched a movement to raise productivity above official goals, claiming that one Donets coal miner, Alexei Stakhanov, had exceeded his quota more than 14-fold by mining 102 tons of coal (his quota was 7) during a single shift. Special teams of "Stakhanovite" workers went to factories and plants, and set new production records. Higher quotas were set and bonuses paid to those who met and exceeded them. Such policies made sense within the goal of raising productivity, but created resentment and rivalry among workers.

But there is evidence that the management and workers of individual factories and plants were often successful in resisting external interference in setting productivity targets. Their success in this respect led many managers to fall victim to the purges in 1937 and 1938. Absenteeism was endemic, reaching a peak in 1937, but there was little that managers and foremen could do about it. In sectors where there were shortages of skilled labor, like mining, workers had the upper hand. Mine managers explained that if they fired workers for lateness or being absent without an excuse, the workers would quit and take a job in another mine.

The limitations of central authority were also clear in agriculture. In order to persuade the peasants to enter collective farms the government had conceded them the right to own private plots, a little less than an acre in size, which they could use to grow produce for private profit. Peasants devoted a disproportionate amount of time to these plots, making them more productive than the collective land. No central policy was able to alter the peasants' attitudes and behavior, despite its negative impact on Soviet agriculture, which suffered enough disabilities without passive resistance from the farmers themselves.

There is no easy generalization about the impact of an authoritarian regime like the Soviet Union's in the 1930s. That there was persecution, repression, and murder on a wide scale is indisputable, as is the dominance of the Communist Party and the police. But within the context of the formal centralized system of control and organization, there was a more complex reality. Stalin ensured his own position, but in so far as his regime's prime goals were to marshal women, workers, and peasants to raise birth rates, industrial productivity, and agricultural output, respectively, the regime fell short and revealed the limitations of its power.

The Nazi State: Coercion and Consent

It is clear that there were also limits to the success of the Nazi regime in forcing Germans to follow its policies. No matter how often the leadership stressed the importance of increasing the "Aryan" population, Germans were reluctant to raise the birth rate significantly. In broader terms, however, the Nazis were able to impose control over the general population, and they did so by coercion, manufactured compliance, and consent. The role of Hitler himself in the process was far from negligible; one way or another, the Führer constantly cast his shadow over Germans. For those unable to participate in the great Nazi rallies, or who missed one of Hitler's public appearances, images of the Führer were hung in public buildings, schools, and factories, not to mention many homes. Hitler's voice blared out of radios, which more than doubled in number between 1932 and 1939, when there was one in every second household. Newsreels and documentary films, geared to propaganda purposes, showed Hitler orating, inspecting his armed forces, and mingling with ordinary folk. The Nazi salutation, "Heil Hitler!" and a raised hand, ensured that the Führer's name came regularly to the lips (although there were places, like lavatories, where it was deemed inappropriate to use it).

Small girls give the Nazi salute at a party rally in Coburg, Germany.

The omnipresence of Hitler was a key trait of the regime, which invoked what was called the "leader principle" to elevate Hitler far above the level that claimed by contemporary dictators elsewhere. Hitler was portrayed as almost a godlike figure, the embodiment of the German people, as enunciated in the often-repeated slogan "One People, One Germany, One Leader" (*Ein Volk, Ein Reich, Ein Führer*). Complete and unquestioning obedience was expected of Germans at the highest levels, no less than of ordinary men and women. Political leaders had to swear "eternal allegiance" and "unconditional obedience" to the Führer, although perhaps because he was concerned about his subordinates' commitment to eternity, Hitler required the oath to be made on an annual basis.

Hitler and his associates set out to create an image of the Führer for public consumption. This carefully crafted Hitler (part of what historians call the Hitler myth) was a man of the people, the "people's chancellor" as the Nazi press styled him in 1933. Hitler was portrayed as an ascetic bachelor who devoted his total energy to Germany; he put the national interest above sectional interests and stood for law and order; he was a genius, in economic terms for having engineered Germany's recovery from the depression, and also in the diplomatic and military spheres; he had led Germany to the front ranks of European powers, and (until 1943, at least) his military strategy seemed almost flawless.

The ubiquity of Hitler's image, and the fact that all the Nazi regime's policies and actions were executed in his name, give the impression that from 1933 Germany was a dictatorship in which one man determined policies that were then faithfully carried out by descending ranks of loyal subordinates. This was far from the case, for the Nazi regime was a complex system in which party and state apparatus had indeed merged to a large extent, but where there were extensive quasi-autonomous sectors and hierarchies.

Within the complex intricacies of state and party links there developed particular empires, often headed by prominent Nazis. The most extensive was the SS, which had been formed in 1925 to be an elite bodyguard for Hitler within the SA paramilitary force. Hitler used the SS to wipe out the leadership of the SA in 1934, and by the late 1930s its head, Heinrich Himmler, had built it into an organization exercising vast repressive, military, and political functions.

The SS was responsible for all security matters and had its own military regiments. During the war it expanded its military forces, creating rivalry and frequent conflict with the regular army. The SS operated the concentration camps and, using slave labor, created a massive economic empire of more than 150 factories and plants. Himmler's domain also included the Gestapo, the state secret police, and the ordinary uniformed police that dealt with day-to-day crime and public order. As chief of German police, Himmler was able to exercise vast power, and it is clear that in some respects he did so autonomously.

The question of the organization of the Nazi state is important because it shapes our understanding of responsibility for the crimes perpetrated by the Nazis. It has been suggested that Hitler knew nothing of the extermination campaign that commenced in 1941, but that it was initiated and carried through by subordinates. Certainly, Hitler signed no order to begin the mass murders, but then Hitler signed very little. He tended to indicate his wishes in broad terms and vague words, leaving it to others to interpret his will. To this extent it is frequently difficult to link a specific policy to Hitler directly, although there may be no doubt that those in charge of executing policy believed they had been ordered to do so. Nor is there doubt that such policies accorded with the broad lines of Hitler's intentions and expectations.

To varying degrees and by various means, including physical force, coercion, and the simple elimination of alternatives, the Nazis impinged on the daily lives of most Germans during the 1930s. As we would expect, their experiences varied not only according to class, gender, and region, but also to their attitudes toward the Nazi ideological agenda.

Class distinctions are vital, for it is clear that industrial workers were markedly less supportive of Hitler than the middle class. As we have seen, workers fared poorly in the 1930s, but they were unable to express their grievances collectively because the Nazis had destroyed their institutions and undermined their culture. Labor unions were banned early on, and the freedom to negotiate wages and conditions was replaced by imposed regulations and restrictions, including limits on the freedom to leave one job for another. The regime fostered competition among workers, with rewards for the most productive, in order to dissolve solidarity.

Workers' autonomous sports, cultural, and leisure associations were also suppressed. Instead, a state organization, Strength Through Joy, sponsored sports, travel, cultural, and other activities. Sports played an important role in the state, especially after 1936 when athletics were declared an aid to military training and racial improvement. According to official statistics, 10 million people participated in organized sports in the four years to 1938. In that year the International Olympic Committee awarded Strength Through Joy a cup for special achievement in sport.

Tourism had its role, too, and subsidized travel ranged from breaks and holidays within Germany to trips abroad and even ocean cruises. Strength Through Joy constructed its own fleet of white cruise ships (they were later used as troop carriers), and passengers enjoyed, or at least participated in, mass calisthenics, singing, and other organized activities while they cruised off Madeira or the Norwegian fjords. Although the official purpose of Strength Through Joy was to benefit workers, most could not afford the more ambitious programs like foreign travel. A week in Italy cost almost a month and a half's income for a worker, and few can have had enough disposable income. Fewer than a fifth of the passengers on the cruise ships were workers, the rest being white-collar workers, Nazi party officials, and secret police agents.

Workers were encouraged to believe they were sharing the new prosperity when the possibility was held out that they might all own a new car. A "people's car," the Volkswagen, was designed by the industrialist Ferdinand Porsche to sell for 990 marks, about six months' wages for an industrial worker. The leader of the German Labor Front urged workers in 1938 to start making installments of 5 marks a week toward a new car: "A Volkswagen for every German—let that be our aim. . . . Will all of you help in that; it shall be our way of saying 'thank you' to the Führer." The Führer promptly returned workers' gratitude by diverting Volkswagen resources to the production of military vehicles.

Other sectional interests were co-opted into the Nazi scheme of things in particular ways. Roman Catholics were placed in a difficult position when in July 1933 the Vatican signed a concordat with Hitler, pledging the Church to refrain from political activities. In return the Church was permitted to retain its youth organizations and schools, and its property was protected. By 1936, however, Church publications had been suppressed, youth groups disbanded, and schools closed, as the regime eliminated all rivals to Nazi institutions.

Hitler planned to replace the Lutheran church by an official Reich church, but it was a difficult process because a breakaway group tried to establish a church in opposition to the regime. In 1937 it was suppressed and the leaders imprisoned. More generally the Lutheran clergy cooperated with the Nazi regime, in part because of their church's traditions of patriotism and obedience to authority.

The Nazis established their own "Positive Christianity," a religion with its own liturgy and ceremony drawn from Christian and pagan traditions and Nazi ideology. On the Nazi altar rested *Mein Kampf* in place of a Bible and a swastika in place of the crucifix. Hitler's name was invoked in services and catechisms more often than God's.

Within the constraints of the regime, both Catholic and Protestant churches continued to operate, and regular services were held. Some clergy rallied enthusiastically to the

Adolf Hitler examines the chassis of the Strength Through Joy people's car, the Volkswagen. On Hitler's left is the car's designer, Dr. Ferdinand Porsche.

Nazis, declaring that Hitler was as much a messiah as Christ, or that Hitler had been sent to carry out a divine mission. Some high-ranking church officials got into the swing of things by insisting they be greeted with the salutation "Heil Bishop!"

Youth organizations were a particular source of tension between the Nazi state and churches because of the premium placed on access to young minds. Several Nazi organizations were established for young people. By the end of 1933, when all except Catholic youth bodies were banned, the Hitler Youth contained 47 percent of boys between ten and fourteen, and 38 percent of those between fourteen and eighteen. In contrast, the parallel girls' organizations had enrolled only 15 and 8 percent of girls in those age groups. In 1939 membership in the organizations became mandatory. Like other youth organizations, such as the Scouts and Guides in liberal democracies, the Nazi organizations provided leisure activities and sports within a context that stressed military qualities of discipline, loyalty, and patriotism.

In all these categories—workers, the clergy, young people—there were patterns of willing cooperation with the Nazis, grudging compliance, and outright resistance. The first two are often difficult to separate, for the outward behavior in each case was often identical. Outright resistance, however, is well documented in the activities of the police agencies.

Informal alternative youth movements developed outside and in opposition to the approved Nazi organizations. One, the "Edelweiss Pirates," formed in the late 1930s in western Germany, was composed of a number of groups having distinctive badges (an edelweiss flower) and clothing (generally a checked shirt, dark shorts, and white socks). "Edelweiss" gangs went off to the country on weekends, camped, and frequently ambushed and beat up Hitler Youth detachments.

The other main alternative youth movement was the Swing Youth, whose members were mainly middle class. Swing culture centered on jazz, which was associated in the Nazi mind not only with blacks but also with Jews. With their jitterbugging, "hot" dancing with overtly sexual overtones, outrageously casual dress, and adoration of non-German bands, the Swing Youth represented everything the Nazis considered decadent. Police raids were carried out on all nonconforming youth movements at various times. Members were coerced into the Hitler Youth, beaten, had their heads shaved and branded, and were imprisoned. The movements persisted right into the war, however, evidence of the resilience of youth resistance.

To resist the Nazi regime in any way carried considerable risks. There was a multiplicity of police forces, including the SS, the Gestapo, the criminal police, and the ordinary uniformed force. In some senses, however, the forces of repression loomed larger than life, for the Gestapo, which became synonymous with repressive cruelty, numbered at its largest only 33,000 members. In 1937, there were 43 Gestapo officials in Essen, which had a population of 650,000, and that was a relatively high ratio. Yet accounts of life in Nazi Germany give the impression that whether at work, school, play, or home, among strangers, friends, and family, no one felt safe.

Such anxieties appear to have been justified, for if the Gestapo was able to stretch its thin resources as effectively as it did, it was because large numbers of ordinary citizens filed reports or denunciations on family members, neighbors, friends, colleagues at work, and strangers. The great majority of Gestapo investigations started this way.

It is hazardous to generalize about the responses of Germans to the Nazi regime. There were young people who hung on to the Führer's every word, and those who regarded him as a clown; workers who labored for the glory of the Reich, and those who labored at the same bench just to keep food on the family table. Attitudes varied not only by class, gender, and region, but within them. Any individual, too, might support the Nazis' foreign policy achievements, but draw the line at the race policies. The problem was that Nazi policies formed a coherent whole, and one could not pick and choose among them.

Nazi Germany: Social and Racial Revolution

Before and after they came to power, the Nazis portrayed themselves as a force for radical change in Germany. The kind of revolution implied by Nazi rhetoric was a return to an earlier time (as when a wheel completes a revolution), for they presented themselves as wanting to reverse modern trends in order to recover an earlier social order. Nazis deplored urbanization, the paid employment of women, the decline of artisans and small businesses, the rise of department stores and industrial conglomerates, the class division of society, and liberal democracy—the main lines of change in the previous hundred years. They deplored, too, the rapid expansion of Jewish participation in Germany's political, economic, social, and cultural life since the nineteenth century.

The Nazis were heirs to the late-nineteenth-century intellectual movement that the historian Fritz Stern has described as "cultural despair," which rejected what was portrayed as soul-less modern society and evoked a mythical age of community and harmony with nature. Nazi rhetoric and propaganda, shot through with a mishmash of symbols drawn variously from antiquity, paganism, and Nordic mythology, evoked a golden age when the German Volk, or people, were not "contaminated" by contact with other races. Blond and blissful, Germans in Nazi propaganda lived and worked together harmoniously in the countryside, on farms and in small villages, all rooted spiritually to the soil. Theirs was no egalitarian society, but a community of men, women, and children who knew their places in the hierarchy of power and functions.

But rather than implement policies that reversed the odious social changes that were in place, the Nazis supervised their continuity during the short life of the Third Reich. Observing a military rather than a cultural agenda, the regime encouraged rapid industrialization, and cooperated with large combines to increase their share of production. Small enterprises continued to decline, and the number of self-employed continued to shrink. Women, although a reduced proportion of the workforce, were employed in ever greater numbers in industry. The trends intensified as war placed greater demands for productivity and efficiency on Germans.

The Nazis' much-vaunted respect for the countryside was little in evidence. Many farmers were forbidden to subdivide their farms, and they chafed under government controls. The regime's emphasis on building a strong and self-sufficient industrial economy accelerated the movement of population to the cities. By the mid-1930s there was such a labor shortage in agriculture that more than 50,000 foreign workers were employed on the land. Respect for the sanctity of the countryside was not evident in the new autobahns that cut through pastures and forests.

Nazi policy had little effect on the fundamental organization of the German economy or the broad experience of social groups. Industry generally remained in private ownership and was largely unregulated. The military needs of the state in such areas as chemical, fuels, steel, and aircraft and automobile production were met cooperatively; state and industry worked together to see that labor, fuel, and raw materials were available to ensure production targets were met. The expropriation of Jewish businesses and private banks benefited only big industry and banking interests, and furthered the concentration of ownership in fewer hands.

These policies drew the traditional landed and industrial elites into a close relationship with the Nazi regime. This does not mean that they enthusiastically supported all Nazi policies. But industrialists benefited from being able to acquire former Jewish concerns, from government contracts, and from the destruction of trade unions. The landed elites were guaranteed that their estates would not be broken up, and they also benefited from rising prices for their produce.

Small businesses did not benefit as they might have expected. The government did not close existing department stores (because of the unemployment that would result), although it forbade the construction of new ones and limited some of the services they could provide, like hairdressing. The expulsion of Jews from many professions opened up vocational opportunities for middle-class "Aryan" children, as vacancies occurred for doctors, lawyers, chemists, and veterinarians. Young men were particular beneficiaries because, in the first years at least, women were limited to 10 percent of university places.

Of the three broad classes, workers fared worst. Outside skilled trades in the military industries, where there was a scarcity of labor, industrial wages fell behind price increases until 1938. When real wages did improve (in 1938 they reached 1929 levels), it was because workers were putting in longer hours; the average work week lengthened from forty-three hours in 1933 to forty-seven hours in 1939.

In general terms, Nazi policies tended to reinforce preexisting tendencies in Germany's economy and society, but in one important respect the Nazis did carry out a sort of revolution: their attempt to create a racial state. Criteria of race were established and individuals who fell into proscribed non-Aryan categories were progressively excluded from the German polity, society, economy, and culture. It must be stressed, however, that the racial revolution was superimposed upon the strong lines of social and economic continuity. The elimination of Jews from retailing, wholesaling, and banking gave greater racial homogeneity to Germany's corporate and commercial elite, but it only intensified the trend toward the concentration of ownership in fewer and fewer hands.

Jews were the first group targeted in the creation of the racial state. As we have seen, laws were enacted between 1933 and 1935 to limit the civil rights, employment, and personal relationships of Jews. After a brief relaxation in anti-Semitism during the 1936 Olympics, the pace of discrimination and exclusion accelerated. In isolation, many of the measures appear trivial, more a nuisance than seriously disabling or harmful. For example, persons married to Jews were forbidden to fly the German flag, Jews were forbidden to hold hunting permits, and were banned from using public swimming pools, sitting on park benches, and owning pets. The cumulative effect of such rules, however, was to draw a line, tighter and tighter, around the lives of Jews. Petty restrictions destroyed the texture of normal life.

Jews were also excluded from more and more professions: In 1936 and 1937 cattle dealers, veterinarians, currency dealers, notaries, and chemists were among the prohibited occupations added to the list. Finally, in 1938, a total ban was placed on all academically trained Jewish professionals. Deprived of work, Jews were also restricted in their leisure time when laws forbade them to visit cinemas, galleries, theaters, and eat in certain restaurants. Social benefits were withdrawn as Jews were ruled ineligible for child allowances and health insurance.

Jews began to disappear from German cultural life, too, as librarians researched the racial origin of authors, and then removed books written or edited by Jews from library shelves. Jewish names became problematic: University professors could not mention

Einstein or Hertz in physics lectures; streets and squares named after Jews were renamed. In order to ensure that Jews could be identified by name, a list of recognized Jewish first names was published. Any Jews who did not have one of those on the list had to add either Sara or Israel to their existing names.

The effect of the Nazi legislation was to make Jews readily identifiable and to prevent Jews and non-Jews from coming into contact with one another. The official restrictions were accompanied by persistent harassment and violence that was sanctioned by the Nazi authorities at all levels. Jewish-owned stores were daubed with paint, and individual Jews humiliated, roughed up, seriously assaulted, and in some cases killed.

Life for Jews became increasingly untenable, and by 1938 some 150,000 Jews, about a quarter of the Jewish population, had left Germany. The flow of Jewish refugees from oppression in Germany, as well as other Central and Eastern European countries, persuaded most European governments to close their doors. The effect of immigration restrictions there and elsewhere (both the United States and Canada placed limits on Jews) was that Jews found it harder to leave Germany just at the time persecution intensified in 1938. It was a terrible irony that anti-Semitism prevented the Nazi government itself from expelling Jews from Germany.

In October German police arrested and tried to deport 17,000 Jews with Polish citizenship, but the Poles refused to admit them. The Polish government had attempted to deprive Polish Jews of citizenship the previous March, and had no desire to increase the number of Jews under its jurisdiction. The 17,000 Jews at issue, denied entry to either state and left destitute in camps in a no-man's land, included the family of a seventeen-year-old student, Hershel Grynszpan. To avenge his family, Grynszpan assassinated an official in the German embassy in Paris, an act that provided the Nazis with an excuse for a full-scale attack on Jews.

On the night of November 7, 1938, hundreds of synagogues were vandalized and burned, other Jewish-owned buildings destroyed, and thousands of Jews killed, beaten, or arrested. This phenomenon is known as *Kristallnacht,* or Crystal Night, after the glittering broken glass that littered the streets of German towns after the windows of Jewish stores were smashed. The Nazis portrayed Kristallnacht as the spontaneous outpouring of Aryan anger at the assassination in Paris, but in reality it was a carefully coordinated attack, though primarily on property rather than on persons. Confidential Nazi documents reported that 191 synagogues and 14 community centers were set on fire, 815 retail shops, 29 department stores, and 171 private dwellings wrecked, and some 7,500 stores damaged. Despite the emphasis on property, 36 Jews were killed, and an equal number seriously injured. In the following weeks some 25,000 were arrested.

November 1938 marked the beginning of a new wave of persecution of Germany's Jews and the enactment of further laws to limit their freedom. Jews were encouraged to abandon their property and leave Germany. About 150,000 did so in the following nine months, so that by the time war broke out in September 1939, more than half Germany's Jews had emigrated. Those who remained were collectively required to pay a fine of 1 billion marks, and were prevented from claiming any insurance or compensation for losses incurred as a result of attacks on their property. In addition, some 20,000 Jews were imprisoned in concentration camps. By the eve of World War II, Germany's remaining Jews lived a tenuous existence at the pleasure of the Nazi regime.

Jews are generally highlighted among the victims of Nazism because during the war they were singled out for annihilation in the program of systematic killing called the Holocaust. Other groups within the German population were also systematically persecuted, and later killed in massive numbers, for failing to conform to the racial and ideological requirements of the government.

Sinti and Roma (Gypsies) historically experienced discrimination and persecution for their mobile lifestyle and alleged criminality, and in the Third Reich racial impurity was added to their putative offenses. Although Sinti and Roma were not mentioned specifically in Nazi race policies, legal commentaries stipulated that they were to be treated like Jews and subjected to the same laws of citizenship, marriage, and personal relations.

In 1936 the Reich Central Office for the Fight Against the Gypsy Nuisance was established. Using 19,000 files inherited from the police in Bavaria, where in 1926 a law had been passed allowing the authorities to confine Sinti and Roma to workhouses, the Nazis arrested Sinti and Roma and subjected them to compulsory sterilization. In the same year a major research project on Sinti and Roma was set up, a collaborative effort of the ministry of health, the criminal police, and the SS. The psychologist who headed the project hypothesized that Sinti and Roma were Aryans who had interbred with "inferior races" and developed criminal tendencies as a result.

No specific legislation was enacted against Germany's 30,000 Sinti and Roma until December 1938, when Himmler ordered all Sinti and Roma, as well as vagrants "living a Gyspy-like existence," and anyone looking or behaving like Sinti and Roma, to be registered with the Central Office. Himmler observed that the "Gypsy question" was part of the Nazi task of "national regeneration," and added that the aim must be "the physical separation of Gypsydom from the German nation."

The reference to national regeneration is a reminder that Nazi race policy had dimensions other than the exclusion of non-Aryan races. It aimed to create a nation of perfect men and women, portrayed in visual propaganda as tall, youthful, muscular, handsome, and often (but not always) blond. It is a mark of the power of the Nazi message that it was able to override the reality that few Germans—and certainly none of the Nazi hierarchy—looked anything like the Aryans depicted in official art.

Germans who demonstrably fell short of the ideal, the disabled, were subjected before the war to policies even more drastic than those directed at most Jews and Sinti and Roma. Drawing on the eugenics ideas that were widespread in Europe, the Nazis focused on hereditary illnesses as harmful to the national interest. Healthy parents were said to have one or two children as a rule, but the unhealthy "are producing unrestrainedly while their sick and asocial offspring burden the community." The reference to "asocial" highlights the connection between biological and social characteristics that was embedded in Nazi thought.

The contraction of public funds during the Great Depression raised, for many eugenicists generally and Nazis specifically, the question of the costs of sustaining the lives of people regarded as "unfit." A 1933 law stipulated that anyone with a hereditary illness could be sterilized to prevent them from reproducing. The list of hereditary illnesses included "congenital feeble-mindedness," schizophrenia, manic depression, hereditary epilepsy, Huntington's chorea, hereditary blindness, hereditary deafness, serious physical deformities, and chronic alcoholism.

An estimated 320,000 to 350,000 people, or half of 1 percent of the population, were sterilized under these guidelines. This was considerably less than the usual estimates bandied about by Nazi doctors and leaders, who suggested that 20 to 30 percent of the population might need to be restrained from breeding. The process of reducing the "unfit" population went further when in 1935 abortions were encouraged on women who were (or whose sexual partners were) "hereditarily ill." Abortions could be performed up to the seventh month of pregnancy.

In the years before the Second World War the Nazis also began a program of euthanasia. Euthanasia, which generally means the painless killing of terminally ill persons at their own request (or the request of relatives when the ill person is unable to consent), had an entirely different meaning for Nazis. As early as 1929 Hitler suggested that Germany might be strengthened by the removal of the weakest 70 or 80 percent of all children born, a proportion that clearly has nothing to do with euthanasia in the usual sense, and everything to do with mass killing for other reasons.

As soon as the Nazis were in power, tours of asylums by party officials were organized, and between 1933 and 1939 one asylum in Munich received 21,000 such visitors, including 6,000 members of the SS. It was noted that some of the SS visitors recommended that machine guns should be set up to kill the patients. Initially, actual policies fell short of these suggestions, although the resources devoted to such institutions fell. The chronically ill were given minimal care, those discharged were first sterilized, and the doctor-patient ratio rose until it reached 1:500, at which point real treatment was impossible. When a program of killing the unfit was launched (the so-called euthanasia program), it focused on children. Doctors and midwives reported newborn infants and children with deformities, and between 1934 and 1939 more than 5,000 were transferred to special clinics where they were starved to death or given lethal injections. After the beginning of the war, a broader program of killing patients in mental asylums was inaugurated.

Male homosexuals, regarded as degenerate and "racially destructive," also attracted Nazi attention early in the 1930s, as conventional homophobia was amplified by racial arguments. Germany had lost 2 million men in the First World War, it was argued, and the estimated 2 million homosexuals in Germany in the 1930s prevented the population from recovering. Persecuting and killing homosexuals would not increase the population, but the refusal of homosexuals to act like proper Aryan men, by impregnating Aryan women, identified them as abnormal and unfit. Homosexual bars, bath houses, and other meeting places were regularly raided, and the number of prosecutions rose from 766 in 1934 to over 4,000 in 1936 and 8,000 in 1938. Beginning in 1937, most homosexuals were sent to concentration camps after they had served a prison sentence. Lesbians were not subjected to formal persecution, although lesbianism was sometimes included with other charges against women imprisoned or sent to concentration camps.

If the Nazis' plan was to eliminate from German society the "unfit" and "harmful"— Jews, Sinti and Roma, the disabled, and homosexuals—they also attempted to strengthen the able-bodied and heterosexual Aryan population, both in terms of its numbers and its health and physical strength. In October 1935, the Marriage Health Law forbade anyone marrying who was suffering from any physical or mental illness; men and women had to get a certificate of health before marrying. The Nazis encouraged marriage in order to stem the decline of fertility rates and to increase population.

A new Nazi divorce law, enacted in 1938, added to the racial policies designed to Aryanize marriage and promote fertility. Refusal to have children was made a ground for divorce (some Nazi judges had already allowed divorces in these circumstances), as was any attempt to use an illegal means to prevent a birth. Divorce could also be had when one spouse suffered from premature infertility or a mental or physical disorder. The 1938 law also allowed husbands and wives who had lived apart for three years or more (in "useless and barren marriages," according to one Nazi newspaper) to divorce so they could remarry and have children.

It is likely that most of the divorces in Nazi Germany reflected quite conventional personal problems, like incompatibility and adultery, rather than any widespread desire to breed pure Aryan children for the Fatherland. But some divorces were clearly political. One Nazi official divorced his wife when she insisted on shopping at Jewish stores, while one women divorced because her husband expressed indignation when his son gave the

Hitler salute. The German Supreme Court ruled that "disparagement of the Führer by a wife entitles the husband to claim a divorce."

Nazi race policy took marriage and sexuality out of the private realm and made them state property. Himmler, rejecting the view that sexual orientation is a purely private matter, told SS leaders that "all things which take place in the sexual sphere are not the private affair of the individual, but signify the life and death of the nation." Nor did Nazi ideas of the family conform to notions of the "traditional" family. The regime cared little whether children were born inside or outside marriage, as long as the stock of Aryans increased. The state provided financial and other assistance to unmarried pregnant women as long as they and the man responsible for the pregnancy were Aryans. Children identified as pure Aryan were later abducted from conquered territories and brought to Germany to increase the racial stock.

Clearly these policies had far-reaching implications for women, who were seen primarily in terms of their reproductive potential. Goebbels, the minster of propaganda, put it best: "A woman's primary, rightful, and appropriate place is in the family, and the most wonderful task she can perform is to present her country and people with children."

Women were discouraged from working in paid employment, although the reality of Germany's labor supply made women an essential part of industrial growth. The campaign to increase fertility was, however, pursued vigorously. Aryan women's access to abortion and contraception was restricted, and a cult of motherhood promoted. Any woman who bore three children received honor cards that gave her preferential treatment in shops. Women with larger families were awarded the Honor Cross of German Mothers.

The birth rate in Germany did indeed rise during the 1930s, but it is unclear how much Nazi policies contributed to it. It is quite possible that it resulted more from improvements in the economy and the greater willingness of couples to have children once the worst economic times had passed. Whatever the reason, the increase in the birth rate in Germany contrasted with nations like Britain and France, where the birth rate continued its long-term decline even after their economies picked up. Even so, the German birth rate remained far lower than the regime wanted. Family size fell from 2.3 children in 1920

A "Mother and Child Home" for unmarried "Aryan" mothers, established in the interest of increasing the births of children who were racially acceptable to the Nazi regime.

to 1.8 in 1940. It was particularly distressing that married SS men, who ought to have been model fathers of large families, had on average only one child each.

Although an emphasis on women's roles as mothers was combined in many European legal codes with greater sexual equality, in Nazi Germany it accompanied a deterioration of married women's status. A husband could prevent his wife from working outside the home, and women lost many rights to control their property and income. Farms could be inherited only by males. Children came under the primary control of their fathers. Men, like women, found themselves with explicit tasks in the making of Nazi society, generally the mirror-image of women's. Men were to produce and reproduce for the Fatherland, and be the financial support of their families. In many respects the Nazi regime presented itself as collectives of men, typically soldiers in martial formation. Nazi art focused a great deal of attention on the male body as it did on the female. Aryan men were portrayed as muscular and quintessentially virile, usually holding a substantial sword or other weapon. There was a deliberate effort to exploit homoerotic imagery (without crossing over to overt homosexuality) in order to promote male bonding in the context of a military brotherhood.

The racial state, which required the mobilization of the law, the civil service, and all the forces of coercion, lay at the center of the Nazi enterprise. It is conceivable that had the Nazi regime not failed in the Second World War, a racial hierarchy might have challenged Germany's economic class structure. The SS, membership of which was limited to the racially "pure," had the potential to dominate important sectors of the German economy.

By the outbreak of war, however, only modest progress had been made in the task of building the racial state. Some of the steps necessary to its completion were so dreadful in their character and intended scope that it was difficult to carry them out in peacetime, and their fuller realization had to be postponed. The mass killing that the Nazis called euthanasia is an example; Hitler told the leader of the German physicians' organization that in the event of a war he planned to take up the euthanasia policy and enforce it, because "such a problem would be more easily solved in war-time."

The European Road to War, 1936–39

Mid-1936 saw Nazi Germany host the pacific Olympic Games and send the first of its combat forces to Spain. Thereafter, with Germany's economy strengthening and the dictatorship apparently unassailable, Hitler began to move even more forcefully in both domestic and foreign affairs. In October 1936, reflecting their partnership in the Spanish civil war, Germany and Italy formed an alliance. Mussolini referred to it as a Rome-Berlin "axis," a new pivot around which European affairs would revolve, and before long Germany and Italy became known as the Axis powers. Italy's alliance with Germany shifted the balance of power in Europe, and the prospect of another fascist state in Spain boded ill for the future. Elsewhere in Europe, too, right-wing regimes were developing that had ideological affinities with fascism.

The only significant counterweight to the growth of these fascist regimes was the Soviet Union. The British, even more concerned about Stalin than about Hitler, spurned the idea of a Soviet alliance. Between 1936 and 1939 they persisted in futile attempts to woo Mussolini away from Germany by offering to accept Italy's influence in the Mediterranean and to recognize its authority in Ethiopia.

The French, more concerned than the British by the spread of fascism because they faced the prospect of being surrounded by fascist states, held negotiations with the Soviet

Union in 1936 and 1937. The idea of a French-Soviet pact echoed the French-Russian alliance before World War I. The ideological reserve felt by Britain's conservatives about communism was less strong in France, which was governed by a left-wing Popular Front administration led by Léon Blum.

Throughout this period, Germany prepared for territorial expansion by attempting to achieve economic self-sufficiency. A four-year plan was put in place in September 1936. Underlying Hitler's policies was a plan to create a Greater Germany populated by the German Volk (Aryans) that would be the heart of a European New Order. Other parts of Europe and their inhabitants would provide the resources and labor for German prosperity.

It has been argued that Hitler did not so much plan the series of territorial acquisitions in the late 1930s as much as he seized opportunities as they presented themselves. From either point of view, the acquisition of additional territory was necessary if Germany was to bring ethnic Germans in other states within the borders of the Reich, and control access to the raw materials, oil, and grain that would make Germany self-sufficient.

Hitler's first target was his native Austria and its predominantly ethnic German population. After the failure of the German attempt to overthrow the Austrian government in 1934, Austria's chancellor Kurt Schuschnigg relied on Italian opposition to German designs on Austria to balance pro-German forces, especially the Austrian Nazi Party. By 1937, however, when it was clear that Italy was more concerned with expanding into Africa, Schuschnigg was forced to make concessions by bringing a Nazi, Artur von Seyss-Inquart, into the government. In February 1938, Hitler met Schuschnigg, harangued him for three hours, and ordered him to legalize the Nazi Party and make Seyss-Inquart minister of the interior, a key post that carried with it control over the police. The alternative Hitler offered was invasion by German forces.

Schuschnigg capitulated to the demand, but as pressure for the incorporation (*Anschluss*) of Austria into Germany mounted in the following weeks, he attempted to fend it off by announcing a plebiscite on Austrian independence for March 13. A vote for independence would have set back Hitler's hope that Anschluss could be portrayed as the will of the Austrian people.

Unwilling to risk having his plans derailed by Austrian sentiment, Hitler prepared to act. Schuschnigg canceled the plebiscite on Hitler's demand, but that was not enough. Nor was it enough that the Austrian president dismissed Schuschnigg as chancellor and replaced him with the Nazi Seyss-Inquart. Mussolini, currently preoccupied with Ethiopia and Spain, signaled his consent to Anschluss, and a grateful Hitler ordered German forces into Austria on March 12. There they were met by large, jubilant crowds, giving the Nazi salute and conveying to the world the impression that Austrians wanted nothing more than to be subjects of the Führer.

It was certainly accepted as such by foreign states, and despite a few formal protests there was no real objection to the disappearance of Austria as a sovereign state. There was a sense that this is what most Austrians had wanted after the First World War, but that they had been prevented from realizing their aim by the prohibition on German-Austrian union in the Treaty of Versailles. The inclusion of Austria increased the size of Germany and added almost 7 million inhabitants to the Reich, including Austria's 200,000 Jews. It also contributed a significant industrial region to the German economy.

Once the Austrian precedent was established, Hitler turned his attention to other ethnic German populations living outside the borders of the Reich. One of the largest concentrations, more than 3 million, lived in the Sudeten region of Czechoslovakia, bordering Germany (and what had been Austria). The German minority's resentment at

Nazi troops, watched by civilians, humiliate Jews by forcing them to scrub sidewalks in Vienna, following the German annexation of Austria in 1938.

minority status in Czechoslovakia, which had focused on language and education issues, grew during the depression as unemployment among Germans outpaced that of other groups. The leader of the Sudeten Germans, Conrad Henlein, was encouraged by Hitler in April 1938 to present an impossible set of demands to the Czechoslovak prime minister, Eduard Beneš. The Karlsbad Program, as it was called, demanded self-government for the German minority and reparations for their sufferings under Czechoslovak rule. The government responded with some concessions.

The volatility of the situation, following the Anschluss, was evident in May 1938 when, following reports of German military activity on the border, the Czechoslovaks mobilized their army. France and the Soviet Union reaffirmed their treaty obligations to Czechoslovakia, and Britain declared its support for the Prague government. Despite a denial of territorial ambitions in Czechoslovakia, Hitler was determined to destroy the country. The British government, seeing the problem as primarily an internal one, was anxious to avoid war. Prime Minister Neville Chamberlain secretly offered to persuade the Czechoslovak government to agree to concessions that would satisfy the Sudeten Germans and therefore, he assumed, Hitler as well. The Beneš government was reluctant to give the minority German population special status in Czechoslovakia, the only Eastern European state to have preserved its democratic institutions largely intact. Hitler denounced the

Beneš government at the Nazi Party's congress in Nuremberg on September 12, and promised to help the Sudeten Germans, whom he described as "these tortured creatures." When riots promptly broke out in the Sudetenland, the Czechoslovak government imposed martial law. The leader of the Sudeten Germans fled to Germany, where he declared that his people wanted to join the Reich.

So tense was the situation that France and Britain began to mobilize their armies. The Soviet Union was in favor of appealing to the League of Nations and wanted to join Britain and France in guaranteeing Czechoslovakia's sovereignty. They, however, were distrustful of the Soviet Union and rejected any idea that the Red Army should be involved in a war in Central Europe. Poland, for its part, refused to allow Soviet troops to cross Polish territory in order to assist Czechoslovakia.

Armed conflict was averted partly by the intervention of Neville Chamberlain, who shuttled to meet Hitler three times in the second half of September 1938. At the first meeting they agreed that the Sudetenland should be "detached" from Czechoslovakia and transferred to Germany; this was more than Hitler had asked for, and not the self-government the Sudeten Germans had initially requested. Chamberlain accepted Hitler's assurance that this was the last major demand he intended to make. Chamberlain did not have a mandate to negotiate Czechoslovakia's territory, and prime minister Beneš agreed only after Britain and France threatened to withdraw their support.

When Chamberlain communicated the agreement at his second meeting with Hitler, on September 21, Hitler had increased his demands; now he wanted the Sudetenland to be ceded in three days and German troops to occupy it immediately. Believing the peace effort had failed, the French and British mobilized their armies. The French brought troops to defend the Maginot line, and in London Chamberlain bewailed the fact that the British were preparing for war "because of a quarrel in a faraway country between people of whom we know nothing." He seemed as puzzled as Hitler was that Britain should contemplate war over an issue that did not affect it directly.

But again war was avoided, this time by the intervention of Mussolini, who (at Chamberlain's request) proposed a four-power conference of Germany, Italy, France, and Britain. Czechoslovakia was excluded from discussing its own fate, and the Soviet Union was not invited. The meeting, held in Munich on September 29, 1938, produced what is known as the Munich Agreement. All regions of the Sudetenland with a more than 50 percent German population were to be transferred immediately to Germany, and in areas with substantial German populations plebiscites were to be held to decide whether they would remain in Czechoslovakia or be transferred to Germany. Hitler agreed to respect the integrity of the rest of Czechoslovakia.

Although the Munich Agreement was later condemned as a sellout to Nazi aggression and came to symbolize the whole bankrupt policy of appeasement, it was greeted as a great success in Germany (which had won territory) and in France and Britain, where there was relief that war had been prevented at no cost to themselves. Arriving home, Chamberlain waved a piece of paper that carried the text of the agreement, and announced "peace in our time." He was praised by much of the mainstream press and by the king.

Having furthered his racial policies within the Reich, Hitler set out to expand it even more in 1939 by completing the destruction of Czechoslovakia that the Munich Agreement had begun. The incorporation of the Sudetenland into Germany (including areas where plebiscites were supposed to have been held) was followed by Polish and Hungarian annexation of Czechoslovak territory on their borders. Czechoslovakia had lost almost half its land, critical defenses, more than 5 million inhabitants, most of its raw materials, and considerable industrial infrastructure. Agitation among Slovaks for separation from the Czechs

Reactions to German conquests. The top picture shows part of the enthusiastic crowd of Austrians who welcomed Hitler to Vienna in March 1938. The other photograph shows an angry crowd in Prague when German troops completed their invasion of Czechoslovakia.

increased, and Hitler acted to oblige them. Czechoslovakia's considerable army and air force were by this time deprived of their fortifications and the Skoda armaments works, and German troops easily occupied what was left of the country after the Munich Agreement. In contrast to the rapturous, flag-waving crowds of Vienna almost exactly a year earlier, angry but muted crowds watched German troops roll through the streets of Prague on March 15, 1939. Czech areas of the country were designated the Protectorate of Bohemia-Moravia, and the Slovak areas were established as an independent state of Slovakia.

In the full flush of this victory, Hitler embarked on yet another conquest, this time of Memeland in Lithuania, contiguous with German East Prussia. The Lithuanian government had been given an ultimatum and had ceded the territory rather than face German troops. On March 23, Hitler arrived at Memel and declared the region part of the Reich.

Next on Nazi Germany's agenda of aggression was Poland, like Czechoslovakia set up by the Treaty of Versailles and having a substantial German population in the free port of Danzig and in its western regions. Scarcely had Prague been occupied when Germany demanded the return of Danzig and free access to East Prussia by road and rail across the Polish Corridor. Coming so soon after the breach of the Munich Agreement, these demands provoked a stern response from Britain and France, which guaranteed assistance to Poland if its independence were threatened.

It is not clear why France and Britain abandoned the policy of appeasement, which they had practiced over the Rhineland, Austria, and Czechoslovakia, when it came to Poland. In 1938 Chamberlain had written off the Sudetenland as "a faraway country" and it was hardly likely that he felt any closer, geographically or otherwise, to the Poles. Public opinion in both countries was against war, and neither was militarily well prepared. But appeasement was based on the belief that Hitler had limited and, in geopolitical terms, reasonable demands. It was reasonable that Germany, a strong, populous country, should be allowed to play an appropriately prominent role in European affairs, and various unilateral revisions of the Treaty of Versailles could be tolerated to help Germany achieve this. It also seemed reasonable that Germany might include ethnic Germans outside Germany; these were the arguments that justified Anschluss and the Munich concessions.

But the total destruction of Czechoslovakia called into question Hitler's trustworthiness and the extent of his territorial ambitions. Had Hitler abided by the terms of Munich and limited German acquisitions to German-populated Sudetenland, perhaps his demands for access to East Prussia and control of Danzig would not have evoked the same response from Britain and France. After Hitler had occupied the rest of Czechoslovakia, Chamberlain had asked rhetorically if this was his last attack or if there were to be more, if "this [is] in fact a step in the direction of an attempt to dominate the world by force?"

By definition, policies of appeasement have their limits: Either the behavior requiring continual appeasement ends, the patience and goodwill of the appeasers are exhausted, or the appeasers are destroyed by their own policies. The point at which the patience of appeasers runs out generally appears arbitrary. In the case of Europe in the 1930s, we might ask why Britain and France drew the line at Poland and not at Czechoslovakia. In fact, most arguments about appeasement revolve not around the question of whether concessions ought to have been made to Germany, but at what point the concessions ought to have stopped.

The policies adopted by Britain and France toward Nazi Germany are often condemned as having encouraged Hitler to pursue aggressive policies. If they did have any justification, it was because Hitler was regarded as a conventional leader who, if not entirely transparent, would at least honor open agreements that he himself had made. When those assumptions proved wrong, as they clearly did when Hitler broke the Munich Agreement, the policy of appeasement was abandoned.

It was impossible to undo the damage the policy had done. Territorial gains had strengthened Germany economically and demographically. Austria and the Czech part of Czechoslovakia were highly industrialized regions, and the latter included important arms industries. It was not clear how Britain and France could possibly guarantee Polish sovereignty. Poland's defenses were weak and its army poorly equipped, and a concerted German attack would almost certainly succeed well before British or French assistance arrived. Even a French attack on Germany would probably be too late to save Poland.

The Soviet Union, which bordered Poland's east, loomed as a critical variable. In April 1939, the Soviet Union again proposed a three-power pact. If Britain and France were allied with the Soviet Union, any German move against Poland would risk a war on two fronts. Negotiations for an alliance began in the spring of 1939, but proceeded at glacial speed during the summer. The British, more than the French, were suspicious of Stalin's intentions and doubted whether his purged army was any longer an effective fighting force. Although the chiefs of staff were arguing for an alliance with the Soviet Union (or at least an arrangement securing Soviet neutrality), the British government dragged its feet. Instead of sending high-level diplomats to Moscow, Britain dispatched low-ranking officials; they traveled by sea rather than air.

Meanwhile Hitler was also active diplomatically. On May 22, Germany and Italy signed a military treaty called the Pact of Steel. It obliged each country to come to the other's assistance in any war, even if it was against its interests and wishes. In the course of negotiations Mussolini stressed that Italy would not be prepared to participate in a European war until 1943 at the earliest. By signing the pact, however, he theoretically surrendered control over Italian foreign policy. Clearly it was Italy that would follow Germany into war, rather than vice versa.

Hitler's real diplomatic coup was not the pact with Italy, however, but a nonaggression treaty with the Soviet Union. Stalin had been negotiating with both sides, and had decided that not only was Germany more serious about reaching an agreement, but also had more to offer than Britain and France. Stalin expected Germany would attack Poland, so that an alliance with France and Britain would soon involve the Soviet Union in war. Stalin was not convinced that Britain or France would render much assistance to Eastern Europe, leaving the Soviet Union to fight Germany alone.

A treaty with Germany, however, offered neutrality in the event of war and, in a secret protocol, Germany offered even more: In the event of a war Germany would get the western part of Poland and Lithuania; the Soviet Union could occupy eastern Poland, as well as Estonia and Latvia. The Soviet-German nonaggression treaty not only saved the Soviet Union from going to war but also rewarded it with territory that had been part of the Russian Empire.

The announcement of the German-Soviet pact stunned the international community. It radically altered Germany's position in Europe and made Poland much more vulnerable. It was stunning, too, to Communists throughout Western Europe, who now found themselves ordered by the Comintern not to oppose Nazi Germany's policies.

Well aware of the implications of the pact, Britain formally guaranteed its support for Poland on August 25, and Chamberlain announced that Britain would declare war if Poland were threatened. Hitler approached Mussolini for support, only to be told that despite the terms of the Pact of Steel, Italy was too weak to join a war. Hitler waited only a few days before attacking Poland on September 1, 1939. Even then the British and French declarations of war were not immediate. They gave Germany until September 3 to withdraw its forces, and declared war when the ultimatum expired. Italy and the Soviet Union declared their neutrality. There was none of the public or official enthusiasm for war that had broken out in London and Paris in August 1914.

Conclusion

There is no doubt that in the critical period between the depression and the outbreak of World War II, Germany set the direction and pace of international developments. By adopting policies that brought Germany out of the depression more quickly than the other main powers, Hitler gained a degree of respect even from European leaders whose ideologies were quite unlike those of the Nazis. Germany also benefited from the policies implemented by Stalin (who was far more murderous than Hilter in the 1930s), which weakened the Soviet Union militarily and eventually gave Hitler a free hand in Central Europe. Historians have debated whether the policies adopted by the German government in this period (and during the war) were predetermined or whether they were the result of Hitler seizing opportunities as they occurred. But although issues of timing may be debated, there seems little doubt that Nazi policies like revision of the Treaty of Versailles and the persecution of political opponents, Jews, and others designated undesirable, followed well-planned lines.

It is important to recognize that the policies adopted by the Nazi regime, which eventually led to the outbreak of war in 1939, were not purely political and economic. Racial, sexual, demographic, and gender elements were integral to them, such that the new order envisaged by the Nazis entailed a thorough transformation of fundamental aspects of European society.

·8·
The Second World War, 1939–1945

Introduction

The war that broke out in 1939 easily exceeded the grim statistics of the Great War. Combined military and civilian deaths in Europe alone totaled some 50 million, with another 30 million wounded or injured. (In Asia and the Pacific, the other main theaters of the war, there were 30 million additional casualties.) The Second World War in Europe does not conjure up the horrific images of trench warfare that are part of the legacy of the Great War, but it left instead memories of immense suffering and mass murder deliberately inflicted on civilian populations.

Directly or indirectly, civilians have almost always been involved in wars, suffering the effects of taxation, requisitioning, and conscription. But attacks on civilians have generally been deplored as unavoidable or as necessary to weaken the economic infrastructure of the enemy's war effort. In 1939–45, however, civilian populations were drawn into strategic planning in their own right, with appalling results. Unlike the 1914–18 conflict, in which most of the millions of dead were soldiers in the terrible battles like the Somme and Ypres, most of the many more casualties of the Second World War in Europe were civilians.

The majority were victims of German policies. Tens of millions of civilians under German occupation, particularly Eastern Europeans, were brutally mistreated, deported, forced into labor camps, killed, or allowed to die. Millions more, especially Jews, Sinti and Roma, and others considered by the Nazis to be subhuman or expendable, were systematically murdered in what we know as the Holocaust. Many of Nazi Germany's allies endorsed and participated in these policies.

The treatment of civilian populations as legitimate elements in strategic planning was not confined to Germany and its associates. The Soviet regime deported and killed millions of civilians in the parts of Eastern Europe it occupied in 1939–41 and 1944–45. British and American policy included the mass bombing of German cities, just as Germany had bombed British, Eastern European, and Soviet cities that had marginal military significance in the strict sense.

A conflict of this scale and character had immense effects on European society, economic structure, and political systems. By 1945 much of Europe was in ruins. The infrastructure of transportation, industry, and agriculture had been largely obliterated between the Rhine and the Volga. Collaboration with Nazi Germany, together with the near destruction of political elites by the Germans and Soviets in turn, left a power vacuum in much of Central and Eastern Europe. Millions of people had been uprooted or had fled one or more approaching armies, and at war's end roads were clogged with people either trying to get home or fleeing from their homes. Families and communities had been dispersed, and the scale of mortality was such that many were never reconstituted. In the midst of this chaos, the Allies positioned themselves as best they could in Europe for a postwar global confrontation dominated by the Soviet Union and the United States.

This chapter looks at the political and military conduct of the war, and the general civilian experience and the specific phenomenon of the Holocaust as facets of the same event. The case of Germany, where foreign, domestic, and racial policies from the mid-1930s were closely integrated, is particularly clear. The war those policies generated was intended to achieve Nazi military, political, economic, and racial goals across the board, and to create a "New Order" in Europe. The Holocaust, integral to the broader Nazi enterprise, was yet influenced by the course of the war.

Like other events of its magnitude, aspects of the Second World War have provoked vigorous debates among historians. Certain questions come up again and again: Was the Nazi policy of attempting to kill Europe's Jews decided upon before the war or did it arise from circumstances as the war developed? Why did some people and groups collaborate with the Nazis, and why did others resist? How should the role of the Soviet Union in the war be understood?

The Not So Phony War:
September 1939 to March 1940

Although German annexation of Austria and Czechoslovakia might be considered part of the war, the act that led to a declaration of general war was Germany's invasion of Poland. On September 1, 1939, German forces staged a sudden strike (*Blitzkrieg*, or lightning war), employing dive-bombing Stuka aircraft, conventional bombers, 2,000 tanks, and a million and a half infantry supported by artillery. Poland had not mobilized its reserve forces until August 31 for fear of antagonizing Hitler, and fielded an army of 600,000, less than a third its full strength. Years of neglect and mismanagement of the military by Marshal Pilsudski's regime resulted in armed forces that were quite unprepared for mid-twentieth century warfare. Frontline forces were poorly equipped and in some battles German tanks confronted Polish cavalry regiments armed with lances. The Polish air force, denied modern aircraft for years because Pilsudski could envisage it having little more than a reconnaissance function, was largely destroyed on the ground in the first days of fighting. The contest was so unequal that Poland's border areas were taken in five days, and by September 8 German forces had begun to subject Warsaw to artillery and air bombardment.

The speed and size of the assault on unprepared defenses were decisive, but the success of the German invasion was ensured by the refusal of Poland's allies to come to its assistance. Although Britain and France declared war on Germany soon after the invasion, both countries overestimated German military strength and adopted a passive defensive policy. In Britain the government was so reluctant to become embroiled in a war over Poland that the House of Commons had virtually to force Prime Minister Chamberlain to declare war—two days after the invasion. When the French government followed suit it did so by cabinet decree for fear that the National Assembly would not support a war with Germany.

The Polish town of Rozan after bombardment by German artillery, September 1939.

Poland's treaties with Britain and France obligated them to provide air support immediately and ground forces no later than fifteen days afterward. Yet although German forces on France's border were inferior to their French counterparts, the French did no more than stage a brief incursion into the German Saar on September 8, before withdrawing. Britain went no further than dropping leaflets over Germany, warning Germans of the dire consequences of aggression. A proposal that the Royal Air Force should bomb the Black Forest outraged the British secretary for air, who responded: "Are you aware that it is private property? Why, you will be asking me to bomb Essen [a major industrial city] next."

Other European states did no more to assist the Poles. Italy remained neutral and in any case had a treaty with Germany; Switzerland, the Scandinavian states, and the Low Countries were neutral; and in Spain General Franco remained grateful to Hitler for German assistance during the civil war.

The Soviet Union, bound by a nonaggression pact with Germany, not only failed to help Poland but participated in its destruction. Secret clauses in the 1939 Soviet-German treaty provided for a division of Poland, and on September 17, alarmed at the stunning German successes (to which the Soviet Union had contributed by providing directional beacons for the Luftwaffe), Stalin ordered Soviet troops into Poland. They quickly captured more territory than the Germans. The Soviet Union now had a common border with German-controlled territory, but Soviet-occupied Poland provided the buffer zone that Stalin wanted between German forces and the Soviet Union proper.

In the final week of September Warsaw was captured by the Germans. Surrounded by German forces, the city was bombarded by more than a million pounds of high explosive and hundreds of thousands of incendiary bombs. The smoke from the fires was so dense that at times the Luftwaffe was forced to suspend bombing raids. Toward the end of the devastating assault on Poland's capital, high-ranking German officials and politicians were ferried to its outskirts to admire the awesome display of the Third Reich's military power.

The destruction of Poland as a political entity was accomplished in little more than a month. Part of German-occupied Poland was incorporated into the greater Reich while the rest was designated a "Government-General," outside the Reich but under direct German control. Soviet forces occupied the eastern half of Poland. Lithuania and Slovakia annexed small parts of Poland—mere nibbles compared with the vast areas swallowed by Germany and the Soviet Union, but they completed the disappearance of Poland from the map of Europe once again.

While the Germans and Soviets consolidated their gains in Poland, Stalin began the process of protecting his country against the possibility of attack by its German ally. In late September and early October 1939 the three Baltic states (Latvia, Estonia, Lithuania) were pressured to allow the Soviet Union to garrison troops within their borders. The Germans waived their claim on Lithuania in exchange for more territory in Poland.

Stalin then turned to Finland, a neutral country with which the Soviets had signed a nonaggression pact in 1932. The Soviet Union was anxious to create a buffer zone around the strategically important city of Leningrad (St. Petersburg), which was only twenty miles from the Finnish border. The Finns were asked to cede territory that would increase that distance to fifty miles, and to allow the Soviet Union to construct a naval base on a Finnish peninsula in the Baltic. In exchange, the Finns were offered twice as much Soviet territory as the Soviet Union would gain.

Soviet policy was more concerned with securing the protection of Leningrad than with obtaining Finnish territory for its own sake, but when the Finns refused even reduced proposals, Soviet forces invaded Finland on November 30, 1939. Although the Soviet air force bombed Helsinki and deployed forces that outnumbered Finland's four to one, the invasion was checked. The Finns were assisted by a harsh winter (temperatures fell to minus 50 degrees Celsius) for which the Soviet troops had not been prepared, and by the impact of the purges on the Soviet officer corps. In the temporary lull in German military expansion, public opinion in the west turned on Soviet aggression against what were popularly called "the brave little Finns." Volunteer brigades, reminiscent of the Spanish civil war, were organized in several countries to help Finland against the Soviet Union.

Britain and France gave more serious and sympathetic attention to Finland's plight than they had done to Poland's. They discussed the possibility of bombing Soviet oil fields in the Caucasus, and when Sweden refused permission for their forces to cross its territory en route to Finland, they considered invading neutral Norway so as to cross into Finland through Sweden anyway. This would not only have helped the Finns against the Soviet Union but would also have harmed Germany's war effort indirectly: Sweden exported vitally needed iron ore to Germany through the Norwegian port of Narvik, and a British-French expedition could have cut off the supply route.

The plan had not been implemented when Finland sued for peace with the Soviet Union. Despite early setbacks that did nothing to help their reputation, Soviet forces overwhelmed the Finns, who suffered 70,000 casualties. Under the Treaty of Moscow (March 12, 1940), the Soviet Union gained Finnish territory that included industries, power stations, and forests; 400,000 Finns (more than 10 percent of the population) were uprooted and relocated. But the most important acquisition for the Soviet Union was additional territory for the defense of Leningrad against possible German attack.

Between September 1939 and March 1940, then, Germany and the Soviet Union expanded their frontiers without serious interference from Britain or France. The Allies adopted an essentially passive and defensive posture with respect to Germany, the country with which they were officially at war; they more seriously contemplated hostilities against the Soviet Union, with which they were not. Such armed conflict as there was between Germany and the two Western European allies occurred mainly at sea. German submarines and surface ships attacked British merchant shipping and even fishing boats. One of the raiding battleships, the *Graf Spee,* was pursued to the south Atlantic where it was scuttled rather than allowed to be sunk by British naval forces.

These skirmishes apart, the French and British tried to replicate their success of 1914–18 by isolating Germany commercially. But it was a futile policy. Italy and the Soviet

Union were conduits for supplies into Germany, and neutrals like Norway and Sweden would not cooperate in any economic blockade.

As the Allies tried to undermine Germany's economic and military strength, they sought to increase their own. War production was stepped up in France and Britain, and they increased the size of their armed forces. In Britain all men between eighteen and forty-one were made liable to conscription under an act passed the day war was declared. Actual registration began in late October, starting with unmarried men in the younger age groups. Many men also volunteered, but in the fall of 1939 there was little sign of the enthusiasm for war in Britain—or elsewhere in Europe—that had been so evident in the summer of 1914. An English bishop described the mood of the troops as "a half cynical boredom, as remote as possible from the high crusading fervour which their situation authorizes and requires. . . . Religion makes little appeal, and patriotism no appeal at all. They have neither the enthusiasm of youth, nor the deliberate purpose of age, but just acquiescence in an absurd and unwelcome necessity."

In the four months between the declaration of war and the end of 1939, the British armed forces increased from 400,000 to more than a million and a half. More than 40,000 women—all volunteers—were enrolled in the Women's Auxiliary Services (one for each of the army, navy, and air force) or the nursing services. Yet for all that was done to ready the armed forces in Britain, it was expected that civilians would bear the initial brunt of war in the form of air raids on industrial and urban centers. Hundreds of thousands of children were evacuated from London and other large cities to be billeted with families in the countryside and small towns. Many inner city schools were closed or became civil defense centers, while schools in the reception areas were overwhelmed by the evacuees.

The British government made myriad other preparations. Almost 150,000 patients were discharged from hospitals to clear beds for expected air raid victims. Thousands of short-term prisoners were released from jails to save the costs of their upkeep. Air raid shelters were built, gas masks distributed, barrage balloons put in place above cities, and taxis requisitioned to serve as ambulances. The snakes in the London zoo were killed for fear they might escape if the zoo were bombed.

But the air raids did not occur, and the six months following the declaration of war seemed like an anticlimax; war had been declared, preparations made, but nothing happened. People became blasé about the war to the point of forgetting that it had been declared. Many stopped carrying the gas masks that had been issued, and complaints arose about the new restrictions. When the government reduced speed limits to 20 miles per hour in cities to conserve gasoline, it was condemned for its "Nazi methods." This phase of the conflict later became known as the "phony war," but at the time the British called it the "Bore war" (a pun on Boer War) or the "funny war."

The French government followed similar policies. The armed services were increased, and war production was stepped up: At the outbreak of war there were 82,000 workers in the aircraft industry, but nine months later there were 250,000.

The start of hostilities made little impact in Germany. The Nazis' control over society had left few liberties to be suspended. Conscription was implemented, but it had only a modest effect on the civilian labor force, thanks mainly to the arrival of more than 100,000 forced workers from occupied Poland in October 1939. The German government intended no repetition of World War I, when the home front had been squeezed and exhausted. The government expected to be able to exploit the human and material resources of occupied territories to sustain its armies in the field. Even though their country was actively at war, it is possible that the first months of conflict seemed even more "phony" to Germans than to the British and French.

But in Eastern Europe it was impossible to think of the war as phony, let alone boring or funny in any sense of those words. The German invasion created chaos as millions of civilians took to the roads, fleeing east and south and frustrating the already collapsing defense. German dive-bombers strafed the columns of refugees, killing thousands. Hundreds of thousands escaped ahead of the German advance into the Soviet zone. Others, including many soldiers, found refuge in Romania and Hungary before making their way to Western Europe where they formed the Free Polish Forces to fight with the Allies.

The Nazis considered all Poles inferior, and tens of thousands were deliberately wounded and killed, but as a group Jews were treated particularly harshly. Two-fifths of Poland's 3.3 million Jews lived in the regions occupied by Germany, and many lived in towns, villages, and *shtetls* (communities) directly in the path of the German advance. German forces, SS and regular military units alike, destroyed whole villages, burned synagogues, and killed and injured thousands of Jews for no military purpose. At Sazalas, in the Government-General, all 300 males over the age of fifteen were seized by German troops; many were machine-gunned, the rest were locked in a school that was then set on fire. Although not the systematic and comprehensive policy of annihilation that the Nazis later directed at Jews, Sinti and Roma, and other groups deemed subhuman or undesirable, early German actions in Poland followed official directives, and the protests some officers lodged with Berlin were brusquely overruled.

The anti-Jewish campaign quickly took on more formal characteristics. On September 21, 1939, the commander of the annexed territory ordered rural Jews to move to the cities and certain areas to be cleared of Jews entirely. Jewish property was to be Aryanized (expropriated by ethnic Germans), and Jews over the age of twelve were to wear a Star of David on their clothing. Temporary ghettos were set up in many towns, and in Warsaw the Jewish section was declared off limits to non-Jews.

In October a plan was put into effect to reduce the mixing of populations in German-controlled Poland. Poles who were ethnic Germans were to move to the annexed part of the country, and Jews there were to be relocated in the Government-General. At this point, German policy focused on expelling Jews from the Reich, and the creation of the Government-General provided the first destination outside the Reich over which the Nazis had control. Beginning in October 1939, Jews from other parts of the Reich, including former Austria and Czechoslovakia were also sent there, 45,000 by early November. The conditions in which they traveled were such that a third died in transit, many from typhus that raged in the insanitary conditions.

Non-Jewish Poles also figured in Nazi population policies. They were regarded as an underclass fit only for manual labor, and on October 26 all Poles between eighteen and sixty were made subject to compulsory labor service. Hundreds of thousands were transported to Germany to work in factories and on farms, the first of millions of deportees and prisoners who would form an army of forced labor for the German war effort. Polish workers were paid, but charges for camp accommodation and other deductions left them such a meager surplus that essentially they worked solely to survive. Their involuntary departure, dividing families and depriving those left of vital economic support, triggering the descent into poverty that, together with terror and degradation, would be the Polish experience of life under German occupation.

Most Poles—soldiers and civilians, Jews and non-Jews—were powerless to resist the fate the Nazis had decided for them, but thousands escaped capture or arrest. Between 1 and 2 million, including 300,000 Jews, escaped to the Soviet sector. Many of those who remained took to the forests where they formed armed bands of partisans that harassed German forces throughout the war.

German soldiers execute Poles in retaliation for the killing of a German officer. The ratio of Poles killed in reprisal for the deaths of Germans was often higher than a hundred to one.

Although considered by many Poles a lesser evil, the Soviet occupiers were often as brutal as their German counterparts. Whereas the Germans persecuted and killed primarily on the basis of race, the Soviets concentrated on destroying Poland's leadership elites: In the first months of war hundreds of politicians, church leaders, and intellectuals were killed and thousands imprisoned. Some 15,000 Polish military officers were abducted and murdered, and many of the bodies were later discovered in mass graves in the forest of Katyn, near Smolensk.

The Soviet Union also engaged in massive ethnic deportations. To facilitate their control of occupied Poland, the Soviet government transported hundreds of thousands of Poles, perhaps as many as a million and a half by mid-1941, to Soviet Asia and Siberia in atrocious conditions that many did not survive. Following the Soviet occupation of the Baltic states, more than 50,000 inhabitants, most drawn from the elites, were deported to Siberia.

Jews, Ukrainians, and Belorussians in the annexed Polish territory were given Soviet citizenship so as to weaken the position of the remaining Poles. Many Polish Jews, in fact, gave the Red Army an enthusiastic welcome in 1939. They saw the arrival of Soviet forces as liberation from Polish and Ukrainian persecution and attacks that increased as social order broke down following the German invasion.

The German and Soviet governments often cooperated in the matter of ethnic reorganization of their territories. Ethnic Germans left the Soviet Union and Soviet-occupied Poland for the Reich; Ukrainians and Belorussians there moved to Soviet territory. In 1940 the Soviets even returned to Germany hundreds of German political refugees, including a number of Jews, on the ground that they were enemies of German-Soviet understanding.

It is clear that the early months of conflict were a phony war only from the point of view of the British and French. In Eastern Europe the war was all too real. Tens of thousands of non-Jewish and Jewish Poles were killed and millions more, together with hundreds of thousands of Finns, had been uprooted from their homes. Before the conflict in the west began, one of the essential characteristics of the Second World War was starkly defined: that it would be waged as much against civilians as armed forces.

Germany Attacks West: April 1940 to June 1941

When the fulcrum of the war shifted from Eastern to Western Europe, it did so not as a Franco-British attack on Germany, but as further German aggression. The first thrust was into Scandinavia, a strike designed to prevent the British from invading Norway and cutting German access to the much-needed Swedish iron ore shipped through Narvik. On April 10, 1940, German forces invaded Denmark, capturing Copenhagen within twelve hours. Access to Danish airfields assisted a German invasion of Norway the same day, and despite British assistance—too little, too late—Norway fell. The Norwegians had delayed rearmament so long that the Germans discovered American aircraft still in their crates.

The loss of Norway brought down the British prime minister, Neville Chamberlain, whose foreign policy had been under attack for some time, even within his own party. On May 10 he was replaced by Winston Churchill, who headed the British government for the rest of the war. On Churchill's first day on the job, May 10, 1940, German forces invaded Belgium, the Netherlands, and France.

By the spring of 1940, the British Expeditionary Force of more than 200,000 was positioned in northern France to repel a German invasion. But the attack came where it was not expected. Instead of invading France via Belgium (as in 1914), the main German force attacked directly across the French border in the heavily wooded Ardennes region. Believing that an invasion at this point was impracticable, the French had installed only light defenses in the sector.

A secondary German attack was launched simultaneously on the Netherlands, Luxembourg, and Belgium. Dutch resistance was quickly overcome, particularly after the Luftwaffe bombed the center of Rotterdam, killing a thousand civilians. British, French, and Belgian forces held up the German advance in Belgium somewhat longer, but were soon beaten, and by the end of May the Low Countries had succumbed to apparently irresistible German military power.

French and British forces were isolated and being driven closer and closer to the Channel coast. A major rescue effort was mounted, and in early June a massive fleet of ships and boats of all sizes ferried 224,000 British and 114,000 French troops from the beaches at Dunkirk across the English Channel. The success of the operation scarcely concealed the fact that it represented a major defeat: The rescued soldiers left behind all their equipment and 100,000 comrades who were taken prisoner by the Germans.

Despite some attempts to fight on, sentiment in France favored surrender over what was widely seen as a hopeless war. Paris was declared an open city in the hope that it would be spared the devastation of Warsaw and Rotterdam. Millions of French demonstrated their confidence in a German victory by creating the greatest single body of refugees of the war as some 7 million people, a sixth of France's population, fled west and south. Their numbers were swelled by refugees from the Low Countries, including German Jews who had found refuge there and were again trying to escape the Nazis.

France was further threatened, this time in the south, when Mussolini declared war on France and Britain on June 10. Six days later, a French administration headed by Marshal Pétain, the hero of the Battle of Verdun in World War I, signed an armistice with

Hitler after a tour of the Eiffel Tower, in Paris, after Germany had defeated France in 1940.

Germany. Under its terms, Germany occupied the western and northern parts of France (including Paris) and the coastline. The rest of the country, essentially the southeastern third, was to be governed by Pétain's administration, which established itself in the spa town of Vichy. This Vichy government agreed to collaborate with Germany, an arrangement that freed the Germans from having to commit forces to the occupation of much of France. In the south of France, Italy was provisionally permitted to keep the small amount of territory it had seized before the armistice was signed.

Germany's successes in the west were so decisive that Hitler was tempted to turn east again and attack the Soviet Union before Stalin was ready for war. In the aftermath of the German defeat of France, the Soviet Union, increasingly alarmed at Hitler's successes, had invaded and annexed the Baltic states, providing yet another buffer to protect the heart of the country. As in Poland, the Soviet authorities quickly deported the region's leaders. Some 50,000 Balts were shipped to Siberia.

Although an early strike against the Soviet Union was attractive, Hitler was aware that leaving Britain undefeated in order to concentrate on the Soviet Union could mean Germany would have to fight a war on two fronts. He elected to try to force Britain into a settlement with Germany. The Luftwaffe was now able to use French airfields and began to attack British airbases in the summer of 1940, beginning a phase of the war known as the Battle of Britain. In August the air war escalated after a German pilot bombed London against orders, and the Royal Air Force (RAF) bombed German cities in response. Air attacks on civilian populations became standard policy from September 7 when the Luftwaffe began a two-month campaign of bombing London and other British cities on a nightly basis.

British Prime Minister Winston Churchill surveys bomb damage in London during the Battle of Britain.

The thousands of bombers and escort fighters committed to this campaign caused widespread urban destruction. Fires from one night's bombing were scarcely extinguished when the bombers returned the next, and many buildings in the capital, including Parliament, were damaged or destroyed. Some 15,000 people were killed in London alone. Yet the campaign failed as the RAF inflicted massive losses on the Luftwaffe despite suffering heavy losses itself. Unable to secure superiority in the air, Hitler decided in December 1940 to postpone a planned seaborne invasion of Britain (provisionally code-named Operation Sealion), and turned his attention to an invasion of his Soviet ally.

Preparation for the attack began in December 1940, and in the spring of 1941 massive forces were gathered for the assault. In April some German forces were diverted to Yugoslavia and Greece. Italy had invaded Greece in October 1940 but had been beaten back and the Greeks requested British units to reinforce their defenses. When the Yugoslav government proposed helping the Germans and Italians, it was overthrown in a military coup and the new regime announced that it would support the Allies. To forestall the development of a new front in the Balkans that would undermine their attack on the Soviet Union, German forces invaded and quickly defeated both Yugoslavia and Greece in April 1941. The next month German paratroopers paved the way for the occupation of the Greek island of Crete. The Germans might have made more progress in the Mediterranean region if they had persisted: Panzer units were sent to Libya to reinforce Italian troops, and the Germans supported Arab nationalists against the British and French in Iraq and Syria.

Germany was also having considerable success disrupting the flow of supplies to Britain. Food, munitions, and other needed goods were brought from Canada and the United States across the Atlantic, in convoys of scores of merchant ships. They could be protected by air for short distances after they left North America and before they arrived in Great Britain, but for most of the journey they were protected only by small numbers of naval escort ships. These escorts could do little to prevent massive losses to German submarines, which attacked the convoys in packs, sending ships, crews, and supplies to the bottom. In 1942 the Allies lost 8.3 million tons of shipping.

But Hitler was not to be diverted from the invasion of the Soviet Union, Operation Barbarossa. Although the decision is often thought to have been Hitler's greatest single military miscalculation, there were arguments to be made in favor of it. German planners expected the Soviet armed forces, undermined by Stalin's purges, to collapse quickly. They had, after all, had difficulty beating the small Finnish army in 1939–40. A speedy victory would give Germany control of Soviet oil fields, grain, and other resources needed for the longer war against Britain. If attacking the Soviet Union meant that Germany would have to fight a war on two fronts, it would be only for a short time, after which Germany would have the resources to deal more easily with Britain.

The Invasion of the Soviet Union:
June 1941 to February 1943

The German invasion of the Soviet Union on June 22, 1941, by an army 3 million strong, was a political as well as a military watershed in the war. It turned the Axis war into an anti-communist crusade that attracted support from countries and individuals who otherwise had reservations about Germany's policies. The German effort was promptly assisted by Romania, Hungary, and Italy. Bulgaria declared war on the Soviet Union (but not on France and Britain), and Spain abandoned strict neutrality to allow "volunteers" to fight beside German troops. Finland allied with Germany in order to regain the territory lost to the Soviet Union in the 1939–40 winter war. By the same token, many anti-communist conservatives who supported the Allies were alarmed at the inclusion of Stalin's regime in the anti-Nazi coalition.

But the course of the war on the eastern front proved more important than the entry of the Soviet Union per se. Soviet defenses were inadequate and its armed forces apparently caught off guard, and early results seemed to bear out German expectations of a quick victory. Stalin had ignored British and American warnings of an imminent invasion, apparently thinking they were designed to trick him into military preparations that would provoke a German response. He even refused to give credit to warnings from Soviet intelligence sources, and right up to the day of the invasion the Soviet Union continued to provide Germany with the supplies specified in their 1939 treaty.

Not only did discipline and order in the Soviet forces quickly disintegrate under the German attack, but the government fell into disarray. Stalin panicked in the first week of the invasion and disappeared from public view for several days. Soviet civilians in some parts of the country actively welcomed the Germans. In the grain-rich Ukraine, which had experienced Stalin's most brutal policies of deliberate famine and forced population relocation, peasants regarded any enemy of Stalin's regime as a potential ally. They were soon disabused of their illusion that Nazi rule would be an improvement. Others never had the illusion and went along with the hurried evacuation of millions of people from areas about to fall to the Germans, together with the removal of as many industrial plants and other facilities as could be dismantled.

By November 1941, the German forces in all three sectors of the invasion had advanced farther than Napoleon's Great Army had in 1812. In the north the Germans had besieged Leningrad, in the center they had entered the outskirts of Moscow, and in the south they had reached the Don River. Yet even this startling progress was slower than planned, and German troops were not equipped for winter. By early December 1941, Soviet forces recaptured Rostov-on-Don, and in December a Soviet army of 3 million pushed the Germans back from Moscow.

In the middle of the winter campaign on the eastern front, Hitler was so confident of victory in the Soviet Union that he declared war on yet another major power. On December 7, 1941, Japan declared war on the United States and Japanese aircraft attacked the American naval base at Pearl Harbor in Hawaii, killing thousands and inflicting serious damage. Although a treaty of mutual assistance existed between Germany and Japan, Hitler need not immediately have declared war on the United States, but on December 9 he did so, hastening the intervention of the world's strongest economic power in the European war.

Even before the United States entered the war, Britain had begun to provide military equipment to aid the Soviet war effort, and from November 1941 the United States extended lend-lease facilities to the Soviet Union. Such Allied assistance, most transported by convoys around Norway to the Soviet ports of Murmansk and Archangel, was useful but not critical to the Soviet military struggle. Soviet factories, many transferred from western regions occupied by Germany and reassembled farther east, increased production of arms, tanks, aircraft, and vehicles. But the Allies' contributions signaled the importance they attached to keeping the Soviet Union actively in the war to force Germany to fight on two fronts.

Despite massive losses on the eastern front in the winter of 1941–42 the Germans generally held their early gains. In the summer of 1942 they advanced in the southern sector toward Stalingrad, a city they had to take in order to control major Soviet oil and grain resources. During the Battle of Stalingrad that raged for six months from November 1942, the city was surrounded by German and associated forces, bombarded by artillery and aircraft, and subjected to constant infantry and tank assaults. Soviet troops and civilians defended the city building by building. Again the defenders were assisted by winter, and this time by Hitler's intransigence as well, for despite Soviet counterattacks he refused to allow his commanders to retreat an inch. Although most of Stalingrad was at one time in German hands, the city never fell.

At the same time, the northern city of Leningrad had been under a siege that was to last sixteen months. Leningraders suffered terrible privations, and almost 3 million of them died of starvation and disease. But in early 1943, Soviet troops opened a supply route to the city across frozen Lake Lagoda. The denial of Leningrad and Stalingrad to the Germans in the winter of 1942–43 marked a turning point in the eastern war.

Living and Dying in Wartime Europe, 1939–43: Under German Occupation

By the end of 1942, after a little more than three years of war, Nazi Germany dominated Europe from France's Atlantic coast in the west to the suburbs of Moscow in the east, from Norway in the north to Greece in the south. Those parts of continental Europe not under direct German occupation were either neutrals or nonbelligerents, or ruled by regimes allied or having various arrangements or alliances with Germany: Italy, Finland, Vichy France, Hungary, Bulgaria, Slovakia, Croatia, and Romania. The only European states that remained actively at war with Germany were the Soviet Union (much of which had been invaded) and Great Britain.

Hitler's aim in conquering Europe was to create a New Order, a Europe entirely reorganized in political, economic, cultural, and racial terms to serve a new state that would be its core. This Greater Germanic Estate (*Grossraum*) would comprise pre-1938 Germany;

Occupied by Germany

Allied with Germany

MAP 8.1   Europe under Nazi domination.

its annexations in Austria, Czechoslovakia, and Poland; the territory it had lost after the First World War; and other regions like the Baltic states and Crimea where relocated ethnic Germans would replace other populations.

The territorial aspects of the New Order were never implemented, and wartime annexation went no further than parts of Poland, some border areas of Belgium, Alsace and Lorraine, Slovenia, and South Tyrol. But the outlines of economic and racial facets of the New Order were visible early in the occupation of Poland: the relocation of populations, with ethnic Germans being moved to the incorporated part of Poland, and non-Germans (especially Jews) being expelled to the Government-General, together with the designation of Poles as nothing more than a labor force at the disposal of Germany.

These were precursors of the broad policies that the Nazis began to implement throughout occupied Europe. Specific policies varied from country to country according to the character of German occupation. The Nazis treated Scandinavians, Dutch, Flemings, and Walloons, whom they regarded as Aryans, utterly differently from Russians, Ukrainians, and other Slavic groups they regarded as scarcely human. Until 1943 the Danish king and his ministers continued to run certain facets of government, and communication between them and the German occupation forces was carried on through conventional diplomatic channels. Norway (like the Netherlands) was governed by decree by a civilian Reichskommissar who reported directly to Hitler, but at a lower level the country's administration was left intact.

In contrast the Germans eliminated the indigenous leadership in the occupied parts of eastern Europe: Poland, the Baltic states, and the Soviet Union. The German military authorities and SS administered these territories, and their populations were subjected to an occupation far more deadly than in Northern and Western Europe. The occupation personnel sometimes reflected a perverse historical sense on the part of the German government. The commander of occupation forces in northern France and Belgium was the son of the German officer in charge of the German occupation there in the First World War. He took his father's records with him in 1940, and promptly rounded up the children of the men who had given his father the most trouble twenty-five years earlier. As for the occupation forces in the Balkans, they were drawn from Austria in particular because it was thought that their Habsburg background uniquely qualified them to deal with Slavs and other minorities. (The Austrians included Kurt Waldheim, who later became secretary-general of the United Nations and president of Austria, and whose wartime activities and alleged knowledge of atrocities in the Balkans created a political controversy in the 1980s.)

At the most general level, all the resources of all occupied territories were placed at the disposal of the German war effort. Military units with specifically economic functions accompanied each invasion to identify, and when necessary seize, whatever was useful for the German economy. Gold and currency reserves, railway rolling stock, raw materials, and manufactured products were high on the list.

The German leadership had not made economic plans for a long war, and in the first year of conflict there was a severe shortage of productive capacity in Germany. It did not go onto a war economy until 1943, and the effects of delaying were soon felt: In 1940, for example, aircraft production was slashed by 40 percent to allow increased output of tanks and submarines. Later, factories had to revert to aircraft production to build up the strength of the Luftwaffe (diminished by losses in the Battle of Britain) for the invasion of the Soviet Union. The acquisition of territory across Europe gave the Germans access to labor, raw materials, energy, and factories.

In some occupied countries the process of seizing economic resources was given a veneer of legality. Under the terms of the June 1940 armistice, France had to pay Germany the equivalent of 300 million francs a day, a sum that initially "paid for" the goods Germany took from France. When German demands for French resources and products exceeded this, the amount was raised to 700 million francs. In the Netherlands and Denmark the Germans helped themselves to goods and went through the motions of purchasing them; but currency exchange rates were set so much in Germany's favor that German enterprises could buy foreign goods very cheaply.

In Eastern Europe such subterfuges were considered unnecessary. Germany unilaterally claimed ownership of the Soviet and Baltic states, meaning that they claimed ownership of factories, mines, and other resources and could use them as they pleased. In Poland land was confiscated without compensation, and Jewish property everywhere was Aryanized—appropriated outright and sold or transferred to German ownership. Food supplies were obtained by similar means. Farmers were ordered to supply the German authorities with produce and were expected to get whatever payment they could from their own governments.

The longer-term Nazi plan was to restructure non-German societies into primary producers for the core of the Reich: Norwegians would farm and fish, Ukrainians would grow grain. Germans would rule over occupied territories, the farmers living on handsome and spacious farms and the governors in palaces. Populations considered inferior would labor like slaves and be prevented from improving their position; Hitler thought that they should "know just enough to understand road signs, so as not to get themselves run over by our vehicles. For them the word 'liberty' must mean the right to wash on holidays." Should the slaves revolt, Hitler said, "we shall only have to drop a few bombs on their cities and the affair will be liquidated."

The Nazis might fantasize about the quality of life as masters in the New European Order, but millions of Europeans realized their envisaged roles only too soon. Almost all suffered a deterioration in their diets, although the extent varied immensely according to local conditions and the effectiveness of transportation. Even where the occupation was relatively light (a notion to be used with great caution in the case of the Nazis), the populations suffered privations. In the Netherlands the average normal ration provided about 2,000 calories a day in 1941 and 1942, about the same as in Germany. In Norway and Belgium it provided less than 1,400 calories, whereas in the Government-General of Poland it was 1,000 or less. In Athens and some of the Greek islands, the daily adult intake of calories fell to 600 to 800 in the winter of 1941–42; more than half the deaths in Greece due to the war were caused by starvation.

Declining diets were only one facet of the degradation of social and economic life in Europe under German occupation. The structure of everyday life was disrupted. Countless families were affected by deaths, deportations, or absences that rendered them economically vulnerable. Some 790,000 of the 1.6 million French soldiers held prisoner in Germany had wives and of those 616,000 had children, all of whom were placed at risk. Allowances were paid to wives of prisoners of war, but their real value declined and wives were expected to send their husbands two packages of food and clothing a month because the German rations were inadequate.

Employment opportunities were limited as economies faltered or simply ground to a halt under conditions of disrupted trade, labor shortages, and low consumer demand. Health services were nonexistent in many places, schools did not operate, and mail deliveries were sporadic when they were made at all. We need not evoke a golden age before the war to appreciate how grim daily life under occupation was, and that is before we take into account the omnipresent threat of arrest, abduction, and death.

Even before the war Germany had needed labor, and in early 1939, 300,000 foreigners worked in Germany. The raising of massive armies depleted the German labor force even more, and one of the first policies implemented was the seizure of foreign nationals for forced labor. By mid-1941 there were 3 million foreigners working German farms, factories, and mines, and by 1943 that number had more than doubled to 6.3 million.

Many of the foreign workers in Germany were prisoners of war, particularly Soviet soldiers, who were forced to labor in conditions that contravened the Geneva Convention on the treatment of military prisoners. Other foreigners were compelled to work in Germany by methods that ranged from simple abduction to pressure that included withholding ration cards and extending workdays to thirteen hours if they did not comply. A small proportion, perhaps one in twenty, volunteered for work in Germany.

Working conditions of foreign laborers varied, generally according to race criteria. Jews were treated worst of all; able-bodied Jews who were not killed outright were worked to death or until they could work no more, when they were killed. Russians were only slightly above Jews on the hierarchy of ill treatment, and Poles above them. Some of the workers were paid, but once "deductions" were made for accommodations, food, and other costs, little remained.

Workers from Western Europe were generally treated somewhat better. Among the most favored were skilled workers from countries like Denmark, Belgium, Hungary, the Netherlands, and France. The diets of workers from Eastern Europe were so poor that they were more than 1,000 calories less than the lowest German ration. Jewish workers survived as long as they could on 600 to 800 calories a day. The high death rates from malnutrition and disease meant that a constant flow of new workers was needed to replace the dead. Four million foreigners died working for the German war effort.

The absence of such large numbers of workers from their homes added to the economic disruption of national economies under occupation. The Nazis greatly overestimated the resources they would harvest from their conquests. They had an almost mystical belief in the abundance of grain that Ukraine could provide, and anticipated taking an average 7 million tons a year. After a decline in the harvest because of the war, and the consumption of vast amounts by the occupation armies, so little Ukrainian grain reached Germany that it was exceeded by imports from France.

Throughout occupied Europe most indices of agricultural productivity declined. The tonnage of fish landed in Norway and the Netherlands fell as the Germans limited the activity of fishermen, although Danes, who were allowed more latitude, increased their haul. French wine output in the four years of occupation fell to two-thirds the prewar level. The reasons for the decline in the primary sector included shortages of experienced labor, mechanization, fuel, and fertilizer. Export-driven industries like wine were affected by the interruption in trade. Finally, extensive agricultural regions in Poland and the Soviet Union were ravaged by war.

It was not only in the strictly economic terms of land, resources, and labor that Nazi Germany exploited occupied Europe. The idea of race lay at the heart of Nazi policies, and in this respect women of occupied countries were also expected to play their part. Hundreds of Norwegian women judged "racially pure" were taken to Germany to be impregnated by SS soldiers in order to increase the Aryan population. In addition, Himmler approved plans for racially acceptable children in occupied Europe to be abducted to the Reich, given German names, and brought up as children of the Nazi state.

Cultural resources were also exploited. Art collections in Eastern Europe were raided, and hundreds of paintings and other artifacts shipped to the Reich for display after the war. Art historians and curators accompanied German armies of invasion to select works of art to be shipped back to Germany. Some were destined for public display, thus compensating German galleries to some extent for their losses during the purges of "degenerate" art in the late 1930s. Hitler's art advisers earmarked some of the best items for exhibition in an art museum he planned to build in Linz (Austria), near his birthplace, which he intended to turn into a city that would rival Vienna.

The Nazi plan for a European New Order was only partially implemented, but its outlines were clear enough. All the resources of Europe—human, material, and cultural—were to be placed at the disposal of the Reich. Even though various agencies and individuals in the Nazi regime vied for power, established competing priorities, and occasionally worked at cross-purposes—there was no single blueprint for the New Order—the direction of policy was the same, and in all their endeavors Hitler and his followers demonstrated a single-minded preoccupation with furthering the interests of the Reich at all costs.

Collaboration and Resistance

Reactions to German occupation varied from willing collaboration, through acquiescence, to resistance. The great majority of people in German-occupied or dominated regions were opposed to the German presence, but went about their daily lives as normally as possible in highly abnormal conditions. They carried the identity papers the Germans issued, and presented them when required; city dwellers lined up for ration coupons, farmers grudgingly complied with the occupiers' demands for their produce. In each country, however, a percentage of the population actively supported or collaborated with the Germans, and a percentage actively resisted.

Patterns of collaboration and resistance varied from country to country, often depending on the character of the occupation itself. There was little chance for Soviet citizens to collaborate for long, for example, because the Nazis regarded them—even the anti-communists—as enemies of the Reich. Many Ukrainians welcomed the Germans in 1941 as liberators from Stalin's oppression, but their support quickly turned to opposition when the character of German occupation became clear. The racial policies of the Nazi regime made it difficult for Slavs to collaborate directly, although some anti-Semitic partisan groups in Poland and the Soviet Union, which hunted down and killed Jews who had escaped the Germans, did the Nazis' work for them.

In other parts of Eastern Europe, collaboration with the Germans served broader political purposes. Under the New Order, Hungary regained territory it had lost to Czechoslovakia and Romania under the Treaty of Versailles. The Slovaks and Croatians, who had been subsumed into Czechoslovakia and Yugoslavia respectively by the same treaty, gained their independence. Together with the Baltic states and Romania they contributed hundreds of thousands of troops to the German invasion of the Soviet Union.

Collaboration took various forms in Western Europe. The creation of the Vichy government by Marshal Pétain even gave a stamp of legitimacy to collaboration with the Germans. The domestic policies introduced under Vichy had elements common to fascist programs. There was a stress on reviving what were represented as traditional values, and

Russian men and women with pitchforks herd a man accused of collaborating with the Germans. Soon after the photograph was taken he was shot.

the regime replaced the "Liberty, Equality, and Fraternity" motto of the republic with "Work, Family, Fatherland." Marriage and procreation were promoted, and divorce was made more difficult. Penalties for performing an abortion, which had been illegal in France since 1920, were rigorously applied from 1942, and 11,000 people were convicted by the end of the war. The law described abortionists as "dangerous individuals" guilty "of acts harmful to the French nation," and under its terms one woman was executed, a rare exception to the unwritten rule in France that women were not executed.

It is likely that a greater proportion of the French actively assisted the invaders than in any other part of Western Europe. Certainly a proportionally greater number of French men and women were tried for collaboration after the war than Norwegians, Dutch, and Belgians, although that might also mean that the postwar administration in France was less forgiving than its counterparts elsewhere.

The reasons for collaboration were as varied as its forms. There is no doubt that the loyalties of many prewar fascists were torn by the German invasion. On the one hand they had affinities with the Nazis' ideology; on the other, they were nationalists who resented German occupation. Many, however, saw German occupation as a means to achieve the power that they would not have gained otherwise, and opted for German domination rather than government by indigenous liberal or left-wing regimes. For the most part, they were disappointed if they hoped the Germans would install them in office. The Nazis were profoundly suspicious of foreign fascists (who might want to carve out independent policies), and they generally excluded them from power. In Norway the fascist leader Vidkun Quisling was given no more than a token position, and that only from January 1942. In Belgium, Léon Degrelle and his fascist Rexists became influential only when they were able to produce thousands of volunteers for the German war effort in the east. Instead of seeking support from marginal prewar fascists, the Germans tended to look for support to men with political power bases, especially military leaders like Marshal Pétain in France, Admiral Horthy in Hungary, and Marshal Antonescu in Romania. Many Europeans who wanted to collaborate for ideological reasons found themselves less appreciated by the Nazis than they expected.

But the Nazis did find a use for these fellow travelers, particularly after the June 1941 invasion of the Soviet Union. Support for the Germans among conservatives probably grew and became more respectable once it could be represented as an anti-communist crusade. Throughout Western Europe young men volunteered for service alongside the Wehrmacht and SS units. They included some 50,000 Dutch, 40,000 Belgians, 20,000 French, 6,000 Danes, and 6,000 Norwegians. Although these seem like substantial numbers, they represented a small percentage of their respective populations. Even the substantial Dutch contingent was less than 4 percent of men aged between twenty and forty.

Most collaboration took place at home. Men and women willingly assisted the occupation authorities, turned in their friends and neighbors, betrayed members of the resistance, and revealed the hiding places of fugitives from Nazi political and racial persecution. Not all this collaboration was ideologically motivated. Louis Malle's movie *Lacombe Lucien* provides a good account of the way in which a young man in the south of France was drawn to active collaboration, partly as an opportunity to get even with his neighbors (who joined the resistance) for the disparaging way they had treated him before the war.

Many people collaborated because they were called upon to do so. Bureaucrats and people in business had pragmatic reasons to do the Germans' bidding. They argued that nothing was to be gained by refusing, and that it was better for local people to govern than for the Germans to do so. Industrialists often did well under the occupation; not only were they freed from union activities, but German contracts could be very profitable.

Resistance was the mirror image of collaboration: It varied from country to country and took many forms. The most dramatic were the campaigns of violence that included blowing up militarily important installations and transport facilities and assassinating German personnel. Such activities involved huge risks to the perpetrators, their families, and their communities. When the Germans were unable to attribute responsibility precisely, they carried out reprisals on civilians in the localities where the attacks took place.

Even in reprisals there were differences between Western and Eastern Europe. In France the common ratio was fifty civilians shot for each German killed by the resistance; in Poland it was twice that, and in some cases thousands of civilians were killed to revenge a single German death. A notorious example was the destruction of the entire population of the village of Lidice in Czechoslovakia after Reinhard Heydrich, the head of the Nazi Security Service, was assassinated in 1942. The male population of Lidice over the age of sixteen was shot, and women and children sent to concentration camps; pregnant women were allowed to give birth, then their babies were killed and they were sent to death camps; the village itself was obliterated. Such reprisals did not stop the resistance, but they must have deterred many people who, although willing to risk their own lives, were reluctant to put the lives of innocent compatriots on the line.

Campaigns of sabotage and assassination against the German occupation were generally carried out by organized resistance groups like the Maquis in France (named after the scrubby landscape of southern France where they hid out) and the partisans in Poland. Resistance organizations brought together men and women from disparate backgrounds who often had in common only a visceral hatred of the occupiers. In the Maquis, liberals, Catholics, Protestants, and Communists cooperated in a way that was unthinkable before the war.

The resistance is generally associated with men, who were more likely than women to be directly involved in the sensational acts of sabotage and assassination. Women, however, formed the infrastructure of resistance movements everywhere. The sexual division of labor in society at large was replicated in the French Maquis; women at home fed, clothed, and hid fugitives; secretaries stenciled posters and underground newspapers; concierges, famous for knowing everything going on in their neighborhoods, passed on information; nuns concealed documents under their habits; prostitutes provided places of refuge. Because women could circulate more easily and were less likely than men to be searched, they were the bulk of the liaison agents who kept the resistance networks operational. Women were awarded only 6 of the 1,059 highest awards for service in the French resistance movement after the war, but that ratio greatly understated their contribution to it. Nor was France unusual in this respect. Women were prominent as scouts in partisan bands in the German-occupied Soviet Union, especially Belorussia where up to a quarter of partisans were women.

Resistance was motivated by a range of considerations, of which the most important were nationalism and ideological opposition to fascism. A major breakthrough came with the June 1941 German invasion of the Soviet Union. Until that time Communists in occupied Western Europe had been instructed by the Comintern to adopt a neutral stance because of the 1939 Soviet-German nonaggression pact. This had deprived the resistance of an important constituency, but the German invasion freed Communists to participate actively. They became leading members of the resistance in many countries, something that gave them strong claims to share political leadership throughout postwar Europe.

Although only a small number of Europeans were active in resistance organizations (they kept their membership small for security reasons, in any case), countless others carried out other acts in defiance of the occupation. Anti-German graffiti were scrawled on walls; the clandestine press was passed covertly from person to person; overheard information that might be useful to the resistance was passed on. Other Europeans performed small and personal acts of defiance, like walking out of bars and restaurants when off-duty German soldiers entered. In the Netherlands, where the House of Orange is associated with national independence, people saluted traffic lights as they turned orange. Far more symbolic than substantive, such personal gestures prevented people from slipping gradually into total acceptance of the German occupation.

Yet at some point individual and unsystematic acts of resistance like these faded into a general acquiescence in occupation. With an attitude compounded of indifference, an understandable preoccupation with their own and their families' survival, and even a sense of normality as occupation stretched into years, most people went about their lives as best they could, hoping to be left alone by the occupiers. No doubt the mass of people wished the Germans would leave so that things could return to normal, but they were no more prepared to go out of their way to resist than they were to collaborate beyond the extent necessary to keep out of trouble.

It might be argued that acquiescence of this sort was tantamount to collaboration, but we should not make too easy a link between them. Many people had little choice but to acquiesce, especially in Eastern Europe where German domination was severe, unrelenting, and unforgiving. Not to acquiesce there meant to risk almost certain death. In Western Europe the choices were more difficult because more were available, but even there we should not underestimate the consequences of going against the Germans even in small ways.

The French had perhaps the most difficult decisions to make. The Vichy government claimed legitimacy, yet it was itself a collaborationist regime, unlike the Dutch, Norwegian, and Belgian governments whose existence in exile legitimated resistance. The French had to choose between Pétain in France and an administration, headed by General Charles de Gaulle, which was recognized by the Allies as the Free French government. It was a moot point whether cooperating with the Vichy regime—by working in its bureaucracy, for example—was the same as collaborating with the Germans.

There is also the question of resistance and collaboration within Germany itself. The war brought new issues to the fore and led to material hardships and national risks that caused many Germans to reassess their attitude toward the Nazi government. Germans faced decisions that were different from those confronting citizens of occupied Europe. They had no nationalist ax to grind. The Nazis might be said to have occupied Germany in some senses, too, but whatever the Nazis were, they were not foreigners (although many Austrians, Czechs, Poles, and others incorporated into the Reich did not see them that way).

Germans had to face the likelihood that resistance to the Nazis could lead to Germany's being invaded by foreigners, especially the Red Army. Even for staunch opponents of the Nazis this was not a happy prospect in light of Nazi propaganda that had convinced people that the Soviet armies were no more than barbarian hordes bent on killing, raping, and stealing. If these objections to opposing Hitler's regime were not enough, there was the fact that years of Nazi rule before the war had weakened or eliminated the institutions (like political parties, churches, and unions) and individuals who might have provided the core of a resistance.

It is not surprising that wartime resistance to the Nazis in Germany itself was sparse. Most people willingly supported the regime and its war, were terrorized into acquiescence, or focused their attention almost entirely on the problems of daily life and survival and left politics to others. Even so, networks of resistance existed in Germany and, given the sex ratio of the wartime population, it is hardly surprising that women predominated. As in France, German women resisters concealed fugitives (including army deserters), printed leaflets and newspapers, and acted as couriers.

Resistance more directly threatening to Hitler—from within the highest ranks of the military—broke out when a German victory was no longer certain. There was an attempt on Hitler's life in March 1943, and another in July of the following year. The second of these was an attempt to blow up Hitler with a bomb brought into a briefing room in the briefcase of a colonel, Count von Stauffenberg. Hitler was slightly injured, but survived. Many of the conspirators, who had hoped to seek a peace after Hitler's death, were hung up to die on meat hooks. Their agonizing deaths were filmed for Hitler's benefit.

Living and Dying in Wartime Europe: The Holocaust

The Holocaust is the name given to the systematic killing of millions of women, men, and children belonging to groups considered by the Nazis to be racial, social, or political threats to the Reich. The most prominent single group was Europe's Jews, an obsession of Hitler and the Nazis from the earliest days; it is estimated that as many as 6 million died in the Nazi attempt to rid Europe of Jews entirely. Other groups must not be forgotten: millions of non-Jewish Poles and Russians, Sinti and Roma (Gypsies), homosexuals, political dissidents, and the mentally and physically handicapped were systematically massacred.

It is debatable whether the Holocaust should be thought of as a facet of World War II or as a phenomenon with a separate history. Racism generally, and anti-Semitism specifically, were integral to Nazi ideology from the beginning, but historians disagree whether the plan to kill all Europe's Jews was conceived before or during the war. Some historians point to the writings and speeches of Hitler and his most anti-Semitic associates like Joseph Goebbels and Alfred Rosenberg, and to prewar Nazi policies like the Nuremberg Laws, as indicative of a final goal of extermination. In the light of later events, statements like Hitler's January 1939 reference to "the annihilation of the Jewish race in Europe" seem quite unambiguous.

Other historians, however, suggest that such statements were political rhetoric, exaggerated and metaphorical, and that even though Nazism was virulently anti-Semitic, the decision to kill all Europe's Jews was made not before the war but during it. In 1939 and 1940, Nazi policy seemed to focus on the relocation of Jews, specifically their removal from the Reich into areas like the Government-General of Poland. In 1940 the Nazi official directly responsible for Jewish matters, Adolf Eichmann, resuscitated an earlier idea that European Jews should be transported to the French colony of Madagascar, off Africa's east coast. The scheme seemed that much more feasible after the defeat of France gave Germany effective control over the island. The notion of ridding Europe of Jews by killing them, these historians suggest, was adopted only a year or two after the war had begun.

The debate on the origins of the Holocaust is fraught with problems of historical interpretation. There is no doubt that Jews and others considered racially undesirable were killed in large numbers before the establishment of the death camps that are most commonly associated with the Holocaust. Not only did countless Jews die in Nazi actions in prewar Germany, but the killing of Polish Jews was approved of from the first days of the war. The killing rate was stepped up with the invasion of the Soviet Union. Special units of the SS called "action units" (*Einsatzgruppen*) were established to execute Communist officials, political commissars, and Jews, as the German armies swept east. Hitler signed an order for the killing of commissars, its terms so vague that the special units had open license to murder. The action units performed their task with deadly effectiveness, rounding up ideological and racial "enemies" of the Reich, and drowning, burning, or shooting them.

Typically Jews were taken in batches of several hundred, shot, and then thrown—dead and dying alike—into trenches. The largest single action of this type involved more than 30,000 Jews from Kiev in September 1941. The fact that so many people could be killed in a two-day period is grim evidence of the efficiency and deadly purpose of the Nazis. About 300,000 Jews were killed in the Soviet Union in the first six months of German occupation and 2 million by the end, including Jews deported specifically for that purpose from Germany, Austria, and Czechoslovakia.

What prompted the shift from killing some Jews and relocating the others to the attempt to kill them all? It is possible that mass deportation outside Europe was never seriously considered, and that relocation within Europe was nothing more than a prelude to mass murder. Mass relocation was never intended to be benign, in any case; it could be anticipated that a European population of millions deported to Madagascar would experience terrible privations and mortality.

But it is also possible that the decision to murder the entire Jewish population was taken when the other options became less feasible—the Germans suffered from chronic transportation problems for military and economic purposes—and when the escalation in the scale and extent of the killings gave Nazi officials the notion that it would actually be feasible to kill all 8 million Jews under German control.

The outbreak of war and early German successes might have favored this policy. First, the Nazis' fears of enemies within the Reich were intensified by war; second, the outbreak of war made extreme policies more acceptable; third, there was less need for the Nazis to take even the little account of international opinion that they had done before the war; and fourth, the war seemed to focus Hitler and his associates on the most fundamental aspects of their ideology, notably racial purity and the establishment of the racial state. These considerations, combined with the fact that military conquest had placed millions of Jews under German control, might well have contributed to the beginning of the systematic genocide that became known as the "final solution of the Jewish problem."

The decision-making process that led to the Holocaust is difficult to pin down because many Nazi leaders and organizations, often competing with one another, were involved. No written directive from Hitler ordering the extermination of the Jewish population has ever been located, and it is unlikely that one ever existed, but that in itself is not significant: Many of Hitler's orders were not committed to paper, and inferiors were expected to understand what their leader wanted through various euphemisms, verbal signals, and codes, even by the tone of his voice. After Hitler had conveyed a mandate for a particular policy, there was no need for a written order. Those who implemented the policy at the highest levels, like Adolf Eichmann, had no doubt that Hitler knew and approved of the mass murder of Jews. Reports destined for Hitler's eyes, detailing numbers of Jews killed, are further confirmation.

A critical step in the development of the Holocaust was taken on January 20, 1942, at a meeting of high-level Nazis in the Berlin suburb of Wannsee. This meeting did not decide on the policy of genocide but clarified its organization and the role of the various civil and military agencies that proliferated in the Nazi regime. Heinrich Himmler's SS was given overall control, and various agencies concerned with transport, resources, and the labor supply were mobilized in a coordinated effort. The "final solution" was arguably the Nazis' most effectively and efficiently executed policy.

Millions of Jews, and people of other ethnic groups and political and social categories, were killed in SS and army actions throughout occupied Eastern Europe, but the core of the Holocaust was a network of concentration camps. Camps for the internment of "undesirables" and opponents of the Nazis were established in Germany in the first days of Hitler's regime. Mistreatment, forced labor, unsanitary conditions, and inadequate diets led to large numbers of deaths.

Death had therefore been a deliberate consequence of internment in concentration camps, but toward the end of 1941, when systematic mass killing in the east had become policy, it became obvious that if millions were to be killed quickly, a new technology was required. The SS soldiers of the action units had worked effectively with the means at their disposal. But day after day of shooting children, women, and men took its toll even though the perpetrators were dedicated Nazis, and even though their victims were Jews and others considered barely human. The soldiers had to be compensated by high wages and holidays, and they were assisted by quantities of alcohol and drugs.

It was not only the SS that was involved in mass killings. Although there were some early protests from regular army officers about the treatment of civilians, the army was also extensively involved in massacres. This was particularly true after the initial failure of Operation Barbarossa, when the German armies began to suffer extremely heavy casualties. As supplies failed, soldiers were ordered to live off the land, an instruction that legalized theft and indicated an official attitude toward the civilian population that seemed to legitimate rape and murder as well. For some time these activities seemed to shock regular officers, who seemed unable to link them with the fact that the Soviet campaign was predicated on theft, destruction, and murder.

The German army systematically pursued a scorched earth policy: Any livestock and crops the army could not use were destroyed, villages were burned, and their populations driven into the countryside to starve and, in winter, freeze. Some 600,000 Soviet prisoners of war were shot and another 2.7 million died in German captivity.

The killing even drew in the ordinary German police, men normally used for duties like walking the beat in German cities. Detachments of police were drafted to Poland and the Soviet Union to keep order in communities, thus freeing the army and SS to pursue their other activities. Gradually the police were drawn into these other activities themselves. Historian Christopher Browning has chronicled the initiation of one police unit, Reserve Police Battalion 101, to the essence of the Holocaust. These policemen, mostly middle-aged businessmen and shopkeepers from Hamburg—"ordinary men," as Browning calls them—had helped round up Jews for deportation and acted as guards on trains carrying Jews, and in July 1942 were stationed in Poland. That month they were given the task of rounding up Jews in the Polish village of Jozefow about forty miles south of Lublin. After "work Jews" had been selected, the remainder were to be taken to the nearby forest and shot. One policeman recalled how the battalion's doctor gave advice on the most effective way of shooting the victims in the back of the neck. "I remember exactly that for this demonstration he drew or outlined the contour of a human body, at least from the shoulders upward, and then indicated precisely the point on which the fixed bayonet was to be placed as an aiming guide."

The Jews were trucked to the forest in batches of forty, and each paired with a policeman. The group, victim and executioner walking side by side, then went into the forest where the Jews were forced to lie in a row and were shot. Two detachments of police worked a shuttle system all of one day, with a break for lunch. At some point in the afternoon, a supply of alcohol was organized. In all at least 1,500 Jews, including infants, children, and women and men of all ages, were shot.

The amount of coercion applied to the policemen varied. Those of the police who did not want to participate in the shootings were given other duties, like guarding and driving the prisoners; some, reluctant to show their unwillingness, quietly drifted off. Others, who tried to beg off killing children because they were themselves fathers, were told they could join the victims if they did not want to be among the shooters. A number of police participated only for a while before being revolted by it. Many of the police were soon covered in the blood, bone splinters, and brains that sprayed everywhere when bullets hit the skulls of the victims.

What is especially telling about the involvement of the police is that such ordinary men quickly became accustomed to killing. Like most regular army soldiers, they were not ardent Nazis, but in the context of the war they accepted the Nazi notion that Jews (or prisoners of war, or other designated categories) were for killing. The Jozefow massacre was only the beginning of that particular police battalion's contribution to the killing work of the Holocaust; by the end of 1943, its recorded Jewish victims numbered 38,000.

Although individual killings at close range continued right through the war, by 1941 there was concern about the effects on soldiers of shooting women and children in such a way. An alternative method of killing was devised. Victims were loaded into a van, modified to channel the carbon monoxide from the exhaust into the back, which was sealed once the victims were inside. The van was then driven off through the countryside, its human load screaming and scratching at the doors, walls, and each other, for the ten or fifteen minutes it took for them to die.

But even this innovation, which had the advantage of killing in a less personal way than shooting, had limitations. The genocide that the Nazis envisaged demanded larger and more efficient facilities, and for this purpose death camps were created. Most were in Poland, and their names—like Auschwitz, Belzec, Treblinka, and Sobibor—conjure up images of the most barbarous cruelty. It is often thought that they were built so far east so as to prevent Germans from knowing what was happening there, but they were located there also because of the large populations of Jews in Poland, Eastern Europe, and the Soviet Union. Warsaw's Jewish ghetto, which had been completed and sealed by October 1940, alone contained half a million Jews.

The killing process of the death camps seems even more horrendous than the work of the special SS killing units. Victims were brought to the camps packed into railway cars and cattle trucks. In winter they froze, in summer they suffocated; trains were sometimes left at sidings for days at a time, and many victims died of disease and starvation on the way to the camps.

The immediate fate of those who survived the journey depended on their sex, age, and health. The able-bodied, mostly men, were kept alive in barracks and forced to work. A number of large industrial enterprises, like the I. G. Farben chemical works, established plants adjacent to the camps so that they could exploit the inmates' labor. Eventually the labor regime, inadequate diet, cruelty, and sickness rendered the prisoners unable to work, and then they shared the fate of the women, children, and old people on their arrival at the camps.

Most women and children, together with old people, and men judged unfit for work, were killed soon after reaching their destination. They were required to undress and enter chambers made to look like communal showers. Once the victims were inside, the doors to the chambers were closed and poison gas pumped in. It took about ten minutes for all the occupants to die. The bodies were then removed, thrown into trenches, and covered with lime to speed up decomposition. This was an inefficient means of disposal, and at Auschwitz crematoria were built to burn bodies instead.

The camp authorities extracted all they could from their victims before and after death. Clothing was sorted and bundled up for use by forced laborers. At the camp at

Majdanek, hundreds of thousands of victims' shoes were kept in the hope that some process would be discovered for turning the leather to some military purpose. (The shoes were still there in the 1980s.) Watches, jewelry, and money were confiscated for state purposes. Even the naked corpses were looted: Hair was cut off for use in the manufacture of the special slippers worn by U-boat crews, and gold fillings were pried out of teeth for transfer to the German treasury. Nazi denial of the victims' humanity went so far as to give their deaths a decorative as well as utilitarian purpose: Some heads were shrunk and taken as souvenirs by guards, and skin was stripped from bodies, tanned, and used for lampshades.

The camps were also the sites of horrible experiments on Jews, some designed to test the Nazis' genetic and race theories. Jews were kept in freezing water to see how long it took them to die, and subjected to unbearable conditions in air pressure chambers to test the effects of parachuting at high altitudes. When the experiments were done, the victims were killed and autopsies performed on the bodies. Children's eyes were injected with dyes to see if it was possible to change eye color, hideous experiments were performed on identical twins, and pregnant women were cut open without anesthetic.

But it was to mass death, rather than individual torture, that these camps were dedicated. Operating at full capacity, the death camp at Chelmo could kill a thousand people a day, that at Treblinka 6,000. These grim statistics pale against Auschwitz, which could consume 12,000 people a day, and where more than a million people were killed in less than three years. In all, 3 million people—half the victims of the Holocaust—died in the camps located in Poland alone. Two million were killed in the Soviet Union, and the rest in various other locations throughout Europe.

Although most of the victims of the death camps were Polish Jews, many Jews were transported from other European countries. The success of the German authorities in rounding up Jews for deportation—often with assistance from local police and military forces—varied from country to country. In Romania, widespread pogroms took place without German encouragement, and two-thirds of the country's 750,000 Jews were killed. In Bulgaria, in contrast, popular opposition to cooperation with German anti-Semitic policies, was largely successful: No Jews from Bulgaria itself were deported, although the regime did turn over to the Germans some 11,000 Jews from parts of Greece that Bulgaria had annexed. Hungary's Jewish population was largely protected during most of the war; the country's government, although allied with Germany, drew the line at genocide, and it was only when the Germans took direct control in 1944 that Hungary's 800,000 Jews were directly exposed to the Holocaust.

Jews in German-occupied Western Europe were initially interned in their own countries, but in 1943 they, too, were included in the killing process. A third of the Jews in Norway, half those in Belgium, and three-quarters of Dutch Jews were deported and killed, but almost all Denmark's Jews escaped. In contrast, a relatively low proportion, about a quarter, of the Jews living in France were sent to their deaths in Poland, despite the anti-Semitism of the Vichy authorities and the cooperation of the French police in interning Jews in preparation for transportation to Auschwitz. The Vichy prime minister, Pierre Laval, insisted that French Jews, as distinct from foreign Jews who had fled to France before the Occupation, should be dealt with by French authorities, and this slowed the deportation process.

Although the cooperation of non-German governments and police agencies in the "final solution" varied, the overall result was that the Nazis almost achieved their aim. In 1941 there had been some 8.5 million Jews in the parts of Europe occupied or controlled by Germany. By 1945, between 5 and 6 million of them had been put to death.

The immediate responsibility for this dreadful achievement is beyond dispute: The Jewish Holocaust was the implementation of a policy that emanated from the highest levels of the Nazi leadership and was carried out by officials and functionaries at all levels, from military and civilian officials in Berlin and the occupied territories, to death camp commandants and guards, and engineers who designed the gas chambers. Military and police forces—German and foreign alike—were involved in the rounding up of Jews for deportation. Their treatment of the Jews in their custody, and the conditions of internment and transportation, suggest they had few illusions about the fate awaiting Jews at their destination, or that they did not care whether their prisoners lived or died.

Somewhat removed from the operational center of the "final solution" were concentric categories of men and women who participated less directly. The mass killings could not have taken place without the contribution of clerks who arranged camp construction contracts and railway officials who requisitioned rolling stock for the human freight. Such personnel participated at a level different from the enthusiastic anti-Semites of the Nazi hierarchy and the SS. Even further removed were men and women who were responsible for all the details associated with mass deportations and killings. It was not possible to eliminate such a large number of people—whole families as well as individuals—without an immense amount of paperwork that brought large numbers of clerks, secretaries, and other functionaries into the process. Property leases and deeds had to be transferred to non-Jews, insurance policies canceled, mail delivery stopped.

The boundaries of responsibility for and participation in the Holocaust are easily blurred and confused. The secretary in an insurance company who canceled coverage of a Jew clearly carried out a function integral to the Holocaust, but it would be absurd to accuse her of meaningful responsibility for it. The further individuals were from central planning, the less likely they were to be able to know how their task fitted into the broad enterprise. Hundreds of thousands of men and women were thus wittingly or unwittingly implicated in the horror of the Holocaust by those who planned and directed it and who knew exactly what was happening.

Beyond the direct and indirect participants in the Holocaust were millions of ordinary Germans. After the war there were widespread denials that ordinary people, those who went about their lives as best they could in wartime Germany, knew or could have known what was happening to Europe's Jews. But information about the death camps reached Germany from soldiers on leave, and rumors about events in the east circulated. The fact that the phrase "going up the chimney" became a popular expression for being killed suggests a widespread awareness of the death camps' existence. Studies of public opinion and attitudes in Germany during the war suggest that most people were more concerned with private issues of survival than with public and political policies, an area where they had no influence and where criticism could be dangerous.

It is a moot point whether historians ought to attribute moral responsibility, but they ought at least to try to clarify the roles, active and passive, that the Nazis, other Germans, and cooperative non-Germans played in the mass killing of Europe's Jews. It is no easy task to understand how the Jewish Holocaust could have happened. Anti-Semitism had a long tradition in Europe, but by many measures Germany appeared to be one of the least anti-Semitic European countries at the time of the Nazi rise to power. Jews remained far less assimilated in Eastern Europe than in Germany, and French and Polish anti-Semitism was more entrenched than the German expression. Religious and secular traditions of anti-Semitism must be part of any explanation of the inception of the genocidal policies directed at the Jews, as well as of its virtual success.

But anti-Semitism alone is far from a sufficient explanation. The shift from traditional anti-Semitism, which under certain circumstances had led to violence and killing, to its radical Nazi form and then to the implementation of the Holocaust, can only be understood in the terms of the specific conditions of interwar Germany and of the Second World War.

The fact that Jews were the largest single group to suffer systematic killing should not lead us to ignore the hundreds of thousands of non-Jews who died in the concentration camps and other killing places of the Holocaust. The victims included men, women, and children put to death because they belonged to unacceptable religious confessions (like Mennonites), ethnic groups, or because they held political views hostile to Nazism.

The Nazis held Slavs in low esteem and had little compunction about killing them, but there was no attempt to kill them all because they were regarded as a valuable labor force for the Reich. Not so the Sinti and Roma (Gypsies), whom the Nazis regarded as little better than Jews. German Sinti and Roma were deported to the Government-General of Poland in 1940. Although Himmler had wanted to preserve some of them alive as curiosities, in 1942 he ordered their removal to Auschwitz, where they wore the black triangle that identified them as "asocials." An estimated 200,000 died in death camps and elsewhere, 4,000 in one gassing operation at Auschwitz alone.

Among other groups dispatched in large numbers to the death camps were homosexuals, whom the Nazis regarded as socially degenerate and guilty of failing in the duty that German men had to procreate. Gay men in concentration camps wore a pink triangle for identification, and an estimated 10,000 to 15,000 men were killed for reason of their sexual orientation. Among the medical experiments carried out in the concentration camps were attempts to "cure" homosexuals by hormone implants.

The mentally and physically disabled also died in droves. The German government had begun to kill the disabled before the main phase of the Holocaust was under way. Gas chambers, disguised as shower rooms, were constructed at psychiatric hospitals, and thousands of patients killed. The program was suspended after protests from Catholic clergy opposed to euthanasia, and after concern was increasingly expressed by relatives of hospital patients who died mysteriously. It is also possible that the program was stopped because the target figure of deaths had been reached. Up to September 1941, between 70,000 and 93,000 mental patients disappeared.

The Nazis defended killing mental patients, the disabled, and the incurably ill in various ways. Their upkeep was represented as an unnecessary burden on the state, and to make the point mathematics texts for students posed problems such as: "The construction of a lunatic asylum costs 6 million reichsmarks. How many houses at 15,000 reichsmarks each could have been built for that amount?" Fundamentally, the disabled and terminally ill did not fit into Nazi race policies and had to be removed.

It is important to remember the non-Jewish victims of the Holocaust not only for their own sake but also because we cannot appeal to anti-Semitism to explain their deaths. Anti-Semitism undeniably lay behind the desire to annihilate the Jews, but the Nazis had no compunctions about killing any group or individual they defined as a threat to the construction of their racial state.

It is invidious and only marginally helpful to compare the mass killing and attempted genocide by the Nazis with others, such as Stalin's in the 1930s. Mass murders are fundamentally the same, but the way in which the Holocaust was carried out strikes many historians as different from the famines, deportations, and forced labor inflicted by the Soviet Communists on Ukrainians, Cossacks, and other populations. The Holocaust was executed with a cool industrial efficiency that required the participation of masses of quite ordinary people. The killings in the death camps were modeled on production line techniques, as victims were processed from trains to crematoria, being stripped in turn of their remaining possessions, their clothes, their dignity, their lives, and even parts of their bodies. They were not just killed, but treated as commodities. The Holocaust was a denial that its victims were human at all, and how so many people could participate in it continues to challenge our understanding.

The Holocaust raises other questions as well. Why did outsiders not try to stop it, once it became known what was happening in the death camps? There are, of course, degrees of "knowing," and even when news of the mass killing began to filter into Germany, the rest of Europe, and beyond there was in many minds a sort of incredulity, an inability to believe that such a thing could be happening. When the evidence became incontrovertible, some individuals and institutions did try to intervene.

Germans who learned of the Holocaust while it was in progress generally felt powerless to do anything. The Gestapo, the Nazis' domestic police force, was sensitive to any criticism of the regime or opposition to its policies. Any conversation or comment might be overheard by a neighbor or fellow worker and reported. Yet there were examples of defiance and obstruction. In February 1943, several score Jewish men, still employed in Berlin factories, were seized at work and taken to collection points ready for deportation to the east. When the men failed to return home after work, the non-Jewish wives of a number of them (they were married before the law forbidding intermarriage), together with women friends and some male relatives on leave from the army, went to the collection points and confronted the SS guards. Despite a ban on demonstrations, the crowd stayed for several days, calling the guards "murderers" and attracting the attention of other citizens. Afraid of spreading public unrest, the SS ordered the Jews released. Thirty-five who had been transported to Auschwitz were returned to Berlin.

Little could be done from outside German-occupied Europe to slow or stop the killings. The Vatican was probably well informed on the progress of mass murder, but clung to its neutral status. Pope Pius XII refused to denounce the policies or demand an end to the killing, nor would he join the Allies in their condemnations of Nazi war crimes. The most the Vatican did was to encourage priests to render humanitarian assistance and criticize the oppression of unnamed religious and racial groups. Hitler, who was nominally a Roman Catholic, was never excommunicated.

The Allied governments clearly had no moral power over Germany, even of a nominal kind. In 1944 Jewish organizations asked the Allies to bomb Auschwitz to destroy the gas chambers and crematoria. It was realized that prisoners would be killed in any attack, but thought that they were likely to be murdered in any case and that the destruction of the camps would save the lives of victims who could no longer be brought there. The British and Americans refused the request, first because other targets had priority, and second because they insisted that arrivals at Auschwitz had ceased. In fact the camp was receiving train- and truckloads of Jews from Hungary, Greece, and elsewhere.

But there were some successes in reducing the toll of the Holocaust. Jews in many countries evaded capture by fleeing to forested areas (one reason Belgian Jews survived in larger numbers than their Dutch counterparts), and many others were sheltered by non-Jews. Thousands of Polish and French families risked their own lives by concealing Jewish children. Chiune Sugihara, the Japanese consul in Lithuania, acted against his government's orders and issued some 6,000 visas to Polish Jews fleeing from the Germans. The Spanish authorities under General Franco saved 20,000 Jews by issuing them Spanish safe-conduct papers. A German entrepreneur, Oskar Schindler, saved more than a thousand Jews from death by placing their names on a list of needed workers. Toward the end of the war, the Swedish government dispatched a diplomat, Count Raoul Wallenberg, to issue Hungarian Jews with Swedish passports that would protect them from arrest. Such interventions testify to the humanity and often the bravery of individuals, but in the end the process of the Holocaust could be stopped only by the defeat of Germany in war.

In some cases the attempts to help ultimately failed. In one case French nuns who took in dozens of French Jewish children were betrayed, and all their charges were dispatched to Auschwitz. The famous *Diary of Anne Frank* describes the life in concealment of a young Jewish girl and the rest of her family in Amsterdam up to the point of their discovery by the SS.

A final question is why the victims themselves did not do more to help themselves. One of the enduring images of the Holocaust is of lines of people, often whole families that included infants and children being held and reassured by their parents and aged grandparents, patiently waiting to be gassed. Many of them might have wanted to believe what they were told, that they were going to showers or disinfecting rooms, but few of the adults can have had many illusions about their fate, having just disembarked from trains where they left friends, family members, and neighbors dead from suffocation, starvation, cold, or illness. Countless Jews escaped from the trains en route to the camps by prying boards off the sides and roofs of cattle cars. German police traveled in separate cars at the rear of the trains to shoot any escapees, and at each stop along the way repairs were carried out to prevent further escapes.

After such journeys, with camp guards beating them with whips and rifles as they entered the camps, would the prisoners expect anything but the worst, and why did they not rebel? The answer might lie in the realm of sheer hopelessness, for by the time victims reached the death camps they had endured months and years of humiliation, degradation, and debilitating conditions.

But in thousands of cases Jews did resist arrest, deportation, and death. In 1942 the 800 Jews of the Ukrainian village of Lachwa fought the troops sent to arrest them; almost all were killed, but some escaped to join a Soviet partisan unit. In the Government-General, hundreds of Jews escaped arrest in the town of Zelechow in September 1942. In 1943, as the Warsaw ghetto was depleted by deportations, there was a rebellion that kept German troops at bay for several weeks. When the ghetto fell, the surviving Jews were taken to Auschwitz and the ghetto was physically destroyed. In the death camp at Sobibor, 80 Russian Jews, many former Soviet soldiers, rose in September 1943. Ten guards were killed and 400 inmates escaped, but most were recaptured or killed by minefields, German troops, or anti-Semitic Polish partisans.

The tragically thin results of resistance highlight the overwhelming success of the Holocaust, whose sheer enormity lifts it from the broader sweep of twentieth-century history. It is important, nonetheless, to remember that it did occur during the Second World War and that the policy could only have unfolded as it did because of the preeminent position Nazi Germany had attained in Europe by early 1942.

Living and Dying in Wartime Europe, 1939–43: The Home Fronts

It is less straightforward to discuss the home fronts of the Second World War than of the First. In 1914–18 military activity was geographically more concentrated, and the combatants had effective control over all or most of their own territory. The only major European combatants in this position throughout World War II were Britain and Germany, although

German soldiers during the destruction of the Warsaw Ghetto, 1943.

for the most part it was also true of smaller German allies like Hungary, Romania, and Bulgaria. Italy qualified until 1943, and we can also include those parts of the Soviet Union not occupied by Germany. But occupied countries like France, the Netherlands, Poland, Norway, Denmark, and Belgium, many of whose nationals fought against the Axis powers from British bases, did not have a home front in the conventional sense of the term.

The experience of the home fronts varied immensely, but all shared the social and economic effects of large-scale war production. In Italy and the Soviet Union, centralized state control of the economy was in place by the late 1930s. In Britain the war again compelled the government to take control of labor and industry. Essential labor was defined and exempted from military service, and the workforce in areas of the economy not necessary to the war effort, was scaled back. Germany was an oddity, an authoritarian state that exerted relatively little central direction in economic matters. Hitler was so confident of German military success that instead of gearing German industry to increased production, he expected the labor and material resources of conquered territories to provide for the Reich's needs. This was a miscalculation, and it was not until 1942 that serious attention was given to coordinating the economy.

A fundamental problem all combatants faced was labor supply. The creation of huge armies drained men in particular from productive jobs just as war-related industries, from aircraft and tank manufacturing to munitions and shipbuilding, had to gear up to higher production. Before the war there had been 1.5 million British unemployed, but wartime industries added a total of almost 3 million jobs, so that the war provided employment not only for those looking for work (there were only 75,000 unemployed by 1944) but also for millions not registered as unemployed or who had not actively been searching for a job.

The bulk of these workers were women, many conscripted into employment. Beginning in 1941, British women between ages twenty and thirty were required to do war work or serve in the women's branches of the armed forces. Up to May 1942, fifteen women had been jailed for refusing to do designated work, but noncompliance was rare. By 1943 some 80 percent of married women aged eighteen to forty, and 90 percent of single women were in the armed forces or employed in agriculture or industry. A survey showed that about half the married women had had previous experience in their wartime tasks: Many women who had left their jobs at marriage returned to them during the war. In many industries, such as aircraft manufacturing, women's work had been increasing before the war, so that wartime employment accelerated an existing trend rather than established an entirely new direction for women.

The trend was similar in the Soviet Union, where 38 percent of women were in employment in 1940 and 53 percent by 1942. Women quickly accounted for a third of welders and lathe operators, two-fifths of stevedores, and half the tractor drivers. The traditional sexual division of labor was blurred for the sake of the war effort. The Communist Party newspaper *Pravda* portrayed women as winning victory "side by side with men, and shoulder to shoulder, equal with them." Soviet women were also conscripted into the armed forces. In 1942, 8,500 young women were directed into the army and navy, and by the end of the year there were three women's battalions.

In Italy the initial callup of 1.6 million men in June 1940 created an instant labor crisis that was resolved by the abrogation of laws limiting women's work. By 1943 women constituted a large proportion of the industrial workforce.

Germany was again an exception. Nazi ideology insisted that women should stay at home and look after increasing families, not work in paid employment, and there were fears that heavy work contributed to miscarriages that reduced the birth rate. The need for labor quickly became critical once the war began (by February 1940, armaments factories were short 250,000 workers) and a vigorous debate took place within the Nazi government. The military wanted women conscripted into industry; others, true to Nazi ideology or afraid of the unrest that drafting women might cause, prevailed.

The number of employed women in Germany fell slightly, from 14.6 to 14.1 million, between 1939 and 1941, and even though it rose annually thereafter it never exceeded 15 million. On the other hand, the number of German men in the civilian workforce declined steadily as military service and war casualties took their toll. There were 24.5 million German male workers in 1939, 20.4 million in 1940, and 15.5 million in 1943. Without greatly increasing their numbers, then, women significantly increased their proportion in the German workforce from 37 percent in 1939 to 49 percent in 1943.

Nor was it only because the regime discouraged it that women did not seek paid work during the war. The separation allowance paid nonemployed wives of German soldiers was higher than any other country. Designed to alleviate soldiers' concerns for their families' well-being, this policy discouraged many women from seeking employment. Added to this, employers frequently complained that women workers were unreliable; burdened with household responsibilities, they took time off from work to stand in line for goods that were in short supply.

Instead of drawing on the labor potential of its female population, the Nazi regime imported forced labor from occupied or annexed territories and put prisoners of war to work, mainly in industry and agriculture. The importation of laborers, almost all of them male (although thousands of foreign women were drafted to work in German homes) did not compensate for the decline in German men employed in civilian work. Although 6 million foreign workers had been imported by 1943, they did not offset the 9 million

German males drawn off from the workforce from 1939. Nor was the productivity of foreign workers as high—not surprising given their poor working conditions and diets.

Germany was not alone in using forced labor. The Soviet Union exploited the relocated populations from Eastern Europe in forestry and mining in Siberia and Soviet Asia, and later used German and other Axis prisoners of war when they were captured in huge numbers. Britain also used prisoner of war labor in its economy, but it was a less important component because of the relatively small number of prisoners taken until the end of the war.

The food supply was as important as labor, and all governments tried to control its supply and distribution. Britain benefited from imports of foodstuffs during the war, but domestic production also increased. Increased mechanization, the extension of land under cultivation, and a stress on arable over livestock farming led to more than a doubling of the annual output of calories from British agriculture during the war. The fact that Britain had a flexible and efficient agricultural sector meant that even with rationing and increased work demands the population remained in buoyant health.

The British government was anxious to protect the most vulnerable groups, like children and pregnant women, to whom some foods were supplied free of charge. Such policies contributed to a general improvement in the health of the civilian population during the war. A more general concern for the social and economic inequalities highlighted by the war led the government to appoint a commission on social welfare under Sir William Beveridge. The Beveridge Report, published in November 1942, set out a plan for state-sponsored social security, family allowances, unemployment insurance, health care, housing, and education that became the basis of the postwar British welfare state. The report embodied the spirit of common purpose and sharing that the government tried to encourage during the war, and its implementation became almost a domestic war aim for the British.

In Britain, food rationing was introduced early in the war but it excluded basic items like potatoes and bread. The range of food covered by rationing expanded as the war continued, particularly after Japanese conquests in Asia reduced British imports of tea, sugar, and rice. In 1942, when rationing reached its greatest extent, soap and candies were included, and gasoline for personal use was no longer available. Bread was never rationed during the war, although white bread gradually gave way to a coarse, darker loaf that wasted less of the grain—a vital concern in view of declining flour imports and the destruction of many flour mills in German bombing raids. Despite the new bread's patriotic name, National Wheatmeal, consumers found the change hard to swallow. Like bread, wartime beer was neither rationed nor what it had been before the war. To conserve resources, beer was adulterated with oats and potatoes, and to limit drunkenness, it was diluted with water.

In Germany food was a greater problem. It had been anticipated that ample food supplies would come from German conquests in the east (especially Russia and Ukraine), but the expectations were frustrated by a sharp decline in productivity in the occupied regions. Until 1943 the shortfall from the east was balanced by imports from France, Scandinavia, the Low Countries, and southeastern Europe. The result was that German civilians were spared many of the hardships associated with rationing and a black market.

Living conditions in Italy deteriorated quickly, however. Italians had been given a taste of rationing before the war as Mussolini's government attempted to reduce imports and consumption in order to achieve self-sufficiency. In 1939 the sale of meat had been forbidden on two days each week, and by the end of 1940 bread flour was diluted with corn meal. In 1941 both pasta and bread were rationed, and in the winter of 1941–42 there was widespread hunger and such civil unrest that in some instances the militia fired over the heads of crowds of women to disperse them.

In a desperate attempt to prevent civil disturbances, the Italian government cut food prices by a fifth, but the result was that the limited supplies were quickly bought up and disappeared entirely from all but the black market. By the end of 1942, the normal rations for an adult had sunk below a thousand calories a day, and in March 1943 thousands of workers (mainly women) went on strike for higher wages and "peace and bread." The decline in living standards, with its attendant civil unrest, contributed to the overthrow of Mussolini in June 1943.

In the Soviet Union the food supply deteriorated dramatically as a result of the German occupation of much of European Russia and Ukraine, and almost every index of Soviet agriculture declined during the war. The grain harvest available was never more than half the 1940 output, and livestock numbers plummeted. The horse population—vital for military transportation and farm work—fell from 21 million in 1940 to under 8 million in 1943, and the number of pigs fell from 28 to 6 million. Even more than in industry, women provided more and more of the workforce in agriculture and bore the burdens of working without horses or tractors to meet often unrealistic production quotas.

Rationing was introduced throughout the Soviet Union immediately after the German invasion in mid-1941, with varied levels of entitlement to ensure that workers in heavy industry received most, children under twelve least. The daily rations for Moscow's industrial workers in 1943 included 650 grams of bread, about 70 grams each of grain and meat, and some sugar and fats. Office workers received about two-thirds to three-quarters of that, young children a half or less. As for clothing and other needs, Soviet citizens just had to make do, because industries dedicated to consumer goods, including civilian clothing, were all but closed down.

Soviet citizens trapped in the two besieged cities, Leningrad and Stalingrad, suffered far more than their counterparts in unoccupied regions. Leningrad was kept supplied during the siege, but the supplies of food, fresh water, and fuel for cooking and heating were inadequate to see the population through two winters. Starvation, disease, malnutrition, and bombardment combined to kill a third of the city's 3 million inhabitants.

Beyond the material needs of their citizens, wartime governments tried to ensure that morale survived in the face of military attack at worst, and restrictions on normal activities at best. Mass bombing brought the military conflict to the British in a way the First World War had not. More than 60,000 civilians died in bombing raids; some 4 million houses (about a third of the total) were damaged and almost half a million destroyed.

The bombing was intended not only to disrupt industrial production but also to undermine public morale so as to force the British government to sue for peace. Although morale under bombing was not consistently as resilient as it is often portrayed, a grim determination to stay the course prevailed. It was helped by the perception of Britain's leaders sharing the danger. Although the war was directed from well-protected bunkers under Whitehall, Prime Minister Winston Churchill often visited devastated areas of London. Newspapers printed photographs of him, cigar clamped in his jaw, striding over the rubble of bombed-out houses. The royal family also experienced the war firsthand. When Buckingham Palace was attacked, the queen remarked, "I'm glad we've been bombed. It makes me feel I can look the East End in the face," a reference to a severely damaged working-class part of London.

Although the wartime experience of the nation's political elites was not the same as that of ordinary people, the perception of shared dangers was important for morale. Even so there was widespread anger at the authorities over what were seen as shortcomings in defenses and assistance for families whose homes had been destroyed. In some cases they were forced to camp in the open by day without any facilities, and live underground by night. On some occasions Churchill and members of the royal family were booed by crowds. Such variations in reactions were glossed over in postwar recollections of the brave "Blitz mentality," as was the fact that a quarter of London's population fled from the city.

German public morale was also targeted. The British and American air forces launched extensive bombing campaigns against industrial and civilian targets like the Ruhr cities (Essen, Düsseldorf), Hamburg, Leipzig, and Berlin. Loss of life and material damage were far greater than that inflicted on Britain by the Luftwaffe, as more than 550,000 German civilians were killed and 900,000 injured by Allied bombs, and millions of houses obliterated. But the mass bombing did not demoralize Germans or turn them against the Nazis, as the Allies had hoped. As in Britain the leadership was prominent, although it was the minister of propaganda, Joseph Goebbels, rather than Hitler, who was a frequent visitor to areas of destruction, inspecting damage.

Goebbels also orchestrated a media campaign to forestall the growth of defeatism. Radio, newsreels, and movies (the film industry was nationalized in 1943) were harnessed to portray the justice of the German cause and the evils of communism and Jews. Germans were reminded increasingly, after the war began to turn against them in 1943, of the dire consequences that awaited them should the "Bolshevik-Slavic-Jewish hordes" engulf the Reich. The Allied policy that Germany must surrender unconditionally strengthened Nazi propaganda by raising the specter of a devastated Germany in the event of defeat. German society, already regimented at the outbreak of war, became even more so. As the war demanded even tighter control over the media, the number of newspapers shrank.

In the Soviet Union all aspects of life were geared to national survival. Communist Party propaganda began to appeal more to nationalist sentiments than ideological doc-

A crowd of hungry Germans ransack a freight train halted by Allied air attacks outside Frankfurt.

trine, making it easier for citizens opposed to Stalin's regime to participate in what was called the Great Patriotic War. At the same time, membership in the party was made easier, and its numbers grew from 2 to 6 million during the war. Morale on the Soviet home front appears to have held up despite terrible conditions in housing, food supplies, and work. Poor conditions were not unknown before the war, and Soviet citizens were accustomed to extensive state controls over all aspects of their lives. The deteriorating conditions in wartime were perhaps more easily tolerated because they resulted not from internal policies, but from an external threat to the very lives of the Soviet peoples.

Social life on all homes fronts was affected by the war. As in 1914–18, the fundamental change was in the sex and age distributions of the home population as men, especially those in the twenty to forty age group, left on military service. Children were often removed from more dangerous urban centers, disrupting their family life.

Patterns of presence and absence of men affected demographics in a number of ways. It was common to find an increase in marriages shortly before soldiers left (or expected to leave) on service, accelerated marriages that might or might not have taken place in time of peace. In Germany 130,000 more couples married in 1939 than in 1938, a 20 percent increase that was matched by England and Wales. In the Austrian part of the Reich the increase was 31 percent. Marriage in Germany was encouraged by the high separation payments made to wives of soldiers on duty, up to 85 percent of their civilian incomes.

Marriages in Germany and Britain had been increasing in the years before the war, and the start of the war amplified the trend, but where marriages had been declining, as in France and Italy, they declined even further. Once the war was under way the number of marriages fell everywhere, partly because many couples of marrying age had married earlier, partly because of the separation of men and women. The immense casualties suffered by German and Soviet forces deprived many women of prospective husbands and widowed many others.

The increased marriages in 1939 did not everywhere translate into more births. In Germany the increase in births in 1939 and 1940, less than 5 percent higher than 1938, represented another setback to the Nazi policy of increasing the Aryan population. Only Austria obliged; births there shot up from 94,000 in 1938 to 138,000 in 1939 and 146,000 in 1940. In England and Wales, births declined as marriages rose. The failure of birth rates to keep pace with marriages reflected extended periods of separation and also a desire to postpone having children until life seemed more secure.

But the separation of wives and husbands did not mean that they were sexually inactive. Men who committed adultery abroad usually did so without repercussions to themselves (other than sexually transmitted diseases), but women were more likely to be betrayed, generally by gossip, sometimes by pregnancy. Britain was a staging point for millions of troops from the British Empire, from occupied Allies, and, beginning in 1942, from the United States, thus ensuring a constant and changing male population from which British women (married and unmarried) might draw sexual partners. A popular complaint, made only half in jest by British men about the American troops, was that they were "overpaid, oversexed, and over here."

The liaisons that developed with married women laid the foundation for the massive number of divorces in England from 1944 to 1949, most based on the wife's adultery. Relationships between unmarried women and foreign troops often led to marriage; 30,000 British war brides were transported to the United States on a standby basis during the war, along with prisoners of war and wounded American soldiers. Another 70,000 arrived in 1946. It is estimated that, in all, a million American soldiers married foreign women during and immediately after the war.

Neutrality in Wartime Europe, 1939–42

Although the only European states to declare war in September 1939 were Germany, Britain, and France, almost all the rest later became involved either as German allies or by being invaded by Germany or its allies. Only a handful of states, notably Sweden, Switzerland, Spain, Portugal, and the Irish Republic, retained neutral or nonbelligerent status throughout the war.

Neutrality implied that a country would adopt an even-handed policy toward both sides, whereas nonbelligerent status suggested a tilt in one direction without the country's actually committing itself to fight on one side. Either position required a delicate balancing act, and a simple declaration of neutrality proved no guarantee of remaining out of the war. The British had planned to invade Norway, but were beaten to it by Germany, which occupied several other neutrals as well: Denmark, Belgium, the Netherlands, and Luxembourg. The Soviet Union had ridden roughshod over the neutrality of Finland and the Baltic states.

The neutral states that remained found their status difficult to maintain. When the Soviet Union attacked Finland in November 1939, the Swedes were very tempted to assist their neighbor against a traditional enemy. In the end the government declined to send forces to help the Finns, but did dispatch war materiel and allowed 8,000 Swedish volunteers to bolster the Finnish defense.

No sooner had that crisis ended than Sweden faced an ever greater threat, the German invasion of Norway and Denmark in the spring of 1940. The Germans announced that they wanted Sweden to continue to observe strict neutrality; Sweden should not mobilize or threaten German policies, and should continue to deliver iron ore to Germany. The Swedish government accepted the terms, but reserved the right to protect its neutrality, and immediately increased the number of personnel under arms from 85,000 to 320,000. There was evidence of support for the Nazis in the highest ranks of the Swedish military, however, and the government was never anxious to test its loyalty.

The German government (including Hitler personally) repeatedly assured Sweden that its neutrality would be respected, although it was also clear that this policy depended on Sweden's continuing to supply Germany with resources. Understandably skeptical, the Swedish government tried not only to observe the requirements of neutrality but also to avoid actions that would offend the Germans and provoke an attack, especially when Germany appeared certain to win the war. A request to transship German supplies across Sweden early in the Norwegian campaign was declined, but by July 1940, when the German position in Western Europe seemed unassailable, transit rights were agreed to. Even then Sweden permitted only unarmed German soldiers to be moved by train across Sweden and an equal number had to travel in each direction: Sweden's railways would not be used to increase the size of the German army occupying Norway.

Sweden felt compelled to make further concessions after the German invasion of the Soviet Union. Germany was permitted to move forces from Norway across Sweden to Finland, German and Finnish aircraft were allowed to fly over Swedish air space, and the Germans could lay mines in specified Swedish waters in the Baltic.

These concessions were preceded by a vigorous debate in the Swedish parliament. Although condemned by some Swedes as an unprincipled surrender to German interests, the concessions were regarded in London, Washington, and even Moscow (which wanted to prevent a Swedish alliance with Finland against the Soviet Union) as realistic and understandable in light of the fact that Sweden was surrounded by German-controlled territory. In fact the Swedish concessions went further in practice. German warships were regularly allowed to travel through Swedish waters as long as they flew a flag of distress.

Sweden depended on Germany not only for its territorial integrity but also economic survival. Sweden's trade with Germany increased significantly during the war, and although commerce with Allied states continued, it did so at a level much lower than before the war. A pragmatic policy toward Germany kept the Swedish economy viable throughout the war.

Swedish politics during the war were dominated by the policies demanded of a neutral surrounded by a potentially hostile power. In the 1940 elections the Social Democrats swept to power—a confirmation of public support for modest concessions to Germany—and right-wing members of the Second Chamber were defeated. The new government, ideologically hostile to fascism, was pragmatic enough to confiscate and censor some newspapers after official German protests against their anti-German tone. But Sweden also risked German wrath from time to time. Refugees from Norway and other German-occupied countries were given sanctuary, and in 1943 Sweden provided a haven for almost all of Denmark's 7,000 Jews.

Like Sweden, Switzerland was concerned about the fragility of its neutral status, the more so because it was landlocked and entirely surrounded by Axis-controlled territory once France was defeated and Italy entered the war. Military preparations, stepped up in the late 1930s, were increased. The Swiss constitution provided for the appointment of a military (rather than civilian) commander-in-chief in time of emergency, and General Henri Guisan was put in charge of the country's defense. The armed forces (regular, auxiliary, and home guard) were doubled to 850,000, almost a quarter of the total population. Preparations were made to defend the core of the Switzerland in the Alps should it be invaded, and there was a notable movement of population from border areas to the center of the country. Preparations were made to blow up major industrial and transport facilities, including important tunnels through the Alps, should Germany attack.

Why was Switzerland not invaded by Germany to complete Hitler's control over central Europe? No doubt this would have happened had Nazi plans for a New Order not been checked; prewar German military maps showed Switzerland as part of the Reich, and the German army had prepared invasion plans. But Hitler probably thought it unnecessary in the short term to commit forces to the invasion and occupation of a small state without great economic importance to Germany. Swiss plans for defense and the destruction of its economic infrastructure would have left Germany occupying a country with few assets.

The impact of the war on Switzerland's economy was dramatic. It supplied food and manufactured goods to Germany and continued to trade with the Allies, transporting goods across German-occupied territory. Imports slowed, however, and agriculture had to be stepped up to meet domestic demand. Forests were cleared and pastures plowed up for grain production. Rationing was introduced and strict government controls exercised over the country's economy.

The war impinged on the Swiss in other ways as well. The German invasions of 1939–40 produced a flood of refugees trying to board the Swiss "lifeboat." Following the defeat of France, 50,000 French and Polish troops sought refuge in Switzerland, where they were interned in line with the rules of neutrality. Despite opposition from Germany, Switzerland also took in some 100,000 political refugees from various parts of occupied Europe. Included were more than 20,000 Jews, but in August 1942 Swiss authorities announced that "refugees on the ground of race alone are not political refugees." Some 10,000 Jews who tried to enter Switzerland from German-occupied France were turned back.

Switzerland assumed importance as the headquarters of international relief agencies, notably the Red Cross and Children's Aid. Such bodies carried out their activities relatively impartially and the Germans as well as the Allies benefited from their good offices. A Swiss National Fund was also established to provide assistance such as food, housing, clothing, medicines, and seeds, to war-affected parts of Europe regardless of their political status.

Unlike Sweden and Switzerland, Spain had an ideological bias toward the Axis powers, being governed by a fascist regime indebted to Hitler and Mussolini for their assistance during the civil war. Establishment political opinion in Spain was generally favorable toward Germany: The two countries had signed a Treaty of Friendship in March 1939, and Spain had joined the Anti-Comintern Pact. Its embassy in Madrid became Germany's largest diplomatic mission anywhere during the war, and Germany used all means to penetrate the Spanish media and culture. Beyond its intrinsic importance, Spain was seen as a conduit for German influence to Latin America.

Spain was neutral when the war broke out, but after the defeat of France and what appeared to be a certain German victory, General Franco considered joining the Axis war effort. Despite pressure from Mussolini and negotiations that at one point brought Hitler and Franco face to face (Hitler later referred to the Spanish dictator as a "Latin charlatan"), Spain did not join the Axis. But the German invasion of the Soviet Union in June 1941 persuaded Franco, a virulent anti-communist, to abandon neutrality in favor of nonbelligerent status. Some 19,000 Spanish "volunteers" (the great majority regular army and air force personnel) fought under German command near Leningrad. Franco insisted that the Soviet Union was guilty of causing the civil war in Spain and that "the extermination of Russia is required by history and the future of Europe." Spain might have joined the broader Axis war had Hitler agreed to Franco's terms: annexation of Gibraltar and French colonies in Africa, German submarines to defend the Canary Islands, and large amounts of food, munitions, and other supplies. Hitler would not agree, partly because he was considering an alliance with Vichy France and did not want to alienate the French by giving their territory in Africa to Spain. If Spain did not enter the war it was not on principle but because its potential allies thought the price of Spanish participation too high.

The food supplies Franco sought were vital. The harvests of 1940 and 1941 were both poor, and Spaniards suffered widespread hunger. The war had disrupted trade and food imports, and one of the pressures the Allies were able to bring to bear on Franco was the ability to control Spain's food imports by their superior naval strength. Franco's Spain also stood out as an opponent of the Holocaust. Some 3,000 Jews had taken refuge in Spain before the war, the Spanish government was responsible for rescuing thousands more Jews from death by issuing them Spanish papers, and as many as 40,000 Jews were permitted to pass through Spain to asylum outside Europe.

Portugal, the other nonbelligerent on the Iberian peninsula, trod the path of neutrality more consistently. Nationals of all countries were found there, and Lisbon became the spy capital of wartime Europe. Much Portuguese diplomacy centered on tungsten, of which Portugal was Europe's major producer and which was vital for the manufacture of machine tools and armor-piercing shells. Portugal supplied both sides. The Allies attempted to purchase the country's total production to deprive Germany of the resource, but there was an understanding that German submarines would not attack Portuguese shipping as long as exports of tungsten to Germany continued. Demand drove the price of tungsten up fivefold during 1941, leading many farmers to take up small-scale mining in order to cash in on the boom. Trade patterns were disrupted, and Portugal had difficulty disposing of its colonial surplus. On the other hand, rationing was never introduced.

The fifth major neutral power in Europe was the Republic of Ireland (Eire), a relatively new state with no tradition of neutrality. Although there were constant attempts throughout the war from within the country to persuade the government to support the Allies, neutrality was maintained because of residual suspicion of Britain's intentions. Like other neutrals, Ireland's policies responded to the course of the war. Neutrality was relatively uncontroversial during the "phony war," although there was dismay at Germany's invasion of Catholic Poland. If the religious balance was redressed a little in June 1940 by Italy's declaration of war, the strategic importance of Ireland was transformed by the simultaneous German occupation of France. Ireland was a potential site for a German invasion of Britain, and fears that the British might occupy the southern region of the country to forestall a German landing were increased when Churchill complained that the Royal Navy's inability to use Irish ports was hampering the battle against German submarines.

There is no evidence that either side was anxious to draw Ireland away from its neutral stand. For Germany Ireland was potentially useful as a window into Britain, but the extent of German espionage from Ireland was overrated at the time, as were the links between Germany and the Irish Republican Army. As for the British, they were able to protect their important west coast ports on the Mersey and the Clyde from bases in Northern Ireland.

Beyond the main neutral and nonbelligerent states there were others. One was the Vatican, unique in that its potential power was moral rather than military, economic, or strategic. The wartime role of Pope Pius XII, who was elected in 1939, is controversial. As Cardinal Pacelli, Pius XII had negotiated the 1933 concordat with Nazi Germany, and had firsthand knowledge of Hitler's policies in prewar Germany. Despite good Vatican intelligence from bishops and priests throughout Europe, Pius XII did not speak out publicly and unambiguously against German actions in occupied Europe. The Vatican's silence contrasted with the words and deeds of many Catholic clergy who tried to help the Nazis' victims.

Overall, the experience of the neutrals demonstrated that in practice neutrality was not a pure state but could encompass degrees of accommodation with the side that was dominant at any given time. Those states on the fringes of the European theater, especially Portugal and Ireland, had the greatest freedom of action. Those in the center of occupied Europe, Switzerland and Sweden, fashioned their neutrality according to their perceptions of the threats that faced them in each phase of the war.

Toward the Defeat of Germany, 1943–44

The winter of 1942–43 marked a turning point in the war, especially in the Soviet Union where German forces reached the extent of their advance and began to be repelled. The key battle in this process centered on Stalingrad, which had been contested from the end of 1942. Besides its strategic importance, the city had assumed immense symbolic significance for the two dictators. Hitler became obsessive about this city that for so long resisted conquest; he referred to it grandiosely as "Fortress Stalingrad" in order to stress the magnitude of the victory he anticipated. Stalin had given the city his own name, and he was no more keen to see his urban namesake fall than Hitler had been to contemplate the possibility that the battleship *Deutschland* (*Germany*) might be sunk (he had renamed it *Lützow*).

In November 1942, Soviet forces rallied against German, Italian, Hungarian, and Romanian troops that by then occupied most of Stalingrad, and gradually drove them out. The main German force, the Sixth Army, was forced into untenable positions and its supplies began to run low. Despite the soldiers' parlous position (they fought on half rations from mid-November) and huge losses, and in the face of opposing military advice, Hitler refused to allow a withdrawal. The Luftwaffe tried to fly in supplies, but harsh winter weather and shortages of aircraft prevented them from providing more than a fraction of the amount needed. To neutralize the temptation of a Soviet offer of surrender terms, Hitler promoted General Friedrich Paulus, commander of the Sixth Army, to field marshal in the expectation that no officer of that rank would ever surrender. He was wrong. On February 2, 1943, Paulus and the remnants of his force capitulated, giving the Red Army not only a field marshal, but 24 generals and more than 100,000 soldiers. Some 70,000 Germans had died during the siege.

Defeat at Stalingrad dealt a major psychological blow to Hitler, who had already begun to deteriorate physically and, as his policy at Stalingrad showed, lose touch with military reality. Conversely, Stalingrad boosted morale in the Soviet Union and among the Western Allies. Despite the battering the Soviet military had taken from Stalin's purges and Hitler's invasion, it had defeated a whole German army, and Nazi Germany had been shown for the first time to be vincible.

Success on the eastern front was amplified by Allied advances in western theaters, where strategy was not to counterattack the Germans directly, but to open up new fronts where the Axis powers were most vulnerable. In November 1942 (just as the Red Army began its successful resurgence in Stalingrad), United States and British forces landed in North Africa and began a desert campaign against Italian and German forces in Tunisia, Libya, Egypt, and Vichy French territories like Morocco. The success of the campaign by May 1943 broke Axis control of the Mediterranean and created the possibility of an Allied invasion of Europe from the south.

The prospects for a new front were also enhanced by improvements in supplies reaching Britain. In 1942 German submarines had sunk more than 8 million tons of Allied shipping, but in 1943 their losses were halved to 4 million tons. In part the improvement was due to changes in the organization of convoys, more escorts, better anti-submarine strategies, and the use of radar and sonar. The British, using a computer called Ultra, were able to intercept and decipher coded messages from the German High Command, and learned the locations and plans of German submarines and their supply

Tens of thousands of German prisoners of war file through the streets of Stalingrad after their surrender in February 1943.

ships. The contribution of American shipbuilders, who constructed ships faster than they could be sunk, was also vital; they were responsible for the bulk of the 9 million tons of new ships launched in 1943.

Churchill likened Axis Europe to a crocodile, well defended by its tough skin but having a vulnerable "soft belly"—Italy. The decision to move against Germany through Italy was endorsed by Roosevelt in January 1943 at a conference in Casablanca, recently captured by Allied troops. The conference publicly affirmed Allied determination, and the United States and Britain declared that they would accept nothing less than unconditional surrender by the Axis powers.

The invasion of Italy began on July 10, 1943, when an army of half a million, ferried across the Mediterranean in a massive fleet of 3,000 ships, attacked Sicily. The assault quickly paid political dividends: Even as Allied forces fought for control of Sicily, Mussolini was deposed in a coup d'etat led by a former army chief of staff and supported by the king and even some leading members of the Fascist Grand Council. Within Italy's military and civilian leadership there had been growing disenchantment with Mussolini's rule, alarm at civil unrest caused by declining living conditions, and dismay at the way Italian forces had been used by Hitler. But they knew that getting rid of Mussolini and disengaging Italy from the war would incur a German military response. The invasion of Sicily seemed to offer the possibility of Allied support against Germany.

Mussolini's enemies underestimated German determination to keep Italy in the war, at the very least as a buffer between the Reich and Allied forces. German troops were already stationed in Sicily and at other strategic points on the Italian mainland, and the Germans had also prepared an army on the Austrian side of the Alps, ready to act should the Allies launch an attack on Italy. This army sped into Italy and enabled the Germans to occupy the mainland. The discredited Mussolini, freed by a German commando raid, was kept on as a figurehead under German control and allowed to rule a part of northern Italy.

While the western Allies established their beachhead in Southern Europe in mid-1943, the Germans suffered further reverses on the eastern front as Soviet forces moved forward in almost every sector. In July the German and Soviet armies met in a critical encounter near Kursk that involved more than a million troops, with thousands of tanks and aircraft, on each side. Soviet industry had rebounded enough to ensure that Stalin's forces were even better supplied than Hitler's in some respects. That, together with superior leadership and planning and advance knowledge of the German military plans, contributed to the defeat of the Germans, who lost half a million men killed, wounded, or captured before withdrawing.

Significant Soviet successes on the eastern front and modest American and British advances in Italy were the background to a three-day meeting by Churchill, Roosevelt, and Stalin in Teheran in November 1943. The future conduct of the war was discussed, in particular Stalin's concern that a western front should be opened up quickly to take the pressure off his forces. It was agreed that an invasion of Nazi-occupied Western Europe would take place in May 1944.

There was also vague talk of the shape of postwar Europe. Although no definite decisions were made about territorial questions, several implications were drawn that had consequences after 1945. Churchill agreed that Germany ought to be partitioned, and that the 1940 Soviet-Polish border (giving the Soviet Union Polish territory) ought to be recognized, with Poland being compensated with German territory to the west. The discussions at the Teheran conference implied the partition of Europe into two spheres: an eastern one dominated by the Soviet Union, and a western sphere dominated by the United States and Great Britain.

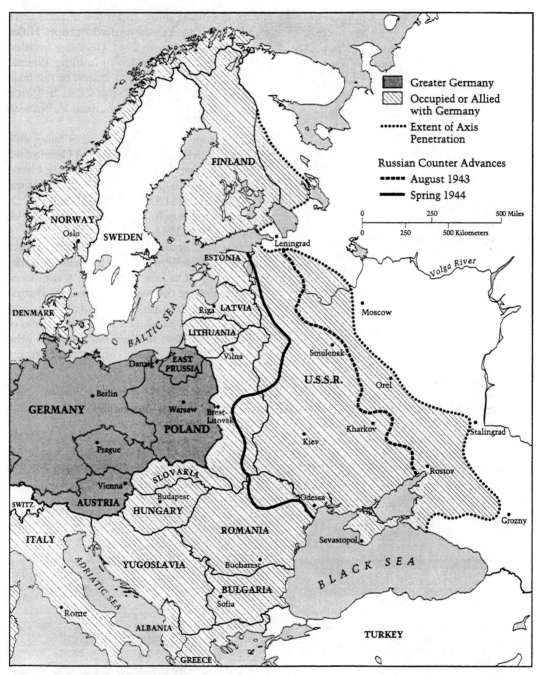

MAP 8.2   The Russian front, 1941–44.

Even as the leaders met, Soviet forces were liberating more and more of their territory, and by early 1944 they were poised to advance into Axis-controlled Europe. Hitler tried to secure his hold over his threatened resources. In March 1944, Germany invaded its ally, Hungary, a pivot of German defense in the east and the key to holding Vienna. Admiral Horthy's regime had allied with Germany in 1940 and participated in the invasions of the Soviet Union and Yugoslavia, but it did not support all Nazi policies. In March 1944, Hitler installed a regime of the Arrow Cross, Hungary's fascist organization, but with effective control resting with Germany.

In Italy Allied progress toward the center of Europe was slower. Instead of being able to move unimpeded to the Austrian frontier of the Reich and to the edges of German-occupied France as they had hoped when Mussolini was overthrown, the Allies were forced to fight their way north against German forces and those Italian units that remained loyal to Mussolini. Beginning with an invasion of the mainland at Salerno in September 1943, a mixed army of American, British, Canadian, Polish, French, Australian, New Zealand, and Indian troops was able to occupy Rome only in June 1944.

The key to ending German domination in the west proved not to be the Italian campaign, which did not open up the second front needed to relieve German pressure on Soviet forces, but the Allied invasion of France in June 1944. On June 6 (D-Day), a combined British, American, and Canadian force of 90,000 landed on the coast of Normandy. During the following weeks artificial harbors and breakwaters were constructed out of old ships and massive purpose-built concrete caissons, enabling the Allies to land enormous quantities of personnel and materiel. In three months more than 2 million soldiers, half a million vehicles, and millions of tons of supplies were transferred from Britain to continental Europe.

The Allied beachhead in Normandy in July 1944. Fleets of United States transports and landing craft swarm close to the beach, bringing reinforcements and supplies.

Allied forces gradually forced their way from the beach heads in Normandy deeper into northern France. By the end of August 1944 Paris had been liberated, and by early September the Germans had been forced to retreat from Belgium as well. In the south, too, Allied forces made gains. After Rome was liberated in June 1944, some Allied forces pushed north as far as Florence, while others invaded southern France and moved north to meet up with the Allied forces that were coming south and east from Normandy.

The recovery of France was deceptively easy for the Allies. German commanders were divided over Allied intentions and responded hesitantly to the D-Day invasion. Hitler had been convinced that the Allies would invade further east, where the English Channel was at its narrowest. Moreover, German forces in France were remarkably few and tended to be either inexperienced or overexperienced—the latter being veterans of the eastern front who were sent to the far less demanding occupation army to recuperate from their ordeals.

Just as the Normandy invasion was taking place, the Soviet army opened a new campaign in the east, and for the first time Germany had to fight actively on two major fronts. On June 10, only four days after D-Day, the Red Army moved toward Leningrad, defeated the Finns, and compelled them to accept an armistice. The Soviets then advanced west, progressively forcing the Germans and their allied forces out of Belorussia, the Baltic states, and parts of eastern Poland.

By the end of August 1944, the German and Romanian armies in southern Ukraine were also beaten. Faced with the approach of the Soviet armies, as Stalin hastened to secure his position in the Balkans, the Axis coalition in Eastern Europe began to unravel. Bulgaria, which had been at war with the western Allies but not the Soviet Union, tried to declare neutrality, but was nonetheless invaded by Soviet forces and compelled to declare war on Germany. In Romania the pro-Axis regime of Marshal Antonescu was overthrown and a new, predominantly communist government, installed; it immediately declared war on Germany. German forces were expelled from Yugoslavia by Yugoslav partisans under Josip Tito. Eastern Hungary was occupied (although Budapest did not surrender until early 1945), and eastern Czechoslovakia and parts of East Prussia also came under Soviet control.

As each Eastern European state was freed from German control, Soviet and local political forces jockeyed for power. In most cases sheer military power favored a Soviet-backed leadership. In Poland there was an extended struggle as the Polish Home Army battled the Germans with little outside help from August 1944. Warsaw was partially taken by the Poles, then recaptured by the Germans who held it until Soviet forces occupied it on the first day of 1945. Many surviving Polish military and political leaders were promptly abducted to the Soviet Union and an administration friendly to Moscow installed in Warsaw.

By the end of 1944, what had been the vast Axis empire still extended north-south from Norway to northern Italy, comprising also Denmark, Germany, the Netherlands, and parts of Hungary, Czechoslovakia, and Austria. But its breadth had shrunk dramatically, from 2,000 miles in 1942 (the distance between France's Atlantic coast and Moscow) to only 400 miles.

Within Germany itself, conditions began to deteriorate in 1943–44. Foreign workers could not meet the demands for increased agricultural and industrial productivity and the German people, women especially, were placed under increasing burdens. In 1943 the food minister announced that "the country woman must add a few hours to her daily work of 14 to 16 hours." Sunday ceased to be a day of rest. Hitler was finally persuaded that women ought to be mobilized to work, and all between seventeen and forty-five were required to register so that authorities could determine if their family responsibilities allowed them to be drafted into employment. So many were able to avoid work that the Armaments Ministry lamented: "We must record a total failure to mobilize German women for work in the war effort."

This was not true, of course. It ignored the fact that more than 14 million women were employed, mostly working-class women who had no option but to work. The number of women in employment rose by 450,000 between May 1942 and September 1944. Middle-class women resisted the labor draft, however, and the regime was not prepared to confront them head-on. Children were mobilized, however. In May 1943, Hitler Youth leader Arthur Axmann announced that 6 million children would enter the labor force. Children ten and older would work in harvesting, teenagers would work in heavy industry after a short training period.

The unwillingness of the Nazis to mobilize their potential labor force contributed to the downturn in economic production in 1944. Steel production fell 15 percent compared with 1943, iron ore production 28 percent. Production among Germany's foreign suppliers of armaments, like Hungary, also peaked in 1943, and imports of vital supplies from Sweden and Portugal slowed as the neutrals tilted their policies toward the Allies. Increased Allied bombing also cut into production and transportation. Losing the war became a cumulative process.

The worsening of the military situation led to a steady decline in German morale. The government carefully monitored public opinion, and the records show a final peak in morale in the summer of 1942. Thereafter, spirits began to fall, and by July 1944 public attitudes were so pessimistic that the surveys were discontinued. Disenchantment with the Nazi regime sometimes led to defeatist talk and opposition. Outspoken critics of the regime were dealt with in various ways, but the numbers judicially convicted and executed rose significantly in 1943 and 1944. The propaganda effort launched by Joseph Goebbels tried less to reassure people that conditions would improve, and more to prepare them for an even harsher war than they had experienced to that point.

The Political Consequences
of the Allied Advance, 1943–44

Just as the extension and consolidation of German control in Europe from 1939 to 1942 had social and economic repercussions, so did its contraction, beginning with the defense of Stalingrad and the invasion of Italy in 1943, and accelerating after the Normandy landings and Soviet offensives of June 1944. Liberation from German occupation control and the collapse of pro-Axis regimes raised thorny questions of national independence, political legitimacy, and the future of the alliance against Germany.

The problems were somewhat less acute in Western Europe, where national governments in exile had retained legitimacy, and where monarchies often provided continuity. In Belgium and the Netherlands, acting civil administrations were quickly reestablished after the liberation. In France a provisional government was established under General Charles de Gaulle, who had commanded the Free French Forces from London. In some parts of the country the evacuation of German forces before the arrival of the Allies created a power vacuum quickly filled by local resistance leaders, many of them Communists. Their authority lasted only until they were replaced by de Gaulle's appointees. De Gaulle's own status was cemented when he led his forces down the Champs Elysées to mark the liberation of Paris.

To the east the situation was more complex. As was to be expected, Soviet rule was reestablished in those parts of Russia, Belorussia, Moldavia, and Ukraine that had been occupied by the Germans. But Stalin took advantage of military liberation to extend the Soviet Union's territory beyond its 1939 borders. Estonia, Latvia, and Lithuania were all incorporated into the Soviet Union as constituent republics, and parts of Poland and Romania were annexed.

Farther west, in Eastern Europe proper, Stalin's policy was to install indigenous governments that would be subservient to the Soviet Union. In Poland, Stalin was confronted by a Polish government in London, headed by General Wladyslaw Sikorski. A truce forged between this government in exile and the Soviet Union in 1941 collapsed two years later when the Poles asked the Red Cross to investigate the mass graves of thousands of Polish officers, discovered in the forest of Katyn. The officers had been murdered in 1940 by Soviet forces, but Stalin, insisting the Germans were responsible, denounced the Poles' attitude as virtual collaboration with Germany. The Soviet Union promptly repudiated the London-based Polish government and established a rival government based in Moscow, together with a new Polish communist grouping called the Polish Workers' Party.

In Romania the pro-Axis regime of Antonescu collapsed as the front arrived in August 1944. King Carol broke relations with Germany and made contact with the Communist Party, which rapidly assumed the powers of government. The following month Bulgaria, which had allied with Germany but had managed to avoid declaring war on the Soviet Union, was occupied by Soviet forces. A Communist government was quickly installed.

The collapse of Axis occupation in Yugoslavia had quite different results. There a 250,000-strong army of partisans led by Josip Tito, a Croatian communist who was president of the Council for Liberation, had established itself in control of substantial parts of the country by late 1943. The partisans fought not only German and Italian occupiers, but also collaborationist groups like Ustashi, Croatian anti-Semitic nationalists responsible for many atrocities against Jews and Serbs. Tito controlled what was so evidently a viable military and political organization that the Western Allies supplied him with vast quantities of military materiel and, from May 1944, air support for ground operations against German troops. Soviet forces teamed up with Tito's partisans to capture Belgrade in October 1944, but withdrew soon afterward, leaving him to form a government.

In Albania and Greece, too, liberation and civil war intersected, though with different results in each case. In Albania various groups of partisans fought one another as well as the German and Italian occupation forces. The Communists prevailed and established a post-occupation regime. But an attempt by the Greek Communist Party to dominate the resistance through its ELAS partisan army, and thus claim legitimacy as the postwar government, failed. In March 1944, the Communists set up a provisional government to rival the government in exile of King Constantine, but it was frustrated by British forces that landed in Greece and paved the way for the return of the monarchy. Stalin did not assist the Greek Communists, probably believing that the Allies would oppose the extension of Soviet influence.

The creation of new governments raised questions about the fate of those who had headed collaborationist regimes. Some fled. The Belgian fascist leader Léon Degrelle sought refuge in Spain (where he died in 1994). Others were captured and eventually tried. The trials of alleged political collaborators began almost as soon as countries were liberated, and continued well beyond the end of the war.

These were not issues in neutral states, but they too were affected by Allied successes in 1943 and 1944, and those that had tilted toward Germany after its 1940–41 victories shifted their policies. By 1944 Spain, which had tried to negotiate an alliance with Germany in 1941, returned to strict neutrality. Franco repudiated Nazism, insisting that his regime had nothing in common with an ideology that did not recognize Catholicism as the first principle of the social and moral order. The other Iberian neutral, Portugal, reduced economic ties with Germany from 1943 and permitted British forces to use bases on the Azores Islands. After June 1944, Portugal agreed to cease supplying Germany with tungsten.

Sweden, too, acceded to Allied pressure to reduce its trade with Germany from 1943, particularly exports of iron ore and ball bearings. Sweden was anxious not to be drawn into another set of concessions that would sit awkwardly with its neutral status, and for the most part the Allies were content with the reduction of Swedish trade with Germany as its contribution to ending the war. In the interests of Scandinavian solidarity, which had been damaged by Swedish policies, Danish and Norwegian police forces were permitted to train in Sweden for the task of keeping order after their countries' liberation.

The Social and Economic Consequences of Allied Victory, 1943–45

It is difficult to separate the social and economic consequences of the collapse of German hegemony from the military and political events. Four years of occupation had resulted in economic dislocation and decline, millions of deaths, and for the survivors widespread poverty, health problems, population dispersal, emotional trauma, and the breakdown of established social relations of all kinds. These broad problems were confronted more systematically in the postwar period, but they emerged as the war drew to its conclusion.

Compared with the relatively rapid expansion of German rule in Europe from 1939 to 1941, its contraction was slow and hard-fought. Some parts of Europe experienced the war twice within a period of four or five years. Warsaw was subjected to a devastating air and artillery assault in 1939 and then became the site of battles between German, Polish, and Soviet forces in 1944; in between it was the locus of further destruction when German forces fought a revolt in the Jewish ghetto in 1943. The city was in ruins by the end of the war. Although far less damaged than the Polish capital, London also experienced the war in two major episodes of attack. The city was bombed extensively in 1940 during the Battle of Britain and again during 1944 and 1945 when German V-1 and V-2 rocket campaigns killed as many Londoners as the Blitz had in 1940.

In other parts of Europe, the German invasion had been so swift that civilians were not initially exposed to the war. France capitulated in 1940 before Paris—or any part of the country much beyond its northeast border—came under attack. In the course of the liberation, however, much of Normandy became a battleground, and cities like Caen and Rouen suffered extensive damage and numerous deaths as a result of Allied bombing. Eastern European states like Romania, Hungary, and Bulgaria were exposed to the military aspects of the war only when the Soviet army advanced in 1944 and 1945.

The Allied armies frequently behaved more like conquerors than liberators, especially the Soviet forces as they entered countries that had participated in the invasion and occupation of the Soviet Union. The arrival of Soviet troops was often accompanied by violence against people and property that had no military purpose. Women of all ages were raped; men, women, and children were gratuitously terrorized, injured, and killed; houses and shops were looted; churches were vandalized. The Soviet soldiers' treatment of civilians in Vienna, the first major city of Hitler's Reich to fall, is infamous.

The western Allies also committed crimes against the civilian populations they liberated, and numerous cases of sexual assault were reported. In many cases soldiers bought sexual intercourse with starving women with a bar of chocolate or some other small item of food. It is arguable that in such circumstances sexual compliance was economically, even if not physically, coercive. In parts of Normandy, the first region of occupied France liberated in mid-1944, some old people still use the saying "The good weather left with the Germans" when they want to decry what they see as the breakdown of social order. The saying reflects one dimension of their wartime experience: that while the Germans were in charge, law and order were strictly maintained and soldiers who behaved improperly toward French civilians were punished. In contrast, the invading Allies bombed not only the ports and other installations but also farms, churches, and markets, and when the ground troops arrived they often did so with the demeanor of conquerors, stealing, raping, and shooting in their exuberance. As perverse as these recollections seem—they overlook the atrocities committed by German forces against local Jews and resistance fighters, and ignore the fundamental difference between Nazi occupation and Allied liberation—they remind us of the way private perceptions can shed different light on public events.

For Europe's surviving Jews the ending of the war often meant an increased exposure to terror and death. The concentration of German power in France, Italy, and Denmark in 1943 and in Hungary in 1944 had extended the scope of the Holocaust. Once German forces occupied Italy, they began to round up Jews who until then had suffered discrimination under anti-Semitic legislation enacted by Mussolini in 1938, but had generally been protected from the Holocaust. Some 8,000 of the 60,000 Italian Jews were transported to their deaths before the whole of Italy was liberated by the Allies. The Jews of Denmark were more fortunate than most. Warned by a German official that a roundup was imminent, almost all Denmark's 7,200 Jews were ferried in small boats to safety in Sweden.

But Hungary's Jews did not escape. Tens of thousands had died in forced labor battalions on the eastern front, but Admiral Horthy's regime had refused German requests to deport the rest to German control. Hitler had protested Horthy's "irresolute and ineffective" handling of the Jewish question. With German occupation in 1944, deportations began with sickening efficiency: Almost 300,000 Jews were dispatched to Auschwitz between mid-May and mid-June. If only a quarter of Hungary's 750,000 Jews died, it was largely because they were exposed to the Holocaust only in what was to be the final year of the war.

The Jews of Greece also came within the Holocaust in March and April 1944. Half the country's 10,000 Jews were captured, loaded into cattle trucks, and driven eight days to Auschwitz. In May 1944, the 260 Jews of Crete, together with 300 non-Jewish hostages and 300 Italian prisoners of war, were put on a ship that was sailed 100 miles into the Aegean before being sunk, drowning all on board. The 1,800 Jews on the Greek island of Corfu were deported to Auschwitz in June 1944, all but 200 being gassed immediately on arrival.

It is evidence of the centrality of the mass murder of Jews to the Nazi enterprise that so much effort was dedicated to collecting, transporting, and killing Jews when the Allies were exerting increasing pressure on all fronts. The various labor and death camps continued to operate until the last minute, and were closed only as the Allies approached. In some cases the inmates were killed. As Soviet forces neared labor camps at Klooga and Lagedi in Estonia in September 1944, for example, almost all the prisoners, including women and babies, were killed. In other cases inmates were moved. From October 1944, thousands of prisoners were taken from Auschwitz to locations farther west, but the gassing of others continued until late November.

Elsewhere in the east, special units of slave workers were created to try to destroy evidence of earlier mass murders by digging up the bodies, burning them, and scattering the ashes. There were also attempts to conceal other anti-Jewish activities. In 1942 a plan had been drawn up to establish a collection of Jewish skulls and skeletons in the Reich

In April 1945, as the war ended, SS troops herded 1,100 slave laborers into a barn at Gardelegen, soaked the straw with gasoline, and set fire to it. Those who tried to escape were shot, including the man who tried to burrow under the wall.

Anatomical Institute in Strasbourg, and the following year 103 Jewish men and women were selected at Auschwitz, then sent to be weighed and measured before being gassed and the bodies sent to the Institute. In October 1944, Himmler ordered the collection destroyed, but the documentation survived.

From late 1944 until the end of the war, as German transportation began to break down, hundreds of thousands of Jews were forced to march across Europe. In November 50,000 Jews were forced to leave Budapest and march toward Vienna. Some 4,000 were saved by the intervention of a Swedish diplomat, Raoul Wallenberg, but another 10,000 died of exhaustion or were killed by guards on the way. Death marches became common in early 1945 as the concentration camps were emptied and their inmates moved west. When the concentration camps were liberated by the Allies, they contained few living prisoners but abundant evidence of what had gone on. In Belsen the British found 10,000 unburied bodies, most victims of starvation.

The Jews forced to walk west were one constituency in a mass of people uprooted by the war who took to the roads as the Germans were forced back to Germany. German conquest and Nazi policies had relocated millions of people, and as the war receded many tried to return home. Others fled their homes, heading west with the Germans, to avoid the Soviet forces. The roads and highways of Eastern Europe were clogged with a mass of humanity—complete families and scattered individuals of all ages, some trying to take small amounts of property, others with nothing. They had no resources and lived as best they could off the impoverished land. Hundreds of thousands died, their bodies left at the side of roads by the survivors.

There was a similar pattern in Western Europe. As France was liberated people who had fled south in 1940 began the return journey, and hundreds of thousands of refugees of other nationalities prepared to return to their homes. In all it is estimated that some 15 million Europeans were on the road as the war came to an end.

The flood of refugees was one aspect of a general breakdown of what economic and social order had survived German occupation. Normality had all but disappeared. Economic activity had all but ceased, depressing even sedentary populations deeper into

A scene from the liberation of the concentration camp at Belsen.

the desperate starvation and poverty that had intensified during the war. Staple crops failed. In Bulgaria the all-important wheat harvest in 1945 was only two-thirds the 1944 yield, while the production of potatoes fell to less than a quarter.

The figures for Belgium were similar; livestock numbers fell dramatically as horses, cows, and pigs were killed for food. In the neighboring Netherlands, conditions deteriorated into famine in late 1944 and early 1945. Nutrition had been adequate until September 1944, but in October the daily intake of calories dropped to 1,600, and by April 1945 it had fallen to 1,300. People were driven to eating tulip bulbs. Malnutrition made people, especially infants and children, vulnerable to diseases like diphtheria and diarrhea. The infant mortality rate doubled, and life expectancy for women at birth fell from 68.5 years in 1939 to 60.6 years in 1945 (and from 66.8 to 50.1 years for males).

The Defeat of Nazi Germany: January to May 1945

The final months of the war, from January to May 1945, saw a complex mixture of military and political calculation as the Western Allies and the Soviet Union fought their way to the core of Nazi Europe. Again the leaders of the three major Allied powers met, this time in February 1945 in the Soviet resort town of Yalta, on the Black Sea. In the sixteen months since the meeting in Teheran, the Allies had reached a point at which victory seemed certain and when more concrete consideration had to be given to the shape of postwar Europe.

Stalin and Churchill had already met in Moscow in October 1944, and it is often thought that they agreed there to divide the Balkans into areas of British and Soviet

MAP 8.3 The defeat of Germany, 1944–45.

influence: the British to have Greece, the Soviet Union to have Romania and Bulgaria, and the two to share Yugoslavia and Hungary. One account has it that Churchill took a scrap of paper on which he wrote a list of countries and suggested percentages of British and Soviet influence in each, and then pushed it across the table to Stalin, who signified approval by ticking it with a blue pencil.

It is debatable whether that transaction ever took place, but the silence of the Yalta conference on territorial matters implicitly conceded much influence to the Soviet Union in Eastern Europe. Soviet power was by then a fact, as the Red Army had swept across Eastern Europe to within fifty miles of Berlin. The Americans were not anxious to alienate Stalin: Roosevelt wanted guarantees that once Germany had surrendered, the Soviet Union would assist in the defeat of Japan. The Americans were also more concerned to get broad agreement on a new international organization to replace the League of Nations than to discuss territorial matters in great detail.

What was decided was that Germany should be partitioned, with Britain, France, the United States, and the Soviet Union each occupying their own sectors. Berlin, which would be in the Soviet zone, was also to be partitioned four ways. The question of reparations—Stalin demanded $10 billion for the Soviet Union alone—was left unsettled. As for Eastern Europe, new governments were to be elected under the supervision of three-power Allied Control Commissions. The Soviet Union had already established and formally recognized a compliant administration in Poland, but agreed to add some non-communist members to it and eventually to allow free elections.

The Yalta agreement has been much criticized for giving Stalin control over Eastern Europe. According to other assessments, it represented an attempt by Churchill and Roosevelt to preserve their wartime alliance with the Soviet Union while limiting Soviet domination of Eastern Europe. British and American preferences for postwar Europe were compromised by major military considerations. The Americans believed that without Soviet assistance the final assault on Japan could cost hundreds of thousands of American lives. Moreover, by the time of the meeting at Yalta, the Soviet Union not only occupied Eastern Europe but could quite conceivably invade and occupy almost all of Germany. Faced with an unpalatable situation in February 1945, the British and Americans agreed to an unpalatable compromise.

The defeat of Germany came less than three months after the Yalta meeting, as German forces were squeezed between Allied advances. In Italy senior SS officers unsuccessfully sought a negotiated surrender at the beginning of 1945, and although the actual surrender did not take place until May 1, it was clear that the battle there was all but won. On the main western front American forces crossed the Rhine in March. To the east, Soviet forces captured Budapest in February and Vienna in April, and entered Germany proper.

The progressive invasion of Germany itself largely followed the Teheran agreement on the zones of Germany that each power would occupy. The Soviet Union was to control about 40 percent of the country, including Berlin. The final Soviet assault on Hitler's capital began on April 16, and pitted an attacking force of 2.5 million troops, supported by more than 6,000 tanks and 7,500 aircraft, against a million defenders with 1,500 tanks and 3,300 aircraft. Within a week Soviet forces were fighting in Berlin's streets. Young boys and old men were drafted to defend the capital.

Germany itself suffered extensively in the final weeks of the war. Hitler refused to allow his forces to surrender and seemed prepared to defend what was left of the Third Reich to the last German. In his political testament, written hours before his death, Hitler blamed "international Jewry" for the war and condemned the German people for letting him down in his struggle. This frame of mind no doubt explains why he compelled Germans to fight to the end with such terrible consequences: In the logic of Hitler's mind the German people deserved to survive no more than the Jews.

As Germany fell town by town, millions of refugees took to the roads. Millions were Germans fleeing the oncoming Soviet forces. Millions were foreign nationals, workers, and prisoners of war who had performed forced labor for the Reich. Many were concentration camp inmates, still forced by their guards to keep moving: only two weeks before Germany's surrender, 40,000 men from the camp at Sachsenhausen and 17,000 women from Ravensbrück were forced to march west; thousands died in the process.

Allied bombing created thousands more refugees and added to the civilian death toll. In February 1945, Dresden, with its beautiful medieval core, was bombed for two days by more than a thousand British and American aircraft, ostensibly because German armor was being transferred through the city's rail junction. It was learned in advance that this was not the case, but the raids went ahead. Estimates of the number killed in the city, whose population was swelled by refugees, range between 100,000 and 130,000. In the ten separate raids to which Dresden was subjected between 1940 and 1945, some quarter-million civilians were killed.

In the final weeks of the war, Berlin itself was ruined in the futile attempt to defend it from the Red Army. Hitler himself spent the last weeks of the Third Reich cooped up

Benito Mussolini, his mistress Clara Petacci, and some of their associates were shot and their bodies hung up by Italian partisans in April 1945.

in his bunker under the streets of Berlin with his longtime companion Eva Braun and members of the Nazi elite like Martin Bormann and Joseph Goebbels. Hitler, by then a physical and emotional wreck, was still convinced that German forces might yet rally; he issued order after order to armies that had long since ceased to exist. Of all the hundreds of thousands of deaths in the last month of the war, two seemed to bring Hitler to the realization that his cause was lost. After President Roosevelt died on April 12, Hitler expected that the United States would ally with Germany against the Soviet Union. He was disappointed. Then the news reached Berlin that Mussolini and his mistress had been captured by partisans on April 28, quickly tried, shot, and strung up by their feet. On May 1 Hitler married Eva Braun, and hours later they committed suicide. To prevent the bodies being mutilated or displayed, aides carried them outside the bunker, poured gasoline over them, and set them on fire. Goebbels and his wife also committed suicide after killing their children. The rest of the entourage and staff tried to escape, some successfully.

On May 2 the commander of the Berlin garrison surrendered and the red Soviet flag was raised over what remained of the Reichstag and other major buildings in the capital. The formal and unconditional surrender of Nazi Germany's forces to the Allies took place on May 8, 1945, V-E (victory in Europe) Day.

Conclusion

World War II had repercussions as broad and deep as those of World War I. In terms of international relations, it raised the United States and the Soviet Union to unprecedented prominence in European affairs. The Soviet Union occupied most of Eastern Europe, and in 1945 it was unclear how long its forces would remain there. The gradual breakdown of the alliance against Hitler, as the differences between Soviet and the Western Allies' policies became evident, paved the way for the cold war, which would be the context of international relationships for half the twentieth century.

Like the earlier world conflict, the 1939–45 war cast the European states into economic and financial disarray from which they emerged only slowly. Again, the extent of human and material losses varied from country to country and within individual states. Even so, losses in Central and Eastern Europe, particularly in the Soviet Union, were immense: In strictly human terms, the war had cost the Soviet Union 20 million lives. The Nazi war against Jews and other populations defined by ethnicity, religion, social standing, sexual orientation, disability, and political belief, took many more millions of lives.

The unprecedented scale of devastation was reflected in the cultural reaction to the war. In spite of the appalling and unnecessary carnage of the First World War, battles, fear, death, and boredom could still be described in heroic terms, as thousands of poets on all sides showed. There was something of the amateur about the conflict, illustrated by thousands of men dashing hopelessly across no-man's land into deadly machine-gun fire. The point has often been made that the generals in the Great War directed it so badly because they insisted on fighting it as wars had historically been fought, instead of recognizing the impact of new technology. It might be said that the poets of the Great War similarly wrote in anachronistic terms. Their perspectives on the mass deaths were often refracted through ideas of national glory and individual heroism more commonly associated with soldiering in earlier times.

In the Second World War, however, generals and poets seem to have caught on at last. There were huge blunders in war planning, as Polish defenders discovered in 1939 and their French counterparts found the next year. But, on the whole, the generals were realistic about the war. So were the poets or aspirant poets, for they kept their pencils in their pockets for the most part. Perhaps there was nothing new to say about war after the 1914–18 conflict. As the British poet Keith Douglas wrote in 1943, "Hell cannot be let loose twice: it was let loose in the Great War and it is the same old hell now." It is equally likely that the Great War killed off the notion that war was a glorious event, an opportunity for individuals to demonstrate their finest qualities. Instead, the Second World War was pursued with industrial-quality grimness and cruelty on many sides. Paradoxically its unprecedented devastation and catastrophic effects on Europe's peoples inspired after 1945 a revival of Great War poetry and novels, but primarily of those that embodied an antiwar message.

·9·

The First Postwar Decade, 1945–1955

Introduction

From 1945 it becomes both easier and more difficult to discuss Europe as a single entity. In many respects there had been "two Europes" from the nineteenth century on: The west was industrial and the east agrarian; the west was urban and the east rural dwelling; the west experienced earlier and more rapid fertility and mortality declines than the east; the east was more religious and its social structure more traditionally hierarchical and authoritarian than the secular and more often democratic mass societies of the west.

Of course these are broad generalizations. There were vast areas of rural settlement and agriculture in the west, as there were intensively industrial regions in the east. Some west European states became authoritarian, whereas in the east Czechoslovakia remained essentially democratic.

From 1945, with the defeat of Germany, a new political distinction was superimposed on Europe by the advent of what became known as the superpowers. Most of Eastern Europe fell within a sphere of interest dominated by the Soviet Union. Much of Western Europe formed a bloc in its own right, not controlled by the United States directly but to a large extent in its economic and military thrall. The cold war, the enmity between the two great powers and their respective partners, conditioned international relations in Europe and influenced domestic politics, economics, and social policies for decades.

The long-term division between the two Europes widened in many respects as the populations in the western states experienced increasing prosperity and liberty while their eastern counterparts suffered chronic austerity and deprivation of civil liberties. Again this is a crude distinction that understates the extensive poverty in the west and the significant national and social variations within the east. In other respects, however, the two Europes began to merge. An important dimension was economic change, as Eastern Europe went through a rapid course of industrialization. Within a decade of the end of the war, much of Eastern Europe was urbanized, and the historic distinction between an urban west and agrarian east was far less sharp.

When considering postwar Europe, it is important to bear in mind that the cold war provided the political context of many of the developments, not only in politics but in social policy and culture. But it is equally important not to allow the distinctions between the east and the west to impose a false homogeneity on each. Within each half of Europe

MAP 9.1 Territorial changes after the Second World War.

there were immense variations in such spheres as national policies, population trends, and social structure. And although the emphasis everywhere was on building anew, many of the trends represented easily recognizable continuities with prewar Europe.

The Immediate Social Problems: Food Supplies and Refugees

The immediate challenge that faced tens of millions of Europeans in 1945 was sheer survival. In the last years of the war, food supplies declined markedly throughout Europe, and there was no hope that productivity would soon return to levels that would sustain the population. Inadequate diets were the lot of millions of Europeans for a year or more after the conflict ended, and often the immediate postwar official rations were little improvement on the wartime allotments.

Overall, agricultural output in 1946 was little more than half prewar levels. Destruction of farm buildings and land, neglect of fields during the war, and the lack of labor, machinery, and fertilizers were obstacles to rapid agricultural recovery. Livestock numbers were dramatically reduced as families were forced to kill their animals for food and as armies—the Allies advancing and the Axis retreating—took what they needed. In France three-quarters of a million farms were destroyed, and in Hungary half the livestock and a third of the machinery were gone.

Climatic variations exacerbated the situation in some areas. In France a cold spring in 1945, following a hard winter, helped reduce the wheat harvest to half the prewar average. The harvest of 1946 was an improvement, but even so the consumption of bread (an important element in the French diet) until 1948 was only two-fifths what it had been during the 1930s, and bread rationing remained in place until 1949. The Hungarian wheat harvest of 1945 was only 30 percent the prewar level.

Conditions varied greatly depending on each region's experience of the war. In July 1946, Italians consumed an average of 1,650 calories a day, compared with 2,650 before the war. In Central and Eastern Europe, where there were vast areas of utter devastation, conditions were often appalling, and there was widespread famine. Although Austria had not suffered food shortages during the war and had maintained average intakes of 2,700 calories a day, it fell to only 800 calories in mid-1945 and did not rise above 2,000 again until late 1948. In Poland food shortages in 1945 led to riots. In contrast, the Swedish diet contained 3,715 calories in 1945, only a little lower than the 3,921 Swedes consumed in 1939.

One sign of hardship in some countries was an increase in infant mortality. Compared with rates in the late 1930s and early 1940s, the frequency of infant mortality doubled in the famine-stricken Netherlands in 1945, when 80 in every 1,000 children died before reaching the age of one. The infant death rate almost doubled in Austria (to 162 in every 1,000), and it rose substantially in countries such as Hungary, Bulgaria, France, and Czechoslovakia.

It was not only food but also housing that was in desperately short supply as the war ended. Large cities, medium-sized towns, and villages throughout Europe were destroyed or heavily damaged. In France more than 500,000 houses were destroyed, and in Germany more than 3 million, most in the last phases of the war. In the Soviet Union, where 1,710 towns and 70,000 villages were classified as destroyed, an estimated 25 million people were homeless. By mid-1947, 80 percent of Warsaw was still rubble, and tens of thousands of corpses remained to be recovered. Throughout Europe, refugees returning home often found nothing but streets bordered by piles of rubble. Housing became a particular

Bomb damage in the commercial center of Berlin, 1945.

problem in the immediate postwar winters, when there were unusually high levels of rain and cold temperatures in many regions.

Aggravating these fundamental problems was a widespread dislocation of Europe's population. When the war receded, it left an estimated 30 million people where they did not want to be, and the great majority promptly took to the road. Individuals and families, small groups and massive crowds, all streamed throughout Europe, some pushing small carts loaded with their belongings, most having so few possessions that they could carry or simply wear them. They lived off the land, poaching, begging, stealing, sometimes being helped by passing military detachments and by relief organizations that played an increasing role in alleviating the postwar misery.

Millions of these refugees were adrift in their own countries and wanted only to return to their homes, like the millions of French citizens who had fled in advance of the Germans in 1940. Refugees in their own countries were the least problematic because there was usually no question where they belonged or of their right to go there. Others found themselves in foreign countries, so that to get home meant crossing one, two, or more borders. Known to the relief agencies as "displaced persons" (or DPs), they included Belgians and Dutch who had taken refuge in France, Danes who sought asylum in Sweden, and Germans who had escaped to Britain before the war. The great bulk of DPs were located in Germany, however, where they constituted almost a quarter of the population at war's end. Germany and its former annexed territories poured forth millions of women, men, and children who had been forced laborers, racial and political prisoners, and prisoners of war.

But many of these displaced persons did not want to return home. This was especially true of Eastern Europeans who were desperate to avoid living under Soviet occupation. Millions of Poles, Bulgarians, Albanians, and others sought refuge in Greece and Italy. Those countries also became common destinations for Jews, who crowded Mediterranean ports hoping to find a place on a ship that would take them away from Europe to Palestine.

In addition to all those who had been uprooted and moved during the war, 1945 witnessed millions more fleeing from their homes to other parts of Europe, especially Eastern and Central Europeans heading west to escape occupation by the Red Army. As many as 10 million ethnic Germans, those who survived the terrible Soviet onslaught in heavily German-populated regions like East Prussia, set out for Germany and Austria.

Germans also fled, or were expelled from, Poland, Czechoslovakia, Hungary, and Romania. Once the war was over, a formal policy was adopted to move some millions of ethnic Germans from the territory where they had lived before the war. Although this was intended to be an orderly transfer of population, it had all the signs of revenge; people were dispossessed of their land and property, assaulted, and some estimates of the number of Germans killed during the process range into the millions.

Nazis and their collaborators fled from their homes throughout Europe in fear of the vengeance they could expect to suffer. They included not only prominent members of the German Nazi government but low-ranking officials, camp guards, and police of all nationalities. Many took advantage of the chaotic situation caused by the floods of refugees, adopted new identities, and settled in localities where they were not known. Many left Europe altogether and established new lives in North and South America and Australia, where they escaped detection for decades.

There was a general distinction between the experiences of Western and Eastern European populations, whether displaced or not, because the war in Eastern Europe (including Germany and Austria) was far more devastating on people and property. Not only did the retreating Germans practice a scorched earth policy, but Soviet forces were often as brutal when they arrived, especially in areas with ethnic German populations and in countries that had supported Nazi Germany. Immediately after the war, the Soviet Union experienced its own severe food shortages, and in Ukraine, which had been devastated by the Germans, there was famine and a high incidence of dystrophy. Under these conditions the welfare of Eastern Europeans, particularly in countries that had provided forces for the invasion and murderous occupation of the Soviet Union from 1941, was not given a high priority.

This period of uncertainty and movement of ethnic populations gave Stalin an opportunity to crack down on non-Russian populations in the Soviet Union, often on the pretext that whole peoples had collaborated with the Germans. Among others, the Volga Germans, Chechens, Ingush, and Crimean Tartars were dispatched to Siberia. The total deported in this way during 1944 and 1945 was probably about 5 million, and the expulsions continued beyond that period and up to Stalin's death in 1953.

In contrast to the fate of many Soviet citizens and Eastern Europeans, the immediate needs of many refugees and displaced persons in Western Europe were met by efforts to move them home as quickly as possible. A massive operation was mounted by the Allied armed forces (which often regarded the refugees as a nuisance and an obstacle to the real work that needed doing) and relief agencies like the Red Cross and United Nations Relief and Rehabilitation Administration (UNRRA). By mid-1945 some 1,500 transport aircraft and bombers, as well as army trucks, barges, and trains were ferrying up to 80,000 refugees each day. By the end of 1945 only 2 million refugees and DPs remained within the jurisdiction of the Western Allies. Astonishingly, there were no major epidemics among the wandering hordes in the West, although there were outbreaks of typhus in parts of Eastern Europe. In this respect the Second World War was different from the First, which was accompanied and followed by severe outbreaks of typhus and other infectious diseases. (The 1918–19 influenza epidemic that was far more deadly was not a consequence of the war.)

But among the successes, there were dark sides to the resolution of the refugee problem. In mid-1945 more than 2 million Soviet nationals were located in the zones of Germany occupied by the Western Allies. Many were prisoners of war, who had suffered a mortality rate of 50 percent while in captivity, whereas most others were either volunteer or forced laborers. At Yalta the Americans and British had undertaken to return all Soviet nationals within their jurisdiction, not only because they wanted to reinforce the alliance (the United States wanted Soviet help to defeat Japan) but also to guarantee the rapid repatriation of their own nationals from Soviet-controlled areas.

Many Soviet "nationals" did not want to return, however. Many were citizens of the Baltic states that had been annexed by the Soviet Union, and whose status as Soviet "nationals" was at least debatable; they began the war as, and still considered themselves, Estonians, Latvians, and Lithuanians. Others were ideologically opposed to returning, particularly those who had volunteered for work in Nazi Germany and those who had joined military formations to fight with the Nazis against the Soviet communist regime. The latter included many members of national populations, like Ukrainians, and also some 40,000 Cossacks who had been mobilized by the German army and had fought the Red Army wearing German uniforms.

Despite the reluctance of so many to return, the Western Allies proceeded with repatriation, using force where necessary. By July 1945, 1.5 million had been handed over, and by October, when the reorganization of the occupation zones in Germany was complete, a total of 2,272,000 had been transferred to Soviet authorities. Most were Soviet soldiers who had been taken prisoner. A small number were emigres from the early Bolshevik period, who had lived in Western Europe for decades and had technically never been citizens of the Soviet Union. An estimated half million eligible for repatriation were able to avoid it by one means or another.

Most of those who returned or were returned to the Soviet Union were sent to prison camps and a substantial number executed for treason. Of one group of Cossacks numbering between 1,500 and 2,000, only 250 were alive by 1948. Even the Soviet prisoners of war who had been forced to work in Germany were treated badly on their return home. Instead of being honored, as Western POWs were, they were regarded by Stalin's regime as traitors for not having fought to the death. Other Soviet soldiers who had served in Central Europe, especially in the divisions that met up with American forces on the Elbe, were suspected of having been affected by Western ideas and impressed by the relative wealth outside the Soviet Union. Hundreds of thousands were sent to labor camps. There were also repatriations to Yugoslavia where, according to some accounts, tens of thousands were soon killed by Tito's government.

Although the challenges facing Europe's populations in the first years after the war reflected their actions and experiences during the war, they also resulted from the new political reality. Most of Central and Eastern Europe in 1945 was occupied, either by international agreement or simply in fact, by the Soviet Union. Many facets of postwar reconstruction, which encompassed economies, social institutions, political systems, and cultures, would be influenced by the political division of Europe. Basic problems of food supply, housing, and resettlement would be solved only by the more general recovery of economies and stable political administrations. Where those processes were delayed, as they were in Eastern Europe, not only did people continue to suffer but the problems deepened and even expanded.

The Cold War Begins, 1945–48

The calculations that the Western Allies and the Soviet Union made in 1945 about the return of their nationals from each other's jurisdiction was evidence of the weakening of the wartime alliance. The British and Americans feared that if they allowed Soviet "nationals" to stay in Western Europe, Stalin would prevent the return of Western Europeans in

Soviet-occupied Europe. Stalin was anxious to have all "his" people back to prevent the development of a large anti-communist emigre community in the West. In a short time the mutual suspicions each had about the other turned to hostility, and within three years Europe and the world were divided by the cold war, which pitted the Western states, democratic and undemocratic alike, against the Soviet Union and its Communist partners.

In a sense the cold war needs less explanation than the wartime partnership. Since its foundation in the 1917 Bolshevik Revolution, which was followed by armed intervention by a number of Western states and Japan, the Soviet Union had been regarded as a pariah nation, outside the international community. The Marxist ideology that the Soviet regime claimed to represent was a threat to the economic and political systems of the United States and Western Europe, and they saw the Comintern as an agent of worldwide communist revolution. For its part, the Soviet regime looked upon the West as irreconcilably hostile. The evidence lay in the military intervention of 1918–22, and in the perceived willingness of European states in particular to allow the rise of fascism and Hitler in the 1930s rather than seek an accommodation with the Soviet Union.

From this perspective, the cold war can be seen as part of a long-term continuity that was disrupted for a short four-year period between 1941 and 1945 when the interests of the Western states and the Soviet Union coincided and they joined to fight a common enemy. It is noteworthy that the Soviet Union not only stood by as Germany committed aggression in 1939 and 1940, but actually invaded Poland itself and continued to provide Germany with vital supplies under the 1939 German-Soviet pact. The Soviet Union joined the anti-Nazi war only when it was itself invaded, but it then felt betrayed when it was left to bear the brunt of German military power until the Normandy invasion belatedly opened a second front.

Nor was the commitment to the wartime alliance equally strong on both sides. The Western Allies not only appreciated that the Soviet contribution to the war was vital to the final victory, but they seemed willing to change their minds about Stalin's regime and treat it as one that could be trusted to abide by agreements it entered into. There was a great deal of praise for the Soviet war effort in the West, although much of it was self-serving in that it drew attention away from the failure of the Western Allies to make headway against Germany for several years. In the Soviet Union, on the other hand, there was little acknowledgment of the Western contribution, and American and British military assistance was never publicly acknowledged. When in 1945 thousands of Muscovites gathered in Red Square to show their gratitude to the Western Allies, they were dispersed by the police.

Not only did each side have a different view of the other, but their experiences of the war varied dramatically. Without understating the suffering of their populations and military forces, the Western Allies (especially the United States) emerged lightly scathed compared with the Soviet Union. The Soviet population had been subjected to a systematically murderous invasion and occupation that cost an estimated 20 million Soviet lives. More Soviet citizens had died from battle, starvation, and cold during the siege of Leningrad alone, than the combined military and civilian deaths of Britain, France, and the United States.

With different experiences of war, different ideologies, and a history of mistrust and enmity, it is hardly surprising that the alliance of convenience began to unravel once the common enemy had been defeated. The vastly different ideas each side had about the shape of the postwar world began to emerge as soon as the abstract principles enunciated at the wartime conferences had to be translated into concrete terms.

They emerged at the first postwar conference, held in Potsdam in July 1945. Although there was agreement on a number of issues, such as the demilitarization of Germany, the prosecution of war criminals, and the restoration of democracy in Germany, sharp tensions emerged over territory and reparations. The Soviet Union insisted on its right to retain the Polish lands it had seized in 1939, and wanted Poland compensated from German territory to the west; the disagreement centered on how far west Poland should extend. In the end a final agreement was left to the peace treaty with Germany, when its boundaries would be fixed.

On reparations, the Soviet Union was understandably anxious to recover what it could to compensate for its immense wartime losses. The Soviet demand for half the $20 billion that had been proposed at Yalta was rejected as unrealistic, but the Western Allies finally agreed that Soviet forces could take goods and material from the zone of Germany they occupied, plus a quarter of the industrial equipment from the Western-occupied zones to the extent that it was not necessary for Germany's economic recovery. This was a formula tailor-made for conflicting interpretations.

Other issues at Potsdam drew attention to emerging conflicts elsewhere. The Soviet Union complained about Western intervention in a civil war that had broken out in Greece, and demanded that Communists, who were trying to overthrow the monarchist administration, be included in the government there. There were also Soviet demands for control over former Italian territory in Northern Africa and over the Dardanelles, the straits between the Black Sea and the Mediterranean so important for the Soviet Union's navy and maritime trade.

In the years following the Potsdam conference, relations between the Soviet Union and its wartime allies deteriorated rapidly. The latter were dismayed by Soviet policies in Eastern Europe, where agreements to carry out democratic elections had not been fulfilled. Even though multiparty coalitions held formal power until 1948, it was clear that Communists, with the backing of the Soviet Union, were actually in control. There was particular horror in Western capitals at the Communist takeover of Czechoslovakia, the only Eastern European state with a democratic tradition.

Stalin's priority was clearly to ensure that the Eastern European states provided a buffer between the Soviet Union and the rest of Europe, especially Germany. The only way to guarantee that they remained friendly to the Soviet Union was to control their governments, and that meant making sure that Communists were in control. As we shall see in the next section, this aim was achieved gradually by indigenous Communists who often used physical coercion but who rarely needed the direct intervention of Soviet occupation forces.

American policy in Western Europe was similarly concerned to promote friendly governments, and Washington was alarmed at the popular support for Communist parties in France, Italy, and Belgium. The economic coercion they employed to ensure more compatible governments was of a quite different order than that brought to bear in Eastern Europe—the difference between banks and tanks. As early as 1946 it was becoming clear that Europe was divided into two hostile camps. In March Britain's wartime prime minister, Winston Churchill, made the speech that popularized the way in which Soviet domination of Eastern Europe would be referred to throughout the cold war: "From Stettin on the Baltic to Trieste on the Adriatic, an iron curtain has descended across the continent." Within months Stalin was denouncing his former partners in the struggle against Germany as imperialists and aggressors. Although the cold war broke out in earnest only in 1948, it is clear that the temperature of Soviet-Western relations, never as warm on the Soviet side in any case, began to cool from the moment victory seemed assured. These chill winds blew across the devastated landscape as Europeans bent to the tasks of rebuilding their homes, farms, factories, and lives.

Political Reconstruction
in Western Europe, 1945–55

In the immediate postwar period, most European states reaffirmed or reestablished democratic political systems. This was not an issue in Britain and Sweden, where democratic government (modified by wartime limitations) remained continuous during the war. In a different sense, democracy was not an issue on the Iberian peninsula either, where two authoritarian states had sat out the war. In Belgium, the Netherlands, Norway, Denmark, and Finland, it was largely a matter of reactivating pre-occupation constitutions. In Italy and France (the latter occupied by Germany, although partially controlled by the quasi-fascist Vichy regime for some of the war), new constitutions had to be drafted.

The reaffirmation of democratic principles in most of Western Europe was accompanied by a general shift of political support toward the left. Parties of the nationalist right had been discredited by their association with fascism, and even conservative parties were tainted by the suspicion that they had not opposed Germany with a great deal of strength. Mainstream political parties were also suspect for having led their economies into the Great Depression.

The left did not gain support simply by default, however, for there was a generally more positive attitude toward progressive socialist policies. In place of the mainstream prewar conservative parties, a new political movement developed: Christian Democracy. This was a generally progressive Catholic movement that embraced liberal and even moderately social democratic policies rather than the nationalistic and reactionary authoritarianism that political Catholicism had tended to support in the 1930s. Christian Democrats were generally in favor of European unity and the extension of social welfare programs.

The greater acceptance of socially progressive ideas in Western Europe was also reflected in a general sense that there should be more long-range planning in the economic and social spheres. Before the war, such planning was associated with centralized and bureaucratic states like the Soviet Union and Nazi Germany. The failure of free enterprise in the 1920s and 1930s, coupled with the experience of greater state activity during the war, convinced even moderate conservatives that central planning could coexist with fundamentally private and free enterprise and a free citizenry.

There was also a more positive attitude toward Communists, especially in formerly occupied countries where their prominence in the resistance had won them considerable prestige. Nor, for a short time at least, was the Soviet Union quite the bogeyman it had been in the 1930s. In the first postwar years it was widely considered a heroic ally whose sacrifices had made the defeat of Hitler possible. This attitude dissipated as Soviet actions in Eastern Europe and the advent of the cold war made the Soviet Union an official enemy once more, but for two years or more national Communist parties in Western Europe benefited from the afterglow of the Communist contribution to victory.

These varied trends are evident in postwar Britain, where in 1945 Winston Churchill's Conservatives were defeated and replaced by a Labour Party government. The election was an embarrassment to Churchill, who was attending the Potsdam conference when the election result became known. He might have been expected to benefit from the immense prestige his wartime leadership had won him. But the election result reflected a widespread desire for improvements in employment, housing, health, and education. Churchill was associated with victory, but the Conservative Party was associated with the 1930s, persistently high rates of unemployment, extensive poverty, and class distinctions.

Even though Britain's wartime government had begun a program of reforms, including the 1944 Education Act that made some form of secondary schooling generally available, Labour's program of comprehensive welfare responded to the mood of the electorate. The results were less than people hoped for, however, not least because Britain's weak trading performance limited the government's ability to provide employment or to fund social welfare programs fully. Food and raw materials had to be imported and even coal, formerly an export, had to be purchased abroad when temperatures plummeted well below normal in the winter of 1946–47.

The Labour government did take some measures to support ailing industries and bring essential sectors under state control: Coal mining, steel manufacturing, long-distance trucking, and the railroads were brought into state ownership. In 1948 it laid one of the cornerstones of the welfare state, the National Health Service (NHS), which guaranteed free medical services to all. Although it coexisted with private health services that enabled people to pay if they wished—some believed medical care was better if it was paid for, while a few objected in principle to socialized medicine—almost all patients in Britain were registered with the NHS within two years.

Policies like these were expensive and they were paid for by increased taxes, which added to growing dissatisfaction in the late 1940s as Britain recovered only slowly from wartime conditions. Basic foods like bread, butter, and eggs were rationed for years after 1945 (sugar until 1954), and living standards began to decline. Workers who went on strike for higher wages found themselves opposed by a Labour government elected on a pledge to look after the interests of ordinary people; they were not mollified that tax increases bit especially deeply into the higher income brackets. The Labour government's

Labour Party posters during the 1950 general election. They include a number of important historical themes, such as unemployment, health, and the family.

financial problems were aggravated by heavy defense spending and British participation in the Korean War. The Labour Party itself was divided over foreign and domestic policy, its left wing accusing the government of starving the welfare state of funds in order to prop up an anachronistic colonial empire and to support American foreign policy. Aneurin Bevin, who had created the NHS, resigned from the government in 1950 over the introduction of fees on some services, like glasses.

In 1950 the Labour Party was returned to power but with such a small majority that another election was held the following year. Even then the party received more of the popular vote than the Conservatives, but the latter won more seats and formed a government with Winston Churchill as prime minister again. They remained in power until 1964. Although they campaigned on a program of returning nationalized industries to private ownership, the Conservatives privatized only iron and steel and some elements in the transport industry. They maintained and even extended many of the Labour Party's social policies.

The path of political reconstruction in France was far more littered with debris from the war, and as in other states that had been occupied, resistance forces had a legitimate claim to a role in shaping the postwar settlement. But the preeminent indigenous force during the liberation was the military, the Free French Forces, led by General Charles de Gaulle, that participated in the Allied invasions. De Gaulle had headed the French government in exile, and by 1944 had achieved unassailable influence over the French forces and the resistance. From mid-1944, he dispatched representatives to take control of administration in newly liberated regions, not only to ensure social order but also to forestall any attempts by local resistance leaders, many of whom were Communists, to create power bases for themselves.

De Gaulle himself became head of a provisional government that administered France during the next two years. His provisional government wasted no time in setting the pace of reform. It created a state airline (Air France) and nationalized the Bank of France, the armaments industry, and the Renault automobile company (because Louis Renault was indicted for supplying tanks and other vehicles to the Germans). Social security was extended: Retirement pensions were improved, and a medical care plan established that paid 80 percent of patient costs. Health and safety standards for workers were improved, and employees of large enterprises were given the right to examine their employers' accounts.

The provisional government also oversaw the reconstruction of France's political system. In an October 1945 referendum, 96 percent of voters opted not to revive the Third Republic, which was identified with economic problems and defeat in 1940, and they elected a constituent assembly to draw up a new constitution. De Gaulle resigned as head of the government in January 1946 in protest at party quarreling over the constitution and the refusal of the constituent assembly to provide for a stronger executive in the new constitution. De Gaulle believed that party divisions and a weak executive had undermined the Third Republic, but like their counterparts elsewhere in Europe, the architects of the new constitution were wary of executive power after the experience of fascism. The constitution of the Fourth Republic, completed in 1946, placed power firmly with the legislature, but unlike its predecessor it enfranchised women. It was approved in a referendum, in which women voted, by 9.2 to 8.2 million votes.

The Fourth Republic was the creation of three main political groupings, all left and liberal-center parties, that had cooperated in the resistance: the Communists, the Socialists, and the Popular Republican Movement (MRP), a Catholic party that sought to reconcile the church and the republic and in many respects resembled Christian Democratic parties in other European states. The Radicals and conservative parties had been compromised by favorable or ambiguous attitudes toward the Vichy regime.

In elections in 1946, the Communists won 29 percent of the vote, the MRP 26 percent, and the Socialists 18 percent, giving them a combined three-quarters of the ballots cast. The rest were won by Radicals, conservatives, and various independents. The three large parties attempted to cooperate in a policy called tripartism, and the government formed in January 1947 was broad-based, comprising nineteen Socialist, Communist, and MRP ministers, and seven from other parties. The appointment of a Communist as minister of defense was especially sensitive, in light of the growing division between the Western Allies and the Soviet Union. In recognition of this, the premier created separate ministries for the army, navy, and air force, leaving the minister of defense with an uncertain jurisdiction which he administered from a house that initially had no telephone.

The Communists remained in the French cabinet only for five months. Following the breakdown of U.S.-Soviet relations in early 1947, and in light of French dependence on U.S. aid, the premier responded to a hint from the Americans that the presence of Communists in government was preventing the Americans from being as generous as they might. When the Communist ministers voted against a government bill, they were dismissed, and at the same time the radio service was purged of Communists, and Communist army officers were moved to marginal posts. There is no direct evidence that the expulsion of the Communists actually influenced American policy, but when the U.S. aid strategy for Europe (the Marshall Plan) was announced the next month, France received a fifth of it, a larger proportion than any country other than Britain.

Tripartism, which had ensured a government majority, died with the expulsion of the Communists, and from mid-1947 until 1951 there were ten distinct administrations, starting the pattern of government instability that eventually destroyed the Fourth Republic in 1958. The period 1947–51 saw the political reappearance of General de Gaulle as the motivating force behind a new movement, the Union of the French People (RFR), a parliamentary partnership open to all deputies except Communists. Insofar as its adherents could retain their own party affiliations, it was designed to reduce interparty rivalry and foster broader national interests.

The rise of this conservative force coincided with a decline of support for the French Communists. The isolation of the Communists made them less attractive to voters than when they were participants in government. The party was tainted by association with some unpopular and unsuccessful strikes, and it found itself on the defensive over Soviet policies like censorship and political repression in Eastern Europe. By 1951 and 1956 the Communist share of the popular vote in France slipped to 26 percent, still the largest bloc of votes, but a step toward a situation in which the Communists would attract a solid but politically impotent 20 percent of the national vote from the late 1950s through to the 1980s.

Italy's postwar political reconstruction was similar to France's in some respects. The committees of liberation that had fought the Germans, many of them headed by Communists, were quickly shunted aside. As in France, three parties dominated postwar politics: the Communists (illegal before the war, but with nearly 2 million members by 1946), Socialists, and Christian Democrats. Together these parties won three-quarters of the vote in the 1946 election (Christian Democrats 35 percent, Socialists 21, and Communists 19). In the same ballot, 54 percent of voters opted for a republican form of government, a result that led to the reluctant abdication of Humbert II, the son of Victor Emmanuel III, who had abdicated a month earlier. The vote demonstrated the continuing division of Italy: A majority in the south voted for the monarchy (79 percent in Naples), the north for a republic.

The three main parties dominated the process of writing a new constitution. In many respects a revival of the one abolished by Mussolini, it differed in enfranchising women, making the upper chamber elective (rather than appointive), and being republican. It was also carefully designed to prevent a concentration of power in the hands of one party or person: Representation was proportional to the popular vote, governments were made responsible to parliament, a constitutional court was established with the power to strike down unconstitutional laws, and a series of freedoms guaranteed, including speech, assembly, the press, and freedom from house searches.

The assembly that drafted the new constitution was so anxious to distance Italy from the Fascist period that it designed a weak government that would make Italian politics after the Second World War as volatile as they had been before the First. The weakness of the state was confirmed by a clause that embedded the 1929 Lateran Accords as the basis of church-state relations. This gave the Catholic Church special status in Italy, because no other denomination or religion had its position guaranteed by the constitution. Moreover, the constitution undermined central government by recognizing regionalism; certain regions, including Trentino-Alto Adige in the north and Sicily in the south, were granted their own assemblies with autonomy over language, economic matters, and welfare.

Italy's first postwar cabinet was formed by the Christian Democrats under Alcide de Gasperi (a member of the pre-Fascist Popular Party), but because of the distribution of seats in parliament he had little choice but to include Socialists and Communists. As in France, however, the participation of the Communists in Italy's government concerned the Americans. It also angered the pope, who was not entirely happy about some of the more progressive aspects of Christian Democratic policy, like free health services and religious liberty. Under pressure from both the Vatican and Washington, the Christian Democrats excluded the Communists from the governing coalition in May 1947, the very month Communists were dismissed from their ministries in France. In the run-up to Italy's first elections under the new constitution, in April 1948, the United States provided food, promises of aid, weapons for the police, and anti-Communist leaflets and posters. The pope's contribution included warning Catholics against supporting atheistic parties, while individual bishops and priests threatened to excommunicate parishioners who voted Communist. In the deepening shadow of the cold war the combined Communist-Socialist vote fell to 31 percent (from 40 percent two years earlier), while the Christian Democrats won 48 percent of the vote and an outright majority of seats in the assembly.

During the 1950s, however, the Communists gained electoral support, winning 23 percent of the vote in 1953, and increased it steadily until the 1970s, for reasons examined in the next chapter. An important factor was the commitment of the Communist leader, Palmiro Togliatti, to working with other parties, which prevented the Communists from becoming too marginalized. For this he was criticized by the Soviet regime. The Communists were elected to power in a number of regions, where their social reforms, like health care and sanitation projects, proved popular.

In contrast, support for the Christian Democrats declined as alternative parties developed on its right wing. In the 1953 election it won only 40 percent of the vote, compared with 23 percent for the Communists, 13 percent for the Socialists, and a combined 13 percent for the Monarchist Party and the neo-Fascist Italian Social Movement (MSI). Echoing the pattern of interwar politics elsewhere, the center had begun to decline and the extremes (which in 1953 garnered two in every five votes) increased. The diffusion of votes in 1953 ushered in a long period of political instability in Italy.

In the Scandinavian states, politics resumed rather as they had been left off at the time of the German invasion in 1940. In both Denmark and Norway, the provisional administrations that governed following liberation were composed of resistance leaders; but after October 1945 elections in both countries, left-wing governments took over. Throughout Scandinavia, Communists earned record votes in the first postwar elections, and they were included in governments in Iceland and Finland.

Communists also participated in Belgian administrations, and, as in France and Italy, they were excluded during 1947. But the main political problems there centered on ethnic rivalries between the French-speaking Walloons and Dutch-speaking Flemings. Walloons accused the Flemings of having actively or passively collaborated with the Germans; the reaction against collaborators had focused on Flemings, and there were allegations that the Walloons had taken advantage of the moment to undermine the Flemish nationalist movement. Flemings and Walloons were also divided over the behavior of King Leopold III during the war. Instead of accompanying his government into exile, he had stayed in Belgium, surrendered to Germany without consulting the government, and negotiated with the Nazis over Belgian prisoners. He had also remarried during the war, an act seen as inappropriate in his realm's tragic circumstances. Just before Belgium was liberated, Leopold was taken by the Germans to Austria, but when he was freed by the Americans public hostility prevented him from returning to Belgium. In a 1950 referendum 58 percent of Belgians supported the king, but there were such divisions between Flemings (of whom 72 percent supported him) and Walloons (about 45 percent), together with serious outbreaks of violence, that the government forced him to abdicate in favor of his son, Baudouin.

The Belgian case exemplified a trend throughout Western Europe from 1945 to 1950, when the restoration of politics to what was thought of as a normal footing also required facing the recent past. In occupied states there were Nazi collaborators to deal with. In France, for example, there was the tangled problem of the Vichy regime, which had collaborated with Germany but had been accepted by most French people within its jurisdiction as the legitimate government. In Italy the Fascists had been in power for more than two decades, long enough for almost all adults to have been associated with them in some way.

Postwar administrations responded in various ways to the tens of thousands of denunciations that poured in to government offices after each country was liberated. Many of the reports detailed serious war crimes, others economic collaboration, and many described nothing more than acts like purchasing a collaborationist newspaper or serving drinks to occupation troops in a bar. Thousands of women throughout Western Europe were denounced for having had sexual relationships with German soldiers.

In Belgium some 634,000 files on collaboration were opened, one for every seven adults, and in the end 87,000 people were tried and 77,000 convicted. In the Netherlands more than 150,000 collaborators were arrested, and in Norway, 18,000. In both countries, as in Belgium and Denmark, collaborators were deprived of the right to vote and to work in their professions. The Norwegian fascist leader, Vidkun Quisling, was executed, but his Belgian counterpart, Léon Degrelle, escaped. Retribution was wider ranging in France, where there were 170,000 trials, resulting in 120,000 convictions. Of these, 4,785 collaborators were sentenced to death, and about 2,000 were finally executed. Of the leaders of the Vichy government, the prime minister Pierre Laval was tried and executed, while 89-year-old Marshal Pétain had his death sentence commuted to imprisonment because of his age. Italy was among the most lenient states in its treatment of Fascists. Special tribunals set up after liberation tried the prominent Fascists, but few of the lower-ranking of-

Women accused of collaborating with the Germans are paraded through the streets of Paris after the liberation of the city. Women who had had sexual relationships with Germans frequently had their heads shaved, and one here has a Nazi swastika painted on her forehead.

ficials were bothered by arrests or even affected by the modest purge of the civil service. As early as October 1946, an amnesty was announced, and fewer than 4,000 Fascists or war criminals remained in prison at the beginning of 1947.

Official action was only part of the campaign against collaborators, however, because during and immediately after liberation many were punished informally by the resistance and the communities in which they lived. Women known or suspected of having had sexual relationships with the enemy had their heads shaved and were driven naked through the streets. They included prostitutes who might be said to have done no more than carry on business in the same way as a shopkeeper who sold a newspaper to a German soldier. Other collaborators were beaten and driven out of their homes. In France at least 5,000 people, especially police chiefs and those whose cooperation with the Germans had caused French deaths, were lynched. Mussolini and his companion Clara Petacci, shot and then strung up by the feet, were only the most prominent of thousands of Fascists killed by Italian partisans in the wake of the liberation. Although the official figure of such deaths is 1,732, an estimated 12,000 to 15,000 Fascist officials, factory managers, and landowners were killed between April and June 1945 alone, 3,000 of them in Milan.

Political Reconstruction in Eastern Europe

Unlike the West, much of Eastern Europe came under hostile military occupation in the postwar period. Where there was a Soviet occupation, the presence of the Red Army shaped the course of political reconstruction; where there was not, its shadow sometimes had the same effect. Soviet domination did not take the form of blanket repression, however. It varied in intensity and form from country to country, and was nuanced according to specific circumstances and concerns. Initially, at least, there was more concern to keep control of Poland, which lay between Germany and the Soviet Union, and Romania, which had participated in the 1941 invasion, than to keep a firm grip on strategically less important countries like Hungary and Czechoslovakia.

By 1948 Soviet-supported Communist regimes had been installed in Poland, Hungary, Bulgaria, Romania, and Czechoslovakia, generally after each state had gone through a similar three-phase process. In the first phase, a general coalition of center-left political groups, including Communists, assumed power. Second, the Communists gradually neutralized the non-Communist elements while maintaining the appearance of plurality. Third, the facade was either abandoned as the Communists took sole power, or it was partially maintained as the Communists absorbed other parties and ruled under a new composite name.

The Soviet occupation administration assisted the whole process in various ways, including abducting opponents and strengthening Communist-controlled police forces. But although the simple presence of the Red Army as the ultimate coercive force in Eastern Europe goes some way to explaining how small, indigenous Communist parties were able to seize and maintain power, it alone does not explain the success of Communists in Czechoslovakia, which was not occupied, or Bulgaria, which had only a small occupation force. Other considerations included the ability of national Communist parties to impose themselves by force, the introduction of policies to attract specific sections of the population, and a broad acceptance that socialism of some kind was the way of the future after right-wing nationalists had been discredited by association with fascism and Nazism, and capitalism compromised by the prewar economic disasters.

The provisional governments established immediately after liberation from German occupation generally included Communists, Social Democrats, and representatives of the prewar agrarian parties. In Bulgaria, for example, the 1945 government consisted of Communists, agrarians, and Social Democrats, together with independents; in Hungary it was drawn from the Communist, Social Democratic, Smallholders, and National Peasant parties.

The absence of significant parties representing other class interests and ideologies can be explained partly by the fate of those classes by 1945. For the most part the landed aristocracy had its estates seized in a crash program of land redistribution in 1945 (discussed below). Many members of middle and lower-middle classes in prewar Eastern Europe were Jews or ethnic Germans, and neither survived there in large numbers by 1945. Germans who did remain were generally disenfranchised, along with wartime collaborators. Members of the middle classes who were neither Jewish nor German were often either ruined or compromised by collaboration. The net effect of the war in Eastern Europe was to leave the peasantry as the only group that remained reasonably intact. The absence of conservative parties in some places was the result of deliberate policies. In Bulgaria an estimated 30,000 to 100,000 anti-Communists were killed, most by the militia but many also after trials for war crimes and collaboration. The result was the virtual disappearance of the right wing of Bulgaria's political spectrum.

Although there was a general transformation of left-center coalitions into one-party Communist states throughout Europe, there was no typical case. An example is Hungary, where it was quickly evident that the Communist Party would not achieve power by electoral means. In the Budapest municipal elections of October 1945 the combined Social Democrat–Communist list won 43 percent of the vote, and in national elections in November it attracted only 34 percent, compared with the 57 percent won by the centrist Smallholders Party. The Smallholders did not form a government in their own right, however, because of an all-party agreement before the election that the four-party coalition should remain in office no matter what the election result. Within the coalition, Communists occupied key posts, one being the Ministry of the Interior, which ran the security police.

Throughout 1946 and 1947, with the backing of the Soviet army, the Hungarian Communist Party engaged in "salami tactics," removing their opposition one slice at a time. Factions of the Smallholders Party were expelled from parliament after being accused of fascist tendencies, and there were allegations that the Smallholders and the Catholic Church were involved in anti-Soviet activities. Leaders of the Smallholders Party were seized by the secret police, and the prime minister was forced to resign while he was on vacation in Switzerland. Covert communists in the Smallholders and Social Democratic parties were appointed to office.

Before the next elections were held in 1947, the now-ascendant Communists enacted a law that removed 350,000 of the 5 million voters from the electoral lists. Even so, they attracted only 22 percent of the vote, a result suggesting that the election was either honest or defectively rigged. Their allies, including the Social Democrats, won 23 percent, giving the Communist-led bloc 203 of the 411 seats in parliament. Using various means, the Communists had several smaller parties dissolved, and by 1948 only the Social Democrats remained as a viable alternative to them. That year Social Democrats were coerced into a merger—really their absorption by the Communists—and a new Hungarian Workers' Party was formed. In 1949 new elections were held to give the Communist government an appearance of democratic legitimacy, and a new constitution drawn up to put the arrangement on a permanent basis.

The parallel process in Poland was somewhat more complicated. A "Lublin Committee" of Communists that acted as a government in exile during the war was recognized by the Soviet Union as Poland's provisional administration in January 1945, two days after Warsaw was liberated. In June a broader administration was formed, with a majority of Communists with other ministers from the Socialist, Democratic, Labor, and Peasant parties. Other key non-Communist leaders, including several Socialists, missed the election after they were abducted to the Soviet Union, tried, and jailed.

Opposition to the Polish Communists and Soviet occupation took armed form at the end of 1945, when as many as 35,000 anti-Communists, many former Home Army soldiers who had fought the Germans in the Warsaw uprising, took to the forests and marshes of eastern Poland. There were a number of serious clashes, and what looked like the beginning of civil war enabled the government to expand its security services and create a volunteer militia of 100,000 men.

The other major challenge to the Polish Communists came from a regenerated peasant movement. In 1946 the Peasants' Party was formed and, with 600,000 members, soon became the largest political grouping in Poland. It called for social reform, local autonomy, and observance of the terms of the Potsdam agreement, including elections by July 1946. Failing to persuade the Peasants' Party to join a common list (called the Democratic Bloc) that they dominated, the Communists set about rigging the election, which was finally held in January 1947. There was widespread intimidation, thousands of Peasants' Party supporters were arrested, and the party was denied full access to the radio. Just to make sure of the result, Peasants' Party candidates were disqualified in almost a quarter of the voting districts. The result of the election was that the Democratic Bloc, dominated by the Communists, won 80 percent of the vote. A new constitution was passed in February 1949, and a series of political transformations put in place. The Communist leader Wladislaw Gomulka announced that Polish workers needed only one party to represent them, and the Socialist and Communist parties (the latter was called the Workers' Party) were merged to form the Polish United Workers' Party.

Similar processes took place in Romania and Bulgaria, but Czechoslovakia was different. It had an established democratic tradition before being dismembered by Nazi Germany, and after the end of 1945 Soviet forces withdrew from its territory. The wartime leader in exile, Eduard Beneš, had signed a friendship treaty with the Soviet Union. On returning in 1945, Beneš announced the resumption of democratic government, along with extensive autonomy for the Slovaks (to preempt a resumption of Slovak separatism) and state control of major enterprises and services. A National Front coalition government was formed from the Czech and Slovak Communist parties, Social Democrats, National Socialists (who were not Nazis), the People's (Catholic) Party, and others. Communists held about half the posts, including the important ministries of the interior and defense. In elections in May 1946, they won 38 percent of the vote and became the largest single party in parliament.

From the spring of 1946, there was relative quiet as the work of reconstruction continued, but in July 1947 a crisis developed over Marshall aid. The government, including the Communist members, wanted to accept American assistance, but the Soviet Union objected. The Communists had already suffered some setbacks in the legislature, and the Soviet veto on aid cost them further support. An opinion poll suggested that they had the support of only 25 percent of voters. In order to reverse their declining fortunes, the Communists used their control of the police to intimidate smaller parties. In February 1948 "action committees" of Communist trade unionists were set up and armed, creating an instant militia of 15,000. In order to force Beneš's hand, the non-Communist ministers resigned, but instead of forming a new government without the Communists, Beneš agreed to a Communist administration. He had little choice: The Czechoslovak army could not be counted on to oppose the Communists, and the Soviet army had mobilized forces on Czechoslovakia's borders. The opposition was neutralized, and in May 1948 new elections gave a veneer of legality to Czechoslovakia's Communist regime.

At the same time that Communist parties throughout Eastern Europe repressed the opposition, they attempted to provide reasons for important sectors of the population, if not to support them, at least not to oppose them. The most important social group was the peasantry, who still comprised most of the population. Despite programs of agrarian reform put into place in the 1920s and 1930s, peasants were still hungry for land, and the Communists set about satisfying their demands. In Poland it was decreed that all estates of more than 100 hectares were to be subdivided into small plots of 2 or 3 hectares. The beneficiaries included not only the landless and those with very little land, but even peasants with quite substantial plots of 20 hectares. With the expansion westward of the Polish border and the expulsion of the ethnic German population, even more land became available for redistribution, as well as buildings, implements, and livestock in some cases.

In Hungary, land reform took place under the provisional government. Almost a third of the country's arable land, more than 3 million hectares, was divided among 642,000 families, providing each with about 5 hectares. Most of the beneficiaries were farm laborers or domestic servants, who owned either very little or no land at all, and by the time the redistribution was complete, more than 90 percent of Hungary's rural population owned land, even if in many cases it was insufficient to support a family.

Land reform was such an important step in appeasing peasants or rallying them to the new governments that in Bulgaria, where land redistribution had progressed much further before 1939, the postwar Communist leadership regretted not still having large estates it could break up. The creation of small landholders distanced the European

Communist regimes from their Soviet counterpart and its policy of collectivization, and created a class of small landowners with a tangible debt to the new regimes. At the same time, the subdivision of large estates broke the economic and political power of the traditional landed elites, such as the Hungarian magnates.

What was the relationship of the early Eastern European Communist regimes to Stalin's Soviet government? Many of the postwar Eastern European Communist leaders had spent the war in the Soviet Union and had been dispatched to their own countries specifically to take power afterward. But they proved to be not necessarily mere puppets, as they were often portrayed during the cold war. The extent to which the regimes acted or could act autonomously varied not only from country to country but from issue to issue. The Polish leader Wladislaw Gomulka had defeated the pro-Soviet wing of his party, which wanted to make Poland an integral part of the Soviet Union. He openly praised the Western Allies for their role in defeating Hitler, resisted Soviet pressure to collectivize agriculture, and argued against the trade bloc that the Soviet Union established in Eastern Europe.

There were, of course, Eastern European states that differed from those discussed above. One was Yugoslavia, where the Communist-dominated resistance army under Josip Tito was so effective that it expelled the Germans. In doing so, it avoided an occupation army and administration by the Allied Control Commission. It was only due to Soviet insistence that Yugoslavia went through the process of coalition government before becoming a one-party state. Stalin, concerned about the reaction of the Western Allies to a Communist state in Yugoslavia, persuaded Tito to add non-Communists to his government and even bring back the king.

The regime formed in 1945 consisted of three regents (a Serb, a Croat, and a Slovene) who took the king's place until a referendum was held on the monarchy. An apparently broad-based coalition of Communist and non-Communist partisans, Croatian and Serbian parties, and former members of parliament was formed. It widened the franchise to include women and lowered the voting age to eighteen. When an election for a constituent assembly was held in November 1945, however, there was only one list of candidates, Tito's, and it received 96 percent of the vote. The new assembly proclaimed a republic and made Yugoslavia a federal state composed of Serbia, Croatia, Slovenia, Bosnia-Herzegovina, Montenegro, and Macedonia.

Tito was by no means a puppet of Stalin, however. He established his own domestic and foreign policies, which did not coincide with Soviet policies. He pursued the idea of a Balkan federation with Albania and Bulgaria, and not only declined to force collectivization on Yugoslavia's peasants but allowed them to leave the cooperatives they had joined. When Tito refused to toe the Soviet line, Yugoslavia was expelled from the Soviet-led Communist movement in 1947. The justification was Yugoslavia's insistence on building socialism without the support of other Communist states, including the Soviet Union.

Finally, there were two cases in which Communist regimes were not installed in partly or temporarily Soviet-dominated states. In Finland, which was partly occupied by the Red Army, the constitution continued to function, but the Soviet Union seized territory in the south as well as in the north, where Finland lost nickel mines and its corridor to the Barents Sea. A full 12 percent of the population had to be relocated from the Soviet-annexed territory, putting great pressure on the Finnish economy. Finland also had to pay large reparations to the Soviet Union, and in 1947 was forced to agree to lease the Porkkala naval base, located on the Baltic Sea only twelve miles from Helsinki.

Austria was a special case. Absorbed into the German Reich by the 1938 Anschluss, it could be seen either as Hitler's first victim nation or as a willing accomplice in the war. Austrians were prominent in Nazi organizations: They included not only Hitler himself but also Ernst Kaltenbrunner, the head of security services after 1942, and many members of the SS. The Allies had agreed to a four-power occupation of Austria, but at first only Soviet forces, which had defeated the German army, were present. In April 1945, a provisional government was formed, with equal representation of the Communist, Socialist and Christian Social parties and under the leadership of Karl Renner, who had been the first chancellor of the Austrian republic in 1919. The Anschluss was annulled and Austria declared a "democratic republic" with the 1920 constitution as its interim framework. Six months later, the three Western powers moved their occupation forces in, and four zones of occupation were established. Vienna, located in the Soviet sector, was also partitioned among the Allies.

In November 1945, free elections were held, the first since 1930, although former Nazis and the thousands of Austrians in prison camps were not permitted to vote. The conservative Christian Socials, who had renamed themselves the People's Party, won almost 50 percent of the votes, the Socialists 45 percent, and the Communists a mere 5 percent. Renner was elected president. In deference to the occupying forces, a coalition government of People's and Socialist party representatives governed, along with one Communist minister, until 1947. Thereafter, although the Soviet occupation authorities treated the Austrian government in a generally hostile manner, they did not try to overturn it.

Like other Central and Eastern European states, Austria acted against Nazi collaborators, though only under strong pressure from the Allies. In all, some 525,000 people were affected, almost all men, so that the measures involved about one adult male in every three or four. As comprehensive as this was, the penalties were generally light—imprisonment and fines—and although former Nazis were disenfranchised in 1945, they were again permitted to vote in 1949.

In 1955, after repeated Soviet delays, a treaty was signed that ended Allied occupation of Austria. It provided for reparations in addition to what the Soviet Union had already taken, and stipulated that Austria was not to merge with Germany or allow a restoration of the Habsburg monarchy. In 1955 Austria declared its permanent neutrality, forswore future military alliances, and forbade the establishment of foreign military bases on its soil.

The Problem of Germany

In Germany the postwar conflict that divided Europe between the Soviet Union and the Western states was expressed in a single country. During the war itself, when the defeat of Germany was the prime goal of all the Allies, there was broad agreement on how Germany ought to be treated. It was to be demilitarized, de-Nazified, and made to pay for the war its policies had produced. There were even proposals that it should be deindustrialized and turned into a pastoral country, and broken into smaller states to prevent it from again disturbing the peace in Europe. By 1945, however, these last notions had been abandoned as unrealistic and even undesirable. Britain wanted a united Germany as a counterweight to the Soviet Union. The Soviet Union wanted to use German industry for its own reconstruction, for despite widespread damage less than a fifth of German industrial capacity had been destroyed.

The immediate plan, as the war ended, was that Germany would be occupied by the major Allies, with the United States, Britain, France, and the Soviet Union each having its own zone of occupation. The three Western zones contained 70 percent of Germany's 1946 territory, and 72 percent of its population. Berlin, which fell entirely within the Soviet zone, was similarly divided among the four Allies. A single body, the Allied Control Commission, composed of representatives of each state, would coordinate policies in each zone.

Although it soon became clear that the Soviet Union and the other Allies would pursue different political and economic objectives in Germany, they were generally at one in their determination to put Nazis and their accomplices on trial. In November 1945, a court was convened in Nuremberg. The city had been the site of the great Nazi rallies in the 1930s, and gave its name to the race laws Hitler announced there in 1935; ten years later it lay in the U.S. occupation zone.

The war crimes trials, of which the Nuremberg trial of the most prominent German Nazi leaders is the best known, compelled the Allies to innovate. The trials were held before an international panel of judges, each from a different legal tradition. The rules of procedure and evidence had to accommodate practices that differed widely. Not only was this kind of international tribunal unprecedented, but so were some of the crimes with which the defendants were charged. There were three categories of indictment: crimes against peace, which included preparing and carrying out a war of aggression; war crimes, which included murdering civilians and prisoners of war and the wanton destruction of property; and crimes against humanity, which encompassed the deportation, enslavement, and extermination of people for political, racial, and religious reasons.

Although some of the acts alleged in 1945 were offenses against conventions that governed the treatment of civilians and prisoners of war, others, like some of the crimes against humanity, did not appear in formal international law. One of the objections raised to the Nuremberg trials was whether anyone could justly be tried for an act that was not a crime when it was committed. There were other objections. One was that this was a victors' tribunal that focused only on the deeds of the losers. The defendants' lawyers attempted to bring to the court's attention acts committed by the Allies that might fall within the scope of the indictments: the bombing of German cities, the Soviet massacre of 15,000 Polish soldiers at Katyn (which Germany was charged with in the original indictment), and the treatment of civilians and German prisoners of war by Soviet occupation forces. The Soviet Union denied responsibility for the Katyn massacre (but it disappeared from the list of charges), and the court ruled that it was only the German government's policies that were on trial.

Despite these and other criticisms that might be made of the Nuremberg trials, they had a value and purpose that overrode their shortcomings in a strictly legal sense. They were a clear statement that policies such as the Nazis pursued were repugnant to international law and opinion. To have done nothing—to have allowed leading Nazis to resume normal lives after the horrors of the war, occupation, and the Holocaust—was simply unthinkable.

In the main Nuremberg trial, twenty-one former Nazi civilian and military leaders were arraigned, including Hermann Göring, Julius Streicher, Joachim von Ribbentrop, Albert Speer, and Wilhelm Keitel. Hitler's deputy, Martin Bormann, was tried in his absence, as he had escaped the Allied advance, while Hitler himself and Joseph Goebbels had committed suicide. Nazi organizations such as the SS, SA, SD, the Gestapo, and the Nazi Party itself were also charged at Nuremberg for the crimes committed by their members collectively. The evidence produced at the trial was almost entirely from the Nazis' own documents: interviews, memoranda, diaries, photographs, records of meetings, documentation of imprisonments, deportations, and mass killings. Eighteen of the defendants were convicted and three acquitted, and the Nazi organizations were declared to be criminal. Of the individuals convicted, eleven were sentenced to death and seven to prison terms ranging from ten years to life. The death sentences were carried out on all except

for Göring, who committed suicide. After the trial of principal Nazis, other trials were held in Nuremberg and elsewhere in Germany, but the number was relatively small. By 1960 some 10,000 Germans had been convicted and sentenced in the Soviet zone, and about the same number in courts administered by the Western Allies and by the Germans after the creation of sovereign German states in 1949.

There was also an extensive de-Nazification campaign to convince Germans that Nazism was wrong. A generation of Germans had grown up thinking that Hitler was a kind of god, and there was concern that even the German defeat might not have demonstrated otherwise. In Hitler's eyes, after all, the defeat only proved that he was right about the power of the Jewish-Communist conspiracy and the extent to which it had weakened the Aryan race. De-Nazification, which often involved purging the civil service and professions of those who had supported the Nazis, necessitated difficult assessments of motivation and commitment; it was never easy to determine whether an individual had joined a Nazi professional association by conviction or simply in order to keep a job. Other cases were more straightforward; membership of any Nazi organization deemed criminal was proof enough.

In the zones occupied by the Western Allies, those who had held specific offices in the Nazi government were removed from their positions and made to take menial jobs, although in some cases job titles and descriptions were demoted to satisfy the requirements. Even so, the result by 1946 was to reduce the availability of experienced personnel, and thereafter cases were examined on an individual basis. The three Western Allies applied different standards, with the British being most lenient and French least. There were clear injustices, as minor functionaries were punished and high-ranking Nazis exonerated. Most of those investigated claimed that they acted as they did reluctantly, under duress, and with no inner conviction.

Overall, the Soviet authorities were more assiduous in rooting out Nazis than their Western counterparts. They were particularly energetic in dismissing teachers with a Nazi past, less sweeping when it came to the medical profession because of the shortage of doctors. De-Nazification also provided an opportunity for the Soviet authorities to confiscate land belonging to members of the Junker class and expropriate the property of German industrialists who had done business with the Nazis, which was just about all of them. The campaign in the Soviet zone was to this extent an integral part of the restructuring of society in that part of Germany.

It was not only in the matter of de-Nazification that the occupying powers pursued divergent policies in 1945. All began to dismantle the German arms industry in their respective zones, for example, but France and the Soviet Union also began to seize other industrial equipment and facilities to help their own industrial reconstruction. Until May 1946, when the Americans put an end to it, Soviet troops also helped themselves to industrial facilities in the Western zones, as agreed at Potsdam. Britain, which had suffered

Opposite: Germans confront war crimes. In the top photograph, men and women brought by U.S. military police from Weimar to the concentration camp at Buchenwald are forced to look at a cart loaded with some of the bodies of prisoners found when the camp was liberated. The bottom photograph shows top German officials in the dock during the war crimes trials at Nuremberg. Left to right, back row: Dönitz, Raeder, Shirach, Saukel, Jodl, von Papen, Seyss-Inquart, Speer, von Neurath, and Fritsche. Left to right, front row: Göring, Hess, Ribbentrop, Keitel, Rosenberg, Frank, Frick, Streicher, Funk, and Schacht.

less material damage, and the United States, which had suffered none, opposed the weakening of German industry, not least because they believed that economic recovery was the best way of weakening the attraction of communism.

There were also divergences in the Soviet and Western Allies' political policies in their respective zones. The Soviet authorities announced in June 1945 that any anti-fascist party dedicated to democracy could be active in their zone. This enabled the German Communist Party, led by Walter Ulbricht, who was flown from Moscow to Berlin just as the German capital was being liberated, to play an active role in German reconstruction. Communists were placed in most key positions. The other powerful political force was the Social Democratic Party, but under pressure it "merged" with the Communists in 1946 to form the German Socialist Unity Party (SED), in which the Communists were dominant.

In the Western Allies' sectors, political parties were licensed from late 1945, but carefully vetted to ensure that they were committed to democracy; the SED was banned but the Communist Party permitted to function. The most important groupings were the new conservative Christian Democrats, soon dominated by Konrad Adenauer, the Social Democrats, and the conservative Free Democrats. As there had been during the Weimar Republic, there was also a multiplicity of small parties. The three Allies followed varying courses of political regeneration. The British and Americans adopted a paternalistic approach, gradually giving provincial assemblies control over such matters as housing and economic development. The French, on the other hand, continued to govern their smaller zone more directly. Occasionally democratization and de-Nazification clashed, as when a former Nazi mayor was reelected, and the Allied authorities were faced with the dilemma of letting the democratic choice stand or overturning it in the interests of democratization.

One of the most important aspects of reconstruction was the economy. In the Soviet zone, economic recovery was set back by the removal of perhaps a quarter of productive capacity, mainly plants that were dismantled and transported to the Soviet Union. The Soviet Union also imposed immense reparations burdens and occupation costs on their sector. Most of what remained, as well as banks and insurance companies, was taken into state ownership or turned into German-Soviet joint-stock companies in 1945–46, and by the end of 1948 private enterprise was responsible for about a third of industrial production. In the rural areas, some 7,000 large estates were seized from Junkers and former Nazis, the area being so immense that it comprised almost a third of the Soviet occupation zone. Some of the land was distributed in small parcels to farmers and the rest converted to state-owned farms.

In the zones administered by the Western Allies less infrastructure was seized as reparations, but there was concern that industry should not recover too quickly and exceed the level of other European economies. It was to be reduced to about half the 1938 capacity. There was, in general, less interference with the structures of economic ownership. There were few large estates that could have been subdivided, and although some large banks and industrial cartels were broken up into smaller companies, the concentration of ownership in German industry was hardly diluted. In 1947 the deterioration of Western-Soviet relations produced a change in policy. The British and Americans merged their zones of occupation into a single economic unit (the "Bizone") and began to stimulate economic recovery, allowing German industry to rise to three-quarters of its 1938 level.

Economic recovery necessitated a currency reform, and in 1948 a new deutsche mark was introduced in the Western zones that was much stronger than the currency circulating in the Soviet zone. In protest at the new currency, as well as the Western Allies' plan to draw up a new constitution for their now united zones, the Soviet Union withdrew from the Allied Control Commission. This signaled the end of Allied cooperation in institutional terms. It had never really existed in the economic or political spheres except, arguably, in the prosecution of war criminals at Nuremberg—and that might be said to have been unfinished business from the war that had united the Soviet Union and the Western Allies in the first place.

In March 1948, the Soviet authorities restricted rail traffic from the west to the Western Allies' sectors of Berlin, and in June they sealed off all land routes from the west across the Soviet zone to Berlin, claiming that closures were needed so that repairs could be made to the roads. They hoped that, faced with a besieged Berlin, the Western powers would abandon their control over their zones and permit the whole city to become part of the Soviet zone. The Western powers declined to read their lines in this script, however, and mounted an airlift of supplies through the air corridors over the Soviet zone that Western aircraft were permitted to use. The airlift lasted 324 days, as hundreds of aircraft made 277,000 flights to ferry food, supplies, and coal to Berlin's civilians and the Western occupying forces.

In May 1949 the Soviet Union lifted the blockade, but the event had far-reaching consequences. In the West, Berlin was portrayed as a symbolic flame of freedom burning in the dim light behind the iron curtain. The blockade also made it clear that there could no longer be cooperation between the Soviet Union and the West over the future of Germany. On their side, Britain, the United States, and France proceeded to establish a new German state from the territory in their zones of occupation. The Federal Republic of Germany, or West Germany as it was usually known, became a sovereign state in September 1949, with its capital in Bonn. The following month the Soviet Union responded by declaring its zone to be the German Democratic Republic (or East Germany). Berlin itself remained a separate political entity. When the notion of two Germanies became accepted as virtually normal, as did the division of Europe into two camps, the anomaly of Berlin was a reminder of the immediate postwar conflicts.

The Berlin blockade, 1948: a plane being loaded with supplies for the besieged city.

The Soviet Union After the War

The tasks of postwar reconstruction were nowhere more formidable than in the Soviet Union, which between 1941 and 1945 had suffered 20 million deaths and whose cities and countryside had been laid waste. On this desolate landscape Stalin planned not only to rebuild Soviet industry and agriculture but to surpass prewar levels so as to match the Soviet Union's economic strength to the great-power status it had gained from the war. The successes of wartime production showed Stalin what Soviet workers were capable of: Despite far worse conditions, over 40,000 aircraft were produced in 1944, four times the output in 1940. Stalin, who saw his country under siege as much by the West after 1945 as it had been by Germany before 1945, intended to give Soviet workers no respite from their labors.

Unlike Western Europe, reconstruction in the Soviet Union took place without massive American assistance. A United States offer of aid was declined, probably because it would have restricted Stalin's freedom of political action. It is not certain, however, if the Soviet Union would have received Marshall Plan assistance even if it had accepted, because the plan was sold to Congress as an anti-Communist measure. Stalin did accept United Nations aid to help recovery in the most devastated areas. There were also benefits from the industrial infrastructure, railroad equipment, and rolling stock seized as reparations from Germany and Eastern Europe. Although the precise contribution of reparations to Soviet reconstruction is debatable, it was less than expected. Some was damaged while being transported to the Soviet Union, and some was not easily usable once there without spare parts and specific expertise, even though foreigners were brought to train Soviet workers. As in the earlier Five-Year Plans, Stalin fell back on the labor and capital generated within the Soviet Union, although the war-depleted labor force was supplemented by forced labor from Eastern and Central Europe and from prisoners not repatriated after the war.

In political terms it was not reconstruction that was required—there was no question of changing the regime—but some adjustments. Internally there was anxiety about the extent of Western influence during the war, not only on Soviet soldiers who had liberated Central Europe, but also on soldiers and civilians who had had contacts with British and Americans in the Soviet Union itself, such as those bringing supplies to Archangel and Murmansk. The government had also relaxed its control on religion during the war to allow citizens to attend church services, and individuals had been permitted to cultivate private plots to help overcome food shortages. The regime had played a nationalist theme during the war, rather than an ideological one. Now it was time to curtail these dangerous tendencies.

Although victory might have legitimized the Soviet system in the eyes of more of its citizens, and might even have raised Stalin's prestige, it is also likely that Stalin's preeminent position was less secure after the war. New elites had been promoted during the conflict, and they often threatened the status of those who had gained power in the 1930s. All these trends tended to weaken Stalinist control and orthodoxy just at the time the Soviet Union was extending its authority over Eastern Europe and needed to enforce control in the newly annexed Baltic states and those parts of Czechoslovakia and Romania it had seized. From 1945 Stalin's regime began to reimpose rigid rules governing all aspects of Soviet political, economic, social, and cultural life.

In politics there were renewed purges of Communist Party officials, although on a much smaller scale than in the 1930s. Still, the entire party leadership in Leningrad was shot for treason, and the commander of the Soviet army, Marshal Zhukov, was removed from his post. The establishment of the state of Israel in 1948 appeared to give Soviet Jews an alternative focus of loyalty, and anti-Semitic measures were intensified. The arts and literature fell under strict censorship and were approved only insofar as they supported Stalin and the task of economic recovery.

Within the economy, emphasis was given to heavy industry and scientific research and development that supported the modernization of the Soviet armed forces. The military possessed 25,000 frontline tanks, and 19,000 aircraft, but there were dangers of obsolescence as the war had promoted advances in military technology. By 1948 long-range units had been added to the air force and the first of a series of MiG jet fighters was in production. A variety of guided missiles was being developed with the assistance of German scientists abducted after the war, and in 1949 the Soviet Union tested its first atom bomb.

Overall, however, the economy progressed against massive obstacles. Plants had to be converted from military to nonmilitary production, and the labor force had to be retrained. The armed forces were reduced by two-thirds in 1945 to provide industrial labor. Many workers relocated to their home regions, and others, such as older workers who had been drafted or had volunteered for war work, retired (or retired again). Diets and housing were poor, particularly in those regions that had been occupied. These conditions, aggravated by an understandable relaxation of discipline after four years of exhausting work, when vacations were suspended, led to a decline in industrial output by almost 17 percent between 1945 and 1946.

From 1946, however, production increased impressively. Despite the flooding and destruction of the Donets coal mines by retreating German armies, more coal was mined there in 1950 than had been in 1940. The Dnieper Dam, disabled in 1941 to deny it to the Germans, was operational again by 1947. There were even big improvements in the supply of some consumer goods like cotton and sugar, although overall the textile and footwear industries lagged behind. By 1950 the industrial side of the Soviet economy had rebounded.

Agriculture proved more problematic, for there were shortages of machinery, labor, fuel, seeds, and, in many places, housing. In 1945 and 1946 the area under cultivation was only three-quarters that of 1940. The 1945 harvest was 47 million tons, but in 1946 it fell to 40 million, thanks in part to a drought that year. The results were widespread food shortages and the continuation of rationing, and the situation was exacerbated by the government's policy of exporting grain to purchase foreign goods needed for industrial growth.

Discipline on collective farms was tightened, as private cultivation was restricted and emphasis given to delivering produce to the state. Additional burdens were placed on the collective farms; they were to plant forests, build canals, expand livestock herds, and increase dairy production. Many of these demands proved utterly unrealistic, although state procurements did increase. But because the prices paid by the state did not change in line with rising costs and consumer prices, the peasants' real incomes fell steadily. By 1950 it took a year's wage on a collective farm to purchase a suit, or twenty days' work to buy a bottle of vodka, which was probably more useful. Farmers avoided the cash economy and resorted to bartering goods and services.

Lack of capital investment, administrative confusion, the imposition of deterrent taxes, and shortages of all kinds led to persistent weaknesses in agricultural production. After the harvest disasters of 1945–46, grain output rose to 70 million tons in 1949 and 92 million tons in 1952, but even though that was a good year it was less than the 1940 harvest. The potato crop rose in 1948, but then declined into the early 1950s. The number of cows in the Soviet Union, 28 million in 1940, stagnated at 23–25 million between 1945 and 1952.

Living conditions in the immediate postwar period improved very slowly. Building domestic housing was given lower priority than industrial construction, and there was also emphasis on rebuilding some historic cities and provincial capitals. Food supplies were poor as well, and rationing at fixed prices remained a feature of Soviet life until 1947, although goods were available on the open market at much higher prices. In 1946, for example, a kilogram of beef cost 90 rubles on the ration and 140 rubles in commercial stores. The prices of rationed goods were raised, with wage supplements provided for the lowest paid. From 1949, however, general wage rates improved and prices fell, and there was a broad increase in real wages.

A currency reform in 1947 affected many people. All cash in the old currency could be exchanged for the new in the ratio of 1:10, although better rates were given on small savings accounts and on bonds. Two effects of the reform were to reduce the value of bonds (and thus the state's indebtedness) and wipe out 90 percent of the value of cash that had been saved privately rather than deposited in banks; this affected peasants in particular.

Pronatalism raised its head again. Not only had the Soviet Union lost massive numbers of people, but the marriage and birth rates had plummeted during the war as might be expected. In Moscow the birth rate fell from twenty-two to nine per thousand between 1941 and 1943. The government responded by encouragement and coercion. In 1944, as victory became certain, an edict removed the last traces of the liberal family laws of the Bolshevik period. Legal recognition was withdrawn from de facto marriages, and the notion of illegitimacy was reintroduced in respect of children born outside marriage. Divorce was made even more difficult to obtain, on the interesting assumption that forcing wives and husbands to stay married would lead to their having more children. Couples who produced fewer than three children suffered fiscal penalties, while those who produced large families were rewarded with generous benefits and state honors. The results were not impressive. In the early 1950s there were about 26 births per 1,000 population in the Soviet Union, well below the rates of 40 and above in the 1920s and the 35 to 40 births per 1,000 in the late 1930s. As ever, people declined to have children to order, but adjusted their family size to social and economic circumstances.

At the same time as women were urged to bear children for the state, they were expected to bear the burden of economic recovery. The massive male mortality and maintenance of a large standing army created a manpower shortage that womanpower had to fill. By 1945 women comprised 51 percent of workers in large-scale industrial enterprises (compared with 41 percent in 1941). In agriculture there was a massive gender imbalance, as 80 percent of workers on collective farms were women. Not only had millions of peasant men been killed during the war or imprisoned after it, but many soldiers who had acquired skills in the army took industrial employment rather than return to farming. Women's agricultural work was even more arduous than before the war because of the lack of tractors and other farm machinery.

Although the structural problems in the Soviet economy were worked out slowly, and even then imperfectly, the political structure began to change more quickly after March 1953, when Stalin died of a stroke. Shortly before his death, in January, it seemed that Stalin was planning another purge. A number of Jewish doctors were arrested amid allegations of a "doctors' plot" to kill high Soviet officials. It was a sign of change that they were freed after Stalin's death.

For the next four years, the Soviet Union was governed by a collective leadership as individuals jockeyed for dominance. One by one, contenders were elbowed aside, some with little ceremony. The head of the secret police, Lavrenti Beria, was arrested and executed in June 1953. The competition ended only in 1958, when Nikita Khrushchev, whose posts under Stalin included administering Ukraine and overseeing agriculture, became both head of the Communist Party and premier of the Soviet Union. Under Khrushchev, who remained in power until 1964, the Soviet Union remained a one-party state, but there was a distinct reduction in the repressive control that Stalin had exercised.

Economic and Social Reconstruction in Western Europe

The formidable challenges posed by Western European economies after the war were met by a variety of policies, most of which mixed state intervention with free enterprise. In Britain and France, as we have seen, the first postwar administrations carried out extensive programs of nationalization, but for the most part they affected only essential services and products. The British Labour government nationalized coal mines and the iron and steel industries, railroads, trucking, electricity, gas, and the Bank of England. In some of these cases nationalization meant that state corporations were established to run the enterprises, whereas in other cases companies continued to operate under the same names and management as before even though they were owned by the state and were, in the final analysis, answerable to it as to a majority shareholder.

In the immediate postwar period the British economy foundered. In order to finance growth and the nationalization program the government borrowed heavily, but the markets for British exports were weak, and within two years of the war's end Britain faced a major financial crisis. It was aggravated by a severe winter that produced coal shortages not only for generating power but for industry as well. A rash of strikes reduced coal production further, and as production fell and the balance of payments worsened, the government was forced to borrow from the United States and devalue the pound by almost a third against the dollar. In order to reduce domestic demand and stimulate exports, a series of new taxes was imposed and wartime rationing was extended.

Over the next three years, however, the economy picked up steam. By 1948 industrial production was restored to its prewar level, and it grew another quarter by 1950. There was a period of decline in the early 1950s, but by 1955 the economy was probably healthier than at any time since the war.

The financial problems of the 1940s prevented the Labour government from moving ahead as rapidly as it wanted with the process of social reconstruction. Important innovations like the National Health Service (NHS) proved expensive, particularly after doctors demanded and won a fee increase in 1956. Within two or three years, exceptions were being made to the "free" services offered by the NHS. Charges were introduced for glasses and false teeth, and patients had to pay a shilling toward the cost of each prescription. Even though such levies contributed only a small proportion of the costs of the NHS, and the mass of Britons had better medical care than ever before, the gradual imposition of charges was resented as an infringement of what was quickly perceived as a right to free health services.

The French government also nationalized key industries as the beginning of its economic strategy, including electricity, gas, coal mines, and some banks. The state also took control of any enterprise that had collaborated with the Nazis. Reflecting the growing popularity of long-range planning in Western democratic states, the French established a Plan for Modernization and Equipment to assess France's human and material resources and set goals for economic development. Rather than take direct control of the economy, the French government offered incentives in the form of tax concessions, loans at preferential rates, and subsidies to enterprises that worked within the economic plan.

The first plan, which ran from 1947 to 1952, stressed heavy industry, fuel, tractors, and transport, all fundamental to growth. French industry had recovered to its prewar level by 1947, and agriculture by 1948, so that any increases were real advances, not merely a recapturing of historic levels of productivity. Improvements in productivity were made possible by longer workweeks and the modernization of plants and equipment, especially in enterprises destroyed during the war, which were rebuilt from scratch with state-of-the-art technology. The whole recovery was funded by United States aid and capital generated at home, and guided by the state planning commission. By 1952 the targets of the first plan were almost met, and France's GNP was 14 percent higher than in 1938. Although its industrial growth rate was lower than those of Germany, Italy, and Austria, these countries had suffered much more war-related damage and their economies started from lower levels, allowing higher initial growth rates. The French recovery was better than those of Britain, Belgium, and even Sweden.

In Italy the means of economic recovery differed from France's and Britain's, not least because during the various economic crises of the 1920s, and especially during the Great Depression, the state IRI agency (Institute for Industrial Reconstruction) had invested in the economy to prevent unemployment from rising. By 1945, for example, the IRI controlled a third of the steel industry, three-quarters of cast-iron output, and most shipping. In the late 1940s the IRI carried out a thorough modernization of Italy's steel industry and in the 1950s played a key role in the major public works program that underlay more general economic recovery.

In the short term, there were serious economic problems. The first years of peace were accompanied by high inflation; prices rose 150 percent between 1945 and 1947, and the value of the lira against the dollar fell by more than a third. Poor harvests in 1945 and 1947 led to food shortages and higher prices, conditions that raised support for the Communist Party. Under these conditions the Christian Democratic government, which had adopted a laissez-faire policy, intervened to stabilize the economy. Helped by improved harvests from 1948 on, prices began to fall. As the lira stabilized, industrial production began to rise and unemployment declined. By 1949 industrial output exceeded the prewar level. In the first two-thirds of the next decade (1950–57), the economy grew quickly, not as fast as Germany's but faster than in Britain and France.

A great deal of the success of Italy's export economy in the 1950s rested on low-paid labor. Wages were depressed by the ready availability of workers, as unemployment remained high in Italy when it began to fall elsewhere. In addition, trade unions had been weakened in the late 1940s and were unable to maintain wage rates, and there was also a large supply of cheap labor in the southern agricultural regions of the country.

Some effort was made to promote the development of the south, which contained a third of the population but produced only a fifth of Italy's GNP. In 1950 a Fund for the South was set up to provide investment in agriculture, industry, tourism, communications, and sanitation. In addition, the government enacted a modest land reform program, distributing 40,000 hectares in Calabria and breaking up some large estates elsewhere. In the first five years (1950–55), the Fund for the South provided the basis for agricultural reform by aiding projects like land reclamation. The general effect, however, was to reinforce the differences between north and south, rather than to reduce them.

The other major economy to be considered is the Federal Republic of Germany. West Germany, as it was more commonly known, was now treated as part of Western

Austerity in Italy after the war. In 1947 a British magazine carried a story on the Renzi family, all but one of whom was unemployed. The family was described as living on macaroni, paprika, and a few vegetables.

Europe; the division of the continent into two blocs in the cold war led to the virtual disappearance of Central Europe as a political notion. Germany's economy is generally held up as the success story of postwar Europe, an "economic miracle" that rose from ashes to riches. Ironically, much of the physical devastation that Germany had suffered, together with the hordes of ethnic Germans and other refugees that crowded its cities, proved to be the basis of the country's recovery. A greater proportion of German industry than in France and Italy had been destroyed, and much of what survived the war was seized as reparations, some by France and most by the Soviet Union. To this extent German industry had no choice but to rebuild from the ground up, and was able to install the most modern technologies and plant layouts. As for the vast number of refugees, they were initially a great burden on social services and housing budgets, but they soon constituted a large pool of labor for German industry. A steady wave of refugees from East Germany and other parts of Eastern Europe in the 1950s provided additional workers, and the fact that many were skilled workers and professionals helped to reduce education and training costs.

United States aid, in the form of investment capital and trade credits, helped the German economy, but it is important to note that the economy had begun to recover before assistance arrived. Moreover, it is quite likely that West Germany paid more in reparations and occupation costs than it received in assistance. The presence of American aid was important psychologically, too, in encouraging domestic investment in what seemed to be an American-backed economy. Unlike its major Western counterparts, West Germany's Christian Democrat government, led by Konrad Adenauer, shied away from overt state intervention as too reminiscent of the Nazi period. In principle, freer rein was to be given to market forces, with the state providing a context favorable to productivity without controlling the economy. Among the limited roles the state was to play was the provision of social services to protect the vulnerable from unrestricted market forces. In fact, however, the West German government intervened in the economy in significant ways. It acted to thwart attempts to restore the prewar German system of cartels, in which supposedly rival companies cooperated in setting production and prices. It also forced large enterprises to accept employee participation in their management through supervisory boards.

Industrial growth in West Germany was impressive. The index of industrial production, set at 100 in 1950, was 61 in 1948 and 165 in 1954. Coal production rose fourfold between 1945 and 1955, steel output more than eightfold between 1946 and 1955, and private automobiles from 104,000 in 1949 to 762,000 in 1955. The value of exports rose from 8.4 billion marks in 1950 to 25.7 billion in 1955.

As it did elsewhere in Europe, broad measures of economic recovery and aggregate prosperity in West Germany conceal the fact that broad sections of the population did not fare so well. The wages of self-employed in nonagricultural enterprises had incomes well above wage earners and farmers. Unemployment was high throughout most of the 1950s; there were 1.6 million jobless (10 percent of the workforce) in 1950, 930,000 (5 percent) in 1955. Those without work lived on barely adequate benefits, as did war widows and old-age pensioners. In contrast, many middle-class Germans who had been public employees under the Nazi regime and who had lost their jobs in the de-Nazification process, had their employment rights and pensions restored in 1951.

Throughout Western Europe there was also concern for social renewal after the war, and policies were adopted to improve living conditions, health, housing, and education. Demands for some of these facilities, like housing, reflected the material damage done during the war, but in some cases they were reinforced by a significant increase in births.

The persistent concern about population was reawakened in France as the war ended, when in 1945 General de Gaulle pleaded with his compatriots to produce "in ten years, twelve million beautiful babies." The French had heard and ignored such pleas before, and there is no evidence that de Gaulle was actually instrumental in persuading them to reproduce; the birth rate shot up, but so it did in a number of countries as a postwar baby boom got under way. Marriage and birth rates in France rose after 1945 and even though they dipped a little in the 1950s were still significantly above the prewar levels. French women and men failed to meet de Gaulle's target, but more than 8 million children were born between 1945 and 1955. Most of this growth was a result not of new marriages but of couples deciding to have an additional child. Britain followed the same pattern—a sharp increase in births from 1946 to 1948 as servicemen returned home, then a decline to a lower level that was still higher than in the 1930s. The British birth rate began to rise again in the late 1950s.

In other countries there was no evidence of a baby boom right after the war. Germany's birth rate remained fairly constant until the late 1950s, while in Italy the prewar decline persisted until the early 1960s, when there was a slight rally. Among the smaller Western European countries, Belgium, Denmark, and the Netherlands experienced high postwar birth rates with reduced but historically high levels sustained throughout the 1950s.

If the increase in marriage and births pleased the authorities in a number of states, they were alarmed by a simultaneous rise in divorces. Throughout Western Europe, countries involved in the war showed a sudden rise in divorces, peaking between 1945 and 1947. In contrast, there was little or no change in divorce rates of nonbelligerent countries like Sweden, Switzerland, and Portugal. The reasons for increased divorces after the Second World War are probably similar to those that explained the rise in divorces between 1919 and 1921: wartime adultery, the effects of separation and the difficulties of adjustment to married life, and the inherent instability of marriages contracted just before or during the war. Eleven of every 1,000 marriages formed in England between 1942 and mid-1943 ended in divorce within five years, four times the frequency for marriages contracted in 1946–47. Two percent of all wartime marriages ended in divorce within seven years, a very high rate for the time. As had been the case after the First World War, there was a particular increase in divorces based on the wife's adultery. Again, there is no reason to suppose that married women were more adulterous than their husbands. Rather, they were more likely to be caught and less likely to be forgiven than their husbands.

Demographic trends promoted the notion of a "crisis" in the family in several countries. A 1949 royal commission on population in Britain expressed alarm that the baby boom would collapse and bring population decline in its wake. Strengthening families and support services was proposed as a means of preventing it. In Germany there was widespread concern in 1945 because of the sexual imbalance of the population; the 1946 census showed 126 females for every 100 males, while in Berlin it was 146:100. From the perspective of those who wanted to encourage marriage, the situation was even worse when only those in marriageable categories were considered: There were 224 women for every 100 men.

The growing population reinforced the need for more housing, educational facilities, and social services. In France a target of half a million new dwelling units by 1950 was set, but only 175,000 were actually built. In the 1950s, however, the rate of construction rose and the target of the second economic plan (1954–57) was exceeded. The number of children in French primary schools rose from 4.8 to 5.9 million between 1951 and 1955 as the first baby boomers started their formal education.

The French government also provided for growing consumer demand. One indicator, automobile ownership, rose steadily, fueled in part by the mass production from 1948 of the light and fragile-looking Citroën 2CV. The number of private automobiles on the road in France rose from 975,000 in 1945 to 1.7 million in 1950, then to 3.1 million in 1955. In West Germany automobile ownership tripled between 1950 and 1955; in Great Britain it increased by only 50 percent.

Economic and Social Reconstruction in Eastern Europe

Economic reconstruction in Eastern Europe was a massive task. Cities and towns were destroyed and damaged, and with them factories, plants, and mines, and transport infrastructure like bridges, roads, and railroads. Hungary can serve as an example, even if it is not typical. All the bridges over the Danube and Tisza Rivers were destroyed, as were all ships used on the Danube, a third of the railroad installations, and 80 percent of rolling stock. Half the country's factories were destroyed, and in mid-1945 industrial production was about 30 percent of the prewar level.

Destruction of this scale was to be found to a lesser or greater extent throughout Eastern Europe. The region had all the appearance of having gone through a phase of deindustrialization, forcing people back to the land and making agrarian reform that much more important. But the new regimes had no intention of letting their countries slide back to reliance on agriculture, and set about restoring as much industry as possible. The Hungarian communist leader vowed to pull his country out of agrarian backwardness and make it a country "of iron and steel."

They were both urged on and hampered in this enterprise by Soviet policy, which gave priority to industrial recovery in the Soviet Union. In Hungary this entailed the dismantling of factories and plants and their transportation to the Soviet Union. Hungary agreed to pay reparations that amounted to more than a quarter of total expenditure in 1946, and 18 percent in 1947. Goods sent to the Soviet Union as reparations accounted for 71 percent of Hungary's total exports, giving the country a narrow range of movement within which to sustain its own economic recovery. The Soviet Union was also short of labor because of the carnage of the war and its policy of occupying much of Eastern Europe, and large numbers of Eastern Europeans were deported to perform forced labor in the Soviet Union.

As the flow of reparations slowed in 1949, the Soviet Union locked the Eastern European economies into trading relationships by creating the Council for Mutual Economic Assistance (Comecon). Mutual the trade might have been, but it was imbalanced. Under this arrangement the Eastern European states sold their goods to the Soviet Union at favorable prices below world levels, and in turn the Soviet Union sold goods to them at high prices. The result was to deprive the Eastern European economies of much of the export income they might have earned on the world market, and to slow their development. On the other hand, the Soviet Union did provide its partners with cheap oil and natural gas from its own reserves.

To the extent that national governments had an economy to administer, they put in place programs of nationalization: mines and power stations in Hungary; most banks and all businesses that employed more than fifty workers in Poland; the coal, rubber, fur, alcohol, soft drink industries in Bulgaria; all enterprises "necessary to the public interest" in Czechoslovakia.

All the Communist states of Eastern Europe embarked on crash programs of industrialization. In the late 1940s they adopted three-year economic plans to build infrastructure, and from about 1950 inaugurated five- or six-year plans to extend industrial production. The initial growth rates in some countries were impressive, although they began from very low levels and could be expected to achieve high growth rates in the first years. Under Poland's three-year plan (1946–49), annual growth rates of 37, 39, and 22 percent were achieved.

The benefits of industrialization were mixed, however. Such was the rush to build plants and factories that little time was given to overall planning, and even less attention was paid to environmental impact than in Western Europe. Despite the notion that the Communist states formed an economic bloc, planning was done on a national basis, so that each country forged ahead with massive steel mills. There was duplication of effort within individual countries, plants were constructed without proper regard to transportation facilities, and manufacturing capacity in some sectors outstripped the supply of raw materials. As a result many plants and factories stood idle or underproduced.

The emphasis on heavy industry created imbalances within economies, which were too often starved of consumer goods. In Poland the first plan achieved a good balance, and by 1949 the real incomes of industrial workers had increased by 33 percent, the standard of living was rising, and rationing was discontinued. But the six-year plan, begun in 1950, undid all the progress. Because of pressure from the Soviet Union to increase heavy industrial output, less attention was given to consumer goods. In addition, the obvious benefits of industrial work led a million peasants to migrate to the towns between 1950 and 1953, swelling the labor force to the point that industry absorbed perhaps 500,000 more workers than it needed. The new migrants placed immense burdens on state budgets for housing and food, needs that peasants satisfied for themselves in the country. The sudden increase in wage earners, together with the decline of consumer production, led to price inflation, and the real income of workers, which had risen so steadily up to 1949, began to decline from 1950. To make things worse, rationing was reintroduced in 1951. Just as conditions were beginning to improve in the West, Eastern Europeans were still mired in austerity.

If workers failed to derive benefits from industrialization, peasants in several countries were deprived of what they had gained from Communist ascendancy after the war. The initial distribution of land had served to pacify small farmers, but small-scale farming was inefficient. It could not take advantage of mechanization and produce the amount of food needed to sustain increasingly industrial and urban populations. A number of regimes began campaigns to collectivize agriculture on the Soviet model, although others, like Poland, declined to do so.

In Hungary peasants were encouraged to join cooperatives. They would at first keep their private land but would progressively turn it over to the cooperative (along with livestock) until all land was held collectively, apart from a small plot of up to half a hectare that each family could keep. Peasants, wedded to their farms, resisted the idea, and from 1950 the government began to use coercion. Even so, by 1953 only 300,000 families had entered cooperatives. Many peasants chose instead to leave the country and enter the industrial workforce and the resulting labor shortage, combined with other factors, had a disastrous effect on Hungarian agriculture. From having been an exporter of agricultural products, Hungary began importing food to satisfy domestic demand.

As we can see, economic reforms implied changes in Eastern Europe's social structure, but some of the modifications that the Communists desired had already been accomplished by the end of the war. The Polish middle class—professionals, managers, and military officers—had been effectively wiped out by the German or Soviet authorities. Where a middle class did survive, its members came under increasing pressure as "class enemies" in wide-ranging social purges between 1949 and 1953. The scope and intensity of repression varied greatly from country to country; it was relatively light in East Germany and Poland, severe in Hungary and Czechoslovakia. In Hungary it is estimated that 700,000 people had been arrested by 1953. Of that number, almost 100,000 were convicted of being spies or saboteurs, and of those some 5,000 were executed.

Although these purges affected people of all social groups, they fastened on those who could be expected to be enemies of the regimes: better-off peasants, professionals, managers, members of the clergy. By 1953 there were an estimated 8,000 monks and nuns in prison camps in Czechoslovakia. In 1951 some 38,000 middle-class citizens of Budapest, including 14,000 Jews, had their property confiscated and were forced to move to the country and work as agricultural laborers. Some 30,000 middle-class people from other parts of the country might have been relocated in this way, as the regime killed two birds with one stone: destroying the middle classes and providing much-needed agricultural labor.

Not only did the repression have immediate effects on those concerned and their families, but it had far-reaching implications. Tens of thousands of managers, administrators, professionals, trade union officials, and civil servants were removed from their jobs. They were replaced by younger people, often untrained and certainly inexperienced. Not only did they often prove less efficient than those they replaced, but their youth ensured that they would hold their positions for decades. The longer-term result was a blockage in the employment and promotion prospects of later generations, which contributed to their alienation from the Communist system.

The purges also struck the ruling Communist parties themselves, particularly individuals identified as being too nationalist in outlook. It is estimated that between a quarter and a third of party members throughout Eastern Europe were expelled by 1953. Expulsion often meant losing positions in the state service. The purges extended to the highest ranks of Communist parties and governments, and across the region ministers and party leaders (especially Jews) were demoted, imprisoned, or executed.

The churches came in for particular attention before and during the repression of the early 1950s, especially the influential Catholic Church, which was believed to have immense power over Eastern Europeans. From the very beginning there was a running battle involving the Hungarian church, led by Cardinal Mindszenty, who denounced the "Marxist evil" and urged Hungarians not to support the Communists. After the Communists took sole power, the state took control of all religious schools, including 3,000 Catholic institutions. When Mindszenty ordered all 2,500 priests and nuns in the schools to stop teaching immediately, which would have caused chaos in the educational system, he was arrested, tried for crimes against the state, and sentenced to life imprisonment. In 1950 the state seized most religious houses and expelled 12,000 monks and nuns, and later tried Catholic and Protestant bishops and sentenced them to long prison terms.

The Bulgarian regime was equally forceful and had effectively destroyed the Catholic Church by 1952 when it tried a bishop and twenty-seven priests on charges of spying for the Vatican. The Orthodox Church, which had been more docile, was brought under secure control by more subtle means. In Orthodox ecclesiastical terms, Bulgaria was a province of the church in Turkey, but in 1951 its status was raised to that of a patriarchate, making it independent of the church in Turkey and more easily controlled by the Bulgarian regime. Again, the Polish government was notably moderate in its church policy, a realistic approach given the prestige of the Catholic Church as a nationalist force in Poland. Although the 1925 concordat was canceled, the church was initially permitted to retain its property, and religious instruction was retained in schools. The Communist president even took a religious oath when he assumed office.

The Eastern European regimes also focused attention on ethnic minorities. This was less an issue than in the past, because the work of the Nazis, together with mass migrations and expulsions after the war, had created national populations that were more ethnically homogeneous than ever. Czechoslovakia and other states had expelled almost all their Germans, but some other minorities were no more wanted. In the early 1950s Bulgaria deported more than 160,000 Turks, all reported to be in appalling physical condition, across the border into Turkey.

Most of what remained of Eastern Europe's Jewish population after the war had migrated. Of the almost 3.3 million Jews who lived in Poland before the war, only 80,000 survived by the end. Of the Jews left in Bulgaria in 1946, 90 percent had left within ten years. Perhaps half a million Sinti and Roma (Gypsies) lived in postwar Eastern Europe, where they were subjected to various policies. The Polish and Czechoslovakian authorities attempted a campaign of assimilation that included offers of housing, schooling for children, and cooperative workshops based on traditional skills like coppersmithing. In Hungary, where there was concern at the growing Sinti and Roma population, various forms of discrimination were practiced, while in Bulgaria they were included in the population expulsions to Turkey in the early 1950s.

Integration and Division, 1948–55

After 1945 it is even less possible to discuss Europe in isolation from the rest of the world. Non-European regions had always impinged on Europe in one way or another, whether in the imperial ambitions of European states, the importance of non-European markets, or the assistance received from outside Europe in time of war. But in 1945 the United States was the world's strongest economic and military power, and within three years of the end of the war its government had committed the United States to an active role in world politics, reversing the isolationist policies it had pursued for most of the first half of the twentieth century. The unprecedented existence of a dominant global power that was not European had a profound effect on Europe.

The imposition of a Communist government in Czechoslovakia and the 1948–49 Berlin blockade accelerated both the deterioration of relations between the West and the Soviet Union and the desire of some European governments to establish arrangements for collective defense and security. Britain and France signed a treaty in 1947, and they were joined the following year by Belgium, the Netherlands and Luxembourg, but a much broader defense pact was set up in 1949 to encompass both European and non-European nations. The North Atlantic Treaty Organization (NATO) included the United States, Canada, Britain, France, the Benelux states, Norway, Denmark, Iceland, Italy, and Portugal. Greece and Turkey joined in 1951.

The NATO charter stipulated that an attack on any one member, whether in Europe, North Africa, or North America, would be tantamount to an attack on all. The member states agreed to integrate their armed forces, and a NATO command was established in Paris, with U.S. General Dwight Eisenhower as its first commander. The NATO charter also established political and cultural goals, aiming to bring greater cooperation within the North Atlantic region and to foster what it called "the freedom, common heritage, and civilization" of the peoples of the region. Its prime purpose, however, was military and it was designed specifically to confront the Soviet Union.

By 1951, when Turkey and Greece joined NATO, the map of its membership resembled wide open jaws (with Norway and Turkey at their extremes) ready to snap shut and swallow Eastern Europe and the Soviet Union. Soviet policy was not simply reactive to that of the West, but the creation of NATO confirmed the long-held view that the West aimed to destroy the Soviet Union. That perception had already been reinforced by the enunciation of the "Truman Doctrine" by U.S. President Harry Truman in 1947, committing the United States to support anti-communist forces anywhere in the world.

The Soviet Union and its Eastern European partners were not becoming isolated, however. In 1949 following a long civil war, the Communist Party led by Mao Zedong came to power in China, and established the People's Republic of China. The anti-Communist forces under General Chiang Kai-shek took refuge on the island of Taiwan. China formed an alliance with the Soviet Union, Taiwan with the United States. In 1950 the Korean War provided another site for the cold war to heat up. The North Koreans had the military support of China and the Soviet Union, the South Koreans of the Western countries led by the United States. After three years of fighting, an armistice was reached and the peninsula was divided at the 40th parallel. A simultaneous nationalist struggle for independence against the French in Vietnam was soon perceived by the United States as yet another Communist revolution. French forces were defeated in a major battle at Dien Bien Phu in 1954, and by 1955 the United States was beginning to supply one side, the Soviet Union and China the other.

As the cold war deepened, a movement for broader European cooperation developed. Originally a reflection of the desire to prevent another European conflict, the idea of an economic and political union in Europe was soon reinforced by the desire to present a common front to the Soviet-dominated bloc. It is telling that three of the prime movers of what was to become the European unity movement came from parts of Europe ravaged in both wars. Konrad Adenauer, West Germany's first chancellor, came from the Rhineland; Robert Schuman, the French foreign minister, was from Lorraine (and had

MAP 9.2 Political division of Europe after 1955 between NATO and Warsaw Pact members.

actually fought in the German army in the First World War); Henri Spaak was prime minister of Belgium, a country that had been invaded twice in thirty years.

The first step toward European unity was the creation of the Council of Europe in 1949, located appropriately in the city of Strasbourg in Alsace. The council was composed of delegations from national parliaments, at first from France, Germany, Britain, Luxembourg, and Iceland, later from sixteen states. But the council was literally a "parliament," a place where talking went on, and there was resistance, from Britain especially, to the notion that it ought to be given any legislative powers. For it to have the power to pass binding laws would, of course, have diminished the authority of national parliaments. This tension, pitting national sovereignty (which so many nations had fought to gain) against the authority of a supranational body, lay at the heart of debates over European unity for the rest of the century.

In order to circumvent national objections to any substantial form of integration, the French and West German governments agreed in 1950 to coordinate all coal and steel production in their countries. This was a major initiative, not only insofar as two countries surrendered sovereignty over such sensitive sectors of any industrial economy but also because of the two countries involved. With each dependent upon the other, war between France and Germany would become very difficult, if not the impossibility much vaunted at the time.

In 1951 the broader-based European Coal and Steel Community (ECSC) was set up, drawing in France, Germany, Italy, and the Benelux countries. It had the power to regulate prices and promote or discourage investment so that the most efficient use of resources was made to the benefit of all. Although it had limited scope, the ECSC provided a model for supranational economic unification and regulation, and was a critical stage in the later development of the European Economic Community.

One aspect of these developments deserves particular note, and that is the role played by West Germany. Unlike its Weimar predecessor, the Federal Republic of Germany was not treated as a pariah state after the war. Not only had politicians learned something from the past, but they needed Germany in what was believed to be the coming conflict with the Soviet Union. There were, of course, reservations about reintegrating Germany so quickly, especially on the part of the French. When a supranational European armed force was proposed, it raised questions about German participation and, more to the point, command. Although the proposal was supported in several European countries, it was rejected by the French parliament in 1954. That year, however, West Germany was admitted as a full member of NATO. Although limited in the kind of arms it was to possess (nuclear and biological weapons were forbidden), West Germany was playing an important political and military role in Europe within ten years of the devastating defeat of the Nazi Reich.

The institutional framework of the cold war was completed in 1955 when the Soviet Union and its partners in Eastern Europe formed their answer to West Germany's entry to NATO, the Warsaw Pact. It provided for a unified military command (based in Moscow) and obliged all members to assist one another in the event of an attack on any one or more of them in Europe.

Conclusion

The breakdown of the alliance between the Western Allies and the Soviet Union by the end of the war, and the division of Europe into two political blocs by 1948, created the political context of Europe for more than forty years. Between the late 1940s and 1989, for almost half the twentieth century, it was common and sensible to think of two Europes, west and east. The differences between them, in broad political, economic, and social policies, were institutionalized to an extent they had not been during the first half of the century.

In some respects there were continuities in the distinctions between east and west. For example, Eastern Europe, as a whole, had never embraced democratic institutions to the extent that Western Europe had. But the postwar conditions, in which the Soviet Union was able to absorb some of Eastern Europe and dominate most of the rest, were a new phenomenon.

The division of Europe into two hostile political spheres can too easily divert our attention from trends that were, if not countervailing, yet not entirely congruent. The development of the cold war did not see Western European populations rush to embrace conservative political parties out of fear of the Communists to the east. Rather, the whole of Europe tilted toward the left in political terms in the immediate postwar period, partly in reaction to the actions and inactions of right-wing parties in the 1930s and early 1940s.

In part, however, postwar political preferences (soon eliminated in Eastern Europe) also reflected widespread perceptions of the best ways to achieve the recovery that all economies and societies sought following the devastation of the war. Different states adopted different means of rebuilding their economies, creating social order, and encouraging population growth, means that reflected their ideological aims. Europeans of all social classes found themselves affected, directly or indirectly, by the broad political division that descended over Europe.

· 10 ·
Prosperity and Change,
1953–1970

Introduction

Within ten years, the meeting of the armies of the Soviet Union and its Western Allies in 1945 had turned into what appeared a permanent division of Europe. The core Western European states and the Soviet-dominated countries of Eastern Europe formed respective military, economic, and political organizations. Bearing in mind the variations within each region, each half of Europe went its own way, politically, socially, and economically. For the most part, Western European countries were liberal democracies with economies that mixed the free market with state activity. In Eastern Europe, in contrast, the dominant Communist parties repressed their opponents and extended the authority of the state in the social and economic spheres.

There were, nonetheless, similarities. This was generally a period of rising prosperity throughout Europe, and people everywhere had better diets and living conditions by 1970 than they had had in the early 1950s. To be sure, there was a great difference between East and West in terms of the absolute levels of prosperity achieved, but there were also variations within them. Standards of living in the least well-off parts of Western Europe, such as Portugal, were little different from the better-off parts of Eastern Europe, such as Hungary and Czechoslovakia. The overall disparity of wealth between East and West was, moreover, a historical continuity, not simply a product of this period: For centuries, Western Europeans had enjoyed a higher standard of living and a more equitable distribution of resources.

In political terms, too, there were differences between East and West within a broad trend of reform. Most Western European states pursued policies that reinforced liberal and socially progressive trends. Liberal law reforms affected issues such as racism, homosexuality, abortion, divorce, and censorship. In the Soviet Union and Eastern Europe, the end of the Stalinist era introduced a period of relaxation of repression and censorship. As in the West, there was concern that reform should not go too far or too fast, and when reform movements in Eastern Europe threatened basic principles of Soviet policy, they were harshly repressed.

It is both misleading and useful to compare the pressures for change in Western and Eastern Europe. The political, social, and economic contexts in the two Europes were entirely different, and yet similar issues of state control, individual rights, law reform, and the status of the family arose in both. Coincidentally, protest movements came to a peak in both Paris and Prague in 1968; in both cases students were prominent, and in both the authorities—domestic in France, external in Czechoslovakia—repressed the revolt. To say that each of the two Europes went its own way in this period does not mean that they necessarily went in entirely different directions.

Politics and Economies in Western Europe, 1955–65

The Fourth French Republic, which oversaw France's recovery from the war, collapsed after only twelve years. The reasons included economic problems and a series of setbacks in colonial policies, but an overriding weakness was the instability of governments. The system of proportional representation and the distribution of votes among several parties prevented any one party from forming a majority government, and ad hoc coalitions had a short life span. A specific problem for centrists was that the Communist Party kept winning the single largest share of the vote; determination to keep the Communists out of power, and the refusal of the Communists to work with the Socialists, meant that administrations had to be put together from several groupings, each with a small share of the vote.

In the 1956 elections the Communist Party won the support of 26 percent of the voters, the Socialists 16 percent, Radicals and their partners 14 percent, the MRP (Christian Democrats) 11 percent, and various smaller conservative parties 17 percent. When General Charles de Gaulle, France's leader after the liberation, announced his withdrawal from politics in 1955 and there seemed no likelihood that he would ever lead France again, the Gaullist vote fell to 4 percent. But a new movement, the Poujadists, won an impressive 2.5 million votes, 12 percent of the total. Led by Pierre Poujade, a prewar fascist who had rehabilitated himself by flying in the Royal Air Force during the war, this grouping represented artisans and small shopkeepers, whose fortunes declined as the economy improved, and small farmers. It was especially popular among distillers and wine producers threatened by a government campaign against alcoholism. Poujadism was backward looking, anti-communist, and anti-Semitic.

Among the nonpolitical weaknesses of the Fourth Republic was its economic policies, despite all the signs of industrial and agricultural growth. Industrial production increased more than 50 percent between 1952 and 1959, contributing to an unprecedented annual growth rate for France of 6 percent. The main growth sectors were chemicals (plastics and artificial fabrics), metallurgy, and automobiles. A sign of growing prosperity was the increase in automobile ownership. By 1958 there were half a million private vehicles (most less than five years old) on French roads, vying for space with more than 5.5 million mopeds, the choice of the younger French until they could afford four wheels.

Agriculture was also successful, even though most French farms were small (90 percent were less than fifty hectares) and used little machinery or chemical fertilizer. Production rose steadily, even in the face of the massive migration of rural population to the cities. Output rose too steadily in some sectors; wine was produced faster than the French could drink or export it, and by 1958 France's stock of alcohol equaled two years' consumption. Agricultural incomes were low, however, and farmers were excluded from the much-vaunted postwar prosperity.

Housing was particularly problematic, for although there were, on paper, more dwellings than households in 1955, urban migration left hundreds of thousands of unoccupied houses in rural areas and created a desperate shortage in the cities. A third of dwellings with one to five rooms, and half those with one or two rooms, were reported over-crowded. Not only were many dwellings old (85 percent of housing in Paris dated from before 1914), but they were run-down and lacked what were becoming regarded as necessities by the 1950s. Some 41 percent lacked running water, 73 percent had no inside toilet, and almost 90 percent lacked a bath or shower. By the mid-1950s homelessness was becoming a national scandal as shantytowns sprouted in some districts of Paris. France's housing record was the worst in Western Europe, partly a result of the failure of successive governments to accord housing a high priority in a period of rising population and urbanization.

The foreign policy setbacks that France experienced reflected the worldwide movement of decolonization as Africans and Asians sought independence. In 1954 French forces were routed in Vietnam, and negotiations were begun to end French control over Indochina. Plans were soon in place, too, for national independence in French possessions in Morocco, Tunisia, and equatorial Africa. But Algeria became a sticking point because the French had long regarded it not as a colony but as part of France proper; since 1871 Algeria had elected deputies to the National Assembly. Geographical separation was no more a bar here than for the United States with regard to Hawaii and Alaska, or for Spain with regard to the Canary Islands. Equally important, 1.5 million French settlers and their descendants lived in Algeria. Although they represented only 1 in 6 of its 9.5 million people, they dominated Algeria's political, economic, and cultural life.

Algerian Muslim nationalists formed a political and military organization, the National Liberation Front (FLN), and in 1954 began a campaign of violence and terror. The French government dispatched additional forces—a total of 400,000 by 1956—in order to maintain French control. Settlers formed their own armed organization to combat both Algerian nationalists and any French government that might make concessions to the FLN.

France also participated in military action elsewhere in North Africa when, in 1956, combined French, British, and Israeli forces occupied the Suez Canal area in Egypt. In July the Egyptian premier, Colonel Gamal Abdel Nasser, a nationalist sympathetic to the Soviet Union, had announced his intention to nationalize the Suez Canal, which was controlled by an international company. Egyptian control would threaten British, French, and Israeli communications and oil imports from the Persian Gulf, and there was general concern about the growth of Egyptian power in the Arab world. In October and November 1956, the three states attacked Egyptian installations and landed troops. Within weeks, however, the weight of world opinion—notably economic pressure from the United States—forced a humiliating withdrawal.

The years 1956 and 1957 saw French domestic and foreign fortunes reinforce each other and decline in tandem. The Suez crisis produced oil shortages and price increases. A general shortage of labor was aggravated by the commitment of forces to Algeria (an additional 100,000 were dispatched in 1957). Wages increased, and their pressure pushed prices even higher, so that compared to 1953 wholesale prices had risen 2 percent by 1956, 8 percent by 1957, and 21 percent by 1958. The government response—raising interest rates and freezing prices—managed to harm all sectors of the economy. Real incomes of workers stagnated and producers were hurt by freezes; an increasing number of companies (44 percent by late 1957) reported cash-flow problems. To relieve the labor problem, the number of immigrant workers, notably Portuguese, Algerians, Tunisians, and Moroccans, was quadrupled to over 150,000 a year.

Broad social discontent was the background in May 1958 when the government, pressed by rapidly rising military expenses, called for negotiations with the FLN in Algeria. The French effort had not gone well, and there was increasing public dismay at reports of air attacks on nonmilitary villages and the use of torture by French troops. But in order to forestall any concessions to Algerian nationalists, units of the French army in Algeria occupied government buildings in Algiers and formed a Committee of Public Safety, echoing the committee that had governed France during the period of emergency in the French Revolution. The Committee of Public Safety declared its loyalty not to the government, but to General de Gaulle. De Gaulle was hardly surprised by the announcement, but he was reluctant to lead a military coup. Instead, he declared his willingness to assume power if he were constitutionally invited to do so, and sat back to await the invitation. But events forced his hand. On May 24 paratroopers from Algeria seized the French island of Corsica, and paramilitary forces sent by the government to regain control capitulated immediately. Claiming that he wanted to prevent a civil war, de Gaulle declared on May 26, 1958, that he had begun to form a government to ensure the unity and independence of the country.

Faced with the reality that de Gaulle had more control over the army than it did, the government resigned and the French president invited de Gaulle to form an administration. The general appeared before the National Assembly on June 1, 1958, and was given its blessing by a vote of 329 to 224. In the following days the Assembly gave him full powers to govern for six months to restore order, and authority to draw up a new constitution. The end of the Fourth Republic was seen by many as a merciful release after a long terminal illness. In twelve years France had twenty-four distinct administrations, and vast amounts of time had been spent on forming and propping up coalitions instead of governing. It seemed that de Gaulle's objections to the 1946 constitution had been borne out, and now he had been given the opportunity to do the job properly.

The result was the Fifth Republic in which the office of the president was invested with far more extensive powers and independence from the legislature. On the other hand, the new constitution retained the full range of civil liberties, as well as universal suffrage. In a referendum held in September 1958, four-fifths of French voters supported the new arrangement, and in the first elections of the new regime the Gaullist parties, calling themselves the Union of the New Republic (UNR), won 42 percent of the seats. Communist support fell to 19 percent (from 26 percent in 1956), but after the two ballots required under the new system, the Communists were left with only 10 seats (2 percent) in the new Assembly, rather than the 145 in the old. With allies in other parties, de Gaulle easily controlled the legislature and could appoint his own man as premier.

Developments elsewhere in Western Europe were by no means as dramatic, and in Britain, West Germany, and Italy there were broad continuities as the ruling Conservative and Christian Democratic parties entrenched their policies. In West Germany the Christian Democrats remained buoyant on a tide of economic prosperity, as average disposable income increased steadily. They were able to attract a constant 45 to 50 percent of the total vote between 1953 and the mid-1980s, and usually formed the government in alliance with the conservative Free Democrats. Economic well-being seemed to rally the population to the political system (voter turnout in national elections was consistently above 85 percent) and toward moderate parties, a reversal of the polarizing tendencies of the interwar period. Unemployment declined steadily in the 1950s and 1960s: It was 5.1 percent in 1955, 1.2 percent in 1960, and 0.6 percent in 1965. West Germans became so well off in comparison with other Europeans that envious complaints were voiced about their materialism and greed. Many French and British, in particular, were offended by the apparent injustice of West Germany's prosperity so soon after Germany had brought so much misery and devastation to Europe. Having constructed a stereotype of a well-fed, corpulent German man, earning a large salary in strong marks, and driving an equally large Mercedes, the French and British then proceeded to be offended by it.

Germany's postwar recovery was aided by strong exports of automobiles and technology. Here a trainload of Volkswagens waits at the Hamburg docks.

It was not that the British were suffering. The Conservatives, who held office until 1964, generally maintained the social welfare policies that the Labour government had enacted in 1946–51. The National Health Service continued to provide a high level of care that was mostly free. Unemployment was low, ranging between 1 and 2 percent, real incomes rose steadily, and by 1960 consumer spending was two-thirds higher than it had been in 1950. As elsewhere in Europe, increasing automobile ownership was a sign of prosperity: There were 2.3 million cars on the road in 1950, 5.5 million in 1960, and 8.9 million by 1965. There was one television set for every three households, and increasing numbers of Britons took holidays abroad, especially in Spain where their pounds went further.

But there were serious weaknesses in the British economy, including relatively poor productivity, low rates of capital investment, and high levels of state expenditure on social welfare. In the late 1950s, after the Suez crisis, there were problems with the balance of payments and industrial output began to sag. Wages, which doubled between 1951 and 1961, outpaced production, and taxes were reduced in 1958 and 1959. In 1962 the government imposed limits on wage increases, but there was widespread anger when civil servants and workers in nationalized industries were exempted. There was also growing discontent over standards of housing and education.

In 1963, the year before a general election, the government was caught up in a scandal in which the secretary of state for war, John Profumo, was discovered to have had a sexual relationship with a prostitute who in turn was involved with the naval attaché at the Soviet embassy. Allegations that Britain's military security had been compromised were mixed with more general allegations of sex orgies involving high-ranking Conservatives and members of Britain's social elite. The years 1962–63 also revealed evidence of Soviet spies in high places, such as Kim Philby, who fled to Moscow in 1963. Added to discontent over economic and social policies, the scandals were enough to bring the Labour Party to power in 1964.

Meanwhile, across the Channel the Gaullist government was disentangling France from its relationship with Algeria. Instead of stepping up the war against the FLN, as he was expected to do, de Gaulle accelerated secret negotiations with the aim of disengaging France with the least possible political disruption. In January 1960, a revolt by units of the

French President Charles de
Gaulle is acclaimed by crowds
at Bone during his June 1958
visit to Algeria.

French army in Algeria was suppressed, but the rebels formed a Secret Army Organization (OAS) that began a terror campaign, including planting bombs in the National Assembly and the Paris stock exchange. In April 1961 the OAS seized control of Algiers and tried to organize an invasion of France, but the revolt ended when de Gaulle went on television and ordered soldiers to ignore orders by rebel officers.

By 1962 de Gaulle's government had reached an agreement with the FLN that recognized Algeria's sovereignty but guaranteed the safety of French settlers and their property. It also set about dealing with France's economic and political problems. In the economic sphere, policies of austerity were activated. The franc was devalued by almost a fifth to lower the cost of French exports and reduce imports, and taxes were increased and government spending cut, partly by ending subsidies to state enterprises.

Reforms to overcome the chronic instability of French politics focused on giving the government more authority at the expense of parliament. The time parliament could take to debate the budget was limited by law; legislation was generally discussed by parliament only in broad outline, leaving the details to civil servants and government lawyers; and the length of time parliament sat was reduced to about 500 hours a year. The government could also seek parliamentary permission to legislate by ordinance for a fixed period, a facility used by de Gaulle's administration seven times between 1959 and 1967.

De Gaulle's personal prestige continued to climb, not only as he was seen to confront problems that his predecessors had shied away from, but also after a spectacular but unsuccessful assassination attempt. In August 1962, gunmen of the OAS fired scores of bullets into his car, but although de Gaulle escaped unharmed (the plot was the basis of Frederick Forsyth's novel *The Day of the Jackal*), there was widespread alarm at the thought of having to find another president of de Gaulle's stature. Later that year, a hotly debated referendum changed the method of choosing the president from an electoral college to election by direct popular vote; if no candidate won an absolute majority, a second ballot would be held in which voters chose between the two leading candidates in the first.

In the parliamentary elections of 1962, Gaullists won 55 percent of the seats in the National Assembly, although their share of the vote on the first ballot was 36 percent— still the largest share of any political grouping in any French election since the war. The Communists, in contrast, won 22 percent of the vote and 9 percent of the seats. The referendum and election reinforced a split down the middle of French politics between Gaullists and their main opposition; the latter included the Socialists, the Radicals, the MRP (Christian Democrats), as well as the Communists. Although there were great ideological differences within this group, they were united in their anxiety about the government's antiparliamentary measures and also de Gaulle's negative attitude toward European cooperation (discussed below).

In Italy during the period 1955–65, the Christian Democrats dominated politics by attracting almost 40 percent of the votes in both the 1958 and 1963 elections. The left wing maintained a similar share, but it was split between the Communists and Socialists, who would not work together. Governments were always coalitions that had the Christian Democrats as their core but included parties to the right (until 1962) or left (after 1962), depending on circumstances.

Like other Western European states, Italy's economy prospered in these years, but also like them it had serious weaknesses below the surface. Industrial output grew at a rate of 8.1 percent annually, faster than any other country except West Germany and Japan. Various factors came into play: Wages were low and strikes infrequent because migration from south to north and from country to town produced an abundance of labor and relatively high unemployment rates, at least until 1960. The costs of raw materials like steel were low, while reserves of natural gas in the Po valley gave Italian industry access to the cheapest energy in Europe and sheltered it from the costs of imported oil. The state played an important role in economic development. It ran companies as diverse as the Alfa Romeo automobile company and Alitalia, the state airline, and it also provided communications services and, through banks and other financial institutions, it financed state-owned, mixed ownership, and private companies.

Beginning in the early 1960s problems arose, partly as a result of falling unemployment as the number of official jobless fell by two-thirds between 1956 and 1962. As labor became less abundant, employers came under pressure to raise wages and there was increasing industrial unrest; the first major strikes since 1948 took place in 1962 and 1963. But although inflation began to rise from the early 1960s and private investment fell away, the government continued to prop up the whole system, underwriting companies with their growing wage bills, relatively slowly growing productivity, and low reinvestment rates. The result was that the Italian government began to run up large budgetary deficits, and these in turn would eventually weaken the economy and lead to political instability.

Italy also saw the growth of an extensive secondary economy of workers outside the institutional framework of unions, labor standards, taxation, and social security. Many of the millions involved in this shadow workforce were women employed in small workshops or at home. They paid no taxes and received no social benefits. Some textile manufacturers returned to a virtual preindustrial putting-out system that was inefficient but saved on overhead, union wages, and employers' social security contributions.

Italian agriculture was still very much a small-scale enterprise. The Christian Democrats pursued rural reform on a very modest scale, allocating land to about 110,000 landless peasant families by 1962, only 1 percent of the rural population. The plots were often too small and the land too poor to provide for a family's needs, and the program did little more than reinforce rural poverty. Many peasants left the countryside to work in the industrial cities. An average 175,000 a year left the south during the 1950s, 230,000 a year in the 1960s.

Elsewhere in Western Europe there was a general pattern of political stability linked to economic prosperity, whether it was in the authoritarian states of the Iberian peninsula or the democracies of Scandinavia. In Spain the dictatorship of General Franco remained secure, but the policy of economic self-sufficiency was gradually abandoned. This meant giving up the tariffs and subsidies that not only protected Spanish industries and encouraged self-reliance but also retarded more general productivity. The opening of Spanish industry to foreign investment in the late 1950s gave a boost to production, and soon Spain was experiencing its own little miracle. In 1960 foreign investment totaled $40 million, but it grew to $322 million by 1965 and $697 million by 1970, most from the United States and Switzerland. Other sectors also grew, notably tourism after the devaluation of the peseta in 1959 made Spain an extremely cheap vacation destination for other Europeans. In 1960, some 6 million tourists arrived, the vast majority heading to the beach resorts, bringing in almost $300 million.

Prosperity in Spain was even less equitably distributed than in other countries, however. The provision of land to the landless benefited only 50,000 people in the long period from 1939 to 1965. That, plus the growth of industry, produced large-scale urban migration during the 1960s that reduced the agricultural workforce. Workers appear to have fared no worse than their counterparts in France and Belgium, but they typically worked longer hours. A sign of growing expectations, as well as of a sense of political change, was an increase in illegal unions and strikes from 1958 when economic policies altered course.

In Scandinavia social democrats governed or dominated administrations throughout the 1950s and 1960s, and the few major political changes were in the direction of further democratization. The use of referenda was extended, and the Swedish institution of the ombudsman, which gave individuals some recourse against the state, was adopted in Denmark and Norway. In economic terms the period saw virtually uninterrupted prosperity, both in the industrial and primary sectors (the latter including agriculture, forestry, and fishing). Equally important, the Scandinavian governments adopted measures to ensure that the prosperity was broadly shared, and there was a greater degree of economic equality there than anywhere else in Europe. Taxation on higher incomes was raised, the comprehensive system of social benefits was reinforced, and apart from Denmark in the late 1950s, unemployment was low.

Gender: Work, Family, and Sexuality in Western Europe

The period of economic prosperity that began in the mid-1950s did more than stabilize support for the political center of gravity in Western Europe's democracies: the moderate left in Scandinavia and the moderate right in Italy, for example. It also seemed to stabilize society more generally, strengthening existing class structures, and reinforcing inequalities and disparities where they existed.

The family seemed to stabilize as the high postwar divorce rates declined, as marriage rates rose, and as women and men married at younger ages. Women were bombarded by exhortations to marry, get pregnant, and stay home and look after the house and the children. Women's magazines, many of which achieved record circulations in the 1950s, purveyed all the supposed necessities of domestic consumerism from laundry powder and diapers to household appliances, as well as information on fashion, cosmetics, and recipes. Even when women learned a trade it was one traditionally associated with women.

In 1956, for example, 46 percent of young women in French apprenticeship programs were being taught to sew, despite the fact that the clothing industry that might employ them was in decline.

The fact that there was a baby boom, a short-term increase in fertility, seemed to underline a greater commitment to family. As we have seen, fertility rose dramatically in some countries in the immediate postwar years when men returned home from the war, but it generally fell in the late 1940s and 1950s, even though it remained higher than might otherwise have been expected. From the mid-1950s, however, it began to pick up again, lasting until the mid-1960s when the postwar baby boom officially ended.

Most of the baby boom was due to a decline in the age at marriage and the sustained popularity of marriage as prosperity spread and the war and postwar austerity receded. There were increases in the marriage rate in most Western European countries in the second half of the 1960s and early 1970s. In Britain, women who married in the years around 1960 bore an average 2.4 children, compared with 1.8 for women married in 1945, and 1.96 for women married in 1954. In France the postwar fertility increase had continued in a less interrupted manner than most other countries, but women there were also having 2.4 children around 1960, as were women in West Germany.

But the deceptively calm surface of European society concealed swiftly moving currents and some turbulence. Despite the ideological stress in many societies on women's roles as mothers and wives, an increasing number of women, especially married women, were in paid employment. In Britain, for instance, there were 800,000 more women in the workforce in 1947 than before the war, and in the postwar years the proportion of married women in paid employment rose steadily: From about 10 percent in the 1930s, it rose to 22 percent by 1951, 30 percent by 1961, and over 40 percent by 1971.

Similar trends occurred elsewhere to varying degrees. Between 1950 and 1960 the number of employed married women doubled in Norway, rose 20 percent in Sweden (to 44 percent), 10 percent in Switzerland, and 5 percent in France, where in 1962 some 53 percent of employed women were married. All these figures understate actual employment rates because many women were employed informally or did paid work at home, which was not included in official statistics. The figures also excluded women's work in family businesses and on farms, where they were seldom paid cash wages.

Nor was the baby boom everywhere a reflection of commitment to the family on the part of women and men. In France much of it could be attributed to lack of family planning, and surveys in maternity hospitals in 1959–62, at the peak of the baby boom, indicated that a third of children were not wanted. In the early 1960s, two-thirds of French couples depended for contraception on the unreliable system of premature withdrawal by the male (coitus interruptus), while a quarter used "the safe period" (restricting intercourse to the phase in the woman's menstrual cycle when ovulation was least likely). Only 6 percent of sexually active French men used a condom and 4 percent of women used a diaphragm or spermicide. In contrast, more than half of British couples used a device of some kind, a third practiced withdrawal, and a tenth the safe period. The popular English name for a condom, "French letter," seems particularly inappropriate given the infrequency of its use in France. The first family planning clinic was set up in France in 1961, but it was not until 1967 that contraceptives could legally be sold in pharmacies.

Underneath the high birth rate that many governments found gratifying were other alarming statistics. An estimated 20,000 French women died each year from back-street or self-induced abortions, many of which employed knitting needles, pencils, and household disinfectants. After abortion was legalized in Great Britain in 1967, there were 22,000 legal abortions in 1968 and 75,000 by 1970.

Other trends took hold that reinforced the dynamism of Western European society. The number of divorces began to rise in most countries during the 1960s. The divorce rate in England doubled between 1960 and 1970, whereas in France divorces began to rise later, but were significantly up by the early 1970s. While there are many factors involved in changes to the divorce rate, rising expectations and economic independence were crucial. It is likely that expectations did rise during the relatively prosperous 1950s, not only in terms of material comfort but also in terms of behavior within marriage. Among other things there was a growing expectation that marriage should be emotionally fulfilling. During the 1960s discussion of sexuality became more common and open in the mass media, including women's magazines, and stress was placed upon the importance of sexual satisfaction within marriage. Expectations also rose as male adultery, domestic violence, and emotional cruelty—all historically tolerated to a large extent in law and practice—became socially less acceptable. In Spain, where the double standard of sexual morality was especially entrenched, male adultery was made legally equivalent to female adultery, and men were deprived of the right to kill a wife or daughter who stained their family's honor (meaning their husband's or father's honor) by being caught in an illicit sexual relationship.

It is an oversimplification but still essentially true that as expectations in marriage rise, so does the likelihood that marriages will fail to meet them. In the 1960s, a rising proportion of couples became dissatisfied with their marriages. Historically, women have initiated most divorces when they have been legally able to, and that was the case throughout Europe in the 1960s, too. What made the rising divorce rate possible was the availability of paid work for women, giving them a source of independence, as well as expanding social welfare programs. Women continued to be paid less than men (the ratio remained pretty constant throughout the twentieth century), but they were at least able to escape intolerable marriages.

One by one Western European countries liberalized their divorce laws. The main trend was to replace specific grounds for divorce, like adultery and cruelty, with no-fault divorce. Couples had only to live apart for a certain period (generally two years) after which either spouse was entitled to have the marriage dissolved. By 1975 divorce legislation on these lines was enacted in England and Wales, Denmark, Finland, and Norway (1969), Italy (1970), the Netherlands (1971), Sweden (1973), Belgium (1974), and Portugal and France (1975).

Legal changes reflected more positive social attitudes toward divorce. Surveys in France showed a big change between 1969, when about 33 percent of people thought marriage should be indissoluble, and 1972, when only 20 percent thought so. A major breakthrough occurred in Italy, where divorce had been resisted by governments for decades and where, as late as 1962, 69 percent of people surveyed were opposed to it. But when the Socialists entered the government coalition in 1962, they began to promote the legalization of divorce, and in December 1970 they narrowly succeeded in getting a restrictive divorce law through both the Chamber of Deputies and the Senate. Although the law went into force, the Christian Democrats pressed for a referendum to repeal it, but in 1974 Italians voted 59 percent in favor of retaining divorce.

Changes in behavior and government policy raised a storm of debate about the status and future of the family. Conservatives made their usual argument that the basic institution of Western society was under threat. What was often at issue was the status of women, because the 1960s saw the beginnings of the modern women's movement that would mature in the 1970s and later. The initial demands were for women to be given equality of opportunity with men in areas such as education, law, health, and employment. Feminism and its responses are discussed in more detail in the next chapter.

Social Reforms and Their Limits

During the 1960s, governments in a number of states reformed legislation and regulations to provide for greater diversity in many areas of political, social, and cultural life. One area has already been touched on: the liberalization of divorce laws so as to allow individual married women and men themselves, rather than legislators and judges, to define the point at which their marriages had broken down. Similar reforms extended to issues that bore on sexuality and women's health. In Britain abortion was legalized in 1967, enabling women to terminate their pregnancies under the National Health Service on the recommendation of two doctors.

The British experience in the sphere of abortion law reform was ahead of some Western European countries and behind others. Sweden and Denmark had liberalized abortion before the Second World War; Norway did so in 1965. France legalized abortion during the first ten weeks of pregnancy in 1975, and West Germany allowed abortion in specific circumstances in 1977. In the sphere of contraception, France permitted the establishment of family planning clinics and the sale of contraceptives in pharmacies in 1967.

Where abortions were not legal, of course, they were obtained illegally. Women who could afford to travel to countries where abortion was legal often did so, but those who could not obtained abortions from compliant doctors or took their chances with backstreet practitioners. It is estimated that in 1969 there were between 350,000 and a million abortions in West Germany and some half million in France, most performed in conditions that put the woman's health or life at risk.

Homosexuality also became an issue. In 1957 a committee set up by the British government recommended that homosexual activity between consenting adults in private should not be illegal (as it was under an 1885 statute). Actual law reform took a decade, but in 1967 parliament passed legislation that decriminalized homosexual activity between consenting adults.

Social reforms took place in realms other than the sexual. Censorship, for example, was eased in Britain as the power of the Lord Chamberlain to ban or censor plays and books was curtailed and then abolished entirely. There had been pressure against censorship for years, but a crucial test case arose when highly respected Penguin Books was charged with publishing obscene material by bringing out an edition of D. H. Lawrence's novel *Lady Chatterley's Lover*. This was the story of the relationship between a gamekeeper and his employer's wife, and it seemed all too appropriate when, in the course of the trial, one of the prosecuting attorneys asked the jury, in all seriousness, "Is it a book you would want your wife or servants to read?" The question seemed only to highlight the anachronism of censorship in such cases, and the publishers were found not guilty. Censorship declined in other countries as well, sometimes earlier, sometimes later. In Denmark censorship was abolished entirely in 1969, and very quickly Copenhagen became the "pornography capital" of Europe. Cinema censorship was abolished in France in 1976.

In many cases, law reform was in line with public opinion. Public attitudes toward divorce, for example, appear to have become increasingly liberal. In other cases, legislatures enacted reforms at odds with voters' sentiments. In Britain public opinion was generally in favor of maintaining the death penalty, but parliament abolished it anyway, in 1966. In contrast, the French parliament, although believed to be in favor of abolition, was prevented from voting on the matter because the government feared reaction from a pro-death penalty electorate. Even so, by the mid-1960s capital punishment had been abolished in all Western European countries except for France and Spain.

There was, of course, opposition to many of the reforms. Pressure groups, political parties, and many churches resisted legalizing homosexual activity, abortion, and other behavior, as variously immoral, contrary to God's laws, or harmful to society. Churches were often in the vanguard of opposition, and the fact that the reforms were passed over their objections testifies to their weakened position in postwar society. In England church attendances fell markedly during the 1960s, although the great majority of English people continued to express a belief in God.

The churches themselves were not immune from successful reform movements in the 1960s. Pope John XXIII convened a council in the Vatican from 1962 to 1965 that made significant changes in the church's structure and liturgy. Vatican II, as the council is known, permitted the use of national languages in the mass, rather than Latin, and encouraged dialog between the Catholic Church and other Christian denominations. In his 1963 encyclical *Pacem in terris*, Pope John called for social justice and for the participation of workers in matters that affected their lives.

This was a far cry from the often reactionary positions the papacy had adopted during the twentieth century. Even so, neither John XXIII nor his successor Pope Paul VI was willing to modify the church's positions on such issues as the ordination of women as priests, the celibacy of priests, and contraception and abortion. Many individual Catholic clergy in Western Europe, particularly in the Netherlands, did adopt more liberal ideas that brought them into conflict with church authorities. A few reactionary clergy resisted Vatican II's reforms.

An important point about the 1960s is that the desire to reform laws, policies, doctrines, attitudes, and practices was not confined to young people. It was the older generations that sat in parliament, staffed commissions, and enacted the wide range of reforms that took place in the areas of sexuality, gender, the family, race, and culture. It can be argued, as it was at the time by many activists, that the reforms were often half-hearted compromises and incomplete. Women did not have an absolute right to abortion, and homosexuals did not have the same rights as heterosexuals (who could be sexually active legally at a younger age). The reforms were indeed compromises between conservative and progressive forces, but they indicated a marked tilt toward progressive positions.

At the same time there were changes that tested the extent of Western Europeans' tolerance, such as the arrival of large numbers of immigrants. Europe had historically been an exporter of people, and emigration, especially by Britons, Greeks, Italians, and Dutch to Australia and New Zealand, generally increased after the war. Some European countries also began to receive immigrants. During the 1960s large numbers of North Africans entered France to join those already there. By the early 1970s more than a million had settled (three-quarters of them Algerians, the rest Moroccans and Tunisians), especially in Paris and southern cities like Marseilles. In the 1960s West Germany also encouraged immigrants to come as "guest workers," particularly from the Mediterranean countries. By the early 1970s they made up nearly 10 percent of the West German workforce, a tenfold increase since 1960. At first it was expected that the guest workers would be males who would come alone, work, save, and then return to their countries of origin after having contributed to the West German economy, paid taxes, and cost nothing in benefits. The very name "guest workers" implied a short stay, but many came with their families, or sent for them later, and settled in Germany. As in France, their presence would be made an issue in the following decades when economies declined and unemployment rose.

From the mid-1950s Britain began to receive large numbers of immigrants from the empire, notably from Jamaica, India, and Pakistan, and later Asians who were forced to

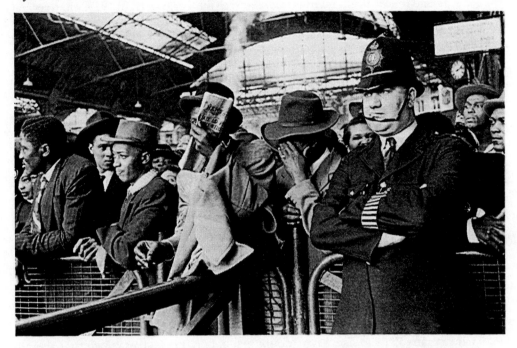

In 1956 some 30,000 immigrants from the West Indies took up residence in Great Britain. In this photograph, people wait at Victoria Station, London, for relatives and friends arriving by train from the port at Southampton where they had disembarked. Two in front shield their faces from the press photographer.

leave African states (notably Kenya and Uganda) after they achieved independence. As citizens of the empire they were entitled to enter Britain, take up residence, and work. Although the immigrants (mostly males who were later followed by family members) took jobs not wanted by the British, they were not brought in specifically to compensate for a shortage of workers as immigrants were in France and Germany. There was widespread resentment at the newcomers, and from 1958 there were violent clashes in areas of London and other industrial cities in the Midlands where immigrants settled in distinct communities, as newcomers historically have. The Labour government elected in 1964 responded to the situation by passing the Race Relations Act (1965) that forbade race discrimination, and setting up a Race Relations Commission (1968) to deal with complaints of discrimination in access to housing, services, and employment. By that time there were almost 700,000 people of Caribbean, Indian, or Pakistani origin in Britain.

There were political repercussions to Asian and Caribbean immigration, however. In the 1950s Sir Oswald Mosley, who had founded the anti-Semitic British Union of Fascists in the 1930s, attempted to revive his movement by appeal to anti-immigrant sentiment. Other movements, like the neo-Nazi White Defence League, joined in, and in 1967 the fascist National Front was formed, with repatriation of nonwhite immigrants as one of its principal policies. In 1968 a prominent Conservative politician, Enoch Powell, made a series of inflammatory speeches in which he predicted that the presence of immigrants would provoke violence and "rivers of blood" in the streets of England.

Historically the British had coexisted on a large scale with people of color only when Britain invaded and colonized their lands, and the only occasions when blacks had been in England in significant numbers were during the world wars. In 1919, when several thousand blacks from the Caribbean remained in Britain after serving in the British armed forces, there were riots and some deaths, and the government repatriated 2,000 of the blacks to Jamaica. In the Second World War the United States forces in Britain included many blacks, but they were clearly a transient population. Many British people expressed outrage at the racial segregation imposed by the American military authorities: Some villages near U.S. bases were designated for whites only to spend recreational time in, others for blacks. The emergence of race and immigration as political issues did not cause a major upheaval in British politics in the 1960s or later, but it added a new dimension to underlying problems within society and the economy.

Students and Politics: Paris, May 1968

Young people also posed a challenge to the status quo. The 1960s have entered late-twentieth-century lore as a time of youthful rebellion against accepted conventions, despite the fact that many of the events and phenomena associated with the sixties took place in the following decade. The scale and effects of youth culture in the 1960s have often been exaggerated for commercial purposes, like selling new releases of music that was not very good when it was first recorded and has not improved with age, or to inflate the importance of individual lives—a habit many people who were young in the 1960s share with war veterans. Even so, there is no doubt that important changes in behavior and attitudes did take place in the 1960s

Young people, particularly university students, were so prominent because there were unprecedented numbers of students in society. Between 1960 and 1970 the number of students in French universities rose more than threefold, from 211,000 to 651,000, while in Great Britain, West Germany, and Italy they doubled. In Britain nine new universities were opened in the 1960s. These increases were due only in part to the fact that the children born in the first phases of the baby boom, from 1945 to 1949, reached university age from the mid-1960s.

The expansion of university attendance was also driven by the demands of the new economy for a well-educated workforce and by rising material and occupational expectations on the part of Western Europe's middle-class citizens. Most of the students who attended university in the 1960s were the first members of their families ever to do so. In the mid-1960s about 20 percent of students in Britain, where there was a system of financial grants, came from working-class families, but in France a mere 2 percent came from the industrial or agricultural working classes.

From the early 1960s, currents of radical thought, often forms of Marxism, began to swirl through Western European universities. They reflected disenchantment with the materialism of the classes from which the students sprang, and were increasingly expressed in the form of public demonstrations. The student movement had several dimensions. Much of its impetus was anti-American, not merely because of the economic domination that the United States exercised over Europe, but because of American foreign policy elsewhere. The United States was blamed for having brought the world to the edge of nuclear catastrophe by confronting Soviet ships bringing missiles to Cuba in 1962, and by the mid-1960s the United States had begun to send troops to Vietnam.

The other main focal point of student political activity was the universities themselves. Generally ignoring the fact that they themselves were drawn from the economically most prosperous sections of society, students condemned institutions of higher learning as bastions of elitism and hide-bound relics of an undemocratic past. French students were especially agitated over conditions. University enrollments increased by 62,000 between 1967 and 1968 alone, without any corresponding growth in facilities or the number of faculty. Lectures were overcrowded and libraries hopelessly inadequate.

It was, in fact, in France in 1968 that the Western European student movement had its most powerful expression. Not only were there unparalleled numbers of students, many espousing radical causes and resentful of the conditions they were compelled to study in, but the French economy underwent a slight recession in 1967. The number of registered unemployed rose by a third between 1966 and 1967, then by a third again in 1968. The recession was in part responsible for the influx of students in 1968, which increased student numbers by 13 percent. Students grew anxious over their employment prospects after graduation.

In April 1968, students at the new University of Paris campus at Nanterre, in the dreary suburbs of the city, demonstrated when a German student leader was the subject of an attempted assassination by a right-wing group. When the government closed the Nanterre campus because of the unrest, the students moved their activities to the city center, near the Sorbonne, the main campus of the University of Paris. As April turned to May, there were days and nights of confrontations between students and police, and as the government closed other faculties, moderate students came to the support of the radicals. As the conflict deepened, the Socialist leader François Mitterrand announced his support for the students, as did the main socialist union organizations.

Although there is little doubt that what became known as "May 1968" was sparked primarily by anxiety over job prospects, once the movement was under way it provided a context for the discussion of all manner of issues, notably feminism, gay rights, and the environment. It also had an anticapitalist tone that provided a tenuous link to industrial workers, many of whom were also discontented in 1968. Not only were workers anxious for their jobs as unemployment rose, but they also worked hours essentially unchanged since the 1930s, and their wages, which were low in European terms, had been effectively cut in 1967 by increases in social security contributions.

Seeing the state under pressure from the students, workers in a number of sectors realized they had an opportunity to press their own claims. A general strike was called for May 13, and on that day an estimated 650,000 to 700,000 students and workers took to the streets and demanded, among other things, the resignation of President de Gaulle. Adopting an imperial posture of disdain for people in the streets, de Gaulle left on a scheduled visit to Romania, but his attitude only accelerated the protest and strike movements. The Sorbonne was occupied, and an astonishing 10 million workers, almost 60 percent of the national workforce struck at some time in the following days. They included the state railroad, post office, airlines, state-owned factories, and private enterprises. As services and supplies were interrupted, people began to stock up on food and gasoline.

It was enough to force de Gaulle to cut short his Romanian visit and return to deal with the crisis. The heat was taken out of the strike movement by wage concessions on May 27: an immediate 7 percent increase with another 3 percent in November. Although there was some resistance to accepting what seemed like paltry monetary offerings when there were no improvements in hours or other conditions, workers gradually returned to their jobs. On May 29, following the agreements with the unions, de Gaulle disappeared for a day. It was later discovered that he had flown to Baden to visit the commander of French forces in West Germany. It is possible that he wanted to be reassured that he could count

Expressions of protest in Paris, May 1968. The top photograph shows some of the results of riots in the Latin Quarter. Cars have been burned, barricades erected, and cobblestones torn up for use as weapons. The bottom photograph, of 1968 posters, shows students' concerns. Some of the posters criticize the growth of bureaucracy, rising unemployment, and the government's spending on the military rather than education. The bottom poster reads "We are power," which was temporarily true.

on the support of those forces if they were needed to suppress a revolt, although the armed forces within France were already prepared for this eventuality; tanks had been placed at the ready on the outskirts of Paris.

On May 30, de Gaulle addressed the nation on radio and announced an election to test public confidence in his government. De Gaulle's supporters, buoyed by his evident determination to carry on, took to the streets (half a million gathered in Paris alone) in celebration. The result of the election, held in the last week of June when almost all strikes had ended and student occupations had been terminated, was an overwhelming victory for the Gaullists. Running under the new and meaningful name Union for the Defense of the Republic, they won 46 percent of votes in the first ballot, but the second ballot assured them of 74 percent of the seats in parliament. The Communists ended up with 7 percent of the seats, despite winning a fifth of the popular vote in the first round.

Despite their electoral defeat, the students' protests led to wide-ranging reforms in higher education. The number of universities was increased to reduce their average size to 15,000 students. They were to be governed by elected councils with equal representation of faculty and students, and the councils would elect their own presidents from among the professors. Despite these changes to administration, the form and content of university education remained essentially unaffected by May 1968. Workers also found that their gains were less than they had hoped. Only small wage raises were granted after 1968, although profit sharing became more common in industry, giving workers a stake in the well-being of their companies.

Although the energy of the protest movement had dissipated, de Gaulle wanted to take advantage of his apparent popularity to push through some constitutional reforms. One was to abolish the Senate as a legislative body, a proposal that was unpopular; the other was to devolve some central powers to regional governments, which most French people supported. De Gaulle held a referendum on both issues, indicating that he would resign if his proposals were defeated. In the referendum on April 1969, 53 percent of the voters called his bluff, and as soon as he received the result de Gaulle issued the statement, "I am ceasing to perform the functions of President of the Republic. This decision takes effect at midday today." He promptly disappeared from public life for the remaining eighteen months of his life.

The Economic Community and European Unity

De Gaulle had put his stamp not only on France but on Europe more generally, not least because of his nationalist distrust of the process of European union that accelerated in this period. Beginning with the European Steel and Coal Community, and spurred by the 1956 Suez Canal debacle, which threatened the security of Europe's oil supplies, economic cooperation expanded in Western Europe. In 1957 six nations (France, West Germany, Italy, Belgium, the Netherlands, and Luxembourg) signed the Treaty of Rome that created a free trade zone called the European Economic Community (EEC, or Common Market). Goods produced in any of the countries could enter any of the others at duties or tariffs that would be reduced to zero in the following twelve to fifteen years. Their citizens could move from one country to another and take up employment without visas or other restrictions, and their national businesses operate freely on the same basis. All the EEC countries imposed a standard tariff on goods entering from non-EEC countries.

Although the EEC was initially a limited economic entity, many of its sponsors hoped it would encompass the whole of Europe and become a political partnership, perhaps a federation of states. Even in its early stages it had a full range of political and other institutions. Apart from a permanent bureaucracy, located in Brussels, it had a principal decision-making body in the form of a Council made up of the foreign ministers of the six nations. It had a consultative body, an Assembly that sat in Strasbourg, composed of appointees in rough proportion to the parties in national parliaments, and a European Court of Justice that sat in Luxembourg, mainly to hear disputes between member states.

The EEC would only work equitably if all the member states followed similar policies in terms of wages, subsidies, social security benefits, and the like. So it was that economics led the way to a broader harmonization of policies across the board. One stipulation of the Treaty of Rome was that men and women doing the same work should receive the same pay.

The major exclusion—by choice—from the EEC was Great Britain. The British retained a historic suspicion of Europe, and feared that membership in any kind of free trade association might reduce British sovereignty. Winston Churchill was not necessarily unrepresentative of Britain when he remarked to his doctor in 1952, "I love France and Belgium, but we must not allow ourselves to be pulled down to that level." In addition the British government felt a responsibility to the Commonwealth, especially to New Zealand, which exported the bulk of its agricultural produce to Britain. Joining the EEC would require the British to turn their backs on Commonwealth countries only a few years after they had made sacrifices by supplying the British with armed forces and essential food supplies during the war.

In the short term the countries of the EEC flourished. Trade within the Community boomed, quadrupling in ten years. Germany did particularly well, and its exports alone almost equaled those of the other EEC countries combined. A 40 percent increase in French-German trade in that period helped France reduce its foreign exchange deficits. One of the most important elements of the EEC, however, was the Common Agricultural Policy (CAP), which was designed to increase productivity, stabilize markets and supplies, and provide farmers with a good standard of living and consumers with goods at reasonable prices. The CAP was one of the EEC's most contentious policies, not least because financial support to farmers to ensure their well-being came at the expense of taxes and high consumer prices. Common prices for agricultural goods were set down between 1962 and 1967. Because prices within the EEC were high, the EEC also compensated exporters who lost money by selling produce on the international market. This practice not only imposed a cost on EEC taxpayers, but provoked protests from competitors that Europe was "dumping" goods on the world market.

No sooner had the EEC got under way than a number of excluded states formed their own trading bloc, the European Free Trade Association (EFTA). Its members were Britain, Denmark, Norway, Sweden, Switzerland, Austria, and Portugal. EFTA went no further than free trade, however.

By 1960 the European states outside Soviet influence were interlocked in a number of economic and military arrangements. Although there was broad support for close ties among these states in the context of the cold war, there was also concern about the effects of increasing European union on national economies and national sovereignty. The formation of the EEC had encouraged the formation of large multinational corporations that were able to achieve economies of scale by operating across national borders. As the harmonization of policies proceeded, states gradually lost control over their policies. All this was music to the ears of Europeanists, who saw every step toward union as a step away from the possibility of another European war, but it rang alarm bells in the ears of nationalists.

Among those with anxieties was the French president, Charles de Gaulle. Although a supporter of the EEC, de Gaulle saw its core as a close relationship between France and Germany with the other members tagging along. De Gaulle attempted to direct EEC policies to assisting France primarily: Because France was the Community's largest agricultural economy, he thought it should absorb all France's agricultural surpluses. He also wanted the bulk of EEC overseas development funds invested in French Africa. In 1963 France vetoed a British application to join the EEC on the ground that it was too closely tied to the Commonwealth and the United States.

The United States was a particular anxiety for de Gaulle, who was concerned that France was losing its status as a great power by being only one of the several European states in NATO. France declined to be sheltered under the American and British "nuclear umbrellas" and set about its own nuclear arms program, testing weapons in the Sahara Desert and the South Pacific. In 1959 French naval forces were withdrawn from NATO's Mediterranean Command, and in 1966 all French participation in NATO's military forces was terminated. NATO headquarters were moved from Paris to Brussels.

There were other critics of large multinational economic and military organizations. The left wing in Europe regarded NATO as essentially an American organization that made its European members parties to American foreign policy. As for the EEC and its implications of European political union, it was opposed by many nationalists because it was internationalist, and by many internationalist left-wing parties because it looked like a capitalist club. There were also complaints that the transfer of jurisdiction to institutions abroad would make it even more difficult for ordinary citizens to make their voices heard.

Nonetheless, the impetus toward European union that was in progress by the 1960s seemed irreversible. In 1967 the EEC was merged with the Coal and Steel Community and became the European Community (EC), a significant change indicating that more than economic matters were involved. The following year, well ahead of the schedule set down in the Treaty of Rome, the last tariffs on trade among member countries were removed. The way was set for increased membership and increased integration.

The Soviet Union: Politics and Economy After Stalin

The death of Joseph Stalin in 1953 ended an era in the history of the Soviet Union. It was not that Stalin personally and directly ran every aspect of Soviet politics, economy, and society, but that the cumulative weight of his quarter century in power was a burden that made changes of course difficult. Even at the end, in the months before his death, Stalin was at the center of what promised to be yet another set of purges sparked by an alleged "doctors' plot." The essence of this imaginary conspiracy was that Soviet doctors were engaged in undermining the health of the Soviet people, and of the Communist leadership in particular. Nine prominent doctors were arrested—six of them were Jews—and many others detained, questioned, or in some other way caught up in the investigation. It is significant that they were released soon after Stalin's death, a signal that although not everything would change after Stalin, the repression would moderate.

A number of prisoners were released from Soviet prison camps, and members of the families of top party members were allowed to return from exile. The chief of Stalin's secret police, Lavrenti Beria, was executed in 1953 for alleged crimes ranging from being a British agent, fomenting dissent among nationalities, disrupting the economy, and sexual perversion. In the following three years a further thirty police officials were executed, but they represented the end of official political killings in the Soviet Union.

In the years immediately after Stalin's death, the Soviet Union was governed by a collective leadership of the most senior members of the Communist Party, but gradually Nikita Khrushchev emerged as the first among equals. He had been prime minister of Ukraine and had had increasing influence over agricultural policy in Stalin's last years, and it was his supposed expertise in the latter that gave him the edge over his rivals. There was broad recognition that Soviet living standards had to be improved, and Khrushchev argued that this goal was best achieved by increasing food production. More grain would improve the food supply, as well as provide fodder for larger herds of cattle, which in turn would provide more milk, meat, and leather for shoes, which were in chronically short supply. Increased production of sugar beets and cotton would also benefit consumers. It was not a matter of running heavy industry down, but of giving due emphasis to consumer goods.

In 1954 a program was launched to increase the area under cultivation by using land that had never been planted before (virgin land) or that had not been used for years (idle land). The original goal was to bring an extra 13 million hectares under cultivation, but it was raised to 28 to 30 million hectares by 1956. To encourage collective farmers, the compulsory deliveries they had to make to the state were reduced, prices paid by the state were raised, and the produce from private plots could be disposed of for private gain.

Attempts were made to improve Soviet foreign relations, and Khrushchev advanced the principle of "peaceful coexistence," the notion that instead of the anticipated war between the Soviet Union and the capitalist powers, there would be economic and technological competition. The battle of ideologies would be won by that which proved itself best able to provide for people's economic, social, and cultural needs. Soviet technological superiority in some areas was demonstrated when it launched the first space satellite, *Sputnik,* in 1957. Khrushchev aimed to catch up with the per capita production of meat, butter, and milk in the United States by 1961.

There was a mending of fences with Yugoslavia, although Tito maintained his independence from the Soviet Union, and Yugoslavia did not join the Warsaw Pact. In 1955 diplomatic relations were established with West Germany, and the release of almost 10,000 German prisoners of war, held in the Soviet Union for more than a decade, began.

Khrushchev realized that reforming Soviet policies across the board—internationally and domestically—meant changing many of the institutions and practices that had developed under Stalin, and that reforms would be resisted by those whose power was threatened. Although Stalin had not been attacked directly after his death, personnel and policy changes were tantamount to a repudiation of much of his legacy. But in 1956 Khrushchev went much further, when in a closed session of the Twentieth Congress of the Communist Party, he attacked Stalin's personality and policies. It was not just a matter of pointing to errors; Stalin was condemned for developing a "cult of personality" by making himself seem more important than appropriate for any one individual in a socialist society, and for committing crimes against the Soviet people by his repression and persecution. Stalin's wartime leadership was criticized and downgraded. Under Khrushchev, some victims of the purges were rehabilitated, prison camps began to close, the powers of the police were curtailed, foreign tourism into the Soviet Union grew, and cultural and academic exchanges with Western states were developed.

It was more difficult to translate this renunciation of Stalinism into more substantial economic achievements, for the expected abundance from the virgin lands failed to materialize. Even so, the grain harvest and other crops increased in 1955 over 1954, and continued to do so in the following years. By 1958 gross agricultural production was 50 percent higher than it had been in 1953. Translated into concrete terms, that meant 135 million tons of grain in 1958 (compared with 82 million in 1953), 7.7 million tons of meat (versus 5.8 million), and 120 million sheep (versus 94 million). These represented satisfactory gains that improved living standards.

In international affairs, the policy of de-Stalinization was tested and shown wanting by revolts in East Germany, Poland, and Hungary, which are discussed in a later section. Following a challenge to his leadership, Khrushchev embarked on policies that were more confrontational. The relationship with China broke down after the Soviet Union withdrew its support for the Chinese nuclear weapons program, and a fissure developed in the world communist movement over the principle of peaceful coexistence. Ironically, Soviet-U.S. relations deteriorated at the same time as the Chinese condemned the Soviet leadership for cozying up to the imperialists. U.S.-Soviet relations took a nosedive in 1960 when an American U-2 espionage aircraft was shot down over the Soviet Union and its pilot, Francis Gary Powers, put on trial. In the early 1960s, Berlin emerged once again as an issue in the cold war, as the Soviet Union threatened another blockade. In 1961 construction began on the Berlin Wall, and the pressure on Berlin provoked a visit from U.S. President John Kennedy. He symbolically identified with Berlin in his famous "I am a Berliner" speech. In the same period, the Soviet Union established relationships with states in Africa, the Middle East (Syria, Egypt), and with Cuba. The decision to install Soviet ballistic missiles in Cuba, where they could be used against the United States, raised cold war tension to its highest point ever. After a confrontation in 1962, the missiles were withdrawn, but the misconceived Soviet policy contributed to Khrushchev's downfall.

The main weaknesses within the Soviet Union, however, were economic. Although agricultural production rose, it fell far short of the targets that were set. Partly for climatic reasons, the 1963 harvest, 107.5 million tons, was less than two-thirds the planned 170 to 180 million tons and actually below the 1958 level. It forced a decision whether to slaughter all the livestock that could not be fed, or import grain from the West. As humiliating as the step was, the government decided to import supplies (20 million tons that year), setting a precedent for the following years. The inability of the Soviet Union to produce enough food for its population on a steady basis was a fundamental failure in economic policy.

Industrial performance was not a lot better. A Seven-Year Plan put into effect in 1959 placed emphasis on energy (especially oil, electricity, and natural gas) and chemicals. But the funds available for investment were inadequate, partly because large amounts were dedicated to maintaining the Soviet lead in the space race with the United States. The lead was demonstrated by the first manned space flight in 1961. It was, however, achieved at the expense of investment in more fundamental areas of research and development, particularly automation and computerization. Soviet shortcomings in these spheres became especially critical in the 1980s.

One of the basic weaknesses of the economic system was its planning structure. Even though decision making was decentralized to some extent after 1957, the imposition of an overall plan with specific targets and quotas produced inefficiencies, as managers and directors sought to achieve their individual goals without reference to the broad enterprise. Thus, because the plan called for so many tons of chandeliers, manufacturers produced heavy chandeliers in order to fulfill the target, and because targets for the road transport sector were set in ton-kilometers, trucks were sent on pointless journeys in order to meet them.

Attempts were made to overcome such problems in the early 1960s when there was a series of economic reforms. Consultative committees were set up, the implementation of planning was devolved to 100 regional agencies (reduced to 47 in 1963), and the Communist Party itself was divided into industrial and agricultural sections. A certain desperation was evident in the extension of the death penalty to cover a range of economic offenses. In the end it was the confusion of economic plans, projects, schemes, the interminable tinkering and interference, and the unfulfilled promises and arbitrary methods, as much as the chronic economic problems, that brought Khrushchev down.

The rest of the explanation lies in the sphere of defense and foreign policy. By 1964 the world communist movement was split. The Soviet Union had backed down when confronted by the United States over the installation of Soviet missiles in Cuba, and Soviet control over Eastern Europe was at its weakest point since 1945. The military was embarrassed by the Cuban missile crisis and dismayed by cuts in defense spending. In 1960 the personnel of the armed forces were reduced by a third, from 3.6 to 2.4 million, and modernization of the air force and navy given second place to increasing nuclear missile strength. Discontent over these matters combined with concerns about the failing economic policies. In October 1964, Khrushchev was accused of a range of political, economic, and personality shortcomings, and forcibly retired.

A collective leadership again replaced a leader, and again one man rose to prominence within a few years, this time Leonid Brezhnev, who headed the Soviet government until 1982. While pursuing the goal of peaceful coexistence, Brezhnev began a program of rearmament so as to negotiate with the West from a strong position.

A military parade in Red Square, Moscow, in November 1965, celebrates the forty-eighth anniversary of the 1917 Bolshevik Revolution.

In economic affairs the new regime gave particular attention to agriculture, which had suffered from the oscillating policies and experiments (like the virgin lands campaign) of the previous ten years. It tried to establish stability for both farmers and planners, and gave particular attention to deficiencies in livestock and machinery. Industries that supported agriculture, like the fertilizer-producing chemical sector, were also promoted.

The results of the first five years were disappointing, however, partly because weather conditions led to poor harvests in 1965 and 1967. Average grain harvests between 1966 and 1970 were 168 million tons, a 29 percent improvement over the average 130 million tons a year in the first half of the 1960s. In the same period the production of other goods also rose: potatoes (a 16 percent increase), meat and milk (24 percent).

Although production trends were heading in the right direction, they were unsatisfactory in part because of the disproportionate cost to the economy. By 1966–70 the Soviet Union was devoting almost a quarter of its total economic investment to agriculture, and the percentage was growing. State subsidies rose as farmers were paid more for the produce they sold to the state but retail prices were held steady to help consumers. As a result of these changes, the role of agriculture in the Soviet economy was transformed. Instead of being the sector that accumulated the capital needed for investment in industry (as it had been in the 1920s and 1930s, when industrialization was paid for by agriculture), agriculture became a burden on the rest of the economy.

Industrial policy itself was reformed after 1965. The decentralization of planning was reversed, but local managers were given more control over production. These two tendencies proved contradictory at times, when jurisdictions crossed, and before long the additional managerial powers declined. By 1970 administrative control from the center had been reasserted. The official statistics showed an increase of 50 percent in Soviet industrial production between 1966 and 1970, but external assessments place it somewhat lower. There were particular improvements in the output of consumer goods such as shoes; 676 million pairs were produced in 1970 (almost 3 pairs per person), compared with 486 million in 1965.

In terms of domestic politics, there were scattered signs that the new regime wanted to rescue Stalin from some of the odium poured upon his memory by Khrushchev. In 1966 Brezhnev became secretary-general of the Communist Party, a title that had been held by Stalin until it was abolished by the 1934 congress. In 1969 there were plans to celebrate the ninetieth anniversary of Stalin's birth by an article and photograph in the official newspaper, *Pravda*, and to erect a statue at his grave near the Kremlin wall, where Khrushchev had demoted Stalin's body after having it moved from the Lenin mausoleum. But these projects were abandoned after pressure on the Soviet government from Eastern European leaders and from within the Soviet Union itself.

Toward the end of the 1960s, foreign policy began to dominate the Soviet government's agenda. As we shall see later in this chapter, there were persistent problems for Soviet dominance in Eastern Europe, culminating in the Soviet-led invasion of Czechoslovakia in 1968. In spite of this, the Soviet Union sought accommodation with the Western powers that resulted in the policy of détente by the early 1970s. This did not lead to any reduction of Soviet spending on defense, partly because relations with China became so bad that many observers predicted all-out war between the two major Communist states. Between 1960 and 1970, Soviet defense expenditure rose by 95 percent, and there were substantial increases in the navy, the air force, and the stock of nuclear missiles.

Social Change in the Soviet Union, 1953–70

The process of de-Stalinization that began as soon as Stalin died led to broad, if often slow and irregular, changes in the material and cultural lives of the Soviet people. The abandonment of the forms of repression current up to 1953 led to a gradual reduction in the level of anxiety about persecution for minor breaches of the law or political rules.

Changes in the economy that gave emphasis to consumers led to a steady rise in the standards of living from the deep poverty that was widespread up to the mid-1950s. Even so, the gains were modest in absolute terms, and only by the 1960s was the poverty level being exceeded by substantial numbers of Soviet citizens. Some sections of the population did better than others. There were disparities among the various republics of the Soviet Union, with the Baltic states clear leaders in most salary scales. In general, state employees—industrial workers, bureaucrats and office staff, and workers on state farms—did better than collective farm workers, but during the 1960s the wage gap narrowed substantially. In 1968 a minimum wage of 60 rubles was established; it represented an income that was just adequate for an individual to keep above the poverty line.

Collective farmers were able to boost their income by selling produce from their private plots, a supplement that in many cases exceeded their wage income. In Lithuania private plots provided 76 percent of a collective farm worker's income, in Georgia 66 percent, and throughout the Soviet Union 53 percent. Although the financial significance of private cultivation declined during the 1960s, it remained evidence of the failure of the government to turn farmers to social labor.

Collective farmers remained outside many of the benefits of the Soviet social security system until the 1960s. Only in 1965 were they eligible for state retirement pensions and women for maternity benefits, and it was not until 1970 that they could receive sickness benefits. Overall, the collective farm workers were a cheap population, for they did not qualify for subsidized housing, and had to make do with educational and medical services that were far inferior to those in towns and cities, although disparities between country and town in these respects were not confined to the Soviet Union. Even so, conditions in the countryside persuaded many people to leave, and between 1960 and 1965 collective farmers and their families declined from 31.7 to 24.5 percent of the labor force.

Not only did incomes rise across the board, but working conditions generally improved, with extensions to social security. In 1967 the five-day week was introduced, and the basic entitlement for paid holidays was increased from twelve to fifteen days. The housing stock also improved, thanks largely to the development of prefabricated concrete units that could be fitted together to make large blocks of apartments. They were not elegant inside or out, and eventually they became terrible slums, but the immediate problem in the 1960s was to ease the overcrowding that forced many families to share dwellings with married children. The bulk of housing was constructed by the state, but as it rose slowly during the 1960s private construction of housing declined more rapidly, with the net result that less housing was built in 1965 (80 million square meters) than in 1960 (83 million square meters). It was, however, an improvement on 1955, when only 33 million square meters of housing were constructed.

The housing situation improved partly because there was no massive increase in the Soviet population. The birth rate registered a steep decline. Having remained at about 25 or more births per thousand population throughout the 1950s, it fell to under 20 in 1965 and to 17 by 1970. There were reductions in the big variations in fertility between the high rates in the country and low rates in towns, as well as among the republics; in 1965 the fertility rate was 15.8 per thousand in Russia and 34.7 in Uzbekistan. The overall decline of fertility represented a loss of some 2 million births each year, which relieved pressure on a wide range of services from housing and health to day care and education.

In part the decline of fertility was a result of more general and increasing prosperity, but it also reflected the high rate of female employment. By 1970 the proportion of women aged sixteen to fifty-four in the paid labor force was close to the biological maximum, at 89.7 percent. The official rate of women's employment in the Soviet Union was a more accurate representation of the real situation than in the West, where women's work in family farms or businesses, often unpaid, was frequently excluded from official statistics. There were scarcely any such enterprises in the Soviet Union.

Women were, however, employed in low-status and low-paying jobs. They were concentrated in a limited number of occupations, including certain sectors of industry (textiles, clothing) and services (telephone operators, cleaners, catering), as well as retail selling, clerical work, teaching, and medicine. They were poorly represented among managers in industry, however, where they declined from 7 to 6 percent between 1956 and 1964. Even where women appeared to predominate in high-status occupations, it proved illusory: Most doctors were women, but the Soviet health care system was poorly funded, with doctors afforded little social prestige and their rates of pay well below those of skilled workers and professionals in industry.

There was some official concern for the relatively low participation of women in politics, a phenomenon at least partly explained by lack of time and energy. State women's organizations pointed out that shopping, cooking, cleaning, and other tasks consumed at least four hours a day. Under socialism, both economic and political differences between women and men were supposed to disappear. Although success in erasing economic differences seemed to be demonstrated by the high employment rates of women, failure in the political sphere was evidenced by the slow growth of female membership in the Communist Party: In 1961 a fifth of the members were women, and by 1976 a quarter were. During the 1960s there was an implicit recognition that Soviet women often carried a double burden of paid and household work. Although it was in the context of concern about declining fertility, the 1961 party congress called for women to be given lighter, adequately paid work, longer maternity leave, and more household appliances.

Among the changes that did affect women was the legalization of abortion once again in 1955. (It had been legalized in 1920, but banned in 1936 in order to halt the decline of fertility.) The new 1955 policy was not designed to depress fertility further, but reflected a wish to curtail the number of unsafe illegal abortions. As they had historically done, women in that part of the world used abortion as the main means of family planning, and it was not until the 1960s that other means, such as intrauterine devices, were promoted. Many back-street abortionists so damaged their patients that hospitals put pressure on the government to do something to rectify the situation. The government was receptive, and made the point that the availability of abortion gave women "the possibility of deciding the question of motherhood themselves." To this extent the legalization of abortion was integral to the de-Stalinization process, for Stalin had abolished abortion on the ground that the social needs of the state outweighed the selfish wishes of women to limit their families.

Notwithstanding the decline of fertility, the number of children in education grew substantially. Students in higher education (mainly universities and polytechnics), rose from 2.4 to 4.6 million between 1960 and 1970. A large proportion of high school graduates went on to university, increasing the number of educated people in the workforce and providing a high rate of social mobility in Soviet society.

The easing of Stalinist restrictions from the mid-1950s was also evident in cultural terms. There was a broader toleration of diversity in literature and the arts, largely as a reaction against the rigid conformity enforced during Stalin's regime. But the gains in cultural freedom, like those in living standards, were measured in Soviet terms, and the limits were soon discovered. Painting that diverged from the principles of socialist realism was tolerated, but abstract art was criticized. Among writers, Boris Pasternak had his novel *Doctor Zhivago* published outside the Soviet Union, and when he was awarded the Nobel Prize for literature in 1958, he declined it in the knowledge that if he traveled abroad to receive his award he would not be allowed to return. On the other hand, works by Alexander Solzhenitsyn—such as his novel on life in a labor camp, *One Day in the Life of Ivan Denisovich*—were published in the Soviet Union until 1967 before they were stopped. In 1969 Solzhenitsyn was expelled from the state-run Union of Soviet Writers.

The pattern of toleration followed by renewed repression is observable in religion, too. Fear at the growing influence of the churches, especially the Russian Orthodox Church, led to the closing of churches and religious houses. There were 20,000 operating churches in 1959, but 11,500 in 1962, and a mere 7,500 later in the decade. The eight theological seminaries in 1958 declined to three by 1964. Many churches were turned over to collective farms for use as communal buildings; where there was opposition to this, the buildings were simply destroyed.

Finally, there was the question of nationalities. Under Khrushchev, concessions to the Soviet Union's nationalities were made in the spirit of de-Stalinization. People banished to Siberia, labor camps, or Central Asia simply on the basis of their nationality were released and gradually rehabilitated from the mid-1950s to the mid-1960s. They included Volga Germans, as well as Chechens and Crimean Tartars who had been exiled by Stalin in 1944–45 because of alleged collaboration with the Germans.

Specific political programs also gave greater status to nationalities, such as the reform of economic policy toward decentralization, which gave more influence to the republics because of the predominance of Russians in the centralized agencies and ministries. This process was reversed in 1962, when centralization was reimposed. There were persistent problems over language policy, but by the 1960s Russian was well established in Soviet schools outside Russia. Though unpopular, this was a realistic measure within a Soviet Union where the language of law, the economy, and administration was increasingly Russian, for it prevented the marginalization of non-Russians.

One nationality decidedly not marginalized during Khrushchev's time in government was Ukraine, with which he had particular affinities. From the mid-1960s until Khrushchev's fall in 1964, the proportion of Ukrainians in the Communist Party and its main political bodies increased steadily, although the process really did little more than rectify the previous underrepresentation of Ukrainians. In 1954 the 300th anniversary of the incorporation of Ukraine within the Russian Empire was celebrated by the gift of the Crimea to Ukraine. This transfer of jurisdiction overrode nationality, because only a fifth of the Crimea's inhabitants were Ukrainians. At the same time, Russians remained fully in control of the Soviet Union's central political, economic, and military organs. Discontent among non-Russian populations (who by 1970 constituted a majority of the Soviet Union's population) would contribute to the collapse of the Soviet Union in 1990–91.

De-Stalinization in Eastern Europe, 1953–57

The death of Stalin appeared to bring a deep sigh of relief across Soviet-dominated Eastern Europe. But hints that there would be a relaxation of political controls and more emphasis on consumer goods rather than heavy industry raised expectations and demands for more rapid changes than were envisaged or immediately possible. One manifestation of pent-up discontent was a wave of strikes throughout the socialist countries, involving groups as diverse as tobacco workers in Bulgaria, automobile workers in Czechoslovakia, and steel workers in Hungary.

The most troublesome area for the Soviet Union, however, was East Germany, where in 1952 the regime had settled on a policy of intensifying its power by nationalizing more of the economy and giving even more emphasis to heavy industry, extending collectivization in agriculture, further centralizing government, and strengthening the police forces. Early in 1953 the food supply problem worsened and price increases were decreed for basic items like sugar and meat. These policies led to an increase in emigration as many entrepreneurs, farmers, and professionals, judging that their prospects in East Germany were dim, headed to West Germany. From an average of 60,000 a year up to 1951, emigration rose to 130,000 in 1952 and 300,000 in 1953.

Faced with growing economic problems, the East German government of Walter Ulbricht asked the Soviet Union to cancel further reparations demands, and tried to stimulate production by raising production quotas by 10 percent without raising wage levels. But instead of helping their colleagues, the new leaders in Moscow suggested they do a policy about-face and adopt more pragmatic approaches to the economic and political situation. The East German leadership was divided on the course to take. Ulbricht himself was opposed to liberalization but, bowing to reformers in his government, made a public announcement that admitted errors in the past and promised more consumer goods, less interference in religion and culture, and freer communications with West Germany. State demands on farmers would be reduced, taxes would be cut, and there would be more scope for private enterprise.

As welcome as these concessions were, they did not go far enough for workers because the increased productivity levels, which were tantamount to a wage cut, were maintained. In June 1953, construction workers went on strike, and even though the government quickly agreed to cancel the new quotas it was too late to stop the workers' demands from broadening to include the resignation of the government and free elections. The next day the strike movement spread to hundreds of other towns and cities, where rallies drew some 300,000 to 400,000 people, mostly workers who represented about 6 percent of the labor force. In some towns, buildings of the ruling party were burned, portraits of Ulbricht were torn down, and prisoners were released from jails.

The revolt was quickly ended when Soviet occupation troops were called out against the strikers. Major buildings in Berlin and some other towns were taken over by Soviet troops, and on June 17 a state of emergency was declared. In battles in Berlin between East German civilians and Soviet forces, which deployed tanks, many civilians were killed; the official number was 21, but estimates range as high as 3,000. There were 20,000 arrests and 40 subsequent executions.

The Berlin Uprising, as it is known, demonstrated to Walter Ulbricht that liberalization could lead to the destruction of the regime. The ruling Socialist Unity Party (SED) was purged of reformist-minded members at all levels, and in 1954 the original plans to intensify the regime were reactivated, although the most contentious 10 percent increase in quotas was not. There were also concessions to improve the standard of living of East Germans. Prices on thousands of items, including many basic foods, were reduced by 10 to 15 percent; pensions and social security benefits were increased; commuter fares reduced for low earners; and credit facilities extended to allow people to buy furniture and automobiles.

In order to assist the East German regime, the Soviet government canceled reparations, reduced the charges it made for occupying the country, provided a loan of almost 500 million rubles, and took steps to assist economic growth. It also established full diplomatic relations between itself and East Germany, a sign that there was no longer any expectation that the two Germanies might be reunified, and that East Germany was now the equal of other Eastern European states in the Soviet sphere.

Over the long term, the signs of discontent that broke out in Germany in mid-1953 served to warn Eastern European governments of the dangers of reform in a liberal direction. In the short term, however, they tended to follow the course set by the new leadership in Moscow, which under Nikita Khrushchev tended to be a reaffirmation of Stalinist economic policy combined with the easing of political restrictions. Khrushchev encouraged the Eastern European regimes to set their own policies, while maintaining their relationships through trading, political, and defense arrangements, such as Comecon and the Warsaw Pact.

To demonstrate the new spirit of cooperation and partnership and the abandonment of the puppeteer-puppet relationship, in 1955 the Soviet and Yugoslav governments patched up their differences and declared their "mutual respect" and commitment not to interfere in each other's affairs. What looked like Soviet approval of a renegade socialist state, which had been excoriated for a decade as a dupe of Western imperialism, shocked the other Eastern European Communist regimes. They received yet another blow from Khrushchev's secret speech at the Soviet Communist Party congress in February 1956, denouncing Stalin for his persecution and "cult of personality." In addition to urging a policy of peaceful coexistence between the Communist and anti-Communist blocs, Khrushchev declared an end to the slavish emulation of Soviet policies in other countries, and recommended his Eastern European counterparts be more sensitive to conditions in their own countries.

These policy changes created turmoil. Eastern European governments were not prepared for the significant changes in policy that were now required of them as they prepared to obey Moscow's instructions to be more independent. More important was the effect of expectations of reform on their populations, for although conditions varied, there was general unrest over standards of living, political repression, and domination by the Soviet Union. Khrushchev's secret denunciation of Stalin was meant to be confined to Communist leaderships, but it was soon leaked by the Polish regime and became widely known throughout the West and in Eastern Europe. In Poland and Hungary, popular sentiment welled up into real challenges against their governments.

In Poland, as we have seen, living standards declined in the early 1950s following improvements in the late 1940s, and by 1955 real wages had fallen 36 percent against 1949. There was also widespread opposition to increasing Russification. Some cultural liberalization had already been permitted in the early 1950s, but after Khrushchev's speech political restrictions began to be lifted as well. The Sejm was given more powers, as a result of which Catholic deputies voted against a government abortion bill, and 30,000 to 40,000 political prisoners were freed, many of them members of the anti-Communist Home Army.

In June railway workers in Poznan went on strike over wages and quotas, but extended their demands to include political freedom and independence from the Soviet Union.

When they believed their leaders had been arrested, the strikers attacked a prison and the police shot and killed about fifty of them. The regime's response was to offer further concessions, but it was too little and too late to quell the unrest. Workers throughout Poland set up councils to provide popular democratic leadership, and called for the reinstatement of Gomulka as leader of the country.

The Soviet leadership was alarmed at the course of events in Poland, which was of immense strategic importance to the Soviet leadership, and in October tried to persuade the Polish regime to halt further concessions. Soviet troops were moved toward the Polish frontier. But the Polish government responded by placing its own forces on alert, and the Communists reelected Gomulka as party leader. He promptly made further concessions, notably concerning the Catholic Church, that satisfied most grievances. The following month an agreement was reached by which the Soviet Union promised not to interfere in Poland's affairs and offered Poland an improved trading relationship.

The significant result was that Poles retained a Communist regime, albeit more nationalist and less repressive than its predecessor. There was a general recognition that to go further risked direct Soviet intervention and more bloodshed, and there was also awareness that Poland's western border with Germany had not been fixed. Hatred of Soviet domination vied with fear of Germany.

In Hungary the background to the revolt was similar to that in Poland, but the results were utterly different. While Stalin was alive, Hungary's Communist regime was far more repressive than Poland's, and far more compliant with Soviet economic requirements, even to the detriment of its own citizens' well-being. Much agricultural produce, which had in any case been affected by collectivization and other agricultural policies, was exported, and the standard of living in Hungary had declined. After Stalin's death a new leader, Imre Nagy, had introduced reforms that included a reversal of collectivization, more consumer goods, and an easing of political controls.

Nagy was replaced by his rivals in the Hungarian Workers' Party, the national Communist Party, in 1955, but the following year de-Stalinization began, and there was an increase in agitation for change and repeated calls for Nagy to be reinstated. Pressure on the government peaked in October, when demands for reform in Hungary intersected with support for the dissidents in Poland. On October 23, a large demonstration in Budapest called for political freedom, economic reform, an equal relationship between the Soviet Union and Hungary, and for Nagy to be made premier. To show support for Polish workers, 100,000 Hungarians demonstrated and laid wreaths at the statue of General Bem, who had fought the Russians in Poland in 1830 and in Hungary in 1848.

After honoring one statue, the crowd moved on to demolish another, this one the massive bronze statue of Stalin in the center of Budapest, constructed from melted-down images of Hungary's monarchs. This was the first violent act of the rising tide of dissent, and it was wholly symbolic, but it marked a point of no return. When the demonstrators gathered outside the parliament, they were addressed by Imre Nagy, who led them in singing the national anthem. Later that evening, the prime minister addressed the nation on radio and condemned the demonstrators, and when they went to the radio service's building to demand air time for themselves, they were fired on by security police guards.

By October 24, Budapest was in a state of civil war as the security police and Soviet forces confronted workers and students who had been joined and armed by units of the city's police and military forces. The Communist Party agreed that Nagy should be made premier. In his first radio address, however, he admitted not having objected to the government's request for support from the Soviet army, and in so doing destroyed any hope that meaningful political reform could be carried out in cooperation with the ruling party. The reformists had no

The Hungarian revolution, 1956: A worker, armed with a submachine gun, stands guard outside a factory on the outskirts of Budapest.

choice but to reject the party and look for alternatives elsewhere, and in this sense Hungary was quite different from Poland, where Gomulka was able to contain and channel reform.

Throughout Hungary, the rejection of the Communist Party was expressed in the formation of revolutionary national councils. They demanded free elections, a multiparty system, withdrawal of Soviet forces, and independence for Hungary. Heavy fighting broke out in Budapest as protesters, joined by almost all units of the Hungarian army, battled Soviet tanks in the streets. Nagy promised more reforms and admitted that the regime had committed mistakes and crimes. He approved the various councils that had been established, and announced the creation of a Patriotic People's Front to govern Hungary.

By the end of October it seemed that the Hungarian revolt had been successful. The security police were disbanded, and the Soviet Union agreed to withdraw its forces from the country. But Nagy's popularity had waned dramatically. His Patriotic People's Front was rejected by an ad hoc committee representing the insurgents, and on October 30 the government announced the end of the one-party system and the creation of a government by the coalition of parties that had existed in 1945. The agreement was given Soviet approval on condition that capitalism was not restored and that Hungary did not become a base for anti-Soviet forces.

In the following days, old political parties like the Smallholders and Social Democrats began to reconstitute themselves, and new parties such as the Christian Democrats were formed. In contrast, the ruling Hungarian Workers' Party began to splinter; reformists rallied on Nagy, while those who had wanted to hold the line against excessive reforms that threatened the dominance of the party began to coalesce around the party leader János Kádár. Political prisoners, including Cardinal Mindszenty, were freed, and dozens of news sheets and political papers began to appear.

These events went too far for the Soviet leadership, which came under pressure from China and other Eastern European Communist regimes to stop the slide toward democracy in Hungary. All were fearful that it would provide an inspiration for dissidents in their own countries. Poland's reforms they could live with, because there the Communists remained in control. The Soviet military authorities were alarmed at the thought that Hungary might withdraw from the Warsaw Pact, and their fears proved right when, on November 1, Nagy announced that Hungary would become neutral. The Soviet leadership was suspicious of the commitment of Hungarians to neutrality; they had twice before allied with Germany against Russia. Hungary was also a major supplier of bauxite and uranium, both vital to Soviet industrial and military strength.

The Soviet Union was determined to stop Hungary's imminent departure from the Soviet fold, and it was assisted by the French-British-Israeli intervention in the Suez Canal zone on October 30, which deflected attention from events in Eastern Europe. On November 4, more than 6,000 Soviet tanks rolled into Hungary. Nagy and his colleagues took refuge in the Yugoslav embassy, and Kádár took control of the process of reversing the political reforms. He was opposed by the councils, which tried to form an alternative administration, and by workers, who went on strike and continued fighting in the streets until mid-November. By the time their ammunition ran out, the revolt had cost more than 3,000 dead and 13,000 injured, as well as 4,000 buildings destroyed.

Although Kádár had wanted to avoid harsh retaliation, the Soviet Union insisted on a crackdown. More than 20,000 insurgents were imprisoned, and thousands more were sent to Soviet forced labor camps. Between 2,000 and 2,500 insurgents were tried and executed. An estimated 200,000 Hungarians fled to Austria, including large numbers of miners, engineers, and others vital to Hungary's industry.

The Communist authorities condemned the Hungarian revolt as the work of reactionaries and fascists, but in fact there were few demands for the restoration of capitalism and the end of state ownership of the economy. It is likely that demands for more fundamental economic change and the introduction of a market economy would have followed before long, however. In this respect the farmers proved more radical, for as the revolution appeared to succeed in October 1956, more than half of Hungary's collective farms dissolved themselves. As the reaction set in, they were recollectivized.

Politics and Economy
in Eastern Europe, 1956–70

After the turmoil in East Germany, Poland, Hungary, and to a lesser extent elsewhere between 1953 and 1956, the various Communist regimes of Eastern Europe attempted to achieve a new equilibrium between, on the one hand, maintaining firm control of politics and society, and on the other, relaxing the repressive and oppressive policies associated with Stalinism. The Hungarian example had demonstrated that even officially sanctioned reform could easily get out of control, and there was nervousness about any kind of political experimentation.

The Soviet Union itself sought to balance greater independence and sensitivity to national conditions among its Eastern European partners with the maintenance of regional unity. They adopted a policy of "polycentrism," the notion of many centers of power in the region rather than one (Moscow). Each state was to have certain latitude in its domestic policies while being bound to the other states and the Soviet Union through multilateral economic and military ties like Comecon and the Warsaw Pact.

The system had inherent tensions, however. From a regional economic perspective it made sense for each country to specialize in the kinds of production for which their resources were best suited, and a plan on these lines was proposed by Comecon in 1962. But this would have created a set of interlocking and interdependent economies with overarching central planning, which ran counter to the notion of polycentrism and decentralization. The problem of integrating ideological and national impulses dogged the Soviet Union and its Eastern European partners to the end of their relationship in 1990.

The Soviet connection was a dominant influence in the development of Communist Eastern Europe's political, economic, and social policies. The pursuit of the cold war and other international events involving the Soviet Union reverberated in Warsaw, Prague, Budapest, and other capitals. Among the important events were the 1962 Cuban missile crisis, when a confrontation between the United States and the Soviet Union over the delivery of Soviet missiles to Cuba brought the two states to the brink of war. There was also a rift between China and the Soviet Union over domestic and foreign policy. Mao Zedong accused the Soviet leadership of "revisionism," betraying Marxist-Leninist principles, and selling out to the Western imperialist powers.

There was a striking diversity in the responses to the various challenges that faced the Communist regimes. Romania, for example, pursued a determined nationalist policy without, however, formally breaking from its treaties and ties with the rest of Eastern Europe. Soviet troops were withdrawn in 1958, which gave Romania's leader, Georghiu-Dej, confidence to strike independent postures in economic and foreign policies. He refused to have anything to do with the Comecon proposal that each nation should specialize in economic terms, particularly because mineral-rich Romania was allocated the role of providing raw materials and agricultural products. This would have undermined the regime's industrialization program. In foreign affairs, Romania adopted a neutral stance in the Chinese-Soviet dispute. Under Nicolae Ceausescu, who became leader of the Romanian Communists in 1965, nationalist policies continued. Ceausescu attacked the interference of Moscow, through Comintern, in the affairs of the Romanian Communist Party during the interwar period, and resisted plans to centralize command over Warsaw Pact forces even further. In 1967 Romania was the only Eastern European state to reestablish diplomatic relations with Israel after the Six Day War, and it became the first to establish relations with West Germany.

Bulgaria's government fell rather more into line with Soviet economic requirements, not least because it was dependent on the Soviet Union for raw materials and fuel. Even so it pursued a program of intensive industrialization. The Bulgarian Communists attempted to improve relationships with the peasantry, but accelerated collectivization, and in 1958 declared that theirs was the first state after the Soviet Union to achieve full collectivization. Indeed, Bulgaria outdid the Soviet Union by collectivizing the collectives: The 3,450 farms were amalgamated into 932 massive units averaging 4,200 hectares, the largest in Eastern Europe. The aim was to create economies of scale so as to triple agricultural output in the space of two years. The labor surplus created in the process was to be directed to a new industrialization campaign that would quadruple industrial output by 1965. Industrial enterprises were also amalgamated, their number falling from over 6,000 in 1947 to only 1,650 in 1960.

Bulgaria's economic targets were later revised to more realistic levels, and in 1961 and 1962, when food output plummeted, partly because of poor harvests, concessions were made to farmers. The prices the state paid for products like eggs, milk, and poultry were raised, and the costs to farmers of fuel and fertilizer were lowered. Taxes on collective farms were reduced and a minimum wage introduced, the first in Eastern Europe for collectivized workers. Perceived as favoritism toward farmers, these concessions provoked unrest among urban workers, particularly when the black market was suppressed. Rationing was introduced on basic goods like potatoes, rice, and beans.

From the late 1950s, leadership devolved increasingly on Todor Zhivkov, who secured his position partly by a close association with the Soviet leader, Nikita Khrushchev. By 1965 Zhivkov was well installed in power (which he held until 1989), having survived an attempted coup by some army officers who opposed his reliance on the Soviet Union. But despite these close ties, Bulgaria began to open up to the non-Communist world. During the 1960s mass tourism on the Black Sea coast brought in valuable hard currency from the West.

Hungary went though greater changes between 1956 and 1970 as a result of the 1956 revolution. At first the government was concerned to reinforce its position, which it did by abolishing the various bodies that had sprung up in 1956, including the national councils and alternative political parties. The Communist leader, János Kádár, had a strong position with the Soviet Union, which regarded him as able to control the rebellious Hungarians more effectively than a conservative who might provoke further revolts.

Even when Kádár's government pursued what seemed like repressive policies, like collectivization, it did so using persuasion and concessions rather than outright coercion. The state played a diminished role in running the farms, and private plots were more tolerated. Not only was three-quarters of agriculture recollectivized by 1962, but it was more productive than it had been before the revolution. During the 1960s there was a debate on restructuring Hungary's economy, and in 1965 a New Economic Mechanism was announced. Under it, Hungary would move to a mixed state and private enterprise system, with less central control.

The government also moved cautiously toward political reform. In 1961 the number of labor camps was reduced, torture was made illegal, and the obligation of Hungarian citizens to inform on disloyal relatives was repealed. The following year most of the 1956 insurgents still in prison were released, and leading Stalinists expelled from the ruling party. More democracy was permitted within the Workers' Party and in the general polity. It became possible, in principle, for more than one candidate to run in an election, and parliament was encouraged to debate government policies more critically and vigorously.

But if in Hungary reform staged a remarkable revival after being crushed in 1956, Poland failed to achieve the same dynamism. The government of Wladislaw Gomulka began promisingly enough, by removing Stalinists and adopting more conciliatory policies across the board. Agriculture was not recollectivized after peasants broke away from the collective farms in 1956, more freedom of intellectual expression was permitted, and the influential Catholic Church was allowed greater latitude than elsewhere in Eastern Europe.

Yet Gomulka, very much in the thrall of the Soviet Union, remained opposed to reforms of the political system, a stance which set him at odds with nationalists within his own party. Opposition to Gomulka, particularly in the police and security forces, coalesced around his minister of the interior from 1964, Mieczyslaw Moczar. Moczar appealed to Polish patriotism, bolstered by illiberalism and anti-Semitism. In the later 1960s the regime became increasingly anti-Semitic; Jews were dismissed from positions in government and universities, and many fled Poland entirely.

Poles generally derived few material benefits from the Gomulka regime, and during the 1960s their wages rose more slowly than anywhere else in the region. In terms of the consumer goods that became increasingly the measure of a population's prosperity, the Poles lagged well behind their comparable neighbors in the northern half of Eastern Europe. By 1970 they were behind Czechoslovakia, East Germany, and Hungary in per capita ownership of televisions, automobiles, telephones, and washing machines. Nor could it be said that what they lacked in material comforts they made up for in other ways, for food was often scarce, and there were fewer doctors per capita in Poland than the other three countries.

The sentiments of Polish workers by 1970 are suggested by the strikes and riots that broke out when price increases were announced that year. Workers in a number of centers, especially in the Baltic ports such as Gdansk (formerly Danzig), became especially strident in their demands, and an unknown number of them were killed in confrontations with the police and army, and even by machine guns fired from helicopters. They were unexpectedly successful insofar as they contributed to Gomulka's having a stroke, and to his being replaced by Edward Gierek, who canceled the price increases.

In East Germany the position of Walter Ulbricht was strengthened in the late 1950s after some challenges from within the Socialist Unity Party (SED), and his regime was one of the most repressive in the region. In economic terms the stress was on central planning and control. Agriculture was collectivized in several phases, and by 1960 about 85 percent was in the form of cooperatives. Resistance to this program took the form of farmers leaving for West Germany, a trend that had such an impact on output by 1961 that food rationing on some goods was reimposed.

By 1961 the steady emigration to West Germany (usually via East Berlin, where people could cross quite easily to West Berlin) had cost East Germany 3 million people if we take into account the half million who returned. In the beginning the outflow could be tolerated, not least because it got rid of dissidents and potential troublemakers. But many, perhaps most, of the refugees were educated and skilled women and men whose career prospects in East Germany seemed poor. Their departure not only deprived the East

Despite the efforts of the East German government, thousands of refugees poured into West Berlin until the Berlin Wall was constructed. Here a nun provides food and drink to some of the 1,600 East Germans who crossed the border during the night of August 11–12, 1961.

German economy of their skills but also represented a considerable loss of return on educational investment. To this extent East Germany was subsidizing West Germany's skilled workforce. In 1961, determined to halt the flight of people and their talents, the East German government began to construct a wall to separate East Berlin from the West. Initially a barrier of barbed wire, bricks, and concrete that snaked across the city, dividing families and neighborhoods alike, the Berlin Wall came to represent the captivity of the East Germans.

It was accompanied by some improvement in the economy as a result of reforms that reduced the level of centralization and increased flexibility. Industry was to become profitable, which meant controlling costs and quality, and investment was made available for research and development. These developments provided more opportunities for employment and advancement of skilled workers and professionals, those who were now unable to look to West Germany. There remained serious problems, however, and even though a wider range of consumer goods was available, the quality was often poor.

In political terms there was little relaxation of controls, and in 1968 the status of the SED as the country's only legal party was embedded in a new constitution. Elements of the 1949 constitution, such as the right to strike and rights of free speech and assembly, were either absent from or qualified in the new constitution.

In contrast to East Germany, whose citizens were prevented from traveling during the 1960s, Czechoslovakia made it easier: In 1963 47,000 Czechoslovaks visited the West; in 1967, 258,000, a small 2 percent of the population but a striking number. This policy, which diverged from that of other Eastern European states, reflected a general liberalization of politics from the late 1950s. There was a partial rehabilitation of those purged in 1949–54, and the massive statue of Stalin in Prague was taken down. In the mid-1960s censorship was relaxed and American and Western European radio and television programs aired. Parliament became more involved in governing, even rejecting some legislation submitted to it, and changes to the electoral law in 1967 allowed the possibility of rival candidates in elections.

In the economic sphere Czechoslovakia began to decline, and there was virtually no growth at all by 1963. Poor planning, the failure of the Soviet Union to provide promised food and supplies, and the severe winter of 1962–63 were blamed, as living standards slipped below those of Hungary and Poland. One day a week was decreed meatless. In order to revive the economy, a new decentralized system was put in place in 1965. Some private enterprise was permitted, factories were allowed to purchase their own raw materials, and they could retain their profits for sharing among their workers or for reinvestment.

These reforms whetted appetites for more. In 1967 there were open challenges to the one-party state from intellectuals. Slovaks, who were adversely affected by some of the economic reforms, also resented the only partial rehabilitation of the victims of the purges. The Slovak section of the Communist Party was led by Alexander Dubček, who in 1967 criticized the share of investment being directed toward Slovakia. To these grievances were added those of students over the rigid structure of party youth organizations, housing, and study conditions. When a group of students marched into Prague to protest conditions, they were dispersed by the police using batons, tear gas, and water cannons. Under growing pressure, the prime minister resigned in January 1968 and was replaced by Dubček.

Although Dubček's first act was to reassure the Soviet leaders that Czechoslovakia would remain faithful to Communist principles and the Warsaw Pact, his second, third, and subsequent acts hardly followed logically. Farmers were told that they themselves should decide what crops to grow, the press was allowed to flout censorship regulations, and pressure groups and organizations sprouted up on all sides. The flowering of political and cultural activities became known as the "Prague Spring."

In April 1968, an Action Program was promulgated to set out the country's path to socialism. It included a reduced role for the state, more freedom for industry and agriculture, a relationship of equality between Czechoslovakia and the Soviet Union, and the withdrawal of all Soviet military advisers. It anticipated a wide range of civil liberties (but excluded freedom of association, or political parties) and a strengthening of parliament and the courts. In foreign policy it called for recognition of Israel. On the other hand, the program envisaged that the Communist Party should maintain its leading role, while being more sensitive to the needs of specific interest groups.

Through the middle of 1968, Czechoslovakia experienced a ferment of reform, some of it going further than envisaged. Unions of peasants (a quarter-million strong), veterans, and artisans were formed. Concessions were made to the churches, allowing them to offer religious education and reestablish youth organizations. Councils were set up in many factories to look after workers' interests during the transition to the new economy. The government even made some concessions on political parties, although it refused to allow the reestablishment of the Social Democratic Party, which it had absorbed in 1948.

By August, reform seemed unstoppable, and new laws promulgated that month introduced a level of democracy within the Communist Party that was unprecedented. Party and state offices were to be separated, a limit was placed on the number of terms an officeholder could serve, and secret ballots were introduced. Even though the leading role of the party was reaffirmed, the policies it had sponsored in the preceding months had already deprived it of influence in many spheres of economic and cultural life in Czechoslovakia.

The scale and speed of these changes produced alarm both within Czechoslovakia, where conservatives could see their whole system sliding away, and throughout Eastern Europe, where leaders who purported to believe that material conditions were the driving force of change expressed hysterical fear of the effects of reformist ideas on their own citizens. They had other grounds for anxiety as well. Citizens of other Eastern European states were traveling to Czechoslovakia, then using the lax travel policies to escape to the West. There was concern that Czechoslovakia might ally with independent regimes in Yugoslavia and Romania or, alternatively, leave the Soviet bloc entirely. The Soviet Union feared West German influence in a liberalized Czechoslovakia, which by its geographical position could act as a conduit for German access to the Soviet Union.

Mindful of all these scenarios, the leaders of the Soviet Union, Poland, Hungary, East Germany, and Bulgaria met in Warsaw in July 1968 to assess the situation in Czechoslovakia. They issued a demand that the reforms be rescinded, but Dubček refused. He later held his ground in face-to-face talks with the Soviet leader, Leonid Brezhnev—meetings held in Czechoslovakia because so many Eastern European Communist leaders summoned to Moscow had discovered that their tickets were one-way only. The result of the talks in late July and early August 1968 was a joint statement reaffirming Communist principles and solidarity that neither side really subscribed to; Dubček did not mean it, and Brezhnev knew it.

Weeks later, a more genuine Soviet response was issued in the form of a military invasion by thousands of infantry, 7,500 tanks, and a thousand aircraft. The force included small units of East German, Polish, Bulgarian, and Hungarian troops to make it look like a Warsaw Pact operation rather than solely a Soviet initiative. The Czechoslovaks resisted only by refusing all cooperation, removing highway signs, and arguing with the invasion forces. In isolated incidents of more determined defense, an estimated 200 civilians were killed.

A poster that appeared at the time of the Soviet invasion of Prague in 1968. Many Czechs remained committed to communism, and the poster implies that Lenin would have wept had he known that the Soviet Union sent tanks into Czechoslovakia. The letters being crushed by the tank stand for Czechoslovak Socialist Republic.

The leaders of the Communist Party were taken to Moscow, where they were browbeaten and threatened, but the popular support they clearly enjoyed at home forced the Soviet Union to reach an agreement with them. Dubček remained in office, a censorship law was passed, and the Czechoslovak government signed an agreement allowing Soviet troops to be stationed temporarily on its territory. In April 1969, however, anti-Soviet protests led the Soviet Union to intervene and remove Dubček from office.

In political and economic terms, the Eastern European states linked to the Soviet Union represented genuine variations on a theme. Apart from Yugoslavia, none broke formally with agreements like Comecon and the Warsaw Pact, but some acted as if those arrangements did not exist. Some regimes tried faithfully to emulate the contortions in Soviet domestic policies, whereas others developed their own plans for reform. Some aped Soviet foreign policy stances; others pursued independent foreign policies. There was, in short, no typical Eastern European state, any more than there was a typical Western European one, although the former did vary within narrower limits.

Social Change in Eastern Europe, 1955–70

When looking at social change in the Eastern European Communist states, it is important to distinguish between actual and apparent changes. All the regimes were anxious to emphasize the ideological point that the working class had come to power there, and in some cases a statistical sleight of hand was used to buttress the argument. In Hungary, for example, workers in agriculture and workers in industry were all counted as workers so as to give an impression of a large working class; in East Germany after 1963, statistics no longer distinguished manual from nonmanual workers, with the result that the great majority of the workforce could be described as working class.

It was not that these statistics were utterly wrong, but that they exaggerated a social trend, for throughout Eastern Europe one result of postwar industrialization was the growth of the working class. Conversely, the proportion of the population involved in agriculture declined; between 1950 and 1970 the percentage fell from 38 to 19 in Czechoslovakia, from 24 to 13 in East Germany, and from 49 to 25 in Hungary. In Poland the decline was somewhat less pronounced: 56 percent of workers were agricultural in 1950, and 39 percent still in 1970. Even in the more intensively agricultural economies of southern Eastern Europe the trend was clear. In Bulgaria the proportion of the workforce in agriculture fell from 70 to 57 percent between 1956 and 1966.

The transformation of Eastern Europe from a predominantly agrarian to an industrial economy must rank as one of the most important social changes in the postwar period. Although there had been a gradual movement in this direction for decades, the trend was accelerated in the 1950s and 1960s. The most important area of social mobility during the late 1960s occurred as peasants became industrial workers. As new manual workers entered the labor force, they made possible the movement of other manual workers into nonmanual occupations.

The reasons for the flight from the country varied immensely. Programs of collectivization, usually accompanied by compulsory state purchasing and limits on private cultivation, antagonized many peasants, who left the land in protest. But the better and more varied standards of living made possible by industrial employment were attractions in their own right, particularly for young people. Towns and cities offered better educational facilities—which in turn permitted people to improve their employment prospects—as well as broader cultural and social outlets.

Expectations were often disappointed, however, because goods and services were not always available. The rural exodus placed burdens on all manner of facilities and services, particularly in Hungary and Poland, where urban populations grew by about a third between 1950 and 1970. Housing was especially problematic, and construction fell well below demand to the point that in Poland many farm workers who opted for industrial employment had to live in hostels or commute long distances to work each day.

The pressure on housing and other facilities was at least not a result of rapidly increasing population, for birth rates generally declined steadily through the 1950s and 1960s. There were short-lived periods of increase—in the mid-1950s in Hungary and the late 1960s in Romania, for example—but overall, Eastern European fertility fell substantially. Poland had a rate of 29 births per 1,000 population in 1955, but only 17 per thousand by 1970; in Bulgaria the decline was from 20 to 16, and in Hungary from 21 to 15. Although there were numerous influences on the birth rate, the most important were the shift from agriculture to industry and within agriculture the collectivization of farms, both of which made children less important as workers and heirs.

No less important was the high rate of women's employment in Eastern Europe's economies, which was a deterrent to having additional children. In East Germany, women were 45 percent of the paid workforce in 1960, and 49 percent by 1970, being concentrated in the manufacturing and service sectors. In Hungary their representation rose from 35 to 41 percent in the same period. Such rates were considerably higher than in Western European states.

Governments in the East, like their counterparts in the West, made affirmations about the equality of women and men but treated them differently. Despite their high rate of paid employment, married women were expected by governments, as well as husbands in general, to look after children and the home. A great deal of women's out of work time could not be devoted to leisure because it was absorbed by shopping, cooking, and child-care. The East German government recognized this by allowing women time off to look after sick children, and there was also a statutory day off for housework. This partially relieved the burden of most women who effectively worked at two jobs. In all Eastern European countries, extensive provision was made for day care.

Women also benefited from the extension of educational opportunities as many of Eastern Europe's regimes created a stratum of technicians, professionals, and managers, many of whom were needed to replace those purged in the early 1950s. University enrollments surged throughout the region between 1960 and 1970, rising by 50 percent in Czechoslovakia and Bulgaria, doubling in Poland, Romania, and Hungary, and more than doubling in East Germany. But there were great variations in the proportion of the population in higher education, with East Germany far outstripping Hungary and Czechoslovakia. Education was emphasized at all levels, and by the 1960s states required all children to have a minimum eight years in school, with East Germany requiring ten.

Despite fostering education, the communist regimes did not eliminate financial barriers, and many qualified students were unable to get the education they wanted. Even in the late 1960s, only half of Hungary's students received any financial aid from the state. Housing and other conditions were often poor and, as we have seen, they contributed to student unrest in Czechoslovakia in the late 1960s.

Housing remained a more general problem throughout the region, both in terms of the quantity and quality of dwellings. Even in the mid-1960s, each dwelling (most of them apartments) in Poland and Czechoslovakia was inhabited on average by about four people, although the situation in Hungary was a little better. The best-housed population was East Germany's, with fewer than three people per dwelling, about the same as in France and Sweden. But the pressure on housing was low in East Germany because, in addition to the very low birth rate, the country had lost millions of emigrants to West Germany before the Berlin Wall stemmed the flow; neither of these trends was particularly welcomed by the government.

It is difficult to generalize about the standards of living in Eastern Europe's societies. Real incomes rose slowly but steadily during the 1960s, but economic priorities and poor planning often prevented people from using their additional income to purchase consumer goods. In some cases consumer and state priorities coincided. Televisions were in high demand, and because they were increasingly used for propaganda and other state purposes, they were produced in satisfactory numbers at affordable prices. Television ownership rose rapidly, 4-fold in Czechoslovakia and East Germany, but 200-fold in Bulgaria, where between 1960 and 1970 the number of television sets in use rose from 5,000 to over a million. Rates of television ownership were not greatly different from those in Western European states. By 1970 there was one television for every four people in East Germany and one for every eight in Bulgaria. Domestic conveniences like telephones and washing machines also became more common, but there were great variations among Eastern European states. It was the same story with automobile ownership, which increased dramatically from very low levels in 1960; in East Germany, the most motorized of the countries, there were 68 private vehicles for every thousand people in 1970, and in Poland there were 15 per thousand.

There were, of course, great variations in prosperity within each country as well. In Hungary, for example, professionals were far more likely than manual workers to own a telephone. Within the new societies that developed between 1950 and 1970, there emerged elites, notably in government administration and industrial management. People in these occupations earned higher incomes than manual workers; but compared with Western Europe, the range of income inequality was relatively narrow, and there were attempts to guarantee a minimum standard of living. This does not alter the fact that a political, economic, and cultural elite began to develop that would later attract a great deal of resentment.

A more general change occurred in diet, which became more varied. Between 1950 and 1970 per capita consumption of cereals fell throughout the region, and people consumed more meat, dairy products, and sugar. Between 1950 and 1970, for example, per capita consumption of meat rose 50 percent in Hungary and Poland, doubled in Czechoslovakia, and more than doubled in East Germany. Consumption of sugar rose between 50 and 100 percent throughout the region.

Although there are currents of dietary thought that argue that such commodities as meat, dairy products, and sugar do not contribute to good health, food has important cultural values that may override nutritional value. In Eastern Europe cereals, in the form of coarse bread, soups, and gruel, were the basis of the peasant and preindustrial diet and are associated with backwardness, while meat and sugar are thought of as modern. To this extent, the access people had to these foods was an indicator of how their living standards were changing and a measure of how well their governments were performing. For this reason, some foods were subsidized, and the Communist regimes, aware as governments have been for centuries that the food supply and social order are intimately related, increased food prices only as a last resort.

The relative prosperity that Eastern Europeans experienced in this period was not great enough to produce a baby boom, or at least not great enough to cancel out countervailing factors like high rates of female employment and overcrowded dwellings. The shift of population from agriculture to industry elsewhere in Europe was associated with the decline in fertility that we have already noted. By 1970 only Romania had a birth rate over 20 per thousand, and all the rest fell in the range 14 to 17 per thousand. There were small baby booms in East Germany in the early 1960s and in Bulgaria, Czechoslovakia, Hungary, and Romania in the late 1960s, but they were all modest and short lived.

A related trend was a steady decline in infant mortality, such that by 1970 the rates in Communist Eastern Europe as a region varied in roughly the same way as in the West. Czechoslovakia's and East Germany's levels of infant mortality were comparable to those of Belgium and West Germany; Bulgaria's was the same as Austria's; and, at the high end, Romania and Hungary had affinities to Greece and Portugal.

The spread of prosperity began later than the rise in the standard of living in Western Europe, and although it paralleled the Western experience, it certainly did not match it. On the whole, however, it is not very enlightening to compare the two regions (although many Eastern Europeans did), because they emerged from quite different sets of conditions: Eastern Europe suffered far more material damage and human loss during the Second World War, and had always been poorer than Western Europe no matter how material wealth is measured. It is more useful to compare Eastern European countries with one another and to look at the progress of each over time. The sluggishness of economic recovery can then be explained in terms of the effect on long-term structural conditions of national government policies, like purges and collectivization, and their relationships with the Soviet Union.

One socialist country was able to develop independent of the Soviet Union. Yugoslavia, under the leadership of Josip Tito, had declared its autonomy earlier, and during the 1950s was branded as a renegade socialist state by the Soviet leadership. "Titoism" was one of the great political crimes of the period, and generally meant the failure to follow Soviet policy. Not only did Yugoslavia diverge by adopting a neutralist foreign policy (it became one of the nonaligned states), it also abolished state economic planning in the early 1960s. In 1962 Yugoslav citizens were able to travel freely to the West, and tens of thousands did so as foreign workers. A seasonal influx of foreigners as tourists to the country's Adriatic coastal resorts brought hard currency and created work for those who stayed behind. Foreign newspapers, books, and films circulated with few restrictions. By 1965 further reforms allowed private enterprise, permitted foreign investment of up to 49 percent in Yugoslav businesses, and abolished price controls. Within a short time, political controls were also loosened, and the identification of the state and ruling party was severed at all levels apart from the presidency.

One of the expectations of the reformers was that decentralization of economic and political power would undermine the appeal of nationalism within Yugoslavia's constituent ethnic populations. The Serbs represented 41 percent of the country's 21.5 million people, and because of the role of Serbia in south Slavic unification and the fact that the national capital, Belgrade, was located in Serbia, there was a tendency to identify centralization of any kind with Serbian domination. It was a reasonable perspective, because the army, police, and security forces were mainly Serbian.

In the late 1960s the language issue arose once again, when Croats demanded that Serbian and Croatian be recognized as separate languages and that the latter be used in Croatian schools. Other national groups, including the Serbians, chimed in with their own linguistic demands, and in 1967 the use of languages other than Serbo-Croat was permitted in the federal parliament and simultaneous translation was provided. This was more than symbolic, because language policy was a substantive issue, but the success of linguistic nationalism marked the beginning of greater problems for the supranational Yugoslav unity Tito had fostered.

It is worth noting that in the rest of Eastern Europe, nationality conflicts had all but disappeared. As we have seen, they surfaced in Czechoslovakia because the country was essentially a union of two different national groups, and the Bulgarian regime oppressed its Turkish minority. But by the 1960s, just as immigration and foreign labor were making Western European states ethnically more heterogeneous, Eastern Europe was more homogeneous than ever before. Populations other than the Czechs and Slovaks represented less than 5 percent of Czechoslovakia's inhabitants; minorities accounted for less than 5 percent of the population in Hungary, and under 2 percent in East Germany and Poland.

Conclusion

The period from the early 1950s to the late 1960s saw what might be called a tendency of convergence that narrowed the differences between Eastern and Western Europe in many spheres. The most remarkable changes took place in the East, where rapid industrialization sharply reduced the dominance of agricultural workers in the labor force, as had happened half a century earlier in much of Western Europe. General living standards improved in the East, although they remained considerably lower than in the West, and fertility rates fell to the ranges found in the various regions of Western Europe.

While there remained striking differences between the predominantly democratic governments of Western Europe (with the persistent exceptions of Spain and Portugal) and those of the East, there was evidence of some liberalization, however tentative and modest, throughout much of Soviet-dominated Europe. This trend was sometimes contradicted by authoritarian nationalist tendencies that emerged when the post-Stalin regime in the Soviet Union relaxed control over its Eastern European partners. Ironically, individual Eastern European states gained the possibility of following more individual socialist paths (within strictly demarcated limits, as the East Germans and Czechoslovaks discovered), just as key Western European states embarked on policies of harmonization that implied the partial surrender of national control over spheres of policy. As the European Economic Community gave way to the European Community, cooperation was expanded from the economic sphere to include the harmonization of social policies and law.

Clearly, the tendencies of Eastern and Western Europe to converge should not be exaggerated, nor should the fundamentally different contexts of change in each region be overlooked. The trends do provide, nonetheless, an important corrective to the all too easy view that Europe in this period was composed of two blocs, radically different in all respects, facing each other from different sides of the cold war.

· 11 ·

Challenge and Decline, 1970–1985

Introduction

Between 1970 and the middle of the 1980s, much of Europe, East and West, went through a similar experience although in vastly different contexts. Standards of living had generally risen during the 1960s, but in 1973 they were suddenly interrupted by rising energy prices. Western Europe entered a recession, with rising prices for manufactured goods, falling productivity, and growing unemployment. Eastern Europe was sheltered from the recession for some years, but by the end of the 1970s economies there began to experience difficulties for reasons both related and unrelated to the economic problems in the West.

Declining living standards almost everywhere had varying impacts. Some governments in Western Europe fell, while Eastern European regimes came under increasing consumer pressure. Some made concessions to popular demands for not only economic but also political reform, while others asserted their authority more vigorously. The 1970s also brought to light a range of deep-seated social and economic problems. One was the status of women, which in Western Europe produced a vigorous feminist movement that had implications throughout society, the economy, and culture. Women in Eastern Europe experienced many of the same problems as in the West, but the debate on women's status there was carried on mainly by the ruling regimes and in quite distinct contexts. Other issues that came to the fore, mostly in Western Europe, included the widespread damage to the environment that had resulted from decades of unregulated industrialization.

The European Economy, 1970–85

In the late 1960s and early 1970s, the prosperity that Western Europe had begun to experience from the mid-1950s reached its peak. Real incomes had grown impressively as wages rose in conditions of low annual rates of inflation in the range of 4 to 5 percent in France, Great Britain, Italy, and most other countries, but under 3 percent in West Germany. Unemployment was also low, only 2 or 3 percent in most states, with the exception of Ireland where it was 7 percent. In Germany unemployment rose above 2 percent in just a single year during the 1960s, and by 1970 was only 0.7 percent.

Western Europeans were better nourished than they ever had been. There were variations, of course, and still extensive pockets of poverty, but the expansion of social welfare reduced the poor to historically low proportions of the population. Infant mortality rates had slid to record low levels, ranging from Italy's 27 per thousand births in 1972 to 11 per thousand in Sweden. At the material level, the numbers of automobiles on the Western European roads was such that new and wider highways had to be built. In the major states there was one private automobile for every four people, and even where cars were less common they were not much so: There was one automobile for every six Austrians, for example.

But by the early 1970s there were signs of structural problems behind the facade of Western European prosperity. It had rested in part on the demands of postwar reconstruction, but by then the pace of urban rebuilding, housing construction, and industrial recovery began to decelerate, and there was a slackening of demand. Inflation began to rise as wages in some countries outpaced productivity and increased labor costs and profits were translated into higher prices. The consumer shopping spree made possible by higher incomes led to increased imports and balance of trade problems. By 1971 inflation and unemployment began to rise perceptibly.

There was another weakness in that much of the prosperity experienced in Western Europe since the 1950s rested on abundant supplies of oil imported from the Middle East. Since World War II, oil had replaced coal as the main form of energy, and by the early 1970s oil produced almost two-thirds of Western European energy. Not only did many power stations run on oil, making oil vital to the functioning of industry, but the mechanization of agriculture and the production of fertilizer made the primary sector dependent on oil, too.

The material well-being of Western European consumers was also oil based. Cheap goods of all kinds relied on cheap energy, and oil produced much of the power to run the increasing number of household appliances. The immense numbers of private and commercial vehicles on the road—some 85 million in all—guzzled billions of gallons of gasoline each year. Much domestic and commercial central heating, which had become more popular as people's wealth and expectations of comfort rose, was oil-fired. It was clear that any dramatic change in the supply or price of oil was bound to have an immediate and far-reaching impact on Western European economic and social life.

In October 1973, such a change occurred when the Organization of Petroleum Exporting Countries (OPEC), which included all the major oil-exporting countries, raised its prices by 70 percent. The Arab oil-exporting states went further and for a while cut off supplies to the Netherlands in retaliation for that country's allowing its territory to be used for the transfer of American supplies to Israel during the 1973 war in the Mideast. The initial oil price increase was followed by others, including a second major increase in 1979, until by the end of the 1970s oil cost $30 a barrel, three times the 1972 price.

Such price increases had profound effects in Western Europe. At the individual level, the cost of running an automobile rose dramatically, and the price of heating fuel rose. The centrality of oil as a raw material, and as energy for the production and distribution of industrial and agricultural goods, meant that the oil price increase was quickly reflected in wholesale and retail prices. The cost of oil imports became a heavy burden on the balance of payments; in Spain energy accounted for 13 percent of the cost of imports in 1973 and 42 percent in 1981. Inflation began to rise, reaching 16 percent in Great Britain and Italy, and double digits in other states. Germany again did better: Inflation had reached 5 percent by 1972, and it rose to 7 percent in 1973 and 1974.

Although the rise in oil prices was itself responsible for the jolt Western European economies felt in the mid-1970s, the other weaknesses added to the malaise that affected them in the following ten years. In part the reason was the success of non-European in-

During the OPEC oil boycott of the Netherlands in 1973, there were occasional bans on the use of automobiles in order to prevent depletion of the nation's fuel stocks. People resorted to bicycles, and occasionally to more traditional horse power, to get around.

dustrial development. Western European industry failed to invest as much in updating its plant and technology, or in research and development, and it fell behind new industrial powers, notably Japan. Asian producers quickly dominated the new electronics, communications, and computer industries. In addition, Western European workers were relatively highly paid and beneficiaries of expensive social security benefits that made their goods far more expensive than those produced in Asia and Latin America. Wages there were low, benefits often nonexistent, and industry not subject to the environmental and other regulations that became increasingly required in Western Europe.

The effects of oil prices and non-European competition on longer-term weaknesses in world markets sent Western Europe's economies into a tailspin. Sectors of the European economy that had led the rise in prosperity, like steel and automobiles, went into decline. The automobile industry was hit by both Japanese competition and the impact of higher gasoline prices, and from 1973 production fell in all Western European countries. Italy was especially affected, and the Alfa Romeo plant near Naples was reported to have recorded greater losses than any other automobile plant in the world.

The general European recession affected countries differently, according to their economic structures and the policies their governments adopted, but none escaped. By the mid-1980s, after another round of oil price increases, unemployment stood above 20 percent in Spain, 15 percent in Italy, 13 percent in Britain, and 9 percent in Germany. The impact was hardest on young people, and across Western Europe a quarter of employable men and women under the age of twenty-five were out of work. The hardest hit were young Dutch men and women, Italians, and Spaniards; by the end of 1984 some 800,000 young people in Spain were unemployed.

Inflation also continued to rise, despite increased unemployment and declining production, which themselves ought to have reduced demand. What kept prices up was the steady and at times increasing cost of oil and oil-based products and services, and the fact that the unemployed were more protected financially by social security plans than they ever had been. Inflation went into double digits throughout Western Europe, and exceeded 20 percent in Italy during 1980. Retail prices in Britain doubled between 1973 and 1978.

The new economic situation posed various challenges to Western European governments. One was to reduce oil consumption or locate new sources of oil or oil substitutes. Conservation measures were adopted in all countries, including lower maximum speeds on highways, days when driving automobiles was forbidden, and campaigns to increase the use of public transport and reduce the level of heating in homes and offices. In the winter of 1973–74, the British government responded to shortages of both oil and coal (caused by a ban on overtime work by miners' unions) by imposing a three-day workweek on industries and large stores.

Medium-term solutions to energy-supply problems were met by developing North Sea oil fields. Although oil reserves had been recognized for some time, the costs of drilling and extraction made North Sea oil uneconomical until Middle Eastern oil prices rose and there was a political desire to escape dependence on non-European sources. By 1980, Great Britain and Norway had become not only self-sufficient in oil but also exporters. The Netherlands recovered natural gas from the North Sea. Italy also turned to its gas reserves, but they proved quite inadequate for its requirements in the 1970s. Another option was nuclear power, which had been developed on a small scale in the 1950s. Advocates of its use had to contend with anxiety about its safety, but nonetheless a number of nuclear power stations were built in several countries in the 1970s and 1980s. By the mid-1980s they generated half of France's electricity. Energy projects that were less contentious environmentally, like harnessing wind, sun, and waves, were tested but had little practical impact. As North Sea oil and nuclear power became available and as economies adjusted to the cost of imported supplies, the drive to find alternative fuels declined.

The effects of the various crises in the Western European economies remained by the mid-1980s, however. Even though inflation rates had been reduced, unemployment was high and Europe had a diminished role in the global economy. Real incomes had declined after the two oil price increases in 1973 and 1979. Western Europe's postwar age of prosperity, if a decade and a half can be called an age, seemed to be over.

Politics and Policies Under Economic Stress

The weakening of Western Europe's economies placed existing governments under stress. Even though recessions such as the one that began in the 1970s were international in scope and to some extent beyond the control of any one national government, voters turned against administrations they judged were not doing as much as they could.

In Great Britain the energy crisis intersected with other problems facing the Conservative administration of Edward Heath. Even before oil prices rose, inflation and unemployment had increased. The government tried a confusing array of solutions that included cutting taxes and increasing spending, nationalizing distressed companies (such as Rolls Royce) and subsidizing others (such as Scottish shipbuilding), and finally trying to impose limits on wage increases.

This last policy led to widespread industrial unrest, and the 23 million working days lost by strikes in 1972 represented the highest level of industrial action since the general strike of 1926. By the time the oil price increase took hold, Britain's society and economy were in a parlous state, and Heath decided to add politics to the mixture. In a 1974 general election the Conservatives won slightly more of the popular vote (37.9 percent) than the Labour Party (37.1), but the Labour Party won more seats (301 to 297) and was able to form a minority government under Harold Wilson.

Labour, which had historic links to the union movement, formed a "social contract" to control wages and prices. After only eight months Wilson called a new election, believing that he could secure a majority. He did, but only just, winning 319 seats in the 635-seat House of Commons, a vulnerable majority of three. The government faced a number of problems, including rising support for Scottish nationalism and the question of British membership in the European Economic Community, but the economy demanded immediate action. Inflation rose to 17 percent in 1974 and 27 percent in 1975. Cuts in spending and a policy to restrict wage increases helped reduce inflation to 13 percent by 1977, but at great social cost: Unemployment rose to 1.2 million and the purchasing power of workers fell by 7 percent in two years.

Sharpened conflicts with organized labor over wage restraints and loss of its majority by defeats in by-elections brought the Labour government down in 1979. The ensuing election was easily won by the Conservatives, for although their share of the popular vote actually fell (to 44 percent), they won 339 seats out of 635. The Conservatives had been led since 1975 by Margaret Thatcher, the first woman to head a major British political party, and who became, in 1979, the first British woman prime minister.

The victory of the Conservatives under Thatcher represented more than the usual shift of emphasis between the moderately socialist Labour Party and the moderate Conservative Party that not only did not shy away from the welfare state, nationalization, and state subsidies, but actually implemented such policies from time to time. Under Thatcher the Conservatives moved to a different policy plane. Their initial aim was to bring inflation under control by a policy known as 'monetarism,' which involved attempting to control price increases by limiting the money in circulation. Deflationary measures like tax increases and cuts in government spending had the effect of reducing inflation, but at great cost. Fifty years after the Great Depression, Britain recorded its worst economic figures since the 1930s: Unemployment in January 1982 exceeded 3 million, some 13 percent of the workforce, and the gross national product fell by 3.2 percent. An estimated 25 percent of British manufacturing capacity was destroyed in the space of a few years.

The "Thatcherite" Conservatives argued that radical restructuring had to take place for the long-term health of the British economy. If this meant short-term hardship on entrepreneurs and workers, then that was the price they had to pay for the prosperity they had squandered in the 1960s. Industrialists were faulted for failing to reinvest and modernize their plants, workers for taking unrealistic wage increases. The determination of the Conservatives to curb organized labor was demonstrated in 1984, when miners went on strike over wages and new restrictions on union activities. A long strike, marked by widespread violence, police repression, and the arrest of 12,000 miners, was won by the government, which had prepared by stockpiling coal supplies. Under the impact of government policies, unemployment, and the recession, union membership fell from 13.5 to 10.8 million between 1979 and 1985.

In the first years of the Conservative government, there was less sign of the major attacks on the welfare state, education, and the state's role in the British economy and society that

British mine workers and supporters rally at Trafalgar Square in February 1985, during a strike that lasted more than a year.

were to become the hallmark of Thatcherism. They became more prominent from the mid-1980s once Thatcher had consolidated her leadership and control of Conservative Party policy. This was achieved in various ways, not least by the government's decision to go to war with Argentina when that country invaded, occupied, and annexed the Falkland Islands, an island colony in the South Atlantic populated by 1,200 people and thousands of sheep, all of British origin. A British task force of 28,000 troops recaptured the islands, and by turning the Falklands War into a major nationalist crusade, the government rallied support. Thatcher herself adopted the demeanor of a latter-day Churchill, with high-flown speeches evoking patriotism and the defense of democracy and freedom. It was just the sort of thing many Britons wanted to hear after decades of declining power in the world.

Military victory cost 255 British lives, two frigates, and made a huge hole in government spending plans, but it contributed to a political victory. The Conservatives won a carefully timed election in 1983 with 61 percent of the seats in the House of Commons (and 44 percent of the popular vote). The way was clear for a full-scale assault on the state's role in Britain.

German politics were less affected than British by the oil price shocks, partly because the wealth that they generated in the Middle East provided a market, albeit limited, for prestigious German automobiles. German companies were also able to sell technology and expertise as the oil-exporting states used their new revenues to develop their own economies. Moreover, Germany was not embroiled in economic conflicts when the energy crisis arose.

In Germany it was the Social Democrats (SPD) who held power in the most troubled economic period, from 1969 to 1982. Initially led by Willy Brandt, a progressive reformer, the SPD governed in a coalition with the liberal Free Democrats and planned to expand social welfare and reform the tax system. After a challenge from the Christian Democrats (CDU), Brandt called an election in 1972, in which for the first time more Germans supported the SPD than the CDU. Encouraged, Brandt began to put his reforms in place, only to have them shunted aside by the first oil price increase. In 1974 Brandt, who was being criticized within his own party for his economic policies, was edged out of the chancellorship after it was discovered that one of his closest consultants was an East German spy. Brandt was replaced by Helmut Schmidt, from the more pragmatic wing of the SPD.

The government's main achievement was to hold inflation to lower levels than elsewhere in Europe. Control of inflation was especially important in Germany because social memory of the disastrous 1923 inflation was still strong. Prices rose by nearly 8 percent in 1974, which was less than half the rate of some other states, and support for the SPD slipped in the 1976 election. But by the end of the 1970s inflation was under 3 percent, and in the 1980 elections it was the CDU vote that fell substantially.

But the understanding between the liberals and social democrats, made possible by the prosperity of the 1960s, that allowed the Free Democrat–SPD coalition to work, weakened under the pressures of economic downturn. In 1980 the Free Democrats gained support at the expense of the SPD and CDU, attracting more than 10 percent of the votes. Free Democrats became increasingly disturbed by deficit budgeting, and warmed to the financially more conservative policies advocated by the Christian Democrats. In 1982 several Free Democrats left the coalition, and the government lost a vote of confidence in Parliament. The CDU leader Helmut Kohl became chancellor, and in 1983 elections the CDU won almost half (48.8 percent) of the votes. Kohl was easily able to form a coalition with the Free Democrats, an arrangement that lasted into the mid-1990s.

In France conservatives governed during the economic problems of the 1970s, first Georges Pompidou (who took over after de Gaulle resigned in 1969, but who died in office in 1974) and then Valéry Giscard d'Estaing (1974–81). The French economy did better than many others. Both inflation and unemployment rose, but policies protected the incomes of the employed: Real incomes of workers rose by a quarter between 1975 and 1981. A high level of personal saving permitted by improved incomes partly offset the decline in investment on the part of industry itself, and France took advantage of opportunities to develop new areas of industry, particularly electronics. Even though the French balance of payments ran a deficit from 1973 to 1977, it returned to a surplus by 1978, and by 1979 France had improved its position among the major exporting nations. The government was reelected in 1978, partly because the Communists and Socialists could not form a united front. Left-wing parties won 49 percent of the vote on the first ballot, but only 42 percent of the seats in parliament after the right unified for the second ballot.

It was not a wholly rosy picture, however. The poor were penalized by the comprehensive indirect tax on virtually all purchases that consumed a higher percentage of the budgets of the poor than of the better off. Relatively low rates of personal income tax and the reluctance of parliament to institute a capital gains tax worked to the benefit of the wealthy. There was anxiety as unemployment rose steadily from under 3 percent to nearly 8 percent. Even that was artificially reduced when many Algerian immigrants took advantage of a government offer of 10,000 francs to any who would leave France. Finally, because the great majority of French families rented their homes, there was widespread concern when rent controls began to be phased out.

Disenchantment with Giscard's government was expressed in 1981 when he was defeated in the presidential election by the Socialist leader, François Mitterrand. Because the national assembly had a conservative majority, Mitterrand promptly called an election.

Many conservatives, opposed to Giscard but unable to vote for the left, appear not to have voted, and the low voter turnout contributed to the Socialist Party's winning 55 percent of the seats in the national assembly. The Communist Party won 16 percent of the popular vote on the first ballot, its poorest showing since the Second World War. Even so, Mitterrand appointed four Communist deputies to his cabinet, although none was given a post that had any responsibility for defense or domestic security.

In 1981 the French government inaugurated economic programs to stimulate economic recovery and employment. Government investment was planned to provide employment and raise low wages so as to strengthen domestic demand and promote production. A program of nationalization began, encompassing all French-owned banks as well as major companies involved in chemicals, electronics, communications, and textiles. Extensive, sometimes majority, holdings were purchased in other aeronautics, computer, and communications companies. By 1985 the French state had doubled its control of France's industrial productivity to 30 percent. The financial cost was enormous: 39 billion francs in capital and 47 billion in interest over fifteen years.

Mitterrand's government also raised wages at the lowest levels (which had repercussions among the better paid whose incomes were geared to benchmarks at the lower levels) and attempted to give tax relief to workers. A wide range of income improvements was provided for the worse off. Family allowances and housing subsidies were raised, and medical benefits under the state scheme were improved. Although unemployment remained persistently high, it was alleviated a little by extensive government hiring (200,000 extra employees in the first year) and by encouraging early retirement to provide work for young people.

The problem with these policies was that France was exposed to the rest of the European economy through the EEC. There could be no tariffs to protect French industry, and industrial production rose at only half the rate of purchasing power. Instead of buying French products, people bought imports, especially automobiles and electrical appliances.

Financial pressure forced the Socialist government to abandon its spending policies as early as 1982 and replace them with curbs on wages and a reduction of social benefits. By 1985 inflation had been brought down to 4 percent, less than a third the 1981 rate, but unemployment was again high, almost 11 percent. In the 1986 parliamentary elections, the Socialists, although the largest single party, won only 36 percent of the seats to the 48 percent of the two conservative blocs. The Communists slumped to 9.8 percent, only a tenth of 1 percent more than a new extreme right-wing party, the National Front.

The fourth major European state, Italy, faced mounting political and economic difficulties in the 1970s and early 1980s. The sudden rise in the cost of oil in 1973 led to an elongated recession and rising prices. Wages in Italy were indexed to the cost of living, however, and as prices and wages rose, they pushed up industrial costs. Production fell, and in 1975 Italy's GNP declined (by 3.7 percent) for the first time since the Second World War. The response of Christian Democratic governments was to increase spending on regional development, subsidies for industry, and social welfare.

The Christian Democrats, who had governed since 1945, began to show signs of wearing out. In the mid-1970s evidence began to come to light of financial corruption in high places, including payments to political parties by oil companies in exchange for tax concessions. The challenge to the Christian Democrats came not only from the Socialists, who had been included in the governing coalitions from 1962, but also from a rejuvenated Communist Party. Led by Enrico Berlinguer, Italian Communists abandoned their principled isolation in the early 1970s and adopted a pragmatic set of policies dubbed the "historic compromise." They accepted the principles and implications of electoral democracy (that a party once elected might later be dismissed by the voters) and sought to cooperate with other political groups, including the left wing of the Christian Democrats.

By the mid-1970s the Communists, who had always been strong in the main industrial centers, had been elected to office in most major cities and half the regional administrations. In the 1976 national elections they won 34 percent of the vote, only slightly less than the Christian Democrats, and between 1977 and 1979 the Communists joined governing coalitions. There they supported such unlikely policies as Italy's membership of NATO. Thereafter, however, the Communist vote declined (to 30 percent in 1979) for a variety of reasons that included growing tension between the Church and Communists everywhere following the election of a Polish pope, John Paul II, in 1978. It made no difference that the Italian communists generally supported the Solidarity movement in Poland, which opposed the Communist government there. The historic compromise began to fall afoul of many anti-Communists and Communists alike.

Among the other Western European states, the experience of economic problems varied, as did their policies. Almost all implemented policies to reduce public-sector spending in order to reduce the level of inflation. This trend placed particular pressure on governments committed to high levels of investment in social security. In Belgium and the Netherlands, state spending was cut, and for the same reasons the Social Democrats who seemed to have an unassailable position in Scandinavia found themselves rejected by the electorates as their economies foundered.

Sweden proved to be particularly vulnerable because it had no domestic source of fuel to offset the increased price of oil, but was committed to heavy state spending to fund its comprehensive social welfare system. The Social Democrats had come to power in Sweden to cope with the depression in 1932, and they were thrown out for failing to deal with the recession in 1974. The centrist government that governed for the following eight years followed policies of austerity, but generally maintained the social welfare system intact. In 1982 the Social Democrats under Olaf Palme were returned to power, but even they began to look more critically at social spending in the cold light of rising deficits.

Even in Norway, which began to reap the benefits of revenues from North Sea oil, the Social Democrats were replaced by a centrist party in 1981. In Denmark the governing Social Democrats were threatened in 1973 by the rise of the Progressive Party that represented a tax revolt. In 1982 a centrist coalition took power and imposed wage controls and reduced the social spending that by 1980 accounted for more than a quarter of all government expenditure.

Spain and Portugal stand out from the rest of Europe because the period of economic difficulty coincided with major political changes. The authoritarian regime of Antonio de Oliveira Salazar, who had been in power in Portugal in one form or another since the late 1920s until he died in 1970, was overthrown in 1974. The dictator next door, Francisco Franco, who had ruled Spain since leading his army to victory in the civil war in the late 1930s, finally died in 1975.

The catalyst for the revolution in Portugal was a colonial war in Angola and Mozambique that convinced many army officers that thoroughgoing changes needed to be made at home. In May 1974, a Supreme Revolutionary Council deposed the government and extricated Portugal from Africa, granting independence to the colonies. On the domestic front they implemented socialist policies, seizing large agricultural estates and turning them into cooperatives, and creating worker councils in factories. In 1976 a new constitution prescribed a socialist society for Portugal, but for the next ten years there was persistent political instability.

In Spain the death of Franco in 1975 represented a sharp break in some respects, but there was a relatively easy transition to the post-Franco period. Franco had prepared for the restoration of the monarchy, in the person of Juan Carlos, grandson of Alfonso XIII who had abdicated in 1931. General elections, including the Communist Party, which was legalized after Franco's death, were held in 1977 and brought a coalition of moderate socialist parties to power. In 1978 a new constitution created a liberal democratic state. Although there was residual support for a more authoritarian regime, its weakness was demonstrated in 1981 when a group of Civil Guard officers attempted a coup. Members invaded parliament, and shots were fired. There were few echoes throughout Spain, however, and all but one army commander pledged support to the king. In 1982 an election gave the Socialist Party power in its own right.

Spanish administrations in the five years before and the ten after Franco's death had to contend with serious economic problems. The country was dependent on imported oil for fueling its economy, and the 1973 price rise helped produce 25 percent inflation by 1977. Unemployment was high, particularly among young people. The post-Franco governments invested in energy and attempted to restructure industry and agriculture, and by the mid-1980s both sectors showed steady growth.

Clearly the economic and political developments of Western Europe between 1970 and 1985 were closely related. Economic policy, in fact, dominated agendas for much of the period, as governments attempted to balance three main considerations. First, there were ideological commitments, such as the maintenance of social welfare systems. Second, there was the impact of short-term policies, particularly insofar as they bore on public support for the government. Third, there were long-term considerations; if the government did stay in power, it would eventually have to confront the consequences of its short-term policies, perhaps in the form of massive debts. Most governments (Mitterrand's in France during 1981–82 was an exception) worked within a narrow range of options in which compromises could be made among all three categories of imperatives.

The commander of the forces that invaded the Spanish parliament gives orders to deputies during an attempted military coup in February 1981.

Social Change and Politics
in Western Europe, 1970–85

The downturn in the Western European economy and the policies governments adopted could not but have social consequences. The return of high unemployment and increases in the price of basic goods and services put pressure on the most vulnerable sections of society, and to varying degrees poverty expanded. Poverty in the 1970s was not the same as during the depression of the 1930s, however. In the intervening years, social safety nets had been woven, and policies like universal health care established in many countries. It is notable that indices of social suffering like infant mortality rates did not show even the slight increase in the 1970s and 1980s that they had during the early 1930s.

Relative poverty increased as the gap between the poor and the wealthy widened, particularly from the late 1970s. Until the 1970s there had been a tendency toward greater equality, even though income was still heavily concentrated within the higher earning strata everywhere. From the late 1970s, however, the trend went into reverse in many countries because of the recession and specific economic and fiscal policies. An example was Britain. In 1979, when the Conservatives led by Thatcher came to power, the top 20 percent of wage earners had received 37 percent of all income after taxes, but by 1988 they received 44 percent. At the other end of the scale, the bottom 20 percent of wage earners received 9.5 percent of all income in 1979, but only 6.9 percent by 1988.

To a large extent, the changes in British income distribution were the result of changes in taxation. After Britain joined the European Economic Community in 1973, a wide-ranging sales tax (Value Added Tax, or VAT) was introduced. Under Thatcher the Conservatives cut the top rates of income tax proportionally more than the lower rates, and deductions for health care were increased. The overall result was that low earners paid a much greater proportion of their wages in taxes than high earners. Britain had by no means the highest degree of income inequality in Western Europe; it was higher than the Scandinavian countries but lower than France, Italy, and Greece.

The growth of poverty in Europe that began in the 1970s can be expressed in various ways. The EEC defines poverty in terms of the percentage of households or persons receiving half or less of the average national income. In 1985 the highest rate of poverty was in Portugal, where a third of the population received less than half the national average wage. In Greece, Spain, and Ireland, around a fifth of the population qualified as poor, in Britain and Italy 14 to 15 percent, and in West Germany 11 percent. The lowest rates were in the Benelux states and Scandinavia.

The signs of growing poverty were increased demands on social welfare and services, as well as homelessness, begging, and a rise in crime typically associated with poverty. The number of homeless in Britain more than doubled in the ten years from 1979. The facilities and services offered by state welfare systems, as well as private charities, came under growing pressure and all governments had to increase the proportion of the budget devoted to such items as unemployment and welfare, benefits, housing assistance, and medical care.

Attitudes toward social welfare varied among countries, classes, and according to the specific question at issue. A 1985 survey of people in Britain, Austria, West Germany, and Italy showed that there was a general consensus in favor of increased government spending on health. This was the view not only of the poor among those who were surveyed but also of the wealthy, four-fifths of whom agreed with the notion in Britain and Italy, and three-fifths in Austria, although only a third of well-off Germans agreed. But when it came to fundamental social change in the form of reducing the gap between high- and low-income earners, the consensus broke down. It was favored by three-fifths or more of the poorer people who were surveyed, and by almost two-thirds of well-off Austrians and Italians. But only 52 percent of wealthy Germans were in favor and 37 percent of their British counterparts. The income gap that existed in all countries was reflected in the sharper attitude gap in Britain, reinforcing the view of the British as more committed to class distinctions than many other Europeans.

Unemployment and poverty affected some social groups more than others. Britain's 700,000-strong black population, most of Caribbean origin and many born in Britain, remained a marginal population underrepresented in education and employment. The young people, born in Britain of immigrant parents, and speaking with the accents of the regions and localities where they grew up, were neither fully accepted in Britain nor felt any great affinity to their parents' country of birth. Extensive unemployment, discrimination, and poverty underlay the serious riots that broke out in the predominantly black Brixton area of London in 1981. It was followed by outbreaks in black communities elsewhere in Britain, including Liverpool and Manchester, and there was another wave of violence in these communities in 1985.

Race became an issue in other Western European states in this period. Historically, French immigration policies reflected employment requirements, and just as in the 1930s, so in the 1970s rising unemployment turned public and government against immigrants. In 1974 the government offered foreign workers 10,000 francs to leave France, but there was no great rush to take it up. Between 1977 and 1980 the immigrant population fell by only 112,000, less than 3 percent. The immigrants facing greatest discrimination were North African, most of them Muslims from France's former colonies in Algeria, Tunisia, and Morocco. A new fascist party, the National Front, included the repatriation of immigrants among its policy priorities, and it received almost 10 percent of the vote in the 1986 elections and thirty-five seats in the national assembly.

The Socialist government of François Mitterrand adopted tolerant policies, however. The situation of illegal immigrants was regularized, immigration was resumed even though unemployment in France was rising, and the government implemented policies to integrate immigrant populations into mainstream society. Similar policies of integration were tried in other states, generally without success. Throughout Western Europe, immigrant populations tended to live in concentrated areas or ghettos. Sometimes the people themselves wanted this or needed to settle where they could be close to mosques or temples. Newcomers were understandably drawn to localities where they could shop for familiar foods, speak to neighbors and retailers in their own language, and watch movies that embodied their own cultural values. In other cases ghettoization was not by choice. The ethnic or racial homogeneity of a number of areas of London resulted not from the arrival there of blacks and Asians, which would have produced mixed communities, but from the subsequent departure of whites.

The 1970s and early 1980s also saw the continuation of demographic trends that had taken root during the 1960s and sometime earlier. Fertility, in steady decline apart from a few postwar upturns, continued to fall and by the 1970s was below replacement level. As a general rule, couples in a given society need to produce an average of about 2.1 children to ensure that population does not decline. By 1970 Western European states hovered around that number, but by 1975 all had fallen below it except for Ireland (where the average completed family size was 3.4), Spain (2.8), Portugal (2.6), and Italy (2.2). The lowest figure was 1.45 in West Germany, whereas most other states registered completed family sizes of between 1.6 and 2.0. Within ten years, by 1985, all the exceptions except

Ireland had fallen below replacement levels, and even in Ireland the average completed family had fallen to 2.5 children.

The rapid decline of family size reflected the spread of the two-child ideal, together with a greater trend toward childlessness. The trend had political implications. First, it produced a growing demand for family planning and the availability of contraception and abortion. Second, the recognition that immigrant groups frequently had higher fertility rates than the indigenous population sometimes fueled ethnic and racial antagonisms. The sentiment was perhaps most acute in West Germany, where the indigenous population was failing to replace itself. Right-wing elements there expressed anxiety that the 4 million or so "guest workers," notably Turks, Yugoslavs, and Eastern Europeans—all from states with relatively high fertility levels—would begin to swamp indigenous Germans. No matter how carefully this fear was expressed, it echoed Nazi race attitudes, but some movements explicitly embraced neo-Nazi ideas.

Not only did indigenous Western Europeans increasingly spurn having children, but they also married less often, which in itself helped lower the fertility rate. The marriage rate decline in the 1970s compared to that of the 1960s, and the proportion of people married and ever married (including the divorced and widowed) fell. Put another way, an increasing proportion of Western Europeans never married in their lifetimes. That did not mean that those who failed to marry would not form relationships that were as stable and long term as formal marriages. In Scandinavia and other parts of Western Europe, the decline in the marriage rate was virtually offset by an increase in cohabitation or de facto marriage.

In contrast to the declining popularity of marriage was the rising popularity of divorce. Divorce rates began to rise in the 1960s, but in the 1970s divorce became a common experience for Western European societies. That did not mean that most marriages ended in divorce, for about three-quarters lasted until either the wife or (more often) the husband died. But divorce did end a higher proportion of marriages than ever before in European history. To illustrate this point, Table 11.1 shows divorces per 1,000 existing marriages in four Western European states; Figure 11.1 relates divorce rates to overall population in various countries of both Western and Eastern Europe.

During the 1970s and early 1980s, more states liberalized their divorce laws: Italy (1970), the Netherlands (1971), Sweden (1973), Belgium (1974), Portugal and France (1975), Scotland and West Germany (1976), Austria (1978), Luxembourg (1980), and Spain (1981). In all cases the trend was to remove the concept of fault from divorce and to transfer the regulation of marriage to the individuals directly involved. Because evidence of offenses like adultery or cruelty was no longer relevant to the actual dissolution of marriage, divorce was increasingly transferred from the court system and became a bureaucratic matter.

TABLE 11.1   Divorces per 1,000 Existing Marriages

	1965	1975	1985
France	3.1	4.5	8.4
Great Britain	3.1	9.6	12.9
The Netherlands	2.2	6.0	9.9
Denmark	5.4	10.6	12.6

Source: Data from *United Nations Demographic Yearbook* (New York: United Nations, various years).

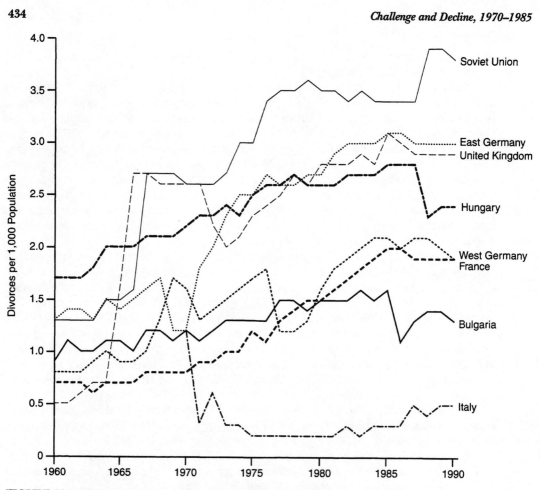

FIGURE 11.1   Divorces in selected European countries, 1960–90.

Source: Data from *United Nations Demographic Yearbook* (New York: United Nations, various years, 1962–92).

For all that, marriage and divorce remained important moral issues throughout the region, and there were allegations that modern legislation and family policies were tantamount to an attack on the family that would eventually destroy morality and the social order. Such issues came to the fore in Italy when divorce, although legalized in 1970, was put to a referendum in 1974 (see Chapter 10). The debate that preceded the vote pitted an anti-divorce coalition of the Catholic Church, Christian Democrats, and fascists against a pro-divorce front composed of feminists, liberals, Socialists, and Communists.

The success of the Italian law reform gave impetus to changes in Portugal and Spain. The socialist government that came to power in Portugal after the 1974 military coup put divorce law reform high on its agenda, and a new law was passed in 1977. It was not as liberal as in most of Western Europe, but mixed fault and no-fault provisions made divorce far easier than it had been. In Spain it was a matter of legalizing divorce, for although a divorce law had been passed in 1932 in the republic, it had been abrogated by Franco during the civil war. The issue raised political passions, however, and in 1980 and 1981 public meetings in favor of divorce were bombed. Divorce was legalized in 1981, but as in Portugal and Italy, it was a restrictive law in terms of contemporary European trends.

Divorce is legalized in Italy in 1970. In the background is St. Peter's, in the Vatican City, heart of the Catholic Church's opposition to the legal reform.

The main holdout in terms of divorce by the mid-1980s was predominantly Roman Catholic Ireland, where it was actually prohibited by a clause in the 1937 constitution. There was evidence of increasing marriage breakdown, however: Applications for annulments of marriage clogged the Church's tribunals, and the number of deserted wives receiving benefits and allowances was rising steadily. Pressure to legalize divorce rose during the 1970s, but it was opposed by the Church and personally by Pope John Paul II, who, on a 1979 visit to Ireland, praised the country's devotion to the sanctity of marriage. In 1986 a referendum to amend the constitution to allow divorce was held, but it was defeated by a margin of two to one.

Challenges to Economies and States

During the 1970s challenges to established authorities and conventional modes of behavior, the hallmark of the youth revolt of the 1960s, were channeled into a number of well-defined movements. The most significant were feminism (which is discussed separately in the next section), environmentalism, and nationalism. Young people were often the leaders of these movements, which employed a wide range of orthodox and unorthodox means to press their point. At one end of the spectrum they lobbied politicians and stood for election themselves; at the other end they engaged in acts of violence and terror. Their impact on Europe was significant.

Concern for the environment was not novel in the 1970s. Centuries earlier, there had been sporadic attempts to limit pollution of water supplies, and the word *ecology* had been coined in the nineteenth century by a German philosopher, Ernst Haeckel, who founded a movement based on nature. But the various back-to-nature movements that in the twentieth century included nudists, hiking groups, vegetarians, and opponents of industrial society, lacked the coherent ideology espoused by ecologists in the 1970s.

By the beginning of the final third of the century, it was becoming clear, not only in Western Europe but throughout the industrial world, that great damage had been done, and was still being done, to the environment. Rivers, lakes, and seas were so polluted that they were no longer safe to swim in or drink from. The air was polluted by factories, automobiles, and domestic fires; acid rain was killing trees; and wildlife was in retreat from pesticides, urban sprawl, industrialization, and highways that cut through the countryside and interfered with animal migration. New environmental organizations sprang up and old ones were reinvigorated by new membership, whether they were concerned with conservation of birds, animals, or trees, or took a broad approach, like Friends of the Earth and Greenpeace.

A number of trends promoted concern for the environment to critical levels. One was the emphasis on economic growth that lay behind government policies throughout the 1960s. The severe recession triggered by the rise in oil prices in 1973 reversed or reduced economic expansion, but only made governments more determined to recover. Environmentalists pointed out that growth could not be sustained indefinitely, and that unrestrained industrialization and consumerism were having disastrous effects on the environment.

Industry was clearly a prime culprit: Many plants poured toxic or inadequately treated chemical waste into rivers or the sea. Municipalities were often no better, allowing untreated sewage to run into natural waterways. Farmers were accused of having lost contact with the land; not only did they treat animals increasingly like inanimate industrial products, but they treated their pastures with dangerous herbicides and pesticides that endangered plants and wildlife. Environmentalists pointed to the damaging behavior of private citizens, particularly to their attachment to automobiles. By the 1970s the pollutants emitted by the leaded fuel of tens of millions of automobiles added to the chemicals emitted from factories and other sources. There was also a massive problem of waste; few products were recycled and most unwanted packaging and goods found their way into garbage dumps often containing toxic waste that leached into the soil.

The scenario of destruction progressively sketched out by ecologists was enhanced by the spread of nuclear power plants, particularly after 1973 when generating electricity by oil became uneconomical. Nuclear power had long been regarded as unstable, and there had already been accidents. A major leak of radioactivity occurred at Sellafield in northern England in 1957, but it was kept secret by the government. The 1979 accident at Three Mile Island in the United States was another demonstration of the apparent weaknesses of nuclear energy. A far worse case occurred in 1986 when a Soviet nuclear reactor at Chernobyl in Ukraine overheated and blew up. Wind currents distributed radiation across broad areas of Northern and Eastern Europe, leading to boycotts of agricultural produce and dairy products from many areas. The injuries and longer-term illnesses that resulted from the Chernobyl case gave insight into potential consequences of a major nuclear disaster.

The energy crisis that provoked the construction of a new generation of nuclear power stations in several Western European states was seen by ecologists as an opportunity to reverse or at least divert some existing trends. Restrictions on fuel purchases, the soaring price of gasoline, and lowered speed limits gave public authorities the chance to wean people from their private automobiles and set up efficient mass-transportation systems. There was some movement in this direction, and municipalities encouraged carpooling by commuters. Governments also sponsored research into alternative fuels. The use of natural gas (propane) was extended to fleets of vehicles, and experimentation with automobiles powered by electric batteries and solar panels was accelerated. The interest lasted only as long as the energy crisis, however, and when gasoline prices settled, governments and people returned to their old oil-consuming habits.

The pressure from the ecology movement nonetheless had an impact on policymakers in many areas. The French government was the first to recognize the political significance of ecology, and in 1971 created a Ministry for the Protection of Nature and the Environment. In 1975–76 the government of Giscard d'Estaing legislated against unrestricted development of green spaces; laws protected coastlines from unregulated resort building, and alpine regions from being lost to a profusion of ski lifts and chalets. The construction of skyscrapers and inner-city highways in Paris was slowed. Such measures tended to be piecemeal, however, and as useful as they were in their specifics, failed to address the broader and, in the eyes of the ecologists, increasingly urgent issues of global catastrophe.

Frustrated by their inability to convert mainstream parties to their policies for more fundamental economic and social change, ecologists in Germany formed the Green Party in 1979 and in the 1983 elections attracted enough votes (2.2 million, or 5.6 percent) to win twenty-seven seats in the Bundestag. In regional elections in Hesse and West Berlin, the Greens participated in governing coalitions. They were also successful in elections in Sweden, Austria, and Switzerland in the 1980s, and in the French presidential election of 1981 the ecology candidate scored a creditable 3.9 percent, a larger share than any other candidate not of a major party.

Environmentalists were directly concerned about the effects of pollution on the health of Western Europeans. Studies were made of patterns of disease in populations close to nuclear power stations, and evidence of abnormally high rates of leukemia, other cancers, and fetal abnormalities were made public. Such concerns paralleled growing anxiety within and outside the medical profession and health policy makers about Western European diets and narcotics use. It is often difficult to separate environmental from lifestyle factors in the incidence of specific diseases, but it seemed evident that high rates of heart disease and lung cancer in particular had to do with diet and tobacco smoking.

The encouragement of less harmful diets produced a trend toward health foods in Europe, as elsewhere. Vegetarianism was encouraged not only because it eliminated animal fats from the diet but also because vegetables and cereals were a more efficient use of land and resources from an ecological perspective. Although many middle-class Europeans changed their eating patterns to a greater or lesser extent, and began to exercise by jogging, cycling, or by aerobic exercises (health clubs and athletic clothing became small growth sectors during the recession), the health movement had a limited impact.

Closely linked to environmentalism was the peace movement; the two overlapped in their opposition to the use of nuclear energy for both military and nonmilitary purposes. Anti-war sentiments had a longer and more defined history than environmental concerns, and had emerged strongly after the war. The anti-nuclear movement was quite precisely focused, however, because far from all its adherents were complete pacifists. They were opposed to nuclear weapons testing (common ground with environmentalists because of the fallout), the possession of nuclear arms by European states, and the stationing of nuclear-armed American forces on European territory.

Such reductions as there were in nuclear armaments and proliferation resulted from international agreements that are discussed in a later section. The anti-nuclear lobby in Britain had one significant if transient victory, which was the 1981 adoption of a policy of unilateral nuclear disarmament by the Labour Party. It was part of an unusually left-wing agenda that also included a large program of nationalization and British withdrawal from NATO. Called by some "the longest suicide note in history," the manifesto made an important contribution to Labour's overwhelming defeat in the 1983 election. Anti-nuclear activists were not deterred, however; in the same year tens of thousands formed a fourteen-mile human chain through the countryside around the U.S. air force base at Greenham Common, and women kept a vigil outside the base for months afterward.

The environmental movement drew support throughout Western Europe, as did the anti-nuclear protests because a nuclear war would have effects far beyond the borders of the nuclear powers. Some protest movements, however, gathered strength in particular regions as centralized government and even the integrity of some states were challenged. In many states demands for the devolution of power and planning to the regions, even federalism, were reactions against the centralization that became popular after the war. They were reinforced in some countries by the growth of supranational entities like the European Community, which removed decision making even further from the people directly affected. Such sentiments were given further impetus by the recession, which struck some regions harder than others and fed longer-term resentments.

In more than one case demands for autonomy were reinforced by other issues. In southern France the movement for self-government and language rights in the ancient province of Occitanie was galvanized into action when the government announced plans in 1971 to extend its tank-firing range on the Larzac plateau from 7,000 to 42,000 acres. The local sheep farmers, whose property was to be appropriated with compensation, resisted the plan and were supported by ecologists, anti-war activists, and Occitan nationalists, who saw it as yet another attempt by the Paris-centered French state to despoil their land. The slogan *Gardarem lo Larzac* ("Save Larzac," in the Oc language of the Occitans) was written on walls, rock faces, and buildings across the south of France. The affair dragged on for years, during which there were regular marches and other protests, until the plan was canceled by President Mitterrand in 1982, a decision facilitated by reductions in the military budget.

The emergence of an Occitan nationalism took various forms, many of them cultural, and drew on the sense that the south of France had been treated by successive administrations in Paris almost as a colony. Occitans often drew on the memory of the Cathar (or Albigensian) heresy, suppressed in a bloody crusade in the thirteenth century, to demonstrate the continuity of their oppression. Like southern Italy, southern France tended to be deprived of industrial and commercial development, its economy resting on agriculture and, increasingly, on tourism.

The natives were also restless in other regions of France, notably in Brittany, and particularly after unemployment rose from 1973 and the prosperity built up during the 1960s looked vulnerable. The Bretons are Celts, and many autonomists took inspiration from the success of their brethren in Ireland who had broken away from the United Kingdom; Brittany had been incorporated within France only in the sixteenth century, not long before Ireland was colonized by England.

Pressure for the recognition of Breton political and cultural claims bore some fruit. In 1977 the French government issued a "cultural charter for Brittany" that made the Breton language an option in state schools, where it could be taught for up to three hours a week. A very limited amount of time on regional state-owned radio and television stations could be devoted to broadcasts in Breton. In economic terms, development was more substantial. Because of its geographical location in the extreme northwest of France, Brittany's trade with Europe, based on agriculture, drew the region toward the center of France. In part to avoid that, and to reestablish commercial links with other Celtic regions, the Breton farmers' cooperative developed the region's ports and in 1973 launched a shipping company to ferry freight and passengers to Britain and Ireland. It became the very successful Brittany Ferries company.

Ethnicity became an issue in Belgium, too, in the form of more episodes in the chronic tension between the French-speaking Walloons and the Dutch-speaking Flemish population. By the late 1960s Belgium's main political parties were split on linguistic lines, and by the 1974 election nationalist Fleming and Walloon parties attracted a fifth of the vote and 45 of the 212 seats in the legislature. The central government made progressively larger concessions at its own expense. In 1970 regional authorities were given responsibility for economic development, and regional committees empowered to set cultural policy. By 1980 the constitution was revised further toward federalism when two regional governments were established, one Flemish and the other Walloon, each with its own administration.

Devolution was less straightforward in Spain, which in the 1970s was confronted by demands for autonomy from two important industrial regions: Catalonia and the Basque provinces, both of which had long-standing grievances about their status in Spain. Catalonia had received regional autonomy under the Second Republic and the Basques expected to, and both areas had been centers of republicanism during the civil war. Under the Franco regime centralization had been rigorously enforced, and Catalan and Basque nationalism became identified with demands for democracy.

During the 1960s a new Basque separatist organization was formed, Basque Land and Freedom (ETA), and in that decade began a campaign of terror against the institutions and personnel of the Madrid government. In 1968 the assassination of a police inspector provoked widespread house searches and a three-month state of emergency. Sixteen members of ETA were tried and nine sentenced to death (although the sentences were later commuted to jail terms). In 1973 ETA had its most spectacular success when it blew up the car of the prime minister (and Franco's designated successor), Admiral Carrero Blanco.

The constitution drawn up after Franco's death declared that the unity of Spain was indissoluble, but it recognized that "nationalities and regions" had rights to autonomy. These rights were quickly ceded to Catalonia and the Basque provinces in 1979, and later to other regions. They enabled the autonomous regions to provide for language instruction in their schools, create their own administrations, operate radio and television facilities, and have their own police forces. Such concessions largely satisfied nationalists, but ETA wanted full sovereignty for the Basque region, and continued its campaigns of terror, now against the democratic government. Reflecting the change since Franco, Basque nationalists formed a political party in 1978. In regional elections in 1980 and 1986 it won about a fifth of the Basque vote, indicating that separatist feeling was not confined to the few hundred paramilitary members of ETA.

Of all Western Europe's states, it was Great Britain that came under the most sustained pressure from its ethnic minorities, the Welsh, Scots, and Irish. As elsewhere, nationalism was spurred by the recession, which created extensive unemployment in Scotland and Wales, both of which were centers of heavy industry. There were sporadic arson attacks against English-owned cottages in Wales, whereas the discovery of North Sea oil gave Scottish nationalists a boost; British oil reserves could be claimed by an independent Scotland and provided an economic basis for sovereignty. The impact of these tendencies was clear in the October 1974 election in which the Scottish National Party won a third of the vote in Scotland and eleven seats in the House of Commons. The Welsh nationalist party, Plaid Cymru, won three seats. Together the two parties held the balance of power in Parliament.

In 1979 referenda were held in Scotland and Wales for devolution, which would have transferred many powers over the economy and culture from the central government. Scotland had maintained its own legal and education system distinct from the rest of Britain. The referenda went against the nationalists in Wales by a margin of four to one.

Scots voted in favor, but the majority of 51.6 percent was too small to satisfy the requirements of the referendum legislation, under which at least 40 percent of all registered voters (not actual voters) had to favor devolution. From that point, electoral support for nationalist parties declined.

Ireland was a far more dangerous issue for the British government. In the 1920s Ireland had been partitioned between the Irish Free State (later the Republic of Ireland), with a predominantly Catholic population, and Northern Ireland (or Ulster), whose mainly Protestant inhabitants remained within the United Kingdom. The Catholics of Northern Ireland experienced chronic discrimination in such vital areas as employment and housing, and in the context of the late 1960s, when protest movements of all kinds gained mass support in Europe, a Catholic civil rights movement developed. After clashes between Catholics and Protestants and between demonstrators and police, the Labour government sent British troops to Northern Ireland in 1969.

Although the troops were at first welcomed by most Catholics as neutral, their presence angered the nationalists, who wanted a united Ireland governed from Dublin and who regarded the British troops as an army of occupation. The Irish Republican Army (IRA) began a campaign against the British and their supporters in Ireland, and in 1971 the first British soldier was killed. On "Bloody Sunday" the following year (January 30, 1972), British forces killed thirteen people at a demonstration that had been banned, an act that alienated Catholic opinion. The conflict escalated as Protestant paramilitary organizations joined the fray and more than a thousand people—soldiers, IRA and Protestant paramilitaries, and civilians—had died by 1974. In 1973 Britain imposed direct rule over Northern Ireland.

The IRA also waged its campaign outside Northern Ireland. During the 1970s and afterward, it planted or detonated bombs in taverns, railway stations, government buildings, and shops throughout England. Strict security measures were quickly implemented. In 1974, threatened by attacks from the IRA and experiencing the three-day workweek and streetlight and shop-window blackouts designed to conserve energy, Londoners might

British paratroopers round up suspects in Londonderry, Northern Ireland, on Bloody Sunday, January 30, 1972. That day troops killed thirteen civilians during civil rights demonstrations.

well have believed they had been plunged back to World War II. By the mid-1980s the Northern Irish question seemed far from resolution. Many Catholics supported the principle of union with the Irish Republic, while Protestants refused to countenance a united Ireland in which they would be a minority. The British government refused to discuss any change to the constitutional status of Northern Ireland within the United Kingdom.

Terror was not confined to the IRA and Protestant armies in Britain and the ETA in Spain, for there was a general upsurge in terrorism in Europe in the 1970s. It reflected a worldwide trend in which small, well-organized groups hijacked aircraft, bombed airports and buildings, and carried out other acts of terror for a wide range of nationalist and political causes. Germany and Italy produced several terrorist groups, such as the Baader-Meinhof gang, the Red Army Faction, and the Red Brigades. Some terrorism was imported, as with the attack by Palestinian nationalists on Israeli athletes at the 1972 Olympic Games in Munich, in which nine Israelis and five terrorists were killed.

Italy experienced the most intensive wave of terror, from organizations of both left and right. The student disturbances of 1968–69 had provoked a reaction in the form of increased support for fascists, and fascist terror squads appeared. Their acts included an attack on the Rome-Munich express in 1974, which killed 12 people, and bombing the restaurant in the Bologna railway station in 1980, which left 84 dead and 200 injured. In 1977 alone in Italy, there were more than 2,000 attacks on people or property, 76 political abductions, and more than 40 law enforcement officers killed. In 1978 a former Christian Democratic prime minister, Aldo Moro, was kidnapped by the Red Brigades and murdered.

Women in Society, Economy, and Ideology

One of the most influential movements to emerge from the late 1960s and to mature in the subsequent decades was feminism. The term has many meanings and by no means represents a monolithic or homogeneous ideology. This was less clear in the 1970s, however, when the women's movement brought about extensive changes in law and social policy that provided the framework for the slow transformation of women's social and economic standing in Western European society. The women's movement that emerged around 1970 is sometimes referred to as the "second wave," heir to the first that spanned the long period from the mid-nineteenth century to the mid-1920s. The movement of the early 1970s was multifaceted but focused on a number of concrete issues of equality—equal employment and educational opportunities and equal pay—as well as free contraception and abortion on demand.

Proponents of women's rights used a wide range of methods and tactics to press their arguments before politicians and the public. The 1970s saw a burst of publishing about women's issues, in the form of books, articles, magazines, journals, and newspapers. Academics turned to the study of women in history, society, politics, the law, literature, and art. There was a receptive audience and readership among young middle-class women, particularly those in university or with a university education. Women's bookstores, resource centers, and meeting places were set up. More direct action included demonstrations, protest marches, and sit-ins. The campaign to legalize abortion in France included a declaration, published in one of the country's leading newsweeklies in 1971, by hundreds of women who acknowledged having had an abortion; the signatories of the "Manifesto of the 343 'sluts,' " as it was titled, included prominent writers and actresses. The variety of tactics achieved a variety of results.

Women had been increasing their participation in the workforce since the war, but there was little evidence of their moving out of the low-paid and low-status jobs in which they were concentrated. Women were the overwhelming majority of workers in clerical and secretarial work, primary school teaching, nursing, food services, textile manufacturing, cleaning, and libraries. Where men were employed in these sectors, they were more likely than women to be in positions of responsibility, as principals, foremen, supervisors, and the like. In France in 1981, for example, women represented 63 percent of teachers, 23 percent of school inspectors, 44 percent of primary school principals, and 23 percent of secondary school principals. In Great Britain the respective percentages were 59, 23, 44, and 15, and in Italy 72, 15, 34, and 28.

Employment patterns varied from country to country and also according to marital status and whether a woman had children. Women, especially married women, were also far more likely than men to be employed part time. Most parttime work in industrial economies was in the service sector (such as retail assistants, waitresses, and cleaners), and in most countries part-time workers were not eligible for such benefits as pensions, maternity leave, training for promotion, vacations, and holiday pay.

To some extent the work women did was dependent upon their education. Women generally dropped out of education at the higher levels, often because of pressure to work and the enduring belief that women did not need to be educated beyond a secondary level. In most of Western Europe female and male 15-year-olds were evenly represented in school in the early 1970s, but at age 20 males outnumbered females three to two, and at age 24, when students were in advanced studies, men outnumbered women more than two to one. Women were especially underrepresented in professional schools of law, medicine, engineering, and business, and were thus underrepresented as workers in those professions.

Feminist organizations rallied support and lobbied governments for legislation that would prevent discrimination against women in school and work. Most Western European states adopted policies and enforcement agencies and some created ministries devoted to women's affairs. Britain's equality legislation was fairly typical of much of Western Europe in the 1970s; the 1970 Equal Pay Act and the 1975 Sex Discrimination Acts forbade discrimination on the basis of sex in education, hiring, and promotion, and gave women equal rights to pensions.

Britain, however, did not create a ministry for women, unlike France, which established a Ministry of Women's Rights in 1981. Other states, including Austria, West Germany, the Netherlands, Sweden, and Denmark, set up agencies whose task was to promote and monitor the progress of women's equality. They included the Equal Status Council in Denmark (1975) and the West German Central Office for Women's Equality (1979).

There were improvements in education. Women began to close the gap at the higher levels by increasing their representation faster than males. In European Community countries in 1970–71, 7.8 percent of 24-year-old men were in full-time education compared with 3.5 percent of women of that age. By 1981–82 both proportions had risen, men to 11 percent and women to 7.7 percent, but women's presence had risen more quickly. The most dramatic gains in education, however, were made among 16- to 18-year-olds, suggesting that by the early 1980s young women were much more likely to finish high school than their predecessors had been a decade earlier.

Ten years of equal opportunity made little difference to the kinds of jobs women performed in the economy. Women remained concentrated in the service sector, which employed 72 percent of women in 1986 compared with 50 percent of men. Women were most commonly employed in the food, banking, and insurance industries. About the same proportion (8 percent) of women as men worked in agriculture, but whereas 42 percent of men had jobs in industry, only 21 percent of women did. Within these sections of the economy, women held management or supervisory positions considerably less often than men, and in fact the proportion of women with such responsibilities fell from 16 to 14 percent from 1980 to 1985.

The progress of women in employment presents a mixed picture. The simple image of an increasing number of women in the workforce hid a complex pattern of segregation among and within the various parts of the economy. Women's progress out of poorly paid, low-status jobs with few opportunities for advancement proved to be much slower than many had expected. Where the segregation of work by gender did begin to break down, it was more often by the entry of men into hitherto female-exclusive professions, rather than the other way around. From this perspective many men benefited more than women from the women's movement's attacks on the gender divisions in society.

In other areas women made more definitive progress, not only in law and policy but also in terms of practice. Most women calling themselves feminists in the late 1960s and 1970s argued that abortion ought to be freely available in order to give women control of their bodies. As we have seen, abortion was legalized in several states by 1970, but in the next decade and a half even further progress was made. The only states not to have legalized or liberalized abortion by 1985 were Belgium, Ireland, Portugal, and Greece.

Spanish women demonstrate in Madrid after the Socialist government's bill to legalize abortion was rejected by the Constitutional Court. The court's decision delayed reform but did not stop it.

The actual accessibility to abortion varied from country to country. Many, including Denmark, Austria, France, Italy, the Netherlands, and Sweden, allowed abortion at the request of the woman; all permitted it on medical grounds. Some required a compulsory waiting period; some required applicants for abortion to be given advice on alternatives to it. While almost all included abortion within state health insurance schemes, West Germany and Austria did not, making abortion more difficult for poorer women to obtain.

Beyond legal and institutional limitations, there were others. Abortion was not evenly available in all parts of any given country, for most states allowed doctors to refuse to perform abortions for reasons of conscience. This often meant that women in rural areas, where there were fewer doctors, had to travel to a town or city for an abortion. Social class was clearly an important factor in the accessibility to abortion, and even where it was not available (as in Ireland and in Italy until 1978) the well off could travel to where it was: Great Britain, the Netherlands, Austria, and Switzerland all permitted non-nationals to obtain abortions in their hospitals and clinics.

The actual frequency of abortion also varied from state to state and reflected not only differences in law but also age structure, marital status, and social traditions of family limitation. Expressed as a percentage of women in the childbearing age range from fifteen to forty-four, abortion rates were high in Scandinavia, West Germany, and France, and low in the Netherlands. Across most of Western Europe there was a tendency for the rate of abortions to fall in the early 1980s.

Other legal changes, such as the changes in divorce discussed in an earlier section, affected women in the family. For example, a 1976 law in Italy ended the right of fathers to marry off their daughters once they had reached the age of twelve.

By the end of the 1970s, the feminist agenda had grown beyond equality of opportunity and abortion rights to include financial and legal independence, women's ability to control their own sexuality and reproduction, and their freedom from the threat or use of violence and sexual coercion. Campaigns were begun against domestic violence, most of which was wife beating. Although a historical continuity, wife beating was seldom discussed publicly for centuries and was usually represented as something that happened only among the working class and poor. The police were reluctant to be drawn into violent marital disputes and treated male violence of this kind with lenience approaching understanding. The courts gave little comfort, let alone redress, to the few women who were able to get their complaints taken that far. In the early 1970s, however, the extent of domestic violence was brought to public attention by books such as Erin Pizzey's *Scream Quietly or the Neighbours Will Hear*, published in 1974. Refuges for women victims of domestic violence began to open throughout Europe: in England (London) in 1972, France (Paris) in 1974, and in Spain (Barcelona) in 1982.

Rape also became an issue in the 1970s. Long considered a sexual act committed by sexually frustrated or provoked men—an act for which women were usually made to bear some or all of the responsibility—rape came increasingly to be viewed as a particular category of physical assault by which men exercised power over women. In France the issue was brought to public attention by the 1971–72 trial of a 17-year-old woman who had an abortion after being raped and impregnated. She was charged with illegal abortion when the young man who raped her notified the police, and although *she* stood trial, he was never charged with rape. The double standard attracted widespread attention and spurred the formation of organizations focusing on abortion and rape.

Legislators began to pass more effective laws dealing with physical and sexual assault against women. In France rape was reclassified as a crime, instead of a misdemeanor, in

1980. Even so, rape remained a greatly underreported offense. There were an estimated 15,000 rapes each year in Spain, but from 1977 to 1981 only 235 charges were filed, and they tended to be particularly serious cases when the woman died, or when gang rapes or incest were involved. By the mid-1970s 24-hour women's information phone lines were operating and the first rape crisis centers opened.

Whatever progress was made in the legal status of women in this period was achieved by the pressure of women on men. The majority of writers, demonstrators, and lobbyists on women's issues were women themselves. Those they tried to influence were mainly men because politics and high civil service posts were dominated by men. By the early 1980s women constituted only a quarter of representatives sitting in national legislatures in Scandinavia (the highest rate was Finland, where a third of deputies were women), a fifth in the Netherlands, a tenth in West Germany, Austria, and Portugal, and a twentieth in France, Belgium, Spain, and Great Britain.

Although much progress was made in reforming laws and policies relating to women during the 1970s and early 1980s, the social and economic conditions that most women experienced meant that their lives were little affected by feminism. The great majority of married women were either financially dependent on their husbands or earned wages that were inadequate to support them and their children. Although there was some movement in employment patterns, working women earned far less than men and were less likely to be in full-time jobs. Women continued to face harassment and violence in the home, at work, and in society at large. The women's movement brought women's issues to the attention of women and men to an unprecedented degree, and forced a wide range of legal and policy reforms. The struggle to change the contours of one of the fundamental structural divisions in European society—gender—proved to be arduous and long.

Western Europe: Looking Inward and Outward

Just as the recession that began with the oil price increase in 1973 brought underlying social and economic tensions to the surface in each European state, so it revealed international divisions that had often been obscured. It showed how vulnerable the collective policies of the European Community were: When the Arab states placed an oil embargo on the Netherlands because of Dutch cooperation with U.S. aid to Israel, none of the European Community partners offered assistance. All feared that the embargo would be extended to them.

As the recession deepened, governments discovered that the traditional trade policies, cutting imports to protect domestic producers, could no longer be implemented because the European Community allowed no tariffs on goods coming from other member states. French primary producers became especially exercised about competition from other countries, and at one point in 1978 the French tried to halt the importation of wine from Italy. When the government was forced to relent, French producers took direct action, ambushing trucks carrying wine and pouring the freight onto the road.

It proved difficult for the European Community to establish a common policy to deal with the recession because each member experienced it differently. While Britain suffered high unemployment and inflation throughout the 1970s, Germany did not feel the full effects until the early 1980s. There were attempts to shore up industries in some countries and to rationalize production, but they foundered on national interests. Agriculture proved an even more bitter issue. Although rising prices were good news for countries that were producers, such as France and the Netherlands, major food importers like Britain and Germany found prices steadily rising. Behind some prices lay subsidies paid to producers by the European Community, and the debate on reducing them—which would benefit consumers at the expense of producers—divided the European Community for years.

The recession tested the economic and political links that bound the members of the European Community to one another. In 1973 Britain had joined the Community, but there was a large body of British political opinion reluctant to form too close a relationship with Europe. The Labour government elected in 1974 raised the possibility of withdrawing, but a referendum in 1975 confirmed British membership by a margin of two to one. When the Conservatives came to power in 1979, they were anxious to avoid loss of British sovereignty and adopted a strong line of protecting British interests.

The European Community now contained two powerful members, France and Britain, that seemed determined to put their own interests consistently before those of Europe more generally. Germany, in contrast, had a much healthier economy and could afford to be more magnanimous on many issues. The Thatcher government in Britain took a particularly hard line on British payments to the Community, which were disproportionately large because Britain was a large importer and minor exporter of agricultural products. The country's contributions to subsidies under the Common Agricultural Policy were far greater than its receipts, whereas in France the balance was reversed. As a temporary solution, British contributions were limited for a short period, but this compromise contributed to a crisis in the Community's budget. It also fueled anti-European Community sentiment in Britain, and in the 1983 the Labour Party made withdrawal part of its election program.

During the 1970s the Community had become a larger entity when not only Britain joined but also Ireland and Denmark. (Norwegians voted against membership in a referendum.) In 1981 Greece became a member, but it took nine years before applications by Spain and Portugal were approved; they joined in 1986. Italy and France were opposed to the entry of two more agricultural members that would provide domestic farmers with competition. Thus the recession caused friction within the European Community, but it did not destroy the compact.

In other spheres there was a reduction of friction within Europe. A notable shift in German policy was adopted by the Social Democratic government that remained in office from 1969 until 1982. Under Chancellor Willy Brandt, a former mayor of West Berlin, West German external affairs were dominated by an "eastern policy" (*Ostpolitik*) designed to settle outstanding disputes between West Germany and the states of Eastern Europe. In 1970 a treaty was signed with the Soviet Union that recognized existing frontiers, an important step that amounted to German renunciation of any claims to land lost after the Second World War. Notably the treaty recognized the line along the Oder-Neisse river as the border between Poland and East Germany, and thus Poland's right to former German land to the east of it.

A subsequent treaty with Poland put the settlement on a bilateral basis. During a visit to Warsaw in 1970, Brandt made a symbolic gesture toward reconciliation when he laid a wreath at the memorial to Jewish victims of the Nazis. Another treaty, signed with Czechoslovakia in 1973, renounced any future German claim on the former Sudetenland. These treaties aroused great indignation among German nationalists who believed that Germany had a right to reclaim its lost territories. Brandt also attempted to normalize relations with East Germany. He visited East Germany in 1970, and in 1972 arrangements were made for West Germans with relatives there to visit them at Christmas 1972. Some half-million West Germans took advantage of the opportunity, staying in the East for up to a month. In 1973 the two Germanies formally recognized each other.

These moves toward the normalizing of relations between the two Germanies were not only substantive in their own right; because of the centrality to the cold war of Germany—a country physically divided, its capital rudely split by a wall—the new relationship accelerated the pace of improving relations between Western and Eastern Europe and between the United States and the Soviet Union. Already by 1972 the two superpowers had agreed to limit the number of missile launchers each nation would be able to deploy. This Strategic Arms Limitation Treaty (SALT) was important to Europe, which would inevitably be involved in a war between the United States and the Soviet Union.

The European states were more directly involved in subsequent sets of discussions, however. In 1972, thirty-three nations from Western and Eastern Europe (including the Soviet Union), plus the United States and Canada, met in Helsinki to begin the Conference on Security and Cooperation in Europe. Three years later, the participants signed a far-reaching agreement in which all recognized the existing frontiers of Europe. In the military sphere all recognized the NATO and Warsaw Pacts—effectively legitimating Soviet control over most of Eastern Europe—and agreed to notify one another of any major military exercises so there should be no misunderstanding of either side's intentions. The final declaration called for increased trade and cultural contacts between the West and East, and all signatories committed themselves, with varying degrees of sincerity, to upholding civil liberties within their respective borders. These Helsinki Accords would become a reference point for dissidents in Eastern Europe and the Soviet Union to justify subsequent attempts to speak against their governments.

In some respects the agreements in the early 1970s accelerated a process that had already begun, namely the growth of trade between Western and Eastern Europe, and especially between Western Europe and the Soviet Union. Total exports had been worth under $5 billion in 1970, and they had risen to $8 billion by 1972 when various talks got under way. By 1976 they had risen to $20 billion, and at the end of the decade stood at almost $30 billion. The largest single importer was the Soviet Union, but Poland also bought extensively. Because the Eastern European states had limited foreign currency reserves, Western European banks advanced them loans, drawing on the vast deposits made by the oil-exporting states after the oil price rise. Eastern European states seemed good credit risks; they were politically stable and had centralized economies.

The process helped limit the effect of the recession in Western Europe, but it led to the growing indebtedness of the East. Because of the recession, the markets for Eastern European goods contracted, and instead of trading their way out of debt, those countries were forced to borrow more deeply. The total foreign debt of Eastern Europe (excluding the Soviet Union) was $19 billion in 1975, but by 1981 it had risen to $62 billion. Almost half that amount, $28 billion, was owed by Poland alone.

Nevertheless, these commercial and financial relations were supported by advocates of reconciliation in Western Europe as the best way of breaking down the barriers between the two blocs. It was expected that as standards of living rose in Eastern Europe and people became accustomed to an increasing supply and variety of goods, the governments would be unable to weaken the economic links for fear of a popular backlash.

But the growth of economic ties did not automatically improve East-West political relationships. The development of new strategic weapons led to a renewal of the nuclear arms race and the installation of new missile systems in both Western and Eastern Europe. Events outside Europe created greater international tension, such as the overthrow of the pro-American government in Iran and Soviet intervention in Afghanistan in an attempt to prop up a pro-Soviet government there. By 1980 superpower relations had deteriorated to the point that the United States led a boycott by many Western states of the Olympic Games held that year in Moscow. Such events could not but affect Europe, but as the United States and the Soviet Union rattled sabers over their heads, their respective allies in Western and Eastern Europe pursued closer economic and political ties.

Politics and Economy in the
Soviet Union, 1970–85

Throughout the 1970s, the government of the Soviet Union was dominated by Leonid Brezhnev, who consolidated his position after the 1968 invasion of Czechoslovakia. There were hints of a "cult of personality" around Brezhnev in the mid-1970s; he was given the top military rank of marshal of the Soviet Union in 1976, and his autobiographical writings were treated as if they were of great significance. At the same time there was greater consultation among top party and state officials under Brezhnev than there had been under Khrushchev, who had often made military and economic decisions without informing the officials most concerned. The diffusion of control from the later 1970s was enhanced by the fact that, from 1975 on, Brezhnev was so often and seriously ill that there were numerous reports of his death before it actually happened in 1982.

Under Brezhnev's leadership, renewed emphasis was placed on foreign policy after earlier setbacks that included an increasingly independent Eastern Europe and the split with China that had weakened the Soviet Union's primacy in the international communist movement. Particular stress was given to expanding Soviet influence in Africa, where the Soviet Union often competed with China to assist national liberation movements. Aid was given to guerrillas in the former Portuguese territories following the 1974 revolution in Portugal, and treaties were eventually signed with Angola and Mozambique. In 1979 the Soviet Union dispatched forces to Afghanistan to support a pro-Soviet regime in Kabul against a Muslim rebellion, and by 1980 the Soviets had stationed 100,000 troops there.

At the same time as the Soviet Union pursued an active policy in the Third World that unnerved many Western European and United States leaders, it also contributed to the progress of détente. This resulted in a number of agreements that dealt not only with arms limitations but also (in the case of the Helsinki Declaration) with political liberties and civil rights. A new Soviet constitution, adopted in 1977 to replace the one drawn up by Stalin in 1936, suggested that debate on government policies might be more tolerated: The principle of "democratic centralism," which allowed debate before a decision but conformity once it had been taken, was extended from the Communist Party to the state as a whole.

There was a similar tension between the Soviet pursuit of arms limitations agreements up to and beyond the mid-1970s and the program of military modernization that followed. To compensate for its inferiority vis-à-vis the United States in intercontinental ballistic missiles, the Soviet Union developed new delivery systems, including a new long-range bomber dubbed "Backfire" by NATO. Between 1975 and 1985 both the Soviet Union and the United States installed, began construction of, or announced the beginning of work on a number of offensive and defensive military projects. These included new surface-to-surface missiles that each country installed in Europe, as well as new systems of defending U.S. missiles from attack. Talks on limiting various categories of military weapons continued throughout the period 1975–85, but with desultory results. On the American side there was suspicion of Soviet intentions, and under the presidency of Ronald Reagan the United States undertook a massive military buildup. A second SALT treaty was signed in 1979 but not ratified, largely because of U.S. opposition to the new Backfire bomber and Soviet opposition to the American cruise missiles.

Against the surge of foreign policy initiatives and increased spending on the military, the Soviet economy stagnated and fell below even the mediocre achievements of the late 1960s. Agriculture performed particularly badly: There was a net decline in productivity up to 1975, followed by a very slight increase between 1976 and 1980. Part of the reason was the climate, which severely damaged harvests in 1972 and 1975; the latter year produced only two-thirds the anticipated 210 million tons. To make up the shortfall, the Soviet Union imported large quantities of grain from the United States, and in 1976 an agreement was signed that provided for continuing imports for the remainder of the decade. This agreement underscored the failure of the Soviet Union to feed its own citizens, despite the fact that between a quarter and a third of all state expenditure in the late 1970s was invested in agriculture. Beginning in 1979, however, the Soviet Union experienced four successive bad harvests, a coincidence that in many ways represented a disastrous turning point in the economy.

Industry performed somewhat better, but also showed signs of slowing down during the 1970s, particularly in the second half. The Ninth Five-Year Plan (1971–75) was notable for being the first to provide for a greater increase in consumer goods than capital production, but in reality it proved no different from the earlier plans, and the consumer sector lagged behind. The failure of agriculture meant that the food industry could not achieve its targets, and there were persistent delays in construction. The shortages of consumer goods were increasingly noticeable because incomes grew more rapidly than anticipated but there was little that people could buy. In almost all respects, industry had slowed by 1980, just as agriculture entered a period of disastrously low yields.

The only sectors that really helped the Soviet economy were natural resources, whose world prices rose considerably during the 1970s. The Soviet Union had extensive reserves of oil and natural gas that not only shielded its economy from the 1973 and 1979 oil price rises but also increased revenues from foreign sales. A new railroad was constructed in the late 1970s to provide better access to Siberian oil fields, and by 1980 the region provided half the Soviet Union's oil and a third of its natural gas. Premium prices enabled the Soviet Union to buy needed Western manufactured goods and technology. The Soviet Union, a major gold producer, also benefited from the rise in the value of gold from 1979.

By the time Brezhnev died in 1982, the Soviet economy had entered a critical phase, and the Eleventh Five-Year Plan (1981–85) gave the impression of being the work of economists going through the motions of setting production targets they knew could not be met. The grain harvest averaged 181 million tons instead of the targeted 240 million; coal output was 726 instead of 785 million tons; and consumer goods production rose 21 percent instead of the anticipated 28 percent.

These disappointing figures concealed even greater problems. There was a decline in investment, aggravated by the large proportion of resources devoted to agriculture and by increased spending on military and space projects. One repercussion of declining investment was that industrial machinery that became obsolete was not replaced or modernized, and constant breakdowns and repairs became an increasing drain on resources. Moreover, the additional labor that might have compensated for technological stagnation was not available; the Soviet birth rate had declined, and women, who were a reserve labor force in many countries, were already employed in the Soviet Union to their fullest extent.

A further drain on investment was the development of natural resources in Siberia. Although the extraction of oil, gas, and minerals from this region was clearly necessary and desirable, it was achieved at great cost because of the distances involved and the difficulty of the terrain and climate. Once obtained, the resources had to be directed toward users, and that involved additional expense. As oil reserves in the Caucasus were gradually exhausted, an increasing proportion of Soviet energy sources existed east of the Urals, while the bulk of industry was located to the west.

By the early 1980s it was possible to point to real economic achievements in the Soviet Union, including a steady improvement in living standards, significant growth in military power, and reductions in the differentials between GNP and worker productivity between the Soviet Union and Western countries. But the problems were equally impressive and for that reason more worrying. Even optimistic statistics showed that the annual rate of growth of the Soviet GNP had slowed steadily with each Five-Year Plan, declining from an average 5.2 percent (1966–70) to 3.7 percent (1971–75), 2.7 percent (1976–80), and then 2 percent in the early 1980s. It is possible that economic growth was even slower (accurate statistics are difficult to obtain), but whatever the actual rate, the rise in Soviet living standards slowed similarly.

The organization of the economy was unable to respond to the crisis that had set in by the early 1980s. Part of the problem was that each sector of the economy worked to achieve targets expressed in quantities, and lacked the flexibility to slow, halt, or divert production when it was clear that bottlenecks were occurring. Inventories rose in some industries, suggesting that there were problems with transportation (the railroads began to become particularly problematic) or that demand had declined, but production continued nonetheless. As the official economy faltered, a black market for all kinds of goods and services developed. Individual consumers, with money to spend but frustrated at the lack of goods on the shelves, paid to have items custom-made. All these trends diverted significant labor and material resources.

Little was done, or could be done, within the existing structure to deal with the stagnation that affected the Soviet economy from about 1979, because the Soviet Union entered a period of political change. Brezhnev, who was 74 in 1980, became progressively more ill and less able to control day-to-day matters, let alone attend to problems of long-term restructuring. Ironically, he was one Soviet leader who might justifiably have retired for reasons of health, but he clung to both power and life until the latter slipped from his grasp in 1982. His successor, 68-year-old Yuri Andropov, died after fifteen months in office, and *his* successor, 72-year-old Constantin Chernenko, died a year later. For five years of economic crisis, the Soviet Union lacked clear leadership. When the new general secretary, Mikhail Gorbachev, assumed office in March 1985, it was evident that drastic changes of course were needed.

Society in the Soviet Union, 1970–85

As we have noted, overall living standards in the Soviet Union rose steadily during the 1970s and to a lesser extent in the early 1980s. Ironically, given the abysmal levels of agricultural production, diets improved significantly and became more varied. Between 1970 and 1985 the proportion of the average diet made up of potatoes and grain declined and the proportion of meat, fish, dairy products, eggs, fruit, and vegetables increased. The main restraint on even greater improvements was availability. The fact that people could have spent more on food is shown by the fact that even though diets improved, food accounted for a declining proportion of a worker's weekly income; in 1970, 35 percent of wages went on food, but by 1986 it consumed only 28 percent. As living standards rose, so did expectations of continuous improvement, and there was growing dissatisfaction about shortages.

The affordability of food was often a reflection of subsidies paid by the state to cover the difference between the price paid to farmers and the price charged to consumers. These subsidies became a heavy burden on state finances, and by the early 1980s were as large as the amount spent on defense.

A better-fed citizenry did not always translate into the statistics that might be expected. For example, the mortality rates began to rise and life expectancy fell, the first time this had happened in Europe outside the context of major catastrophes such as famine and war. In the Soviet Union it happened at a time of rising prosperity. The death rates of adult men aged over forty increased between 20 and 25 percent from 1965 to 1989. The death rates for women aged up to fifty declined, and those for women fifty and older increased by percentages varying by age group. A similar trend applied in the case of infant mortality, which, instead of continuing the steady decline it had begun in the 1960s, started to rise significantly, increasing from 23 deaths per thousand births in 1971 to 32 per thousand in 1976.

It is thought that one of the reasons for the high infant death rate was the level of alcoholism among Soviet women, a characteristic they shared with Soviet men. Other reasons for the decline of Soviet citizens' health included the deterioration of health services as they were progressively starved of funds. In the 1960s health care in the Soviet Union received about 6.6 percent of GNP, but it fell to 4.1 percent in 1970, and under 3 percent in the early 1980s. Some 65 percent of rural district hospitals lacked hot running water, 17 percent had no running water at all, and 27 percent lacked sewerage.

The status of women attracted more official attention in the 1970s than it had for some decades in part because of the declining birth rate. The question was how production and reproduction could be best combined, given women's high participation rate in the Soviet labor force, of which they represented 51 percent. Research showed that women worked in poorly paid jobs and also carried the great bulk of the burden of domestic work, which might include many hours queuing for goods that were in short supply. Suggestions for improving the situation included the provision of part-time jobs, as well as expanding nurseries and other child-care facilities.

Most proposals for improving women's conditions were based on the premise that women would have more children if they had the time to devote to them, but some commentators acknowledged that this was not always so. Under conditions of improving living standards, some writers and researchers noted, the quality of children's lives was important, and parents might prefer to concentrate their resources and time on fewer children. There was little echo in the Soviet Union of the debate going on in Western Europe over women's status in society and the economy. What response there was in the Soviet Union was often hostility at what was perceived as the tendency of Western feminists to blur the distinction between women and men.

In the first half of the 1980s, there was a renewed stress on the responsibility of women to reproduce so as to ensure a constant labor supply. References were made at the 1981 Communist Party congress to the "population problem," and it was proposed to redress it "through greater concern for the family, newlyweds, and women." Support was given to plans for more child-care facilities, part-time work for women, and a year off work after giving birth. There was also limited recognition of the need for men to shoulder a greater share of household work, something it was suggested might not only increase fertility but also make marriages more stable and reduce the high rates of divorce in the Soviet Union. Increasing the supply of labor-saving appliances was also proposed, but that suggestion of course foundered on fundamental economic deficiencies.

In nonmaterial terms, there were also some improvements in Soviet life, but trends were contradictory and difficult to predict. Following the invasion of Czechoslovakia in 1968 there was a period in which dissidents and critics of the Communist regime came under renewed repression and censorship. Many writers were expelled from the Union of Soviet Writers, an action which effectively prevented them from being published, and a number of prominent writers and academics left the Soviet Union entirely. Against the outflow of Soviet dissidents there was an increase in the number of foreign academics and cultural groups entering the Soviet Union following the Helsinki agreements in 1976. As limited and carefully selected as they were, these visitors did increase the exposure of Soviet people to outside influences.

Although most Soviet citizens were not permitted to travel abroad, one group was given an increasing number of exit visas: Jews. Throughout the 1970s the position of Jews in the Soviet Union had been raised in a number of forums. The demand that Jews who wished to migrate to Israel should be allowed to was one of the chronic stumbling blocks to broader cooperation between the Soviet Union and the West. The position of Jews in the Soviet Union worsened in this period. The number of synagogues declined from 67 in 1965 to 60 in 1980 and 50 in 1983; the number of rabbis was even smaller (about 30 to 35 in 1983). During the 1970s more than a quarter of a million Jews left the Soviet Union. Migration peaked at 50,000 in 1979, but fell to under 3,000 in 1983. It is likely that the emigrants represented the more observant members of the Soviet Jewish community, the great majority of which rarely attended services. As a result, the remaining Jews became a more secular and less clearly defined group within the Soviet Union.

Improved relations with Germany also led to the migration of many Soviet Germans to West Germany: 49,000 of them between 1971 and 1978. As far as other national groups within the Soviet Union were concerned, there was increasing emphasis throughout the 1970s on the unity of the Soviet people. To make this point, at the 1971 party congress Brezhnev referred to a "new historical community of people—the Soviet people." When the 1977 constitution was being drafted, there were proposals, not acted upon, that the federal organization of the union be replaced by a unitary arrangement.

The other side of the policy of stressing the integrity of the Soviet people was repression of nationalism among the constituent populations of the Soviet Union. Efforts were made to ensure that natives occupied most of the top positions in the administration of the various republics, a process that went furthest in the Baltic states and Ukraine, where 80 or 90 percent of regional politburo members were members of indigenous ethnic groups. Russians were kept on in regions that were considered troublesome. Central party bodies, like the politburo, which had seen the entry of large numbers of non-Russians under Khrushchev, recovered their Russian predominance under Brezhnev. On the other hand, the promotion of locals to key posts in the republics, including heads of local secret police organizations, served to undermine the effectiveness of central control in Brezhnev's later years.

Poland, 1970–85: Economic Decline and the Rise of Solidarity

The Eastern European states that fell within the Soviet sphere of influence experienced the same kinds of problems as the Soviet Union itself, including stagnating economies with low productivity and dissatisfaction over the supply of consumer goods. They added an extra ingredient to the mixture: a resurgence of nationalist sentiments, not only on the part of non-Communists who wanted independence from the Soviet Union, but also on the part of Communists. The "Brezhnev Doctrine," that each Communist party was responsible not only to its own people but to other parties and the Communist movement in general, had been crudely imposed in Czechoslovakia in 1968. At the same time there were plenty of examples of divergence from the Soviet model: the Eurocommunism espoused by the likes of Enrico Berlinguer in Italy, the distinctive road to socialism built by Tito in Yugoslavia, and the independent lines adopted by Romania in many spheres of foreign and economic policy.

Instead of being cowed by the show of Soviet determination and force in 1968, many of the Eastern European states adopted a broad range of institutional and policy reforms. Some they embraced voluntarily, others were forced on them. The pace of reform varied, and generally reflected the social and economic forces at play in each country. They took place, too, in the context of ever-broadening economic and political relationships with Western Europe.

Poland, however, followed a distinctive political trajectory that proved important for the eventual collapse of communist regimes in Europe. In 1970 it was the site of mass strikes when increases of a third in the price of meat were announced two weeks before Christmas, betraying a sense of timing that only an atheist would consider impeccable. The unrest and the shooting of demonstrators brought the leadership of Wladislaw Gomulka to an end, and on December 20 Edward Gierek became head of the Communist Party. It was the first time since the Second World War that a European administration had fallen because of a spontaneous workers' movement; the workers in this case had limited aims, for they did not wish to repudiate socialism but merely to change the regime's policies.

Under continuing pressure, notably a confrontation with militant women textile workers in Lodz, Gierek canceled the price increases. In the next few years further concessions were made to workers, peasants, and to the Catholic Church. The main guarantor of social peace, however, was a good standard of living, and this Gierek set out to achieve by importing consumer goods and by improving the lot of peasants by making health care and social security more accessible. More important over the longer term, the government set about reviving the moribund economy. On the surface, the policies worked exceptionally well. Poland's industrial growth rates were among the world's highest: Automobile and ship construction flourished, and even agriculture progressed steadily. Real wages rose by 40 percent between 1971 and 1975.

But the economic recovery was built, if not on sand, then on the equally insubstantial ground of loans and credits from Western Europe. Because of the recession in Western Europe the markets for Polish exports, which might have repaid the loans, were weak. Some of the loans had been used to build industries, like steel plants, whose products were in declining demand. Imported goods of all kinds that were needed to satisfy consumer demand, became prohibitively expensive for Poles when the increased oil prices led to a rise in Western European production costs that were reflected in higher prices.

By 1975 Poland's exports were covering the cost of only 60 percent of its imports; its foreign debt rose, and by the next year Poland was unable to service it. To compound problems, there were poor harvests in 1975 and 1976, and farmers could no longer afford high-priced imported fertilizer. The government tried to raise meat prices in 1976 in order to reduce domestic demand and free supplies for export, but it backed down at the first sign of resistance. The economic downturn was accompanied by widespread social discontent. Housing was still in desperately short supply, and in rural areas a third of dwellings still lacked running water. The health services began to break down under the additional pressure when peasants were given access to the system.

As discontent grew, the government found itself increasingly vulnerable. For years the Communist Party had played on Poles' anxieties about a resurgence of German nationalists and their demands for the return of territory now occupied by Poland, in order to justify the close alliance with the Soviet Union. With the visit to Poland of the West German chancellor and the recognition of the German-Polish border, the argument lost much of its strength. The weakening of the regime was demonstrated by its reversal of price increases twice and by its agreement to drop key clauses from a draft constitution in 1975. The clauses, stipulating the leading role of the Communist Party and the centrality of the alliance with the Soviet Union, were opposed by an alliance of the Church and groups of intellectuals.

The vulnerability of Poland's Communist regime increased in the second half of the 1970s. By then, merely paying the interest on the multibillion-dollar foreign debt absorbed 92 percent of export earnings, and Poland was having to raise additional foreign loans and credits to pay for imports. The only way to reduce the debt was by reducing living standards, but that way lay disaster for the regime.

An ill-portent for the government was the coalescence of a number of factions that had until then operated separately. The Catholic Church cooperated with intellectuals, and in the late 1970s both formed links with peasants and workers. By 1976 there were at least two dozen anti-socialist groups of various kinds, and one even announced its intention to contest the 1979 election to the Sejm. Reports circulated within Poland and outside the country, detailing its economic malaise and criticizing the privileges and elevated lifestyles of the political elites. A critical moment in the growth of opposition to the Communist government was the election of the Polish cardinal Karol Wojtyla, archbishop of Cracow, as pope in 1978. Wojtyla had been a prominent critic of the Communist regime, its ideology, and policies. As Pope John Paul II, he returned on a visit to Poland in 1979 and was greeted by large, enthusiastic crowds. Not only was there joy at the fact that a Pole had been elected pope, but there was a sense that the Church might regain its historic leadership of Polish nationalism.

The opportunity for leadership soon arrived, because in 1980 the government once again tried to increase meat prices, this time selectively. As soon as strikes began to break out, meat supplies were rushed to stores and some wage increases quickly granted. The strikes continued, however, and began to center on the shipbuilding workers in the Baltic port of Gdansk (formerly Danzig), where there had been work stoppages over other issues. The increases in food prices had produced a broad-based organization of workers in Gdansk that was no longer committed to socialism but wanted broad changes in Poland's political and economic structure. The twenty-one demands they made in 1980 included the formation of free trade unions, wage increases, less censorship, the broadcasting of Catholic mass on state radio and television, the election of factory managers, and a memorial to the workers killed by police and soldiers in 1970.

Faced with spreading strikes and some uncertainty about the loyalty of the military, the government conceded the right of Polish workers to set up free trade unions, and the workers agreed that the unions would be socialist. To prevent the dissipation of the force they had built up, representatives from factories throughout Poland met in Gdansk in September 1980 and established a national coordinating committee called Solidarity. Its leader and spokesperson was Lech Walesa, an electrician in the Gdansk shipyards who was largely motivated by the wish to commemorate the 1970 deaths. Solidarity was far more than a trade union movement, however; its very existence called into question political and economic constraints across the board. An independent trade union could not operate without the freedom of workers to join it or without freedom of expression. Moreover, it signaled its opposition status by forbidding any member of the ruling party to hold office in Solidarity, even though a million party members had joined the organization.

Following the government's concessions, Gierek resigned, and the new government tried to frustrate the legal registration of Solidarity that was necessary before it could open bank accounts and operate officially. Tensions ran high, leading East Germany and Czechoslovakia to close their borders with Poland, but by November 1980 the organization was duly registered by the courts. There was some concern on the part of Solidarity's leaders and within the Church that extreme nationalists might provoke repression or even invasion from the Soviet Union. There were movements of Soviet troops near the Polish border and suggestions that other Communist parties might come to the aid of the Polish party; this had echoes of Warsaw Pact "assistance" to Czechoslovakia in 1968. Walesa advised workers to obey the law and avoid provocative actions, and the Polish government was also anxious to avoid confrontation that would further disrupt the economy; in March 1981, it admitted it could no longer pay its debts.

During 1981 Solidarity, whose more than 10 million members represented a majority of Polish workers, won increasing concessions. Workers were granted three Saturdays free of work per month. An association of Poland's small farmers, called Rural Solidarity, was finally registered in May after a bitter dispute that included the threat of a general strike. The government had not wanted an organization of small property owners that was inherently not socialist, but it was forced to concede. At the same time that Solidarity won concessions, it did not alter Poland's political or economic structure measurably. The Communists remained in power and in control of the police and armed forces, and under pressure from the Soviet Union, they formed plans for a military coup to reimpose unchallenged authority over Poland.

Their resolve was strengthened by the first Solidarity congress, held in Gdansk in September 1981. Although many resolutions reflected Solidarity's mainstream policies, others went further than Walesa and other moderates wanted. One announced that Solidarity would assist similar movements elsewhere in Europe, an idea that went down poorly in Moscow where the notion of proletarian fraternity was interpreted in a rather more restricted way. Soon after the congress, even Solidarity's moderate leadership embraced more thorough political reforms, including economic restructuring, free local elections, and greater access to the media.

In social policy, especially issues affecting women most directly, Solidarity was conservative. Despite the fact that half its members were women, the leaders were men, and men accounted for 92 percent of delegates to its first congress. Solidarity did take up some women's issues, winning better maternity and childrearing leaves in 1980, but it assumed that women would assume full responsibilities for their families as well as work outside the home. It did not address pay equity, and the wage increases negotiated by Solidarity actually widened the gap between women's and men's incomes. Nor did it address female unemployment, which was higher than men's. Solidarity did not, in its early stages, call for a ban on abortion (as it did by 1990), but expressed the hope that economic improvements would reduce the financial reasons for abortions.

In the wake of the Solidarity congress, there was a further change in the government that brought General Wojciech Jaruzelski, the former minister of defense, to power. He had already decided that military action should be taken against Solidarity, and beginning in November the government used force against strikers. In an emergency secret meeting, Solidarity's leaders discussed their options, and there was talk of setting up a workers' militia and of overthrowing the government. In the end Solidarity went no further than calling for a referendum on the government's methods. But the secret meeting had been bugged by the police, and the talk of revolt gave the government reason to act. On the night of December 13, 1981, martial law was decreed, the borders were

Polish workers strike in 1981 in favor of the Solidarity Union.

sealed, and more than 5,000 Solidarity activists arrested, including the union's entire leadership. Industrial centers were placed under military control and production under military discipline. Civil liberties were curtailed and a government by a military council, headed by Jaruzelski, was proclaimed.

In an address to the nation on Christmas Eve, Jaruzelski referred to the need to choose between "a greater and a lesser evil," which commentators took as meaning that martial law was declared in order to forestall a Soviet invasion. Whether this was so, or whether the Soviet threat was invoked to rally some support to the new regime, is not clear, although it is obvious that the Soviet leadership was glad to have authority restored in Poland. There were attempts, especially by the Church, to forge a compromise that would allow Solidarity to operate as a nonpolitical entity, but they failed, and in October 1982 the organization was dissolved. Paradoxically the success of the military coup demonstrated the strength of Solidarity and the weakness of the Communist government. The latter's inability to manage the economy during the 1970s had forfeited it the extensive, if grudging, support of many workers, and it had been forced to demonstrate that its authority rested on coercion, not consent.

By 1985 attempts had been made to normalize the situation. Martial law was terminated after a year, and Walesa was released from prison. Military government ended in July 1983, although Jaruzelski remained in office. A postponed visit by the pope took place in summer 1983, and two years later a general amnesty of Solidarity prisoners was announced to mark the fortieth anniversary of Poland's liberation from the Nazis—an anniversary that raised the contentious issue of the respective roles of the Polish Home Army and the Soviet Red Army in that achievement.

It was impossible to cram the opposition genie back into its jar, however, and there was persistent tension between government and dissidents. There was a massive outcry when a dissident priest was kidnapped and killed by the secret police in 1984; widespread opposition to price increases in 1985 forced the government to relent to some extent. Although Solidarity had no legal standing, it continued to be an informal force, printing an underground newspaper and running an illegal radio station. By the late 1980s, which were to prove critical for Communist regimes throughout Eastern Europe, Poland already possessed the political and ideological infrastructure for an alternative government.

Society and Economy in Eastern Europe: Prosperity and Decline

Other Eastern European states in the Soviet sphere followed less dramatic paths, but policy changes were generally motivated by the same fundamental concerns as in Poland, notably economic stagnation and threats to standards of living. It became abundantly clear by the late 1970s that a crucial weakness of the Eastern European regimes was their inability to satisfy the basic needs of their citizens or to maintain a steady improvement in living standards. These conditions became particularly acute in the early 1980s because of Eastern Europe's economic ties to the Soviet Union through Comecon, the Communist trading bloc, and the growing dependence on Western finance and imports.

The participation of most Eastern European states in Comecon placed limitations on the development of national economies, but it also helped them until the mid-1970s. The Soviet Union provided cheap energy and raw materials to most of its Eastern European clients, and, together with other Comecon partners, imported finished products that might not have found markets elsewhere. Initially this represented an effective subsidy of Eastern Europe by the Soviet Union, and even when the Soviet Union raised the price of its oil and natural gas in the mid-1970s, it softened the impact in Eastern Europe by phasing in the higher prices over several years. By the time the higher costs were fully charged, however, the benefits of Comecon trade had shifted in favor of the Soviet Union. This reversal of economic fortunes for the Eastern European states intensified the difficulties they began to experience in repaying the Western European loans and credits of which they had availed themselves once political détente began. Retrenchment followed, and a common pattern was for living standards to fall in the first half of the 1980s.

The health of Eastern Europeans in the Soviet sphere also declined markedly between the 1960s and the mid-1980s. While life expectancy at birth rose slightly in this period, it did so less than in the Latin American and Caribbean regions. Insofar as life expectancy at higher ages was concerned, the rates actually fell. In the 1960s, Hungarian men aged 30 had on average another 41.7 years to live, but by the mid-1980s that figure had fallen by almost 4 years. In Poland it had fallen 2 years, and in East Germany eight-tenths of a year. Women's life expectancy had increased, but in no country by more than a year. Death rates of older men and women, from middle age upward, rose. The main reason for the different directions traveled by Eastern and Western European mortality rates (up and down, respectively) was the much higher incidence of cardiovascular disease in Eastern Europe. It is likely that high levels of consumption of tobacco and hard liquor were implicated, but we cannot overlook the failure of health care systems to prevent and deal with the rising level of poor health. These and other social trends were not neatly applicable throughout Eastern Europe—they must be placed in the specific political context and tradition of each state—but they form a common thread linking the fortunes of a number of countries.

HUNGARY, CZECHOSLOVAKIA, AND EAST GERMANY

These three states can be grouped together as the three most prosperous in the bloc within the Soviet sphere of influence. Insofar as Eastern Europe's regimes were able to maintain a degree of consensual social tranquillity by providing satisfactory and rising living standards for their citizens, these had the best chance. Each varied, however, in the degree of political coercion that was applied; each had a different relationship with the Soviet Union and with Western Europe. There were similarities in important respects, however, notably the stagnation of their economies from about 1980, and the social status of women.

In Hungary economic reform was already well under way by the end of the 1960s, and it was enhanced in the following decade and a half. During the whole period (and longer), Hungary was led by János Kádár, who had come to power soon after the failed 1956 revolution. An economic policy called the New Economic Mechanism, implemented in 1968, included the weakening of central planning control and the encouragement of private enterprise in service industries and agriculture. The policies produced a drop in wages, and workers, losing ground against rising prices, were increasingly forced to take two jobs. In addition, the ability of enterprises to import goods raised the level of foreign debt, and when pressure to curb the drift from the Soviet economic model was applied after the Czechoslovak experiment in 1968, the Hungarian government was receptive. Large corporations were brought under central control, and living standards were improved by significant wage increases in 1972 and 1973.

The reassertion of economic control by the state proved to be temporary, however. When oil prices rose from 1973 on, the world price of Hungary's main exports, bauxite, aluminum, and grain, fell. Servicing the foreign debt proved increasingly difficult. The economy lost its protection from high energy costs when its chief supplier, the Soviet Union, raised prices in 1975, and Hungary's expenditure on oil gradually increased more than 100 percent. By 1977 growing difficulties with the economy led to a gradual reversion to the New Economic Mechanism, which was fully restored by 1979. Kádár also allowed the breakup of a number of large state enterprises. Hungary's economic mixture of state and private enterprise was often referred to as "goulash communism" after the national dish, a kind of stew.

Despite discontinuity of policies, the Hungarian economy recorded some notable successes in the 1970s. Agriculture flourished and achieved productivity increases unequaled by almost any other state. Consumer goods and a variety of food were readily available in stores, and automobiles became more common. But structural problems caught up with Hungary in the early 1980s. Like Poland, Hungary had borrowed extensively from Western Europe but was unable to manage the debt, which by 1989 had reached $20 billion; this was more per capita than in any other Eastern European state. In order to deal with the developing financial crisis, the government restricted imports in 1982 and cut subsidies to many businesses in 1983. The economy not only slowed but even declined in some years. As prices rose, the living standards of perhaps a third of the population declined.

A similar evolution in living standards was observable in Czechoslovakia, where the regime of Gustav Husak that came to power after the 1968 Soviet invasion tried to win support by improving conditions for consumers. To assist this goal, the government reduced expenditure on defense and foreign aid. Private consumption rose by 37 percent between 1970 and 1978 and the number of automobiles doubled, from one for every seventeen people in 1971 to one for eight by 1979. By the early 1980s, however, the Czechoslovak economy had begun to slow down, partly because of the rising cost of energy; the country was importing twice as much Soviet oil in 1980 as ten years earlier, and the price had doubled. Austerity measures were adopted in 1981 and 1982, and although they were modest when compared with Poland's after 1981, they frustrated Czechoslovakians' expectations of continuously rising prosperity.

East Germany diverged from the trend toward mixed economies by reversing economic reforms implemented in the 1960s and reasserting central control. Although trade with Western Europe increased, East Germany intensified its commercial links within Comecon and soon surpassed Poland as the Soviet Union's main trading partner. This was made possible by the expansion of the East German economy and the relatively high quality of its manufactured goods.

Economic links with West Germany also became increasingly important, and by the mid-1980s they accounted for a tenth of East German trade. West German banks advanced almost $2 billion in credits in 1983–84, and further income was derived from West German visitors and cash payments made for the release of political prisoners and for family reunifications. Such flows of money contributed to an economy that was strong in Eastern European terms and supported a relatively high standard of living for East Germans. In terms of consumer goods like televisions, automobiles, telephones, and washing machines, East Germany ranked highest or second highest in the region. A considerably higher proportion of young people attended universities and other institutions of higher learning. These standards of living came under pressure from the reversal of the terms of trade with the Soviet Union after oil prices were increased. In addition, loans and credits from West Germany contributed to foreign indebtedness, which rose from $1.4 billion in 1971 to $12 billion in 1981.

In the political sphere the three Eastern European states followed varying policies, as both Hungary and Czechoslovakia broadly liberalized their systems while the East German regime retained tight control. In Hungary there were signs of political liberalization in 1967, when the single-list voting system was ended, making it possible in principle for more than one candidate to stand. Parliament was urged to debate government policies critically. Even though there was a reaction after 1968, and a number of academic and cultural figures were fired and expelled from the party, the losses in the 1970s were outweighed by the gains made in the late 1960s. Most Hungarians were free to travel abroad if they could obtain foreign currency, and political exiles were allowed to make periodic visits to Hungary.

Hungarian political reforms continued into the early 1980s. A constitutional council was set up in 1983, and in 1985 independent candidates were permitted to oppose party nominees in elections to parliament. Even though the independent candidates had to be preapproved, the 1985 elections saw a number of the unofficial candidates elected, while some prominent party candidates, including a former prime minister and former minister of justice, were defeated. There was also greater openness by the regime. At the ruling party's congress in 1985, Kádár admitted that austerity policies had caused a decline in standards of living. By the mid-1980s, Hungary was making steadier progress away from a centralized one-party state than any of its Eastern European counterparts.

In Czechoslovakia the course of political reform was set back when the revolution of 1968 was ended by invasion. Between 1968 and 1971, expulsions and resignations reduced the size of the Communist Party by a third, and many reform-minded intellectuals were dismissed from their university posts. The militia and police were strengthened and rearmed, and reserve forces built up; these security forces could be reinforced by the Czechoslovakian military and the 70,000-strong Red Army contingent that remained in the country. By 1971 all the reforms of 1968 had been rescinded. During the 1970s, however, there was a loosening up. The government sponsored more contacts with Western Europe, and permitted the publication of Western books and the importation of movies and music. The jazz section of the musicians' union forged strong links outside Czechoslovakia, and in 1979 affiliated with the International Jazz Federation. Limitations on political action still rankled, however. After the 1975 Helsinki agreements on civil liberties, a number of prominent intellectuals, including the novelist Václav Havel, formed an organization to press for democratic rights. They issued a manifesto on January 1, 1977, and as a result the organization became known as Charter 77. The great majority of its members were Czechs, a small minority Slovaks. Charter 77 did not set out to become a mass movement, as Solidarity later did in Poland, but it exerted constant pressure by pointing out cases where the regime failed to observe the standards that it itself laid down.

In contrast to Hungary in particular, political freedom in East Germany was extremely limited, the regime distinguishing itself by going so far as to censor material from the Soviet Union. To some extent the attempts to insulate East Germany from external influences, and to intensify the socialist economy, reflected the determination of the Communist regime to make sure that the country was clearly distinct from West Germany. East Germany was portrayed as the heir to a revolutionary tradition in Germany; in 1983 the five hundredth anniversary of the birth of Martin Luther, whose rebellion against the Catholic Church set off the Protestant Reformation, was ostentatiously celebrated in East Germany to make just this point.

During the 1980s, there was growing dissatisfaction over problems in the economies, and other persistent social problems added to discontent. In Hungary in particular, housing remained inadequate: More than a third of a million dwellings were in poor condition, and officials described 100,000 as unfit for human habitation. By 1985 an estimated 350,000 families were looking for improved dwellings, most because they were crammed into small one- or two-bedroom apartments. Such aspirations might be considered signs of rising living standards and expectations, but that was little consolation to those involved. An indication of the magnitude of the problem was that by 1985 a full two-fifths of Hungary's citizens were either homeless or living in accommodations they deemed unsatisfactory. The demand for telephones in Hungary was so great that in the early 1980s it was reported that new subscribers would have a thirteen-year wait for service.

There was evidence of serious environmental damage throughout Eastern Europe because economic growth had been unrestrained and unregulated. The Danube was so polluted that its water could not even be used for industrial purposes, and a quarter of Czechoslovakia's forests were reported dead or dying because of acid rain. Sulfur-dioxide emissions in East Germany and Czechoslovakia were four times higher than in Western Europe, where they were under attack from environmentalists. The development of an ecology movement in Eastern Europe was hampered by restrictions on political activity, and any proposals to shut down or restrict the operation of a polluting plant could easily be construed as opposition to economic growth and prosperity. Nonetheless, there were sporadic demonstrations by environmentalists in all Eastern European states, and in Czechoslovakia Charter 77 added the environmental crisis to its list of charges against the regime.

If growing concern about the environment was something shared by groups in both Western and Eastern Europe, there was less evidence in the East of a women's movement analogous to that which developed in the West in the 1970s. On the surface the reason for the absence of a women's movement seemed obvious: Women in Eastern Europe already had many of the rights their counterparts in Western Europe wanted. Women had full access to employment and education, there were extensive social services like child-care facilities, abortion was readily accessible, and Eastern European societies were generally free of exploitative institutions like beauty contests that Western feminists opposed. But in reality, rather than in legal and ideological terms, the status of women in Eastern Europe was in many ways similar to that of Western European women, although in some respects it was difficult to compare the two populations.

Rates of female employment in Eastern Europe in the 1970s were high. Some 47 percent of the Czechoslovakian workforce was female, and over 90 percent of women in the employable age groups were in paid employment. The same was true of East Germany where 91 percent of women out of school and not studying full time were employed. Although these were much higher participation levels than the increasing rates of women's employment in Western Europe, there was the same tendency in both for women to be concentrated in low-paid, low-status jobs that offered few possibilities of advancement. Women were most often employed in secretarial work, service industries, food services, and in textile and clothing industries, and were paid about half the wages of a male doing similar work. Even in sectors that were dominated by women, women rarely had positions of responsibility. In Czechoslovakia, women accounted for 96 percent of the specialized workers in health care (as doctors, nurses, and technicians) but only 12 percent of managers.

Often, little provision was made for training. Among the grievances of Hungarian women was slow progress in employment: Between 1970 and 1984, the percentage of women qualified for skilled work rose from 4 to 12 percent, but the percentage of men rose from 10 to 28 percent. Although 87 percent of East German women had some formal training for their work, after 1975 there was a steady decline in the employment of women in core technical positions, such as data-processing technicians and electricians, where they had been underrepresented before.

There were also complaints, as there were everywhere in Europe, that women not only worked outside the home but carried the burden of work in the home as well. Promotions, salary scales, and social benefits directed toward women reinforced the notion that men were the prime breadwinners, while women worked full time to earn a secondary wage and also looked after the needs of the family. Czechoslovakian women allocated 62 percent of their nonworking time to the family, men only 21 percent. A 1985 Hungarian survey showed that in 80 to 85 percent of families, the wife alone did all the cooking and laundry, in 75 percent she did all the dishwashing, and in about 60 percent she did all the housekeeping and daily shopping.

The high employment rate of women and the double burden of domestic responsibilities, compounded by housing and other problems, contributed to high divorce rates and low fertility. The number of divorces for every hundred marriages each year rose from 14 in 1960 to 20 in 1970, 29 in 1980, and over 30 in 1985. Low birth rates were a constant worry for Communist regimes. In the 1970s, the Czechoslovakian government spent a full tenth of its budget on measures to encourage couples to have children: family allowances, maternity leave, kindergartens, school meals, tax concessions, and the like. State facilities for child care were more extensive than elsewhere, and the great majority of infants and young children were looked after so that their mothers could be in paid employment.

Contributing to the low fertility rate was relatively easy access to abortion. Unlike women in Western Europe, however, Eastern European women used abortion as a primary means of family planning. This was highlighted by a 1972 East German law that limited women to one abortion every six months. Population policies produced variations in abortion laws over time and among the three states. Although abortion was made illegal in Hungary in the 1950s, a 1974 decree made it available to single, divorced, separated, or widowed women, married women over thirty-five, women who had had three children, or in circumstances of rape, incest, danger to health, or inadequate housing. Few women could not satisfy one of those criteria.

In Czechoslovakia, in contrast, abortion was legalized in 1957, but in the 1970s there were attempts to restrict it to medical grounds. In practice, women who persisted were able to obtain abortions, but full freedom of abortion was not implemented until 1987. Abortion had similarly been restricted in East Germany, when "social" grounds were eliminated and only medical reasons recognized. As a result, an estimated 60 percent of abortions were illegal. In 1972 a reform allowed free abortion during the first three months of pregnancy, and thereafter for medical reasons. Free contraception was made available. Because abortion was used as family planning, the rate of abortions was high. The annual number of legal abortions in Hungary, between 100,000 and 200,000, outnumbered live births, and contributed to a steady decline in the growth rate of Hungary's population; by 1988 deaths exceeded births. Over time, as the use of other forms of family limitation became more widespread, the abortion rate declined.

It was one of the ironies that although the Communist system espoused an ideology of sexual equality, only a minority of political leaders were women, and that minority got smaller the higher one went up the political hierarchy. Some 29 percent of party members in Czechoslovakia were women, but women held only 18 percent of senior posts, and a mere 7 percent of positions on the important central committee of the party. They did somewhat better in the opposition groups that developed from the 1970s. A fifth of the signatories of Charter 77 were women, as was one of its three rotating spokespersons. Women represented half the membership of another group, the Committee for the Unjustly Prosecuted, and accounted for a quarter of those charged in a major trial of dissidents in 1981.

BULGARIA AND ROMANIA

The two southern members of the Eastern European bloc within the Soviet sphere had little in common other than a border. Under Nicolae Ceausescu, Romania pursued an independent foreign policy that included condemnation of the Soviet Union's invasion of Czechoslovakia in 1968 and intervention in Afghanistan in 1979. At the same time, close economic relations were fostered with Western states, and Romania became a member of the General Agreement on Tariffs and Trade and the International Monetary Fund. Ceausescu received visits from U.S. presidents Nixon and Ford, and in turn traveled to the United States and Western Europe. In contrast, the Bulgarian regime of Todor Zhivkov adopted an almost completely subservient posture toward the Soviet Union.

Romania's openness to the West did not reflect a liberalization of political or economic policies; on the contrary, Ceausescu developed a regime reminiscent of Stalin's. In 1974 the leading role of the Communist Party was enhanced, and Ceausescu's position magnified by a cult of personality within which he became the Leader (*Conducator*). Ceausescu's wife, Elena, was portrayed and honored as a great scientist and appointed to powerful state positions, while his son Nicu was prepared to succeed him. Dissidents were ruthlessly suppressed by the Securitate (the security police), who were said to have used five-minute chest X-rays to induce cancer in some opponents of the regime. Strikes, such as one in 1977 by 30,000 miners seeking better working conditions, were suppressed and the leaders fired or killed.

Repression intensified during the 1980s, and fear of dissidents went so far that speaking to foreigners was made illegal. Typewriters (which might be used to prepare illegal literature) had to be registered each year so that their typefaces could be compared with typed material that had been seized by the police. An attempted coup by military officers in 1983 failed, as did sporadic desperate strikes.

Romania's economic policy was equally centralized, and it was assisted during the 1970s by considerable Western aid. Romania had extensive oil fields, and one of Ceausescu's pet projects was the expansion of the country's refining capacity. The plans went awry, in part because by the time the refineries were ready, the price of oil began to fall. The result was that, like other East European states, Romania faced debt problems in the early 1980s. Severe austerity measures were adopted to reduce imports and domestic consumption. Energy use was curtailed to the point that heating was allowed for only four hours a day (often reduced to two), and no room was permitted more than one 60-watt light bulb. The decline of domestic consumption enabled Romania to increase its exports and pay off most of its debt, but the cost to ordinary Romanians was immense.

Bulgaria had begun to decentralize its economy in the 1960s, but threw the program into reverse after 1968 when Czechoslovakia seemed to show how difficult it was to control reform. Western loans were used to promote economic development, but by the early 1980s the results were disappointing and the debt was considerable. As a result, a new policy of decentralization was put in place.

Throughout the 1970s the coercive tendencies of the Bulgarian party grew, but they were intensified in the mid-1980s. Dissidents were roughly dealt with, and a renewed stress on nationalism brought attacks on ethnic minorities. The remaining Turks in Bulgaria,

A 1979 rally in Bucharest, Romania, celebrates the anniversary of the Communist seizure of power in 1944. The banners and photographs of Nicolae Ceausescu reflect the personality cult the Romanian leader created around himself.

who constituted a tenth of the country's population, had already experienced restrictions on their Muslim practices, and were now required to adopt Bulgarian names. The use of the Turkish language on radio or in print was forbidden. The reaction was so vigorous that the army was used to restore order, and hundreds of Turks were reported killed.

As far as women were concerned, the major impact of the Romanian regime was the attempt to force each woman to bear four children. Alarmed at the declining birth rate, in 1966 Ceausescu forbade the use of birth control or abortions by any woman except those over forty-five or those who had had four children. Securitate agents were attached to gynecological wards in hospitals, women were subjected to tri-monthly checks, and severe penalties were imposed on women discovered to have had an abortion. The result of these policies pushed up the number of births from 234,000 in 1966 to 528,000 in 1967, although the number fell in later years when couples found ways of avoiding conception. Because many children were not wanted and others were an intolerable financial burden, the state constructed a network of orphanages. Ceausescu's aim was to increase the population from 22 million in the early 1970s to 30 million by the year 2000.

Ceausescu pressed on with these policies in the 1980s. The legal minimum age for marriage was lowered to fifteen, and women who had not married by age twenty-five were subjected to punitive taxation, as were couples without children. He announced in 1986 that the fetus was "the socialist property of the whole society. Giving birth is a patriotic duty. . . . Those who refuse to have children are deserters." There proved to be many such "deserters," but many women also lost their lives in the illegal abortions to which they desperately resorted.

The lot of Bulgarian women was by no means as dreadful as that of their Romanian counterparts, but it was more difficult than in the states to the north. Nine in ten women of working age were employed in industry, agriculture, services, education, or health, almost all in low-paying professional, clerical, or unskilled jobs. Marriage rates in Bulgaria were high, and there were attempts to encourage Bulgarians to have more than the average two children, in part to compensate for the higher birth rates of Turks and Sinti and Roma (Gypsies). Abortion was not available to married women unless they already had at least two children, and many women resorted to illegal and dangerous procedures. Because abortion was one of the main forms of family limitation, most women had three or more abortions before reaching menopause.

YUGOSLAVIA

Yugoslavia, led by Josip Tito, followed its own course in the 1970s and 1980s. It had pursued a wholly independent foreign policy since the end of the war, often alienating the Soviet leadership. It remained outside both the Warsaw Pact and Comecon. In economic matters it fostered a mixed economy, but suffered a recession after oil prices rose in 1973 and 1979. The regime was propped up to some extent by foreign loans and credits and by funds remitted by Yugoslav migrant workers, many of whom were "guest workers" in West Germany.

Yugoslavia was a multinational federation in which pressures for greater national rights, and even autonomy, were never far from the surface. Populations like Croatians, Bosnian Muslims, Albanians, and Slovenians resented the dominance of the Serbs (40 percent of the population) who were overrepresented in the central administration. The national capital, Belgrade, was in Serbia, so that anti-centralist and anti-Serbian sentiments were intertwined. Tito's declared aim was to make socialism an ideology that would override nationality and unite Yugoslavs, but there was constant tension. In the early

1970s, discontent focused on Croatia, which nationalists believed was receiving a dispro-portionately small share of state investment. Croatia also had one of the lowest birth rates in Yugoslavia and a high emigration rate: In 1971 more than 5 percent of the population worked outside Yugoslavia. Fears that Croatia would be demographically swamped added to anti-Belgrade feelings.

Student demonstrations in 1971 called for an end to Serbian domination and for Croatian independence. When it became clear that the Croatian party was allowing na-tionalist non-Communists to occupy senior posts in some organizations, thus giving pri-macy to nationality over political reliability, Tito purged the Croatian central committee. Some 400 Croatian nationalists were arrested.

The extension of the purges to the Communist parties of the other constituent re-publics of Yugoslavia aroused generally latent nationalist feelings against the central gov-ernment. In order to forestall any serious dissension, the authority of the republics was extended over policy areas not explicitly reserved to the central government, and the re-publics were given virtual veto powers over important state matters. A new constitution in 1974 provided for an assembly with representation not only from the regions of Yugoslavia but also from economic groups such as peasants, workers, and professionals, as well as from the Communist Party and the army. Soon after, Tito (then in his eighties) devised a system of government to succeed him when he died: The presidency of Yugoslavia was to be held for one year in turn by a representative of each of the six republics.

If Tito hoped to perform the difficult task of holding the federation together from the grave, his opportunity came in 1980. That year he died, leaving a fragile national arrange-ment and severe economic problems. Inflation that year rose to 30 percent and unemploy-ment stood at over 800,000. Yugoslavia's foreign debt stood between $15 billion and $21 billion, and payments on it accounted for a quarter of foreign earnings. The new adminis-tration, headed at first by a Macedonian, was forced to impose stringent economy measures. In 1981 and 1985 there were outbreaks of violence among the million ethnic Albanians in Kosovo. Some fifty members of the Serb minority in the province were killed, and relations between the dominant Serbs and Albanians started to deteriorate rapidly. As Yugoslavia ar-rived at the critical mid-1980s, when broad changes would begin throughout the region, it was saddled with growing national tensions on top of economic and social problems. To this extent it bore a burden that most other Eastern European states were spared.

ALBANIA

Albania was the most repressive and controlled of all Eastern European states in the 1970s and early 1980s. Not only was it ruled by Enver Hoxha with a severity Stalin would have approved, but there was a large statue of Stalin in the center of the capital, Tirana, and many factories and towns bore the former Soviet dictator's name. Albania remained re-sistant to changes in the Soviet Union as well as to shifts in the world at large. Having sided with China against the Soviet Union, Hoxha broke that relationship to protest the 1972 visit to Beijing by President Nixon. Albania played no part in the Helsinki Accords and other international agreements that made up détente. The country became isolated and somewhat mysterious, a sort of Balkan Tibet.

Albania's economy, rigidly controlled, provided a subsistence livelihood for its citi-zens. A secret police organization ensured that dissent was curbed, and foreign travel and the importation of foreign books and newspapers were forbidden. The military dot-ted the countryside with thousands of bunkers from which to defend the country against external or internal attack. Religious observances were prohibited, and Albania was declared to be an officially atheistic state. In the 1980s, however, there were signs of problems. In 1981 it was announced that Hoxha's longtime associate, Mehmet Shehu, had been uncovered as a spy, tried, and executed. In 1985 Hoxha himself died.

GREECE

On the southeastern margin of Europe, Greece began to integrate politically and economically a process accelerated in 1974 with the collapse of a military junta that had seized power from the civilian administration in 1967. Before their fall, the "colonels" repressed Greece's strong socialist and communist movements and implemented policies of detention, torture, and execution against their opponents. Civil liberties of all kinds were suspended, and regulations passed on such matters as men having long hair and women wearing short skirts. In economic terms the colonels attracted some support by canceling debts owed by peasants to the Agricultural Bank. Per capita income rose under the dictatorship, but prices rose faster; by 1973 inflation was running at 30 percent annually.

Civilian government was restored largely as a result of the army's failure to prevent a Turkish occupation of half of Cyprus. In 1974 Greeks voted in a referendum for a republic, and in 1975 a new constitution was issued. It provided for a strong president who could appoint and dismiss ministers, dissolve the legislature, and veto bills. A conservative government ruled from 1975 to 1981, but like its counterparts elsewhere in Europe, it supervised an ailing economy. The recession in Western Europe reduced tourist spending, and the downturn in international trade rendered much of the Greek merchant fleet idle. Some relief to agriculture could be expected from Greece's membership in the EEC, which took effect in 1981.

In the 1981 elections, the Socialist Party (PASOK) of Andreas Papandreou won 48 percent of the vote and the Communists 11 percent. Although the Socialists were elected on a platform of extensive social reform, financial constraints limited what they could achieve. There were minor, inexpensive reforms such as the introduction of civil marriage, and plans were announced to improve health care. Closer, formalized links between Greece and the core of Western Europe promised over the longer term to improve social services across the board.

Conclusion

During the 1970s, Europe's brief phase of postwar prosperity was brought to a rude halt. In Western Europe the direct reason was the dramatic rise in the price of imported oil, an event that revealed the reliance of European industry on this vital raw material and energy source, and the vulnerability of Europe to global political and economic forces. The oil price shocks reverberated not only through Western Europe's economies but through its political systems and social structures as well. When funds were drawn off to deal with the economic crisis, living standards and social welfare systems came under strain, and as a result a number of governments fell. Scapegoats, often in the form of immigrants, were identified, and the gap between rich and poor widened.

This was an opportunity for the Soviet Union and its Eastern European economic partners to narrow the gap with Western Europe in terms of economic performance and living standards. Soviet oil and gas resources shielded the Soviet Union and Eastern Europe from the impact of foreign price increases, and loans from Western banks might have enabled the region to position itself advantageously. Ironically, however, just as Western Europe's economies faltered, so did those of the Soviet Union and Eastern Europe. In the latter cases, chronic systemic weaknesses in agriculture and in industrial investment and productivity reached a critical point in the early 1980s.

People in the Soviet Union and Eastern Europe came under the same kinds of pressure as their Western European counterparts, as living standards and basic services declined and their expectations of improvement were frustrated. Where popular pressure could be applied, as in Poland, it was. Elsewhere, Eastern European regimes reacted to economic problems and popular discontent with repressive measures that ranged from forcing women to bear children to more banal restrictions on basic freedoms.

The fifteen-year period from 1970 to 1985 was to prove particularly important for the Soviet Union. The economic crisis that emerged by the early 1980s was so severe that it could no longer be ignored or concealed. Not only did it have a palpable effect on the lives of ordinary women and men, it also disabled the Soviet Union's ability to implement a wide range of domestic and foreign policies. More dramatically than in Western Europe, the economic and social crises that confronted the Soviet government by 1985 had far-reaching political effects. In short order, they would destroy the Soviet Union, lead to the collapse of Communist regimes throughout Eastern Europe, and produce a radical shift in the balance of power.

· 12 ·

Europe and the Post-Communist Era, 1985–1995

Introduction

For almost half the twentieth century, between 1945 and 1990, Europe was divided into two broad regions. The Soviet Union and its Eastern European partners constituted one bloc, Western Europe another. There was, as we have seen, a great deal of variation within each region, but the two regions also varied in significant ways from each other. It was not only a matter of ideology and political structure that differentiated East from West, but also fundamental social systems, social attitudes, and even levels of health.

In 1985 there seemed no reason to think that the division might not endure for many more years, albeit with changes, just as changes had taken place in the preceding four decades. But in 1985, starting in the Soviet Union and quickly spreading to Eastern Europe, the existing political and economic structures began to break down. So fast was the erosion that by 1990 the Communist system that had dominated Eastern Europe since the Second World War seemed to have disappeared entirely. That perception was an illusion, because there remained many continuities between the Communist and post-Communist states in political, social, and economic terms. Moreover, within five years a number of the former Communist parties had been returned to power by democratic election.

The breakdown of the Communist states was widely hailed as the end of communism and a vindication of the capitalist and social democratic systems of the West. It is important, however, to be clear about what it was that collapsed in 1989, for many Marxists and non-Marxist socialists had for years insisted that the political systems in place in the Soviet Union and Eastern Europe were perversions of Marxist socialism. Some historians prefer to describe them as "actually existing communism," to distinguish them from forms of socialism that are not repressive.

However they are described, the changes in Eastern Europe had wide-ranging effects throughout Europe. During the 1980s, trade and other links between East and West had grown, and the collapse of the eastern economies affected their western trading partners. The changes also brought the cold war to an end in Europe, calling into question the character and even the existence of collective security arrangements. In the social and economic spheres, the fall of the Communist regimes had far-reaching implications for all sections of Eastern Europe's populations.

The Soviet Union, 1985–91: Gorbachev and Reform

In 1985 Mikhail Gorbachev became the fourth secretary-general of the Soviet Communist Party to hold office in less than three years; Brezhnev had died in 1982, Andropov in 1984, and Chernenko in 1985. While his two predecessors had been members of the old generation of Soviet leaders and were clearly intended to be no more than caretaker leaders, Gorbachev was younger (he was fifty-four in 1985) and cut from different cloth. Within months of coming to power, he began to behave quite differently from earlier Soviet leaders. He traveled widely inside and outside the Soviet Union and mixed to an unprecedented extent with workers and other citizens, discussing and arguing about social and economic problems. He was remarkably candid about shortcomings in production, shortages of consumer goods, and deficiencies in living standards.

What drove Gorbachev to a policy of openness was a realization that the Soviet economy was in a critical condition—although Gorbachev referred to it as "precritical" because it had not actually collapsed. There had been virtually no growth since 1978, but defense spending continued to rise, drawing off an increasing proportion of resources. Although precise statistics are not available, military spending was estimated to have accounted for 22 to 30 percent of the Soviet Union's GNP in 1987, more than twice that of the United States. It was clear to Gorbachev that only radical reforms in the economy could prevent a complete collapse of the system that would threaten the military security and domestic stability of the Soviet Union.

The program of economic recovery that Gorbachev envisaged was called *perestroika,* or restructuring, a word that became familiar to Western observers of the Soviet Union from 1985 on. Restructuring of the economy came to include a dramatic reduction of centralized planning and control and the introduction of mechanisms associated with market economies, such as adjusting supply and prices to demand, paying attention to quality, using labor efficiently, and applying new technology. New investment in Soviet industry

The Soviet leader, Mikhail Gorbachev, discusses issues with people in a square in Sofia, Bulgaria, October 1985.

was to be directed to modernization and retooling, not to the creation of even more massive plants. Waste of material and labor resources was attacked; it was calculated that Soviet industry required more than three times the resources used by Western industry to produce the same product, and Soviet goods were of much lower quality.

The campaign to improve productivity and quality had many dimensions. One was a struggle against alcoholism, which was widespread in the Soviet Union and blamed not only for the high divorce rate and levels of domestic and public violence, but also low levels of productivity and high rates of absenteeism from work. In 1985 alcohol was made more difficult to obtain. Sales were limited to five hours a day (2:00 P.M. to 7:00 P.M.), the number of retail outlets was halved, and the supply of alcohol, especially vodka, reduced. Vodka lines became as common as lines for other commodities, and men discovered what it was like to stand in line for essentials. Many bars were closed, cafés were forbidden to serve alcoholic drinks, and in Moscow, with a population of 8 million, only seventy-nine restaurants were permitted to serve alcohol. Being drunk at work became a ground for dismissal; being drunk in public was made a crime punishable by fines. From 1986 to 1988 millions of people were charged with breaches of the alcohol law.

The campaign had an immediate impact, and by 1987 consumption of legally produced alcohol fell to 46 percent of the 1980 level. Although there was a rapid rise in home brewing and the production of moonshine liquor, it did not compensate for the decline in legal sales. Alcohol-related diseases, accidents, and crime declined, as did infant mortality. But the increase in productivity that might have been expected from a more sober labor force was not perceptible, and the campaign against drinking had some adverse consequences. In many parts of the country, demand for sugar, used in making alcohol, increased and led to shortages. More serious, workers in all facets of the alcohol industry, from manufacturing to bottling, were predominantly women, so that the slowdown of production threw thousands of women out of work. Most of the illegal distillers who began production were men. Finally, in 1986 alone, the loss of excise taxes on alcohol cost the state 6.2 billion rubles, or 6.3 percent of its revenues, and as a result the Soviet budget fell deeper into deficit.

The economic situation worsened when a 1988 law on state enterprises started to tackle economic structures directly by allowing enterprises to set many prices and wages. The result was a rise in wages above the levels of productivity, and an increase in prices that raised the inflation rate. Unemployment also rose as the government stopped work on a number of large projects and, in the wake of the disaster at the Chernobyl nuclear plant, shut down a number of nuclear reactors. Because the Soviet state had historically guaranteed employment, no means of calculating unemployment was available, and it was not until 1990 that the first official statistics on joblessness were published. In that year a figure of 2 million was given.

To accompany economic reform, Gorbachev embraced the second of the policies associated with his name, *glasnost,* or open information. This involved rolling back the chronic Soviet tendency to keep information secret, and encouraging more open discussion of priorities and problems. Political reform became a higher priority in 1986 after Gorbachev encountered resistance from entrenched interests in the Communist Party and the highest levels of state economic planning, and after the failure of initiatives like the antialcohol campaign.

Realizing that economic change depended on political will, Gorbachev directed his call for restructuring to politics, or "perestroika of the political system," as he called it. Between 1988 and 1990, reforms to the Soviet constitution broke the power of the

Communist Party and unleashed forces that would eventually destroy the Soviet Union itself. The Communist Party voted in 1988 to eliminate the authority of the secretariat, the key decision-making body of the party, over the party itself and the economy. The party also lost its control over the legislative bodies (soviets) of the individual republics. In essence, power in the Soviet Union shifted from the central bodies of the Communist Party to regional governments over which the party had limited influence. In a later step, power shifted more clearly from regional Communist parties to the soviets themselves.

In 1989 elections were held for a Congress of People's Deputies. Two-thirds of the seats were filled by election, either in single-member constituencies or from nationality areas, and one-third were filled by nominees of bodies such as the Communist Party, the Communist youth organization, and the official trade unions. Communist Party candidates were defeated in some key electorates, and in Moscow the former party chief Boris Yeltsin ran against the party and won 89 percent of the votes. Also elected was Andrei Sakharov, a notable physicist and dissident sent into internal exile in Gorky in 1980 but freed in 1986.

Even though the method of selection ensured that the great majority of the deputies were Communists, by 1989 that no longer guaranteed homogeneity of views. The low standing of the Communist Party was confirmed in local soviet elections in 1990. Gorbachev had encouraged party officials to stand, and many were defeated. Some lost even when they were the only candidate, because to be elected a candidate had to win at least 50 percent of the votes cast, and in some districts more than half the voters crossed out the name of the sole candidate.

Rapid political change did not enhance economic performance, however, and by 1990 the Soviet Union was in the grip of a dire and worsening economic crisis. The country's GNP had stagnated in the first four years of perestroika and there were increasing shortages, which by mid-1990 encompassed more than a thousand consumer items from food to clothing and household necessities. Barter became common, the black market flourished, and ration cards were introduced in Moscow. Social benefits were increased by 21 percent in 1990, but because there were no funds to pay for them, the budget deficit increased to over 10 percent of GNP, four or five times the rate in the early 1980s.

The reasons for the continuing economic problems were broadly the same as those that explained its stagnation in the late 1970s. In five years perestroika had made little impact because it had merely tinkered with aspects of the economy rather than undertaking a wholesale reform. There were, of course, major political and structural obstacles to such a thorough restructuring, but progress by 1990 was still disappointing. The state of the economy was not helped by the insistence of the Congress of Deputies on spending money that did not exist, or by the mounting foreign debt. At $80 billion in 1991, the debt stood at three times the level when Gorbachev came to power, and by 1990 the Soviet Union was unable to meet its debt payments on time.

Foreign and defense policies were tailored to reduce expenditure. A series of treaties to reduce arms was signed between 1987 and 1991, providing for the elimination of various categories of nuclear weapons and short- and medium-range missiles. In 1988 Gorbachev announced that the armed forces would be reduced by half a million in the following two years. Soviet intervention in Afghanistan, scaled down by Gorbachev, was terminated early in 1989. In ten years it had taken the lives of almost 14,000 Soviet soldiers and airmen and cost tens of billions of rubles. Later the Soviet Union would face claims by the Afghan government for billions of dollars in reparations payments.

The End of the Soviet Union, 1985–91

The political and economic reforms proceeded erratically and slowly on most fronts, but they had one major effect, namely the rise of nationalism within the Soviet Union's constituent republics and demands for greater autonomy and even independence. The opportunity was provided by the decentralization of power and reduction of Communist Party control that Gorbachev supported as a means of breaking resistance to economic reform. Not only did nationalists became prominent in the governments (soviets) of the republics, but regional Communist parties also came under nationalist influence.

The three Baltic republics set the pace. Integrated by force into the Soviet Union only fifty years earlier, in the first phase of World War II, they retained a keen sense of national identity and had populations that were above the Soviet average in terms of education, skills, and living standards. In 1986 and 1987 there were protests about environmental damage to the Baltic region, and Soviet plans to begin mining phosphate in northeastern Estonia were blocked. The success of the ecological protests in the Baltic states provided encouragement for broader political action, and by 1988 nationalist reformers had gained control of the communist parties there.

Popular Fronts were also formed by reformist groups of all kinds, including Communists. Although they were part of a growing nationalist movement, the Popular Fronts initially envisaged not independence, but greater autonomy within a Soviet Union reformed along the lines set out by Gorbachev. Even so, the ties between the Baltic republics and the rest of the Soviet Union were stretched thinner and thinner. By late 1988, Estonia demanded reductions in the immigration of ethnic Russians that was diluting the ethnic Estonian population, sought greater control over culture and the environment, and declared its right to reject Soviet laws that infringed on its autonomy. In January 1989, Estonian was made the official language, and later that year Lithuania and Latvia followed with their own declarations of linguistic autonomy.

Ethnic Russians in the Baltic states—they comprised about a third of the population of Latvia, a quarter in Estonia, and a tenth in Lithuania—viewed Baltic nationalism with mixed feelings, but the Soviet government was utterly hostile. The possibility that the Baltic states might declare their independence was a particularly serious threat to the Soviet Union because of the strategic and economic importance of the region. With the growing likelihood that Soviet troops would be withdrawn from Eastern Europe, the Baltic republics assumed even greater significance as buffer states within the Soviet Union.

In May 1989, the Lithuanian legislature voted for independence, and in August it declared null and void the annexation of the state by the Soviet Union in 1940. In December a special congress of the Lithuanian Communist Party voted 855 to 160 to separate from the Communist Party of the Soviet Union. The Soviet government tried to check the nationalist movement by exerting political pressure, but in March 1990 the Lithuanian legislature declared independence. It tried to soften the act by declaring that Lithuania wanted "to live in the European common home but in a separate apartment." However, the Soviet government's housing policy was no more generous in metaphorical than in literal terms; Moscow applied economic pressure in the form of an oil embargo that compelled the Lithuanians to suspend their declaration of independence.

The Soviet government tried various methods to halt the process of national disintegration. Gorbachev attempted to devise a lengthy process by which republics could secede from the Soviet Union, then offered special status for the Baltic states. All the while, however, the republics were beginning to act as if they were independent. The three Baltic states began to coordinate their efforts, and in May 1990 their presidents met and renewed the Baltic Entente of 1934. A council was set up to provide for regular consultations. In addition, they began to negotiate with the Russian republic, whose president Boris Yeltsin had declared that "were the Baltic states to finally opt for independence, Russia would be the first to sign treaties with them." In a referendum in February 1991, 91 percent of Lithuanian voters supported independence, and later the same year Estonians and Latvians voted the same way by margins of three to one. Given the magnitude and implications of their independence, the path was relatively smooth. Negotiations, such as took place, were tough, there were long periods of tension, and in 1991 there were sporadic attacks by Soviet military and paramilitary personnel. One such attack, on the television tower in Vilnius, left a number of Lithuanians dead. But there was no sustained use of force to keep the Baltic states within the Soviet Union, partly because the process of secession was taking place throughout the union.

In some other regions of the Soviet Union, nationalism not only challenged the union but also created strife among local ethnic groups. In 1988 armed conflict broke out over the Caucasus region of Nagorno-Karabakh, a part of predominantly Muslim Azerbaijan even though its population was predominantly Christian Armenian. As the possibility of autonomy was raised, the Armenians, wanting to ensure the integrity of their territory, mounted attacks on Nagorno-Karabakh. Fearing a rash of territorial conflicts, the Soviet government dispatched forces to prevent any change in the frontiers, and a three-way conflict raged for two years. In 1989 Azerbaijan declared independence, the first Soviet republic to do so, but the next year Soviet troops were sent in to the capital, Baku, killing scores of civilians in an attempt to restore Soviet control.

By 1990 the most important republics of the Soviet Union, Russia and Ukraine, had joined the secessionist movement. Boris Yeltsin, who resigned from the Communist Party in 1990, was elected president of Russia by a massive majority of votes in 1991. This gave him a strong position from which to challenge Gorbachev, who had never subjected himself to direct election. Yeltsin claimed that Russia had the right to look after its own internal affairs, and to conduct its own foreign policy. Russia, of course, was the core of the Soviet Union, and the assertion of its autonomy was the most serious of all threats to the Soviet federation.

Ukraine moved in a similar direction, unilaterally taking control of internal policy and foreign relations. Its government, a cooperative effort of Communists and non-Communists, also declared Ukraine a nuclear-free zone; the Chernobyl disaster had occurred on Ukrainian territory. Unlike some of the smaller states, like Estonia, Latvia, and Lithuania, where separatism had a decidedly anti-Russian tone, Ukraine's government tried to appeal to all its constituent populations.

By the end of 1990, nationalists throughout the Soviet Union had torn the fabric of the federation beyond repair. States had declared independence or declared their intention to do so, and they had unilaterally seized authority over domestic and foreign policies. They were beginning to negotiate trade and other arrangements among one another, relegating the Soviet government to the sidelines. There was not only a perceptible momentum to the nationalist movement, but a core self-fulfilling logic. Instead of reconstructing the Soviet economy and regenerating Soviet politics, the reform movement begun in 1985 had unleashed all manner of forces that introduced chaos in a system that before had been disabled by mere stagnation. By the end of 1990 the recognizably Soviet aspects of the economy and polity had begun to fade, and the new national entities started to replace them.

The creation of a series of independent states necessarily called into question the Soviet Union, which in principle was no more than a political entity, without a territorial base, that united the various republics. Gorbachev did not give up entirely on the notion of some kind of union, however, and in June 1991 he negotiated a new federation with nine of the republics (excluding the Baltic states, Armenia, Georgia, and Moldova) that provided much reduced power for the central government.

Changes of this magnitude could not take place without some reaction. Rumors circulated constantly about plans to reassert central authority, and the KGB (secret police) and armed forces were known to be alarmed at the security and defense implications of weakening central control. On August 19, 1991, the day before the agreement on the new federation was to be signed, there was an attempted military coup in Moscow while Gorbachev was on vacation in the Crimea. The coup was poorly organized and petered out in part because key units of the police and army refused to participate. But it raised the profile of the Russian president, Boris Yeltsin, who stood atop a tank outside the White House, the Russian parliament, and delivered a defiant speech. When Gorbachev returned to Moscow, his political stature was greatly diminished. Yeltsin banned the Communist Party in Russia, and Gorbachev resigned as its leader. The fundamental institutions of the Soviet Union—its bureaucracy, army, and the Communist Party—had been discredited.

The failed coup was an appropriately impotent final act by defenders of the Soviet Union. In September 1991 the Baltic states became independent; they did not secede because to have done so would have recognized the legitimacy of their annexation by Stalin in 1940. Gorbachev made further attempts to create a new confederation of what was left

A statue of Lenin is dismantled for removal from the Lenin museum in Moscow. The museum was closed to provide accommodation for the city's Duma, or representative assembly.

of the Soviet Union, and in early November seven republics, including Russia, agreed to work toward the formation of a Union of Sovereign States. But on December 1, 1991, Ukrainians voted overwhelmingly in a referendum for independence, and a week later Russia, Ukraine, and Belarus (Belorussia) ignored Gorbachev and became the founding members of a new entity, the Commonwealth of Independent States (CIS). They announced that the Soviet Union had ceased to exist, and to confirm the fact they were joined in the CIS by eight former Soviet republics. The Soviet Union now consisted of its central government, headed by Gorbachev, and little else. The bureaucracy had been appropriated by the new states, as had material assets. In the first half of the nineteenth century, before unification, Italy had been described as merely "a geographical expression"; after December 1, 1991, the Soviet Union might be described as no more than a political expression. Even that ended when, on December 25, Mikhail Gorbachev resigned as its president, bringing the curtain down on the state founded by revolution in 1917.

The Eastern European Regimes: Political and Economic Reform, 1985–90

As the final curtain went down on the Soviet Union, the iron curtain went up across Europe, for as the Soviet state unraveled economically and politically in the six years after Gorbachev came to power, its Eastern European partners experienced a similar process. Progress toward more democratic structures was uneven and often hesitant at first, however, not least because it was unclear how far the new Soviet regime had abandoned the "Brezhnev doctrine" that justified Soviet intervention in Eastern European states; in that respect, the renewal of the Warsaw Pact for another thirty years in 1985 did not seem to promise great change. Nor did the Communist governments of Eastern Europe feel any great hurry to surrender their power, even in Hungary and Czechoslovakia, where reforms had gone farthest by 1985. In 1988, however, Gorbachev renounced the Brezhnev doctrine and replaced it with what a Soviet spokesperson in 1989 called the "Sinatra doctrine" of "letting them do it their way." Within two years the Communist regimes of Eastern Europe had, with varying degrees of willingness, taken their bows. To pursue the theatrical metaphor a little further, some regimes stepped off the stage, others merely moved into the wings.

HUNGARY, CZECHOSLOVAKIA, AND POLAND

The twin rallying cries of perestroika and glasnost reverberated through Eastern Europe and tended to reinforce the trends already in place in each country. In Hungary, perestroika gave retrospective justification to the creation of a mixed economy during the 1970s and pointed the way to even more extensive reforms as the economy deteriorated. Emboldened by reforms throughout the region, economists in Hungary published information on the economy in 1987, including the fact that Hungary had Eastern Europe's highest per capita debt. The same year an opposition movement called Democratic Forum was formed, and in early 1988 groups hostile to government policies began to hold meetings. A special congress of the Communist Party was held in May 1988, but instead of the older conservatives imposing control over younger reformers (some of whom had been expelled for supporting opposition groups), the conservatives were defeated and János Kádár was dismissed from office.

In the following months, the monopoly of the Communist Party over Hungarian politics quickly faded, and toward the end of 1988, two former parties, the Smallholders and the Social Democrats, reestablished themselves. In February 1989, the government conceded what was already happening and agreed that Hungary could become a pluralist democracy. A Christian Democratic People's Party was formed in March 1989, and by September the Communists and most opposition parties agreed on a formula for a transition to democracy. In preparation, the Communists changed their name to the Hungarian Socialist Party.

A referendum in November 1989 forced an even more thoroughgoing reform than the former Communists and main opposition parties had envisaged, a sign that Hungarians wanted to move quickly away from the former regime. Even so, the level of political participation was low. Only half the electorate voted in the referendum, and when parliamentary elections under the new system took place in two rounds in March and April 1990, voter turnout was so low that some areas failed to achieve the minimum 40 percent needed for a valid election. In urban areas only a third of voters participated in the second round. When no single party won a majority, the Democratic Forum formed an uneasy coalition with the Smallholders and Christian Democrats, but the low electoral turnout raised questions about popular support for the new government.

Support was not likely to be increased by Hungary's economic performance and the growth of social problems. Although the economy received a boost from foreign investment—far more than other Eastern European states—the effects were not immediately evident. Industrial production declined in 1991, GDP fell about 7 percent, and unemployment continued to rise (it reached 7.3 percent in 1991). There were widespread complaints about the slowness of privatization, and the government was urged to accelerate it.

As in Hungary, political democratization in Czechoslovakia was relatively straightforward, although there was no echo of trends elsewhere until 1988 when the Communist government announced that it was in favor of the kinds of reform espoused by Gorbachev. But although change occurred slowly and carefully, there was more turbulence below. The twentieth anniversary of the 1968 invasion was marked by a large demonstration, and other expressions of implied and explicit protest took place on other significant occasions, such as the anniversary of the founding of Czechoslovakia in 1918. The government moved hardly at all, however, and even placed Václav Havel, a leader of the dissident Charter 77 group, in detention for several months.

After the fall of the Berlin Wall in late 1989, things moved quickly to produce what has been called Czechoslovakia's "Velvet Revolution." In November student demonstrators were attacked by security police, and soon afterward broad opposition groups were formed to press the government to concede political freedom. Havel and others (most of them Czechs) formed a group called Civic Forum, while in Slovakia a movement called Public Against Violence was founded. Following huge demonstrations and a well-supported general strike, the government resigned at the end of November 1989, and an attempt was made to form a Communist-led coalition. On December 7, this government, which attracted negligible support, gave way to a Government of National Understanding, in which most posts were held by members of Civic Forum, Public Against Violence, and other non-Communist parties. Havel was made president of Czechoslovakia and, in a symbolic act, Alexander Dubček, the leader of the reformist government suppressed by Soviet forces in 1968, was elected chairman of the federal assembly.

In elections held six months later, in June 1990, Civic Forum and Public Against Violence won a majority of seats in the federal and the Czech assemblies, but only a plurality in the Slovak assembly. The federal assembly, now with a popular mandate, reelected

Havel as president. In local elections later in 1990, however, the popularity of the two main groups declined, especially in Slovakia, where nationalists gained strength. Both Civic Forum and Public Against Violence were anti-Communist coalitions, and having achieved their aims they began to break up into smaller parties. Part of Public Against Violence formed a Movement for a Democratic Slovakia. At Slovak insistence, the national question became more pressing after 1991, and was finally resolved in 1993 by the formal division of Czechoslovakia into two sovereign entities. In the meantime, there were pressing disputes over economic policy, which proved more recalcitrant than political reform. Before the "Velvet Revolution," Czechoslovakia's economy had resembled others in Eastern Europe; the only sign of growth was in its foreign debt. During 1990 personal consumption fell by more than a quarter, and production declined by 23 percent. Most of the decline occurred because of the disappearance of Comecon markets in the wake of government changes and a reorientation toward Western Europe.

The situation in Slovakia was worse than in the Czech lands, which goes some way to explaining the rise of Slovakian nationalism. Inflation was 5 percent higher in Slovakia, and unemployment at 12 percent compared poorly with the Czech rate of 4 percent. A 1990 opinion survey showed that Slovakians were much more concerned than Czechs about unemployment, were less keen to accelerate economic reform, and had greater fears about a decline in their standard of living. Half the Slovakians surveyed said they would strike if there was a considerable increase in the cost of basic goods, compared with only a third of Czechs.

The Czechoslovak government elected in 1990 adopted economic policies that included ending price controls, and in 1991 it began a program of privatization. Land was returned to former owners, including those who had lost land during collectivization, and fifty large state companies were offered to foreign investors. Czechoslovak citizens could buy vouchers they could use to invest in privatized companies, and it was intended that private ownership should be broad-based. By the end of 1991, however, plans for economic renewal were faltering. Little foreign investment was forthcoming, and large domestic investment companies began to buy vouchers from individual citizens, leading to a concentration of ownership.

To the north, Poland in 1985 was as weak economically as it had been ten years earlier. The foreign debt rose from $26 billion in 1983 to $29 billion in 1985, then to $39 billion in 1987. Workers' incomes fluctuated, rising in 1986, falling in 1987, then soaring by 14 percent in 1988, but there was widespread poverty; the proportion of people experiencing officially defined levels of poverty in 1987 ranged from 30 percent of single-parent families, to 40 percent of families with more than two children, and 60 percent of people on pensions.

In the context of reform in the Soviet Union and other Eastern European states, the persistent failure of the Polish economy produced increasing disillusionment with the regime, even within the ruling party itself. In order to introduce controlled reform the party proposed limited political and economic liberalization, but only two-thirds of the voters cast a ballot, and of them only 60 percent supported the plan, giving it the overall support of only 40 percent of voters. Forced to make further concessions, the government again legalized the Solidarity union that had been banned in 1981, and in 1989 opened negotiations with it and other moderate opposition groups. The result was a compromise providing for elections in which 35 percent of seats in the Sejm and all the seats in the Senate could be contested by opposition candidates.

The elections, held in June 1989, were a resounding defeat for the government and a victory for Solidarity. Of the 161 seats in the Sejm that it was permitted to contest,

Solidarity won 160, and it also won 92 of the 100 seats in the Senate. Government candidates in contested elections were obliterated, and prominent cabinet members lost their seats. General Jaruzelski offered Solidarity a place in a coalition, but mindful of the experience of non-Communists in Communist-led coalitions after the war, Solidarity declined. Instead it proposed forming a government on its own terms, and after much debate within the Communist Party, Jaruzelski agreed on August 20, 1989. Tadeusz Mazowiecki became Poland's first Solidarity prime minister, and under his leadership the Communist regime was quickly dismantled. The various police forces were reorganized and removed from political control. Changes in the constitution included renaming Poland simply a republic, rather than a "people's republic," and removing the reference to the leading role of the Communist Party. In January 1990, the Communist Party, formally called the United Workers' Party, renamed itself, as Communist parties throughout Eastern Europe were doing, and emerged into Poland's new democratic framework as the Social Democratic Party.

The new government tried to revive the Polish economy by the fiscal equivalent of shock treatment. At the beginning of 1990, almost all price controls and state subsidies were removed and wage controls were imposed. There was an initial sharp rise in prices, and although it was followed by stabilization, the economy continued to founder. By the end of 1990 inflation was so high that food alone consumed 55 percent of household spending, unemployment had risen from half a million to over a million, and production had declined by 30 percent. Other reforms included some privatization and the legalization of foreign ownership of Polish companies to a maximum of 10 percent. All these measures made for even greater precariousness as many small farmers went bankrupt and homelessness increased. As living standards fell even further, there was growing disillusionment over the effects of removing state controls on the economy.

Politically, 1990 saw a division within Solidarity over the pace of economic and political reform, and the election of Solidarity's original leader, Lech Walesa, as president. The Solidarity prime minister, who had opposed him, resigned, and was replaced by Jan Bielecki, a Walesa supporter. This fissure, in what had been a mass organization, began the fractionalization of the anti-Communist opposition into a multitude of political parties. It was not until October 1991, however, that a democratic election was held to replace the Communist-dominated Sejm and Senate elected in June 1989. The elections were held against the background of promises that Poland's foreign creditors would forgive most of its debt. Again the electoral turnout was low (40 percent), and because of a proliferation of parties—seventy registered to participate—the deputies who were elected represented twenty-eight parties. Ten of the parties combined, however, accounted for 78 percent of the votes cast. The largest single party was a Solidarity splinter group, Democratic Union, led by the former prime minister Mazowiecki, which gained 62 of the 460 seats in the Sejm, only 2 seats more than a bloc representing former Communists. With some difficulty a minority coalition was put together, but in economic matters the parties pulled in different directions.

THE DISAPPEARANCE OF EAST GERMANY

The East German regime ruled by the communist Socialist Unity Party (SED) of Erich Honecker resisted the winds of change blowing from the east as long as possible; it went so far as to erect windbreaks in the form of censorship to keep reformist Soviet literature from its citizens. East Germans themselves took heart from the events elsewhere, however,

MAP 12.1   Eastern Europe in the post-Communist era.

and when police arrested scores of demonstrators in January 1988, they provoked a series of protests. That the government responded by releasing the detainees and letting some emigrate suggested that changes were quietly taking root throughout the system. Even so, the local elections of May 1989 produced a 98.55 percent vote in favor of the SED, which showed that the regime intended to maintain as long as possible the fiction that it had the support of its people. The futility of the government's attempts to limit change in a state surrounded by democratic or democratizing nations became clear when, in August 1989, Poland, Hungary, and Czechoslovakia opened their borders and allowed East Germans to seek asylum in the West German embassies in their capitals.

So many East Germans took advantage of the opportunity (an estimated 15,000 in the first three days alone) that the embassies had to close, but the following month Hungary allowed East Germans to travel through its territory to Austria and thence to West Germany. Thousands of East Germans vacationing in Hungary did not bother going home, and one way or another, on foot or in cars loaded with people and belongings, an estimated 225,000 of East Germany's 16 million people left the country in 1989. There was no attempt to prevent people from leaving East Germany itself, which suggests that the regime had by this time given up trying to restrain its citizens. Like the earlier wave of emigration that had been choked off by the Berlin Wall, this one consisted mainly of young skilled workers between the ages of twenty and forty, whose departure was bound to damage East Germany's already ailing economy. Growth rates had declined steadily from 1985 (5.2 percent) to 1989 (2.1 percent), and the foreign debt almost doubled to $21 billion in the same period.

When the Soviet president, Mikhail Gorbachev, visited East Berlin in early October 1989 for celebrations to mark the fortieth anniversary of East Germany, huge demonstrations in favor of reform took place throughout the country, and Honecker was soon compelled to resign on October 18. The new, but still Communist, administration tried to pacify East Germans by promising political and economic reforms, but it was too late to change things from above. Having brought down Honecker, East Germans were determined to destroy the regime from below. Opposition groups had sprung up, representing political and religious tendencies and the environmental movement. One of the most important, New Forum, collected 100,000 signatures on a petition favoring broad political reform. In early November the government resigned and on November 6 permitted unrestricted travel to West Germany through Czechoslovakia. Some 9,000 people a day used the route, effectively making the Berlin Wall redundant. Finally, on November 9 the Central Committee of the SED agreed to end all restrictions on travel to West Germany, and opened the wall. Some 2 million people passed through it the first weekend, and at one crossing point the line of East German cars waiting to make the passage extended thirty miles. If the government had destroyed the purpose of the wall, people set about destroying it physically. For days on end there were massed demonstrations and celebrations on both sides of the wall—and on top of it—and people took turns at chipping bits off it with sledgehammers and whatever other tools came to hand.

As citizens of both Germanies partied and mingled, and as long-divided families reunited, there were growing demands for national reunification. By now there was no stopping the popular movement. In January 1990, a crowd of 7,000 invaded the headquarters of the state security agency, ransacked offices, and took papers and files that revealed the extent to which East Germans had been under surveillance. Files had been kept on 6 million people, a third of the population. By early 1990, the East German regime had run out of options, and was in danger of running out of citizens as tens of thousands streamed across the border to take up residence in West Germany. The West German government was keen to establish a quick but orderly transition to a unified state

The end of the Berlin Wall: Berliners tear down the wall near the Brandenburg Gate in November 1989, after the East German government announced the end of most restrictions on travel from East Germany.

so as to stop the flood of immigration that was placing immense pressures on social services and employment. From the West German point of view, it was important to keep East Germans where they were, not only to reduce pressure on the West but also to rebuild the economic and political structures in eastern regions.

In March 1990, East Germans voted on reunification. Almost half (48 percent) voted for a coalition called Alliance for Germany, which was dominated by the West German Christian Democrats and embraced a policy of rapid national reunification. Twenty-one percent supported the Socialists, who called for a slower process of integration, while 16 percent voted for the former communist SED (renamed the Party of Democratic Socialism), which opposed reunification. The new government, headed by a Christian Democrat, began the move toward reunification by transferring control over East Germany's economic and monetary policies to West Germany on July 1, 1990. Two months later, on August 31, a unification treaty was signed, essentially extending West German law to East Germans.

The reunification of Germany and Berlin required the cooperation of the former wartime allies. In a treaty signed in September 1990, it was agreed that a reunified Germany should be fully sovereign and be free to enter political and military alliances, but that it should not possess nuclear or biological weapons and should reduce its armed forces to 370,000. The Soviet Union agreed to withdraw all its forces from the former East Germany and East Berlin by 1994. In return, the new Germany agreed to provide the ailing Soviet Union with economic assistance and to help resettle the Soviet forces that returned from duty in Germany. The West German economy, which was far stronger than that in East Germany, thus shouldered immense financial burdens, for unification promised to be an expensive process that would last for many years. The process began formally on October 2, 1990, when the two Germanies were reunited. October elections in the former East Germany's five states resulted in one Social Democratic and four Christian Democratic victories, and in December 1990, the first democratic all-German elections since the Weimar Republic returned a Christian Democratic government headed by Helmut Kohl.

BULGARIA AND ROMANIA

In the Balkan Communist states, the revolutions of 1989 took quite different courses. In Bulgaria reform was a relatively uncomplicated series of changes in policy designed to rescue the economy from the brink of catastrophe. By 1989 the Bulgarian economy was in steep decline, foreign debt was rising, and industry was failing because lack of investment had rendered much of it obsolete. To try to inject some investment, enterprises were permitted to issue stock or float bonds. A number of bad harvests and shortages led to a deterioration of living standards.

On the political front, support for glasnost and perestroika led to the formation of political movements, free trade unions, and environmental organizations, although some arrests made it clear that reform movements existed at the pleasure of the regime. As in so many other Eastern European states, it was external events that forced the pace of change. Once the Berlin Wall was opened, Todor Zhivkov, who had been in power since 1956, was replaced by Communist reformers who promptly denounced his regime and began to rehabilitate condemned dissidents. In January a meeting of the new government and opposition groups agreed on a program of reform, which included elections to a new parliament. The Communists changed their name to the Bulgarian Socialist Party (BSP), and in elections in June 1990 they won 47 percent of the vote and formed a minority government. The other main party, a coalition of non-Communist groups called the Union of Democratic Forces (UDF), declined to enter a coalition.

Only when the economy took a nosedive in 1990 did the ex-Communist BSP take radical action to deal with it. By October industrial production had fallen 11 percent, and rationing had been introduced on most basic goods. Opposition to the new economic measures spread to the governing party itself, and when its program was stymied at the end of 1991 it stood aside in favor of a cabinet that contained representatives of all the major parties. This government removed price restrictions, reached an agreement over wages with the trade unions, and secured assistance from the International Monetary Fund and the World Bank. The first elections under the 1991 constitution gave the UDF 36 percent of the vote and the BSF 33 percent. The UDF formed a government and announced plans to establish the institutions of a market economy.

It was in Romania that the Eastern European revolution of 1989 took its bloodiest form. Like several other regimes, Nicolae Ceausescu's appears to have hoped to ride out the wave of reforms. At the end of 1987 some demonstrations were successfully suppressed, and later an open letter by six members of the party, charging Ceausescu with violating the constitution, was met with the usual response: The dissidents were arrested. When the ruling Romanian Communist Party met at its Fourteenth Congress in November 1989, it reasserted its monopoly on power and declared that reform movements elsewhere were irrelevant to Romania.

What brought the apparently secure regime crashing down within a month was a relatively minor dispute concerning a Hungarian pastor in Timisoara, in Transylvania. László Tökés defied a government edict ordering him to leave his community, and when the local Romanian and ethnic Hungarian population rallied to his defense, conflict broke out with the Securitate, Romania's secret police. Demonstrations were soon politicized and became demands for free elections; a state of emergency was declared, and in confrontations from December 16 to 20 the Securitate killed at least seventy civilians, perhaps hundreds.

The day after the killings, Ceausescu addressed a rally in Bucharest, but outrage at the Timisoara killings emboldened the crowd to begin booing him. Clearly perplexed and confused, Ceausescu abandoned his speech, and by the next day a revolt was in full swing. The army sided with the rebels, and a National Salvation Front (NSF) was established. Ceausescu and his wife Elena attempted to escape by helicopter, but they were captured and then, on December 25, 1989, tried and shot. The whole process was filmed, then shown on television to convince Romanians that the dictator was dead. Meanwhile the NSF, led by Ion Iliescu, took over the instruments of government until elections could be held in the spring of 1990.

There were persistent fears that the NSF was nothing more than the Communist Party under a new name, and there were large-scale demonstrations against it. Nonetheless, in the May 1990 elections, the NSF won two-thirds of the seats in both houses of parliament and Iliescu was elected president with 85 percent of the vote. The credentials of the government were highlighted the next month when police were called in against anti-Communist demonstrators, killing at least five and seriously injuring more than 500.

The new regime did, however, start to reform the economy, which had stagnated under Ceausescu even though he had cleared the foreign debt by imposing draconian austerity on Romanians. In July 1990, the government canceled many subsidies and price controls; but because of public reaction, prices were not permitted to rise more than 25 percent. Even so, there were rolling strikes, culminating in September 1990, against the higher cost of living, and in October a six-month freeze was placed on the cost of essential goods and services. A privatization policy was inaugurated, allowing foreign ownership but encouraging investment by private citizens via several large investment funds. In December 1991 Romanians voted 80 percent in favor of a new constitution based on the French model, with two chambers and a strong presidency.

Politics and Society in the Soviet Successor States, 1991–95

The end of the Soviet Union in December 1991 solved one problem for the former republics of the union, but forced them to confront a full range of others. Creating a new political system was perhaps the most straightforward task, although it was not without its problems. There were basic questions of territory insofar as the frontiers of the republics had been determined during the Soviet period, often for political reasons rather than on cultural or ethnic grounds. Russia, by far the largest of the Soviet successor states, was involved in a number of territorial disputes because its vast expanse included, on its margins especially, a number of diverse ethnic and religious populations. Some 30 million (20 percent) of its 150 million inhabitants were not ethnic Russians. In 1992, twenty small republics signed a Federal Treaty with Russia to form the Russian Federation.

Not all entitled to join the federation chose to do so. Chechnia, a small region in the northern Caucasus that had been part of a larger entity, the Chechen-Ingush Autonomous Republic, adopted its own path to nationhood: Ingushetia joined the Russian Federation in 1992, but Chechnia declined to do so and declared independence. Chechens had long-standing grievances against the Soviet Union, and more recent ones against post-Soviet Russia. They had suffered famine in the early 1930s and mass deportation to Central Asia in 1944 as alleged Nazi collaborators. When they were allowed to return in the 1950s, after the death of Stalin, it was to a much diminished territory. In the post-Soviet period there were such serious conflicts between Chechens and the ethnic Russian minority that several thousand Russians emigrated. One divisive issue was religion: The Chechens are Muslims, and there was pressure for the creation of an Islamic state, even though the Chechen nationalist leader, former Soviet air force general Dzhokhar Dudayev, favored a secular constitution. The prospect of an independent Chechnia alarmed the Russian government, not only because it challenged the principle of maintaining the integrity of Russia, but also because Chechnia was economically important. The region was a vital staging point on the Russian oil pipeline system, and loss of control could have led to oil shortages for the industries in Siberia and Russia's distant eastern territories.

Relations between Russia and Chechnia deteriorated after 1991 when the Russian president, Boris Yeltsin, declared a state of emergency in the region. After Yeltsin was forced to lift the emergency decree, Russian troops were expelled by local Chechen forces. Thereafter, there were persistent conflicts among Chechen nationalists themselves. In late 1994 the conflict between Russia and Chechnia intensified when Russian forces, including tanks and aircraft, were deployed to reassert Russian control. By mid-1995 Chechnia's capital, Grozny, and most of its territory had come under the control of Russian forces, but Chechen guerrillas continued their war. A critical point was reached when the war was carried into Russia itself. After Chechen guerrillas took 2,000 hostages in a hospital in Budennovsk, seventy miles inside Russia, the Russian government agreed to negotiations, and by August 1995 a cease-fire was arranged. It left unresolved, however, the central issue of Chechnia's status vis-à-vis Russia.

Tensions also arose involving ethnic Russians who had settled as minorities outside Russia. In the Soviet period all had shared Soviet citizenship, and Russian migration to areas like the Baltic states had been encouraged as a form of Russification, to dilute the proportion of non-Russians and reduce the potential for nationalist separatism. In 1992 some 25 million Russians lived outside newly independent Russia, in the Baltic states, Ukraine, Moldova, and elsewhere.

Ethnic Russians were admitted to Ukrainian citizenship after independence because Ukrainian nationalism tended to be inclusive of the varied populations within its borders: Ukrainians, Russians, Belorussians, Poles, and others. There were attempts to reconcile anxious groups, such as Jews; at a ceremony to commemorate the 1941 German massacre of more than 30,000 Jews at Babi Yar, outside Kiev, Ukrainian President Leonid Kravchuk apologized for the part played by Ukrainians in the Holocaust. But despite the statement in the Ukrainian decree of sovereignty that "the national rights of all peoples" in the new state would be respected, tensions remained between ethnic Russians and Ukrainians. They were reinforced by disputes between Russia and Ukraine over ownership of the Crimea and control of what had been the Soviet Union's Black Sea naval fleet.

A less unequivocal welcome was given to Russians in the Baltic states. Only 52 percent of the inhabitants of Latvia were ethnic Latvians, and 62 percent of Estonia's population was ethnic Estonian. In contrast, the population of Lithuania was 80 percent Lithuanian. The citizenship criteria established in 1991 restricted Latvian and Estonian citizenship to citizens and residents at the time of the Soviet invasion in 1940 and their descendants, thus excluding most ethnic Russians, who had taken up residence later. Those who did not satisfy the residency requirement had to establish long-term domicile and satisfy other criteria. Latvia required sixteen years' residence in the country, the ability to speak Latvian, knowledge of the Latvian constitution, and willingness to swear allegiance to Latvia. Lithuania, which had a much smaller proportion of Russians and other non-Lithuanians in its population, began as early as 1989 to allow all permanent residents, regardless of ethnicity, to register as citizens; by 1991 virtually all had, including 98 percent of non-Lithuanians.

Overlaying the dismemberment of the Soviet Union was the recognition that even after they had achieved independence, the small former Soviet states would not be able to ignore the fact that they existed beside a massive and still-powerful Russia. There were occasional vivid reminders of Russia's historic imperialism. In the 1991 Russian presidential election, one candidate, Vladimir Zhirinovsky, articulated ideas of Russian expansionism, and although he was widely dismissed as a crank, he attracted some 6 million votes. Among his provocative ideas were that Russia should be restored to its 1917 borders, that Latvia, Estonia, and Lithuania should be made administrative districts, and that Finland should be annexed. In an interview with a Lithuanian newspaper, Zhirinovsky said he would bury radioactive waste along Russia's border with the Baltic states so that their populations would die of radiation sickness. However alarming it was, such chauvinism was not Russian policy, and the Baltic and other states gained full sovereignty. In 1994 the last troops of the former Soviet Union were withdrawn from the Baltic states.

One of the Soviet successor states proved much less troublesome to Russia. Belarus, formerly Belorussia, had had such a long association with Russia that it had difficulty establishing its political, economic, and cultural viability as an independent state. In 1994 the presidential elections were won by Alexander Lukashenko on a platform of reintegration with Russia, and within a year Russian was restored as the national language and the Belarus flag modified to a form closer to that of the Soviet period. An agreement was signed to allow Russia to set up military bases in Belarus.

Beyond the important issues of territory and ethnicity were equally fundamental questions of constitutional, economic, and social reconstruction in the former Soviet Union. It was not clear precisely how the citizens of the new states wanted them to develop, although it appeared that they valued certain aspects of the Soviet system and did not want it transformed into a capitalist market system that gave the state a minimal role. People perceived the state, despite all the deficiencies of its Soviet form, as protecting the most vulnerable groups in society. A December 1991 opinion survey in Russia showed that 79 percent of people believed that the future system should guarantee work for all citizens, and 77 percent thought that free health care should be guaranteed. Another survey, in June 1992, found that 68 percent of Russians believed that the government should provide for the "basic material needs" of its citizens.

As for a free market economy, it was considered essential by only 44 percent of Russians who participated in the June 1992 survey. Even among younger Russians, those aged eighteen to twenty-nine who were most in favor of a market economy, only a bare majority of 55 percent considered it essential, but that was much higher than the 37 percent of people in their fifties and the 27 percent of those in their sixties. It is understandable that older people, being economically more vulnerable, might opt for a higher degree of social intervention by the state, but it seemed that older Russians were on the whole less enthusiastic about the attributes of Western-style democracy across the board. Russians in their sixties, those born before 1930 and who grew up under Stalin, were least inclined to think that it was essential in a democracy to have freedom to criticize the government, competing political parties, and protection of minority rights.

Concern about material well-being over abstract political rights was only to be expected in many of the successor states, where economic problems in the early 1990s were overwhelming. They inherited their constituent parts of a Soviet economy that had reached its worst point since the Second World War. Productivity had collapsed, and as governments set about the tasks of reconstruction, which included privatization, unemployment rose. When the Soviet Union disappeared in December 1991, there were some 70,000 registered unemployed; by mid-1992 there were 200,000, and by mid-1993 there were 730,000, plus another estimated 1.5 million men and women working reduced hours or laid off temporarily. In 1993 the Labor Ministry estimated that the real number of unemployed was between 4 and 5 million.

The immediate impact of the collapse of the Soviet Union was a spread of poverty and increased insecurity about employment, income, health, and safety. Despite the massive failures of the Soviet Union to provide a steady increase in standards of living, actual poverty was largely prevented by social security and subsidies on housing and basic necessities. With the advent of a market-oriented economy, many layers of social protection disappeared, leaving large sections of the population exposed and vulnerable. Basic health and welfare services declined or disappeared entirely.

One area of particular concern was the growth of crime after the collapse of the Soviet state. Rates of reported crimes were low before the late 1980s, partly because the chances of detection and punishment of offenders were so high: The police had extensive powers of search and detention, and the criminal justice system was heavily weighted toward the prosecution. Centralized control began to slip in the late 1980s, and the declining effectiveness of the police forces coincided with economic trends that are often associated with criminality: widespread economic hardship, fewer restrictions on personal mobility, and the growth of an unregulated economy. As crime rates rose, shortages of resources prevented the state from responding.

The increase in crime was particularly alarming in a society accustomed to low levels of criminality, and there was growing concern about crime waves in large cities. Street crime increased, especially attacks on foreigners for cash and other personal belongings. Paradoxically, the surveillance of foreigners by the secret police (KGB) in the Soviet period had tended to protect them from crime, but as the KGB's functions were restricted, foreigners came within the jurisdiction of the ordinary police and, like Soviet citizens, they were increasingly subjected to criminal acts. Overall, there was an increase not just in crime rates but in the seriousness of offenses. The breakdown of police and military services made firearms more widely, if illegally, available, and they were increasingly employed in crimes. Murders, aggravated assaults, and rapes increased. In some areas, order broke down to the extent that citizens formed armed vigilante groups to replace regular law enforcement officers. In the main cities, new private security agencies, many of whose employees were former KGB officers, flourished.

Crime rates were spurred not only by economic and political conditions that lowered the chances of detection, but also by reforms of the legal system that reduced the likelihood of conviction and reduced the severity of punishments. Between 1990 and 1991 the number of people in Russia sentenced to death fell by a third, even though the number of reported crimes punishable by death rose by 20 percent. The rehabilitation of offenders and released convicts also suffered: Whereas in the past the Soviet state had guaranteed employment, from the late 1980s the system failed and unemployment grew.

Large-scale economic crime threatened to become endemic in Russia in the post-Soviet era. The chaotic state of the economy fostered corruption and a black market in all manner of goods, including material that could be used in the manufacture of nuclear weapons. Aid from abroad was often channeled into private hands or into luxuries for officials of the new states, many of whom seemed determined to emulate the elevated and much-criticized lifestyles of their Soviet predecessors.

Among the social antagonisms bequeathed by the Soviet era was a generation gap far more significant than any experienced in Western societies. Reference has already been made to the different attitudes of young and old toward the role of the state in the new societies. Preference for an active and protective state reflected the vulnerability of older people (fifty years and older) and a persistent belief in the value of social ownership of essential services. Young people, on the other hand, were more likely to see the market economy in terms of opportunities for wealth and material and social advancement. Others were simply disillusioned with the Soviet system, particularly after revelations of corruption, distortions, and fabrications started to pour out in the late 1980s.

Surveys in 1992 showed clearly that young people had given up on socialism in the Soviet Union. Only a fifth of young people thought that socialism was sound and had a future, compared with 48 percent of those over sixty. One of the issues that alerted young people in particular to the failings of the Soviet system was the extent of environmental damage that had been permitted to occur. The explosion at the Chernobyl nuclear plant in 1986 drew attention to the problem, and environmental groups attracted the support of thousands of young people. Pollution of all kinds was one of the legacies of the Soviet Union to its successors. In Russia virtually all the major rivers, including the Volga, Don, Oka, and Kama, as well as the Kuban and Ob basins, suffered from massive viral and bacterial pollution. An estimated 85 percent of city dwellers breathed air that exceeded levels of pollution considered dangerous to health. Water- and airborne radioactive contamination was so severe in parts of Russia that hundreds of thousands of square miles were unfit for habitation (and would be for generations), and populations in some areas had the high rates of cancer and other illnesses often identified in such circumstances.

Meanwhile, the health services available in the successor states deteriorated from the already deplorable levels of the mid-1980s. The death rate, one of the highest in the world, rose even higher. In 1990 the Russian death rate was 11.2 per thousand, but by 1993 it had leapt to 14.5. In the same period, the infant mortality rate doubled, from 14 to 30 deaths per thousand births. Life expectancy fell accordingly: A boy born in the Soviet Union in 1990 could expect to live 63.8 years, but one born in Russia in 1993 had a life expectancy of only 58.9 years. The deterioration in the life expectancy of girls was less dramatic but still substantial, from 74.3 years in 1990 to 71.9 years in 1993. It is hardly surprising that in these conditions the Russian birth rate fell, and in the mid-1990s there was a steady increase in the number of districts in which the death rate was higher than the birth rate.

Politics and Society in Eastern Europe, 1991–95

Following the dislodging of Communist governments throughout Eastern Europe by 1989, the new regimes had not only to reorganize administrative structures but also to deal with the varied economic and social problems that they inherited. The period of transition was not always smooth and it produced some unexpected results by the mid-1990s, notably the return to power of former Communists—by election this time—in Bulgaria, Poland, and Hungary. Elsewhere there were signs of a right-wing nationalist revival in

Romania, and Czechoslovakia had split into two separate nations, one of which—Slovakia—was led by a potentially destabilizing authoritarian nationalist.

The nationalist issue in Czechoslovakia had become more and more pressing from 1991. Slovakians were aggrieved that their part of the nation fared worse in all economic and social respects, and there were fundamental differences in their expectations of post-Communist economy and society; Slovakians were notably more inclined than Czechs toward a social democratic system. The president, Václav Havel, attempting to find a solution that would preserve the union between the Czechs and Slovakians, argued strongly for a referendum, but the federal assembly was unable to agree on the terms. In the 1992 elections Czech and Slovakian nationalist parties did well, and their leaders agreed that the union should be dissolved. The Slovak national council declared independence in July 1992, and immediately afterward Havel submitted his resignation as president of Czechoslovakia. Both nations worked cooperatively on their divorce, which took place formally on January 1, 1993, when the Czech Republic and the Slovakian Republic came into being.

In the first Slovak election in October 1994, the nationalist Vladimir Meciar won a third of the votes and was able to form a government with the assistance of two small extremist parties of nationalists and communists. Meciar's support was strongest in Central Slovakia, where unemployment was particularly high and seemed likely to rise even higher because former state industries in the region were on the verge of bankruptcy.

In Poland it was the economic crisis that dominated the post-Communist agenda, but progress in attacking it was hindered by persistent political instability. After the 1991 election it took weeks to create a minority coalition government of five parties, but the government's budget was rejected by the Sejm in March 1992. There were three different prime ministers and administrations during 1992, a turnover which tended to increase the authority of the president, Lech Walesa.

Although GNP stopped falling during 1992, unemployment kept rising and real wages declined by 6 percent. A wave of strikes swept through Poland in the summer of 1992. In May 1993 the Sejm carried out a Solidarity-sponsored vote of no confidence in the government. In a fresh election the victors were two parties formed by former Communists, the Union of the Democratic Left and the Polish Peasant Party. Together they won 35 percent of the votes and 70 percent of the seats. The return to government of the reformed Communists so soon after the removal of the Communist regime did not, however, indicate a wish to return to the old days. Eastern Europe in the 1990s was very different from Eastern Europe in the 1980s, and former Communists could be supported in a quite different context. For one thing, they were no longer under the control of a foreign power, and for another, they operated within a broadly democratic system.

Opinion surveys in 1992 showed that Poles considered the economic features of democracy far more important than its political characteristics. For example, 41 percent of people thought that economic prosperity was the most important aspect of a democracy, 18 percent chose government guarantees of the people's basic needs, and 11 percent opted for government guarantees of economic equality among citizens. Against the 70 percent who stressed economic issues, only 21 percent opted for political liberties such as a fair judicial system, freedom to criticize the government, and multiparty elections. Poles were not alone among Eastern Europeans in favoring a social democratic system of government with an interventionist state, rather than a market-oriented system. Ironically the Solidarity union, which had opposed the Communist regime in the 1980s, argued by the mid-1990s against rapid market reform and in favor of more state intervention in the economy. In 1995, official unemployment in Poland exceeded 15 percent.

A contrast was Hungary, where the economy moved more steadily toward an open market system. It was helped by levels of foreign investment higher than those directed toward the Czech Republic and Poland. Western European, United States, and Japanese automobile manufacturers began to set up plants in Hungary, which benefited from location, resources, and cheap labor. Even so, there were continuing problems, including rising unemployment and an overall decline in industrial production. There were also persistent political problems, including the indifference of Hungarians to the political process. Political parties, which had seen their numbers grow rapidly, saw them ebb equally quickly, and voter turnout in some by-elections was so low that they were declared invalid.

In 1994 the reformed Hungarian Communists won 54 percent of the seats in parliament, although they attracted only a third of the popular vote. Choosing not to form a government on their own, they formed a coalition with Liberals. In part their victory was due to the failure of the previous conservative government to distance itself from anti-Semitic extremists and to discontent over its economic policies. Promises of economic assistance from the West had failed to materialize, and Hungary's GNP declined steadily between 1991 and 1993. Even though the rate of decline was smaller than in any other Eastern European state except Poland, Hungarians were not impressed, particularly when they also faced inflation at 25 percent and unemployment at 12 percent. Living standards fell in the early 1990s, and pensions declined below the poverty line.

Bulgaria entered the 1990s under the formerly communist Bulgarian Socialist Party (BSP), but in 1991 an anti-communist coalition was elected. The coalition collapsed when the Turkish minority withdrew its support, and until the end of 1994 Bulgaria was governed by an administration nominated by the president. None of the governments made much progress with the economy, and by late 1994 only 30 medium- and large-scale state enterprises had been privatized. A severe recession appeared to be ending, but standards of living were abysmal: In Sofia there were water shortages and interruptions in heating during the winter. In elections in December 1994, the BSP was reelected, this time with a small parliamentary majority that enabled it to govern on its own.

In some of the Eastern European states, nationalism played an important role in post-Communist politics. Nationalism had never disappeared from Eastern Europe during the Communist period, although it was more often expressed at that time in Marxist ideological terms. With the fall of Communist regimes, however, nationalism could once again be expressed clearly, and the post-Communist period saw the reemergence of ethnic tensions in Eastern Europe as in the Soviet successor states. In the Slovakian Republic, for example (itself the result of the split from the Czechs), there were tensions between the majority Slovakians and the 600,000 Hungarians who represented 10 percent of the population. Although candidates of Hungarian parties were elected to the Slovakian legislature in 1992 and 1994, the prime minister, Vladimir Meciar, accused them of wanting to dismember Slovakia and join their territory to Hungary. The 1.6 million Hungarians in Romania also became embroiled in politics when a 1995 education law gave primacy to the Romanian language. According to Hungarian leaders, the law threatened the viability of Hungarian language and culture in Romania.

German minorities existed in several states, particularly in Poland, where there were an estimated 300,000 to 350,000 in 1993. Although Germans had maintained a low profile for most of the postwar period, the changed political climate and the resurgence of united Germany as a major participant in Eastern European reconstruction led to their taking a more prominent role in public life. Members of a German party were elected to the Polish Sejm in 1991. Their increasing prominence led to some attacks on Germans in

Poland and elsewhere, some provoked specifically by incidents in Germany in which neo-Nazis attacked and killed immigrants.

There were also sporadic signs of traditional popular hostility to Sinti and Roma (Gypsies) in parts of Eastern Europe. In the Czech Republic more than half the 200,000 Sinti and Roma were denied citizenship under a law specifiying that people under the age of forty whose parents were Slovakians in the former Czechoslovakia were to be considered Slovakians and not Czechs. Most Sinti and Roma living in the Czech Republic were members of families that had lived in Slovakia until relocated in the Czech Sudetenland after the war to replace the ethnic Germans who had left voluntarily or had been driven out. (The prewar Sinti and Roma population of the Czech lands was eliminated during the Holocaust.) Thus almost all Sinti and Roma in the Czech Republic in the 1990s had Slovakian parentage, even though two-thirds of them had been born in the Czech region.

Under Czech law, Slovakians could apply for Czech citizenship if they had had a clean criminal record for five years. Many young Sinti and Roma failed to meet this criterion, not least because they suffered an unemployment rate of more than 50 percent, and most lived in extreme poverty. Because being employed also counted toward obtaining a residence permit, there was a likelihood that tens of thousands of Sinti and Roma would be subjected to compulsory relocation. The plight of the population in the Czech Republic was condemned at an international conference on Sinti and Roma rights held in Poland in 1994. One of the sponsors of the conference, the Council of Europe, described Europe's 8 million Sinti and Roma as "one of the most exposed and vulnerable groups" on the continent.

Post-Communist Eastern Europe also provided the opportunity for a revival of the extreme right. For example, the vice president of the anti-Communist Hungarian Democratic Forum in 1992 evoked a conspiracy of "Jews and Communists," a notion that echoed the rhetoric of the prewar nationalist right. In 1995 Slovakia's minister of education opened an exhibition devoted to Jozef Tiso, a priest who led a Nazi puppet state in Slovakia between 1939 and 1945.

In Romania in 1994 there was a movement toward the rehabilitation of Marshal Ion Antonescu, the dictator who had allied with Hitler and participated enthusiastically in the mass murder of 400,000 of Romania's Jews in the early 1940s. After the death of Ceausescu in 1989, dozens of books appeared praising Antonescu as a patriot and military genius, and in 1991 the Romanian parliament observed a minute's silence to mark the forty-fifth anniversary of his execution. The revival of the cult of Antonescu had several dimensions—including an anti-Russian element because he committed thirty Romanian divisions to the Nazi attack on the Soviet Union—but it also resonated with anti-Semitism, a sentiment that began to be expressed in some Romanian political circles.

The first half decade of post-Communist Eastern Europe disappointed widespread expectations in the West that the collapse of Communist regimes heralded the creation of democratic political systems and market economies in the region. Celebrations of what was portrayed as the return of democracy in 1989 ignored the fact that, with the exception of Czechoslovakia, all Eastern Europe's states had soon sloughed off the democratic constitutions imposed on them by the peace treaties after the First World War. An extraneous political system could no more easily be implanted in the social and economic conditions that prevailed in Eastern Europe in the early 1990s than had been possible in the 1920s. Attempts to impose a Western democratic system, of which the region had no tradition, seemed as likely to fail as the Soviet-imposed system.

The Dissolution of Yugoslavia, 1985–95

Separatist nationalism, which had led to the division of Slovakia and the Czech Republic, took its most destructive form in Yugoslavia. From the end of World War II, Yugoslavia had been a federation of several ethnic groups and regions, with the added complication that individual regions, particularly Bosnia and Croatia, had mixed ethnic and religious populations. Josip Tito, Yugoslavia's president until his death in 1980, had generally succeeded in keeping regional rivalries under control by superimposing national institutions and a uniform socialist ideology. During the 1980s, the presidency rotated among representatives of each region. The arrangement gave each an equal share in leading the government, but also gave each president an opportunity to favor his or her region. The revolving presidency, which arguably had the best chance of holding the federation together, also had the potential to weaken it. Economic problems added to discontent. The country was burdened with a massive foreign debt, productivity began to decline, and inflation soared, reaching 88 percent in 1986, 157 percent in 1988, and almost 300 percent in 1989.

During the 1980s the main thrust of political discussion shifted from communism to nationalism, and new nationalist leaders rose to prominence, notably Slobodan Milosevic, who became head of the Serbian Communists in 1987. Two years later, the first steps toward the dissolution of Yugoslavia were taken. Changes made by nationalists to the Serbian constitution deprived the small region of Kosovo of its status as an autonomous province, and resistance was suppressed by Serbian forces. The same year, after clashes between Serbs and Croats living in Croatia, the Serb population there declared its region independent of Croatia.

Although Yugoslavia had stayed out of the Soviet sphere and pursued its own policies, it was influenced by the overthrow or collapse of Communist regimes elsewhere in Eastern Europe. In 1988 the government began a program of economic reforms that included the gradual privatization of state enterprises. In 1990 political parties other than the ruling League of Communists were legalized, and the reference to the "leading role" of the League was removed from the constitution. Within months, the League of Communists, a federal entity, had broken up into regional social democratic parties, and some 200 other parties representing social, ideological, or ethnic interests, were formed.

In the course of 1990, Slovenia and Croatia elected governments dominated by nationalists who were committed to autonomy or outright independence. In Serbia, which had not legalized opposition parties, a referendum in June supported (with a vote of 96 percent in favor) changes to the constitution that removed the word *socialist* from the name of the republic, and gave Serbia control over some small provinces that had previously had autonomous status. In July 1990, Slovenia announced its intention to declare independence. Later in 1990, nationalists won elections in Macedonia, former Communists won in Serbia and in Montenegro, while in Bosnia and Herzegovina ethnic and nationalist parties were returned generally in proportion to their representation within the population.

From late 1990, Yugoslavia dissolved into a series of national and ethnic conflicts as its constituent republics sought independence and ethnic groups within each attempted to improve their position. The Croatian government formed its own army, the Croatian National Guard Corps, following the intervention of the Yugoslav army in Croatia. Slovenian and Croatian declarations of intent to become sovereign provoked an armed response from Serbia. The Serbs opposed the breakup of Yugoslavia largely because they had dominated the federation that represented the aspiration, going back to the nineteenth century, of a greater Serbia. They were also able to justify their military action as necessary to defend the interests of Serbian minorities in other republics, notably the 600,000 Serbs living in eastern Croatia. In the bitter war that followed, thousands of Croatian civilians were killed as the Serb army shelled villages and towns, including the historic resort city of Dubrovnik, which was virtually destroyed. By the end of 1991, Serbia had control of about a third of Croatia, and an armistice was brokered by the United Nations. Slovenia and Croatia were given international recognition as sovereign states in January 1992, an act that marked the de facto end of Yugoslavia.

Encouraged by these successes, despite their costs, Bosnia held a referendum on independence in March 1992. Bosnia's Muslim and Croat populations, respectively 45 and 20 percent of the population, voted overwhelmingly in favor of independence, but the Bosnian Serbs, who formed a third of the population, boycotted the poll. When the result of the referendum was clear, violence broke out between Bosnian troops and police and Bosnian Serb irregulars, supported and equipped by Serbia. With the assistance of the Yugoslav People's Army, by now an arm of the Serbian government alone, the Bosnian Serbs besieged the Bosnian capital, Sarajevo, and soon established control of much of eastern and northwestern Bosnia. By April 1992 there were widespread reports of what became known as "ethnic cleansing," the forced removal or killing of Bosnian Muslims in Bosnian Serb–held territory. Thousands of Bosnian women and girls were raped by the Bosnian Serb soldiers.

In May 1992 units of the Yugoslav People's Army were forced to withdraw from Bosnia, but they left behind equipment and troops for the Bosnian Serb forces, now named the Army of the Serbian Republic of Bosnia and Herzegovina. The aim of the Bosnian Serbs was to prevent the creation of an independent Bosnia in which Serbs would be a vulnerable minority. In Yugoslavia the Bosnian Serbs, although not living in the Serbian part of the federation, had been members of the dominant ethnic group.

The conflict that began in Bosnia in the spring of 1992 was the first protracted war in Europe since the Second World War, and its viciousness attracted international attention and intervention. As fighting developed, European states sought to prevent it from worsening. An international embargo was placed on the shipment of arms to Bosnia, and in response to a Bosnian request the United Nations deployed peacekeeping forces to protect Muslim populations in enclaves surrounded by Bosnian Serb–controlled territory. The notable failure of UN forces to protect Bosnian Muslims led to tensions within the European Union, as France urged a stronger policy against the Bosnian Serbs while other members feared being drawn into an all-out war. NATO air forces were deployed to protect UN ground troops, and there was conflict between the United States and its European partners on how the aircraft ought to be used.

Up to the middle of 1995, the Bosnian Serbs had the upper hand in the conflict and were able to control two-thirds of Bosnia. The UN forces, drawn from countries such as Canada, France, Ukraine, and the Netherlands, were unable to protect Bosnian Muslims in their enclaves, and Sarajevo remained under siege for more than three years, longer than any other European city in modern history. Three years after it began, the war had resulted in widespread devastation and death. Evidence of atrocities led to charges of war crimes being brought against members of the Bosnian Serb forces.

Despite the traumatic sequence of secession and conflict, Serbia insisted on the continued existence of "Yugoslavia," which it confirmed in 1992. This was partly to ensure Serbia's control over Yugoslavia's assets at home and abroad, and its membership in the United Nations and the International Monetary Fund.

Yet the wars that broke out in 1991 wrecked the economies, already in a poor state, and the social fabric of the former federation. Outside Serbia there was serious damage to industry and agriculture, and in many parts of Bosnia the survivors were driven from their villages. The tourist industry, one of the most successful parts of the economy that had drawn millions of foreigners, especially Germans, to Yugoslavia's Adriatic beaches, all but dried up.

The various new states that emerged from the collapse of Yugoslavia sought to increase their ethnic populations so as to strengthen their positions. The resurgence of ethnic nationalism increased consciousness of falling fertility rates. The Serbian government was particularly concerned because the birth rate of its Albanian minority in Kosovo, 28 per thousand population, was much higher than the Serbs' 11.7 per thousand. Serbia introduced legislation to give additional financial help and maternity leave to women who bore three children and to discourage women from working. In Croatia, with its influential Catholic Church, and Slovenia, the governing parties expressed support for making abortion more difficult to obtain. Macedonia adopted a different approach, attempting to drive down the birth rate of its Albanian population by restricting medical care and education to the first four children, and giving parents of small families priority in housing and employment.

Such long-term policies suggested that the territory formerly occupied by Yugoslavia would remain volatile for some time, even when military conflict ended. The turmoil in the Balkans and the expansionist Serb nationalism at the end of the century recalled the earlier phase of these phenomena at the beginning of the century. There was, however, a major difference: None of the major European states now had vital interests in the area. Even so, there were ironies, given the key role of the Balkans in the process that led to the First World War. Russia, which had supported Serbia against Austria-Hungary's policies in Bosnia precisely eighty years earlier, warned the Serbs in 1994 that if they did not cease their intervention in Bosnia, the local conflict could lead to a wider war.

Gender and Sexuality in the Post-Communist States

Among the issues raised by the decline and collapse of Communist regimes in the Soviet Union and Eastern Europe was gender. Almost all the Communist-era states promoted an ideology of the equality of women and men, and it was true that, in principle, women had access to education, employment, and advancement on largely the same basis as men. Equality was seldom achieved in practice, but as the spirit of reform began to spread through the region, the very principle of gender equality was questioned. With the fall of the Communist regimes, the principle was in many instances rejected on the ground that if women's equality was a policy of the Communist period, it should be done away with. Faced with these policies and the deterioration of living standards, which affected women especially, women in Eastern Europe and the former Soviet Union experienced the late-Communist and early post-Communist periods quite differently from men.

A fundamental problem everywhere as economies stagnated was unemployment. High proportions of working-age women were employed in all the socialist societies; typically, about 90 percent of those not in full-time education were in the labor force. Women worked in occupations that had lower pay and status than men, however, and they were concentrated in a small number of sectors, notably textile manufacture, secretarial work, education, health services, and culture. At the same time, women were expected to carry full responsibility for family and child care. To this end, the socialist states had provided extensive maternity leave and other benefits, although women were never systematically relieved of the double burden of work outside and inside the home. In Romania a third burden was added, the positive legal requirement to bear children for the state.

The decline of the socialist economies from the early 1980s had a severe impact on women's employment; they were thrown out of work in greater numbers than men, and formed a higher percentage of the unemployed than men. The reasons included the reduction of state bureaucracies and their clerical staffs, the decline of health services, and the depression in consumer industries that employed large numbers of women. The reduction of alcohol production in the Soviet Union cost tens of thousands of women's jobs. The privatization of state economies intensified the trends. As labor forces were trimmed in the interest of efficiency, women experienced higher rates of dismissal than men. Part of the reason was the entrenchment of attitudes favoring the relegation of women to the realm of home and family. Having lost their jobs, women more often than men experienced difficulty finding work because they were poorly trained for the new economies that began to develop.

It was estimated that of those who lost their jobs when *perestroika* was introduced in the Soviet Union from the mid-1980s, some 80 percent were women. In Bulgaria, 62 percent of registered unemployed in 1991 were women, and that was before extensive privatization, which experience elsewhere indicated would produce much higher rates of female joblessness. The same was true of Hungary, where women outnumbered men among registered unemployed. In Poland women formed about half the unemployed in 1991, but because three times as many jobs were available for men as for women, the proportion of women among the unemployed rose. A particular category of unemployed were women on maternity leave—they numbered 200,000 at any one time in Hungary alone—who found that in the new economic climate there was no guarantee of employment when they were ready and willing to return to work.

Women had worked in the labor force because of financial necessity: their own, their family's, or their children's. Unemployment drove many into poverty, a process accelerated because women received lower unemployment benefits. In Hungary in 1991, 79 percent of unemployed women received less than the official minimum wage, compared with 55 percent of men. Women, allotted primary responsibility for looking after children, found child-care facilities restricted. In Poland about half the kindergartens and infant nurseries had closed by mid-1991. The level of social services, whether expressed in facilities or money, seemed likely to drop throughout Eastern Europe as states steadily withdrew their subsidies.

The overall results were the spread of poverty and the feminization of poverty in particular; as in Western Europe, although in different circumstances, women and their dependent children made up a growing majority of the poor. In Poland, 91 percent of the more than half million single-parent households were headed by women, and of them 23 percent were unemployed and survived by living on social welfare or with assistance from other family members; some 66 percent were living below the poverty line. In Hungary one household in seven was headed by a single parent, a woman in 80 percent of cases.

The growth of poverty among women produced both expected and unexpected results. One was an increase in prostitution, work that was often done with the knowledge and agreement of husbands. The number of prostitutes might well have begun to exceed demand, and there were cases of Bulgarian and Romanian women working in other countries at prices that undercut local prostitutes. Some marginal employment opportunities also developed in the pornography industry that boomed throughout Eastern Europe after the relaxation of strict Communist-era laws against moral "decadence."

The spread of poverty also manifested itself in the growth of an international adoption market. Romania became particularly notorious after the Western news media publicized orphanages housing tens of thousands of children, the result of Ceausescu's campaign to raise the country's birth rate. Many of the children were suffering from disabilities, and they lived in appalling conditions. Not only were many of these children adopted by foreigners, but private adoption agencies also negotiated with poor women for their children, in effect facilitating the purchase of children by foreigners. By 1993 the Romanian government had begun to stop the process, but adoptions by foreigners were taking place elsewhere in Eastern Europe, including Poland, and in Russia.

In institutional terms, women found themselves marginalized in post-Communist politics. Several of the Communist states had set quotas for women's representation in parliamentary bodies, and the disappearance of Communist regimes led to a reduction in the proportion of female legislators. In Hungary the percentage of women in parliament dropped from 21 to 4 by 1993, in Romania from 34 to 4, in Czechoslovakia (before partition) from 30 to 9, and in Poland 23 to 9. Women made up 10 percent of the assembly in the Czech Republic in 1993, and in the 1991 Bulgarian election 8.5 percent of those elected were women.

As a result, women were less represented in the assemblies that made policies with respect to issues like abortion, which also entered the post-Communist agenda. Under the Communist regimes, with the notable exception of Romania, abortion was generally available. In Romania it was fully legalized after the fall of the Ceausescu regime, and it was liberalized in Bulgaria, but in Poland, the Czech Republic, Slovakia, and Hungary, restrictions were either introduced or seriously discussed. A number of post-Communist governments revived the link between nationalism and pronatalism that was characteristic earlier in the twentieth century. Not only was there a recognition that the prevailing birth rates would lead to population loss over the long term, but nationalists realized that minority ethnic groups, like Turks and Sinti and Roma, had considerably higher birth rates that would gradually increase their proportion in some populations.

In this context abortion was debated, above all by men, not as an issue of the reproductive rights of women, but primarily as a population issue, even though it was also promoted as a way of giving greater value to motherhood. The Communists, it was alleged, had degraded motherhood and the family by insisting on gender equality and on women's rights to employment. Many women, on the other hand, saw abortion not in terms of state policy but as a matter of civil rights generally and of women's reproductive rights specifically.

Abortion was an issue of vigorous debate in Poland because of the opposition of the Catholic Church, which had tried on a number of occasions to have abortion restricted or banned. The antiabortion movement included Solidarity, which in 1990 came out in favor of banning abortion. The issue was debated in the Sejm in 1991 and 1992, but there was no resolution on a new abortion law. However, the Polish Association of Physicians adopted a new code of ethics in 1991 that permitted only specialists to perform abortions, and then only when the woman's life or health was in danger or when her pregnancy was the result of a criminal act. A doctor who terminated a pregnancy for any other reason was liable to punishments that included the withdrawal of her or his license to practice medicine. By 1992 doctors in Poland were unable, in terms of this professional code of ethics, to perform most of the abortions to which women were legally entitled.

Abortion was the subject of animated debate in other states, too, with the reinvigorated Catholic Church weighing in on the side of other forces that sought to ban or at least greatly restrict abortions. In all cases there was a practical recognition that abortion has historically proved impervious to prohibition; women who wanted abortions performed them on themselves or turned to women friends, illegal practitioners, or compliant doctors for help. Often the results were damaging to the woman's health, and sometimes they were fatal. In addition, abortion was often used as birth control, and there was some recognition among antiabortionists (even within the Catholic Church) that restrictions on abortion would have to be accompanied by freer access to contraception.

The stress on women's family and reproductive roles may be understood as part of a more general attempt to recapture what were thought of as traditional culture and social relationships. The family lay at the heart of this vision, for it was one of the ironies that in regulated Communist societies the family escaped regulation more than most other institutions. Not only abortion but divorce was readily available, and Eastern European divorce rates were high. Nostalgia for supposedly "traditional" family and gender relationships was stronger among men than among women. In a survey in Bulgaria in the early 1990s, for example, a third of men thought that women should stay at home and not be employed in the labor force; a fifth of women agreed, but only 16 percent said they would do so if they lost their jobs.

Post-Communist reform did not mean, for most women, an extension of liberties; if anything, their liberties contracted as national liberation took place, and when the general standard of living declined, theirs deteriorated faster. In effect, political rights were given priority over economic rights. Changes in ideology and the economy might have given women the option to work or not work, but it was too often not a real choice: Women were dismissed from their jobs whether they wanted to work or not, and even the minority of women who would have preferred to devote themselves to family and home, found that it was financially impossible to do so.

Another issue that arose with the decline and collapse of the Communist regimes was homosexuality. Under the old regimes, homosexuality was generally considered a pathological condition that was associated with "decadent" societies in Western Europe and North America. Manifestations of homosexuality in socialist societies, like the gay clubs and associations formed in East Germany, were generally repressed by the authorities. Under the new regimes, homosexuals were often held up to public scorn, but homosexual intercourse was not illegal. In 1991 the Polish deputy minister of health was forced to resign after stating his view that the homosexual "problem" was limited to a few perverts, and that AIDS could be prevented by acting morally.

AIDS (acquired immunodeficiency syndrome), which cut a swath through Europe's gay population in this period, and increasingly affected heterosexuals, was confronted even less effectively in Eastern than in Western Europe. The case of Romania, where thousands of children were infected after transfusions with infected blood, became infamous. An increase in the number of prostitutes, many of whom did not insist that their clients use condoms, and the frequent difficulty in obtaining condoms, furthered the spread of AIDS. The failure of the Communist regimes and their successors to deal with drug users who reused hypodermic needles also contributed to the spread of the disease among that population.

Gender and sexuality were thus intrinsic themes in the decline of the Communist regimes and in the early years of the post-Communist states of Eastern Europe and the Russian area. Political, economic, and social reconstruction affected sections of the population in varying ways, and gender was one of the most important of these divisions.

The Reunification of Germany

The process of reunifying Germany that began in late 1990 proved to be a difficult process for all Germans. Like the original unification in 1870, it was not a merging of equals but in effect the imposition of the institutions of one state on others: In 1870 the dominant state was Prussia, in 1990 it was the Federal Republic of Germany (West Germany). The West German constitution had provided two possibilities for an eventual reunification of the two states that emerged from the postwar division of Germany. Article 146 stipulated that a new constitution would be drawn up and put to a referendum of all Germans, so that all would become citizens of the new state on an equal basis at the same time. Supporters of this process, mainly on the left, hoped that it would not only give Easterners a stake in the new Germany but also enable some weaknesses in the West German constitution to be removed.

Opponents argued that employing Article 146 would take too long, given the instability of the political situation, especially in the Soviet Union. There was fear that if a new and more conservative government came to power there, it might try to halt the reunification process. The decision was made to unify Germany under Article 23, which essentially allowed East Germany to join West Germany. Thus it was that unification became effectively an enlargement of West Germany, whose official name (the Federal Republic of Germany) was applied to the new state. Similarly, the West German flag became the German flag, and its anthem became the German anthem. In general, the West German constitutional, legal, and administrative systems were transplanted. Personnel were often transplanted, too, as former East German administrators were removed and their positions filled by bureaucrats from the West. Because reunification meant that East Germany was subsumed by the West, the entire diplomatic corps of the former East Germany was dismissed.

There was limited acceptance of the notion that some changes, supported by Eastern and some left-wing Western parties, might be made to the German constitution and legal system. They included more scope for referenda, as well as stronger social rights than provided for in what had been the West German constitution, especially in the areas of employment, gender equality, and protection of the environment.

Transplanting economic and social systems proved to be far more difficult than imposing institutional structures. In July 1990, customs barriers were eliminated, and the process of privatizing the extensive state enterprises of eastern Germany began. By 1993 almost all (95 percent) had been sold or liquidated, the great majority of the buyers being from western Germany. There was a dramatic effect on employment, partly because East German enterprises had been overstaffed, and the new owners quickly began to rationalize production and reduce the number of employees. Between 1989 and 1992, more than 70 percent of agricultural jobs disappeared, 60 percent of manufacturing jobs, 40 percent in mining and energy, and 22 percent in services, including state services. The only sector to show growth was construction, where employment rose 10 percent.

The first years of unification cost the eastern region of Germany 3.1 million jobs, a third of its 1989 total. Unemployment in mid-1993 suggested the differences between the two former Germanies; the west had a 7.5 percent unemployment rate, the east 15.3 percent. Women, who had constituted 50 percent of the workers in East Germany, were overrepresented among the unemployed in eastern Germany after 1990. In 1992, 62 percent of the unemployed were women, and reemployment rates for women were lower than for men. The network of child-care facilities declined, making it increasingly difficult for women—who were still expected to take primary responsibility for children—to work outside the home and to relocate or travel in order to work.

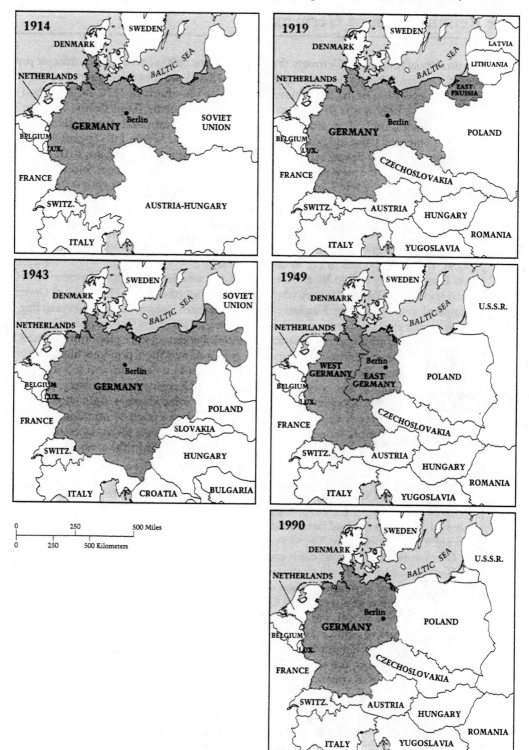

MAP 12.2 Germany's shifting borders, 1914–90.

Moreover, there was evidence of a deep crisis in the eastern German family following reunification, as women in particular rejected marriage and motherhood. Between 1989 and 1992, the birth rate in the east fell by 60 percent and the marriage rate by 65 percent. Changes of this scale in such a short period are generally associated with wartime conditions, which suggests the extent of social disruption that reunification entailed. When free contraception was interrupted, the number of women having themselves sterilized rose dramatically. Despair at conditions in the eastern region of Germany produced a continuous drift of population to the west. Together with the low birth rate, emigration produced a steady decline in the eastern population.

The question of reproductive rights presented the German government with the problem of establishing an abortion policy. Abortion had been available on demand in East Germany, while in West Germany women had to satisfy certain health or social criteria and be professionally counseled first. Under these conditions, women in some parts of West Germany, such as predominantly Catholic Bavaria, had had immense difficulty obtaining abortions. With reunification it was decided that the different laws should remain in force until 1992, and that women from the western region could travel east for easier abortions if they wanted.

In 1992 a new law was passed, giving women the right to abortion after compulsory counseling, with the woman having the final decision. In practice many of the counseling services were religious (half those in the eastern region were, despite the secular character of the population), and rural women continued to have more difficult access to abortion. In order to reduce the number of abortions (estimated at almost 300,000 throughout Germany in 1989), women under twenty-one were given access to free contraception. Such policies echoed the tradition of East Germany more than that of the West, and they were reinforced by a law stipulating that all children aged three to six years had a right to a place in kindergarten. Funds were to be made available to ensure that this policy was in effect by 1996.

The liberal 1992 abortion law was overturned by the constitutional court the following year, however, and it was not until 1995 that Germany got new legislation. Much more restrictive, it made abortion illegal but specified that abortions carried out in the first three months of pregnancy would not be prosecuted.

On political and social levels, the different experiences of the western and eastern regions during almost half a century of division produced differences in culture that showed no sign of disappearing quickly. In general, like citizens in other former Communist states in Eastern Europe, eastern Germans had higher expectations of the state. They expected the state to provide employment and a wide range of social and economic services. Though easterners appeared to be fascinated by the array of consumer goods available in West Germany when unrestricted travel between the divided states first became possible, surveys suggested that after unification they were less materialistic and individualistic, and had a greater sense of social responsibility, than their western compatriots.

Easterners and westerners also reacted differently to the Nazi period. In West Germany there had been official attempts to ensure that the period was understood as integral to the course of German history and a reference point for the construction of a liberal democratic society. The government of East Germany, in contrast, had tended to regard the Nazi period as external, as an ideological aberration from the long-term development of German history that culminated (up to 1990, at least) in the creation of the German Democratic Republic (East Germany). To this extent, East Germans accepted less collective responsibility for their Nazi past.

For this reason, the East German government was less lenient toward those guilty of war crimes. The number of war criminals punished in the East had been higher than in the West, and sentences tended to be tougher. The difference was highlighted by the case of Johannes Piehl, who had commanded a police battalion that killed hundreds of Jews in Poland in the early 1940s. Piehl was sentenced to life imprisonment in East Germany in 1981; but once Germany had reunified, he appealed the sentence on the ground that if he had been tried in West Germany he would have been acquitted or given a much shorter sentence. The Jews were killed, he argued, not for racial reasons but because they were partisans. East Germany regarded the German invasion of Poland in 1939 as illegal and any killings that resulted as criminal. In West German law, in contrast, the killing of partisans was not necessarily regarded as a war crime.

The revision of history was one aspect of broad changes in the eastern educational system that resulted from reunification. Not only were syllabuses and textbooks changed to eliminate their Marxist orientation, but whole institutions and university departments were closed. An estimated 10 percent of faculty members, particularly in political science and law, were purged for political reasons, and many more lost their posts as the education system was restructured. A number of replacement academics were brought in from the western region.

Historical revision extended to place names, too, as more than 100 streets and squares in what had been East Berlin were stripped of names with Communist associations. For example, a street named after Clara Zetkin, a socialist who had fought for women's suffrage and was later honorary president of the Weimar Republic's parliament (in which capacity she called for a common front against the Nazis), was to revert to its former name, Dorothea, which celebrated a seventeenth-century Prussian princess. There were loud protests from many people who lived in the localities affected by name changes. "History was made in both parts of this city," one Social Democratic council leader proclaimed at a public meeting, and others pointed out that there was no plan to change streets and squares named after figures like Hindenburg, the president who had appointed Hitler chancellor in 1933.

Germans in the eastern region had to confront particular problems arising from the Communist past. One was the pervasive influence of the Stasi, East Germany's security police, which had maintained surveillance using millions of informants. Stasi documentation revealed that many prominent citizens had been implicated in repression at various levels, and that hundreds of thousands of ordinary men and women had reported on their spouses, other family members, neighbors, and workmates. Many men and women between the ages of forty and sixty, especially those who had reached positions of responsibility in all manner of hierarchies, found themselves compromised and their careers ruined. On the other hand, it was decided in 1995 that East Germans who had spied on West Germany would not be prosecuted.

Nor was the impact of the former Communist regime on the physical environment negligible. Thousands of miles of rivers were polluted by chemicals and vast tracts of forest devastated by acid rain. Many parts of the eastern region were contaminated by radioactive waste.

The process of reunification by no means spared the former West Germans from its effects. The reconstruction of administration and the extension of social services, such as massive unemployment benefits, placed considerable strain on the western region's economy. During the period of transition and economic reconstruction, the east could be expected to produce far less than it consumed in investment. In contrast to the enthusiastic welcome given to refugees from East Germany when they were a trickle, and even when the first substantial numbers arrived in 1989, many western Germans quickly began to resent the financial burden they represented. A special tax was levied to compensate for the extraordinary expenditure. Easterners, referred to as *Ossis,* became the focus of jokes by *Wessis* that highlighted their perceived naiveté. They were seen by some westerners, particularly unemployed young people, not as fellow citizens but as outsiders taking their jobs.

Rising unemployment in western Germany also focused nationalist attention on non-German immigrants and "guest workers." Despite the domestic costs of reunification, Germany continued to accept large numbers of refugees from Eastern and Southern Europe. In 1992 Germany took 65 percent of all the refugees accepted by Western Europe, and by 1993 had accepted more than 300,000 people fleeing the wars in the former Yugoslavia. The influx was far from universally welcomed, and it was the focus of a number of right-wing, sometimes neo-Nazi groups that became more prominent during the 1980s. In the early 1990s, there were a number of attacks on foreigners, especially Turks and Asians. Immigrant reception houses were bombed, and some immigrants killed.

The prominence given to German nationalist groups, combined with German reunification and the strength of the German economy, gave rise to fears in some parts of Europe that Germany might once again attempt to assert its authority beyond its borders. Germany had the strongest economy in Western Europe, and with the collapse of Communist regimes in Eastern Europe, it began to extend its influence there. German banks and companies were early leaders in the race to establish commercial contacts and

At the bottom of this photo are the coffins of five Turks, killed by neo-Nazis in Solingen, Germany, in June 1993. In the background is the house burned out during the attack.

markets in Eastern Europe. By 1993 Germany was the largest trading partner of most East European countries.

The renewed profile of Germany was indicated by the growing popularity of the German language as Eastern Europeans started to train their populations for the new European economy. The number of Polish students learning German tripled from 500,000 to 1.5 million between 1988 and 1994, and German was being taken by half the schoolchildren in Latvia and the Czech Republic, and by a third in Slovakia and Russia. The German foreign ministry spent half its cultural budget in 1993 on promoting the German language abroad.

The resurgence of Germany resulted in various expressions of alarm. In the Czech border town of Cheb, some 500 Czech nationalists demonstrated in October 1994 against what they alleged was the "Germanization" of their country. Their anxieties reflected concern about the historic vulnerability of the Czech borderlands—formerly the ethnic German-populated Sudetenland—to German expansionism. The Czech residents of the territory, where German place names had been replaced by Czech, were afraid that Germans might buy up property in the area, just as Volkswagen had purchased part of the Czech-owned Skoda automobile company. Their fears were heightened by demands, notably from right-wing organizations in Bavaria representing Germans expelled from Czechoslovakia in 1945, that Germans ought to be compensated for their losses or should be able to buy their properties back.

More general alarm was expressed that modern Germany, with its strong currency and powerful industrial base, would obtain by economic means part of what the Nazis had failed to achieve by military means: a European economy that operated primarily to the benefit of Germany. In Britain in 1990, a former Foreign Office minister in the Conservative government expressed his outrage that Germany had prospered and grown powerful since its defeat in 1945, while a victorious Britain had foundered economically and politically; he described plans for a European economic union as "a German racket to take over the whole of Europe." Fears were expressed within Germany itself. In the 1994 ceremony marking the departure of Allied forces from Berlin, the German army marched by in a torchlight parade at the Brandenburg Gate, the first such performance since the Second World War, and one reminiscent of the Nazi period. It provoked protests from worried Germans who sensed a resurgence of nationalism and militarism. Protests continued the next year when the constitutional court voted to permit German military forces to take part in military actions outside Germany, a practice forbidden since 1945. Germany promptly provided units for a multinational force to be deployed in Bosnia.

Western Europe:
Economics and Politics, 1985–95

In the second half of the 1980s, the Western European economy began to recover from the recession that followed the second oil shock in 1979. Rates of inflation moderated, and many countries saw levels of productivity rise. Recovery was helped by the failure of the oil producers' cartel to maintain its high price levels. The price of oil rose as high as $36 a barrel in 1981, but by 1985 it had fallen to $26, and at points in 1986 was as low as $11. The price subsequently settled around $16 to $19 a barrel, rather higher than it had been before 1973, but a level that was manageable. At the same time the world prices of raw materials declined. The overall effect was to lessen the burden of energy costs and lower the cost of imports needed for Western European industry. There were also sharp reductions in wage settlements. The effects of these developments varied according to national policies with respect to taxation, but in general consumer spending increased and helped the recovery.

One persistent problem was unemployment, which remained high despite the growth in productivity. The lowest average unemployment rate between 1986 and 1990 was the Scandinavian countries' 2 to 4 percent, the highest Spain's 18.7 percent. Most Western European states had rates in the 8 to 10 percent range, whereas West Germany had 6 percent. Part of the problem was that although the labor force was expanding (by about 0.2 percent a year) in this period, the working-age populations, especially women, were growing three or four times faster. This meant that unemployment increased even though jobs were created, and that many young people who came of working age in the late 1980s could expect to face instant and long-term unemployment.

By the early 1990s, a series of European and non-European events disturbed Western Europe's economic stability once again. The collapse of the Communist regimes in Eastern Europe called into question the security of Western European investments in the region and upset trading relationships that had grown steadily during the 1980s. Second, the outbreak of the Gulf War in the wake of Iraq's invasion of Kuwait interrupted oil deliveries and proved expensive for those Western European governments that participated in the U.S.-led intervention. At the beginning of the 1990s, Western Europe experienced another bout of recession, although good progress was made on most fronts by the mid-1990s. By 1995 the level of world trade had increased, and there were signs of rising productivity and even some decline in unemployment.

In Britain the decade from 1985 was dominated by economic and social policies closely associated with the Conservative prime minister, Margaret Thatcher, who had been elected in 1979. "Thatcherism," as the policies were collectively known, entailed reducing the role of government by such means as privatizing state enterprises, cutting taxes and social services, and deregulating many areas of the economy. Underlying the policies was an ideology of self-help, reminiscent of mid-nineteenth-century liberalism, that insisted that the state should play a minimal role in society and the economy. To this extent, "Thatcherism" was in many respects at odds with the tradition of the British Conservative Party, which during the twentieth century had tended to maintain social services and state enterprises when in office, and had adopted a paternalism that often complemented the social welfare policies of its main rival, the Labour Party.

Among the state enterprises privatized in the 1980s were British Airways, airports, the telephone service, gas, the National Bus Company, and Rolls Royce. The government argued that private companies, having to answer to shareholders and without the government to turn to for subsidies, would be more efficient. Opponents replied that the privatized companies were already profitable, which they generally were; the government's motivation was less financial than ideological, although the treasury received one-time benefits from the sales of privatized companies. The government attempted to give the public a stake in private enterprise by setting aside blocs of shares for small-scale investors when state enterprises were put on the market. Nonetheless, large institutional investors bought most shares and were able to control the new companies.

State services of all kinds were encouraged to become independent. Schools were given financial incentives to opt out of local authority control; funding to universities was cut and they were encouraged to turn to corporate sponsors to support expenses like new buildings. Hospitals were treated in much the same way, with the result that wards were closed and waiting lists for operations lengthened. In 1992 many hospitals had exhausted their annual budgets only nine months into the year, and some turned away even patients in serious need of treatment. Other forms of privatization included giving contracts to American firms to run some British prisons, and the hiring of private security companies to guard military installations.

The ideological drive to reduce industry's reliance on the state extended to individuals as well. Under the Conservatives, investment in housing fell and cuts were made in all manner of social services. Thatcher, who as secretary for education in an earlier government had terminated free milk for schoolchildren, took steps as prime minister to freeze child benefits and cut off free school meals to 300,000 children from poor families. The Conservatives also raised fees for medical care, encouraged the growth of the private health sector at the expense of the National Health Service, and deprived some 700,000 old people of housing subsidies.

Although British taxes were reduced across the board, it was high-income earners that did best; the highest rate of taxation was reduced progressively from 98 to 40 percent between 1979 and 1988. Low-income earners also benefited from reductions when the basic rate was reduced from 33 to 25 percent. But while rates of direct tax fell, the rate of indirect tax (Value Added Tax, or VAT), which was levied on a wide range of consumer goods and hit low-income earners hardest, rose to 17.5 percent. Employees' contributions to the National Health Service also rose. On the other hand, various measures were taken to give tax relief to the better off, such as those with mortgages and personal pension schemes.

One tax innovation, a poll tax on property, provoked such resistance that the government was forced to abandon it. Designed to replace property taxes based on the value of property, the poll tax imposed the same tax on all houses, whether they were mansions or small terrace houses, a system that clearly benefited the affluent and penalized the poor. There were not only riots against the tax, but widespread refusal—and sheer inability—to pay it. By 1989, 1.2 million taxpayers in Scotland had been sent sheriff's warrants because of failure to pay, and in 1990 more than half the taxpayers in Liverpool had not paid. Loss of revenue placed strains on municipalities, which were forced to raise taxes each year to compensate for unpaid taxes the previous year, and in this way made nonpayment ever more likely. The tax became so unworkable that in 1991, after Thatcher's fall and when poll tax arrears amounted to 1.6 billion pounds, it was replaced by a more equitable system.

The broad social effect of Thatcherism was to expand poverty in Britain and widen the gap between rich and poor. Persistent high rates of unemployment reinforced poverty, for although inflation fell, unemployment remained high: 11 percent of the labor force was jobless in 1985, and in 1992 it was still over 10 percent. Young people (ages sixteen to eighteen) were no longer able to claim unemployment benefits, and more stringent conditions were imposed on all unemployed. Nor did employment necessarily guarantee a living wage; the great majority of women who worked in the British economy did so on a part-time basis and on low wages. The rate of home ownership did increase during the 1980s, thanks to the government giving tenants of publicly owned dwellings (council houses) the right to buy them; the proportion of families owning their homes rose from half to two-thirds. By the 1990s, however, large numbers of these new homeowners were unable to keep up their payments, and a slump in the housing market meant that many people owed more than their dwellings were worth, even if they could sell them. Between 1990 and 1994 more than 300,000 houses were repossessed, and another 50,000 were seized in 1995. More generally, the number of homeless people in Britain more than doubled between 1979 and 1989, and increased steadily in the early 1990s.

Thatcherism generated much opposition, some from within the Conservative Party itself. In a notable speech a former Conservative prime minister, Harold Macmillan, compared privatizing state enterprises to "selling the family silver." The Church of England was critical of government policies toward the disadvantaged, the House of Lords blocked some legislation, and educators opposed the government's plans to reduce funding and reorganize the educational system. In 1985 Oxford University took the unusual step of voting not to give Thatcher, a graduate of the university, an honorary degree. The continuation of similar policies by Thatcher's successor, John Major, led to revolts within the Conservative Party, as when in late 1994 he attempted to apply the full rate of VAT to heating fuel used by old people.

At the same time as the Conservatives reduced the role of the British state in the social and economic spheres, the state became politically more coercive. Various measures increased police powers over public meetings and protests, and a new Official Secrets Act, passed in 1988 to replace the one enacted in 1911, made it illegal to publish anything the government believed might harm national security. In 1994 the Criminal Justice Act removed many of the rights that had historically protected people accused of crimes, such as the right to remain silent. In the same year, on the other hand, restrictions on travel and free speech that had been imposed as a response to the conflict in Northern Ireland were relaxed when, after a quarter century of resistance to Northern Ireland's status within the United Kingdom, the Irish Republican Army announced a cease-fire. Discussions on the constitutional future of Ireland brought together the British and Irish governments and the main republican and loyalist political groups in Northern Ireland.

Other Western European nations wrestled with their own economic and political problems from the late 1980s on. Italy suffered chronic political instability as governments came and went. In the mid-1980s, evidence of widespread corruption began to emerge, implicating dozens of leading politicians and several former prime ministers. One of them, the Socialist Bettino Craxi, fled abroad to escape arrest. Government instability prevented any sustained attack on fundamental economic problems, such as unemployment rates that remained above 10 percent for much of the period.

The chronic volatility of Italian politics seemed to come to an end with the election in March 1994 of Silvio Berlusconi, a flamboyant millionaire who owned the prestigious AC-Milan soccer club and a business empire that included real estate, department stores, and half of Italy's television stations. Campaigning on a program of cleaning up Italy's corrupt political system, Berlusconi's Forza Italia populist movement was able to form a government with the assistance of other parties. His main partners were the neofascist National Alliance and the Northern League, a party dedicated to autonomy for Italy's northern provinces. One of the National Alliance deputies was Alessandra Mussolini, the granddaughter of the former dictator. The coalition controlled 366 of the 630 seats in the chamber of deputies, and became Italy's fifty-third government since the end of the Second World War less than fifty years earlier. The new government lasted a shorter time than many of its predecessors, however, collapsing after only seven months. From the beginning it was saddled with allegations of corruption and criminality involving the prime minister's business interests. In December 1994, Berlusconi was forced to resign, and the following year officials of his companies were charged with corruption for having attempted to bribe tax officials.

France also experienced some political turmoil, but of a different kind. The Socialist president, François Mitterrand, was elected for a second term in 1988, and would become the longest-serving French president. In elections to the National Assembly in 1994, however, the Socialists were defeated and a conservative majority elected, largely in response to persistent economic problems. As in Italy, the French government—Socialist on this occasion—was tainted by scandals. A minister of health in the 1980s was charged after it became clear that blood transfusion services had negligently allowed AIDS-infected blood products to be supplied to hemophiliacs and others. Other prominent officials with links to the Socialist Party were charged with corruption, and Mitterrand himself became the center of controversy. It was revealed that he had worked briefly in the wartime Vichy government and after the war had maintained contact with prominent Nazi collaborators. On the personal plane, it was discovered that he had fathered a child outside marriage, and that the child and its mother had been living for years in an apartment in the presidential palace.

The Socialist Party seemed to be in electoral decline, not least because it had failed to solve the problem of unemployment that exceeded 12 percent in 1995. Even so, the Socialist candidate in the 1995 presidential elections won a surprisingly high share of the vote in the first round—almost a quarter of the ballots—and conservative votes were split between two candidates. More than a fifth of the votes, however, went to extreme right-wing parties, notably the National Front, that campaigned on nationalist and anti-immigrant platforms. Right-wing support was strong in economically depressed areas and in cities, like Marseilles, with large immigrant populations. In the second round of voting (between the two leaders in the first round), the conservative candidate, Jacques Chirac, won 53 percent of the votes cast to the Socialist candidate's 47 percent. Although this suggested a split between the left and right, an unusually high level of nonvoting suggested that many right-wing supporters were disenchanted with the mainstream parties.

Many of the early policies announced by President Chirac seemed designed to respond to right-wing nationalist concerns. He expressed a more equivocal attitude toward European union than his predecessor had done, and immediately suspended France's participation in a European "open borders" scheme. He also announced, to the dismay of most French people and many of France's European partners, that the testing of nuclear weapons in French Polynesia, which had been suspended by President Mitterrand in 1982, would be resumed. In July 1995 Chirac consolidated his personal power by having the two chambers of the French parliament give him extensive executive authority. He was empowered to bypass parliament in social, economic, political, and international policy, and instead consult the electorate directly by means of referenda.

By this time, many governments in Western Europe faced the task of reducing deficits so as to tackle the massive debts they had built up during the 1980s. Traditional social welfare states faced particular problems because their levels of public spending were so high. In Sweden public spending represented 70 percent of the country's gross domestic product, compared with only 50 percent in Germany, where social services were far less comprehensive. The Swedish deficit of 13 percent was one of the highest in Western Europe. By 1994, after four years of conservative government, unemployment had reached 14 percent, an unprecedented level that followed rates of less than 2 percent between 1985 and 1990. In 1994 Swedes returned the Social Democrats to power, and in a referendum voted to join the European Union.

Persistent economic problems throughout Western Europe in the mid-1990s raised fears of a surge in support for right-wing movements in a number of states. The extreme right did well in the first round of the French 1995 presidential election, garnering one vote in five. In municipal elections the same year, the fascist National Front won control of the Mediterranean port city of Toulon and several smaller towns. In regional elections in Spain in 1995, the conservative Popular Party outpolled the governing Socialists. On the other hand, local government elections in the United Kingdom in 1995 saw the Conservatives lose ground decisively to the now centrist Labour Party. In elections in Belgium the same year, a feared shift to the right failed to materialize, although in Antwerp, which has a large North

African and Turkish population, a quarter of the votes went to parties that advocated repatriating immigrants. Although economic conditions seemed to favor extremist parties, there was no consistent trend in Western European politics.

Western Europe and Social Anxiety: Race, Age, and Sexuality

By the mid-1990s, Europe had experienced two decades of economic uncertainty, as recessions alternated with brief periods of recovery. The spread of poverty and persistent high levels of unemployment, especially of young people, provided the background for what some commentators identified as a *fin de siècle* sense of anxiety. Although it is impossible to describe the mechanism, it seemed possible that as the end of the century approached—and in the 1990s it was also the end of a millennium—people collectively took stock of their recent history and current situation. Whether or not there is anything to this notion, a number of specific issues did provoke anxiety from the late 1980s into the 1990s, and all called into question social relationships that were fundamental to the development of Europe in the twentieth century.

In the 1980s a new wave of racism broke upon many Western European societies. Racism had never been absent from Western Europe, but it had flourished at some times, often during periods of economic hardship, more than others. Traditionally it had been directed at "outsiders within," such as Jews, Sinti and Roma, and Slavs, and the waves of immigration from outside Europe after World War II provided new opportunities for discrimination in housing, employment, and services, as well as outright hostility of various kinds. In the 1980s the most prominent expressions of racism were those of neo-Nazi organizations that focused not only on Jews but to an even greater extent on immigrants or Europeans of non-European ethnic origin: Turks in Germany, North Africans in France,

Neo-Nazi desecration of a Jewish cemetery in Paris. The graffiti on the memorial to some of the victims of the Holocaust read, "Heil Hitler" and "[Jews are] Unworthy to be part of the new Europe."

and Indians and Pakistanis in Britain. By the mid-1990s an estimated 17 million citizens and residents of the member states of the European Union, representing about 5 percent of the population, had ethnic origins outside Europe.

Complaints were renewed that immigrants had taken jobs from indigenous people. In fact, non-European immigrants in many countries were overrepresented among the unemployed from the mid-1980s on, and where that was noted it led to allegations that they were a drain on already overextended welfare budgets. With the growing demand for a skilled workforce, it could be expected that non-European immigrants, who generally reached a lower level of formal education, would remain a pool of unemployed or find unskilled work in service industries. Either way, they seemed unlikely to move beyond the status of an underclass in most European states.

Employed or not, people of non-European origin attracted hostility to the point that in 1994 the European Union expressed concern about the increase in manifestations of racism. Surveying acts of spontaneous or organized violence, its report concluded that "racism and xenophobia have become commonplace, not only in day-to-day neighbor disputes but also in the pronouncements of certain extremist organizations and within certain political parties." There was evidence of supranational networks of racist organizations that comprised neo-Nazi groups in Britain, France, Germany, Italy, Belgium, and elsewhere.

Although they represented a much smaller population than the postwar immigrants from Africa, Asia, and other Third World regions, Jews also continued to attract hostility within Europe. Jewish cemeteries and synagogues were defaced in many parts of Western Europe, and in the 1990s some Jewish centers were bombed. Another manifestation that emerged during the 1980s, within and outside Europe, was a tendency that described itself as "revisionist" history. "Revisionists" argued that the Holocaust, the killing of millions of Jews by the Nazis and their accomplices during the Second World War, had never happened; it was, they insisted, a myth invented and propagated by Jews to generate support for the state of Israel and as part of a Jewish conspiracy to dominate the world. To this end, "revisionists" denied that Hitler's government had set out to kill Europe's Jews and that camps like Auschwitz had been dedicated to this purpose. "Revisionists" of the Holocaust did not seek to offer an alternative interpretation of history, as historians often do when they revise accepted versions; instead, they ignored accepted rules of evidence and interpretation to make a political point. Holocaust revision is not a different point of view or another side of a story; it is the denial of a historical fact for political and ideological purposes. Holocaust "revisionists," who tend to be linked with extreme right-wing or racist organizations and ideologies, have included David Irving, the author of a number of books on World War II, and Jean Marie Le Pen, the leader of the French right-wing National Front movement.

Some of the growing anxiety about non-European ethnic populations in Europe stemmed from concerns about employment and population trends. The fertility decline, which as we have seen began in the late nineteenth century, led to some states dropping below replacement level. Although the population of Western Europe as a broad region was expected to continue to grow until the end of the twentieth century, by the early twenty-first century it was expected to start to decline even faster than it grew in the 1980s and 1990s. A United Nations report noted that "Europe is literally melting away like snow in the sun." In 1984 a former French prime minister, Jacques Chirac (who was elected president in 1995), expressed France's chronic fear of depopulation: "In demographic terms, Europe is vanishing. Twenty years from now, our countries will be empty, and no matter what our technological strength, we shall be incapable of putting it to use."

Although Chirac's scenario was exaggerated, it did reflect the concern of policymakers about demographic trends. One of the perceived problems was the progressive aging of

Europe's population as birth and death rates continued to fall. By the mid-1990s the only Western European country in which the average number of children produced by couples was above replacement level was Ireland, where there was an average of 2.2 children. In Italy, where deaths outnumbered births in 1993, couples had only 1.2 children on average, and in Germany, where the birth rate in the eastern region plummeted after reunification in 1990, the average was under 1.4. Apart from Ireland, the largest families, with an average of 1.9 children, were found in France, a perverse phenomenon in light of the fact that France led the European fertility decline for most of the nineteenth and twentieth centuries. The Western European birth rate was projected to stabilize at the level reached around the year 2000.

Marriage rates, falling from their historic high levels in the 1960s, reached a low point in 1985, after which they stabilized. Some of the decline in marriage rates was a result of postponement, but it was also clear that many couples preferred to cohabit without formal marriage. In the younger age groups, the fall in marriage rates was offset by cohabitation, a trend that began first in Scandinavia but by the 1990s had spread to the rest of Western Europe. As marriage rates fell, divorce rates continued to rise in some countries but stabilized and even fell slightly in others. In general, about one in three or four marriages ended in divorce in the early 1990s.

Like fertility, mortality continued its downward course at the end of the twentieth century. Infant mortality reached negligible levels compared with rates at midcentury. In Western Europe there were 44 infant deaths per thousand births in the early 1950s, but 7 in the 1990s; in Northern Europe the decline was from 28 to 6 per thousand in the same period. A general reduction in mortality helped life expectancy to rise steadily. In the early 1950s Western European females could expect to live to age 70, but by 1985 the age had risen to 78, and it was projected to reach 83 by the third decade of the twenty-first century. Male life expectancy lagged behind the female, but rose over the same periods from 65 to 71 years, and then to a projected 77 years.

The result of a low birth rate and rising life expectancy was that European populations became steadily older. The median age of Europeans was 30.5 years in 1950, reached 35 years in 1990, and was projected to attain 40.3 years by 2010. An associated effect was an increase in the proportion of older people in European populations (see Figure 12.1). Women and men 65 or older constituted 9 percent of the population in 1950, 13 percent in 1990, and were expected to be 16 percent in 2010 and 19 percent in 2020.

The aging population, a phenomenon by no means confined to Western Europe, raised many issues. It was assumed that most of the older people would be consumers rather than producers, and particularly consumers of social services and resources such as pensions and medical care. The cost of caring for the aged could be expected to rise by 50 percent, even assuming no other changes, but in fact it will rise even more because a greater number of people will be in the advanced ages at which most intensive care is often required. The question many policymakers raised was whether adequate levels of services could be provided when the proportion of the population in the most productive (and tax-paying) age groups was shrinking. By 1990 there were 49 people in the so-called "dependent" age groups (0 to 15 years and 65 years and older) for every 100 in the most productive age group (ages 15 to 64); that ratio was expected to rise to 55:100 by 2020. The ratio is, of course, even greater in times of high unemployment when the real dependent population (defined in terms of productivity, not merely age) increases.

No critical point in this trend had been reached by the 1990s, and it was not clear how serious the problem might be. The decline of fertility meant that the proportion of dependent young children declined. In 1950, 39 percent of Europeans were under 15 years of age, but the percentage fell to 29 by 1990 and was expected to reach 26 percent in 2025.

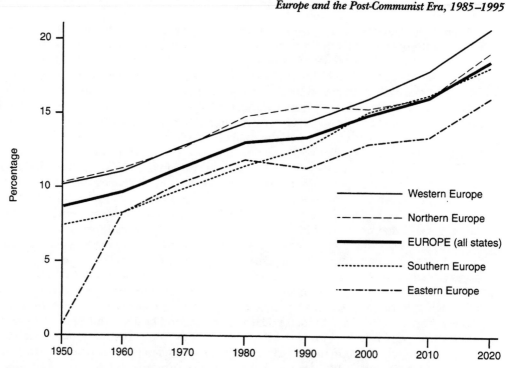

FIGURE 12.1 Europe's aging population: percentage of the population aged 65 and older, by region, 1950–2020 (projected).

Source: Data from Nathan Keyfitz and Wilhelm Flieger, *World Population Growth and Aging: Demographic Trends in the Late Twentieth Century* (Chicago: University of Chicago Press, 1990), pp. 249–53.

Some resources would be transferred from the young (in terms of education, child care, and family benefits) to the old, but there would be little gain from this source after the 1990s, when fertility had stopped falling and had stabilized.

By the 1990s, however, policies were being adopted to accommodate changes in the European age structure. More facilities were being made available by both the state and private sectors for older people. Housing was being constructed, special services extended, and more leisure facilities provided. A University of the Third Age, making education more accessible to older people, had been established in Britain, France, and a number of other countries. At the same time, some governments, including France and Germany, adopted measures to encourage fertility so as to slow down the aging of their populations. These measures included housing allowances, family benefits, and more generous maternity leave provisions.

There were scattered attempts in Western Europe, as in the east, to adopt coercive policies, such as restricting or banning abortion. In 1994 the fascist speaker of the Italian Chamber of Deputies, Irene Pivetti, caused a furor when she told a Roman Catholic youth conference that Italy's 1978 abortion law should be repealed. Meanwhile, the Catholic Church stepped up its campaign against contraception and abortion, and Pope John Paul II unequivocally reaffirmed church policies in these areas.

A third major area of anxiety that arose in Western Europe (and elsewhere) was the spread of AIDS, which drew official and public attention to issues of sexuality and gender.

AIDS spread through Western Europe from the early 1980s and by the 1990s was recognized as a social crisis. Although spread by heterosexual sexual activity as well as through homosexual activity and many other forms of body-fluid transfers, AIDS was concentrated in Europe's male homosexual populations and among drug users who employed syringes that had been infected with the human immunodeficiency virus (HIV). In the 1980s, blood supply agencies in a number of countries failed to eliminate infected donated blood, and passed it on to groups like hemophiliacs who need regular transfusions of blood products. In other instances, hospital patients who needed blood transfusions were infected with the HIV by tainted blood supplies.

Despite the various means by which AIDS can be contracted, it became quickly associated with the male homosexual community. Prevailing attitudes to gay men soon led to AIDS being considered in some homophobic circles as punishment, divine or other, for their sin. Public fear about the spread of AIDS reinforced anti-gay sentiment, and briefly checked what had been slowly but steadily increasing toleration of homosexuals in European society. Fear was even expressed that the merest contact with a homosexual, like shaking hands, could be a conduit for the AIDS virus.

It was soon clear that AIDS would not be confined to the apparently most vulnerable groups, homosexuals and syringe-using drug addicts. Means were adopted to screen blood supplies for the virus, but the number of cases in Europe grew steadily. In 1986, 6,330 cases of AIDS were reported in Western Europe; in 1989, 11,254 cases were reported. There were complaints that governments began to take AIDS seriously only when they realized that populations other than gays and drug addicts were at risk. Nevertheless, during the 1990s anti-AIDS campaigns began.

The campaigns focused on both drug use and sexual contact. In many countries programs were established to provide free syringes for intravenous drug users in order to minimize the repeated use of needles. As for sexuality, campaigns urged people to practice "safe sex," notably by using condoms. Homosexual organizations set up their own self-help services to prevent the further spread of the disease as well as to help its victims, many of whom were rejected by their families and died slow and lonely deaths. There was some resistance to the anti-AIDS campaigns. The provision of syringes was seen by some people as encouraging drug use. Some organizations, including the Catholic Church (but excluding

At the 1993 International AIDS Congress in Berlin, demonstrators call for HIV-positive drug users to unite in order to get more government attention and assistance.

many individual priests), opposed the use of condoms for doctrinal reasons. Others were against urging young people to use condoms on the ground that such campaigns were no more than official endorsement of sexual promiscuity.

By the mid-1990s the number of reported AIDS cases in Western Europe was lower than had been projected, and the main growth regions for the disease in Europe were the former Communist states of Eastern Europe and Russia, where the problem was ignored until the early 1990s. Indeed, AIDS had been fostered in many parts of Eastern Europe and the former Soviet Union by medical practices that included the reuse of syringes without sterilization.

Paradoxically, the AIDS crisis gave Europe's homosexual population a higher profile. Even though the association of gays with AIDS initially provoked a negative social reaction, the subsequent recognition that AIDS was not confined to the gay community led to a broader appreciation of the problems of being gay in a predominantly heterosexual society. The process was furthered by more open discussions of sexual orientation by homosexuals and lesbians, and this trend in itself spoke for a reduction in the level of homophobia. Although widespread prejudice against homosexual men and women persisted in European society, and despite an intensification of it during the early stages of the AIDS panic, the change of attitudes in a more tolerant direction eventually resumed its course.

Supranationalism and Nationalism

The fall of the Communist regimes in the Soviet Union and Eastern Europe had far-reaching implications for the political, economic, and military organizations that from the 1940s to the 1980s drew various combinations of European states together. The first affected were the Soviet-dominated Comecon and Warsaw Pact. The trade agreement was the first to go, once it was decided in 1990 that Eastern European trade should be carried on at prevailing world prices and in U.S. dollars. The decision to dissolve Comecon was taken in January 1991, and was ratified at a meeting in Budapest in June 1991.

In the same year the members of the Warsaw Pact, which had ceased to exist in meaningful terms once the Eastern European Communist regimes had gone, voted to disband and to annul the agreement. The meeting to dissolve it formally took place in July 1991 in Prague, the city invaded by the forces from some Pact members in 1968. By mid-1991 there were no longer any Soviet troops in Czechoslovakia or Hungary. Agreements were made for the withdrawal of all remaining Soviet forces and equipment from Poland by 1993 and from the eastern region of Germany by 1994.

Although the North Atlantic Treaty Organization (NATO) was formed by Western European states, together with the United States and Canada, before the Warsaw Pact, it was above all a collective security defense arrangement designed to counter the Soviet Union. With the collapse of the Soviet Union and the Warsaw Pact, the prime reason for NATO's existence was called into question, but there was little urgency to dismantle the organization. The political situation in Eastern Europe and the former Soviet Union remained volatile and uncertain, and the organization represented the only formal link between North America and Europe. With the end of the cold war, the military side of NATO was given less emphasis, and its role in fostering political cooperation was highlighted. The continuing military functions of NATO were demonstrated in the 1990s when aircraft under its command were used to supplement United Nations ground forces in Bosnia.

There were suggestions that membership of NATO might even be extended to include some former members of the Warsaw Pact. In effect, the continued participation of Germany in NATO after 1990 meant that the former East Germany—which was incorporated into a reunified Germany—became a member of the organization, even while troops from the former Soviet Union were stationed on its territory. Russia, however, opposed any expansion of NATO membership farther east to include states like Hungary, Poland, and the Czech Republic, which would bring NATO right to Russia's borders. Although Russia was not the military power that the Soviet Union had been, Western European states were reluctant to adopt policies that would needlessly alienate the Russian government and create new international tensions.

NATO forces did, however, begin to hold joint exercises with former Warsaw Pact states. The first, which focused on peacekeeping techniques, was held in Poland in September 1994 and involved six NATO countries together with Poland, Ukraine, the Czech Republic, Slovakia, Bulgaria, Romania, and Lithuania. The demise of the Warsaw Pact and the disunity of the Eastern European states increased the importance of the Conference on Security and Cooperation in Europe, which had been established in 1975 and by 1994 had fifty-three member states. It became the principal forum in which all the regions of Europe were represented.

Meanwhile the reorganization of Europe after the end of the cold war gave a boost to the process of European union. The European Community (EC), which had started life in 1957 as primarily a trading bloc of six nations, had in the following three decades steadily expanded its membership and its scope to include the harmonization of many areas of the economy. The European Parliament had been created and was given power to pass legislation on an ever widening range of matters, thus gradually reducing the sovereignty of the individual member states. The direction of all these developments was the creation of a federal arrangement involving a growing number of European states.

The process was taken an important step further in 1991 when a meeting of EC members at Maastricht, in the Netherlands, set the stage for the creation of the European Union (EU) in 1992. Member states agreed to expand cooperation in such areas as health, education, the environment, consumer standards, and energy. There was also to be a higher level of coordination in judicial matters, immigration policies, and closer liaison among domestic police forces, leading to a European version of Interpol.

These were extensions of policies and practices already in place, but in monetary policy the Maastricht agreement pushed forward into new areas of integration. It was agreed that a single European currency should be established in stages starting in 1997; the expectation was that because it would be backed by strong economies, it would become one of the world's key trading currencies. From a European perspective, the single currency would be the leading edge of a broader economic and financial coordination and integration that would include national budgets and national policies on such matters as interest rates and deficits.

Integration continued in other spheres as well. Nationals of EU states were issued EU passports, and in 1995 seven of the EU's states announced plans to abandon border controls for one another's citizens. This meant that a German who wanted, for some reason, to drive into Portugal by the indirect route of the Netherlands, Belgium, Luxembourg, France, and Spain would be able to do so without having to show a passport at any of the frontier crossings. Denmark, Ireland, and Britain chose to remain outside the arrangement.

The Conservative government of Britain was more wary than its European partners about the Maastricht agreement. Important sections of the party (they were called "Eurosceptics") and the public remained profoundly suspicious of the closer ties to Europe,

MAP 12.3   The members of the European Union, through 1995.

particularly the implied steady erosion of national sovereignty in areas of economic, social, and legal policy. The British mass media delighted in drawing Britons' attention to
the latest inanity to emerge from the EU bureaucracy, including (in 1994) specifications
of the degree of "bend" a banana had to have before it could be marketed in an EU-mem-
ber country. At Maastricht the British prime minister, John Major, argued that Britain
must retain control over defense policy and over employment policies such as maternity
leave and gender equality, and Britain also reserved the right not to join the single-cur-
rency scheme. Despite these concessions to Britain, seventy Conservative members of

MAP 12.4 Europe in 1996.

Parliament signed a motion opposing the Maastricht agreement, and opinion surveys suggested that it was supported by no more than a quarter of the population.

Opposition to European union created an unlikely coalition of left and right, conservatives, liberals, and socialists, all of whom were motivated by different reasons. Some were alarmed at the potential effects of the tunnel, opened in 1994, that linked Britain and France under the English Channel and that seemed to end the historic isolation of

Britain from continental Europe. Socialists also opposed the EU for facilitating the growth of vast multinational corporations, while right-wingers often resorted to "little Englander" xenophobia; in 1994 a Conservative junior minister resigned after describing Germany and France, respectively, as nations of warmongers and collaborators. By late 1994, following referenda in Scandinavia on the question of joining the EU, there was talk in both major British parties, Conservative and Labour, of holding a referendum on continued British membership.

Specific conflicts arose among member nations, as they were bound to, given the scope of the EU's activities. In 1994, for example, Germany declared its intention to forbid the use of cheap labor on construction sites, in order to ensure that the same wages were paid for the same work done. This measure was opposed by Britain and Portugal, and less vigorously by Italy and Ireland, many of whose nationals were employed by non-German contractors in Germany. Similar concern for protecting national interests was expressed by German politicians, also in 1994, when the automobile maker Daimler-Benz announced that it would build its new "environment-friendly" two-seater automobile in France rather than Germany. The decision reflected the 30 percent lower labor costs in France, but the company's explanation that it also represented a commitment to a united economic Europe did not mollify German union leaders and politicians concerned about domestic unemployment levels.

The German factor was often important in reservations expressed throughout Europe about the desirability of European union. Although the main proponents of the idea in the first half of the 1990s were the German chancellor, Helmut Kohl, and the French president, François Mitterrand, there was no doubt that Germany would be the strongest single component in a united Europe. The idea of union was uppermost in political rhetoric in the early 1990s, but there were also reminders of conflict. When the fiftieth anniversary of the D-Day landings was celebrated in Normandy in June 1994, the German government was offended that it was not invited to participate in the main ceremonies. It was true that the Germans were present in Normandy in 1944, and that D-Day could not have taken place without them, but the former Allies wished to commemorate the event in their absence. In the interests and spirit of European unity in the 1990s, German representatives were permitted to participate in secondary ceremonies, but the episode underlined the ways in which present realities and future aspirations in Europe would continue to be influenced by the past.

Suggestions for Further Reading

The following pages offer a selection from the immense English-language literature on twentieth-century Europe. The citations include books but not articles in journals. Readers wanting to locate articles on the period should look especially at *American Historical Review, European History Quarterly, Gender and History, The Historical Journal, History, History Today, History Workshop Journal, Journal of Contemporary History, Journal of Modern History,* and *Twentieth Century British History.*

Many of the following books are relevant to more than one chapter. In these cases, the first reference provides a full citation; any subsequent reference gives surname, short title, and the section letter or chapter number where the full citation is provided. Most of the titles listed in Section A cover the whole period and can be consulted for many of the specific periods and themes discussed in individual chapters.

A. GENERAL STUDIES OF EUROPE, REGIONS, OR SPECIFIC COUNTRIES

Europe in General. J. M. Roberts, *Europe 1880–1945* (London, 1989); Paul Hayes (ed.), *Themes in Modern European History, 1890–1945* (London, 1992); Derek H. Aldcroft, *The European Economy, 1914–1990* (London, 1993); Carlo M. Cipolla (ed.), *The Fontana Economic History of Europe* (2 vols., Glasgow, 1976); T. E. Vadney, *The World Since 1945* (London, 1992); Walter Laqueur, *Europe in Our Time: A History, 1945–1992* (London, 1992).

Western and Central Europe. Barbara Jelavich, *Modern Austria: Empire and Republic, 1815–1986* (New York, 1987); V. R. Berghahn, *Modern Germany: Society, Economy and Politics in the Twentieth Century* (Cambridge, 2nd ed., 1987); Mary Fulbrook, *Germany 1918–1990: The Divided Nation* (London, 1991); Martin Pugh, *State and Society: British Political and Social History, 1870–1992* (London, 1994); John Stevenson, *British Society, 1914–45* (London, 1984); A. Dickson and J. H. Treble (eds.), *People and Society in Scotland, Vol. III: 1914–1990* (Edinburgh, 1992); J. J. Lee, *Ireland, 1912–1985* (Cambridge, 1989); Raymond Carr, *Modern Spain, 1875–1980* (Oxford, 1980); Adrian Schubert, *A Social History of Modern Spain* (London, 1992); Martin Clark, *Modern Italy, 1971–1982* (London, 1984); James F. McMillan, *Dreyfus to de Gaulle: Politics and Society in France, 1898–1969* (London, 1985); T. K. Derry, *A History of Scandinavia* (Minneapolis, 1979).

Russia and Eastern Europe. Nicholas V. Riasanovsky, *A History of Russia* (New York, 5th ed., 1993); Martin McCauley, *The Soviet Union, 1917–1991* (New York, 2nd ed., 1993); Alec Nove, *An Economic History of the U.S.S.R.* (London, 2nd ed., 1989); R. J. Crampton, *Eastern Europe in the Twentieth Century* (New York, 1994); Z. A. B. Zeman, *The Making and Breaking of Communist Europe* (Oxford, 1991); Philip Longworth, *The Making of Eastern Europe* (London, 1992); Barbara Jelavich, *History of the Balkans: The Twentieth Century* (Cambridge, 1983); John Hiden and Patrick Salmon, *The Baltic Nations and Europe: Estonia, Latvia, and Lithuania in the Twentieth Century* (London, 1991); R. F. Leslie (ed.), *The History of Poland Since 1863* (Cambridge, 1980); Norman Davies, *Heart of Europe: A Short History of Poland* (Oxford, 1984); R. J. Crampton, *A Short History of Modern Bulgaria* (New York, 1987); Jorg K. Hoensch, *A History of Modern Hungary, 1867–1986* (London, 1988).

B. THEMATIC HISTORIES

Women. Françoise Thebaud (ed.), *A History of Women in the West, Vol. V: Toward a Cultural Identity in the Twentieth Century* (Cambridge, MA, 1994); Gisela Kaplan, *Contemporary European Feminism* (New York, 1992); Gisela Bock and Pat Thane (eds.), *Maternity and Gender Policies: Women and the Rise of the European Welfare States, 1880s–1950s* (New York, 1991); C. Dyhouse, *Feminism and the Family in England* (Oxford, 1989); Barbara Evans Clements, Barbara Lapern Engel, and Christine D. Worobec (eds.), *Russia's Women: Accommodation, Resistance, Transformation* (Berkeley, 1991); Susan Bridger, *Women in the Soviet Countryside* (Cambridge, 1987); James F. McMillan, *Housewife or Harlot: The Place of Women in French Society, 1870–1940* (New York, 1981); Claire M. Tylee, *The Great War and Women's Consciousness: Images of Militarism and Womanhood in Women's Writings, 1914–64* (Iowa City, 1990).

Nationality and Ethnicity. Michael R. Marrus, *The Unwanted: European Refugees in the Twentieth Century* (New York, 1985); Mikulas Teich and Roy Porter (eds.), *The National Question in Europe in Historical Context* (Cambridge, 1993); E. J. Hobsbawm, *Nations and Nationalism Since 1780: Programme, Myth, Reality* (Cambridge, 1990); Benjamin Pinkus, *The Jews of the Soviet Union* (Cambridge, 1988); Steven Beller, *Vienna and the Jews, 1867–1938: A Cultural History* (Cambridge, 1989); Ronald Grigor Suny, *The Revenge of the Past: Nationalism, Revolution, and the Collapse of the Soviet Union* (Stanford, 1993); Walter Laqueur, *Black Hundred: The Rise of the Extreme Right in Russia* (New York, 1993).

Population, Family, and Sexuality. A. J. Coale and S. C. Watkins (eds.), *The Decline of Fertility in Europe* (Princeton, 1986); Michael S. Teilelbaum and Jay M. Winter, *The Fear of Population Decline* (New York, 1985); John Knodel, *The Decline of Fertility in Germany, 1871–1939* (Princeton, 1974); George L. Mosse, *Nationalism and Sexuality: Middle-Class Morality and Sexual Norms in Modern Europe* (Madison, WI, 1985); Wesley D. Camp, *Marriage and the Family in France Since the Revolution* (New York, 1961); Roderick Phillips, *Untying the Knot: A Short History of Divorce* (Cambridge, 1991).

Society and Culture. John Burnett and Derek J. Oddy (eds.), *The Origins and Development of Food Policies in Europe* (London, New York, 1994); Susan Pedersen, *Family, Dependence, and the Origin of Welfare States in Britain and France, 1914–1945* (Cambridge, 1993); Daniel Pick, *Faces of Degeneration: A European Disorder, c. 1848–c. 1918* (Cambridge, 1989); Brian Bond, *War and Society in Europe, 1870–1970* (London, 1984); Arthur Marwick, *War and Social Change in the Twentieth Century: A Comparative Study of Britain, France, Germany, Russia, and the United States* (London, 1974).

Intellectual History. Andrew Vincent, *Modern Political Ideologies* (Cambridge, MA, 1992); Hobsbawm, *Nations and Nationalism* (B); Roger Griffin, *The Nature of Fascism* (London, 1993); F. L. Carsten, *The Rise of Fascism* (London, 1967); Richard Thurlow, *Fascism in Britain, 1918–1985* (New York, 1987).

Statistical Sources. Chris Cook and John Paxton (eds.), *European Political Facts, 1918–1973* (London, 1973); Chris Cook (ed.), *Longman Handbook of Modern European History* (London, 2nd ed., 1992); Chris Cook and John Stevenson, *The Longman Handbook of Modern British History, 1714–1980* (London, 1983); B. R. Mitchell (ed.), *International Historical Statistics: Europe, 1750–1988* (New York, London, 1992); *United Nations Demographic Yearbook* (New York, annually).

CHAPTER 1

Many of the works cited above provide the background to the twentieth century discussed in this chapter. But see also Edward Tannenbaum, *Nineteen Hundred* (New York, 1970).

CHAPTER 2

Robert Gildea, *Barricades and Borders: Europe 1800–1914* (Oxford, 1987); James Joll, *The Origins of the First World War* (London, 1983); H. W. Koch (ed.), *The Origins of the First World War: Great Power Rivalry and German War Aims* (London, 1972); Laurence Lafore, *The Long Fuse: An Interpretation of the Origins* of *World War I* (London, 1966); Norman Stone, *Europe Transformed, 1878–1919* (Glasgow, 1984); Hobsbawm, *Nations and Nationalism* (B); Steven C. Hause with Anne R. Kenney, *Women's Suffrage and Social Politics in the French Third Republic* (Princeton, 1984); Pick, *Faces of Degeneration* (B).

CHAPTER 3

General. Marc Ferro, *The Great War, 1914–1918* (London, 1973); Martin Gilbert, *First World War* (London, 1994); Keith Robbins, *The First World War* (Oxford, 1985); Bernadotte E. Schmidt and Harold C. Vedeler, *The World in Crucible, 1914–1929* (New York, 1984).

Social and Cultural. Richard Wall and Jay Winter (eds.), *The Upheaval of War: Family, Work and Welfare in Europe, 1914–1918* (Cambridge, 1988); Margaret Randolph Higonnet et al. (eds.), *Behind the Lines: Gender and the Two World Wars* (New Haven, CT, 1987); Modris Eksteins, *The Rites of Spring: The Great War and the Birth of the Modern Age* (Boston, 1989); Paul Fussell, *The Great War and Modern Memory* (New York, 1975).

National and Home Front Histories. Jean-Jacques Becker, *The Great War and the French People* (New York, 1986); Patrick Fridenson (ed.), *The French Home Front, 1914–1918* (Providence, RI, 1992); Jurgen Kocka, *Facing Total War: German Society, 1914–1918* (Providence, RI, 1984); J. M. Winter, *The Great War and the British People* (Cambridge, 1985); Arthur Marwick, *The Deluge: British Society and the First World War* (London, 1965); Arthur G. May, *The Passing of the Habsburg Monarchy, 1914–1918* (New York, 1966); John Reed, *War in Eastern Europe: Travels Through the Balkans in 1915* (London, 1994).

The Russian Revolution. Richard Pipes, *The Formation of the Soviet Union: Communism and Nationalism, 1917–1923* (Cambridge, MA, 1964); Richard Pipes, *The Russian Revolution* (New York, 1990); Sheila Fitzpatrick, *The Russian Revolution, 1917–1932* (Oxford, 1982); Riasanovsky, *History of Russia* (A).

CHAPTER 4

Charles S. Maier, *Recasting Bourgeois Europe: Stabilization in France, Germany, and Italy in the Decade After World War I* (Princeton, 1975); Richard Watt, *The Kings Depart: The Tragedy of Germany, Versailles, and the German Revolution* (London, 1969); A. J. Ryder, *The German Revolution of 1918* (Cambridge, 1967); Hans A. Schmitt (ed.), *Neutral Europe Between War and Revolution, 1917–23* (Charlottesville, VA, 1988); Mark Trachtenberg, *Reparations in World Politics: France and European Economic Diplomacy, 1916–1923* (New York, 1980); Fritz K. Ringer, *The German Inflation of 1923* (New York, 1966).

CHAPTER 5

General. Stephen J. Lee, *The European Dictatorships, 1918–1945* (New York, 1987).

France. Philippe Bernard and Henri Dubief, *The Decline of the Third Republic, 1914–1938* (Cambridge, 1985); Antoine Prost, *In the Wake of War: "Les Anciens Combattants" and French Society* (Providence, RI, 1992).

Weimar Germany. E. Eyck, *A History of the Weimar Republic* (London, 1962); A. J. Nicholls, *Weimar and the Rise of Hitler* (New York, 1991); Detlev J. Peukert, *The Weimar Republic: The Crisis of Classical Modernity* (New York, 1993); T. Childers, *The Nazi Voter: The Social Foundations of Fascism in Germany, 1919–1933* (Chapel Hill, NC, 1983).

Fascist Italy. Alan Cassels, *Fascist Italy* (London, 1969); Victoria De Grazia, *How Fascism Ruled Women: Italy, 1922–1945* (Berkeley, 1992).

Soviet Union. Fitzpatrick, *The Russian Revolution* (3).

Women.   De Grazia, *How Fascism Ruled Women* (5); Miriam Glucksman, *Women Assemble: Women Workers and the New Industry in Inter-War Britain* (London, 1990); Wendy Goldman, *Women, the State and Revolution: Soviet Family Policy and Social Life, 1917–1936* (New York, 1993); Mary Buckley, *Women and Ideology in the Soviet Union* (Ann Arbor, MI, 1989); Claudia Koonz, *Mothers in the Fatherland: Women, the Family, and Nazi Politics* (New York, 1987).

CHAPTER 6

Charles P. Kindleberger, *The World in Depression, 1929–39* (London, 1987); Aldcroft, *European Economy* (A); Cipolla, *Fontana Economic History* (A); Eric S. Einhorn and John Logue, *Modern Welfare States: Politics and Policies in Social Democratic Scandinavia* (New York, 1989); Pedersen, *Family, Dependence, and the Origin of Welfare States* (B); Lee, *European Dictatorships* (5); William Sheridan Allen, *The Nazi Seizure of Power: The Experience of a Single German Town, 1930–35* (London, 1965); Robert Conquest, *Harvest of Sorrow: Soviet Collectivization and the Terror-Famine* (New York, 1986).

CHAPTER 7

Nazi Germany.   Detlev J. K. Peukert, *Inside Nazi Germany: Conformity, Opposition and Racism in Everyday Life* (London, 1989); Richard Bessel (ed.), *Life in the Third Reich* (Oxford, 1987); Sarah Gordon, *Hitler, Germans, and the "Jewish Question"* (Princeton, 1984); Michael Burleigh and Wolfgang Wippermann, *The Racial State: Germany, 1933–1945* (Cambridge, 1991); Robert Gellately, *The Gestapo and German Society: Enforcing Racial Policy 1933–1945* (Oxford, 1990); Tim Mason, *Social Policy in the Third Reich* (Providence, RI, 1993); J. P. Stern, *Hitler: The Fuhrer and the People* (London, 1975); Michael Burleigh, *Germany Turns Eastwards* (Cambridge, 1988).

Soviet Union.   Robert C. Tucker, *Stalin in Power: The Revolution from Above 1928–1941* (New York, 1990); Chris Ward, *Stalin's Russia* (London, 1993); Robert Conquest, *The Great Terror* (New York, 1990); J. Arch Getty, *Origins of the Great Purge: The Soviet Communist Party Reconsidered, 1933–1938* (Cambridge, 1985); J. Arch Getty and Roberta T. Manning (eds.), *Stalinist Terror: New Perspectives* (New York, 1993); Nick Lampert and Gabor T. Rittersporn (eds.), *Stalinism: Its Nature and Aftermath* (London, 1992); Buckley, *Women and Ideology* (5); Goldman, *Women, the State and Revolution* (5).

Other.   Lee, *European Dictatorships* (5); Maurice Larkin, *France Since the Popular Front: Government and People 1936–1986* (Oxford, 1990).

Origins of the Second World War.   A. J. P. Taylor, *Origins of the Second World War* (London, 1965); Keith Eubank (ed.), *World War II: Roots and Causes* (Lexington, MA, 1992); Martin Gilbert and Richard Gott, *The Appeasers* (Boston, 1963).

CHAPTER 8

General.   Peter Calvocoressi and Guy Wint, *Total War: Causes and Courses of the Second World War* (London, 1972); Gordon Wright, *The Ordeal of Total War, 1939–1945* (New York, 1968); Michael J. Lyons, *World War II: A Short History* (Englewood Cliffs, NJ, 1989); Paul Fussell, *Wartime: Understanding and Behavior in the Second World War* (New York, 1989); Omer Bartov, *Hitler's Army: Soldiers, Nazis, and War in the Third Reich* (New York, 1992).

Economic and Social.   Alan S. Milward, *War, Economy, and Society, 1939–1945* (Berkeley, 1977); Martin Kitchen, *Nazi Germany at War* (New York, 1995); Angus Calder, *The People's War: Britain 1939–1945* (London, 1969); Alan S. Milward, *The Fascist Economy in Norway* (Oxford, 1972); Louis de Jong, *The Netherlands and Nazi Germany* (Cambridge, MA, 1990); M. R. D. Foot, *Resistance* (London, 1976); Ben-Cion Pinchuk, *Shtetl Jews Under Soviet Rule* (Oxford, 1990); Higonnet, *Behind the Lines* (3).

The Holocaust. Michael R. Marrus, *The Holocaust in History* (Toronto, 1987); Raul Hilberg, *The Destruction of the European Jews* (New York, 1978); Gerald Fleming, *Hitler and the Final Solution* (Stanford, 1984); Christopher R. Browning, *The Path to Genocide* (New York, 1992); Susan Zuccotti, *The Italians and the Holocaust: Persecution, Rescue, Survival* (New York, 1987); Jonathan Steinberg, *All or Nothing: The Axis and the Holocaust, 1941–43* (London, 1990); Bernard Wasserstein, *Britain and the Jews of Europe, 1939–1945* (Oxford, 1979); Burleigh and Wippermann, *Racial State* (7); Christopher R. Browning, *Ordinary Men: Reserve Police Battalion 101 and the Final Solution in Poland* (New York, 1992); Martin Gilbert, *Atlas of the Holocaust* (New York, 1993).

Resistance and Collaboration. Stephen Hawes and Ralph White (eds.), *Resistance in Europe: 1939–45* (London, 1976); Richard Cobb, *French and Germans, Germans and French* (Hanover, NH, 1983); Peter Hoffmann, *The German Resistance to Hitler* (Cambridge, MA, 1988).

CHAPTER 9

Eastern and Central Europe. Geoffrey Swain and Nigel Swain, *Eastern Europe Since 1945* (London, 1993); Paul G. Lewis, *Central Europe Since 1945* (New York, 1994); Hans Renner, *A History of Czechoslovakia Since 1945* (London, 1989); Henry Ashby Turner, Jr., *The Two Germanies Since 1945* (New Haven, CT, 1987); Martin McCauley, *The German Democratic Republic Since 1945* (New York, 1983).

Western Europe. Jean-Pierre Rioux, *The Fourth Republic, 1944–1958* (Cambridge, 1989); Donald Sassoon, *Contemporary Italy: Politics, Economy and Society Since 1945* (London, 1986); Stanley G. Payne, *Franco's Spain* (New York, 1967); John Ardagh, *The New France: A Study in Transition, 1945–77* (London, 1973); Joseph Becker and Franz Knipping, *Power in Europe? Great Britain, France, Italy and Germany in a Postwar World, 1945–50* (New York, 1986).

Social and Economic. Robert G. Moeller, *Protecting Motherhood: Women and the Family in the Politics of Postwar West Germany* (Berkeley, 1993); Charles P. Kindleberger, *Europe's Postwar Growth* (Cambridge, MA, 1967); Gordon Wright, *Rural Revolution in France* (New York, 1964).

CHAPTER 10

General. Josef Korbel, *Détente in Europe* (Princeton, 1972); Stephen R. Graubard (ed.), *A New Europe?* (Boston, 1964).

Eastern Europe. Stephen Fischer Galati (ed.), *Eastern Europe in the Sixties* (New York, 1963); Peter A. Toma, *The Changing Face of Communism in Eastern Europe* (Tucson, 1970); H. Gordon Skilling, *Czechoslovakia's Interrupted Revolution* (Princeton, 1976); Lewis, *Central Europe Since 1945* (9); Swain and Swain, *Eastern Europe Since 1945* (9).

Soviet Union. W. Morton and Rudolph L. Tokes, *Soviet Politics and Society in the 1970s* (New York, 1974); Robert Conquest, *Russia After Khrushchev* (New York, 1965).

Western Europe. Henri Mendras with Alistair Cole, *Social Change in Modern France: Towards a Cultural Anthropology of the Fifth Republic* (Cambridge, 1988); Neil McInnes, *The Communist Parties of Western Europe* (New York, 1975); David Caute, *The Year of the Barricades: A Journey Through 1968* (New York, 1988).

CHAPTER 11

General. Walter Laqueur, *A Continent Astray: Europe 1970–1978* (New York, 1979); Joni Lovenduski, *Women and European Politics: Contemporary Feminism and Public Policy* (Brighton, UK, 1986); Robert Chester (ed.), *Divorce in Europe* (Leiden, 1977); Walter Laqueur, *Terrorism* (Boston, 1977).

Western Europe. Pablo Filo della Torre et al. (eds.), *Eurocommunism: Myth or Reality?* (London, 1979); G. N. Minshull, *The New Europe: An Economic Geography of the E.E.C.* (New York, 1985); Joe Bailey (ed.), *Social Europe* (New York, 1992); Raymond Carr and Juan Pablo Fusi Azpurua, *Spain: Dictatorship to Democracy* (Boston, 1981); J. Earle, *Italy in the 1970s* (Newton Abbot, UK, 1975).

Eastern Europe. Jurgen Tampke, *The People's Republics of Eastern Europe* (London, 1983); Timothy Garton Ash, *The Polish Revolution: Solidarity* (London, 1991).

Soviet Union. Adam Ulam, *Dangerous Relations: The Soviet Union in World Politics, 1970–82* (New York, 1983).

CHAPTER 12

General. Alexis Jacquemin and David Wright (eds.), *The European Challenges Post-1992* (Aldershot, UK, 1993).

Eastern Europe. Anders Aslund, *Gorbachev's Struggle for Economic Reform* (Ithaca, NY, 1989); James R. Millar and Sharon L. Wolchik (eds.), *The Social Legacy of Communism* (New York, 1994); Mary Buckley (ed.), *Perestroika and Soviet Women* (Cambridge, 1992); Nanette Funk and Magda Mueller (eds.), *Gender Politics and Post-Communism: Reflections from Eastern Europe and the Former Soviet Union* (New York, 1993); Timothy Garton Ash, *The Uses of Adversity: Essays on the Fate of Central Europe* (New York, 1989).

Western Europe. John Ardagh, *France in the 1980s* (London, 1982); Peter Jenkins, *Mrs. Thatcher's Revolution* (Cambridge, MA, 1988); Wolfgang Heisenberg (ed.), *German Unification in European Perspective* (London, 1991).

Index